A CONCEPTUAL APPROACH
TO THE MEKILTA

A CONCEPTUAL APPROACH TO THE MEKILTA

by

MAX KADUSHIN

THE JEWISH THEOLOGICAL SEMINARY
OF AMERICA
NEW YORK

Copyright 1969
MAX KADUSHIN

Library of Congress Cataloging in Publication Data

Kadushin, Max, 1895–
   A conceptual approach to the Mekilta.

   Includes "Lauterbach's edition and translation of
the Mekilta de-Rabbi Ishmael, volume I," Tractate
Pisha', and Tractate Beshallah.
   Includes bibliographical references and index.
   1. Mekhilta of Rabbi Ishmael—Commentaries.
I. Ishmael ben Elisha, 2nd cent. II. Mekhilta of
Rabbi Ishmael. Pisha. 1981. III. Mekhilta of Rabbi
Ishmael. Pisha. English. 1981. IV. Mekhilta of
Rabbi Ishmael. Va-yehi be-shallah. Chapters 1-3.
1981 V. Mekhilta of Rabbi Ishmael. Va-yehi be-
shallah. Chapters 1-3. English. 1981. VI. Title.
BM517.M43K3   1981   296.1 '407   81-11740
ISBN 0-87334-014-0   AACR2

Printed in the United States of America

Dedicated To

The Memory of

SOL AND SUZANNE

MUTTERPERL

CONTENTS

PREFACE

The conceptual approach allows us to obtain a deeper insight into rabbinic literature. It shows, for example, how rabbinic concepts differ from the ideas of the Bible, and yet that rabbinic thought is related to biblical thought, that rabbinic concepts always possess biblical antecedents. We are thus enabled to discover how, and in what respects, rabbinic thought represents a development out of biblical thought. Even more important, the conceptual approach solves a major problem of rabbinic literature itself, and especially of midrashic literature. How are the midrashic statements related to one another? They are not united in any logical system, yet this cannot mean that they possess no coherence at all. In this approach rabbinic literature is seen to be informed by a great pattern of concepts, several of which are usually embodied in any particular passage. But the concepts so embodied are not confined to that passage; many other passages contain them as well. In other words, when the conceptual approach is employed, all midrashic statements are found to be related to each other by virtue of the rabbinic concepts they possess in common. On the other hand, the nature of those concepts is such that they also make of any particular non-juristic passage embodying them a discrete entity. These and cognate matters will be discussed in "Part One: General Considerations."

The conceptual approach can also be distinctly helpful in the elucidation of rabbinic texts. In what measure it has proved so may be gathered from a large number of passages analyzed in "Part Two: A Conceptual Commentary on Selections from Tractate Pisḥa' and Tractate Beshallaḥ." That section is based on modern critical editions of the Mekilta, and has profited much from the commentaries in those and other editions. The modern editions are indispensable because their texts are the outcome of critical study of MSS and early editions and compendia; at the same time, they often deal too briefly with a passage and occasionally even leave the text unexplained. What the conceptual approach always requires, however, is the complete and detailed elucidation of a passage. Only if a statement is analyzed in detail will the concepts embodied in it be discerned. Moreover, the analysis is decidedly incomplete unless it explains how the idea in the midrashic statement is derived from the biblical verse or verses on which it is a comment. The conceptual approach acts as a monitor, so to speak, insisting that nothing in a passage is to be left out of account.

A rabbinic concept is a pragmatic concept to the extent that its meaning is revealed when the concept is applied. Now a statement embodying a rabbinic concept indicates how that concept is applied in a given context. To identify a concept embodied in a passage is, then, to elicit at least one of the connotations of that concept. Conceptual analysis of rabbinic literature is thus a process in which we are made aware of the meaning of one rabbinic concept after another. It is not only a method for studying texts but a means, as well, of apprehending the rabbinic mind of which those texts are an expression.

A Conceptual Approach to the Mekilta is intended as an example of the conceptual approach to midrashic literature in general. The section on theory applies, therefore, by and large to midrashic literature as a whole, even though citations from the Mekilta predominate in the illustrative material. The commentary is on segments of the Mekilta extensive enough to afford ample scope for conceptual analysis and to permit the study of various modes of midrashic literary composition. All the haggadic (non-juristic) passages in the segments have been analyzed and, in addition, a number of halakic (juristic) passages have been discussed, those exhibiting the interrelation of Halakah and Haggadah or which throw light on the nature of rabbinic concepts.

The commentary is pegged to J. Z. Lauterbach's edition and translation of the Mekilta, but it departs from both on occasion.

I am greatly indebted to Professor Saul Lieberman for a number of valuable suggestions. Of course, the responsibility for the commentary must rest solely on me.

I also wish to express my thanks to Professor Bernard Mandelbaum for his helpfulness in getting this book published.

Finally, I wish to thank my friend of many years, Professor Max Arzt. Without his interest, manifested in so many ways, this book would not have seen the light of day.

A CONCEPTUAL APPROACH
TO THE MEKILTA

PART ONE:

General Considerations

I. Halakah and Haggadah in Tannaitic Midrashim

The Mekilta is a tannaitic Midrash, and it consists of interpretations of extensive portions of the book of Exodus. Lauterbach has pointed out that the Mekilta, unlike other tannaitic Midrashim, contains more haggadic, non-juristic, than halakic, juristic interpretations. This preponderance of Haggadah is to be accounted for, as he says, by the fact that the Book of Exodus "contains by far more narrative than law."[1]

A fundamental problem, however, is posed by the very presence, side by side, of Halakah and Haggadah. As categories, Halakah and Haggadah are quite distinct from each other, yet this dichotomy is ignored when haggadic and halakic interpretations are presented in tannaitic Midrashim. For example, "And ye shall keep it until the fourteenth day" (Exod. 12:6) is first given

---

1. Mekilta, ed. J. Z. Lauterbach (Philadelphia, 1933), I, p. xix, and see also ibid., p. xvi, n. 6. Unless otherwise specified, all references are to the Mekilta, ed. Lauterbach.

several haggadic interpretations,[2] and then, without any transition whatsoever, a number of halakic interpretations.[3] Evidently in some sense Haggadah and Halakah are closely related; they apparently possess something in common which informs them both. The question is: how is this large common factor to be identified?

II. Midrash and the Plain Meaning

The Rabbis took pains to establish the literal meaning of biblical texts, employing for this purpose sound philological methods.[4] They prove, for example, that *naham* in Exodus 13:17 means "He led them" by pointing to the way in which the root of the verb is used in Psalms 77:21 and 78:14.[5] In this instance the various verses in which the given root is found throw light on the meaning of the word. The Rabbis indicate, however, that sometimes the immediate context alone can be decisive, for the same word may have one meaning in some contexts and a different though related meaning in other contexts; they teach, for example, that *mahar* in Exodus 8:19 and 17:9 means "tomorrow," but that in ibid. 13:14 and in Joshua 22:24 it means "in time to come."[6] Furthermore, a word may possess two distinct and entirely unrelated meanings, either of which is possible in a particular context but one of which is more apt. An example is *ufasahti* in Exodus 12:13, usually rendered "and I will pass (step) over," but which the Rabbis, by comparison

2. Ibid., I, pp. 33ff, ll. 1-71.
3. Ibid., I, pp. 39f, ll. 72-89.
4. S. Lieberman, *Hellenism in Jewish Palestine* (New York, 1950), pp. 49f.
5. Mekilta, I, p. 170, ll. 13-15.
6. Ibid., I, p. 166, ll. 114-18.

with Isaiah 31:5, interpret with a sure philological sense to mean "and I will protect."[7] On the other hand, a word may have two different and equally valid meanings as far as the verse being interpreted is concerned. This is the case with *saf* in Exodus 12:22, a word which R. Ishmael interprets in this context as "threshold" by reference to Ezekiel 43:8 and Isaiah 6:4; and R. 'Akiba, as "vessel" by reference to I Kings 7:50.[8] The ancient translations differ here along similar lines.[9]

Not only do the Rabbis establish and teach the literal meaning of biblical texts but they distinguish between the literal meaning and a nonliteral interpretation, the literal meaning being designated as כמשמעו, "in its ordinary sense." Thus, when R. Eleazar was asked how the word "Rephidim" (Exod. 17:8) is to be understood, he answered כמשמעו,[10] that is, "Rephidim" is a name, as a parallel elsewhere makes plain.[11] In contrast with this literal explanation is an interpretation in the same passage of the Mekilta by "others" who, making a word play on "Rephidim," say that Israel had relaxed their hold on the words of the Torah.[12] In Halakah as well, a distinction may be made between the literal meaning and a nonliteral interpretation, but often there is at least some measure of kinship between the two renderings. According to R. Josiah, *kesutah* (her raiment—Exod. 21:10)

---

7. Ibid., I, pp. 56, ll. 74-77; (57, ll. 87-90); 87, ll. 90-93. See Lieberman, op. cit., pp. 50f., who calls attention to the same rendering in the Septuagint.
8. Mekilta, I, p. 44, ll. 3-7.
9. See S. D. Luzzatto, Commentary on the Pentateuch (Padua, 1872), on Exod. 12:22—his references to Targum Onkelos, the Septuagint, and the Vulgate.
10. Mekilta, II, p. 138, ll. 47-49.
11. Bekorot 5b.
12. Mekilta, II, p. 139, ll. 55-57.

is to be taken literally, כמשמעו, whereas R. Jonathan says that it is to be taken in conjunction with the preceding word and means that he must give her raiment suitable to her age.[13]

These instances of regard for the literal meaning of the biblical text are drawn from among a number of such exegetical comments in the Mekilta. Yet biblical exegesis does not constitute the bulk of the material there, nor is the Mekilta chiefly concerned with elucidating the literal meaning of the Bible text. Still, as comments on biblical verses, the nonexegetical interpretations must in some sense be associated with the plain meaning. What is the character of the association?

A consideration of Targum Onkelos presents another aspect of the problem. Targum Onkelos is the standard rabbinic translation of the Pentateuch into Aramaic, and was used for instruction in the synagogues where it accompanied the reading of the lection of the day.[14] In contrast to the Midrashim, it usually renders the simple, literal meaning. For example, the phrase "beside children" (Exod. 12:37) is translated literally in Targum Onkelos, whereas in the Mekilta these words are said to refer, according to one opinion, to women, children and minors; and, according to another, to women, children and old men.[15] To give one more example from a nearby verse, the words, "they were driven out of Egypt," (ibid. v. 39) are rendered literally in Targum Onkelos, whereas the Mekilta connects them with "and could not tarry,"

13. Ibid., III, pp. 27f, ll. 117-122; cf. also Rabbi's opinion—ibid. p. 29, l. 133.
14. See G. F. Moore, *Judaism in the First Centuries of the Christian Era* (Cambridge, 1927), I, pp. 101f, 174f, 302ff, and the references.
15. Mekilta, I, p. 109, ll. 30-31.

the words immediately following, and interprets the words as thus connected to mean that the Egyptians did not drive out the Israelites of their own accord.[16] On the other hand, it is also true that on occasion Targum Onkelos does not adhere to the simple meaning. For example, it takes *wela-Ger ha-gar,* "the stranger who sojourns" (ibid. v. 49) to refer to a proselyte, an interpretation also given in the Mekilta.[17] Are such departures from the simple meaning only inconsistencies in Targum Onkelos? If not, there must be a connection of some kind between the literal meaning and the rabbinic interpretation.

Apparent inconsistencies of a somewhat analogous type help us to approach the solution of the problem. We noticed that the Rabbis distinguish between literal meaning and nonliteral interpretation by characterizing instances of the former as כמשמעו. Sometimes, however, they characterize in this same manner what is to us a patently nonliteral interpretation. Thus, in the Mekilta, R. Ishmael designates as כמשמעו his interpretation of Exodus 12:36 to the effect that the Egyptian brought forth the requested object and gave it to the Israelite before the latter had finished saying, "Lend me,"[18] an idea obviously not contained in the verse itself. What R. Ishmael regards as the literal meaning is actually, then, a midrashic interpretation, and we are therefore not dealing here with altogether objective literary analysis. Indeed, literary analysis without a conceptual framework is not possible; philological methods do not operate in a conceptual vacuum. A single pattern of concepts informs all the rabbinic comments whether they teach the

---

16. Mekilta, I, p. 110, ll. 46-48. See below, p. 164.
17. Ibid., I, p. 128, ll. 137-141.
18. Ibid., I, p. 105, ll. 129-131. However, see below, p. 147.

simple meaning or are midrashic interpretations. That
pattern of concepts is entirely rabbinic in character, the
dualism of simple biblical meaning and midrashic interpretation notwithstanding. It is no wonder that a midrashic interpretation is occasionally regarded by the Rabbis as the literal meaning of a biblical verse.

III. Biblical Antecedents of Rabbinic Concepts

All rabbinic concepts are rooted in the Bible, that is
to say, have antecedents in the Bible. Yet rabbinic concepts cannot be inferred from their biblical antecedents,
for the rabbinic concepts have characteristics of their
own. At the same time, the biblical antecedents are entirely compatible with the pattern of rabbinic concepts
which grew out of them; they are not outside the range
of the rabbinic concepts. For this reason the literal meaning of a biblical text is not lost for the Rabbis.

Every rabbinic concept is represented by a conceptual
term, a noun which is the name of the concept. The idea
of God's justice, for example, is represented in rabbinic
literature by a conceptual term, *Middat ha-Din,*[19] a purely
rabbinic term. But the idea itself, it is hardly necessary
to say, is written large upon page after page in the Bible,
even though it is not crystallized there in an analogous
conceptual term. No rabbinic statement of the idea ap-
proaches the eloquence of Abraham's plea, "Shall not
the Judge of all the earth do justly" (Gen. 18:25). So
far, then, as the sheer idea of God's justice is concerned

19. Ibid., II, p. 28, l. 75.

there is no difference between the concept of *Middat ha-Din* and its biblical antecedent. Similarly, although the conceptual term *Middat Raḥamim*[20] is purely rabbinic, the idea of God's love which is crystallized in that term is, of course, a biblical idea: "The Lord, the Lord, God, merciful and gracious, long-suffering and abundant in goodness and truth" (Exod. 34:6); "The Lord is good to all, and His tender mercies are over all His works" (Ps. 145:9). Once more, the idea of God's kingship, crystallized in the rabbinic term *Malkut Shamayim*,[21] is also often expressed in the Bible, as in the verses, "The Lord shall reign forever and ever" (Exod. 15:18), and "The Lord reigneth" (Ps. 93:1). The relation between the Bible and the rabbinic concepts is such that the Rabbis could not help being aware, generally, of the plain meaning of the biblical texts.

Because they were aware of the literal meaning, the Rabbis were bound to distinguish between the literal meaning of a verse and their own interpretations of it; in fact, as we have noticed, this is exactly what they do. But they also go further. They lay stress on the simple meaning of a verse as being an entity in itself, something quite apart from its rabbinic interpretation. It is a rabbinic principle that "a biblical verse never loses its literal meaning,"[22] however that verse may be employed in rabbinic interpretation. In consonance with this principle the Rabbis endeavor to elucidate and, especially through Targum Onkelos, to teach the simple meaning of the biblical texts.

---

20. Ibid, 1. 75.
21. Ibid., II, p. 227, 1. 93; p. 230, 1. 13 (see ed. Horovitz-Rabin, p. 219).
22. Shabbat 63a; Yebamot 11b; (ibid. 24a).

IV. Emphatic Trends and Conceptual Development

Rabbinic thought exhibits certain emphatic trends: an emphasis on the individual, an emphasis on universality, an emphasis on love, and an emphasis on the experience of God. Often these emphatic trends are reflected in moving or in striking statements. After declaring that God shares in the trouble of the community, the Rabbis ask, "Whence do we know that He shares in *zarat yahid,* the trouble of the individual?" They answer by quoting, "He shall call upon Me, and I will answer him; I will be with him in trouble" (Ps. 91:15).[23] In this homily embodying the concept of *Middat Rahamim* there is obviously an emphasis on the individual. Again, in the following statement there is clearly an emphasis on universalism. "To three things is the Torah likened: to the desert, to fire, and to water. This is to tell you that just as these three things are free to all who come into the world, so also are the words of the Torah free to all who come into the world."[24] But these statements, and others like them, are only striking evidence of the emphatic trends. Actually the presence of these trends is established not by such arresting statements but by the concepts embodied in rabbinic literature as a whole. The concept of *Malkut Shamayim,* God's kingship, in itself expresses universality, and *Middat Rahamim,* God's love, represents in itself

---

23. Mekilta, I, pp. 113f, ll. 90-92.
24. Ibid., II, p. 237, ll. 98-101. See also Horovitz-Rabin, p. 222 and the note there. On דימוס l. 98, see Lieberman's remarks on the earlier statement, II, p. 198, ll. 80-83, in Shkiin (Jerusalem, 1939), p. 73.

both an emphasis on love and an emphasis on the individual.

Unlike the class of rabbinic concepts exemplified by those just mentioned, there are many rabbinic concepts whose conceptual terms are biblical nouns. In all such cases the term has a dual meaning, one biblical and the other rabbinic, the rabbinic meaning exhibiting the presence of an emphatic trend. Despite this difference, the relation between rabbinic literature and the Bible is such that the biblical meaning of the term is not altogether lost. We are dealing here with folk concepts, as we shall see later on, and folk concepts are always more complex than clearly defined, hierarchically ordered concepts of philosophy and science.

A simple instance is the dual connotation of the word "Israel." In the Bible, Israel is always a collective noun referring to the people as a collective entity,[25] and this meaning is retained in rabbinic literature. Although the verbs and the other parts of speech employed in connection with the noun are now in the plural[26] the word "Israel" still refers to the people as a whole. As used by the Rabbis, however, the word may also designate the members of the people individually as well, and then the parts of speech used in connection with the noun are in the singular, and "Israel" means an Israelite.[27] When, therefore, in rabbinic usage "Israel," though still a common noun, is made to refer to the individual Israelite, we have a clear emphasis on the individual.

An example of a rather more complex development is

---

25. For example, Exod. 5:1,2; 11:7; 17:8,11.
26. For example, Mekilta, I, p. 15, l. 2; p. 18, l. 39; p. 34, ll. 15-17; p. 42, l. 119; and so throughout.
27. Ibid., I, pp. 57f, ll. 89-91; III, p. 5, l. 48.

found in the concept *Goy.* In the Bible the word *Goy* means a people or a nation, and it is applied both to Israel[28] and to other nations;[29] the plural form *Goyim,* too, in most cases conforms to this meaning. Even in the Bible, however, the word has begun to take on another connotation, for *Goyim* is used hundreds of times with reference to other nations[30] and only infrequently with reference to Israel.[31] In the biblical period itself *Goyim* had thus begun to develop a secondary connotation, namely: non-Jews, Gentiles; indeed in Isaiah 8:23 and in Ezra 6:21 *Goyim* does mean Gentiles.[32] This secondary connotation of the word in biblical usage is its usual connotation in rabbinic literature, but it is now strongly affected by the rabbinic emphasis on the individual. As used by the Rabbis, *Goy* is usually no longer a collective noun but refers to the individual Gentile, and as such it possesses not only a masculine form,[33] as in the Bible, but also a feminine form[34] and plurals of both genders which again apply not to collective groups but to disparate individuals.[35] Yet, notwithstanding this development of the concept which emphasizes the individual, rabbinic interpretations indicate that the biblical meaning of the word as a collective noun is not

---

28. For example, Exod. 19:6; ibid, 32:10; Deut. 4:6.
29. For example, Gen. 15:13-14; Hab. 1:6.
30. See the reference in Mandelkern's Concordance, Schocken ed. (1937), pp. 256-8.
31. Gen. 17:4,5; 35:11; IISam. 7:23; Ezek. 37:22.
32. K. Marti, Das Buch Jesaja (Tübingen, 1900), p. 91; H. E. Ryle, The Books of Ezra and Nehemiah (Cambridge, 1907), p. 85. See also I. Heinemann, Darke ha-Agadah (Jerusalem, 1950), p. 113.
33. For example, Mekilta, I, p. 118, l. 20.
34. For example, Yer. Yebamot II, 4a: גויה
35. For example, Yer. Gittin I, 43b: גויים; ibid. Yebamot IV, 6b: גויות.

entirely lost for the Rabbis. The biblical meaning of *Goy* as nation in Exodus 19:6 and in IIChronicles 17:21 is retained in an interpretation in the Mekilta,[36] and its meaning as a collective noun in Proverbs 14:34 is retained in interpretations by various authorities, although limited by them to Israel.[37] There are also rabbinic interpretations of Isaiah 26:15 in which the word *Goy* in this verse is treated both as a term referring to individual Gentiles and as a collective noun referring to Israel.[38]

In the Bible the word *Zedakah* is used in two ways, one usual and the other occasional. The predominant biblical meaning is determined by the root *ẓdk,* "right," but occasionally *Zedakah* is used in the sense of charity.[39] Somewhat similar in that respect to the word *Goy,* this occasional biblical usage of *Zedakah* as charity constitutes its ordinary meaning in rabbinic literature, and now because of the rabbinic emphasis on love. In fact, as used by the Rabbis, *Zedakah* often connotes primarily love rather than any thought of almsgiving. Thus, a passage in the Talmud declares that God "did *Zedakah*" to Israel in scattering them among the nations, for, being scattered, they could not all be destroyed by any one nation;[40] similarly, a passage in a tannaitic Midrash interprets *umaẓdike ha-rabbim* in Daniel 12:3 to

36. Mekilta, II, p. 206, ll. 74-75. See Mekilta, ed. Horovitz-Rabin, p. 209, n. 6, as to correct text.

37. Pesikta de Rav Kahana, ed. B. Mandelbaum (New York, 1962), I, pp. 20ff, and the versions referred to there.

38. Ibid., II, pp. 418f (see n. 2 there pointing out that this section is drawn from another type of Midrash), 421f.

39. See Heinemann, op. cit., p. 114, and the references in notes 74 and 75 there.

40. Pesaḥim 87b; interpreting *ẓidkot pirzono* in Judges 5:11.

refer to the elders who "cause multitudes to love God."[41]
An act of *Zedakah,* therefore, is an act that is done out
of compassion and love, and hence the concepts of *Zedakah* and *Gemilut Ḥasadim* (deeds of lovingkindness) are
not only frequently associated,[42] but may even be inter-
changed with one another.[43] This crystallization of the
concept in rabbinic thought, however, does not prevent
the Rabbis from retaining, at times, the predominant
biblical usage of *ẓdḳ,* as in the case of *Ẓaddiḳ* and *'aẓdiḳ*
in Exodus 23:7,[44] and from employing it even in a rabbinic idiom:צדקתם עליכם את הדין.[45]

Found again and again in the messages of the prophets,
the universalistic outlook of the Bible is likewise expressed in the narratives of the early chapters of Genesis,
and especially in the story of Adam. The very word
'Adam, man, is a conceptual term in the Bible standing
for mankind in general, a term with the widest universalistic connotation. It possesses the same connotation in rabbinic literature, so that in this instance the
rabbinic usage of a conceptual term is at one with the
biblical. Nevertheless, here too, an emphatic trend of
the Rabbis manifests itself, the emphasis on universality.
In the Bible the word *'Adam* is a concept but it is also
a name, and not merely a name but a designation for a
person who is symbolical of all mankind and therefore
not to be classed altogether with the rest of mankind.

41. Sifre Deut., ed. M. Friedmann (Vienna, 1864), p. 83a, and
    n. 9 there. Cf. Midrash Tannaim, ed. D. Hoffman (Berlin,
    1908), pp. 40f.
42. M. Kadushin, Organic Thinking (New York, 1938), pp. 139f;
    hereafter referred to as OT.
43. Ibid., pp. 138f.
44. Mekilta, III, pp. 171ff, ll. 22-52.
45. Ibid., II, p. 67, ll. 5-6.

In rabbinic literature, on the contrary, Adam is classed with the rest of mankind: he is usually called there not Adam but *'Adam ha-Rishon,* the first man,[46] and he is thus referred to by the concept rather than by name. The rabbinic concept brooks no exceptions, so to speak; or, to put it otherwise, the concept man, is so strongly emphasized that all men, even Adam, are simply man.

The concept of *Mizwot* (singular, *Mizwah*) is a biblical concept, but as used by the Rabbis its connotation has been affected by the rabbinic experience of God. In the Bible, while the word often refers to commandments of God,[47] it also refers, as Greenberg has shown, to the commands or admonitions of a king, parent or teacher, or those "of any other superior."[48] But to the Rabbis, the word *Mizwot* stands primarily for commands of God. It has that connotation in rabbinic literature generally because it was used in that manner in living, daily experience. It is a key word in the *Birkat ha-Mizwot.* This type of *Berakah* initiates a mood in which the act specifically named in the *Berakah* is felt to be a direct command of God here and now.[49]

Such acts are those enjoined by either the written or the oral Torah, and include even things which the Rabbis themselves acknowledged to be *Mizwot Zeḳenim,* rabbinical ordinances;[50] all such acts are felt to be *Mizwot*

46. Ibid., I, p. 18, ll. 35-36, 39; II, p. 125, l. 59.
47. For example, Num. 15:39; Deut. 30:11.
48. S. Greenberg, The Multiplication of the Mitzvot, Mordecai M. Kaplan Jubilee Volume (New York, 1953), pp. 381-384, and the references cited there. As Greenberg points out, it is not always easy to determine the meaning of the biblical term since it may refer either to commands of God or of man.
49. M. Kadushin. Worship and Ethics (Northwestern University Press, 1964), p. 214; hereafter referred to as WE.
50. See: The Concept of Mizwot, ibid., pp. 199ff, especially pp. 202f.

of God, although, to be sure, some authorities only *associate Mizwot Zeķenim* with *Mizwot* of God.[51] This daily use of the word *Mizwot* is decisive for its use in general. Thus, for example, the Rabbis speak of "all the *Mizwot* in the Torah,"[52] and the word here obviously cannot mean any kind of command, but only the commands of God. On the other hand, so far as the Bible is concerned, the contexts allow the Rabbis to discriminate between the word as referring to commands of God and its use as referring to commands of any superior. In short, when rabbinic concepts are represented by biblical words, the biblical meanings have not been entirely obliterated.

All the rabbinic concepts have developed out of the Bible and that is especially noticeable when rabbinic concepts are represented by biblical terms. In this conceptual class, a biblical word has acquired a new meaning and yet this new meaning is not entirely new for it . has already been at least adumbrated in the Bible; moreover, the new meaning does not completely obliterate the old one even in rabbinic literature. These new meanings are informed by the rabbinic emphatic trends, and that fact by itself is sufficient evidence that the new meanings were not deliberately forged out of the old biblical meanings, that they were not produced by any logical process. An emphatic trend is established by the effect of a common element repeated in a number of concepts. For example, both the concept of Israel and the concept of *Goy* may refer to an individual and hence exhibit an emphasis on the individual; love is

---

51. Ibid., pp. 202f.
52. Mekilta, I, pp. 26f, ll. 40-44; p. 128, ll. 139-141.

conveyed both by the concept of *Zedakah* and by *Gemilut Hasadim*. Furthermore, the emphatic trends often coalesce, *Middat Rahamim,* for example, exhibiting an emphasis both on love and on the individual, something which is also true of *Zedekah* and *Gemilut Hasadim*. The Rabbis could not have first established the emphatic trends and then have insinuated these trends into the various concepts for, in order to establish the emphatic trends, they would have had to possess the new rabbinic concepts to begin with. We have indicated that rabbinic concepts differ with respect to the mode of their relation to the Bible: some use biblical conceptual terms, others are expressed in purely rabbinic terms, and in the former class the particulars of their relation to the Bible vary. To assume that the Rabbis worked out all these interrelationships in such unimaginable detail is quite like assuming that the grammar of a people's language has been deliberately devised. Not concepts produced by a rationalistic process, the new rabbinic concepts are the result of a genuine emergent development, a conceptual development in which typical characteristics of organic growth appear on a mental level. The concepts are new, yet they have emerged, "grown," out of the old; the concepts are new, yet the old have not been discarded.

The new rabbinic concepts have a much wider range of applicability, another characteristic of conceptual development. *Malkut Shamayim* has biblical antecedents, as we have observed, but the rabbinic term, an abstract term, enables the individual to abstract the idea from Deuteronomy 6:4 and from other biblical statements, to meditate on the idea of God's kingship and, in the *Keri'at Shema',* to transmute its implications—the kingship of God and commitment to the *Miẓwot*—into a twice-daily experience.[53] The concept of *Middat Raḥamim* is embodied in various *Berakot*,[54] and *Berakot* are a purely rabbinic institution. *Ẓedaḳah* is now differentiated from *Gemilut Ḥasadim*,[55] and rules are laid down for its application.[56] These examples demonstrate that, with respect to biblical concepts, rabbinic concepts represent a development not only in idea but in the range of the application of the idea.

V. Organismic Thought in Haggadah and in Halakah

Rabbinic concepts constitute an integrated pattern. They must have crystallized out of their biblical antecedents as a complex or pattern of concepts from their very beginning even though the individual concepts differ in the way they are related to their antecedents. In any case, when we meet these concepts in rabbinic literature, they certainly constitute an integrated pattern. We have already observed that many rabbinic concepts have elements in common and that these common elements, the several emphatic trends, also often coalesce.

The rabbinic concepts, then, are integrated but that integration or unity is not the result of logical, systematic thought. For rabbinic thought is not a system in which each concept occupies a place in a definite hierarchical order. The conceptual terms are only connotative, suggestive, and connotations, of course, are not

---

53. WE, p. 79; for other biblical statements, see ibid., p. 87f.
54. Ibid., p. 66, and see the Index there, s.v. *Berakot*.
55. Ibid., p. 21.
56. Ibid., p. 24; OT, p. 133.

propositions; hence they cannot be connected in a diagrammatic fashion. Indeed, in the literature itself even the connotations as such are seldom actually expressed. As to rabbinic statements, careful modern scholars agree that they cannot be organized into a unified system. Were a hierarchical order the only kind of conceptual order that makes for coherent thought, we should have had no rabbinic thought, and no rabbinic literature.

The problem is resolved when we recognize the true character of rabbinic thought—namely, that it reflects a non-hierarchical, pattern-like coherence of the concepts it employs. This conceptual coherence is not a pattern formed out of the conceptual *terms*, for conceptual terms are but the names of concepts; that is why these terms need be only connotative. This is not to say that they are not important. Indeed, without the terms there could be neither classification nor abstraction, the basic functions of a concept. Important as the conceptual term is, however, it is not necessary that it be always present. For rabbinic concepts possess a decidedly pragmatic quality. They are often embodied in an act or a statement rather than named. "In the twinkling of an eye," say the Rabbis, "the children of Israel travelled from Rameses to Succoth."[57] *Nes,* miracle, is the concept involved here but it is embodied in. the statement, not named.

The coherence of rabbinic concepts is organismic. Besides possessing a name in the conceptual term, the rabbinic concept possesses idea-content, but this idea-content is not given once for all. It is acquired as any single concept interweaves with other concepts of the pattern so that

---

57. Mekilta, I, p. 107, ll. 8-9.

the meaning of that concept keeps growing richer the more it interweaves with the other concepts. The meaning of each concept thus depends upon the pattern of concepts as a whole. This is borne out by some of our earlier analyses, among them a study of passages in the Mekilta containing the concept of *Malkut Shamayim.* "As it combines with other concepts, *Malkut Shamayim,* we learned, signifies that God's dominion is everywhere, that God will ultimately be recognized as King by the whole world, that it negates basically the dominion of the nations of the world over Israel, that it is acknowledged after experiencing God's love or mercy, that it immediately implies the observance of the *Miẓwot.* Had we found it necessary to cite more passages, we should have drawn forth more ideas implicit in the concept of *Malkut Shamayim.*"[58] The idea-content of any particular rabbinic concept is, then, a function of the entire complex of concepts as a whole. If every rabbinic concept depends for its meaning upon all the rest, then all the concepts together constitute an organismic whole.

Almost every haggadic statement reflects the organismic character of the rabbinic concepts. A haggadic idea usually embodies a number of rabbinic concepts. Were the concepts hierarchically related, the idea would be conveyed step by step after the manner of a geometrical theorem. Being organismic, however, all the concepts are

58. M. Kadushin, The Rabbinic Mind (second ed., New York, 1965), p. 23; hereafter referred to as RM. Another such study in the Mekilta is presented in my article, Aspects of the Rabbinic Concept of Israel in the Mekilta (Hebrew Union College Annual, XIX [Cincinnati, 1946]), pp. 57ff.; it treats of the interweaving of Israel with the concepts of God's love, His justice, Torah and *Mattan Torah.* Also discussed there is the manner in which the emphasis on universality, expressed in God's justice, acts as a check on the factor of nationality.

potentially simultaneous and when several concepts are concretized in a haggadic statement or in an act, the concepts concretized are actually simultaneous. Although the idea presented, therefore, may involve a number of concepts the idea is grasped as a unitary entity, as a single idea. To state the matter differently, despite the number of concepts involved, the idea is grasped as a single idea because the concepts are always interwoven. According to the Rabbis, for example, Jonah said to himself: I will go outside the Land of Israel where the *Shekinah* does not reveal itself, for the Gentiles (of Nineveh) are close to repentance (and if they repent) Israel (by contrast) would stand condemned.[59] Integrated in this one statement are the concepts of *Gilluy Shekinah* (revelation of God), Israel, Gentiles, and repentance.

A haggadic idea is not only a unitary entity but an independent entity. Rabbinic thought in Haggadah is coherent because the rabbinic concepts possess an organismic coherence, but the haggadic ideas embodying those concepts are discrete, each of them being a complete idea in itself. They are not related logically to each other precisely because the concepts informing them are not related logically but organismically. Even in those instances in which haggadic statements are connected, they are connected only through an association of ideas. Such an instance in the Mekilta, consisting of a number of statements, begins with one telling that God spoke to Moses in Egypt not in the city but outside of it because the city "was full of abominations and idols," and closes with the declaration that the patriarchs and prophets offered their lives in behalf of Israel.[60] The statements in

59. Mekilta, I, p. 7, ll. 80-82.
60. Ibid., I, pp. 3-11, ll. 35-113.

this passage are connected, to be sure, but the connection
is from statement to statement only, so that the last has
no connection whatever with the first, nor indeed with
any but the one immediately preceding it. Essentially,
each statement in the passage is an independent entity.

Not being part of a logical structure, an independent
idea does not arise without a stimulus of some kind, without a point of departure. For a haggadic idea the stimulus is usually a biblical text. In other words, though haggadic ideas are derived from biblical verses, the ideas
have not been derived through rules of interpretation
but are largely the result of the impact of the verses on
creative minds.[61] As stimulus, however, the verse is not
just a point of departure for the haggadic idea. Instead,
the verse acts as the channel for bringing out the idea and,
by the same token, the idea is a construction or interpretation of the verse. The interpretation is certainly something other than the plain meaning of the verse; nevertheless, in midrash there is an association between the
interpretation and the plain meaning—an immediate and
an ultimate association. The immediate association is obvious: the words of the plain meaning give rise to the
interpretation, but that alone does not make the interpretation midrash. In midrash there is also an ultimate as-

---

61. The thirty-two rules of interpretation given in the name of R.
Eliezer b. Jose, the Galilean, are from the late geonic period; see now Moses Zucker, Proceedings of the American
Academy for Jewish Research (New York, 1954), (Hebrew),
pp. 2ff. See also RM, pp. 129f. This is not to say that Haggadah employed no rules of interpretation at all. A number
of commonly accepted devices for interpreting biblical
verses were often employed, but these devices themselves
were aids to a creative imagination. See S. Lieberman, Hellenism in Jewish Palestine, pp. 68ff, where such devices are
shown to have been current in the ancient world in general.

sociation. Now it is not a matter of the relation between a single biblical verse and its haggadic interpretation; the association is between the Bible as a whole and rabbinic thought as a whole. An intrinsic conceptual bond unites the Bible and rabbinic thought, the bond of relationship between the rabbinic concepts and their biblical antecedents. Jonah's motive given above is a purely rabbinic idea, but the concepts embodied there all have biblical antecedents, and the idea itself is an elaboration of Jonah 1:3. "From before the Lord" in that verse does not mean, according to the Rabbis, that Jonah attempted to flee from God for God is everywhere, but that he sought to avoid receiving a divine communication, *Gilluy Shekinah*.

A biblical verse acting as the channel for a haggadic interpretation is an integral element of the interpretation. But the interpretation is a discrete organismic entity, and therefore the verse also partakes of the organismic quality of that entity. If each of the rabbinic concepts embodied in the interpretation, not being logically connected with the others, can be combined with entirely different concepts, so the verse, too, can be used in other interpretations. A verse, the same verse, can be used over and over again in haggadic interpretations, each of them independent of the others, and thus a feature of haggadic interpretation is multiple interpretation of biblical texts. Psalm 68:7, for example, is given a number of interpretations in the Mekilta, each of them containing a different play on the word *bakosharot* in that verse.[62] Haggadic interpretation, in fine, is altogether nondogmatic. (See also below, p. 125f, on indeterminacy of belief.)

Halakah as well as Haggadah is informed by the or-

---

62. Mekilta, I, p. 140, ll. 157-165.

ganismic complex of rabbinic concepts. Thus, since *Ger* as a rabbinic concept means "proselyte," both Targum Onkelos and the Mekilta take *wela-Ger ha-gar* (in the law concerning circumcision stated in Exod. 12:49) to refer not to the stranger but to the proselyte.[63] Embodying the same rabbinic concepts, Halakah and Haggadah are sufficiently related that no sharp break in thought occurs when interpretations in the one category follow interpretations in the other. That is obviously true when the same concept is embodied in both types of interpretation, as is the case when halakic interpretations dealing, once more, with *Gerim* are followed by haggadic interpretations embodying the same concept.[64] Actually, however, the basic relationship between Halakah and Haggadah stems from their possession in common of the entire complex of rabbinic concepts rather than from having, in a particular instance, a single concept in common. It is this basic relationship, this common ground, that allows halakic and haggadic interpretations to be juxtaposed.

Notwithstanding their basic relationship, Haggadah and Halakah constitute two distinct categories—speech or lore on the one side and acts or law on the other. That dichotomy is reflected in the difference bewteen haggadic and halakic interpretations of biblical texts. In contrast to haggadic interpretation, halakic interpretation often employs rules of interpretation, *middot,* all of which involve logical procedures. A specific application of any one of these thirteen rules[65] demands inferential reasoning. There

63. Above, p. 5.
64. Mekilta, III, pp. 137-141, ll. 1-48. Halakah and Haggadah may even be intermingled, as in the section on theft—ibid., pp. 105-108, ll. 50-94.
65. Ibid., I, p. 128, l. 2, and the sources in the note there.

is, for example, the rule of *kal,* lighter, *vahomer,* and weightier, (i.e., minor and major). This rule enables R. Isaac to infer from Exodus 21:30 that "eye for eye" in ibid. v. 24 means monetary compensation for the injury. "Behold it says, 'If there be laid on him a ransom,' etc. (ibid. v. 30). Now then, by using the method of *kal vahomer,* you reason thus: If even in a case where the penalty of death is imposed (in the Bible), only a monetary compensation is exacted, it is but logical that in this case, where no death penalty is imposed, surely no more than a monetary compensation should be exacted."[66] Again, inferential reasoning enables the Rabbis to establish a *binyan 'ab* on the basis of the words "tooth" and "eye" in ibid. v. 26—that is, a general rule to the effect that the slave is to be freed if *any* chief, visible organ is destroyed by the master.[67] In Halakah, the interpretation of a biblical text is the product of reasoning, and is not, as in Haggadah, an idea merely suggested by the text.

Halakah and Haggadah differ in another respect. A haggadic statement is a discrete, independent entity but this is not true of a halakah, a law. Inherent in the laws is an implicit nexus, a nexus which becomes more and more explicit as a result of logical processes. Classification is one such process, the inherent nexus permitting the laws to be classified in accordance with their subject-matter—tithes in one division, Festivals in another division, damages in still another, and so on. Classification reveals the relatedness of the laws in any one division, and to that extent the Mishnah, which is the product of that classification, made the nexus at least partially explicit. The nexus is made more fully explicit in the Tal-

66. Ibid., III, pp. 67f, ll. 72-75.
67. Ibid., pp. 72f, ll. 40-52.

mud where, in the course of inferential reasoning, a relatedness is exhibited among laws belonging to different
classifications. It is elicited in a discussion, for example,
that an identical principle underlies both a law concerning
acquisition and a law in an entirely different classification concerning the prohibited mixture of animals.[68]

But Halakah, since it, too, embodies the organismic
rabbinic concepts, possesses also some of the characteristics of organismic thought. Organismic thought allows
room for differences of opinion not only in Haggadah but
in Halakah as well. In the Mishnah there are only six
complete chapters in which no controversies are recorded.[69] The halakic Midrashim have a similar character. Although a work emanating from one school, that
of R. Ishmael, the Mekilta nonetheless contains numerous
instances of differences of opinion with regard to the
derivation of laws, and even quite a number of divergent
opinions on particular laws themselves.[70] A feature of
Haggadah is the multiple interpretation of biblical verses.
In a modified form this characteristic of organismic
thought is also to be found in Halakah, for two different
halakot are occasionally derived from the same verse;
moreover, the second interpretation is usually introduced
with the term, *dabar 'aḥer,* "another interpretation,"[71]
the very term which introduces each interpretation after

---

68. Baba Meẓi'a 8b, and see Tosafot, s.v. רכוב עדיף.
69. See RM, pp. 93f, and the discussion there.
70. Examples of the latter: Mekilta, I, pp. 119-120, ll. 25-41 (R.
    Eliezer and R. Ishmael); III, p. 16, ll. 73-76 (R. Judah, R.
    Me'ir and "other sages"); ibid., p. 83, ll. 112-120 (R. Me'ir,
    R. Judah and R. Jose); ibid., p. 86, ll. 152-158 (R. Ishmael
    and R. 'Aḳiba).
71. Examples: Ibid., I, pp. 47f, ll. 52-64; ibid., pp. 155f, ll.
    181-193; II, p. 257, ll. 1-8; ibid., p. 283, ll. 98-103; III, p.
    14, ll. 46-50; ibid., p. 66, ll. 46-56.

the first in a series of haggadic interpretations of a verse. A haggadic statement often embodies several rabbinic concepts, and that characteristic of organismic thought, too, is found in Halakah. Acts of worship, *Berakot*, are governed by Halakah and every *Berakah* embodies at least two concepts—*Berakah* and God's love.[72] Inasmuch as most of the *Berakot* are recited every day, a section of Halakah pertaining to the daily life of every individual is characterized by organismic thought.

VI. Integration of Halakah and Haggadah

Halakah and Haggadah are closely related because they embody the same organismic rabbinic concepts, and as a result both are characterized by organismic thought. In Haggadah, it is a main feature but also, though to a more limited extent, it is present in Halakah as well. This common feature of the two categories is exhibited independently by each of them. Sometimes, however, Halakah and Haggadah are almost fused into a single category, and then they are not merely related but inter-related. In an earlier work we described a number of modes of such interrelationship.[73] Among the examples cited there are several in which a halakah and a haggadah are integrated into a single idea, an idea in which both Halakah and Haggadah are constitutive elements.[74] That type of interrelation in the form of midrashim is to

---

72. See WE, p. 68; cf. ibid., p. 65.
73. WE, "Interrelation of Halakah and Haggadah," pp. 8ff.
74. Ibid., p. 9—the warning given to witnesses, and the two versions of an opinion held by R. Joḥanan b. Zakkai. See also ibid., p. 148f, for an instance in the liturgy.

be found not infrequently in the Mekilta and in the other
halakic Midrashim.

When a halakah is integrated with a haggadah in a
midrash, the haggadah acts as a frame or setting for the
halakah; in other words, the halakah is supplied with
explanatory material. There are various, ways in which
such explanatory material bears on the halakot with
which it is integrated. Thus, there are midrashim in which
a haggadah supplies a reason, in some sense or other,
for a halakah. Midrashim of that character may consist
of several parts, each part containing a different haggadic
reason for the same halakah. For example, with regard
to the law that the paschal lamb is to be purchased four
days prior to its slaughter, two different haggadic reasons are given—one by R. Matia and another by R.
Eliezer ha-Ḳappar who takes issue with R. Matia[75]—
and the midrash accordingly consists of two parts. Again,
both R. Ishmael and R. Jonathan declare that the blood
of the paschal lamb was to be put on the inside of the
house, but each gives his own haggadic reason for that
interpretation of the law.[76] Midrashim containing several
haggadic reasons for halakot are composite midrashim.
In those instances, the integration of Halakah and Haggadah is such that several haggadot are integrated with
the same halakah.

There is another way in which a composite midrash
may exhibit the integration of Halakah and Haggadah.
When different haggadot derive from the same biblical
phrase, each haggadah may involve a different halakic
opinion. That is the case with two contiguous interpreta-

---

75. Mekilta, I, pp. 33ff, ll. 1-55; see below, pp. 72ff.
76. Mekilta, I, p. 44, ll. 8-13; for the third interpretation, see
   n. 78, and see also below, pp. 84f.

tions of "And ye shall eat it in haste" (Exod. 12:11, referring to the eating of the paschal lamb).[77] These interpretations apparently center on the phrase "in haste" but really derive from the entire context. "In haste" in the first interpretation refers to the haste of the Egyptians who were eager to get the Israelites out of Egypt at midnight when the plague of the firstborn occurred; this haggadah therefore involves a halakic opinion, namely, that the Israelites were to eat the paschal lamb only until midnight. "In haste" in the next interpretation refers to the haste of the Israelites when they were permitted to leave their houses at dawn, and that haggadah therefore involves a different halakic opinion, namely, that the Israelites were permitted to eat the paschal lamb until dawn.[78] The halakic opinions here differ in accordance with the haggadot with which they are respectively involved.

Halakah and Haggadah may be integrated in other ways as well. For example, according to R. Ishmael, Exodus 12:2 tells of how Moses taught a halakah to Israel: in order to demonstrate how the beginning of a month is always to be established, Moses pointed to the

---

77. Mekilta, I, p. 52, ll. 5-14; see below, pp. 86ff.
78. In a third interpretation (Mekilta, I, p. 52, ll. 14ff) "in haste" refers to God's haste, for the redemption came long before the end of the period of servitude foretold in Gen. 15:13; that interpretation agrees with the first in the series as to the halakah (see below, p. 89), but now a different haggadic reason is supplied for the halakah. A composite midrash, hence, need not be limited to one type of integration of Halakah and Haggadah. This is also demonstrated in the third interpretation, that of R. Isaac, in regard to the blood of the paschal lamb to be put on the houses (ibid., I, p. 44, ll. 13-15). Unlike the other interpretations there which supply different haggadic reasons for the same halakah, that interpretation contains a haggadah involving a different halakic opinion (see below, p. 85).

new moon, saying as he did so, "This new moon" etc.[79] In this instance a haggadah is a means of teaching a halakah (comp. Rosh ha-Shanah II.8).

Halakah and Haggadah are not only related but interrelated. Indeed, in a number of midrashim Halakah and Haggadah are actually integrated.

VII. Value Concepts

Organismic rabbinic concepts refer to matters which are not objects, qualities, or relations in sensory experience. Furthermore, they are not philosophic or scientific concepts. Philosophic and scientific concepts depend upon definitions, whereas rabbinic concepts are connotative only, and hence are not amenable to formal definition. The organismic rabbinic concepts are value concepts; in fact, a deeper understanding of the nature of value concepts in general may well be an incidental result of a clearer knowledge of the rabbinic concepts.

A value concept endows situations, events, or acts with significance, gives to each of them a distinct value which it would not otherwise have. The act of giving away money, food and clothing can be described in purely "operational" terms; for one who does not possess the concept of charity, however, the act as a whole will have no significance. But in imparting significance to an act, a value concept performs more than an ideational function. An act embodying a value concept conveys emotion as well as meaning, and hence a valuational situation is an experiential rather than exclusively a knowledge-situation. The idea involved in two situations may be the same, yet as an experience the significance conveyed by

---

79. Mekilta, I, p. 15, ll. 1-3; see below, p. 65.

the value concept is more keenly felt on the one occasion than on the other. Both the food one is about to eat and the food one has eaten are regarded as manifestations of God's love; but—as R. Ishmael implies—to a man who is hungry that manifestation is more palpable than to a man who is sated.[80]

In one respect value concepts are fixed but they are dynamic in other respects. Contact with foreign civilizations, notably with the Hellenistic, is mirrored in rabbinic literature in a large new vocabulary—names of objects, proper names, even legal terms.[81] Yet not a single new value term was added as a result of this interaction, the conceptual terminology in the valuational sphere remaining fixed during the entire rabbinic period.[82] This means that the ideas crystallized in that terminology remained the same during the whole rabbinic period, that they were *permanently* characteristic of the people—in other words, that the value concepts reflected, more than any other segment of the vocabulary, the basic character of the people. But that means, in turn, that the value concepts were wide-spread, that they were possessed by the people at large, that they were folk concepts. Now the people at large are not faceless; they are individuals and when viewed from the standpoint of the individual the value concept is seen to be propulsive, dynamic. The

80. Mekilta, I, p. 137, ll. 116-119.
81. See S. Lieberman, How Much Greek in Jewish Palestine, Brandeis University, *Studies and Texts*: Vol. I, (Harvard Univ. Press, 1963), pp. 132ff.
82. RM, p. 44. Lieberman (Greek in Jewish Palestine [New York, 1942], pp. 7-8) demonstrates that some Greek words employed by the Rabbis belong in a category of legal terminology, and that other such words are commercial terms. His discussion of these terms is illuminating. From that discussion we can conclude that, as used by the non-Jews, certain of those words were apparently also value terms, whereas in rabbinic literature they no longer had value connotations.

value concept impels a person to act. Inherent in the abstract value concept is a drive toward concretization. When a person possesses, as part of his folk culture, the concepts of charity and *Gemilut Ḥasadim* and *Berakot,* for example, he will be stimulated to practice charity, to do acts of lovingkindness and to say *Berakot.* This dynamism is not the property of each concept separately. It is the property of the organismic complex as a whole, whose very character calls for the interweaving of concepts, something possible only in a concrete situation. That is why value acts, such as the saying of a *Berakah,* usually embody several value concepts.[83]

A primary condition for a healthy value complex is the interaction of the intellectual leaders and the folk. Since value concepts do not refer to objects or relations in common sensory experience, they need to be cultivated, nurtured. Even more vital is the need to establish norms of behavior ensuring the steady concretization of the value concepts, norms whereby the opportunities for actualizing the concepts discovered by the gifted man, may become similar opportunities for the ordinary man. These needs were met by the Rabbis, the trained intellectual leaders of the people who nevertheless did not constitute a professional class, and whose interests were therefore largely the same as those of the folk.[84] In Haggadah they made the value concepts vivid, and in Halakah they developed the norms which fostered and directed the steady actualization of those concepts in daily life.

---

83. An ethical act is interpreted or grasped not only by the ethical concept involved in the act, such as charity or *Gemilut Ḥasadim,* but also by the concept of *Miẓwot*—see WE, pp. 12f., 206ff.
84. See RM, pp. 85ff.

PART TWO:

A Conceptual Commentary

on Selections from Tractate Pisḥa'

and Tractate Beshallaḥ

NOTES AND ABBREVIATIONS

This Commentary is pegged to selected passages from Volume I in J. Z. Lauterbach's edition and translation of the Mekilta de-Rabbi Ishmael (3 volumes, Philadelphia, 1931). Accompanying our Commentary is a reprint of Lauterbach's Volume I, pages 1-215, for which permission has been obtained from The Jewish Publication Society of America. The catchwords in our Commentary are taken from the translation there. These catchwords are printed in bolder type. The first page in the reprint consists of the key to the abbreviations and signs used in Lauterbach's Apparatus Criticus below the Hebrew text.

Numbers *before* "l." or "ll." (l. = line; ll. = lines) refer to the pages in Volume I of the Lauterbach edition, and numbers *after* "l." or "ll.", to the lines in the Hebrew, e.g., 7, ll. 5-6 indicates page 7, lines 5 and 6 of the Hebrew text.

"Above" or "below" refer to pages in *our* material.

* indicates a new chapter in the text, and **, that some textual material has been omitted.

In references to Volumes II and III of the Lauterbach edition, the Roman numerals refer to the volume and the Arabic numbers to the page; e.g., II, 3 means "Volume II, page 3."

H-R refers to *Mechilta d'Rabbi Ismael,* ed. H. S. Horovitz and I. A. Rabin, Frankfort a.m., 1928.

TE refers to M. Kadushin, *The Theology of Seder Eliahu: A Study in Organic Thinking,* Bloch Publishing Company, New York, 1932.

OT refers to M. Kadushin, *Organic Thinking: A Study*

in Rabbinic Thought, Jewish Theological Seminary of America, New York, 1938.

WE refers to M. Kadushin, *Worship and Ethics: A Study in Rabbinic Judaism,* Northwestern University Press, 1964.

RM refers to M. Kadushin, *The Rabbinic Mind,* 2nd edition, Blaisdell Publishing Company, New York, 1965.

(A) Commentary On Selections From Tractate Pisḥa', Chapters I-XIV

*

1, ll. 1-10

And the Lord Spoke . . . the divine word (*ha-Dibbur*, l. 3) . . . to both Moses and Aaron.

ha-Dibbur or *ha-Dibber* (H-R, p. 1, and n. 2), connotes the idea of a revelation of God in the form of a locution, and in that sense it represents a phenomenal experience of God. This form of divine revelation was experienced by all the prophets and by them alone; accordingly, Aaron is here regarded as a prophet. Our text tells us that *Dibbur* was experienced by all the prophets when it uses the expression *she-nidbar* (5, ll. 58ff) with regard to the communications of God to the prophets in general.

Dibbur is a form of *Gilluy Shekinah,* the revelation of God; hence the concept of *Gilluy Shekinah* may sometimes be employed by the Rabbis to refer to an experience of *Dibbur.* For example, they declare that after the land of Israel was chosen, there were no divine communications outside of that land (4, ll. 42-44), but they also allude to this very idea when they say later on (6, l. 72), "You can learn from the following that the *Shekinah* does not reveal itself outside the land." The concept of *Gilluy Shekinah,* however, refers not only to *Dibbur* but to any sensory experience of God, and especially to a visual experience of that kind. "A maidservant saw at the [Red] Sea what Isaiah (?) and Ezekiel and all the rest of the prophets never saw . . . when the Holy One blessed be He revealed Himself at the [Red] Sea . . ." (II, 24f, and see RM, p. 231, n. 44). "He revealed Himself at the [Red] Sea as a mighty hero doing battle" and at Sinai "as an old man full of mercy" (II, 31).

Since the scope of the concept of *Gilluy Shekinah* includes the concept of *Dibbur,* we may designate *Dibbur* as a subconcept of *Gilluy Shekinah,* provided we bear in mind that *Dibbur* is also a concept in its own right. It is a concept in its own right because, in the first place, it possesses a conceptual term. Moreover, being an organismic concept, it is neither derived from nor dependent on the concept of *Gilluy Shekinah.* On the other hand, the fact remains that the concept of *Dibbur* is an aspect of *Gilluy Shekinah,* and by designating *Dibbur* as a subconcept, we are indicating that particular type of relationship between concepts. This instance demonstrates, too, that the organismic relationship of the concepts does not preclude the existence of supplementary forms of relationship. (On these supplementary forms, see RM, pp. 15f, 26ff).

Gilluy Shekinah and *Dibbur* are value concepts. *Gilluy Shekinah* interweaves with other value concepts in haggadic statements, is usually embodied in a statement rather than named—a primary characteristic of a value concept (above, p. 17)—and, like other value concepts, allows for various and sometimes contradictory concretizations (RM, pp. 228-231). Nevertheless, *Gilluy Shekinah* is not entirely compatible with the other value concepts, for it possesses a feature at variance with them: the other concepts do not refer to phenomena in sensory experience whereas *Gilluy Shekinah* definitely involves visual or auditory sensations. This incompatibility of *Gilluy Shekinah* with the other value concepts prevents it from being used freely, or in the same manner as the value concepts in general. It is employed by the Rabbis to depict events in the past or in the future but, by and large, not in the present, from which we gather that the type of mysticism for which *Gilluy Shekinah* stands was certainly not encouraged by the Rabbis (ibid., pp. 234ff). *Dibbur,* a subconcept of *Gilluy Shekinah,* was likewise employed in a restricted manner; indeed, it was restricted entirely to the past, being an experience only of the prophets (ibid., p. 250f.)

When, however, it says: "And it came to pass . . . land of Egypt" (Exod. 6:28) . . . and not to Aaron.

Exodus 6:28 is here pitted against ibid. 12:1. This type of textual approach is more characteristic of halakic than of haggadic method, though the product in this case is a haggadah. The Mekilta, however, often employs halakic methodology to interpret texts in its haggadic portions as well. Comp. Mekilta, ed. I. H. Weiss (Vienna, 1865), Introd., p. xvii. Of course, there are also a large number of passages where the verse acts only as stimulus, as in Haggadah in general (above, p. 20); for example, the interpretation of Jeremiah 36:32 on 8-9, ll. 93f and of IKings 19:16 on 9, ll. 99f.

If so . . . so was Aaron perfectly fit to receive the divine words *(Dibberot,* l. 7) . . . directly addressed to him.

Dibberot is the plural of *Dibberah,* and refers to specific communications or commands of God, e.g., *'Aseret ha-Dibberot,* the Ten Commandments (II, 229). The *Dibberot* alluded to as those addressed to Aaron alone (ll. 9f) are commands, laws (see Lauterbach, note 1). The communication introduced by Exodus 12:1, the first verse commented on in the Mekilta, similarly deals with laws, those of the first Passover.

According to the comment of the Mekilta here, Aaron was as fit to receive *Dibberot* from God as was Moses. True, because of the honor due to Moses (*kebodo shel Moshe*, l. 8) God generally addressed His *Dibberot* to him, but even so several *Dibberot* were addressed solely to Aaron. The point is not merely that Moses was not the only instrument for *Dibberot*, but that another person was fully as qualified to receive and to transmit them. The true Lawgiver is God. There is no Mosaic religion, not even in the sense that Moses alone was fit to act as God's instrument.

1-2, ll. 10-16

Another Interpretation.

On the use of this expression in the multiple interpretation of texts, see above, p. 24f.

From this . . . Moses was a judge

Moses was like a judge with regard to Pharaoh (rather than "over Pharaoh"). As the passage goes on to say, Moses spoke to Pharaoh without fear, and hence the metaphor "Judge."

Aaron was equal to Moses . . . fearlessly.

He was equal to Moses in courage. Implied once more is the idea that there is no man who is superior to all other men.

2-3, ll. 17-34

A) Rabbi says: "unto Moses and Aaron . . . had precedence over the other . . . as the other.

kodem bema'aseh, the phrase used here (l. 18) and in other passages of this section is variously applied, and it therefore stands in no need of the emendation suggested in Mekilta, ed. Friedmann, p. 1a, n. 5, and assumed in H-R, p. 1, n. 11; in fact, the emendation would obscure the meanings of the passages. Here the phrase means "had precedence over the other in the act (or event)" of redemption. Pitted against "unto Moses and Aaron" of Exodus 12:1 are not only the words "Aaron and Moses" of ibid. 6:26, but that entire verse which reads, "These are that Aaron and Moses to whom the Lord said: Bring out (imperative plural) the children of Israel from the land of Egypt according to their hosts." The Rabbis were thus enabled to teach that Moses did not have precedence over Aaron in the act of redemption from Egypt but that both were equally redeemers, and so once again, this time as redeemer, Moses is not placed in a category by himself. Elsewhere the Rabbis designate Miriam, Aaron and Moses, each in turn, as *Go'el,* redeemer (Exod. Rabba XXVI.1), although perhaps not in quite the same sense as here. In any case, our passage, too, contains the same concept (*Go'el*), although here it is not named but imbedded. We ought also to point out that, as is illustrated by the concept of *Go'el,* a rabbinic value concept is usually not limited to one concretization.

B) In like manner . . . "the heaven and the earth" . . . both were created simultaneously.

A paraphrase of *shekulin* (1. 23), but the idea of heaven and earth being "even balanced" is thereby lost. Still, what does the note of evaluation imply? Precedence in the act of creation, which is the thought expressed in *kodem bema'aseh* here (1. 21), is a mark of rank. Earth and heaven are of equal rank. Earth is the abode of man, and the concept stressed, apparently, is man, his rank being no lower, it would seem, than that of the heavenly angels.

C) In like manner . . . "the God of Abraham, the God of Isaac, and the God of Jacob" . . . all three were equal *(shekulin, 1. 27)*.

Jacob is the equal of the other *'Abot,* patriarchs. The concept of Israel is emphasized, for Jacob was the ancestor of Israel alone whereas Abraham and Isaac were the ancestors of other peoples as well as of Israel.

D) In like manner . . . "thy father and thy mother" . . . the one . . . have precedence over the other . . . are equal.

kodem bema'aseh here (1. 29) refers, apparently, to precedence with respect to filial acts or filial behavior. The phrase is integral to the passage despite its absence in the Oxford MS. The concept here is *Kibbud 'Ab Wa-'Em,* honoring father and mother.

E) In like manner . . . "Joshua . . . and Caleb" . . . they were both equal *(shekulin, 1. 34)*.

"Even-balanced," for in the matter of the spies both acted in the same way and at the same time. In that act (*ma'aseh*, 1. 33), neither preceded the other. The concept embodied here is *Zaddik*.

3-4, ll. 35-42

In the Land of Egypt . . . the argument of *Kal va-homer* . . . the divine word . . . outside of the city.

Inference *a minori ad majus* (*kal va-homer*, 1. 38) is a halakic rule of interpretation (see above, p. 22f). What is usually involved is a matter of law, for it is with respect to a law that one thing is *kal*, less weighty, and the other *homer* or *hamur*, weighty, (another example: 25, ll. 36-39). But here no law acts as the standard of measurement whereby *Tefillah*, prayer, is seen to be *kal* and *Dibbur* to be *homer*, nor is the inference a law. Instead, two concepts are compared, and *Dibbur* is declared to be weightier than *Tefillah*. Now in what sense can one concept be measured against another and declared to be weightier? If all value concepts convey significance, and that is their common attribute, then by this particular *kal va-homer* the Rabbis are saying that *Dibbur* is a matter of greater significance, greater worth, than *Tefillah*. In other words, the concept of *Tefillah* is regarded as of a lower rank than the concept of *Dibbur*.

All this demonstrates once more that the concepts of *Dibbur* and *Gilluy Shekinah* are not really compatible with the other value concepts. Integrated organismically, the value complex as a whole exhibits no hierarchical order (above, p. 16f), and therefore no instance in which one concept ranks higher than another. This organismic, non-hierarchical order does admit of an exception, as we can now see, but this exception concerns *Dibbur*, a concept wholly restricted to prophetic experience, to the past. Were concepts which are applied to daily life also placed in a hierarchical relation, those concepts would lose their flexibility and soon cease to function as value concepts.

And why . . . Because it was full of abominations and idols.

There is no hierarchy of value concepts, but there may be hierarchies in the *halakic concretizations* of a specific value concept. The concept of *Ṭum'ah*, levitical impurity, possesses such hierarchies, and in one hierarchy any idol is the original cause of an entire order of levitical impurity (see WE, pp. 231f). Since *Ṭum'ah* is the antithesis of *Ḳedushah*, holiness, the presence of idols in the city made the city unfit for *Dibbur*, *Dibbur* being a manifestation of God, "the Holy One blessed be He." Embodied in this brief statement, therefore, are, besides *Dibbur*, the concepts of *'Abodah Zarah* (idolatry), *Ṭum'ah*, and *Ḳedushah*.

The same condition which made the city unfit for *Dibbur*, the Rabbis imply, made it also unfit for *Tefillah*. This implication is contained in the *ḳal va-ḥomer*, an expression which assumes there is something in common between *Dibbur* and *Tefillah*, but that it is stronger in the case of *Dibbur*. What is that common element? It cannot be the manifestation of God to the physical senses for that is precisely what constitutes the *ḥomer* of *Dibbur*, and it is thus not a characteristic of *Tefillah*. Common to both, however, is the awareness that God is near. In *Dibbur* God's nearness is manifest to the senses but not so in *Tefillah*; in that respect *Tefillah* is certainly the *ḳal*.

Nevertheless, would prayer be possible without an awareness that He is near, that He hearkens? Prayer is a mystical experience yet, unlike *Dibbur* or *Gilluy Shekinah,* of a kind which does not involve visual or auditory sensations. Because it does not involve such phenomena, prayer may well be regarded as *normal* mysticism (ibid., p. 14).

4-5, ll. 42-57

A) Before the land of Israel . . . all lands were suitable for divine revelations (*Dibberot,* l. 43)

Inherently all lands are suitable for *Dibberot* or *Gilluy Shekinah* for the reason that God is everywhere, and hence the scene of His revelation may be any place in the world. "When R. Gamaliel was asked why the Holy One blessed be He revealed Himself in a bush (to Moses), the answer was: To teach you there is no place on earth not occupied [*panuy*] by the *Shekinah,* that is, there is no place on earth where the *Shekinah* cannot reveal itself" (RM, p. 254). The idea expressed in these statements is an example of the emphasis on universalism, one of several emphatic trends in the rabbinic outlook (above, pp. 8, 12f).

B) Before Jerusalem . . . the entire land of Israel was suitable for altars

Not the whole world, but only the land of Israel was fit for altar-building, for that land alone was the Holy Land. No such limitation is placed on nonsacrificial worship of God.

C) Before the Temple (*Bet 'Olamim,* ll. 48, 49)

lit., "the house of worlds," and referring to the idea

that the Temple was to exist also in the world to come (on this earth).

Jerusalem was appropriate for the manifestation of the divine presence *(Shekinah,* l. 49)... eliminated.

The concept is *Gilluy Shekinah,* and the statement refers to the visible manifestation of God. According to several interpretations of Exodus 23:17 and Deuteronomy 16:16 in the tannaitic Midrashim, the pilgrims who went up to the Temple in Jerusalem went up to see God (RM, pp. 239ff). It must be added, though, that the Mishnah rejects that assumption (ibid., pp. 242ff).

In saying that Jerusalem was appropriate for *Gilluy Shekinah* the Rabbis clearly imply that Jerusalem is a holy city. The holiness of Jerusalem is, in fact, reflected in the halakah that certain sacrifices offered in the Temple may be eaten in any part of the city but not beyond it (WE, p. 217). Yet, since the statement concerns *Gilluy Shekinah* it may also contain an implication regarding *Gilluy Shekinah* itself. If all of Jerusalem was inherently appropriate for *Gilluy Shekinah,* then the visible manifestation of God was not inherently limited to one spot.

"For the Lord hath chosen Zion . . . This is My resting place forever" (Ps. 132:13-14).

Verse 14 continues with, "Here will I dwell; for I have desired it." Psalm 132:13 is taken to refer to God's choice of the city of Jerusalem, Zion standing for Jerusalem. "This is My resting place forever" (v. 14) is then interpreted as relating to the Temple—"forever" because it will also exist in the world to come—and about which God further says, "Here will I dwell; for I have desired it."

D) Before Aaron . . . all Israelites were qualified for the priesthood

Inherently, the people of Israel as a whole had priestly status. In accord with this idea is the tradition which insisted that *ḥullin,* ordinary (non-priestly) food, ought to be eaten in levitical purity, a tradition which thus challenged the demarcation between priests and people (WE, p. 222).

E) Before David . . . all Israelites were eligible to the kingship

A kindred idea is expressed in the Halakah. What is permitted to princes on the Sabbath is, according to R. Simeon, also permitted to all Israelites, for "all Israelites are princes" (Shabbat XIV, end). See also ibid. 67a and Baba Meẓi'ah 113b.

5-6, ll. 57-72

A) You could say: "I cite . . . outside of the land."

A logical objection to the idea in ll. 42f and couched in halakic terminology (*dan 'ani,* l. 58). Although the section in ll. 42-57 consists of essentially independent statements (above, p. 19f), those statements are united by a common formula: "Before . . . was chosen . . . after . . . had been chosen . . . were (or, was) eliminated." That formula integrates the statements into a single literary entity. The objection here raised to the conclusion of the first statement could not be raised before without breaking up that entity.

True, . . . only because of the merit of the fathers (*bi-Zekut 'Abot*, l. 60).

Zekut 'Abot is a subconcept of God's justice, connoting that God rewards children for the good deeds of their fathers. Reflected in this concept is the view that fathers and sons constitute a single personality, a corporate personality. For Abraham's kindness to the angels, for example, God rewards the children of Israel measure for measure (184, ll. 193ff), and yet the word *lo,* "to him," (l. 194) implies that the reward was given "to him," that is, to Abraham. The answer to the objection raised, then, is that because of *Zekut 'Abot* God made several exceptions in which He did speak to prophets outside of the land of Israel. But the proof-text given (Jer. 31:15f) is rather elliptical; it apparently takes for granted an idea not given here. See H-R, p. 3, n. 1.

Underlying the notion of corporate personality is the indubitable fact that society and the individual cannot be set up one against the other; as Whitehead has put it, "The individual is formative of the society, the society is formative of the individual" (A. N. Whitehead, *Religion in the Making* [New York, 1926], p. 257). Concepts like *Zekut 'Abot* reflect the factor of society. On the other hand, the factor of the individual is likewise reflected in rabbinic concepts, so much so that it has the character of an emphatic trend. Emphasis on the individual informs not only concepts like Israel and *Goy* (above, pp. 9ff) but ethical concepts like *Zedakah,* charity, and *Gemilut Hasadim,* deeds of lovingkindness (WE, p. 21). *Zekut 'Abot* is a subconcept of God's justice, but of God's justice itself we are told that God "judges the sons of men, each one according to his ways, and pays to every man according to his deeds" (TE, p. 166, and see the pages following there).

B) Some say . . . near water,

"and because of the merit of the fathers" is not found in the Oxford MṠ, which is the most reliable; this clause, then, is probably an interpolation. Exceptions to the rule regarding *Gilluy Shekinah* or *Dibbur* are sufficiently accounted for by "a pure spot" as the scene of the revelation. "Some say" is another instance of halakic terminology. See, for example, Tamid III.8; Middot II.3.

as it is said, "And I was by the stream Ulai" (Dan. 8:2).

It is assumed here that Daniel was a prophet. There are two traditions concerning Daniel. According to one, he was a prophet; according to another, he was not. See RM, p. 251n.

C) Some say: He had already spoken with him in the land . . . 'and came' . . . the land.

Ezekiel is taken account of in this opinion but not Daniel. According to this opinion, apparently, Daniel was not a prophet, and the communications to him, being indirect, were not instances of *Dibbur*.

D) R. Eleazar . . . says . . . the plain was suitable for divine revelation.

Although the scene of the *Dibbur* on this occasion was not near water, it was in "the plain," outside the city, and thus not in the proximity of idols (cf. ll. 40f).

6-8, ll. 72-88

You can learn from the following . . . outside of the land.

This statement introduces a passage which, like the preceding one, goes back to the idea in ll. 42f, but now, in proof of that idea, namely—that *Dibbur* or *Gilluy She-kinah* does not take place outside of the land of Israel. The passages in ll. 42-44 (a), 57-72 (b), and 72-88 (c) are thus segments of a logical entity: (a) states that *Dibbur* does not take place outside of the land of Israel; (b) accounts for the exceptions; and (c) goes back to prove (a), and hence to confirm (b). Logical thought of that kind being characteristic of Halakah rather than of Haggadah, requires halakic terminology and so these passages too, though consisting of Haggadah, must employ that terminology. But from 8, l. 88 to 11, l. 113, as we shall see, the connecting principle is once more that of an association of ideas just as it is in the case of the passages from 3, l. 35 to 5, l. 57, passages which include ll. 42-44 (a). Since they are connected, all the passages from 3, l. 35 to 11, l. 113 constitute a unified midrashic composition. Although several segments in that composition possess a logical coherence, the composition as a whole, including the first segment of the logical entity, is unified not as a result of logical thought but as the result of an association of ideas.

It is said: "But Jonah rose up to flee unto Tarshish from the presence of the Lord" (Jonah 1:3) . . . "There is no darkness, nor shadow of death, where the workers of iniquity may hide themeslves" (Job 34:22).

God's omnipresence and omnipotence as depicted in biblical verses—Psalm 139:7ff, Zechariah 4:10, Proverbs 15:3, Amos 9:2-4, Job 34:22—make it impossible to assume, according to the Rabbis, that Jonah attempted to flee, literally, from God's presence.

But Jonah thought: I will go outside of the land, where the *Shekinah* does not reveal itself.

"From the presence of the Lord" (Jonah 1:3) means, accordingly, from God's revelation or manifestation in *Dibbur,* and not actually from God's presence. (That this interpretation does not contradict the idea of God's omnipotence is shown in the sequel.) As thus interpreted, Jonah 1:3 is now adduced as evidence from Scripture for the statement in ll. 42-44, the only statement in that section which did not include a proof-text from the Bible. Because Jonah 1:2 does not contain a warning of destruction such as is found in ibid. 3:4, the Rabbis evidently take it to be a call rather than the communication to Nineveh. Compare Ḳimḥi on this verse.

For since the Gentiles are more inclined to repent . . . condemned.

Teshubah (l. 81), repentance, is a concept informed by the emphasis on universality; not only does God desire the repentance of all men—of the Gentiles as well as of Israel—but the Rabbis even teach that on this occasion the Gentiles, not Israel, were close to repentance. However, the emphatic trends, among which is the emphasis on universality, are not the sole type of emphasis possible in rabbinic thought. Characteristic of rabbinic thought is also the type of emphasis that permits one concept to be stressed above other concepts. Here, in the motive attributed to Jonah, the concept of Israel is stressed above all the other concepts involved. (On the concepts embodied here, see above, p. 19.)

They give a parable . . . "But the Lord hurled a great wind into the sea" (Jonah 1:4).

The parable is not simply a restatement of Jonah's predicament. It teaches that God told Jonah He has other agents and that they would cause Jonah to return to the land of Israel. When was he told this? When "the Lord hurled a great wind into the sea." We may generalize and say that a parable always adds a factor not made explicit in the narrative or the teaching. See also below, p. 252. God may employ an agent, as when He "hurled a great wind into the sea" so that, in the end, Jonah was once more in the land where he might receive the *Dibbur* he had endeavored to avoid. God's omnipotence brought about the circumstances for the revelation of the *Dibbur*.

Although employed frequently enough by the Rabbis, the ideas of God's omnipresence, God's omnipotence, God's omniscience and the like are not represented by conceptual terms in rabbinic literature. Such ideas are therefore not rabbinic value concepts, since a rabbinic value concept is always crystallized in a conceptual term (above, p. 6). How, then, are these ideas employed? They are auxiliary ideas, ideas that allow a value concept to stand out more clearly or that make it possible for a value concept to be concretized (see RM, pp. 53f, 220f). In this interpretation of Jonah 1:3-4, it is God's omnipotence which delivers Jonah to a place appropriate for the revelation of the *Dibbur*. The idea of God's omni-

presence plays a role in the rabbinic interpretation of
Jonah 1:3, but the entire purpose of that interpretation
is to provide a text proving that the *Dibbur* is not revealed outside of the land of Israel; the idea of God's
omnipresence is an auxiliary idea in an interpretation
whereby Jonah 1:3 becomes a text embodying the concept of *Dibbur*.

8-10, ll. 88-103

A) Thus you find that there were three types of prophets.

This section on the respective attitudes of the three
prophets is connected with the preceding section through
an association of ideas. Jonah's attitude, a theme of the
preceding section, is now one of the attitudes evaluated.

One . . . the Father . . . the son . . . Father.

In these figures of God as the Father and Israel as the
son there is an emphasis on God's love. (The emphasis
on love is one of the emphatic trends [above, pp. 8, 11]).
By using these figures the passage hints that the Father
will disapprove of a harsh attitude toward Israel, the son.

B) Jeremiah . . . "We have transgressed and re-belled; Thou hast not pardoned" (Lam. 3:42).

In this interpretation of Lamentations 3:42, when
Jeremiah says, "We have transgressed and rebelled," he
is saying that God's punishment was deserved, but when
he says, "Thou hast not pardoned," he is taking Israel's
part, for the words may imply that God ought to have pardoned. The verse is Jeremiah's own lament (see note 11
in text) and is not a prophetic utterance. Similarly, the

attitudes ascribed to Elijah and Jonah are not contained in prophecies but represent, according to the Rabbis, those prophets' personal reactions.

Therefore his prophecy *(Nebu'ato,* l. 93) was doubled . . . (Jer. 36:32).

The term *Nebu'ah* refers to the speeches of a prophet whereas the term *Dibbur* refers to a communication by God, a communication which may consist of a commandment, a law (see above, p. 38f). Every conceptual term has its own distinctive connotation. "However closely related certain concepts may be, the very fact that they are represented by different conceptual terms is an indication that they are to be distinguished from one another" (RM, pp. 39ff.).

C) Elijah . . . "I have been very jealous for the Lord, the God of Hosts" (I Kings 19:10).

As is indicated in וגו׳ (l. 96), the rest of the verse, too, is relevant—"for the children of Israel have forsaken Thy covenant, thrown down Thine altars, and slain Thy prophets with the sword; and I, even I only, am left; and they seek my life, to take it away." The entire verse is not prophecy but Elijah's own words, his own personal attitude, and in what he says about Israel he exhibits, according to this interpretation, no regard for "the honor due the son."

And thereupon . . . I am not pleased with your prophesying.

Rather, I do not want your prophesying. Because of Elijah's present attitude toward Israel, and not because

Elijah's prophecies displeased God, He now dismisses him as prophet. A turn is given here to the expression "in thy room" (I Kings 19:16) which hardly comports with its biblical meaning. In this rabbinic interpretation, so strong is the emphasis on God's love and on Israel that Elijah's later ascension is taken as evidence of dismissal!

D) Jonah . . . "But Jonah rose up to flee unto Tarshish from the presence of the Lord" (Jonah 1:3).

Assumed here is the interpretation of this verse in ll. 79-81 in which Jonah's motive for fleeing was his concern for "the honor due the son."

What is written . . . He spoke with him a second time but did not speak with him a third time.

It is not unlikely that "a second time" is Jonah's meed for his positive attitude toward Israel. Apparently Jonah's attitude did not merit, as did Elijah's, his immediate dismissal as prophet; once more the emphasis is on the concept of Israel.

10-11, ll. 103-113

A) R. Nathan says: Jonah made his voyage only to drown himself in the sea . . . "And he said . . . the sea" (Jonah 1:12).

As the next statement indicates—"and so you (also) find"—Jonah's act illustrates the proposition given there that "the patriarchs and the prophets offered their lives in behalf of Israel." Jonah wanted to drown himself, then, out of concern for Israel, his concern evidently being, as in ll. 79-81, lest he "cause Israel to be condemned." But the motive ascribed to Jonah by R. Nathan is similar only in part to the one in ll. 79-81. Here Jonah 1:3 is not established as the proof-text for the idea that *Dibbur* does not take place outside the land of Israel; that idea is not even mentioned. R. Nathan's statement is connected with ll. 79-81, therefore, only through an association of ideas.

B) As to Moses . . . "And . . . my wretchedness" (Num. 11:15).

Elsewhere Moses is designated as one of the patriarchs (see RM, p. 38, n. 8), and it is possible that he is so regarded here too. In that case, the instance of Jonah is taken as representative of the prophets.

C) As to David . . . "And . . . father's house" (II Sam. 24:17).

See also RM, loc. cit.

D) Thus you find everywhere . . . in behalf of Israel.

Proofs given are not from "everywhere" but only from several specific instances, yet there is no need to give more. Described here is a character held to be common to both patriarchs and prophets, and the instances adduced suffice to establish that contention. By the same token, with respect to that character, the patriarchs and the prophets thus constitute a single category, which is to say that what is true of the part is true of the whole.

II, ll. 114-125

A) Saying.

Literally, "to say." This is the last word in Exodus 12:1. Presented thus far were comments on the preceding words of that verse together with various statements related to those comments through an association of ideas.

This means, go out and tell it to them immediately . . . R. Ishmael . . . "And . . . commanded" (Exod. 34:34).

"To say," according to R. Ishmael, means "go out and say to them," to Israel; that is the entire purpose of the *Dibbur,* to be carried out "immediately." Proof for this interpretation is brought from Moses' general procedure. Exodus 34:34 is adduced to indicate that Moses always "went out and spoke unto the children of Israel that which he was commanded."

B) R. Eliezer . . . go out and tell it to them, and bring Me back word . . . "And . . . the Lord" (ibid. 19:8).

According to R. Eliezer, "to say" has a dual meaning: one which agrees with R. Ishmael's interpretation, and another in which "to say" means to say to God, to bring back word to God. Proof for this additional meaning is ibid. 19:8—"And Moses reported the words of the people unto the Lord"; this verse, too, as interpreted in a later section of the Mekilta, has reference to a general procedure of Moses. The comment on the verse there (II, 207 and see also H-R, pp. 209-10) is as follows: "And was there any need for Moses to report? Scripture merely wishes you to learn proper manners (*Derek 'Erez*) from Moses. He did not say: Since He Who sent me knows anyhow there is no need for me to report back." Good manners demand that an agent report back to the one who sent him, and Moses followed this procedure even when it was God Who sent him. "To say" means, therefore, not only to say or tell God's commands to the people but also to say, to report back, to God. Whereas the first meaning emphasizes Israel, the additional meaning emphasizes *Derek 'Erez*.

The concept of *Derek 'Erez* (literally, "the way of the world") possesses a number of aspects or phases and is used by the Rabbis in the same sense as we use the word "ethics" (see WE, pp. 39ff.). One of the phases of *Derek 'Erez* consists of good manners (ibid., pp. 41f). See also below, p. 85f.

C) And again it says . . . (Ezek. 9:11).

Another instance of an agent reporting back to God.

D) And again it says . . . (Job 38:35). Thy messengers are not like the messengers of human beings . . . whithersoever they go they are in Thy presence and can report . . . (Jer. 23:24).

As is evident from the manner in which this passage is introduced ("And again it says"), it presents still another instance of agents reporting back to God. True, the passage is largely taken up with the idea of God's omnipresence, yet this idea is only incidental to the purpose which the passage serves here, namely, to give further proof that His agents report back to God. Embodied in the passage is the value concept of *Derek 'Erez,* the same concept which is embodied in the two preceding examples or proofs. Since it does not possess a conceptual term in rabbinic thought the idea of God's omnipresence is not a rabbinic value concept but an auxiliary idea enlarging the scope of a value concept (above, p. 51).

11-13, ll. 125-135

R. Josiah says:

This section is connected with the preceding one through an association of ideas. R. Josiah's teaching is a modification of R. Eliezer's teaching that God's agents report back to Him, but a modification which brings into play additional concepts, among them those of God's love and Israel.

When God issues decrees (*Gezerot*, l. 126) concerning Israel,

For another aspect of the concept of *Gezerot* see WE, pp. 210ff.

if they be beneficent their execution is reported back to Him, but if they be for evil it is not

The concept of *Middat Raḥamim,* God's love, is embodied here. It is only of benefits for Israel that God wants to hear, so to speak.

For thus . . . "And, behold, the man clothed in linen . . . all that Thou hast commanded me" (ibid. v. 11).

The full context of this verse takes in almost the entire chapter, and here it is the full context which is interpreted; in the preceding section this verse alone (v. 11) was employed. Modification of the idea of the preceding section thus involves using a verse employed there but in such fashion as also to include its context.

13-15, ll. 135-166

A) Simon the son of Azzai says: *Saying* means:

After an "interruption" consisting of R. Josiah's teaching, the Mekilta resumes the interpretation of "saying," offering now more comments on that word.

Teach in the same manner (*be-ḳol*, l. 136; lit., in the voice) in which you hear.

Moses is told by God to teach Israel in the same tone of voice as that in which he had heard the instruction. (On that idea see the more explicit statement in II, 223.) A factor of importance in oral teaching is the tone of voice in which the instruction is given. The concept here is *Talmud Torah,* study of Torah.

B) R. Akiba . . . Go and say to them; since it was only for their sake

Rather, because of their merit, *Zekutam* (l. 137).

For during all the thirty-eight years . . . He did not speak with Moses,

During the thirty-eight years when Israel had no *Zekut* God did not speak to Moses. R. Ishmael (l. 114), R. Eliezer (l. 116) and now R. 'Aḳiba agree in interpreting "saying" as meaning "say to Israel," but R. 'Aḳiba, by adding the concept of *Zekut* makes the emphasis on Israel even stronger. According to R. 'Aḳiba, were it not for Israel the *Dibbur* would never have come to Moses.

as it is said: "So . . . the Lord spoke unto me, saying"

"saying" is interpreted here too as "say to Israel." Now that the generation without *Zekut* had passed away, the *Dibbur* came again to Moses, and, as always, only because of Israel, "to say to Israel."

C) Said (R.) Simon the son of Azzai . . . but merely adding to his words.

In "adding to his (R. 'Aḳiba's) words," Simeon ben 'Azzai assents to R. 'Aḳiba's interpretation of "saying" despite having already given a different interpretation of that word; indeed, in the sequel his interpretation of "saying" in Ezekiel 3:16 is the same as R. 'Aḳiba's here. This does not mean that he surrenders his own interpretation here but that he entertains both. "In Halakah, a text cannot bear more than one halakic interpretation for the same authority" (RM, p. 129). Such is not the case in Haggadah. "Since each haggadic interpretation is an independent entity (see also above, p. 19), there can be no demand for consistency in the interpretation of Scripture. The same individual may offer more than one interpretation of a verse" (RM, p. 72 and the examples there).

Ben 'Azzai's prefatory statement also occurs twice, and in precisely the same words, in Sifra, Nedabah, Chapter II, ed. I. H. Weiss (Vienna, 1862), p. 4a-b. In the earliest MS of the Sifra, which Louis Finkelstein describes as "the oldest Rabbinic manuscript in existence (aside from fragments deriving from the Cairo Genizah)" the title "Rabbi" does not precede the words "Simeon ben 'Azzai"—see Sifra. According to Codex Assemani LXVI, with a Hebrew Introduction by Louis Finkelstein (New York, 1956), p. 9, and the Hebrew Introduction, pp. 1, 18f, and the quotation on p. 20 there. Ben 'Azzai was never ordained, and hence did not have the title "Rabbi" (W. Bacher, Agadot ha-Tannaim, Hebrew trans., II, 2nd ed. [Berlin, 1925], p. 124, n. 4).

It was not . . . but with all the other prophets, likewise, He spoke only because of Israel,

Rather, again, because of the merit—*Zekut* (l. 144), and see H-R, p. 5—of Israel. Were it not for Israel's *Zekut* there would have been no prophecy. Proof is given from the instances of Ezekiel and Jeremiah.

for . . . it is also written: "And . . . the word of the Lord came unto me, saying" (Ezek. 3:15-16).

"saying" means, once more, "say to Israel"; this is proof that the *Dibbur* came to Ezekiel only because of the merit of Israel. See notes 18 and 19.

D) You will also find it so in the case of Baruch the son of Neriah . . . before God.

In the case of Baruch, the point is made that if there is "no flock, what need is there for a shepherd," (ll. 162-3), but nothing is said about *Zekut*. The existence of the people is obviously a *sine qua non*.

"Thou didst say . . . pain" (Jer. 45:3)—"I have been treated differently from

Rather, [Wherein] have I been different from. See the text in H-R, p. 5, and notice the same phrase here in l. 153. Compare the similar use of the phrase in Pesaḥim X.4: "Wherein is this night different from" etc.

other disciples (*Talmide*, l. 150) of the prophets.

Talmid in the sense of disciple is rabbinic usage; in the Bible the word occurs only in I Chronicles 25:8 where it means "a learner," one who is acquiring an art. As used in early tannaitic literature, *"Ḥakam* was the designation for the ordained scholar fully empowered to decide on all questions of law, whereas *Talmid Ḥakam* referred to the student who was permitted only to answer questions on the sections he had been taught" (RM, pp. 43f and the notes there). Qualifications for the student are not only technical but include ethical qualities ('Abot VI.6, and compare OT, pp. 46f). Analogous qualifications are implied in the term *Talmide ha-Nebi'im* (1. 150), the disciples of the prophets, and apparently Baruch is asking in what respect he failed to measure up to such qualifications.

Joshua ministered *(shimmesh,* l. 151) to Moses,

shimmesh refers to a disciple's attendance on the scholar, the final stage of training (OT, p. 62, and see L. Ginzberg, Meḳomah shel ha-Halakah, Jerusalem 5691, pp. 16, 38f). The analogy to the *Talmid Ḥakam* holds here as well.

and the Holy Spirit *(Ruaḥ ha-Ḳodesh,* l. 151) rested upon him.

Ruaḥ ha-Ḳodesh, Dibbur, and *Nebu'ah* are used interchangeably in this passage. The word *nidbar* in l. 144 relates to *Dibbur,* here the word used is *Ruaḥ ha-Ḳodesh,* and in l. 154 the expression used is *Nebu'ah.* Now each of these concepts has its own individual character, as do all rabbinic value concepts; *Nebu'ah,* prophecy, differs from *Dibbur* (above, p. 53), and *Ruaḥ ha-Ḳodesh* is a

term used in a number of ways (see RM, p. 251, n.
126). However, since all of them refer to divine communication they may sometimes, as in this passage, be
used interchangeably. Such concepts are overlapping concepts (ibid., p. 29).

**"I am weary . . . no rest" (ibid.). "Rest" here is but
a designation for (the spirit of) prophecy . . . (Isa.
11:2).**

Baruch's words, in their literal sense, are the words
of a man depressed not only by the prophecies of doom
he had written "in a book at the mouth of Jeremiah"
(Jer. 45:1, and cf. ibid. 36:1-8) but also, and perhaps
especially, by the vicissitudes in his own life—"I find no
rest." In the rabbinic interpretation the circumstantial
character of the verse is ignored and everything is pitched
in a different key; Baruch's distress is ascribed to his
failure, despite all his longing, to achieve prophecy. The
interchangeable terms in this passage indicate that this
longing for *Nebu'ah* is a longing for the experience of
Dibbur and for that of *Ruah ha-Kodesh,* that is to say,
for the experience of divine communication.

**Now, notice . . . "Thus . . . and seekest thou great
things . . . not" (Jer. 45:4-5). "Great things" here
is but a designation for (the spirit of) prophecy,**

Here, too, the rabbinic interpretation is pitched in a
different key from that of the literal meaning. Taken
literally, the words "And seekest thou great things for
thyself" (ibid.) reveal that Baruch simply desired prefer-
ment, high position (see A. B. Ehrlich, Mikra ki-Phe-
shuto, III [Berlin, 1901], p. 269).

as it is said: "Tell me . . . all the great things that
Elisha hath done" (II Kings 8:4). And again it says:
"Call unto Me, and I will answer thee, and will tell
thee great things . . ." (Jer. 33:3).

The two verses are quoted to prove that the expression
"great things" refers to prophecy. II Kings 8:4, however, is another instance in which the rabbinic interpretation of a verse is pitched in a different key from that
of its literal meaning, the rabbinic interpretation being
concerned with prophecy itself and the literal meaning
only with deeds done by a prophet. "Great things that
Elisha hath done" are made specific in their literal
sense when Gehazi tells how Elisha "had restored to life
him that was dead" (II Kings 8:5). Ignoring the latter
verse, ignoring even the phrase "that Elisha had done"
which qualifies "great things," the rabbinic interpretation
thus minimizes the deed done, and instead, teaches that
"great things" stands for *Nebu'ah,* divine communication.
Brought in to corroborate that interpretation is Jeremiah
33:3—"Call unto Me, and I will answer thee, and will
tell thee great things."

"Baruch son of Neriah! There is no vineyard, what
need is there of a fence . . . what need is there of a
shepherd?" Why? . . . (Jer. 45:5).

It is through no fault of his, Baruch is told here, that
he failed to achieve prophecy. In order to be a prophet
in Israel there is a *conditio sine qua non,* namely, the
people of Israel.

*

15-16, ll. 1-12

A) This New Moon (*ha-ḥodesh ha-zeh*) Shall be unto You.

The biblical meaning of *ha-ḥodesh ha-zeh* (l. 1) is "this month," but the translation properly renders *ḥodesh* as "new moon" here, since the interpretations to follow hinge on this rabbinic usage of the word. In 16, l. 13 the biblical usage is retained, for the Rabbis themselves often employ the word in the sense of "month," as in l. 3 of this passage.

R. Ishmael says: Moses showed the new moon to Israel and said unto them: In this manner . . . by it.

The concept embodied, besides Israel, is *Talmud Torah,* study of Torah, for, according to R. Ishmael, the verse tells of how Moses taught a halakah to Israel. In order to demonstrate how the beginning of a month is always to be established, he pointed to the new moon, saying as he did so: *ha-ḥodesh ha-zeh,* "this new moon"; by this direct teaching method Moses overcame the difficulty of a verbal description of the details of the first appearance of the new moon (see "Integration of Halakah and Haggadah," above, p. 27f).

R. Ishmael's interpretation is consistent with his interpretation that "saying" in Exodus 12:1 means that Moses is to go out and teach them (Israel) "immediately": the very next verse (ibid. v. 2), in R. Ishmael's view, depicts Moses teaching a law to Israel.

B) R. Akiba says: This is one of the three things which were difficult for Moses to understand and all of which God pointed out to him with His finger . . . (Exod. 29:36).

כולן (l. 5), "all of which," is undoubtedly a scribal error for כאלו, "as if" (as if with His finger), as is evident from the related sources. See H-R, p. 6, n. 13. Like R. Ishmael, R. 'Aḳiba, too, says that *ha-ḥodesh ha-zeh*, "this new moon," refers to teaching the halakah concerning the new moon by the direct method, but in his interpretation it is Moses who is being taught by God, not Israel, by Moses. Nor is R. 'Aḳiba inconsistent here with his interpretation of "saying," in Exodus 12:1, an interpretation so similar to that of R. Ishmael (see above, p. 59), for unlike R. Ishmael, R. 'Aḳiba does not take "saying" to mean "immediately," as well. He can therefore maintain that God first taught the halakah to Moses.

C) R. Simon the son of Yoḥai says . . . He spoke to Moses only in the daytime . . . after nightfall.

According to a tannaitic tradition, the *Dibberot* to Moses occurred only by day (Sifra, ed. Weiss, 40c, and see also the other references in H-R, p. 6, n. 16).

**

18-19, ll. 35-42

Shall be unto You. Adam (lit., *'Adam ha-Rishon*, the first man, l. 35) did not reckon by it.

Adam is usually called *'Adam ha-Rishon* in rabbinic literature. On the implication of this use of the concept "man" in place of the name, see above, p. 12f.

"By it"—*bo* (l. 35)—refers to the month, that is to Nisan. *bo* can relate only to *ha-ḥodesh ha-zeh,* and to the way those words are interpreted by the last rabbinic comment on them. That comment reads: *"ha-ḥodesh ha-zeh.* This means Nisan" (16, l. 13). If "unto you" excludes Adam, then for Adam Nisan was not the first month. Up to the Exodus from Egypt (see S. Lieberman, Tosefta Ki-Fshuṭah, V, p. 1018, and the quotation from Naḥmanides there) not Nisan but Tishri was regarded as the first month. So far as counting by years is concerned, Israel retained this original manner of reckoning, but now they are commanded to use an additional way in which Nisan, the month of redemption from Egypt, becomes "the beginning of months." This new manner of reckoning is informed by the concept of *Ge'ullah,* redemption. Incidentally, the concept of redemption, as is evident in this instance, does not connote redemption from sin but from servitude.

You say . . . unto you, and not unto the Gentiles (*la-Goyim,* l. 37).

On the concept of *Goyim,* Gentiles, and its relation to its biblical antecedent, see above, p. 10. The word *'amur* in l. 37, incorrectly translated here and in l. 38 by "is commanded," is a dittography affected by *'amur* in l. 38. It is deleted here (l. 37) by Elijah Gaon (see his note ad. loc. in ed. Malbim) and by Friedmann, 3a, n. 17, and is omitted here in H-R, p. 7. The rendering of the next sentence ought to be as follows:

When it says: "It shall be the first month of the year *to you,*" [the teaching] to you and not to the Gentiles is there referred to (*'amur,* l. 38).

On 52, l. 8 *'amur* is correctly translated. To the Gentiles Nisan is not the first month of the year, nor is Tishri, nor is any lunar month, for the Gentiles do not reckon their months by the moon. It is this second "unto you" which excludes the Gentiles. (On a version which transposes the two interpretations of "unto you," and which Friedmann is inclined to favor, see ed. Friedmann, p. 106a, the reference to n. 17.)

Hence the expression "unto you" used here (i. e., the first "unto you") must aim to teach you that Adam did not reckon by it.

Making of Nisan the first month of the year is, then, a departure from the original mode of reckoning. This additional mode of reckoning serves to remind Israel of the *Ge'ullah,* the redemption from Egypt.

We thus learn that Israel reckons by the moon and that the Gentiles reckon by the sun.

The months of the year may be either lunar months or else divisions of the sun year; since the Gentiles do not reckon by the moon, they reckon by the sun. But Israel always reckons by the moon, no matter which month is "the first month," Tishri or Nisan. Reckoning by the moon provides situations for a religious experience, as the next rabbinic comment indicates.

And the Israelites are not content . . . but once every thirty days they lift up their eyes to their Father in heaven.

The occasion for this act is given in n. 7, but the phrase there should read: "Blessing of the New Moon," meaning the blessing or *Berakah* referring to the new moon. Objects or phenomena are not blessed, but may be *occasions* for saying a *Berakah*.

Described in the statement of the Mekilta is the deliberate cultivation, through a physical act, of a profound inward experience, more specifically, the cultivation of an acute awareness of God's near presence through a physical orientation. The act is one of *Kawwanah* but of a singular type. *Kawwanah* in saying the *Tefillah* or reciting the *Shema'*, both of them forms of worship, is likewise the cultivation of an inward experience, but there *Kawwanah* consists of concentration on the idea contained in the *Tefillah* or the *Shema'* (see WE, pp. 185ff.), an entirely different matter. No ideas at all are involved in an acute awareness of God's near presence resulting from an act of orientation; there is only sheer experience of God, for the moment unconceptualized and hence not communicable. (See the discussion of other instances of *Kawwanah* of this type, ibid., pp. 192ff.) However, such an experience is indeed momentary, and always passes into a communicable experience, one that is mediated by concepts. In this case, what begins as an incommunicable experience leads directly to an awareness of God's love as expressed in the *Berakah* on the new moon. Incommunicable mysticism leads directly into normal mysticism (on normal mysticism, see above, p. 44, and the lengthy discussion in RM, pp. 194ff.).

19, ll. 42-50

And (so) when the sun is eclipsed, it is a bad omen for the Gentiles since they reckon by the sun . . . R. Meir says: If the sun is eclipsed in the east . . . R. Josiah says: If the planets are eclipsed in the east . . . inhabitants of the west.

This passage on astrology basically contradicts the entire rabbinic outlook in which the world is governed by God alone, *Malkut Shamayim,* and where anything that happens is in accordance with *Middat Raḥamim,* God's love, and *Middat ha-Din,* God's justice. Lieberman cites sources which do express the rabbinic outlook, and which forbid astrology and divination by stars and other means (Greek in Jewish Palestine [New York, 1942], p. 97f). But, as he points out, "To deny at that time the efficacy of Astrology would mean to deny a well established fact, to discredit a 'science' accepted by both Hellenes and Barbarians" (ibid., p. 98), and hence such passages as the one here and its parallels.

Analogues carried out the idea of the eclipse as an omen, *siman.* The word for "eclipsed" is *lokah,* smitten, and the idea of suffering is thus conveyed by the word for the phenomenon itself. Where will the suffering take place? The general location is supplied by another analogue—in the east, if the eclipse is in the east; in the west, if it is in the west.

This passage is inherently an independent entity. It is connected with the preceding passage solely through an association of ideas, namely, the idea that Israel reckons by the moon and the Gentiles, by the sun; obviously, the astrological ideas have no logical connection with the idea that Israel lift up their eyes every thirty days to their Father in heaven. The word "so" in the first line of the translation does not refer to anything in the text, and is therefore gratuitous.

R. Jonathan says: All these signs may be left to the Gentiles . . . (Jer. 10:2.)

Lieberman describes this statement as a compromise "between the power of Astrology and the proper Jewish attitude to it" (ibid., p. 99).

** and *

22-23, ll. 1-14

A) Speak Ye . . . Did actually both of them speak? . . . the Holy One.

The answer here does not refer to the question, and the original text cannot be restored. See H-R, p. 9, n. 9. This entire passage is not free of textual difficulties.

B) R. Aḥai the son of R. Josiah says . . . so that the word went forth from among them as if both of them were speaking.

As used here (l. 10) and in the next statement, *dibbur* (l. 13) refers to the words of Moses, although usually *Dibbur* is the communication of God to a prophet. Since Eleazar and Ithamar are named here and not the older brothers, Nadab and Abihu, the text apparently assumes that the latter had died; yet that occurred later in the wilderness, not in Egypt (Lev. 10:1-2). H-R, p. 9, n. 11, cites Malbim who regards this statement as an interpretation of Leviticus 11:1-2, and the next statement as an interpretation of ibid. 15:1-2.

C) R. Simon the son of Yoḥai says: Moses would show respect to Aaron, saying to him, "Teach me," and Aaron showed respect to Moses, saying to him, "Teach me" . . . speaking.

Aaron was as capable, or as fit, as Moses to impart

the divine communication, an idea similar to the one in
1, ll. 6f. Here, however, there is also a further implication. "Teach me" implies that even for Aaron or Moses
who heard the divine communication directly, the sheer
repetition by either would still mean that he was teaching
the other. That idea, though in a reverse manner, reflects
something the Rabbis themselves experienced. A man ac-
quires Torah through the medium of a human being, a
teacher, but another experience may take place as well.
The proper study of Torah, *Talmud Torah,* requires that
such instruction result in an experience akin to that of
hearing the laws from God here and now. See WE, p. 86.

** and *

33, ll. 1-14

**And Ye Shall Keep It . . . Why . . . the purchase
of the pascal lamb . . . four days before its slaughter?**

There are two answers to this question, one by R.
Matia and one by R. Eliezer ha-Ḳappar. Each answer
contains a different haggadic reason for the same halakah
(see "Integration of Halakah and Haggadah," above,
p. 26).

**R. Matia . . . "thy time was the time of love" (Ezek.
16:8). This means, the time has arrived for the
fulfillment of the oath which the Holy One blessed
be He had sworn unto Abraham our father to deliver (redeem) his children.**

"The time of love" is taken as the time of lovers
(*dodim,* l. 4), the lovers being God and Abraham. The

concepts here are God's love, *'Abot,* patriarchs, and *Ge'ullah,* redemption.

But as yet . . . the duty of the paschal lamb and the duty of circumcision.

These two *Miẓwot* (l. 8) are thus joined since only the circumcised could partake of the paschal lamb (127-8, ll. 131-4). On the concept of *Miẓwot,* see above, p. 13.

For thus . . . "And when I passed by thee, and saw thee wallowing in thy blood, I said unto thee: In thy blood live" (Ezek. 16:6).

See Lauterbach's note. But the verse repeats the words "in thy blood live," and it is in this mention of blood twice that the midrash sees a reference to "two bloods" —that of the paschal lamb and that of circumcision— as does Targum Jonathan and as is the case in Canticles R. I.38. Lauterbach's view accords with a view in Pirke R. Eliezer, Chap. XXIX, ed. Warsaw, p. 65a (and see Luria ad loc.). The *Miẓwah* of circumcision was observed on the night of the Exodus from Egypt and hence both *Miẓwot* were carried out on the same day (ibid., 65a, top; and comp. Rashi on Exod. 12:6). All this the midrash draws forth from Ezekiel 16:6. By analogy with *we-'abarti* ("I will go through"—Exod. 12:12), *wa-'e'ebor* ("when I passed by") of Ezekiel 16:6 is taken to refer to the night of the Exodus, and the rest of that verse, to God's seeing the blood of circumcision and of the paschal lamb and protecting the Israelites as He "passed through" on that night. (In R. Matia's interpretation, there is a correspondence between the entire

verse and Exodus 12:12-13.) Failure to recognize that
the verse acts as the channel for the ideas in the midrash
results in the failure to recognize the ideas the midrash
conveys, and that is illustrated in a comment by Friedmann. In his edition, p. 5b, n. 10, he states that according to R. Matia, the circumcision took place on the
tenth of the month so as to allow a four days' interval
for healing.

**For this reason Scripture required that the purchase
of the paschal lamb take place four days before its
slaughter.**

The paschal lamb and the daily communal sacrifices
had to be examined four days before being slaughtered
(39, ll. 78f, and parallels) so as to determine whether
the animals were free from blemishes; if the Israelites
in Egypt were properly to observe the *Mizwah* of the
paschal lamb, the animals had to be in their possession,
then, four days before the fourteenth of the month. A
halakic matter, that of examining the paschal lamb four
days prior to slaughter, is here placed in the framework
of a haggadic idea, namely, that Israel had to perform
Mizwot in order to be worthy of redemption. See also
ed. Weiss, p. 6a, note.

For one cannot obtain reward except for deeds.

Embodied in this statement are the concepts of *Middat ha-Din,* God's justice, and *Mizwot,* deeds. Yet the
very giving of the two *Mizwot* (circumcision and the
paschal lamb) embodies also another concept—*Middat
Rahamim,* God's love.

34-38, ll. 14-55

R. Eliezer ha-Kappar says: Did not Israel possess four virtues—*Miẓwot* (l. 15) . . . language.

R. Eliezer disagrees with R. Matia who said that Israel needed to be *given Miẓwot* to perform in order to be redeemed; on the contrary, says R. Eliezer, they performed *Miẓwot* of their own accord, and of such character that "nothing in the whole world is more worthy." What is translated as "chastity" is the negative value concept of *'Arayot* (l. 16) and tale bearing is, likewise, another negative value concept, *Lashon ha-Ra'* (l. 17), "the evil tongue" (on negative value concepts see WE, p. 25). Both are concepts belonging to the sphere of universal human ethics (ibid., pp. 43ff.). The other two virtues—not changing their names and their language—were safeguards against assimilation, and doubtless suggested themselves to the Rabbis because Hellenistic Jews did change their names (and language) —notice the version in Leviticus R. XXXII.5, ed. Margulies, pp. 747f.

And how do we know that they were above suspicion in regard to chastity? . . . "A garden shut up is my sister, my bride" etc. (Cant. 4:12) . . . the two modes of cohabitation.

Canticles 4:12, interpreted here, is the warrant given in Sifra, 'Aḥare, ed. Weiss, p. 86c, for the idea that Israel was the first people to practice chastity (on p. 390 of the Sifra MS referred to above, p. 60, the reading is פתחתם תחילה). The teaching in the Sifra takes for granted the interpretation here (Mekilta, ed. Weiss, p.

6b, note). In its complete form, then, the thought conveyed is: Israel already practiced chastity in Egypt, and was the first people in the world to do so, although as an element in universal ethics it should have been practiced by mankind as a whole.

And how . . . "But every woman shall ask of her neighbor" etc. (Exod. 3:22). They had this order for twelve months . . . other.

The order was given Moses before he returned to Egypt, that is, before the ten plagues were visited upon Egypt. Twelve months had elapsed between the infliction of the first plague and the last ('Eduyyot II.10; Seder 'Olam R., Chap. 3; and see also L. Ginzberg, Legends of the Jews, II, p. 347 and V, p. 427, n. 174).

And . . . names . . . "The angel . . . and let my name be named in them" (Gen. 48:16).

In these words Jacob designated the sons of Joseph as being his sons too, just as were Reuben, Simeon, Levi and the rest of the brothers. The names of Joseph's sons were thus as authentic and characteristic of Israel as were those of Jacob's own sons, even though Joseph's sons were born in Egypt.

And whence do we know that they did not change their language? "And . . . Abram the Hebrew" (Gen. 14:13).

As the Rabbis interpret them, the proof-texts indicate that Hebrew was the language of Abraham (Gen. 14:13), that it remained the language of Joseph despite his being in Egypt (ibid. 45:12), and that it was the language of the Israelites in Egypt (Exod. 5:3). If the language of Abraham's descendents in Egypt was the same as his, then the descendents did not change their language. H-R, p. 15, omits or deletes Exodus 2:14, nor have we cited it in our list of the proof-texts; however, the Yalḳuṭ (see Apparatus) quotes the verse before it (v. 13)—"two men of the Hebrews were striving together"—which would refer, in conformity with the references to the word "Hebrew" in the other proof-texts, to the Hebrew language, and hence be an indication that it was spoken by the Israelites in Egypt.

Why then was the purchasing of the paschal lamb to precede its slaughtering by four days?

It was not, then, nonobservance of *Miẓwot* that prevented Israel's redemption. The entire matter of the paschal lamb and the laws involved, according to R. Eliezer, had a different purpose from the one stated by R. Matia.

Because the Israelites in Egypt were steeped in idolatry (*'Abodah Zarah*, l. 39), and the law against idolatry outweighs all the other commandments (*Miẓwot*, l. 40) of the Torah . . . It is the law against idolatry.

Although Israel in Egypt practiced *Miẓwot,* they also practiced idolatry and it was that which prevented their redemption, the practice of idolatry outweighing all the *Miẓwot* in the Torah. This point is made in ll. 39-43. Found elsewhere in a purely halakic context, the rest of this discussion down to l. 54 is deleted here by Elijah Gaon (see ed. Malbim ad loc., and comp. ed. Weiss, p. 6b, n. 6), obviously because it interrupts the idea being advanced by R. Eliezer. Even without the interpolation this statement by itself constitutes an example of the integration of Haggadah and Halakah, for the idea that the Israelites in Egypt practiced idolatry is Haggadah and the principle that '*Abodah Zarah* outweighs the practice of all the *Miẓwot* in the Torah is Halakah. The statement also indicates that the rabbinic value concepts, in this case '*Abodah Zarah,* are concretized both in Haggadah and Halakah (above, p. 21f).

'*Abodah Zarah* is a rabbinic concept, the biblical antecedent of which is the term "other gods" (as in Exod. 20:3). Implying the same idea are terms like "the gods of Egypt" (ibid. 12:12). Stigmatizing idolatry as "strange" and wrong worship, the rabbinic concept possesses a more clearly stressed pejorative connotation than does its biblical antecedent (below, p. 94f). Moreover, the rabbinic term refers not only to idols but to the worship of idols, to the acts of worship (ibid.). On how acknowledgment of God is associated with the denial of idolatry, see WE, pp. 231f.

Therefore he [Moses] said to them: Withdraw your hands from idol worship (*'Abodah Zarah,* l. 55) and adhere to the commandments (*Miẓwot).*

Where do we find that Moses spoke thus to Israel? Given here at the end of the lengthy passage of which R. Eliezer ha-Ḳappar is the author, precisely the same statement is also given later (82, ll. 14-15) as a comment by R. Jose the Galilean on Exodus 12:21. The words of the injunction attributed to Moses by both R. Eliezer and R. Jose are a midrashic interpretation of the biblical injunction by Moses in Exodus 12:21—

"Draw out and take you lambs . . . and kill the passover lamb." "Draw (out)," *mishku* of the verse, is interpreted as part of the idiom *mishku yedekem* (38,
ll. 54-55), withdraw your hands or, simply, withdraw;
they are to withdraw from the "lambs," that is, from
the worship of the lambs, characterized in Exodus 8:22
as "the abomination of (pejorative for 'the deity of') the
Egyptians" according to 39, ll. 68-69. Like the Egyptians,
Israel in Egypt, influenced by their surroundings, worshipped the lamb, and Moses demands that they withdraw from that worship, withdraw from *'Abodah Zarah.*
(See also Exodus R. XVI.2, end.) To demonstrate that
Israel had indeed withdrawn from lamb worship, they
were bidden, "Take you lambs . . . and kill the passover
lamb." But "the passover lamb" was a sacrifice, and it
involved two *Mizwot*: the paschal sacrifice itself and
circumcision (as in R. Matia's teaching). When Moses
said, "Take you lambs . . . and kill the passover lamb,"
he was therefore saying, according to this interpretation: Adhere to the commandments (*Mizwot*). Since
the paschal sacrifice had to be examined for blemishes
four days before being slaughtered (above, p. 74), that
halakic rule now too accounts for the interval of four
days between the purchase of the paschal lamb and its
slaughtering.

38, ll. 55-66

**R. Judah the son of Bathyra . . . "But they hearken-
ed not to Moses for impatience (lit., shortness) of
spirit" etc. (Exod. 6:9).**

For the interpretation, the rest of the verse also is

essential—"and because of (their) hard labor, *ume-'abodah kashah.*"

Merely that it was hard for them to part with their idols.

Rather, But it was hard for them to separate themselves from idolatry. The word *'abodah* in the verse is taken to refer to *'Abodah Zarah,* and *kashah,* hard, not as descriptive of *'abodah* but as descriptive of Israel's attitude. As thus interpreted, the verse is to be rendered as follows: But they hearkened not unto Moses because of shortness of spirit ("short" in the sense of "lacking") and because it was hard for them to separate themselves from idolatry. Proof is then given from the plain meaning of Ezekiel 20:7,8.

This is what is meant by the passage: "And the Lord spoke unto Moses and Aaron, and gave them a charge unto the children of Israel" (Exod. 6:13)— charging them to give up (lit., to separate themselves from) idol worship.

Ezekiel 20:7 tells that God commanded the Israelites in Egypt to cease practicing idolatry, and it is that command or charge which is referred to, according to this interpretation, in Exodus 6:13. In quoting also Ezekiel 20:8—"but they rebelled against Me and would not hearken" etc.—the midrash teaches, too, that the charge to cease from idol worship went unheeded.

This midrash is a comment on Exodus 6:9, 13. Why is it placed here? Even though he is an earlier Tanna, R. Judah ben Bathyra's teaching here apparently provides background for R. Eliezer's teaching in the preceding

passage. A full year had elapsed between the time when
Moses had returned to Egypt and the slaughter of the
paschal lamb (see above, p. 76). How is it that during
that entire year God had not commanded the Israelites
through Moses to cease practicing idolatry? The answer
is that God *had* so commanded them, and indeed, immediately after Moses' return, but Israel had not obeyed.
Similarly, the passage may also supply a reason for the
slaughter of the lamb, the object of their idolatry. Since
the Israelites persisted in their idolatry despite God's
command, only such an act could demonstrate their
change of heart. On the other hand, it may well be that
this passage was not thought of as pertaining to the
preceding one and was placed here only because of an
association of ideas, both passages telling that Israel
in Egypt practiced idolatry. After all, the two passages
differ decidedly in their attitude toward Israel. R. Judah's
teaching is informed with both the spirit and the words
of Ezekiel 20:7, 8 and 9, in contrast to R. Eliezer's
teaching in which Israel is extolled, although in that
teaching too, Ezekiel's tradition is reflected in the theme
that the Israelites in Egypt were idolaters.

39, ll. 67-71

**And Ye Shall Keep It . . . "Draw out and take you
lambs" etc. (Exod. 12:21) . . . if we sacrifice the
abomination of the Egyptians before their eyes,
will they not stone us"?**

The lamb is characterized as the deity, "abomination" (pejorative), of the Egyptians. "And ye shall
keep it" is explained in accordance with this midrash by

Targum Jonathan on the verse (Weiss, p. 7a, n. 9): It is to be tied and kept for the four days so that the Israelites may know that they need not be afraid of the Egyptians who have seen all this (and who would presumably resent it). See the next comment.

Then . . . From the miracle—*Nes* (l. 70)—which He will perform for you at its acquisition, you will know what *(Nes)* He will do for you at its slaughtering.

The word *Nes* which we have added in parenthesis is implied in the text—*ha-Nes,* as in l. 70. Moses allays the fear of the Israelites ("If we sacrifice the 'abomination' of the Egyptians before their eyes, will they not stone us?"). They will not be harmed now by the Egyptians at the acquisition of the lambs, obviously a *Nes,* and they can therefore expect that they will not be harmed when they sacrifice the lambs, again a *Nes* which God will do for them.

The concept of *Nes* has two aspects or phases—the phase in which a *Nes* is a spectacular or extraordinary happening, and the phase which encompasses non-spectacular and everyday matters, "Thy *Nissim* which are daily with us" (a phrase in the Eighteenth *Berakah* of the *'Amidah*). Among the spectacular things are the *Nissim* which we describe today as supernatural, and which the Rabbis characterized as changes in *sidre Bereshit;* it is these matters alone to which the word "miracle" really applies, and hence, in order to retain the full meaning of the concept, it is best to leave *Nes* untranslated. In fact, because *sidre Bereshit* is a quasi-scientific concept, something akin to "orders of nature," the phase so qualified is not purely valuational, and there is a marked tendency to curb its application, especially in Halakah. Only pure value concepts function freely; see above, p. 37f, regarding the limited application of the concept of *Gilluy Shekinah.* (On the concept of *Nes,* see RM, pp. 152ff; and on its biblical antecedents, ibid., p. 296.) Of course, there are *Nissim* consisting of extraordinary happenings that are not changes in *sidre Bereshit. Nissim* of that kind took place, according to our midrash, when the Egyptians did not attack the Israelites either at the time the lambs, the deity of the Egyptians, were acquired for slaughtering or at the time of the slaughtering itself.

** and *

44, ll. 1-7

And They Shall Take of the Blood . . . *(ba-saf)* . . . (I Kings 7:50).

On this passage, see above, p. 3.

44, ll. 8-15

A) And Put it . . . "And when I see the blood" (Exod. 12:13), i. e., the blood that would be seen by Me and not by others—these are the words of R. Ishmael.

See n. 2. To the biblical statement "And when I see the blood," there is added the idea that the blood is to be on the inside of the houses (R. Ishmael's interpretation of the law) and that God would see it nonetheless. R. Ishmael gives expression here to the rabbinic emphasis on the otherness of God. God is not like man:

what would be hidden from man is not hidden from God. This idea has nothing in common with the philosopher's aversion to anthropomorphism, for the latter involves metaphysical conceptions which belong to a nonrabbinic universe of discourse. (On this entire matter, see the discussion on "The Otherness of God" in RM, pp. 303ff.) The stress on the otherness of God arises out of the rabbinic consciousness of a relationship with God, a mystical relationship which is like none other. In order to express this relationship the Rabbis are obliged to employ terms of human relationship, but the variety of relationships thus represented gives the terms a certain metaphorical character. It is because no one term of relationship suffices in itself that the Rabbis speak of God as "Father," "King," "Friend," or "Brother," (ibid., p. 270f, and see also ibid., pp. 194ff., "The Conceptual Terms for God").

B) R. Jonathan . . . "And the blood shall be to you for a token" (Exod. 12:13), i. e., a sign to you and not a sign to others.

R. Jonathan agrees with R. Ishmael that the blood is to be on the inside of the houses, but he disagrees in part with him as to the reason. According to R. Jonathan the blood is to be on the inside as a token for Israel, "to you for a token," implying that it is not meant as a token for God at all (see below, p. 97). God needs no token or sign. Like R. Ishmael, therefore, R. Jonathan too stresses the otherness of God.

C) R. Isaac says: Still I say it means on the outside, so that the Egyptians, seeing it, would be cut to the quick.

Since the blood which they will see will be that of their slaughtered deity. The law itself is different in the interpretation given it by R. Isaac from what it is according to the preceding interpretations. At the same time, the reason given in R. Isaac's teaching implies, as does the reason given in R. Jonathan's teaching, that the blood on the house is not a token for God. All three authorities here teach, then, the idea of God's otherness. A common feature of all three opinions, too, is the character of the teachings; in each teaching a halakah is integrated with a haggadah (see "Integration of Halakah and Haggadah," above, p. 26).

** and *

51, ll. 1-4

And Thus Shall . . . This passage teaches you that according to the Torah it is proper (*Derek 'Erez,* l. 3) for people starting on a journey to be alert.

A warning, apparently, for those intending to journey with a caravan. It will leave them behind if they are not ready.

The concept of *Derek 'Erez* possesses a number of phases (WE, pp. 39ff.), among which is that of practical wisdom, the phase referred to here. Literally the term means "the way of the land (or, of the world)." Yet in most of its phases the concept points to the way mankind ought to act rather than to the way it does act —in other words, this concept encompasses what we mean today by ethics. Now the way a person ought to act includes not only fundamental matters like justice, or charity, or deeds of lovingkindness, all of which are subconcepts of *Derek 'Erez,* but also less crucial matters such as taking precautions in regard to earning one's livelihood, as in the rabbinic comment here. Obviously some ethical matters are more important, have larger bearings, than others, but this is not to say that those other matters may be disregarded. When the Rabbis characterize an act as *Derek 'Erez* which is taught by the Torah, therefore, they often characterize in this manner something that does not belong in the category of crucial ethics. On *Derek 'Erez* as referring to good manners, another phase of the concept also characterized in the same manner, see above, p. 57.

52-53, ll. 5-20

A) And Ye Shall Eat It in Haste. This refers to the bustle (correct to: the haste) of the Egyptians.

The word *hippazon* can only mean "haste" in all the views expressed here, not just in the third view where alone it is properly translated; in the catchwords, therefore, we shall render *hippazon* as "haste" throughout.

A halakic opinion is implied in the midrashic statement. The Israelites may eat the paschal lamb until the time when the Egyptians will be "in haste"—that is, until midnight, midnight being the time of the plague of the firstborn when the Egyptians will be "in haste" to have the Israelites leave Egypt. (This accords with the view of R. Eleazar b. Azariah in Berakot 9a. See there also the interpretation of *hippazon,* "in haste," in R. 'Abba's explanation as well as the one in R. 'Akiba's statement.)

You interpret . . . "But against any of the children

of Israel shall not a dog whet his tongue" (Exod. 11:7). The haste of Israel is (already) referred to there.

Meaning, Israel will *not* be in haste, the proof being that the dogs will not bark at them as they do at men who run (not as in n. 2, an explanation given in late midrashic collections). That is how the verse is interpreted in Sifre on Deuteronomy ed. Friedmann, p. 101a in a comment concluding with: "You must say, therefore, that only the Egyptians were in haste." (See ed. Weiss, p. 9b, note; ed. Friedmann, p. 7b, n. 3; H-R, p. 22, n. 13, who also points to another such use of *'amur* ["is referred to there"]). So interpreted, the verse teaches that the Israelites did not flee from Egypt; they were not runaway slaves.

All three interpretations of "in haste" in the passage, of which this is the first, are instances of the integration of Halakah and Haggadah.

B) R. Joshua, the son of Korḥah says: "And ye shall eat it in haste." This refers to the haste of Israel.

When was Israel in haste? At dawn on the day of the Exodus, for it was at dawn that they could leave their houses. According to this interpretation, the Israelites may eat the paschal lamb until dawn. (See, in Berakot 9a, the opinion of R. 'Akiba who interprets *hippazon* in this manner, and Rashi's gloss; and see also ibid., the statement of R. Joshua and the explanation of R. 'Abba, and Rashi's glosses.)

You interpret . . . "Because they were thrust out of

Egypt and could not tarry" (v. 39). The haste of the Egyptians is referred to there.

If the verse (39) is to be taken in its literal sense, the haste of the Egyptians is referred to there only indirectly. As specifically interpreted by the Rabbis in due course (110, ll. 46-47), however, the verse is made to refer directly to the Egyptians, and that is undoubtedly the case here as well (see ed. Friedmann, p. 15b, n. 17, and see our discussion below, p. 164). In that interpretation, "and they could not tarry," literally "and they could not delay," refers to the Egyptians: They (the Egyptians) "could not delay," had no free will in the matter, but were forced by God to drive out the Israelites because the hour of redemption had come. The haste of the Egyptians was no haste at all, for it was not of their own volition. Furthermore, although the redemption began at that hour, i.e., at midnight, the Israelites went forth at God's command only in the daytime. Like the first interpretation, this teaching too says that the Israelites were not runaway slaves, and says so with greater emphasis.

C) Abba Ḥanin . . . It refers to the haste of (the) *Shekinah* . . . "Behold He cometh, etc. Behold He standeth behind our wall" (Cant. 2:8-9).

The *Ge'ullah,* redemption, took place at night, i.e., midnight, although at God's command the actual Exodus was in the daytime (Sifre Deut., ed. Friedmann, 100f; Berakot 9a, bot., and Diḳduḳe Soferim ad loc.). Of the 400 years of servitude foretold in Genesis 15:13, 190 years were still left, and it was only because of God's haste that the redemption occurred when it did (see the reference in n. 3). As to the law, this interpretation agrees with the first one in the passage: the paschal lamb is to be eaten until the hour of redemption which was at midnight. But the haggadic framework here, the "reason," stresses God's love above everything else. Because of His love the redemption took place much before the time for which it had been set, and what the Egyptians did hardly seems to matter. "Behold He standeth behind our wall" (Cant. 2:9) indicates that *Shekinah* here means *Gilluy Shekinah*.

One might think that in the future (*Le'atid La-bo*, l. 18) also the deliverance will be in haste. But it says: "For ye shall not go out in haste, neither shall ye go by flight; for the Lord will go before you" (Isa. 52:12).

Le'atid La-bo is a conceptual term which may stand either for the days of the Messiah or for the world to come; here it refers to redemption from servitude to Rome, the last redemption, and hence to the days of the Messiah. That redemption will not take place "in haste," if by "in haste" is meant before the time which has been set for it. No time has been set. Certain to be brought about by God, it is always imminent.

53, l. 21

It Is the Lord's . . . All work done in connection with it should be in the name of Heaven.

"Heaven" is an appellative for God. See H-R, p. 23. We take the midrash to mean: Every act connected with the paschal lamb (such as the purchase, the slaughter, roasting and eating it—cf. Leḳaḥ Ṭob, ed. Buber, II,

30a)—should be done with the thought in mind that it is a command of God, that is, every such act is to be felt as a *Miẓwah* in itself. Comp. ed. Weiss, p. 9b, n. 2. Embodied in the midrash is the concept of *Kawwanah* which, in one of its aspects or phases, connotes proper intention in the performance of *Miẓwot* (WE, pp. 197f, 231f). Other aspects of *Kawwanah* were discussed above, p. 69.

53, ll. 22-27

A) For I Will Go . . . R. Judah says: Like a king who passes from one place to another.

God's dominion extends over the entire world, over every land, and He can therefore pass through Egypt with no interference. The concept here is *Malkut Shamayim,* God's kingship.

B) Another interpretation. I shall put My wrath and My terror in Egypt. For the word 'ebrah means (only) anger, . . . (Isa. 13:9).

See n. 4. The midrash obviously deviates from the plain meaning ("For I will go through the land of Egypt"), yet the concept embodied in the midrash, God's justice, is none other than that which is expressed in the plain meaning. What is contained in the midrash, however, and not in the plain meaning, is the idea of God's otherness. God will punish Egypt, but not only by actually passing through the land as a man might pass. (On how the idea of God's otherness differs from the philosophic aversion to anthropomorphism, see above, p. 83f.)

53, ll. 28-30

And Will Smite . . . not through an angel nor through an agent.

Why this stress on the last plague as something accomplished by God alone? Because the last plague, the proximate cause of the redemption, is identified with the redemption. The point made is, therefore, that God alone—not an angel nor an agent——was the Redeemer, and the concepts embodied in the midrash are *Middat Rahamim, Middat ha-Din,* and *Ge'ullah.* In a version of our midrash, the same verse, Exodus 12:12 ("And I will go through . . . and will smite"), is the proof-text for the statement, "When *Rahamana'* (God) came to redeem Israel He did not send an agent nor an angel but He Himself (came)"; Yer. Sanhedrin II.1, 20a (ibid. Horayot III.1, 47a), cited by D. Goldschmidt, Seder Haggadah Shel Pesah (Jerusalem and Tel Aviv, 1947), p. 40. This version explicitly identifies the last plague with the redemption (Goldschmidt).

53-54, ll. 31-35

And Will Smite All . . . Even those who hailed from other places . . . Egyptian first-born who were in other places . . . the first-born of Ham, Cush, Put and Lud . . . (Ps. 78:51).

Apparently Egypt is depicted here as an empire, analogous to Rome. That seems to be borne out especially by the manner in which Psalm 78:51 is interpreted, "in Egypt" being equated with "the tents of Ham," Cush, Put and Lud.

54-55, ll. 36-50

Both Man and Beast. He who was first to sin (lit., to commit the transgression—'*Aberah*, l. 36) was also the first to be punished. In like manner you must interpret . . . And so also here you interpret: "And I will smite the first-born in the land of Egypt, both man and beast." He who was the first to sin was also the first to be punished.

This interpretation assumes that the plague upon the first-born came in punishment for their sin, although what that sin was is not specified. Nonetheless, the assumption in itself indicates that the rabbinic concept of *Middat ha-Din*, God's justice, has a wider range or applicability than its bibilcal antecedent. In the biblical account, the plague on the first-born is not related to their having sinned, and to that extent the event is left uninterpreted. On the other hand, even when the midrash does no more than assume such a relation, an added interpretation is thereby already placed on the event. (On the wider range and applicability of the rabbinic concepts, see above, p. 15f. See also below, pp. 134, 142.)

Now, by using the method of *Kal vaḥomer*, you reason:

Correct what follows in the translation to: [When it is a matter of the lesser measure, of punishment, he who was the first to commit the transgression ('*Aberah*, l. 49) was also the first to be punished; all the more certain is it when it is a matter of the greater measure, of reward, (that he who is the first to perform a *Mizwah* is also the first to be rewarded).] (See Judah Goldin, The

Fathers According to Rabbi Nathan [New Haven, 1955], p. 123; we have utilized his translation there of a related passage.) In Tosefta Soṭah IV.1, a homily permits the Rabbis to be more definite and to say that the measure of reward is five hundred times as great as the measure of punishment. Such statements, while embodying at once both the concepts of God's love and His justice, yet stress the concept of God's love. The entire idea is thus in accord with the rabbinic emphasis on love, an emphasis to be discerned not only, as here, in particular statements but also in general value concepts (above, pp. 8, 11f). See also Goldin, op. cit., p. 203, n. 6.

55, ll. 51-58

And Against All the Gods of Egypt I Will Execute Judgments . . . Judgments differing one from the other . . . as it is said: "While the Egyptians were burying," etc. (Num. 33:4).

Numbers 33:4 concludes with, "Upon their gods also the Lord executed judgments." This verse is cited so as to teach that the "judgments" took place, for in the account in Exodus 12:29ff, telling of the execution of the last plague, they are not mentioned (ed. Friedmann, p. 7b, n. 19).

R. Nathan says . . . four judgments . . . We thus learn that the idols were smitten in four ways, and those who worshipped them, in three ways, by affliction, by injury, and by plague.

Rather: We thus learn that an idol is smitten (*'Abodah Zarah loḳah*, l. 57) in four ways, and its worshippers in three ways etc. As is especially indicated by the present tense (*loḳah*), this inference ("we thus learn") is a generalization concerning any and every idol and its worshippers. (In the version in the Yalḳuṭ on Exodus 12:12 the reading is *sheha-'elilim,* "that the idols," but the present tense still obtains—*loḳim*). In other words, the Rabbis assert that this rule was applied not only in Egypt but it also continues to be applied in their own day as well.

By using the word "smitten" in both cases, the Rabbis seem to imply that the idols were no less culpable than their worshippers, indeed were more culpable since they were smitten in four ways and their worshippers in three. Yet the idols were obviously regarded as nothing but stone, metal or wood—they become soft, or hollow, they are chopped down, or burned. If the idols are nothing but material objects, how is it that they are regarded as culpable, even more culpable than their worshippers? The answer is to be found in the connotations of the concepts of *'Abodah* and *'Abodah Zarah.*

To us the word "worship" stands for all forms of worship. It is a generic term for acts and attitudes which we recognize as belonging to a certain type, one broad enough to include acts and attitudes of the most diverse societies. Apparently, but only apparently, that seems, too, to be the meaning of *'Abodah,* for this term is used by the Rabbis not alone as a designation for Jewish worship, especially worship in the Temple, but also for pagan worship. Actually, however, *'Abodah,* when applied to pagan worship, is used in a pejorative sense (WE, p. 124 and p. 271, n. 158). Idolatry is false worship, better, pseudo-worship; by the same token, idols are pseudo-gods. *'Abodah Zarah,* literally "strange worship," connotes the idea of pseudo-worship, of pseudo-gods. Were idolatry no worship at all, idol worshippers would be performing merely meaningless acts, not wicked acts: the negative value concept of *'Abodah Zarah* stigmatizes those acts as wicked. Similarly, *'Abodah Zarah* stigmatizes the objects of worship, the idols, as pseudo-gods, and as such they have the same limited kind of reality as pseudo-worship has. A largely unreal, wicked, miasma-like atmosphere envelops both gods and worshippers, an atmosphere in which the idols have sufficient reality to be culpable and, as pseudo-gods, to be even more culpable than their worshippers. The point here is that when the Rabbis designate idolatry, too, as *'Abodah*—the same word as is used to designate proper worship—that connotation also involves the connotation of *'Abodah Zarah* as a culpable pseudo-deity. These concepts have antecedents in the Bible (above, p. 78). In fact, both the biblical antecedent and the connotation of *'Abodah Zarah* are contained in the verse interpreted by the midrashim here—"And against all the gods of Egypt I will execute judgments." "All the gods of Egypt" can only refer to pseudo-gods, *'Abodah Zarah,* and "I will execute judgments" implies that they are culpable. Nevertheless, the view reflected in these midrashim is probably not the dominant one; see, for example, II, p. 245, l. 115, where idols are characterized as "dead," and comp. 'Abodah Zarah IV.7. (As to how the pagans themselves regarded their idols, see the material cited in WE, pp. 182f and p. 289, n. 98.)

There are laws obligatory for all mankind, according to the Rabbis, and one of them is the law against idolatry.

Called "The Seven *Miẓwot* of the Sons of Noah," these
laws are: To institute law and justice, not to blaspheme
God, and not to worship idols (*'Abodah Zarah*), not to
commit incest, murder, or robbery, and not to eat the
meat of a living animal. To abstain from idolatry is thus,
in the Rabbis' view, to abide by one of the ineluctible
standards of universal human conduct (WE, p. 206; see
also above, p. 75f, with respect to chastity). That is why
idolatry is regarded by the Rabbis as a heinous sin
even when practiced by non-Jews. At the same time, the
Rabbis also realized that idolaters who had had no contact with Jews could not be expected to know that their
worship was sinful. Indeed, a famous statement in the
name of R. Joḥanan goes so far as to declare that such
Gentiles are really not idolaters at all. "The Gentiles
outside of the land of Israel are not to be considered as
idolaters, for they only continue the usage of their ancestors" (Ḥullin 13b).

55, l. 59

I Am the Lord. What flesh and blood cannot say.

Since the verse (Exod. 12:12) tells of *Nissim,* miracles, and these can be done only by God. Comp. ed Malbim ad loc.

55, ll. 60-63

**I Am the Lord . . . Now, by using the method of
Kal vaḥomer, etc.**

See the rendering above, p. 92, of the similar passage.
The conclusion here is: [All the more certain is it when
it is a matter of the greater measure, of reward, (that the

Holy One blessed be He acts when He says that He will
act).]

56, ll. 64-65

**And the Blood . . . A sign to you and not to Me, a
sign to you and not to others.**

This is R. Jonathan's interpretation already given on
44, ll. 11-13. The supplementary comment here—"A sign
to you and not to Me"—makes explicit the idea of the
otherness of God which is there implied (above, p. 84).

** ** **

56, ll. 70-77

**And When I See the Blood . . . R. Ishmael used to
say: Is not everything revealed before Him . . .
"Even darkness is not too dark for Thee," etc. (Ps.
139:12).**

R. Ishmael's interpretation here of Exodus 12:13 is
not wholly at variance with his interpretation of the
same verse on 44, ll. 8-11, where he takes the verse to
teach that the blood is to be put on the inside of the
houses and that God will see it nonetheless. That interpretation, too, expresses the idea of the otherness of
God (above, p. 83f). Aside from this, the interpretations
diverge. In the one given earlier, the blood is still a
sign for God, whereas now it has no such function. Moreover, although the earlier interpretation expresses the
idea of the otherness of God, it does so by means of a
specific instance. Now, however, in the question, "Is not
everything revealed before Him?" this idea is expressed

in a less specific manner. The question is, in fact, tanta-
mount to the idea of God's omniscience, but neither that
idea nor the more inclusive one of God's otherness is
crystallized in a conceptual term in rabbinic thought. (On
the relationship between those two ideas, see RM, pp.
319f.)

**What then is the purport of the words: "And when
I see the blood *(we-ra'iti 'et ha-dam,* l. 73)?" It is
only this: As a reward for your performing this
duty *(Miẓwah,* l. 73) I shall reveal Myself and protect you,**

The *Miẓwah* referred to here is, apparently, the act of
putting the blood on the houses, in reward for which,
God promises, He will reveal Himself (*Gilluy Shekinah*)
and protect the Israelites. The derivation of this idea
from the text appears to be as follows: *we-ra'iti* (and
when I see) is taken as *we-nir'eti* (and I will be seen),
while *'et ha-dam* is interpreted as "with the blood," that
is, at the time the blood is being put on the houses.

We ought not be surprised that R. Ishmael gives two
different interpretations of Exodus 12:13. A feature of
haggadic interpretation is multiple interpretation of biblical texts (above, p. 21), and the same authority may,
therefore, offer more than one haggadic interpretation
of a verse (RM, p. 72). Besides, these interpretations
by R. Ishmael possess an idea in common, namely, the
idea of God's otherness. Both interpretations, incidentally,
demonstrate that this idea is not to be identified with an
aversion to anthropomorphism. The earlier interpretation speaks of God seeing the blood even though it will
be on the inside of the houses, and the present interpre-

tation speaks of God's promise to reveal Himself to man's *sight*.

. . . as it is said: "And I will pass over you *(ufasaḥti,* l. 74)" . . . (Isa. 31:5).

See above, p. 2f.

57, ll. 78-82

And When I See the Blood. I see the blood of the sacrifice of (lit., the binding of, *'aḳedato,* l. 78) Isaac . . . "God will Himself see the lamb" etc. (Gen. 22:8).

On the basis of a number of sources, H-R, p. 24, rightly prefaces the passage with the words, "Another interpretation."

This passage, too, contains the idea of the otherness of God, but here that idea is implied rather than actually expressed. God's otherness is implied because, instead of taking "I see" literally, the passage treats those words almost as pure symbol. "And when I see the blood" means, according to this interpretation, "I see the blood of the sacrifice of Isaac." That is, God says that He will protect the Israelites for the sake of the sacrifice of Isaac. This interpretation is derived by placing "And when *I see* the blood" in conjunction with Genesis 22:14, the verse telling that Abraham called the place of the sacrifice *"Adonai-jireh,"* "The Lord *will see.*" Corroboration is found in another event: " 'And as He was about to destroy, the Lord *saw* and He repented Him,' etc. I Chron. 21:15). What did He see? He saw the blood of the sacrifice of Isaac, as it is said: 'God will Himself *see* the lamb for a burnt-offering, my son' (Gen. 22:8)." By thus interpreting "And when I see the blood" symbolically, that verse, which would seem to contradict the idea of God's otherness, is practically interpreted away. In other words, though the question of God's otherness is not actually raised in the passage, that idea is nonetheless taught, even if indirectly.

What does "the blood of the sacrifice of Isaac" refer to? In a brilliant study, Shalom Spiegel demonstrates that this passage is one of numerous rabbinic vestiges of a very ancient legend, a legend that Isaac's blood was shed, that Isaac was actually sacrificed by Abraham and then revived by God (see the discussion in RM, p. 318f, and the notes there). Now ancient legends are folklore, tales transmitted orally from generation to generation and hence reflect early, even primitive, levels of a people's culture (see the reference to Spiegel, ibid.). But the legend here has not been preserved by the Rabbis for its own sake. Incorporated in an interpretation which concretizes the concept of *Zekut 'Abot,* the merit of the fathers, the legend in this context is an example of how the Rabbis utilize an ancient folk tale in order to cultivate the rabbinic value concepts. Such utilization of folklore by the Rabbis indicates that there was an interaction between the Rabbis and the folk. That interaction, indeed, was a primary condition for the entire development of both Haggadah and Halakah (above, p. 30).

In retelling the story of the sacrifice of Isaac, the Rabbis say that Abraham informed Isaac of God's command and that Isaac asquiesced with joy (L. Ginzberg, Legends of the Jews, I, p. 279f, and V, p. 250, n. 240). A characterization of Isaac as well as of Abraham is thereby given

in this interpretation of the biblical story, a characterization of Isaac not found in the Bible. This accords with
the rabbinic emphasis on the individual (above, p. 8
and see OT, p. 223). Paradoxically, however, the story
is often associated with *Zekut 'Abot,* merit of the fathers,
and that concept involves the idea of corporate personality. The passage we have been discussing is a case in
point. It concretizes the concept of *Zekut 'Abot,* the connotation of which is that children receive reward for the
good deeds of their fathers; for according to that passage,
God says He will protect the Israelites because of the sacrifice of Isaac. In this view, the patriarchs and the Israelites are regarded as members of a corporate personality, so that the patriarchs' obedience to God is, so to
speak, attributed to the Israelites. The association of the
story of the sacrifice with the concept of *Zekut 'Abot*
shows how the Rabbis emphasized the individual even
when they employed concepts involving the notion of
corporate personality. See also above, p. 47.

57-58, ll. 83-93

A) R. Josiah says: Do not read *ufasaḥti* (I will protect) but *ufasa'ti* (I will step over). God skipped
over the houses of His children in Egypt . . . "Behold, He standeth behind our wall" etc. (Cant.
2:8-9).

From this comment it appears that in tannaitic times
the generally accepted meaning of *ufasaḥti* was "I will
protect" (cf. 56, ll. 74-77); a change in a consonant
had to be made in order to have the word mean, "I will
step over." Whether the one meaning is taken or the other,
the concepts embodied are the same: *Middat Raḥamim*

(God's love) and Israel. Citing this midrash as one of several examples, Naḥmanides makes the point that the letters *ḥet* and *'ayin* were interchangeable (Commentary to the Pentateuch, Deut. 2:23, and his reference to ibid. 2:10).

B) R. Jonathan . . . This means, you alone will I protect but I will not protect the Egyptians . . . "And there shall no plague be upon you . . . the land of Egypt."

It is taken for granted here that *ufasaḥti* means, "I will protect," no proof being given. There are textual difficulties; see H-R, p. 25, n. 9.

58, ll. 93-95

Another Interpretation. When I smite the land of Egypt (Exod. 12:13), there will be no plague upon you, but there will be at some future time.

The words in the verse are taken here as a warning to the Israelites that they will not be exempt from the plague later, should they deserve punishment. The concepts embodied, therefore, are *Middat ha-Din* (God's justice) and Israel. In contrast to the particularism of the preceding passage, in this passage there is an emphasis on the universality of God's justice.

**

67, ll. 97-99

(That soul shall be cut off) From Israel (Exod. 12:15). I might understand it to mean . . . but go to live among another people. But it says: "From

before Me; I am the Lord (Lev. 22:3). My dominion is everywhere.

(The relevant phrase in Lev. 22:3 reads in full: "That soul shall be cut off from before Me; I am the Lord.") The text here is *be-kol makom hu' reshuti* (lit., "in every place it is my domain"), and the words represent God Himself as teaching that His kingship extends over the whole world. But in H-R, p. 29, l. 10 (and in the parallel, ibid., p. 35, l. 2) the last two words of this phrase read *she-hu' reshuti,* and now the phrase must be rendered, "in every place which is My domain," so that the entire phrase refers to *Malkut Shamayim,* God's kingship, in quite a different manner. He who heard this comment on Exodus 12:15, the whole commentary being oral Torah, was bound to add, mentally, the inference demanded by the phrase—namely, that God's domain is everywhere. In doing so he really made an acknowledgment of *Malkut Shamayim.* (For the text, compare Rashi on Exod. 12:15; on the study of Torah as affording opportunities for the acknowledgment of *Malkut Shamayim,* See WE, pp. 87ff.)

** and *

68, ll. 1-3

And in the First Day there Shall Be to You a Holy Convocation . . . Honor the festival by food, drink and clean garments.

The comment is derived from the words, "holy convocation," *mikra' kodesh* (ll. 1,2), but the text as given here does not allow us to see the derivation, nor to realize its implications. Instead of *kabbedehu* (l. 2), "honor it," the best MSS read *'are'em* (see the Apparatus) and the rabbinic teaching here, together with its implications, hinges on the relation of *'are'em* to the biblical *miḳra'*. Targum Onkelos translates *miḳra' ḳodesh* as *me'ara' ḳaddish,* "a holy occurrence," or "a holy occasion," and that is also what this comment takes those words to mean. "Make them (i.e., those days) [holy] occasions—*'are'em* —by food, and by drink, and by clean garments" (see also Sifre on Numbers, ed Horovitz [Leipzig, 1917], p. 194 and the note there). A comment on the verse in another source expresses the same thought and conveys the same halakic rule: "With what should you make it holy? Make it holy with food, make it holy with drink, make it holy with clean clothes" Mekhilta D'Rabbi Sim'on b. Jochai, ed. Epstein-Melamed [Jerusalem, 1955], p. 18).

We ought, first of all, to recognize that whereas the biblical verse itself is addressed to the many (notice the plural form of "to you" and, in the verse following, the plural forms of verbs and nouns), the rabbinic halakah is addressed to the individual, as the second person singular of the verbs in both sources indicates. This is patently an emphasis on the individual, and that emphasis is here related to the role of the individual in making the Festivals holy. *Kedushah,* holiness, in this instance is held to be a quality by virtue of which those days are regarded as God's own in a special sense (see the discussion of this type of *Kedushah* in WE, pp. 216f, 220f). At the same time, the individual himself must make those days holy, and do so through acts of an entirely normal character, acts of a kind which in other contexts have no such mystical association. Resulting from acts by the individual, and such as are altogether free from theurgic implications, the felt mystical quality of the holy days is thus an experience in keeping with what we have described as "normal mysticism" (see ibid., pp. 13ff., and see above, p. 44).

**

70-71, ll. 34-47

No Manner of Work Shall Be Done in Them. This means, neither you nor your fellow-Jew shall do any work, nor shall a non-Jew *(Goy,* l. 35) do your work . . . as you are against your own work.

As is apparent from the Apparatus, the text of this passage is uncertain. See, too, the text in H-R, pp. 30f, and the notes there. According to all versions, however, both halakic opinions, that of R. Josiah and that of R. Jonathan, embody several value concepts: Israel, *Goy,* and *Ḳedushah* (the Festival and the Sabbath). Both halakic opinions exhibit, therefore, a characteristic of organismic thought (above, p. 24f, and comp. ibid., p. 18f).

**

74, ll. 86-89

And Ye Shall Observe . . . R. Josiah . . . "Ye shall observe the commandments *(ha-miẓvot)*" . . . But if a religious duty *(Miẓwah,* l. 89) comes your way, perform it immediately.

An element in the observance of a *Miẓwah* is promptness of performance. The statement can also mean that when several *Miẓwot* are involved, the one that is nearest in space or in time is to be done first (Yoma 33a and Megillah 6b).

74, ll. 90-91

For in This Selfsame (*be-'ezem*, l. 90) Day, etc. This tells that they went out of Egypt in the daytime.

be-'ezem is taken to mean "in the essence of," i.e., broad daylight. They were not runaway slaves who needed the cover of night to escape. See also 58, ll. 102-104.

74, ll. 92-97

Have I Brought Your Hosts Out. These are the hosts of Israel . . . Perhaps this is not so, but it means the hosts of the ministering angels? . . . of Israel.

How could it have been even tentatively supposed that "your hosts" refers to the ministering angels, implying that, in some sense, the hosts of angels belonged to Israel? This tentative interpretation of "your hosts," however, but reflects in an exaggerated form the tendency in tannaitic sources to regard the angels as lower in rank than Israel (see, WE, p. 149). More beloved of God (ibid.), Israel is also holier than the angels (ibid., p. 279, n. 112). Angelology thus acts as background for bringing into stronger relief God's love for Israel and the holiness of Israel.

** and *

81-82, ll. 1-12

Then Moses Called for All the Elders of Israel. This tells that he constituted them a court.

Nahmanides regards this statement as part of the com-

ment by R. Josiah: the elders were constituted a court
that they might gather (summon) the people for the purpose of hearing the commandment directly from Moses
(Commentary to the Pentateuch on Exod. 12:21).
When R. Josiah, in the sequel, speaks of Moses showing
respect for the elders, he apparently refers to this use
of the elders by Moses (see H-R, p. 36, n. 7).

And Said unto Them . . . telling it to all Israel—
these are the words of R. Josiah. R. Jonathan says:
. . . the elders were to tell it to all Israel. Said R.
Josiah to him: Why distinguish this commandment
from all the other commandments *(Dibberot,* **l. 6)**
in the Torah? Here, too, . . . telling it to all Israel.

There is obviously an emphasis on Israel in R. Josiah's
interpretation. All the *Dibberot,* God's communications to
Moses, this one included, were transmitted by Moses directly to Israel. So far as the relation to *Mattan Torah*
(the giving of Torah) is concerned, there was no distinction at any time between Israel and its elders; in this sense
Israel had no superior class or spiritual elite.

What then is meant by: "And said unto them?"
Simply, that Moses showed respect to the elders.
. . . "And Moses and Aaron . . . of Israel" (Exod.
4:29).

See the first paragraph of the remarks on this passage.
Another explanation given in H-R, loc. cit., and based
on the Mekilta de R. Simon (ed. Hoffman, p. 21): Although Moses spoke to all Israel, he directed his gaze
upon the elders.

**

85, ll. 61-65

**And None of You Shall Go Out etc. This tells that
the angel, once permission to harm is given him,
does not discriminate between the righteous and
the wicked . . . "Behold . . . and will cut off from
thee the righteous and the wicked" (Ezek. 21:8).**

An ancient folk belief has been reinterpreted here, but
in a manner that does not really overcome its amoral character. Instead of the folk belief that there are evil demonic
spirits whose purpose it is to wreak harm on everyone
indiscriminately, the comment here speaks of an angel
who has been given permission to destroy; but having
been given this permission, the angel too, according to
this comment, does not discriminate between the righteous
and the wicked, an idea incompatible with the concept
of God's justice. A version in the Sifra (ed. Weiss, p. 3b),
indeed, reflects the old folk belief despite the rabbinic
reinterpretation. In connection with several verses, the
statement is made there: "This teaches that permission
was given to the destroyers to destroy—*la-mehabbelim
le-habbel*" (that is the correct reading; see the reading
in the commentary of R. David b. Abraham ad loc.; in
the Sifra MS ed. Finkelstein, p. 4; and in Yalkut Shime'oni,
I Kings, par. 189). Referring to angels, since they need
permission, "the destroyers" is nevertheless a term more
than reminiscent of demons, evil spirits. Although not
really compatible with the value complex, still the idea
enabled the Rabbis to account for communal disasters
which spared no one, such as pestilences, marrauding
soldiers, and the like (comp. Baba' Kamma 60a-b).

And it further says: "And it shall come to pass, while My glory passeth by" etc. (Exod. 33:22).

The relevance of this supporting verse is to be seen from the aforementioned version in the Sifra. The verse concludes with: ". . . and will cover thee with My hand until I have passed by." This part of the verse is quoted by the version in the Sifra, and there it is followed by the comment, "This teaches that permission was given to the destroyers to destroy." "My Glory" is taken to refer to *Gilluy Shekinah,* a visual revelation of God (comp. "His Glory" in the verses of the *Kedushah*—WE, p. 144), and "will cover thee with My hand" as meaning that God will protect Moses during that revelation; it is therefore inferred that on this occasion Moses was in danger of his life because of the destroying angels.

86, ll. 66-77

Until the Morning.

H-R, p. 38, n. 6, points out that the expression *dabar 'aher,* "another interpretation," should have prefaced this text.

This is to teach you that you should come into a place or leave it only in the daytime. And you also find that the patriarchs and the prophets observed this as a custom.

Rather, "observed this as a rule of *Derek 'Erez*" (ll. 68, 72). Leaving and coming to a place only in the day-time is practical wisdom, and practical wisdom is an aspect of *Derek 'Erez,* "the way of the world" (above, p.

85f). Travelling at night was dangerous both because of armed robbers and because of prowling beasts.

For, it is said: "And Abraham rose early in the morning" (Gen. 22:3) . . . "And Jacob" . . . "And Moses" . . . "And Joshua" . . . "And Samuel" . . . If the patriarchs and the prophets, who went to carry out the will of Him by whose word the world came into being . . . how much more should all other people

Where there is imminent danger, say the Rabbis, "we do not rely on a *Nes*." This principle is applied even in the case of those who are engaged upon a *Mizwah*, and it modifies R. Eleazar's dictum that persons so engaged are kept from harm (RM, p. 163).

And thus it says: "Thou makest darkness and it is night" etc. (Ps. 104:20) . . . "How manifold are Thy works, O Lord," etc. (v. 25).

The description of nature in Psalm 104 portrays God's love or beneficence in providing for His creatures, and is not intended, as Yehudah Ha-Levi assumes (Kuzari V, 8-10), as an example of teleology. In the verses selected here the concept embodied is likewise God's love, but more is made of the demarcation between the temporal spheres of beasts and man. Night is the time when the beasts "creep forth" (v. 20). It is then that the young lions "seek their food from God" (v. 21). By interposing verse 28 at this point, the passage applies that verse specifically to the beasts—"Thou givest it (the food) unto them, they gather it," etc. The proper order of the verses is now resumed for the passage continues by quoting verse 22, the verse which tells that "when the sun ariseth" the time alloted to the beasts is over. Verse 23 follows, but in order to emphasize that the daytime alone is given over to man the passage introduces that verse with, "From then on"—"From then on, 'man goeth forth unto his work and to his labor until the evening' (v. 23)." A man ought to know, therefore, that when he ventures forth at night, the time given over to the beasts, he is imperilling his life; that is the implication of this section of the comment, an implication which also refers back to the rule of *Derek 'Erez* in the first part of the comment.

Unlike the preceding comment, the comment here is thoroughly consistent with the rabbinic value complex. The wild beasts are not "destroyers," but have been allowed the nighttime by God in order that they may obtain their food (God's love). A man who ventures out at night violates a rule of *Derek 'Erez* and therefore deserves what befalls him (God's justice).

86-87, ll. 78-84

See above, p. 90.

87-88, ll. 85-96

See above, pp. 97-101.

88-89, ll. 97-105

And the Lord Will Pass . . . Behold, by using the method of *Kal vahomer* . . . The *Mezuzah* . . . since it contains the name of God ten times . . . should all the more be the cause of God's not suffering the destroyer to come into our houses. But what caused

**it to be otherwise? Our sins . . . "But your iniquities
have separated between you and your God . . . and
your sins . . . He will not hear" (Isa. 59:2).**

There are two factors in this passage—a theurgical factor and a value concept (*'Awon,* sin), and the value
concept nullifies the theurgical factor. When the Rabbis
make the assertion about the efficacy of the names of God,
they are expressing a theurgical idea; but a valuational
attitude, the consciousness of sin, displaces that theurgical
attitude. As a consequence, a *mezuzah* is regarded as
having no theurgical potency.

There are some opinions and passages elsewhere, however, which do maintain that a *mezuzah* guards those
within the house from harm, and which thus retain the
theurgic idea nullified here. (Menaḥot 33b—R. Ḥanina
as against *Rabbanan;* 'Abodah Zarah 11a; Yer. Pe'ah
I.1, 15d). Now a *mezuzah* ranks third in a hierarchy of
holy objects to which, in general, no theurgical potency
is ascribed (WE, pp. 221f). The comment here in the
Mekilta is in accord with the general character of the
hierarchy, therefore, whereas the view ascribing a theurgical potency to a *mezuzah* is obviously not so. Maimonides
denounces those who treat a *mezuzah* "as if it were an
amulet" (Mishneh Torah, Hilkot Tefillin, V.4).

** and *

89, ll. 1-2

**And It Shall Come . . . Scripture stipulates that this
service be observed only after the time of their coming into the land.**

There is a difficulty here, for they did observe it, on

God's command, during their second year in the wilderness (Num. 9:1ff.). For attempts at harmonization, see Tosafot to Ḳiddushin 37b, s.v. הזאיל, and Ibn Ezra on Exodus 12:25.

89-94, ll. 3-64

A) According as He Hath Promised. And where did He promise? "And I will bring you in unto the land" etc. (Exod. 6:8). In like manner . . . And where had He spoken? "And it shall come to pass on the sixth day that they shall prepare" (ibid. 16:5).

This begins a long passage which is directed, apparently, against the contention of sectarians that the Decalogue alone was given to Moses by God (on this contention, see Yer. Berakot I.8, 3c, and L. Ginzberg, Commentary on the Palestinian Talmud, I [New York, 1941], p. 166). To disprove this contention, the Rabbis adduce numerous verses which enable them to ask, "And where had He spoken," or "And where had He said it," the answer in every instance being supplied in the form of a verse from a Book of the Pentateuch. The result is that verses in all the Books of the Pentateuch are "pointed to" as having been said by God, which means that the entire Pentateuch was given by God.

The verse adduced together with the verse from the Pentateuch it is said to point to constitute a unitary entity, a rabbinic interpretation embodying value concepts. The verses on God's promise to bring Israel into the land embody the concepts of God's love and Israel, and the verses on the Sabbath embody the concepts of *Miẓwah* and *Ḳedushah* (the holy day). In these instances, the midrashim retain the literal meaning of the verses. There are other such midrashim in the passage, and we shall discuss them only when they need some elucidation.

In like manner . . . "This is it that the Lord spoke, saying: Through them that are nigh unto Me, I will be sanctified" etc. (Lev. 10:3). And where had He said it? "And there I will meet with the children of Israel and it shall be sanctified by My glory" (Exod. 29:43).

The word for "by My Glory" is *bi-kebodi* (1. 8), and it is interpreted as though it read *bi-kebudai,* "My honored ones," so that the verse is taken to say: And there I will meet with the children of Israel, and [My Name] shall be sanctified through My honored ones (see Rashi on Exod. 29:43, and see Lev. R. XIII.2, ed. Margulies, p. 256f, and the notes and references there). Exodus 29:43 is thus regarded as a warning by God, and it is that warning, according to the Rabbis, which is pointed to in Leviticus 10:3.

The concepts embodied in this midrash are God's justice and *Ḳiddush ha-Shem* (sanctification of the Name). When Nadab and Abihu died because they had transgressed and "offered strange fire before the Lord" (ibid. vv. 1-2), their punishment was *Ḳiddush ha-Shem,* for a manifestation of God's justice is one of the ways through which God's Name is sanctified (TE, p. 70f. For other aspects of *Ḳiddush ha-Shem,* see ibid., pp. 69-70; and WE, p. 231f and the pages referred to in the notes there.).

B) In like manner . . . "The Lord your God . . . as He hath spoken" (Deut. 11:25). And where had

He spoken? . . . And where had He spoken? "And
ye shall be holy unto Me" (Lev. 20:26).

Various concepts are embodied in the midrashim here,
but each midrash also embodies the concepts of God's love
and Israel.

C) In like manner you interpret: "Hear, O heavens,
and give ear, O earth, for the Lord hath spoken"
(Isa. 1:2). And where had He spoken? "Give ear, ye
heavens, and I will speak" (Deut. 32:1).

When a prophet declares that "the Lord hath spoken"
or that "the mouth of the Lord hath spoken it," the
phrase in its literal sense usually refers to the words the
prophet has uttered or is about to utter. This is true of
the phrase in Isaiah 1:2 (see Kimḥi on the phrase there)
and wherever it occurs in any quotation from a prophetic
book to be found in this entire passage. In its literal
sense the phrase stamps the words of the prophet as being
the words of God in exactly the same way as does the
phrase, "Thus saith the Lord." But the Rabbis do not
take the phrase literally, either here or in the other quo-
tations cited in this passage; instead, they teach that it
points to verses in the Pentateuch where "the Lord hath
spoken." It is not a matter only of adducing more instances to prove that the Pentateuch was given by God,
but of finding evidence from the prophets, the messengers
of God, to that effect.

This midrash has a conceptual kinship with the literal
meaning of Isaiah 1:2, one of the two verses here interpreted. In that verse, Isaiah calls upon heaven and earth
to hear, for what he is about to say "the Lord hath
spoken." According to the midrashic interpretation, God

commands heaven and earth to hear when He speaks
through the prophet, and Isaiah, in calling upon them to
hear, reminds them of God's command. Both the literal
meaning of Isaiah 1:2 and the midrashic interpretation
embody the concept of *Nebu'ah* (prophecy); the midrashic
interpretation, in addition, embodies the concepts of
Gezerah (decree), or *Mizwah.*

**In like manner . . . "And the Glory of the Lord
shall be revealed, and all flesh shall see it together
. . . (Isa. 40:5). And where had He spoken it? "See
now that I, even I, am He" (Deut. 32:39).**

Isaiah 40:5, according to the interpretation here, refers
to the world to come, and the other concepts embodied
in this midrash are *Gilluy Shekinah* (the visual revelation
of God) and man ("all flesh").

**In like manner . . . "He will swallow up death for-
ever . . ." (Isa. 25:8). And where had He spoken it?
"I kill, and I make alive" etc. (Deut. 32:39).**

Deuteronomy 32:39 ("I make alive") indicates, in this
interpretation, that Isaiah 25:8 is taken as speaking of the
resurrection of the dead. On the resurrection as a rabbinic
dogma, see RM, pp. 361ff.

**In like manner . . . "Then . . . I will make thee to
ride upon the high places of the earth . . ." (Isa.
58:14). And where had He spoken it? "He maketh
him ride upon the high places of the earth," etc.
(Deut. 32:13).**

This refers to the days of the Messiah ("then"). Connected in consecutive order, the days of the Messiah, the

resurrection, and the world to come are not true value concepts, but matters of belief, dogmas. Value concepts are never connected in consecutive order. Nonetheless, like value concepts, these dogmas too, allow for a wide variety of views. (See RM, pp. 362ff.) Wherever we have not specifically indicated otherwise, all the midrashim commented on below likewise refer to the days of the Messiah. In such midrashim, the proof-texts brought forward contain biblical antecedents of that concept.

In like manner . . . "Behold it cometh, and it shall be done, saith the Lord God; this is the day whereof I have spoken" (Ezek. 39:8). And where had He spoken it? "And I will make Mine arrows drunk with blood, (and My sword shall devour flesh)" (Deut. 32:42).

A comment in the Sifre on Deuteronomy 32:42 asks: How is it possible for arrows to be drunk with blood, or for a sword to devour flesh? The comment answers by saying, "I will make others drunk with what My arrows do," and "I will give others to eat from what My sword does," and it refers to Ezekiel 39:17ff as an example— "Speak unto the birds of every sort, and to every beast of the field, . . . The *flesh* of the mighty shall ye eat . . . and drink blood till ye be *drunken*." (The words italicized show how the verses in Ezekiel relate to the verse in Deuteronomy.) Our midrash is based on this comment in the Sifre; however, it quotes an earlier verse from the same chapter in Ezekiel (v. 8) because that verse contains the words, "This is the day whereof I have spoken," words which prompt the question, "And where had He spoken?" Other midrashim in the passage are likewise based on earlier tannaitic interpretations; compare, for example, ll. 14-16 ("For the Lord God will bless thee" etc.) with Sifre on Deuteronomy 15:6. Obviously, the earlier interpretations have been recast for a purpose. That purpose, as the common form of the present midrashim reveals, is to supply evidence that the Pentateuch was given by God.

In like manner . . . "But they shall sit . . . and none shall make (them) afraid . . ." (Micah 4:4). And where had He spoken? "And I will give peace in the land" etc. (Lev. 26:6).

Leviticus 26:6 continues with: "and ye shall lie down, and none shall make (you) afraid," and hence the correspondence with Micah 4:4.

In like manner . . . "And there shall not be any remaining (sarid, l. 38) of the house of Esau . . ." (Obad. 1:18). And where had He spoken? "And out of Jacob shall one have dominion, and shall destroy the remnant (sarid, l. 40) from the city" (Num. 24:19).

Numbers 24:18, the preceding verse, speaks of Edom (Esau).

D) In like manner . . . "And the Lord remembered Sarah as He had said" (Gen. 21:1) . . . "Unto thy seed have I given this land" (ibid. 15:18).

The concepts embodied here are: God's love and patriarchs (*'Abot*). From this point on nonprophetic evidence is interspersed with prophetic evidence.

In like manner . . . "And I will sell your sons and

**daughters . . ." (Joel 4:8). And where had He
spoken? "And He said: Cursed be Canaan" etc.
(Gen. 9:25).**

"Your sons and daughters" refers back to "Tyre and
Zidon" (Joel 4:4), and Zidon was the firstborn of Canaan
(Gen. 10:15). Apparently Noah's curse is taken as being
really God's words.

**In like manner . . . "Forasmuch . . . return no more
that way" (Deut. 17:16) . . . "For . . . ye shall see
them again no more (Exod. 14:13).**

"Ye shall see them again no more" was said by Moses.
These words are explicitly declared to be a command of
God on 213, ll. 118-121, and in other sources (see H-R,
p. 95, n. 10). Apparently the present midrash is based
on an earlier source. This is probably another instance
of an earlier statement recast for the purpose of this passage. The concept here is *Mizwah.*

**In like manner . . . "Then spoke Solomon: The
Lord hath said that He would dwell in the thick
darkness" (I Kings 8:12). And where had He said
it? "For I appear in the cloud upon the ark-cover"
(Lev. 16:2).**

This refers to *Gilluy Shekinah,* sensory experience of
God. It took place not only in the Tabernacle but also in
the Temple built by Solomon (RM, p. 226, and see
Rashi on Lev. 16:2).

**In like manner . . . "And . . . whoever shall call
on the name of the Lord shall be delivered; for in
mount Zion and in Jerusalem there shall be those**

that escape . . ." (Joel 3:5). And where had He said it? "And all the peoples of the earth shall see," etc. (Deut. 28:10).

Deuteronomy 28:10 continues with "that the name of the Lord is called upon thee." The next verse as well is to be included, and that verse (ibid. 28:11) is to be rendered practically in accordance with Targum Jonathan: "And He will leave you (plural) a remainder . . . in the land which the Lord swore unto your fathers to give you."

In like manner . . . "And of them also will I take for the priests and for the Levites . . ." (Isa. 66:21). And where had He said it? "The secret things belong unto the Lord our God," etc. (Deut. 29:8).

The midrash refers to the days of the Messiah, as is indicated in a longer version in Midrash Tehillim, ed. Buber, 190a (see also the notes there and the references to Rashi and Kimḥi). At that time "they shall bring all your brethren out of all the nations" (Isa. 66:20), and among them will be priests and Levites whose true lineage will not be known then except, of course, to God ("the secret things belong unto the Lord our God"). It is of men of proper lineage, therefore, that Isaiah 66:21 speaks when it says, "And of them also will I take for the priests and for the Levites." The functionaries of the Temple in the days of the Messiah will be authentic priests and Levites.

E) So also here you interpret:

From this point on the text ought to read as amended in several commentaries (see the Apparatus and H-R, p. 41, n. 14): "And it shall come to pass, when ye be come to the land which the Lord will give you, according as He hath promised," etc. (Exod. 12:25). And where did He promise?

"And I will bring you in unto the land," etc. (ibid. 6:8).

This return to the point of departure of the entire passage (89, ll. 3-4) is deemed necessary because what followed was a long digression.

94, ll. 65-69

And It Shall Come to Pass, When Your Children Shall Say Unto You.

The two interpretations of this verse which follow are a striking illustration of how the same verse may be interpreted in diametrically different ways (see above, p. 21). In such cases the interpretations differ with respect to some of the concepts they embody.

Evil tidings . . . that the Torah would ultimately be forgotten.

The reasoning seems to be: If, at some future time, "your children" will have to say, "What mean ye by this service" (v. 26), it will be because they will have no knowledge of all the matters recorded in the Torah concerning the Exodus; this will be true of the parents as well, since they will be performing the paschal service and will not have taught their children the reason for it. The concepts here are Torah and Israel.

But some say it was good tidings . . . that they were destined to see children and children's children;

It is assumed that the children of the generation of the Exodus would have no need to ask about the reason for the paschal service, and therefore that "your children" must refer to the grandchildren. The concepts here are God's love and Israel.

for it is said: "And . . . worshipped."

These words are to be deleted (see H-R, p. 41, n. 18 on these words; and see also Elijah Gaon in ed. Malbim here). In general, however, the text, from this midrash to the end of the chapter, as given in Lauterbach's edition, is to be preferred to the texts in the other editions.

94, ll. 70-74

That Ye Shall . . . Sacrifice of the Lord's Passover . . . and Delivered (*hizzil*, l. 71) Our Houses . . . R. Jose the Galilean says: Until the last one of them finished his paschal sacrifice . . . "That . . . passover," etc.

The words "and [He] delivered our houses" are redundant. *hizzil*, lit., "he saved," is taken, therefore, to refer not to God but to the Israelites, that is, to each individual Israelite. If the people was not safe from destruction until after every Israelite had slaughtered a paschal lamb, then it was only after the last Israelite had completed his paschal sacrifice that the safety of the people was assured. But what relation was there between the destruction of Israel and the failure to engage in the paschal sacrifice? R. Jose's statement here is undoubtedly connected with his statement on 82, ll. 14-15, which we discussed above, p. 78f. According to R. Jose (and to R. Eliezer ha-Ḳap-

par), the Israelites in Egypt were lamb-worshipping idolaters, and now each Israelite, by sacrificing a lamb, demonstrated that he was no longer an idolater. The concepts
embodied here are *Miẓwah* (the paschal sacrifice), God's
justice, Israel and by implication, *'Abodah Zarah* (idolatry). Although the midrash expresses the idea of corporate personality, in the very expression of that idea
here, there is an emphasis on the individual. See also
above, p. 101.

95, ll. 75-78

**And the People Bowed the Head . . . This is to teach
you that whoever hears [about] these miracles (ha-
Nissim, l. 75) . . . should give praise, as it is said,
". . . And Jethro said: Blessed (baruk, l. 74) be the
Lord" (Exod. 18:8-10).**

In its biblical context, as well, the phrase telling that
the people bowed their heads refers to an act of obeisance
to God out of gratitude to Him, but the interpretation of
that act is purely rabbinic. According to the biblical narrative, the people realized, after hearing Moses' words,
that their deliverance was at hand, whereupon they expressed their gratitude to God in an obeisance (U. Cassuto,
A Commentary on the Book of Exodus [Jerusalem,
1951], p. 98f). The midrash here, however, interprets
this expression of gratitude to God differently, taking it
to teach "that whoever hears about these *Nissim* . . .
should give praise." Notice two things more. On the one
hand, the thanksgiving prescribed in the rabbinic rule is
to consist of words ("give praise"), whereas the biblical
instance which illustrates the rule consists of an obeisance;

evidently, then, thanksgiving in rabbinic experience consists of words rather than of an obeisance. On the other hand, it is apparently also true that in the Bible, too, thanksgiving *usually* consists of words; in the proof text brought forward (Exod. 18:8-10) it is told that, after hearing "of all the goodness which the Lord had done to Israel," Jethro said "Blessed (*baruk*) be the Lord."

Factors in rabbinic religious experience are reflected in this passage. One of the rabbinic value concepts embodied in this midrash is *Berakah,* a term connoting thanksgiving to God. Now an expression of thanksgiving by an individual may become, under guidance, an opportunity for bringing into play a larger self, a form of self-awareness which includes awareness of mankind or of Israel (WE, pp. 7, 108f, 171). A *Berakah* is thus governed by Halakah, and therefore not only is thanksgiving expressed in words but it is couched in a formula, the formula depending upon the occasion or situation. All these *Berakot,* and the concept that informs them, are rabbinic. Still, the idea of thanksgiving connoted by the term *Berakah* is a biblical idea. Indeed, even words with which all the *Berakot* begin are already found in the Bible and are used in a similar manner—"And Jethro said: Blessed (*baruk*) be the Lord."

The occasions for the *Berakot* are likewise governed by Halakah. "Whoever hears about these *Nissim* . . . should give praise," is a teaching which has halakic bearing. At the Passover Seder, after the rabbinic discussions related to "these *Nissim,*" praise is given in two forms: in the first part of the *Hallel* (Pss. 113-114), the introduction to which refers to "these *Nissim*" by that very phrase (contained also in the original version—see Goldschmidt, op. cit., p. 48, n. 1); and in the *Berakah* on the redemption following those two psalms. Similarly, one *Berakah* on the redemption is recited every morning and another, every evening, the occasion for both being the last verse in the Shemaʿ (Num. 15:41) just preceding it —"I am the Lord, your God, Who brought you out of the land of Egypt, to be your God" (WE, p. 92f).

95, ll. 79-88

And Worshipped. Why did they worship?

According to this midrash, just as "bowed the head" implies thanksgiving, so does the next expression "and worshipped"—*wa-yishtaḥawu* (l. 79), literally, "and prostrated themselves." Besides "these *Nissim*," there was also another matter for which they thanked God.

Because of the following . . . one out of five . . . not even one out of five hundred . . . a woman would give birth to six children at one time. And you say one out of five hundred went up!

"Six children at one time" is derived from *wa-yishreẓu* (l. 84, translated "and increased abundantly"), and taken to imply the fecundity of *shereẓ,* creeping things (see Exod. R. I.7). R. Nehorai's argument is certainly not of the kind admissable in Halakah, for there arguments from *Nissim* are specifically excluded (RM, p. 164). Nor, despite his vehemence, is his own haggadic derivation more valid than the haggadic derivations derived from *ḥamushim* (l. 79), for in Haggadah even the same event is subject to different and, occasionally, to contradictory interpretations (ibid., pp. 73ff). This means that those who heard the various opinions here were not required to accept one and reject the others. The attitude toward haggadic teachings was characterized by indeterminacy of belief, an attitude fairly analogous to the frame of mind in which the metaphors in a poem are today apprehended. As we have shown elsewhere, Haggadah and poetry are but different modes of one great category, the category of significance, Haggadah communicating valuational significance, and poetry, esthetic significance (RM, pp. 111ff; on indeterminacy of belief, ibid., pp. 131ff; cf. also, on poetry, OT, p. 215f).

When did all the others die?

This accounting for the death of the "others" accords with all four opinions.

During the three days of darkness, of which it is said (rather, as it is said): "They saw not one another (rather, no man saw his brother)" (Exod. 10:23).

"No man saw" refers to the Egyptians, that is, no Egyptian witnessed the burial of an Israelite by "his brother." There were Israelites who were wicked and rebellious and who wished to remain in Egypt; these men died during the three days of darkness (Exod. R. XIV.3).

They then . . . thanked (*we-hodu*, l. 87) . . . rejoice over them.

Two value concepts, God's justice and His love, are intermingled in the idea that God punished the wicked among Israel but at a time when the Egyptians could not know that Israelites had died. Other concepts embodied in the midrash are *Hoda'ah* (*we-hodu*), thanksgiving which is not necessarily expressed through a *Berakah, Nes* (the fecundity of Israel), and *Ge'ullah* (redemption). Attached here to "and worshipped," the midrash is primarily an interpretation of Exodus 13:18, and it is found on 175, ll. 75ff as a comment on that verse.

96, ll. 89-90

And the Children of Israel Went and Did. This indicates that reward is given . . . performing it.

"And went," according to this interpretation, would otherwise be superfluous. The concepts are God's love and *Mizwot.*

96, ll. 91-92

And Did So. And had they already done so? . . . once they undertook to do it . . . had already done it.

All these things were told them on the first of the month, and the implication here is that the Israelites immediately "went and did so" (see Rashi); "did so" therefore, the midrash says, means that Scripture credited them with having already performed the *Mizwah,* although they had only undertaken to do so. The concepts are, again, God's love and *Mizwah.*

96, ll. 93-96

This makes known the excellency of Israel . . . as Moses and Aaron told them.

An emphasis on Israel.

Another Interpretation . . . that Moses and Aaron also did so.

Moses and Aaron, too, observed the *Miẓwah* of the paschal lamb, despite being occupied with another *Miẓwah,* that of the redemption of Israel (Mechilta de-R. Simon b. Jochai, ed. Hoffmann, p. 22, and the notes there; cited by H-R, p. 42, n. 12). The concepts are: *Ẓaddik* (a righteous man) and *Miẓwot.*

*

96, ll. 1-5

And It Came to Pass at Midnight. The Creator of the night divided it exactly. . . . Because it is said: "And Moses said: Thus saith the Lord: About midnight will I go out" etc. (Exod. 11:4). For, is it possible for a human being to fix the exact time of midnight? . . . R. Judah b. Bathyra says: He who knows its hours and its fractions divided it.

The text presents difficulties (comp. the text in H-R, p. 42f and see the notes there). With the help of the variants and versions, however, the thought stands out rather clearly. In Exodus 11:4, the prefix *ka,* "about," is used, whereas here (ibid. 12:29) the prefix is *ba,* "at," and this difference is made the subject of interpretations. "About midnight" (see Rashi, ed. Berliner, p. 53b, on Exod. 11:4) is said by Moses ("and Moses said") who, although speaking in the name of God, must, nevertheless, use the indefinite expression since, as a human being, he cannot presume to know the exact moment of midnight. That is not the case when it is Scripture itself which speaks, and hence "at midnight" is the expression em-

ployed here (Exod. 12:29). God divided that night into
two equal halves, and He could do so because He created
that night (just as He creates every night and every
day—WE, p. 94); this opinion takes "at midnight" to
imply the idea of the omnipotence of God. According to
R. Judah b. Bathyra, "at midnight" implies the idea of
God's omniscience; that night was divided into two equal
halves by Him Who knows the exact limits of "its (i.e.,
the night's) hours and its fractions." (On the divisions and
subdivisions of night and day, see Yer. Berakot I.1, 2d,
and L. Ginzberg, Commentary on the Palestinian Talmud,
I, pp. 57ff, and see S. Lieberman, Tosefta Ki-Fshuṭah,
I, p. 2).

Not represented by conceptual terms in rabbinic literature, the ideas of God's omnipotence and of His omniscience are not rabbinic value concepts but auxiliary
ideas (see above, p. 51). Here those ideas are employed
in order to make vivid the concept of *Ge'ullah* as concretized in the redemption from Egypt. Israel was redeemed from Egypt by God at midnight (above, p. 88;
on the last plague as identified with the redemption, see
ibid., p. 91). The redemption was precisely at midnight.
There was not even a moment of transition between
slavery and freedom.

97, ll. 6-8

**R. Eliezer . . . "night" used there (v. 12) . . . not
later than midnight.**

It is more likely that "there" refers to v. 8 ("And they
shall eat the flesh in that night"), and that R. Eliezer
teaches here that the paschal lamb may be eaten only
until midnight (see the anonymous opinion and that of

'Abba' Ḥanin in the name of R. Eliezer in the discussion
above, pp. 86ff.). Compare 46, ll. 40-43 with the text
in H-R, p. 19, ll. 7-8 and the notes there and see ibid.,
p. 43, end of n. 1. The concepts embodied in this halakah
are *Miẓwah* and *Ge'ullah,* redemption.

97, ll. 9-17

See above, p. 91.

97-98, ll. 18-25

**From the First-Born . . . Scripture comes to teach
that Pharaoh himself was a first-born . . . He alone
was left of all the first-born, and referring to him
Scripture says: "But in very deed for this cause."
have I made thee to stand," etc. (Exod. 9:16).**

The rest of the verse, too, is decidedly relevant—"to
show thee My power, and that My name be declared
throughout all the earth." Although in the simple meaning the words "that My name may be declared" do not
relate to Pharaoh (cf. Ibn Ezra on the verse), according
to the midrashic interpretation here it is Pharaoh who
will tell of God's Name so that God may be acknowledged
everywhere. This midrashic idea is also expressed in
Targum Jonathan on Exodus 9:16—"in order to show
thee My power, and in order that thou mayest tell of
My holy Name in all the earth," the phrase "My holy
Name" implying that God alone is holy and hence is to be
acknowledged.

This midrash embodies the concepts of God's justice
and *Kiddush ha-Shem,* the sanctification of God's Name.
As is the case with all the other plagues (see TE, pp.

189f), the plague on the first-born was regarded by the Rabbis as having its own justification. The first-born are characterized earlier as "the first to sin and thus the first to be punished" (54, ll. 46-47, and cf. above, p. 91), and we shall soon see that the Rabbis view the death of the first-born of the captives and servants as punishment for sin. Against this background, the sparing of Pharaoh, even though he was a first-born, calls attention to another concept embodied here, *Kiddush ha-Shem,* sanctification of God's Name. When the concepts of God's justice and *Kiddush ha-Shem* are combined, the aspect of *Kiddush ha-Shem* described is not sanctification of God's Name by man but by God Himself (see below, pp. 245ff, and the discussion there). Pharaoh's role is to be that of making the nations aware of the punishment of Egypt by God, and hence that God alone is holy, which is to say that God alone is to be acknowledged.

In a comment on Exodus 14:29 (246, ll. 46-47), R. Nehemiah teaches that all the Egyptians at the Red Sea were destroyed except Pharaoh. R. Nehemiah then goes on to quote Exodus 9:16, and he obviously interprets it as does the midrash we have just discussed, namely, that Pharaoh was spared so that he might make the nations aware of the punishment of the Egyptians by God. Possessing the same theme and embodying the same concepts, the two midrashim are certainly akin, yet because their backgrounds are different, each is undoubtedly independent of the other. Perhaps in an attempt to connect the two, Rashi on Exodus 12:29 says that Pharaoh was spared when the rest of the first-born were smitten "to show thee My power" at the Red Sea (see ed. Berliner, p. 55b and the note there).

98, ll. 25-27

Baal-Zephon was left of all the deities (*ha-Yir'ot*, l. 26)

All the other idols were destroyed at this time (see the discussion above, p. 93). *Yir'ah,* literally "fear," is used here and elsewhere in the sense of "idol," and is therefore a pejorative term in such contexts. As thus used, it has an ironical connotation since an idol is actually powerless, a connotation all the more striking when the Rabbis have idolaters themselves refer to their idol in this fashion (l. 40). *Yir'ah* refers to the idol alone, whereas *'Abodah Zarah* refers both to idols and to idol worship. This midrash follows the preceding one because, like Pharaoh, Baal Zephon "alone was left."

to mislead the minds of the Egyptians.

For, as idolaters, they reasoned that this idol was left because it was so powerful as not to be affected by the visitation. (See Mechilta de R. Simon b. Jochai, ed. Hoffman, p. 23; in our text, no explanation is given, but see the remarks following. See also Rashi on Exod. 13:2 and Job 12:23.)

Referring . . . "He misleadeth the nations and destroyeth them" (Job 12:23).

The simple, nonmidrashic meaning of Job 12:23 is: "He increaseth the nations," etc. However, the rendering in the translation conveys the idea of the midrash, *masgi'* (he increaseth) being taken as *mashgi'* (he misleadeth). Likewise to conform to the interpretation, *la-Goyim* (l. 27, "the nations") ought to be rendered "the Gentiles" in accordance with the rabbinic meaning of the word, for the word is taken here to refer to non-Jews in the sense of pagans, idolaters. (It does not always or necessarily refer to idolaters; see RM, p. 41.) In ll. 40-42, the teaching is just the opposite, since the point there is that the Egyptians were prevented, by the death of the first-born of the cattle, from saying that their deities, the cattle, were so powerful as not to be affected by the visitation. But the reasoning which the Rabbis attribute to the idolaters is the same in both teachings, and such reasoning by idolaters was not merely a figment of the Rabbis' imagination. When an idol was left standing in the midst of ruin brought about by fire or another catastrophe, the Rabbis actually heard idolaters laud their idol in these very terms (see II, p. 245, ll. 109-112, and comp. 'Abodah Zarah 54b).

98-99, ll. 28-38

Unto the First-Born of the Captive. But how did the captives sin? (It was only . . . "Our deity . . . did not prevail over us.")

What we have placed in parenthesis is practically repeated in ll. 40-42 where the idea has far more relevance. Moreover, this idea is not found in Targum Jonathan on the verse, although the idea which follows is found there; (see also H-R, p. 43, n. 13 and ed. Friedmann, p. 13b, n. 8).

Another Interpretation:

This expression is not found in the best MSS. Its absence there indicates that the answer to the question, "But how did the captives sin?" properly begins with, "This is to teach you," etc.

This is to teach you that the captives used to rejoice over every decree . . . "He that is glad at calamity shall not be unpunished" (Prov. 17:5) . . . And not the captives alone acted thus but also the Egyptian menservants and maidservants . . . "even unto the first-born of the maidservants" (Exod. 11:5).

A rabbinic concept, we noticed above (p. 15f), has a much wider range than its biblical antecedent, and here is a prime example. To the Rabbis it was unthinkable that the first-born of the captives and the slaves would be destroyed without cause. They ask, "But how did the captives sin?" Their answer is given in terms of *Middat ha-Din,* God's justice, whereas the biblical antecedent of that concept allows these aspects of the plague to be uninterpreted. (See also above, p. 92, and OT, pp. 221ff.) As to the idea in the midrash, the Rabbis, it seems, take it for granted that approving an evil deed is like doing the deed oneself.

99, ll. 39-42

And All the First-born of the Cattle. But how did the cattle sin? . . . "Our deity . . . did not prevail over it."

See the remarks on the two preceding passages.

99, ll. 43-48

And Pharaoh Rose Up . . . after the third hour of the day . . . But Scripture says: "in the night" . . . but the passage: "He"

Rather, but Scripture says: "He". See the text in H-R, p. 44. Instead of his usual kingly habit of late rising, and instead of being awakened by courtiers, Pharaoh on this occasion awakened by himself.

"and all his servants, and all the Egyptians" tells that it was Pharaoh who went . . . and aroused everyone from his place (literaly, and made each and every one stand up from his place).

wa-yaḳam (and he rose up, l. 43) is carried over, but taken now as though it read *wa-yaḳem* (and he raised up). Pharaoh himself rose and then he raised up "all his servants and all the Egyptians," that is, he literally made each and every one stand up from his place. See also Rashi on the verse. In this humiliation of Pharaoh there is manifest God's justice.

And There Was a Great Cry. Just as it had been said: "And there shall be a great cry," etc. (Exod. 11:6).

Exodus 11:6 is quoted here because it tells about the character of this "great cry"—"such as there hath been none like it, nor shall be like it any more" (Zeh Yenaḥamenu, cited by Friedmann, p. 13b, n. 18).

99-100, ll. 51-60

For There Was . . . R. Nathan says . . . they would make a statue of him . . . on that night such statues were crushed, ground and scattered . . . on that day.

"Crushed, ground and scattered"—what Moses did to the golden calf (Exod. 32:20), and in the manner in which an idol is destroyed; see ʿAbodah Zarah III.3 (B.

Mandelbaum, in his ed. of Pesikta de Rav Kahana, I, p. 127, note; see also the preceding note there). "As though they had just buried him on that day"—see S. Lieberman, Some Aspects of After Life in Early Rabbinic Literature, in Harry Austryn Wolfson Jubilee Volume (Jerusalem, 1965), p. 523, n. 72.

100, ll. 61-63

And He called for Moses and Aaron. This tells that Pharaoh ... where does Aaron dwell?

The simple meaning of the verse is that Pharaoh called for Moses and Aaron to come to him, but the verse is elliptical and does not actually say that they came at his call. This enables the midrash to take "And he called for Moses and Aaron" as a statement complete in itself, and hence to interpret the words as meaning that Pharaoh kept calling, kept on asking for Moses and Aaron. Pharaoh's humiliation is far greater in the midrashic interpretation than in the verse interpreted, and at the same time he is also shown to be bewildered and helpless. Pharaoh's condition now is in contrast to his former arrogance and is an instance of God's punitive justice.

100, ll. 64-66

And said: Rise Up, Get You Forth. Moses, however, said to him: "We are warned not to go out except in broad daylight (literally, in public—*be-farhesya'*, l. 65)," as it is said: "And none ... the morning" (v. 22).

"And he called for Moses and Aaron by night" precedes the words commented on here. Pharaoh told them to go immediately, and thus "by night." The answer attributed by the midrash to Moses embodies the concept of *Ge'ullah,* redemption. If the people of Israel are in truth being redeemed, this means that they are not to leave by night, to steal away, as it were. See the remarks above, pp. 87, 88.

100-102, ll. 66-86

A) Another Interpretation. And He called for Moses and Aaron. Why is this said?

The question refers to the entire verse. The verse tells of how Pharaoh capitulated and gave the Israelites permission to leave, but this permission was not necessary since it was God who redeemed Israel from Egypt. The entire verse is therefore interpreted as depicting how the words uttered by Moses to Pharaoh were fulfilled. Among these words, the midrash says, was a hint that Pharaoh would come down to Moses, and that hint, too, was now fulfilled. According to this midrash, Pharaoh did not "call *for* Moses and Aaron" but called out, exclaimed *to* Moses and Aaron, an interpretation involving a different but entirely possible meaning of the prefix *le* (l. 66). (Indeed, the verse actually continues with exclamatory phrases—"Rise up, get you forth.") But if Pharaoh called out to Moses and Aaron without calling for them, he must have come down to speak to them. The midrash goes on to tell when it was that Moses hinted Pharaoh would come to him.

Because it is said: "And Pharaoh . . . Get thee from me," etc. (Exod. 10:28). "And Moses said . . . I will see thy face again no more" (ibid. v. 29) but "all these thy servants shall come down" etc. (Exod. 11:8).

The Rabbis take Exodus 11:4-8 to be continuous with ibid. 10:29, apparently regarding ibid. 11:1-2 as a *Dibbur* to Moses before he delivered God's message to Pharaoh and v. 3 as parenthetical. See Rashi on Exodus 11:4.

The purpose of saying "these" was none other than to imply: "You yourself will ultimately come down leading them." Moses, however, showed respect to royalty.

See note 4—Moses only hinted that Pharaoh himself would come down. Several medieval compendia read: "For he (Moses) did not say, 'Thou and all thy servants',", and they omit the interpretation on "these" (cited by H-R, p. 45, n. 5); according to this reading Moses did not even hint that Pharaoh himself would come, so great was the respect he showed to royalty. See Zebaḥim 102a (and Rashi's gloss there) which probably affected this reading.

For so . . . "And the Lord spoke unto Moses and unto Aaron, and gave them a charge," etc. (Exod. 6:13)—He charged them to show respect to royalty.

Exodus 6:13 describes the charge as being "unto the children of Israel, and unto Pharaoh king of Egypt," whence the midrash derives that the charge included an admonition to respect Pharaoh as king. H-R (loc. cit.) says that this statement represents another version of "Moses showed respect to royalty," the preceding statement, and that one or the other ought to be deleted.

Two value concepts are mentioned by name in the phrase, "he showed respect to royalty"—*Kabod* (ll. 72, 73, 74) and *Malkut* (ibid.). As the phrase indicates,

Malkut (royalty, kingship) is a status which calls forth the attitude of *Kabod* (respect, honor).

B) And so we find that Joseph . . . "It is not in me; God will give Pharaoh an answer of peace" (Gen. 41:16).

This midrash regards "God will give Pharaoh an answer of peace" as constituting a prayer by Joseph; in praying thus he showed respect to royalty (R. David Moses Abraham of Rohatyn, Mirkebet ha-Mishneh [Lemberg, 1894], p. 25a). Beginning with this midrash, there is a digression consisting of examples of respect for royalty. The digression is connected with the preceding section through an association of ideas, of course.

And we also find that our father Jacob . . . "And Israel . . . sat upon the bed" (ibid. 48:2).

See note 5.

And we find that Elijah . . . "And he girded up his loins, and ran before Ahab" (I Kings 18:46).

"Elijah did not hesitate to challenge and defy the king when an issue was involved, but now when there was no such issue, he did not allow Ahab to go home alone, but made use of his supernatural strength to show deference to the king" (L. L. Honor, Book of Kings I, A Commentary [New York, 1955], p. 268). On "supernatural strength" see Targum Jonathan to the verse.

And so we find that Hananiah . . . "Then . . . said: 'Shadrach . . . come forth and come hither' . . . came forth" (Dan. 3:26) . . . Daniel . . . "Then said Daniel . . . 'O King, live forever' " (ibid. 6:22).

Hananiah, Mishael and Azariah did not come forth until they received permission from the king to do so.

This digression probably served a specific purpose. By giving example after example, it teaches respect for royalty over and over again. Represented here is, most likely, the view of those who advocated cooperation with the Roman government of Palestine.

102, ll. 87-96

**And Said . . . I had said . . . And you had said . . .
"Rise up . . . serve the Lord, as ye have said" . . .
"Take . . . as you have said and be gone;**

The Rabbis resume the theme of how the words uttered by Moses to Pharaoh were fulfilled, a theme interrupted by the digression. But now the simple meaning too is made a factor in the rabbinic interpretation. "As ye have said" (v. 31) and "as you have said" (v. 32), obviously referring to statements by Moses, indicate—according to the simple meaning—Pharaoh's capitulation to those demands of Moses. All this is included in the rabbinic interpretation, except that the capitulation is underscored by showing how Pharaoh refers to each demand of Moses in order to reverse his own previous stand. Yet it is not just Pharaoh's capitulation which constitutes the midrashic theme but how the words uttered to him by Moses were fulfilled. The midrash says, accordingly, that Pharaoh also fulfilled Moses' words, "Thou must also give into our hand sacrifices and burnt-offerings" (Exod. 10:25). Embodied in the rabbinic theme are the concepts of *Nebu'ah* (prophecy) and *Ge'ullah* (redemption).

and bless me also." Pray for me that this visitation may cease from me.

"Bless me" is interpreted as pray for me, for in rabbinic thought a blessing which has as its object another human being is a prayer, a petition to God. That is to say, a blessing in that sense is really a *Bakkashah* (petition), rather than a *Berakah,* since a *Berakah,* by contrast, is an acknowledgment of gratitude to God, a thanksgiving (WE, pp. 14, 106). Not consisting of incantations or spells, neither *Berakah* nor *Bakkashah* partakes in the slightest degree of magic or theurgy. In the literal sense, however, "and bless me" may not refer to a *Bakkashah* at all. Addressed by Pharaoh, a pagan, to Moses and Aaron, who now appeared to him so efficacious, these words may have been conceived by the Bible as a pagan's plea for an incantation by powerful magicians. (On spells and incantations, as contrasted with the word of God, see Y. Kaufmann, Toledot ha-'Emunah ha-Yisre'elit, I [Dvir, 1938], pp. 477ff; English translation and abridgment, The Religion of Israel, by Moshe Greenberg [University of Chicago Press, 1960], pp. 84ff.)

103, ll. 97-98

And the Egyptians Were Urgent upon the People, etc. This tells that they hurried and rushed them to go out.

wa-teḥezak (l. 97) in the verse could be taken to mean that the Egyptians forcibly expelled the Israelites, and the midrash says that the Egyptians but urged and pressed them to go. When Israel did go out of Egypt, it was not at Egypt's behest but at God's (see above, pp. 86f).

103, ll. 99-107

For They Said: "We Are All Dead Men." They said: This is not according to the decree of Moses . . . They thought that if a man had four or five sons, only the eldest (lit., the first-born) of them would die.

According to this midrash, the Egyptian people knew that Moses had announced the plague of the first-born but were willing to overlook those deaths. (This is made more explicit in the reading of the Oxford MS—see the Apparatus in our text, and see the comment on that reading in H-R, p. 45f, n. 19, where the suggestion is also made that this is the basic reading.) It is thus taught here that the Egyptian people, although knowing that the death of all the first-born was imminent, remained unmoved, and took action only when their own lives appeared to be at stake ("We are all dead men"). This interpretation characterizes the Egyptians as selfish and callous and hence embodies the concept of *Rasha'* (wicked man). Furthermore, this interpretation ascribes to the Egyptian people as a whole a desire to keep the Israelites in slavery: they were willing to have their first-born die rather than allow the Israelites to go. The Rabbis thus interpret what the Bible leaves uninterpreted, namely, the affliction of the Egyptian people as a whole by the plagues. We have here another example of how the rabbinic concept of *Middat ha-Din* (God's justice) is made to apply in a situation where the biblical antecedent of that concept has not been applied. (Other examples: the first-born sinned—above, p. 92; the captives sinned—ibid., p. 134.)

But they did not know that their wives were guilty of adultery . . . a different bachelor for his father.

This statement probably reflects the sexual immorality of the pagan women in Hellenistic times, especially in Rome. (On the condition in Rome, see W. E. H. Lecky, History of European Morals, II [London, 1910], pp. 302f.) The concept is *'Arayot* (l. 103).

These women had done wrong in secret but God exposed them. Now by using the method of Kal va-ḥomer you argue:

Correct what follows in the translation to: [When it is a matter of the lesser measure, punishment, God makes public the deeds done in secret; all the more certain is it that when it is a matter of the greater measure, reward, (God makes public the deeds done in secret).] See the remarks above, p. 92f.

103, ll. 108-112

And the People Took Their Dough before It Was Leavened. This tells that they had kneaded their dough but had not sufficient time to let it leaven before they were redeemed.

At first glance, the comment seems to convey merely the literal meaning. The words "before they were redeemed," however, identify the idea in the comment as rabbinic. It was because of the Israelites' redemption by God, not because they were driven out by the Egyptians, that they "had not sufficient time to let it leaven." See below, p. 164f.

You also find the same said about the future (*Le-'atid La-bo'*, l. 110) . . . "Who ceaseth to stir . . . sick" (Hos. 7:4-5).

The redemption in the days of the Messiah will come just as suddenly; the people then, too, will knead their dough but will not have suffiicent time to let it leaven before their redemption. What is quoted from Hosea 7:5 should probably be rendered here: "On the day of our king (that is, on the day of the Messiah) the princes (of the world) will be weak" (that is, they will be conquered suddenly). It was expected that the downfall of Rome, ushering in the days of the Messiah would be sudden, for the redemption from Egypt was regarded by the Rabbis as a paradigm for the redemption from Rome. The concepts here are *Ge'ullah* (redemption) and the days of the Messiah.

104, ll. 113-117

Their kneading-troughs (*Mish'arotam*). This refers to the "left-overs" of the unleavened bread and bitter herbs . . . Perhaps . . . the left-overs of the paschal sacrifice? . . . Hence . . . of the unleavened bread and bitter herbs.

It is taught here that the first half of Exodus 12:34 refers to one thing and the second half, to another. What the Rabbis take the first half to mean has been explained in the preceding passage: the people took with them unleavened dough although it had been their intention to let the dough leaven (see H-R, p. 46, n. 5). To this the comment here adds that they also took with them the left-overs of unleavened bread and bitter herbs remaining from the Passover meal (see note 6). However, the comment also teaches that the people did not carry with them the left-overs of the paschal sacrifices; these were burned. To be sure, they had been commanded to do so ("And ye shall let nothing ,of it remain until the morning; but that which remaineth of it until the morning, ye shall burn with fire"—Exod. 12:10), but the Bible does not say that they fulfilled this commandment. The midrash, therefore, makes it a point to teach that this commandment was fulfilled. Sometimes, as in this case, a teaching in a midrash given apparently in support of another idea is really the major teaching of that midrash. (The left-overs of the paschal sacrifices in Egypt were burned immediately— R. Judah Najar, Shebut Yehudah [Leghorn, 1801], p. 18b; and cf. R. Abraham of Slonim, Be'er Abraham [reprinted Warsaw, 1927] p. 89.) The concept embodied is *Mizwot*.

104, ll. 118-122

Being Bound . . . R. Nathan says: And were there no beasts of burden there? . . "And . . . flocks and herds even very much cattle." . . . the Israelites cherished their religious duties (*ha-Mizwot*, l. 122).

R. Nathan bases his interpretation on the conclusions of the preceding midrash. He accepts the latter's interpretation of *mish'arotam* (l. 113) as the leftovers of the unleavened bread and bitter herbs, for he associates what the Israelites carried on their shoulders with *Mizwot* (see Exod. 12:8), implying thereby that what the Israelites carried in that manner were those leftovers. This also involves the underlying idea that the Israelites had already burned the left-overs of the paschal sacrifices. To these ideas R. Nathan adds that the verse as it continues indicates how the Israelites cherished, loved, the *Miẓwot.*

104, ll. 123-125

And the Children of Israel Did according to the Word of Moses . . . Behold, it says "Speak now in the ears of the people," etc. (Exod. 11:2). And so the children of Israel did.

The comment emphasizes that "the word of Moses" was an express command of God given in Exodus 11:2. Taking all those things from the Egyptians was not a trick on the part of Israel. "And so the children of Israel did" —they carried out the command of God. The concepts embodied are *Miẓwah* and Israel.

105, ll. 126-128

And They Asked . . . Silver . . . Gold, and Raiment. There would be no purpose in saying "and raiment" except to indicate that garments were more precious to them than silver and gold.

Although raiment is not mentioned in the command of God as given in Exodus 11:2, it is mentioned in the communication of God to Moses in ibid. 3:22; the Israelites therefore did not ask for raiment of their own accord. But the order in which the objects are named, says this comment, does indicate the value attached to them by the Israelites, the last named, the garments, being more precious to them than silver and gold (see Rashi). Deliberately underplaying "silver and gold," the comment stresses the Israelites' need ("raiment"). Their need was uppermost in their mind, not the valuables.

105-106, ll. 129-141

A) And the Lord Gave the People Favor, etc. This is to be taken literally.

Correct what follows in the translation to: [The Israelite had not finished saying, "Lend me," when the Egyptian brought forth the article and gave it to him—these are the words of R. Ishmael.] By saying here, "This is to be taken literally," R. Ishmael is enabled to enlarge upon what is indeed the literal meaning; he construes literally a phrase that is usually an idiom. "The Lord gave the people favor in the sight of the Egyptians." How? "They let them have what they asked" before they actually put their requests into words. According to R. Ishmael, then, it was through an intervention by God, through a *Nes,* that the property of the Egyptians came into the hands of the Israelites. (The text as given here may not be entirely correct. In the MSS and in the printed editions, "these are the words of R. Ishmael" follows immediately after "This is to be taken literally," and the rest is a new and an anonymous opinion—see the Apparatus. After calling attention to this textual variant H-R, p. 47, n. 1 nevertheless goes on to say that the text as given in the H-R edition is the correct one, and that text is practically the same as the text given here.)

B) R. Jose the Galilean says: They trusted the Israelites . . . during the three days of darkness . . . shall they now be suspected?

Given an unparalleled opportunity to take the property of the Egyptians with impunity, the Israelites proved to be above suspicion, and hence the Egyptians trusted

them. R. Jose certainly does not mean to say here that
the Israelites deliberately tricked the Egyptians into be-
lieving them trustworthy in order to take advantage of
that trust later; when the plague of darkness took place,
the command about taking the property of the Egyptians
had not yet been given (see Exod. 11:1-2). The implication is, therefore, that the Egyptians assessed the character of the Israelites correctly, and that it was only because of God's command that the Israelites took the
property of the Egyptians. Since the three days of darkness were a *Nes,* the Egyptians' trust was ultimately due
to God. "And the Lord gave the people favor in the sight
of the Egyptians, so that they let them have what they
asked."

**C) R. Eliezer . . . The Holy Spirit rested upon the
Israelites . . . "And I will pour upon the house of
David . . . the spirit of grace" (Ḥen) etc. (Zech.
12:10).**

According to this comment, too, the property of the
Egyptians came into the hands of the Israelites through
an intervention by God. "I will pour . . . the spirit of
grace" (ibid.) is apparently taken in conjunction with
"I will pour My spirit" in Joel 3:1 where the phrase
refers to prophecy.

**D) R. Nathan . . . they let them have even what they
did not ask for . . . "Take it, and here is another
one like it."**

Not only is this a comment on "so they let them have"
(see note 8) but also, of course, on "And the Lord gave

the people favor in the sight of the Egyptians." This generosity of the Egyptians was not really voluntary but a *Nes.*

Every interpretation in this passage constitutes a graphic way of teaching that the property of the Egyptians was given to the Israelites by God. Less graphic but also containing the same idea is the biblical verse on which the interpretations are based—"And the Lord gave the people favor in the sight of the Egyptians, so that they let them have what they asked." So far as the sheer idea is concerned, the rabbinic interpretations and the biblical text are thus in accord. Now the Bible views this "surrender" of the Egyptians' property to the Israelites as a just recompense for the years of slavery, as Cassuto points out. A law concerning the Hebrew slave states, "And when thou lettest him go free from thee, *thou shalt not let him go empty; thou shalt furnish him liberally* out of thy flock," etc. (Deut. 15:13-14). Precisely the same phrase—"not go empty"—is contained in God's words to Moses: "And it shall come to pass, that, when ye go, ye shall *not go empty;* but every woman shall ask of her neighbor" etc. (Exod. 3:21-22) (Cassuto, op. cit., p. 27). How this act of justice is to be achieved is described there, again, precisely as in Exodus 12:36: "And I will give this people favor in the sight of the Egyptians" (ibid. 3:21). If the rabbinic interpretations but enlarge upon, make more graphic, the idea in Exodus 12:36, then those interpretations, too, embody the concept of God's justice.

106, ll. 142-149

A) And They Despoiled the Egyptians (*wa-yenaẓẓelu 'et Miẓrayim,* l. 142). This means that their idols

(*'Abodah Zarah*, l. 142) **melted, thus ceasing to be idols and returning to their former state.**

The idols had melted, so that their substance, now that it had cooled and hardened, was nothing but metal, and its use was therefore no longer forbidden (on the halakic views, see H-R, p. 47, n. 8). But the verse itself does not speak of idols, much less that they had melted and that their substance was now hard metal, and the entire idea including, of course, the halakah involved, is solely rabbinic. Representing so wide a departure from the text, the idea can be related to it only by means of an ingenious derivation. *wa-yenazzelu* is taken to refer to *nezel*, decayed, mucilagenous flesh (from a corpse) that had become hard, brittle, and by analogy here, to the melted substance of the idols which had hardened. (See R. David Moses Abraham of Rohatyn, op. cit., p. 26a, who cites on *nezel* Nazir 50a and Rashi's gloss there. As far as we know, the only other commentator who attempts to relate the verse directly to the idea in the rabbinic comment is Weiss, p. 18a, n. 70; according to his explanation, *wa-yenazzelu* refers to "inferior things," hence the idols.) The whole biblical clause is interpreted to mean, "And they removed the *nezel* (i.e., the melted substance of the idols that had become merely hard metal) from Egypt"; in this interpretation the linguistic construction of the biblical expression is regarded as being the same as that of a mishnaic phrase like *ha-mesakkel 'et sadehu*, "he who removes stones from his field" (Shebi'it III.7). A different interpretation is given in the version in the Tanḥuma, and we shall deal with that version shortly.

When the Rabbis explain the verse to mean that the Israelites removed the metal from Egypt, they are teaching that the Israelites thus lessened the possibilities for idol-making in Egypt, and also, therefore, the opportunities for idolatry there. But the real bearing of the interpretation lies in what the Rabbis evidently wish to imply rather than in what they actually teach. By interpreting the biblical clause as they do, they are able to ignore its simple meaning—"and they despoiled the Egyptians." What remains of the verse, then, is a description of God's justice alone, namely, the idea that the property taken from the Egyptians represented a just recompense for the years of slavery, and no more. To put it differently, the Rabbis deny that the Israelites took more than their due by interpreting away "and they despoiled the Egyptians," words which could be taken to mean that the Israelites took far more than just recompense. (See the penetrating article on וינצלו את מצרים by J. T. Radday in ספר יאיר כ״ץ [Haifa, 1965], pp. 34-40. Because this article came to my attention after this commentary had already been written, I could not take account of it here.)

B) And how do we know that the plunder at the sea was greater than the plunder in Egypt? It is said . . . Egypt.

The interpretation of Ezekiel 16:7 relates, apparently, to the interpretation above in which ibid. verse 6 is made to refer to the Israelites in Egypt, and the interpretation here continues the narrative, so to speak (34, l. 10). For the interpretation of Psalm 68:14, see Targum Jonathan to that verse, and for that on Canticles 1:11 see Canticles R. to that verse. It is because there is no mention anywhere in the Bible of any plunder at the sea that the Rabbis have had to employ, or to devise, such far-fetched interpretations. But why did the Rabbis compare the plunder at the sea with the plunder in Egypt in the first place? So as to indicate that much more wealth remained in Egypt than was taken out by the Israelites. Nor must "and" in the word meaning "and how do we know" be left out of account. Found in all the MSS and printed editions, it links the statement about the plunder at the sea with the interpretation about *nezel*. Even including the precious metal of the former idols, the wealth taken out of Egypt was much less than the wealth kept by the Egyptians and now become "the plunder at the sea." What the Israelites had taken with them from Egypt was a just recompense, and no more.

A briefer version of this entire section of the Mekilta is found in the Tanḥuma. In that version *wa-yenazzelu 'et Miẓrayim* is interpreted as follows: "Even the idols of silver and of gold melted and returned to their former state, and they took everything." This version patently combines the interpretation in the Mekilta with the simple meaning. However, the statement in the Tanḥuma immediately continues with, "And the plunder at the sea was greater than the plunder in Egypt, as it says, 'And thou camest to the ornament of ornaments' " etc. (Ezek. 16:7). The question obviously is: If "they took everything," how could there have been any plunder at all at the sea? Friedmann has described the version in the Tanḥuma as textually unsound (p. 14b, n. 44); certainly the passage we have quoted is no more than a later explanation. Apparently, both that explanation and, especially, Rashi's gloss have led the commentators to adopt Targum Onkelos' rendering of *wa-yenazzelu* as "and they emptied out," which is the literal meaning. As a result, they have had to attempt to reconcile that rendering with the "plunder at the sea," an unsuccessful attempt, we must say. As to the plunder at the sea, the Rabbis evidently regarded it as booty of war given the Israelites by God who fought for them.

*

107, ll. 1-10

And the Children of Israel Journeyed from Rameses to Succoth. From Rameses to Succoth was a distance of a hundred and sixty miles, forty parasongs.

In a long note, H-R, p. 47, n. 13, also concludes that the correct text here is "a hundred and sixty miles." After the words "forty parasongs" there is an abrupt break in thought, and the comment on the verse (Exod. 12:37) is resumed only in l. 8—"In the twinkling of an eye," etc.

Moses' voice traveled the distance of a forty days' journey.

See note 1. The converging of the Israelites at Rameses was thus made possible by a *Nes*. According to this view, what is said about Moses' voice is a parenthetical statement, and that is the view of the commentaries in general. But the major problem remains. If the *Nes* was necessary, it was because the Israelites were scattered over the entire land of Egypt; how then, could they all have arrived at Rameses in time for the Exodus, even if Moses' call did reach every one of them? We shall return to this matter soon.

This need not surprise you . . . "And . . . handfuls

**of soot of the furnace . . . and it shall become small
dust over all the land of Egypt" (Exod. 9:8-9) . . .
Kal vaḥomer . . . If dust . . . how much more could
the voice do so!**

The Rabbis resort to an inference because there is no
biblical warrant, no proof-text, for this *Nes.*

**In the twinkling of an eye . . . "I bore you on
eagles' wings" etc. (Exod. 19:4).**

This statement completes the thought broken off in l. 3.
Uninterrupted, the comment on Exodus 12:37 reads:
"From Rameses to Succoth was a distance of a hundred
and sixty miles, forty parasongs. In the twinkling of
an eye did the children of Israel travel from Rameses to
Succoth. This confirms what has been said: 'I bore you
on eagles' wings,' etc. (Exod. 19:4)." The concepts embodied are God's love, *Nes,* and Israel.

In another tractate of the Mekilta, a different interpretation of Exodus 19:4 accounts for the convergence of
the Israelites *at* Rameses. " 'And I bore you on eagles'
wings'—R. Eliezer says: This refers to the day of Rameses. For they were all gathered and brought to Rameses within a little while" (II, p. 202, ll. 19ff.). Neither
this statement nor the one apparently based on it and
quoted in the Yalḳuṭ (Ma'se, beg.; cf. Midrash Tehillim,
ed. Buber, p. 34b and the note there) makes any mention
at all of Moses' call. There was, indeed, no need of any
call by Moses. What is said there about Moses' voice reaching to all parts of Egypt is not a parenthesis but an interpolation. Almost word for word that statement, in-

cluding the inference from the "small dust," is found in Yer. Pesaḥim V.5, 32c, except that there we are also told that Moses was enabled thus to instruct the people regarding the slaughtering of the paschal lamb. In its proper setting, then, the *Nes* of Moses' voice reaching every part of Egypt serves a purpose, whereas here not only has that purpose been omitted but no other is even hinted at. It is hard to say whether the interpolation was deliberate or merely due to the resemblance between "forty parasongs" and "forty days"; in any case, it is the work of a copyist.

108, ll. 11-12

A) To Succoth, to the place where they actually put up booths (*sukkot*, l. 11), as it is said: "And Jacob . . . made booths for his cattle" (Gen. 33:17)— these are the words of R. Eliezer.

The proof-text continues with, "Therefore the name of the place is called Succoth." On the basis of this earlier instance, R. Eliezer says that Succoth received its name in Exodus 12:37 as well, because it was the place where *sukkot,* booths, were built, although the locale and circumstances were different. This is an endeavor to arrive at the simple meaning by employing an analogy.

B) But the other sages say: Succoth is merely the name of a place, for it is said: "(And the children of Israel journeyed from Rameses and pitched in Succoth.) And they journeyed from Succoth, and pitched in Etham" (Num. 33:5-6). Just as Etham is the name of a place, so also is Succoth.

And Etham is the name of a place because it refers to a locality—"which is in the edge of the wilderness" (ibid. v. 6). Gesenius explains the word Succoth in Exodus 12:37 and Numbers 33:5-6 as the hebraization of *Thuku,* the name of a district in Egypt and of that district's capital (Handwörterbuch, s.v.).

C) R. Akiba says: Succoth here means only clouds of glory, as it is said: "And the Lord will create . . . a cloud and smoke by day . . . by night; for over all the glory shall be a canopy. And these shall be a pavilion (*sukkah*, l. 18) for a shadow in the day-time" (Isa. 4:5-6).

The Israelites journeyed from Rameses covered by clouds of glory, according to R. 'Akiba. This interpretation hinges on the meaning given to *sukkah* (literally, booth, not pavilion) in Isaiah 4:6; that word refers back to the phrase of the preceding verse (v. 5) which speaks of "a cloud and smoke by day and the shining of a flaming fire by night," and to the next clause which is rendered as, "for over all there shall be (a cloud of) glory (as) a canopy." The verbs in Isaiah 4:5-6 are in the future tense, but here those verses are employed only in order to demonstrate that *sukkah* means "a cloud of glory." In keeping with this meaning, Succoth, the plural, means "clouds of glory"—Israel journeyed from Rameses covered by clouds of glory. (There is no clear indication of how the proof-text is connected with the word Succoth without including Isa. 4:6 in the proof-text—see the Apparatus.) A major difficulty remains, however; see the remark in D) below. The concepts embodied in R. 'Akiba's interpretation are God's love, *Nes,* and Israel.

As in the journey from Rameses, clouds of glory will cover "the ransomed of the Lord" on their journey from the Diaspora to the land of Israel when the redemption from Rome will take place in the days of the Messiah. The redemption from Egypt was regarded as a paradigm for the redemption from Rome. See above, p. 144, and also the text, 103, ll. 108-112 (and the parallel, 110, ll. 38-41). On the other hand, it was felt that, unlike the redemption from Egypt, no time was fixed for the redemption from Rome, and that, instead, this final redemption is always imminent. See above, p. 89, and notice there the explanation of the term *Le-'atid La-bo'*.

So far I know only about the past. How about the future (*Le-'atid La-bo'*, l. 19)? Scripture says: ("And there shall be a pavilion—*sukkah*—for a shadow in the daytime" [Isa. 4:6].) And it also says: "And the ransomed of the Lord shall return . . . and everlasting joy shall be upon their heads" (ibid. 35:10).

To facilitate the discussion we shall designate Isaiah 4:6 as (a), and ibid. 35:10 as (b). Though omitted from the translation, (a) is given in the text itself, and rightly so, for it is found at this point in all the MSS and early editions (see also 182, ll. 175-176). Since it refers back to the verse which precedes it (Isa. 4:5), that verse too, as rendered above in our first paragraph on R. 'Akiba's comment, is part of the proof-text. Here, however, the future tense of the verbs in these verses is decidedly relevant, for the future tense here indicates that the matter spoken of, the cloud of glory, relates to the future, *Le-'atid La-bo'*. As for (b), "and everlasting joy shall be upon their heads" is taken to refer to a cloud of glory. Targum Jonathan on the verse gives this meaning only to the words "upon their heads," whereas Rashi apparently finds it in the clause as a whole. He explains *simhat 'olam* as "the joy that was of old" (on their heads) when they journeyed from Egypt.

D) R. Nehemiah says: "To Succoth" . . . a *he* is appended at the end of the word.

This grammatical principle is assumed both in the interpretation of R. Eliezer and in that of "the other sages." R. 'Aḳiba, too, apparently assumes this principle, since he does not give the *he* a midrashic interpretation. On this basis, R. 'Aḳiba's interpretation implies that Succoth was a place which was designated by that name because Israel was there given clouds of glory. Comp. Targum Jonathan to Exodus 12:37. In our discussion of R. 'Aḳiba's interpretation in C), we did not take the *he* into account because R. 'Aḳiba himself does not mention it at all, and because the problem does not even arise in the parallel found in the Sifra on Lev. 23:43, ed. Weiss, p. 103b.

108-109, ll. 23-30

About Six Hundred Thousand Men (*ha-gebarim*, l. 23) on Foot. Sixty myriads—these are the words of R. Ishmael. For when it says: "Behold, it is the litter (*miṭṭato*, l. 24) of Solomon . . . about it," it means, behold the litter [correct to: the tribes] of Him who is the possessor of peace, sixty myriads of mighty men (are about it) "of the mighty men of Israel. They . . . are expert in war" (Cant. 3:7-8). And it

says: "Wherefore . . . the Wars of the Lord" (Num. 12:14). And it is written: "Let the saints . . . To execute vengeance . . . To execute upon them the judgment written" etc. (Ps. 149:5-9).

In both the Oxford and the Munich MSS the statement "these are the words of R. Ishmael" is found as given here, and there is no reason to delete it, as some of the commentators do. R. Ishmael's comment begins with "Sixty myriads," and it refers to "six hundred thousand men" in Exodus 12:37, but he reads *ha-gebarim*, "men," as *ha-geborim*, "mighty men"—sixty myriads of mighty men. Corroboration is had from Canticles 3:7 where "three score mighty men" is understood as elliptical for "three score myriads of mighty men," this verse being taken to refer to the Israelites upon their exodus from Egypt. In the comment interpolated in that verse here ("it means," etc.) *mittato* is rendered *mattotaw*, His tribes (*not* "litter")—"behold the tribes of Him Who is the Possessor of Peace" (comp. the interpretation of that verse in Canticles R. III.14, and see H-R, p. 48, n. 14). This interpolated comment does not contain the phrase "are about it"; so far as we can see, the interpretation has not taken account of it (see another example above, p. 64).

"He Who is the Possessor of Peace" is a name of God, an appellative, yet it is different from other appellatives of God, although similar in its clausal form to "He Who Spake and the World Came to Be" (86, l. 72). It occurs primarily as the interpretation of *Shelomoh* (Solomon) in Canticles, an interpretation which allows the Rabbis to expound that Book as an allegory. But it is not an appellative alone. By implying that peace is a boon given by

God, the appellative characterizes peace as well and extols it. (Peace is often extolled by the Rabbis; see, for example, II, 290, ll. 83-92, where R. Johanan b. Zakkai speaks of peace between individuals, between man and wife, between cities, nations and governments.) Though they extol peace, the Rabbis are not doctrinaire pacifists, as indeed the context here indicates. According to this passage, the Israelites of the Exodus were mighty men expert in war, warriors of the Lord who went forth "to execute vengeance" and to execute "the judgment written," that is to say, they were a mighty army which was to be employed to execute God's justice. The occasions when it was so to be employed are not specified.

The passage exhibits a rather unusual aspect of organismic thought, that of dual emphasis. Besides the emphatic trends, other types of emphasis are also characteristic of rabbinic thought, notably the type which permits one concept to be stressed above other concepts (see above, p. 50f). Here, likewise, the concept of God's justice is obviously stressed above that of peace, but this is only half the story. Peace, too, is emphasized for it is extolled, and this means that, in most circumstances, peace is to be made a prime standard of conduct. In this dual emphasis, the nature of emphasis in organismic thought is brought into sharper focus. Emphasis is seen to be a valuational mode which does not rule out what is, for the moment, *not* emphasized (cf. WE, p. 12). What makes this phenomenon possible is the potential simultaneity of the value concepts (see above, p. 18f).

109, ll. 30-31

Beside Children. That is, beside women, children

and little ones [rather, and minors—*u-ḳeṭanim,*
l. 31]. R. Jonathan says: Besides women, children
and old men.

The readings of the MSS do not have "old men." In
any case, by listing those who were patently noncom-
batants, both opinions imply that all the rest were warriors. R. Ishmael is apparently the author of the first
opinion.

109, ll. 32-34

**And a Mixed Multitude Went Up Also. A hundred
and twenty myriads . . . Two hundred and forty
myriads . . . Three hundred and sixty myriads.**

On the basis of even the smallest number given here
the mixed multitude far outnumbered the Israelites. The
inference seems to be that, by sheer force of numbers, the
mixed multitude exercised an influence over Israel and,
in view of Israel's backslidings in the wilderness, an
influence not for good. Without the mixed multitude, there
would not have been the sin of the golden calf, according to a rabbinic comment on Exod. 32:7. Designated
by God there as "thy (i.e., Moses') people" because
Moses had insisted on accepting them as proselytes, the
mixed multitude, idolaters that they had been, made the
golden calf and they caused "My people" to sin (Exod.
R. XLII.6; Tanḥuma, Ki Tissa, 21). Similarly, with reference to the "lusting" in Numbers 11:4, an anonymous
statement in the Sifre (ed. Horovitz, p. 86) declares it
was "the proselytes gathered from everywhere" who led

the Israelites to commit that sin. See also Targum Onkelos and Rashi on that verse. On the derivation of the various numbers, see H-R, p. 49, n. 2.

From the passages just cited, it is evident that the Rabbis regarded the mixed multitude as *Gerim,* proselytes (see also Rashi on Exod. 12:38), and hence the concept embodied in the Mekilta passage here is *Gerim.* Despite the condemnation of the mixed multitude, the attitude of the Rabbis toward proselytes is, on the whole, decidedly favorable; see the long passage below, III, pp. 137-141, ll. 1-48, and the many statements in Numbers R. Chap. VIII. On the rabbinic character of the concept, see RM, pp. 290ff.

109, ll. 35-37

And Flocks and Herds even Very Much Cattle. All these were implied in . . . "And afterward . . . with great substance" (Gen. 15:14)—at their going out from Egypt I will fill them with silver and gold.

kabed (l. 35) literally means "heavy," and the interpretation is based on that meaning: the cattle were heavily laden with silver and gold (ed. Friedmann, p. 15a, n. 12, and the references there; H-R, p. 49, n. 4). We saw above, p. 149, that in the Rabbis' view the wealth taken from Egypt was a just recompense for the labor of the Israelites, and thus a manifestation of God's justice. That God had long before informed Abraham of this act of justice was, however, a manifestation of His love for him, and so the concepts embodied here are God's justice, His love, patriarchs, and Israel.

110, ll. 38-41

**And They Baked . . . This tells that they had knead-
ed the dough . . . (Hos. 7:4-5).**

See above, pp. 143f.

110, ll. 42-45

**Cakes (*'Ugot*). *'Ugot* . . . baked on coal, as it is
said: "And . . . as barley cakes" (Ezek. 4:12) . . .
"But . . . a little cake first" (I Kings 17:13). A great
miracle (*Nes Gadol*) . . . They kept on eating of it
for thirty days until the manna came down for them.**

On the number of days and meals, see H-R, p. 49, n.
9. This *Nes* is different from the biblical one in IKings
19:6-8 in that here the cakes supplied the Israelites with
meals day after day, just as did the manna later. Before
the *Nes* of the manna, this midrash says, there was one
of similar character, so that during the entire journey
from Egypt to Canaan the sustenance of the Israelites
was a matter of palpable *Nissim,* extraordinary manifestations of God's love.

Although it does so here, *Nes Gadol,* a great *Nes,* does
not always imply something supernatural. When, for example, R. Joshua b. Levi says that God's giving sustenance to man is a greater thing than was the cleaving of
the Red Sea, "greater" refers to the range of the *Nes,*
for the cleaving of the sea was in behalf of Israel only,
whereas sustenance is given to the whole world (Bereshit
R. XX.9, ed. Theodor, p. 193, and the note there). Were
Nes Gadol limited to supernatural miracles, the term
Nes by itself would characterize everyday *Nissim* alone,

and that is not the case. See above, p. 82f, and RM,
p. 161, n. 42.

110, ll. 46-47

**Because They Were Thrust Out of Egypt. I might
understand this to mean that they hurried out of
their own accord . . . get out.**

The translation relates "of their own accord" to the
Israelites, and so do R. David Moses Abraham of Rohatyn
(op. cit., p. 26b) and Weiss (p. 19a, note). But Friedmann (p. 15b, n. 17) cites Zayit Ra'anan, a commentary
on the Yalkuṭ by R. Abraham Abali Gumbiner, which relates "of their own accord" to the Egyptians—the Egyptians did not thrust out, drive out the Israelites of their
own accord—and this explanation appears to be correct.
In an interpretation further on, the same expression un-
questionably relates to Pharaoh, again in the context of
the redemption. " 'And it came to pass when Pharaoh
would hardly let us go' Exod. 13:15)—I might understand this to mean of his own accord, but Scripture says,"
etc. (167, ll. 135-136). "Of their own accord" and "of
his own accord" refer to the enemy, not to the Israelites.
If this is so, then the Rabbis take "Egypt" to refer not
to the land but to the people, the Egyptians—that is, the
verse is interpreted to say: "Because they were thrust
out by the Egyptians." (Notice that in the simple rendering as well, the word *Miẓrayim* often has to be construed
as meaning "the Egyptians"—see, for example, 86, l.
78; 103, l. 79; 105, l. 126.)

In consonance with this interpretation, the phrase with
which the verse continues, translated "and could not

tarry," likewise refers to the Egyptians, as Friedmann (loc. cit.) points out. It is to be translated, however, as "and they could not delay" (comp. Ps. 119:60)—the Egyptians could not delay in driving out the Israelites, for it was not a matter of their own will but of God's, since the hour of the redemption had come. This, in turn, involves reading: not *'ad she-nig'alu* (l. 47) but *'al she-nig - alu,* a slightly different reading found in one of the compendia (see the Apparatus and also H-R, p. 49, n. 10), and meaning "since they (i.e., the Israelites) were redeemed."

On the basis of these explanations, the midrash as given is to be translated as follows: " 'Because they were thrust out by the Egyptians'—I might understand this to mean that they (the Egyptians) did so of their own accord but Scripture says: 'and they (the Egyptians) could not delay,' since (at that moment) they (the Israelites) were redeemed (by God)." But it is quite possible that *'ad she-nig'alu,* awkward even when amended, crept in here because of the somewhat similar clause in line 39; indeed, Elijah Gaon (ed. Malbim ad loc.) deletes those words here. The midrash would then state explicitly that the Israelites were only apparently driven out by the Egyptians, and the reason for the involuntary character of this act by the Egyptians would be implied rather than stated. See above, p. 87f.

110, ll. 48-53

Neither Had They Prepared for Themselves Any Victual. This proclaims the excellence of Israel, for they did not say to Moses: How . . . without having provisions for the journey?

"They did not attempt to provide provisions, not now and not earlier, but trusted in the Lord"—Weiss, p. 19a, n. 4.

But they believed in Moses and followed him.

Rather: But they trusted—*he'eminu* (1. 50)—[in God]; and they followed Moses. This is how Weiss, whom we have just quoted, seems to understand the passage; so also does Midrash Sekel Ṭob, II, ed. Buber, p. 142. We wish merely to add the following considerations:

(a) The word *bo* ("in him," l. 50), translated "in Moses," is not found in the version of this passage below, II, p. 84f, ll. 9-13; moreover, it is not found here in any of the versions of the compendia, or in Rashi on the verse, or in the text as given in H-R, p. 50. Rendered literally, the phrase which follows, translated "and followed him," would be "and went after Moses" or, more smoothly, "and followed Moses." Although without provisions for a journey, they followed Moses into the wilderness. But even if *bo* is retained, this pronoun refers to God and not to Moses.

(b) *he'eminu* here means "they trusted." Were it to mean "they believed," it would have to refer to a statement or to something equaly definite (see RM, p. 347, and the examples there in n. 32). *'Emunah,* the noun, always has the connotation of "trust" in rabbinic literature, and so also, most often, do the verb forms. (See 252ff., ll. 124ff., and see the discussion in RM, p. 42ff., and in WE, p. 255, nn. 79 and 80.) Because of their trust in God, this passage says, they deliberately did not prepare provisions for the journey in the wilderness, "a land that was not sown."

Of them it is said in the traditional sacred writings: "Go and cry . . . saying," etc. (Jer. 2:2).

In the words, "How thou wentest after Me in the wilderness, in a land that was not sown" this verse extols, according to the Rabbis, Israel's trust in God when they went into the wilderness without provisions. The term *Kabbalah* ("the traditional sacred writings") refers in rabbinic literature to the Books of the Prophets and the Hagiographa.

What reward did they receive for this? "Israel was God's hallowed portion," etc. (ibid. 2:3).

As reward for trust in Him, God conferred holiness upon Israel; the concepts embodied here, therefore, are God's justice, holiness and Israel. Jeremiah 2:3, however, goes on to say that "all that devour" Israel, all that harm him, will be punished, and hence the punitive phase of God's justice is expressed here as well. The other concept embodied in the passage is that of *'Emunah,* trust or faith.

In the Bible as well as in rabbinic literature, what is holy is regarded as belonging to God in a special sense, as being God's own—"Israel is God's hallowed portion." With respect to Israel, it must be added, this idea means to the Rabbis that because the people of Israel are God's own, it is incumbent upon them to be holy. Instead of being just a status, the holiness of Israel constitutes an obligation, something the individual is called upon to achieve through effortful personal conduct. Thus, below (III, 157, ll. 1-2), the verse "And ye shall be holy men unto Me" (Exod. 22:30) is interpreted by R. Ishmael to say, "When you are holy men, then you are Mine."

111, ll. 54-63

A) Now . . . Four hundred and Thirty Years . . . One passage says: "Four hundred and thirty years" (Exod. 12:40), and another passage says: "And . . . they shall afflict them four hundred years" (Gen. 15:13). . . . Thirty years before Isaac was born the decree (*Gezerah*, l. 58) was issued at the covenant between the parts.

See note 2. "Thy seed" in Genesis 15:13 is taken to mean the generations that began with Isaac, and "a stranger in a land that is not theirs" (ibid.) to refer to the sojournings that began with him and culminated in the sojourn in Egypt (Rashi on Exod. 12:40). According to this interpretation, which harmonizes Exodus 12:40 with Genesis 15:13, the "extra" thirty years in Exodus 12:40 are associated with the decree concerning the seed of Abraham, the first of which was Isaac.

A *Gezerah* of God is a command of God the reason for which is not apparent (see WE, pp. 210ff. on the difference between a *Gezerah* of God and a *Mizwah*). A decree of God may also be a *Gezerah* under similar circumstances, i.e., when the reason for that decree is not given or apparent. When Scripture states, "For the iniquity of the Amorite is not yet full" (Gen. 15:16), a reason is given for the delay in granting the promised land. On the other hand, no reason is given for "they shall afflict them four hundred years" (ibid. v. 13), and so these events-to-be as a whole were designated by the term *Gezerah*.

A striking concretization of the concept of Israel is to be found in this midrash. Usually the concept of *'Abot*, patriarchs, is quite distinct from that of Israel, but not so here. (Another instance is in Bereshit Rabba LXIII.3, ed. Theodor, p. 680). In this midrash, the concept of Israel is made to extend backward in time and to include Isaac, for one of the verses harmonized, Exodus 12:40, specifically speaks of "the children of Israel," who begin, according to this harmonization, with Isaac.

B) Rabbi . . . "And shall serve them . . . four hundred years" (Gen. 15:13) . . . "And in the fourth generation they shall come back hither" (ibid. 15: 16) . . . If they repent (lit., do *Teshubah*, l. 62) I will redeem them after the number of generations, and if not . . . the number of years.

Like A), this passage is a harmonization involving Genesis 15:13, and it is therefore linked with A). Otherwise the passages are so much unlike that, in contrast to A), this passage contains a lesson for the Rabbis' own times.

Concerned with religious attitudes rather than just with chronology, B) regards the "four hundred years" mentioned in Genesis 15:13 as referring simply to the sojourn in Egypt; if they will not repent, their slavery there will last four hundred years. But "the fourth generation" mentioned in ibid. 15:16 also refers to the sojourn in Egypt. "If they repent I will redeem them after the number of generations," that is, in the fourth generation from those who went down into Egypt. Since they were redeemed in that generation (see Rashi on ibid.), the inference is that they did repent. Clearly implied is the lesson that the sooner the Jews of the Rabbis' own day repent, the sooner will they be redeemed. The concept of

Teshubah, repentance, in this passage may not involve repentance for specific misdeeds for no such misdeeds are mentioned. "Doing *Teshubah*" here, as often elsewhere, may mean the resolve and the subsequent constant endeavor, to live the good life (see TE, pp. 122ff.). Other concepts embodied in the passage are God's love and *Ge'ullah* (redemption).

111-112, ll. 64-77

Now . . . the Children of Israel Dwelt in Egypt . . . Canaan . . . Goshen . . . Four Hundred and Thirty Years. This is one of the passages which they changed when writing the Torah for king Ptolemy.

"When writing the Torah for king Ptolemy" refers to the Septuagint. (See the version of this Mekilta passage in Megillah 9a which contains the legend of the seventy-two elders who translated the Torah into Greek [*septuaginta,* seventy], and see also the other versions cited in H-R, p. 50, n. 10.) The rendering here of Exodus 12:40 is similar to the rabbinic interpretation of that verse in section A) above, for here, too, the concept of Israel ("the children of Israel") is extended backward in time to include the patriarchs. But here even Abraham is designated as Israel—"in the land of Goshen," the last of the inserted phrases, obviously relates to the sojourn of the Israelites in Egypt, and hence "in Egypt," the first sojourn, must relate to Abraham's stay in Egypt, Abraham thus being, so to speak, the first of "the children of Israel." When the rendering here of Exodus 12:40 is quoted in another midrashic work it is, in fact, introduced with the words, "Abraham is called Israel" (Bereshit R., loc. cit.). Nevertheless, the rendering listed here is so similar to **A)** that it is associated with that interpretation. It is followed by the rest of the tradition, of which it was an element, concerning the changes made "when writing the Torah for king Ptolemy."

This Greek translation of the Bible constituted a representation of Judaism to the Hellenistic world. Had the Bible been rendered throughout in accordance with its literal meaning, it would not have served properly as such a representation. Could non-Jews, or Jews so Hellenized as not to know Hebrew, possibly apprehend how the Bible functioned for the Palestinian Jews? For the latter, the Bible possessed a creative role from the earliest rabbinic times. All the rabbinic concepts grew out of the Bible (above, pp. 6ff.); rabbinic interpretations were the products of the never ceasing stimulus supplied by the biblical texts (ibid., pp. 20f); new laws were developed or inferred by applying hermeneutic rules to the Bible (ibid., p. 22f and RM, p. 123). Regarded as representing Judaism and yet conveying none of these things, a translation of the Bible in accordance with its literal sense would simply result in wrong impressions. The only alternative, therefore, if a translation was necessary, was to make such changes here and there as might obviate flagrant misconceptions of Judaism or, to put it differently, changes that would be in harmony with the spirit of rabbinic Judaism. This alternative was chosen "when writing the Torah for king Ptolemy." Most of the changes made are in harmony with rabbinic thought, some of them, as in the case of the one already presented, being similar to rabbinic interpretations; in several instances, indeed, what appears to be a bold change is an addition which makes the verse congruent with a rabbinic idea.

A translation which gives the simple meaning for the most part and yet, because of the changes made, is also in keeping with the rabbinic outlook, is the Aramaic version known as Targum Onkelos (see OT, p. 318f; RM, pp. 325ff.; and above, p. 4f). Characterized in the Babylonian Talmud as "our Targum (Ḳiddushin 49a), it was held to be practically on a par with the original (see the glosses in Rashi and Tosafot ibid., and see also Lieberman, Tosefta Ki-Fshuṭah, V, p. 1223). Toward the Septuagint the attitude of the Rabbis varied, being at times favorable and at times unfavorable. (See the sources cited in Weiss, Dor Dor we-Doreshaw, I [4th ed., Wilna 1904], pp. 90f; however, Yer. Megillah I.11, 71c, refers not to the Septuagint but to the Greek translation of the Bible by Aquila—see Lieberman, Greek in Jewish Palestine, p. 17f.) It was doubtless connected with their attitude toward Greek education in general. "The attitude of the Rabbis toward Greek education varied according to individuals, places and times" (Lieberman, ibid., p. 16, n. 11). The Mekilta exhibts a favorable attitude toward the Septuagint inasmuch as it associates the tradition about changes in the Septuagint with a rabbinic interpretation. See also A. Geiger, ha-Miḳra' we-Targumaw (Hebrew trans.) (Bialik Foundation: Jerusalem, 1949), pp. 281ff.

Likewise they wrote for him: "God created in the beginning" (Gen. 1:1);

The literal translation is "In the beginning created God," and Rashi (to Megillah 9a) states that the change was made "lest he say 'In the beginning' is a name, and that there are two Powers and the first created the second." This explanation is not at all far fetched; rather, it accords with the rabbinic approach. *Bereshit* ("in the beginning") is a word that the Rabbis themselves noun-ized, using it as a conceptual term (RM, p. 35f), and sometimes equating it with the concept of *'Olam,* world (ibid., p. 150f). Since the Rabbis themselves thus used *Bereshit* as a common noun, it was conceivable to them that others might use it as a proper noun. As to the Rabbis' need for reckoning with sectarians who gave allegiance to two Powers, see RM, p. 344f. The explanation of Tosa-fot (to Megillah, loc. cit.) is really the same as that of Rashi, despite the objection there to Rashi's idea that the word *Bereshit* might be taken to be a name. Fried-mann (p. 15b, n. 25) says that the honor of God de-manded that He be mentioned first, and he points to the comment in Bereshit R. I.16 bearing on this matter.

"I will make a man according to an image and a likeness" (Gen. 1:26);

Rendered literally ("Let us make man in our image, after our likeness"), this verse was employed by sec-tarians as biblical evidence that there were two Powers. R. Simla'i answers them by directing them to the next verse (v. 27), which reads, "And God created man," and in which the verb "created" is in the singular (see Bereshit R. VIII. 9, ed. Theodor, p. 63 and also the en-tire note there). In a different interpretation given to his pupils, R. Simla'i takes into account as well the plural in "our image, after our likeness" (ibid.). The purpose of the change made in Genesis 1:26 and the purpose of these rabbinic interpretations of that verse is the same, namely, lest it be said "that there are two Powers." As we shall see, this is the purpose, too, of still another of the changes made for "king Ptolemy."

"A male with corresponding female parts created He him (*bera'o*, l. 69)" (Gen. 1:27 or ibid. 5:2);

This rendering (comp. also Friedmann, p. 15b, n. 27 and H-R, p. 50, n. 12) does not seem to us to be correct. The explanation of the change here requires several steps. (a) "Male and female created He them" occurs as a literal clause both in Genesis 1:27 and in ibid. 5:2; and the question is whether the change was made in regard to the former or the latter verse. As recorded in the Mekilta, the change was made in Genesis 1:27, for in all the versions the changes made are given in accordance with the order of the verses in the Bible, and the change in question is found in the Mekilta after the one in Genesis 1:1 and before the one in ibid. 2:2 (H-R, loc. cit.). (b) The correct text here is *bera'o* ("created He him"); this is the reading in the Oxford MS. In the cognate versions —Yer. Megillah I, 71d, and Bereshit R. VIII.11, ed. Theodor, p. 64 (and see his note there)—the reading is *bera'-am* ("created He them"). (c) The change made as recorded in the Mekilta is to be rendered: "a male and his orifices created He him" (see the Ḳorban ha-'Edah to Yer. Megillah loc. cit., and also Theodor, loc. cit.). Emphasis on the creation of man's orifices accords with the rabbinic idea that they constitute a *Nes* (Bereshit R., I.3, ed. Theodor, p. 5; cf. Berakot 60b). The change was made apparently because of the context of the words "male and female created He them" in Genesis 1:27— "in the image of God created He him, male and female created He them," a conjunction of clauses that might be taken to mean that "the image of God" is "male and female" (Korban ha-'Edah, loc. cit.).

As recorded in Talmud Babli Megillah 9a (and parallel; see H-R, loc. cit.), the change made consists of "male and female created He him," the change being only "him" instead of "them," as the Talmud itself remarks. This remark of the Talmud indicates that the change was made in Genesis 5:2 (*bera'o* instead of *bera'am*), and not in ibid. 1:27, something which is again indicated by the change being given after the one in ibid. 2:2 and before the one in ibid. 11:17. Conveyed by the change is the idea that God created Adam with two bodies, one male and the other female. That idea, too, is rabbinic ('Erubin 18a; Bereshit R. VIII.1, ed. Theodor, p. 55). The change was made because "male and female created He them" in Genesis 5:2 might be taken to contradict the previous account which tells that just Adam was created (Fried-mann, p. 15b, n. 27).

"And God finished on the sixth day . . . and rested on the seventh day" (Gen. 2:2);

Instead of "And on the seventh day God finished His work which He had made" etc., which more than implies that God was still engaged in the work of creation on the seventh day, the Sabbath. A rabbinic interpretation explains this verse by saying that the world still lacked one thing, namely, rest, and that the Sabbath completed the creation, for when the Sabbath came, rest came (Bereshit R. X.9, ed. Theodor, p. 85 and the note there). Citing this interpretation, Rashi (loc. cit.) states that "since he (Ptolemy) would (doubtless) not accede to this midrash of the Ḥakamim," the change was made

here so as to obviate the objection. The change was made
here in lieu of a rabbinic interpretation.

"Now I will go down and there confound their language" (Gen. 11:7);

Instead of "let us go down." This is the change we
referred to above as being another change that was made
lest it be said that "there are two Powers."

"And Sarah laughed among her relatives" (Gen. 18:12);

Instead of "within herself," a change that involves only
several vowels in one Hebrew word. This change was
made, according to Rashi (loc. cit.), "lest he (Ptolemy)
say" that God did not mind when Abraham "laughed and
said in his heart" (Gen. 17:17) but did mind when it
was Sarah who did so; there was cause to mind, however,
if Sarah, unlike Abraham, laughed about it among her
relatives, openly. Berure ha-Middot, a commentary on
the Mekilta, adds that "saying" (ibid. 18:12) which follows the word in the biblical text does not properly apply
to an unexpressed thought (cited by Friedmann, p. 15,
n. 30). All this leads Friedmann (loc. cit.) to suggest
that perhaps the change here implies that, in general, there
is no punishment for what is merely thought and not expressed. This would be in line, indeed, with rabbinic law
and teaching (see WE, p. 191 on *mahashabah* and the
notes there on p. 291, and see also Kiddushin 39b and the
parallels). Weiss, in his commentary (p. 19b), declares
Rashi's explanation here to be far-fetched, and he suggests an emendation likewise involving only vowels which
would make the change agree with a midrash that Rashi

employs in his Commentary on the Pentateuch to this verse.

"For in their anger they slew an ox and in their selfwill they tore up a stall"(Gen. 49:6);

An ox instead of "a man," and *a stall* instead of "an ox." The objection raised by Albeck (Bereshit R., ed. Theodor-Albeck, p. 1256, n. 6) against Rashi's explanation of this change seems to be a valid one; according to Rashi (to Megillah, loc. cit.), it was made "lest he say, 'Your ancestors were murderers, for their (own) father testified concerning them that they killed a man,' " but unless what was written about Simeon and Levi was changed not only here but also in Genesis 34:25-26, the change made here could not avail against the charge that they murdered the men of an entire city. Albeck (loc. cit.) suggests that the change made here may be connected with a calumny of the Jews invented and spread by their enemies about which Josephus tells in his Against Appion. In that accusation the Jews are described as capturing a Greek every year, fattening him in the Temple and then killing him; and lest the enemies say, "Your ancestors, too, killed a man as a sacrifice," changes were made in the text of Genesis 46:9. Since the basic change was the substitution of *ox* for the word "man" of the text, the word "ox" was already preempted, and hence the substitution of *stall* for the word "ox" of the text (Albeck). As Albeck notes, other changes, too, may have been made because of a current defamation of the Jews (see the remarks on the change following).

"And Moses took his wife and his sons and set them upon a carrier of man" (Exod. 4:20);

Instead of "and set them upon an ass." The next change recorded consists once more of a substitution for the word "ass," and Friedmann (p. 16a, n. 33) and H-R (p. 51, n. 2) say, therefore, that a single reason may underlie both substitutions. This reason, suggests Friedmann (loc. cit.), was the canard that the Jews worshipped the form of an ass in the Temple, another defamation which Josephus tells about in his Against Appion. It is not unlikely, of course, that the translation of the Bible was in some places affected by current calumnies of the Jews. Still, it is hard to see what was gained by avoiding mention of the word "ass" in these two instances when the word is not avoided elsewhere in the translation, not even in the stories about Abraham, the first patriarch; moreover, the mention of an ass in connection with its function as a common beast of burden would, if anything, tend to give the lie to the canard. Rashi (loc. cit.) states that the change was made in Exodus 4:20 "lest he say that your master Moses did not even possess a camel or a horse," that is, Moses was a lowly, unimportant person.

"I have not taken any desirable thing from them" (Num. 16:15);

"Any desirable thing" instead of "one ass"; the change here involves only a slight stroke in a single letter of one Hebrew word. See the remarks immediately above on the reason suggested by Friedmann. According to Rashi (to Megillah 9b), the reason for the change here was "lest he say, 'He did not take an ass but another desirable thing he did take.' " Although the current defamations of the Jews do not figure in Rashi's explanations of the changes made in Genesis 49:6, Exodus 4:20, and here in

Numbers 16:15, his explanations of those changes certainly imply that the translators expected a carping attitude on the part of the non-Jews. In any case, unlike the many changes which consist of teachings inherently rabbinic, the changes made in these three verses evidently but reckoned with the animosity of the non-Jews.

"Which the Lord thy God hath alloted to give light unto all the peoples" (Deut. 4:19) ;

A word which means "to give light" has been inserted here, and that insertion makes the verse completely congruent with a rabbinic interpretation of this verse. "R. Jose the Galilean says: Since it says, 'Which the Lord thy God hath alloted unto all the peoples' you might think that He alloted them (i.e., the sun and the moon and the stars etc.) to the nations [to worship], therefore Scripture teaches, 'Gods that they knew not, and that He had not alloted to them' (ibid. 29:25)"—Sifre on Deuteronomy, par. 148, ed. Friedmann, p. 104a. What is explicit in the insertion is implicit in this interpretation, namely, that the heavenly bodies were "alloted to give light" only; conversely, what is explicit in the interpretation is implicit in the insertion, namely, that the heavenly bodies were "not alloted" as deities to the nations. The rabbinic interpretation also implicates a halakah. Embodied in the interpretation are the concepts of idolatry—the worship of heavenly bodies (WE, p. 184)—and the nations of the world, and we saw (above, p. 95f) that idolatry, in the rabbinic view, was a prohibition laid on all mankind, the nations included. So consistent with this entire rabbinic approach is the insertion that Rashi employs it as a comment on the verse in his Commentary on the Pentateuch.

"Which I have commanded the nations not to worship them" (Deut. 17:3);

Rather, and perhaps no more awkward: "Which I have
not commanded the nations to worship them." This rendering indicates more clearly that the change consists of
an addition to the verse and not of an insertion, the addition being "the nations to worship them." The addition
was made, apparently, to forestall a misconstruction of
the text, for the text reads: "And hath gone and served
other gods, and worshipped them, or the sun or the moon,
or any of the host of heaven which I have not commanded." Had they not made an addition to this text, explains
Rashi (to Megillah 9b), the phrase "which I have not
commanded" might be construed to mean that God had
not commanded the sun or the moon or the other heavenly
bodies to be, a construction allowing "him (Ptolemy) to
say" that the heavenly bodies are gods, "since they were
created against His will." Rashi's gloss is on the change
as recorded in Megillah 9b where the addition consists
only of "to worship them." However, the reading of "the
nations to worship them" is attested to not only by the
printed editions but also by all the MSS of the Mekilta as
well, and it is also the reading of the parallels in Yer.
Megillah I.9, 71d and Tanḥuma, Shemot, 22. The change
was made to forestall construction of the verse by an
idolater so as to make it appear to condone idolatry;
naturally, therefore, the change would consist of a prohibition of idolatry, specifically alluding to such idolaters,
namely, "the nations." Embodying the concepts both of
idolatry and the nations, the change as recorded in the
Mekilta clearly teaches the rabbinic idea that the prohi-

bition of idolatry is laid upon all mankind, the nations included. On the other hand, when only "to worship them" is added, and thus no reference made to the nations, the context permits the addition to be applied to Israelites only; in fact, it is so applied in a rabbinic interpretation which, strangely enough, takes "to worship them" to be an integral part of the verse (Sifre on Deut., loc. cit., preceding the statement by R. Jose).

"And the slender (*ze'irat*)-footed" (Lev. 11:6).

Instead of "And the hare." H-R (p. 51, n. 3) calls attention to *se'irat* (hairy), the reading of the Munich MS, i.e., "hairy-footed." M. L. Margolis (The Story of Bible Translations: Jewish Pub. Society, Philadelphia 1917, p. 35f) states that of the changes enumerated by "the talmudic tradition" only a few "may be verified from the extant manuscript of the [Septuagint]." He goes on to say: "The most interesting case is the circumlocution 'rough-foot' for 'hare' in Leviticus 11:6, because the ordinary Greek appellation of the hare (*lagos*), it was feared, might be offensive to the royal family, the first Ptolemy being surnamed Lagi. As the Rabbis expressed themselves, the king's wife [according to the Babli] (or the king's mother [according to the Yerushalmi]) bore the name of hare." Here, then, is another instance of a change due to a circumstance of the times, and not because it was inherently a rabbinic teaching. This change is given last instead of in its proper order, and Friedmann (p. 16, n. 37) attempts to account for that.

112-113, ll. 78-84

And It Came to Pass at the End of Four Hundred and

Thirty Years, etc. This tells that as soon as the designated time came, God did not delay them an instant.

Correct "the designated time" to: "the designated time of redemption" (*ha-Ḳez̧*, l. 79). The redemption from Egypt took place on the fifteenth of Nisan. God did not delay them an instant for, according to this midrash, the specified years of wandering and servitude began also on a fifteenth of Nisan; that is to say, the day of the redemption was precisely at the end of those specified years. This was the case, the Midrash teaches, with respect both to the four hundred years spoken of in Genesis 15:13 and to the four hundred and thirty years specified here.

On the fifteenth of Nisan . . . at the covenant between the parts.

The very thing to be established—that the event occurred on the fifteenth of Nisan—is here merely stated. A similar statement, but deriving that day from a text, constitutes the last section of this midrash. Apparently the statement here is a scribal insertion. Rashi's comment on the verse, a quotation from this passage, begins not with this statement but with the one following; moreover, this statement is not found in the printed edition (see the Apparatus).

On the fifteenth of Nisan the ministering angels came to bring good tidings to our father Abraham. On the fifteenth of Nisan Isaac was born.

Both of these statements relate to "the designated time" implied by the four hundred years spoken of in Genesis

15:13. The four hundred years began with the birth of Isaac (see above, p. 168). But how do we know that he was born on the fifteenth of Nisan and hence that this day, four hundred years later, was "the designated time?" A tradition is here stated, details of which are given elsewhere. The angels came to Abraham on Passover, that is, on the fifteenth of Nisan, an interpretation derived from the word *'uggot,* cakes, in Genesis 18:6 (Bereshit R. XLVIII.12, ed. Theodor, p. 490, and n. 1 there). On that occasion Abraham was told, "When the season cometh around, and Sarah shall have a son" (Gen. 18:14), and this refers back to the word *la-mo'ed,* interpreted as meaning "at the Festival"—in other words, Abraham was told that Isaac would be born on the Festival of Passover a year later (see Pesiḳta Rabbati, ed. Friedmann [Wien, 1880], p. 24b, and Tosafot to Rosh ha-Shanah 11a, s.v. אלא).

On the fifteenth of Nisan it was decreed at the covenant between the parts, for it is said: "And it came to pass at the end (of four hundred and thirty years)." There was one date designated for all of them.

Correct "date designated" to "designated time of redemption" (*Ḳeẓ,* l. 84). The "extra" thirty years simply indicate that the period of wandering and servitude is now reckoned as beginning with the decree issued at the covenant between the parts, thirty years before the birth of Isaac (see 111, ll. 57-58). This implies that the decree, too, was issued on a fifteenth of Nisan; in other words that the four hundred and thirty years period began on a fifteenth of Nisan—and this is the point made here. If the specified years of wandering and servitude, both in the case of the four hundred years and in the case of the four hundred and thirty years, began and ended on a fifteenth of Nisan, then the redemption, the moment when the servitude ended, could have taken place without the lapse of an instant. See also the first remark on the next passage.

Kez here and in other instances in rabbinic literature means "the designated time of redemption," and is thus, in such instances, a subconcept of *Ge'ullah,* redemption. However, the word is also used in the related sense of "season, term, time," a usage for which there are biblical precedents; see H. L. Ginsberg, The Composition of the Book of Daniel, Vetus Testamentum, IV, 3 (1954), p. 273.

The concepts embodied in this passage are redemption, God's love, the patriarchs, and Israel.

113-114, ll. 85-99

A) Even the Selfsame (*be-'ezem*, l. 85) Day It Came to Pass, that All the Hosts of the Lord Went Out from the Land of Egypt.

In the Oxford MS and in two compendia this verse is prefaced by "And thus it says" (see Apparatus). With this preface the verse is a proof-text referring to all the events listed in the passage; that is, "the selfsame day" is taken to mean that the Exodus was only the last of a number of events which took place on a fifteenth of Nisan, "the selfsame day." H-R, p. 51, evidently regards the prefatory phrase as authentic. If the phrase is authentic, the verse itself is to be repeated, for it also serves as the departure for a new interpretation.

The hosts of the Lord are the ministering angels.

Found neither in the MSS nor in the early printed editions, this statement has been inserted here on the basis of 74, ll. 94-95 by all the modern commentators and some of the earlier ones. But the insertion is gratuitous. As we shall see, here the words, "the hosts of the Lord" are taken to refer to Israel, as in the simple meaning.

And so you find

The passage from here on is a long section taken from a still longer one in Sifre on Numbers, piska' 84 (ed. Horovitz, p. 82f). In the Sifre, the words "And so you find" connect this section with what precedes there; here these words are superfluous. For the comments in A), however, our text also made use of the manner in which the versions in Yer. Sukkah IV.4, 54c (Lev. R. XXIII.8, ed. Margulies, p. 637f) associate, by implication, Exodus 24:10 with ibid. 12:41. This association of verses is not given in the Sifre.

that whenever Israel is enslaved the Shekinah, as it were, is enslaved with them,

Correct to: All the time Israel was enslaved *Shekinah,* as it were, was enslaved with them (on *kol zeman,* ll. 86-87, comp., e.g., Shebi'it II.1,3). H-R, p. 51, omits "that."

as it is said: "And they saw the God of Israel; and there was under His feet," etc. (Exod. 24:10). But after they were redeemed what does it say?

"Etc." refers to words which, in this connection, must be rendered in some such fashion as, "the likeness of a sapphire brick." The Israelites saw the God of Israel and they saw that under His feet was the likeness of a sapphire brick. This phenomenon of *Gilluy Shekinah* took place before the Israelites were redeemed from Egypt; that is implied by the question, "But after (rather, when) they were redeemed what does it say?" (In Yer. Sukkah, loc. cit., the version with Levi b. Sisi as authority, after quoting the verse, states explicitly, "This was so long as they were not redeemed," and so does the baraita there by Bar Ḳappara', where the verse is assumed.) But the detail of the sapphire brick just barely suggests that, in sympathy with the Israelites, God Himself, as it were, was engaged like them in making bricks. A comment by R. Berechiah in Yer. Sukkah (loc. cit.) adds, therefore, that together with the sapphire brick there were also implements for brick-making (see also the parallel in Lev. R., loc. cit., Margulies' note, and Lieberman's remarks in ibid., p. 877). On the other hand, Targum Jonathan and Rashi on Exodus 24:10 characterize the sapphire brick as a reminder to God of Israel's servitude and affliction, from which, evidently, the conclusion is to be drawn that the sapphire brick was merely a reminder.

"And the like of the very (*uke'ezem*, l. 89) heaven for clearness" (Exod. 24:10).

The interpretation of this part of the verse answers the question "But after they were redeemed what does it say?" It says, according to this interpretation, that when they were redeemed the heaven cleared entirely. But where does the verse here specifically refer to "after they were redeemed" or, more accurately, "when they were redeemed?" *uke'ezem* is taken by the midrash to be an allusion to *be'ezem* of Exodus 12:41, *'ezem* being thus interpreted as the particular moment when "all the hosts of the Lord went out from the land of Egypt"; *uke'ezem* hence means "and when *'ezem* took place," that is, when the Israelites were redeemed. This interpretation of the second half of the verse implies, furthermore, that the *Gilluy Shekinah* spoken of in the first half had its locale in the sky. Clearing just when the Israelites were redeemed, the sky during their servitude had been the scene of *Gilluy Shekinah* and the sapphire brick, a scene the Israelites saw when they looked upward. We can recognize now that the entire interpretation of Exodus 24:10 hinges on ibid. 12:41, the verse which opens the passage. This connection between the two verses is posited, however, on the assumption that the phrase "all the hosts of the Lord" refers to the Israelites, not to the angels.

Embodied in this section, besides the concept of *Gilluy Shekinah,* are the concepts of God's love, redemption, and Israel. On the concept of *Gilluy Shekinah* and its restriction, see above, p. 37f.

B) And it also says: "In all their affliction He was afflicted" (Isa. 63:10).

Although the prefatory "and it also says" would make it appear to be so, Isaiah 63:10 is not really a corroborative verse. It is the subject here of a comment in its own right and therefore it is not related, primarily, to the preceding midrash.

So Far . . . He shares in the affliction of the community. How about . . . of the individual? Scripture says: "He shall call . . . I will be with him in trouble"

(Ps. 91:15). It also says . . . "But the Lord was with Joseph" (Gen. 39:21).

This midrash lays stress on the individual at the same time that it emphasizes God's compassionate love, a theme somewhat different from that of the kindred midrashim of the passage. The midrash here appears to be an interpolation. Yer. Sukkah, loc. cit., does not contain this midrash whereas it does contain C) and versions of A) and D).

C) And thus it says: "From before Thy people, whom Thou didst redeem to Thee out of Egypt, the nation and its God" (II Sam. 7:23).

See the note. "And thus it says" refers to the second of the two comments interpreting this verse, that of R. 'Akiba.

R. Eliezer says: An idol (*'Abodah Zarah*, l. 95) crossed the sea with Israel, as it is said: "And a rival passed through the sea" (Zech. 10:11).

See the note. The expression "crossed the sea" and the word "rival," it would seem, impute to this idol a kind of vitality or reality. As we pointed out earlier (above, p. 95), however, when a degree of reality is imputed to idols it is of a dim, miasma-like kind, both largely unreal and wicked. Moreover, what is probably the dominant view attributes to idols no vitality whatsoever; they are characterized as "dead" (II, 245, l. 115. Notice also how the passage there expressly denies that God is "jealous" of the idols).

And which idol was it? The idol of Micah.

See the note. "The Mekilta and many other sources presuppose that Micah's activity took place shortly after the death of Joshua" (Ginzberg, Legends, VI, p. 209f, n. 127). "Even before the Israelites left Egypt, he made his idol" (ibid., III, p. 49 and VI, p. 13, n. 72). Our midrash, too, teaches that the idol was not made in the land of Israel, that it derived from Israel's sojourn in Egypt and thus, apparently, that it was a borrowed idea. There is also the implication that, by letting the idol cross the sea, God redeemed the people despite their incipient, or more than incipient, idolatry.

D) R. Akiba says: Were it not expressly written in Scripture, it would be impossible to say it. Israel said to God: Thou hast redeemed Thyself, as though one could conceive such a thing.

See the note, but see also Lieberman's remark in RM, p. 311, n. 25. "And thus it says," the phrase introducing the interpretations of II Samuel 7:23, refers to the statement by R. 'Akiba; the idea expressed in his statement is similar to that of A), for if He redeemed Himself He must have been "in servitude" in Egypt. In this passage, and in Sifre loc. cit., R. Eliezer's and R. 'Akiba's statements appear as independent interpretations of II Samuel 7:23. In Yer. Sukkah, however, R. 'Akiba's statement is called forth by R. Eliezer's and is preceded by a vehement objection to R. Eliezer's interpretation, circumstantial details which indicate that the version there reflects the original source.

When R. 'Akiba says, "Were it not expressly written in Scripture, it would be impossible to say it," he is not, as some would have it, attempting to mitigate the anthro-

pomorphic statement which thereupon follows. Anthropomorphism is an idea which belongs to the philosophical
universe of discourse and not to that of the Rabbis. Notice
that, far from being a mitigation, R. 'Aḳiba's remark, by
calling attention to the anthropomorphism, actually makes
it stand out all the more boldly. What we do have here is
a structural stereotype employed not infrequently by the
Rabbis (see, for example, R. Joḥanan's statement in Rosh
ha-Shanah 17b), a structural stereotype consisting of a
prefatory formula ("Were it not expressly written" etc.)
immediately followed by a concretization of God's love
or of His justice. It is a teaching device which emphasizes,
usually, the concept of God's love by placing a concretization of that concept against the background of the idea
of God's otherness (on the idea of God's otherness, see
above, p. 83f). Thus, R. 'Aḳiba teaches here that, although
God is not like man who may be enslaved and then redeemed from slavery, God nevertheless did this very thing
to Himself out of His sympathy and love for Israel. On
the other hand, the structural stereotype also teaches, even
if incidentally, that God is not like man, that He is other.
This means that, for all the emphasis on God's love, the
specific instance given does not elicit unqualified belief
but rather indeterminate belief, an attitude that permits
shadings in belief. (On indeterminacy of belief see above,
p. 125f and the references there; on the several kinds of
structural stereotypes, see RM, pp. 308ff.)

114-115, ll. 99-112

A) Likewise you find

What follows now is the second half of the passage
taken from the Sifre, and here these connecting words are

relevant in the Mekilta as well (see above, p. 185). They point to another way in which God, out of sympathy for the people of Israel, shares in their affliction.

that withersoever Israel was exiled, the Shekinah, as it were, went into exile with them . . . to Egypt . . . to Babylon . . . to Elam . . . to Edom . . . "Who is this that cometh from Edom," etc. (Isa. 63:1).

Edom stands for Rome—though much more frequently in amoraic than in tannaitic literature, according to Ginzberg (Legends, V, p. 272, n. 19). However, "the use of the names Edom, Seir, Esau, and similar ones, to describe Rome is very old, and was probably coined at the time of Herod, whose designation 'the Idumean' was applied to his masters, the Romans" (ibid.). See now Gerson D. Cohen, Esau as Symbol in Early Medieval Thought (Jewish Medieval and Renaissance Studies, ed. by Alexander Altman. Cambridge, Harvard Univ. Press, 1967 [—Philip W. Lown Institute of Advanced Judaic Studies, Brandeis Univ. Studies and Texts, Vol. IV], pp. 19ff.) Edom represented to the Rabbis the last exile, and the punishment of Rome by God was conceived as being the prelude to the new and perfect world order. To suggest that Edom, Rome, is the last exile the Rabbis adduce here Isaiah 63:1 which relates that God "cometh from Edom" (and hence implies that He had shared that exile with Israel) and that He says, "I that speak in victory, mighty to save."

The concepts embodied in this midrash are God's love, the nations of the world, Israel, and exile, *Galut. Galut* connotes the sense of having been uprooted and a sense of present homelessness.

Shekinah is a name for God, an appellative. Notice that for statements in this midrash concerning *Shekinah* the Rabbis present proof-texts in which the word for God is the Tetragrammaton. "Thus saith the Lord" (ISam. 2:27); "Thus saith the Lord, your Redeemer, the Holy One of Israel" (Isa. 43:14); "And I will set My throne . . . saith the Lord" (Jer. 49:38). *Shekinah* does not refer to the immanence of God, for that idea is a philosophic, not a rabbinic, conception (RM, p. 255f). Because the name *Shekinah* is always used in contexts which speak of God's nearness, the word has been taken to connote the idea of God's immanence by those who believe that rabbinic literature was affected by philosophic thought. As we saw, they also take instances in which the Rabbis express the idea of God's otherness to demonstrate an aversion to anthropomorphism as such. But it requires only a closer view of the midrash here to recognize that when the Rabbis depict the *Shekinah* as having gone into the various exiles with Israel, they are indeed telling of God's nearness, not of His immanence. Had it been God's immanence the Rabbis intended to teach, could they have described God in the proof-text as He "that cometh from Edom?" Immanence, as a philosophical principle, eschews such anthropomorphisms. Again, if during the exile in Edom He was immanent, then at some point toward the end of that exile He apparently ceased to be immanent. Did He become transcendent? How does transcendence accord with mundane victory—"I that speak in victory, mighty to save"?

In keeping with the usage which limits the appellative *Shekinah* to passages that speak of God's nearness is its use in the conceptual term *Gilluy Shekinah*. The concept of *Gilluy Shekinah* connotes sensory experience of God, in other words, visual or auditory apprehension of God's nearness. By the same token, when the Rabbis concretize this concept in a haggadah, the name *Shekinah* is apt to be the appellative there for God. In a midrash at the beginning of this very passage, for example, one of the verses cited is "And they saw the God of Israel," and when the Rabbis interpret this biblical account of *Gilluy Shekinah,* it is by the appellative *Shekinah* that they refer to God. As in this case, obviously the context decides whether or not the name *Shekinah* refers to *Gilluy Shekinah.*

B) And when they return in the future . . . "That then the Lord thy God will return with (*'et,* l. 107) thy captivity" (Deut. 30:3) . . . "He will return" (*ve-shab*).

'et is rightly translated as "with" in accordance with the interpretation. Implied here is the concept of *Gilluy Shekinah;* see the remark on the next comment.

And it is also said: "With me from Lebanon, my bride" (Cant. 4:8) . . . You and I, as it were, were exiled from Lebanon; you and I will go up to Lebanon.

In rabbinic literature Lebanon is often, as here, a designation for the Temple (see Ginzberg, op. cit., VI, p. 395; J. Neusner, A Life of Rabban Yohanan Ben Zakkai [Leiden, 1962], p. 39, n. 5). Since the Rabbis taught that there was *Gilluy Shekinah* in the First Temple (some said even in the Second), they regarded the Temple as, in a sense, the "abode" of God (WE, p. 163). When

Israel will be restored to its land, the Temple will be reestablished and will again be the locale of *Gilluy Shekinah* (ibid., p. 130); that is what is involved in the interpretations here of Deuteronomy 30:3 and Canticles 4:8. Implied in these interpretations, therefore, is the concept of *Gilluy Shekinah*. "Bride" in Canticles 4:8 is taken to refer to Israel. Thus interpreted, the word is not only a metaphorical expression of God's love for Israel but it is also one of the terms which reflect the rabbinic consciousness of a mystical relationship to God (RM, p. 270f; above, p. 84).

If Lebanon stands for the Temple, how is it that Canticles 4:8 speaks of "with me from Lebanon?" Israel will be restored to its land and will once more experience *Gilluy Shekinah,* and hence the thought should have been expressed in the verse that "the bride" will ascend or come *to* Lebanon, and not that she will come *from* Lebanon. But the verse—"With me from Lebanon, O bride, with me from Lebanon thou shalt come"—represents more than a foretelling that the people of Israel will return from exile. It is God Who speaks and He says to them: When you will be exiled from Lebanon you will be exiled with Me for I will go into exile with you ("with me from Lebanon, O bride"). Not actually derived from the verse but implied is the idea that God will return with them. See Rashi on the verse. (An obviously later version in Shemot R. XXIII.5 asks, "Why does 'with me from Lebanon' occur twice?" The first phrase is then given the same meaning as in our text, with Lebanon taken as a designation for the Temple. In the second phrase, according to this version, Lebanon is a designation for "the kingdoms" [i.e., the nations] by comparison with Ezekiel 31:3, and now "with me from Lebanon" is interpreted to mean that they will return with God from "the kingdoms." On the various interpretations of Lebanon, see J. Neusner, op. cit., p. 120, n. 1, and the references there.)

115-116, ll. 113-123

A) A Night of Watching unto the Lord, etc. In . . . that night they will be redeemed in the future—these are the words of R. Joshua. . . . "This . . . watching unto the Lord."

See note 10. According to R. Joshua, the first part of the verse ("A night of watching unto the Lord for bringing them out from the land of Egypt") refers to the night of Passover on which they were redeemed from Egypt, and the second part ("this same night is a night of watching unto the Lord for all the children of Israel throughout their generations") to a night of Passover in the future when redemption from their last exile will take place. As was the case with the night of the redemption from Egypt, so now too, God is watching and waiting for the night of Passover on which they are to be redeemed. The concepts embodied are redemption, God's love, and Israel.

B) R. Eliezer says: In that night they were redeemed;

He agrees with R. Joshua with regard to the meaning of the first part of the verse. God was watching and waiting for this night of redemption, the night of Passover— "A night of watching unto the Lord for bringing them out from the land of Egypt."

in the future, however, . . . in the month of Tishri,
as it is said: "Blow the horn at the new moon," etc.
Why? "For it is a statute for Israel," etc. (Ps. 81:
4-5).

See note 11. The midrash here is elliptical. Elsewhere
Psalm 81:4 is one of two verses conjoined in demonstrating that the future redemption will take place in Tishri, at
the New Year. According to Rosh ha-Shanah 11b, R.
Eliezer associates this verse: "Blow the horn at the new
moon," with Isaiah 27:13: "And it shall come to pass
in that day, that a great horn shall be blown; and they
shall come that were lost in the land of Assyria, and
they that were dispersed in the land of Egypt; and they
shall worship the Lord in the holy mountain at Jerusalem."
The latter verse is interpreted as relating to the redemption in the future, a redemption that will be characterized
by the blowing of the horn; since the horn is blown "at
the new moon" (Ps. 81:4), the redemption of the future
will therefore take place at the new moon. But what is
the ground for saying that "the new moon" in Psalm
81:4 refers to the day of the New Year? This is the question asked by the midrash in the words *mi-pene mah,* l.
117 (translated by "Why"). The question is answered by
quoting the next verse, Psalm 81:5, and which is to be
rendered here as, "When [the day is thus] a statute for
Israel, it is judgment [-day] unto the God of Jacob"; that
is, the day on which the people of Israel observe the
statutes referred to in the preceding verse, v. 4 (to "blow
the horn" and also, as implied in "feast-day," to cease
from work)—that day is made by God His day of judgment, the day, none other therefore, than that of the New
Year. See the Ḳorban ha-'Edah on the version in Yer.

Rosh ha-Shanah I.3, 57b, s.v. אם אינו, and see the version in Pesikta de Rav Kahana, ed. B. Mandelbaum (New York, 1962), I, p. 102f and the references there (in place of *mi-pene mah* the versions have *mah ṭa'ama'*, "what is the reason"). As a parable in the Yerushalmi makes even more evident, the midrash here and its versions exhibit an emphasis on God's love: although they themselves are to be placed in judgment, the people of Israel are nevertheless given the power by God to determine when the day of judgment is to be.

What then does Scripture mean by saying: "This same night is a night of watching unto the Lord?"

The comment requires the following, more literal translation: "This same night (was) the Lord's." R. Eliezer does not relate these words to the future, as does R. Joshua, but to the past.

Merely this: This is the night . . . when He said to our father Abraham: "Abraham, on this night I will redeem your children."

"This same night" refers back to that earlier night of the fifteenth of Nisan, when the covenant was made between the parts.

And as soon as the designated time (*ha-Ḳeẓ*, l. 120) came, God did not delay them an instant.

Thus keeping His promise to Abraham. See above, p. 182.

Watching unto the Lord for All the Children of Israel.

Add: "throughout their generations" (as in H-R, p. 52). But, again, the comment requires this more literal translation: "(A night of) watching for all the children of Israel throughout their generations." The comment which now follows concludes R. Eliezer's interpretation of the verse.

This tells that all the Israelites need watchful protection on that night.

See n. 12, and the suggestion there. However, *le-hish-tamer* (l. 123) is passive rather than reflexive; M. Z. Segal, A Grammar of the Language of the Mishnah (Hebrew) (Jerusalem, 1936), p. 120. Accordingly, the interpretation can only mean that all the Israelites are watched over or guarded by God, as the translation implies. That protection is necessary because the first night of Passover is made dangerous, after the analogy of the night of redemption from Egypt, by "the harmful ones." (In regard to the analogy, cf. the Shebut Yehudah, referred to in the note, who quotes, "And will not suffer the destroyer to come in unto your houses" [Exod. 12:23]; also R. David Moses Abraham of Rohatyn, op. cit., p. 28a, who quotes, "And none of you shall go out of the door of his house" [Exod. 12:22]). On "the harmful ones," see above, p. 108. So far as the idea is concerned there seems to be no difference between R. Eliezer's statement here and the view attributed to him in Rosh ha-Shanah, loc. cit.—"A night which is always guarded against the harmful ones."

R. Eliezer's interpretation represents an instance of the interrelation of Haggadah and Halakah (other examples in WE, p. 9, and cf. above, p. 25), despite containing no allusion to the halakah involved. That halakah, found both in the Mishnah (Pesaḥim X.5) and in the Passover Haggadah, states: "In every generation a man is duty-bound to look upon himself as though he personally had gone forth out of Egypt." This injunction is carried into practice on the first night of Passover; on that occasion the Passover Haggadah is recited, and the various tangible symbols bring the individual further to dwell on the events associated with the Exodus from Egypt (RM, p. 360f). In other words, the injunction directs a man to relive in imagination the night of redemption, and other halakot provide the means to enable him to do so. R. Eliezer's interpretation is, of course, not a halakah but a haggadic idea. For those who entertained it, however, that idea too constituted a factor in the imaginative reliving of the night of redemption.

(B) Commentary On

Tractate Beshallaḥ,

Chapters I-III

CHAPTER I

(Exod. 13:17-22)

169, ll. 1-12

A) And It Came to Pass When Pharaoh Had Let the People Go. "Letting go," *Shilluaḥ*, (everywhere) means escorting,

Pharaoh himself, according to this midrash, escorted the Israelites for a short distance as a means of honoring them. ("Everywhere," which is contained in the text, is omitted in the translation; Lauterbach evidently feels it ought to be deleted. See also H-R, p. 75, n. 1.)

as it is said: "And Abraham went with them to bring them on the way" (Gen. 18:16); "And Isaac sent them away" (ibid. 26:31).

Genesis 18:16 in particular throws light on the statement in the midrash. The verse is relevant, in accordance with the midrashic method, because, like the verse being interpreted (Exod. 13:17), it employs the *piel* form of the root *shlh,* a linguistic feature which the Rabbis here designate by the denominative *shilluaḥ*, a nonbiblical word. Furthermore, Genesis 18:16 relates that Abraham, to honor "the men," personally escorted them for a short distance (see S. D. Luzzatto, Commentary to the Pentateuch [Padua, 1872] on the verse); since *shilluaḥ* describes what Pharaoh did as well, then Pharaoh too must personally have escorted the Israelites for a distance to honor them. In Exodus R. XX.3, Exodus 13:17 is adduced to teach explicitly that "Pharaoh escorted them." See also the first remark in B) below.

Embodied in this midrash is the rabbinic value concept of *Lewayah*, escort. It has a biblical antecedent in one of the usages of the *piel* of *shlh* which, besides being found in Genesis 18:16, is also found in ibid. 12:20 and 31:27 (comp. Gesenius, Handwörterbuch, s.v. שלח). The rabbinic concept, however, is crystallized in a conceptual term whereas its antecedent is not, and this indicates that the rabbinic concept possesses a character of its own, qualities that its biblical antecedent does not possess. Thus, *Lewayah* applies the idea of escorting a person as a means of honoring him in a more inclusive manner than does the biblical antecedent; judging from the biblical instances apparently only notables were so honored, but now the honor is extended to others besides, especially to scholars (Soṭah 46b), and even more inclusively when it comes to honoring the dead by participating in a funeral escort (Berakot 18a). In Genesis 12:20, the purpose of the escort provided by Pharaoh was to guard Abram, as Rashi says (Commentary to the Pentateuch). Escort for the purpose of protection is, likewise, one of the connotations of the concept of *Lewayah*, but now providing escort of that sort is regarded as a paramount duty of every host and, indeed, of the community as a whole (Soṭah, loc. cit., and comp. ibid. IX.6). In fine, the concept of *Lewayah* is rooted in the Bible but has a much wider range of application than that of its biblical antecedent. What is true of this rabbinic concept is true of all rabbinic concepts. Every rabbinic concept has its roots in the Bible, and yet its range

of application is wider than that of its antecedent there
(RM, "Organismic Development," pp. 288ff.).

In teaching that Pharaoh escorted the Israelites so as
to do them honor, the Rabbis imply that *Lewayah* is one
of those concepts which they designate by the collective
term *Derek 'Erez,* the way of the world, their term for
what we describe as ethics. (On *Derek 'Erez* see WE, pp.
39ff., especially p. 47f.) Since he later pursued the Israelites, the Rabbis do not actually say in this passage that
Pharaoh, elsewhere called by them "Pharaoh the wicked"
(e.g., 199, l. 170), had now become a moral or righteous
person, but they do come close to saying so. By attributing
a moral act to a hitherto wicked Gentile, the midrash
exhibits an emphasis on universality, and this note is still
more pronounced in what follows here.

**B) The mouth that had said: "And moreover I will
not let Israel go" (Exod. 5:2), that same mouth
said: "I will let you go" (ibid. 8:24).**

This midrashic statement is integrated with the preceding one. The Rabbis interpret "letting go" also in
these verses as "escorting," and hence take Exodus 8:24
to mean "I will escort you." All the verses employed so
far are therefore integrated; the midrash not only refers
Exodus 8:24 back to ibid. 5:2 but also regards it as containing a promise by Pharaoh which ibid. 13:17 indicates
was subsequently fulfilled. From the presence of the first
person pronoun before the verb, grammatically superfluous
and thus rhetorically emphatic, the Rabbis infer that Pharaoh promised he would escort them personally—"I myself will escort you" (R. Judah Najar, Shebut Yehudah
[Leghorn, 1801], p. 26a).

What was the reward for this? "Thou shalt not abhor an Egyptian" (Deut. 23:8).

This reward relates to Pharaoh's act of courtesy. Deuteronomy 23:8 continues with "because thou wast a stranger in his land," and the status of the Israelites as strangers and guests was demonstrated when Pharaoh escorted them (R. Judah Najar, loc. cit.). Egyptians are placed by Deuteronomy 23:8f in the same category as Edomites. "The children of the third generation that are born unto them may enter into the assembly of the Lord" (v. 9).

Beginning with this midrash the passage does not distinguish between Pharaoh as a particular person and the Egyptians as a whole.

The mouth that has said: "I know not the Lord" (Exod. 5:2), that same mouth said: "Let us . . . for the Lord" (ibid. 14:25). What was the reward for this? "In that day shall there be an altar to the Lord in the midst of the land of Egypt . . . to the Lord" (Isa. 19:19).

"In that day" is interpreted here to refer to the days of the Messiah, a period which will be the prelude to the perfect world order, the world to come. Essential to the interpretation are the verses which follow, Isaiah 19:20f, for they not only tell of how the Egyptians will worship God and sacrifice to Him, but also of how God "will send them a saviour and a defender, who will deliver them" from their oppressors (v. 20), and hence they tell also of a tangible reward; moreover, in the expression "a saviour and a defender" the Rabbis no doubt saw an allusion to the Messiah. This interpretation of Isaiah

19:19ff. can hardly be deemed a departure from the idea
the verses themselves convey. Kaufmann, calling it "the
peak of universalism," describes that idea as the clearest
expression of the vision that paganism will cease to exist
in the world (Toledot ha-'Emunah ha-Yisre'elit, III [Tel
Aviv, 1947], p. 226 and n. 80 there; English trans., The
Religion of Israel, by M. Greenberg [Univ. of Chicago
Press, 1960] p. 391f, and n. 6 there). Altogether congruent with this idea, the midrash here is another indication that a close bond united the prophets and the
Rabbis (on that bond, see RM, pp. 291f, 300). However, what was to the prophet a vision took on, in tannaitic
times, a semblance of reality. Not actually proselytes,
many non-Jews in those days rejected paganism (WE,
p. 57), and the Rabbis probably had in mind such "fearers of Heaven" when they interpreted Exodus 14:25 to
mean that the Egyptians acknowledged the Lord. See
also below, p. 249.

The concepts of the days of the Messiah and the world
to come are not pure value concepts. As we have pointed
out elsewhere, these hereafter concepts refer to specific
events whereas the pure value concept is abstract and indeterminate (RM, pp. 361ff.; on the days of the Messiah,
ibid., pp. 362f).

**The mouth that had said: "Who is the Lord . . ."
(Exod. 5:2), that same mouth said: "The Lord
is righteous, and I and my people are wicked" (ibid.
9:27).**

An expanded version of this midrash (II, 67, ll. 3-7)
adds that in saying "The Lord is righteous" Pharaoh

acknowledged God's punishment to be deserved. Such
an acknowledgment is a virtuous act in itself.

**What reward did they receive for this? A place to
be buried in was given them, as it is said: "Thou
stretchedst out Thy right hand—the earth swallowed them" (ibid. 15:12).**

By so interpreting "the earth swallowed them" as to
have those words describe a mitigation of punishment,
the midrash makes the verse contain a note of mercy. Reflected in this midrash and in other, perhaps more obvious, examples is the rabbinic emphasis on love (OT,
p. 225.)

Common to every midrash in B) is the formula, "The
mouth that had said . . . that same mouth said . . . What
was the reward for this," and that formula therefore constitutes a form uniting those midrashim. B) as a whole is
connected with A) because, as we noticed, the first
midrashic statement in B) is integrated with A). Forms
are an indispensable means for uniting haggadic midrashim, since each haggadic statement is itself a complete
idea and so, essentially, an independent entity. In this
case, it is true, the midrashim are united by a common
idea as well—namely, that Pharaoh's recalcitrance was
later replaced by a proper attitude or act. Nevertheless,
it is also true that here, too, the constituent midrashim
are essentially independent entities, the proof being that
several are to be found singly in other contexts (see the
references below the text).

170, ll. 13-15

That God Led Them Not. The expression "*nihuy*"

can only mean "leading." And thus it says . . .
(Ps. 77:21). And it is written . . . (ibid. 78:14).

Here is an instance of simple commentary, not of midrashic interpretation. Other examples of biblical verses
where *nihuy* means "leading" could have been given; in
fact, Rashi on the verse cites Exodus 32:34 and Proverbs
6:22. Since the corroborative verses quoted in the rabbinic comment are thus merely representative, they indicate that the word here possesses its usual meaning. Elsewhere we show that the Rabbis not only differentiated
between midrashic interpretation and simple meaning but
that they made it their concern to teach simple meaning
(RM, pp. 99ff.).

170, ll. 16-19

**By . . . for That Was Near. That which the Holy
One blessed be He had said . . . (Exod. 3:12), was
soon to be.**

Departing from the simple meaning, the Rabbis interpret "near" in this comment, and in midrashim which
follow, to refer to time and not to "the land of the
Philistines," a place. What God said to Moses in Exodus
3:12 was soon to be fulfilled, for He led the people into
the wilderness, where they were to worship Him "on the
mountain," instead of leading them by way of the land
of the Philistines. The comment as it now reads, though
saying that the event would take place soon, does not
indicate how soon.

170, ll. 19-20

(Another Interpretation . . . a nearer way to return

**to Egypt.) As it is said: "We will go three days'
journey into the wilderness" (ibid. 8:23).**

Exodus 8:23 continues with: "and sacrifice to the
Lord our God," an allusion to ibid. 3:12; the words we
have put in parenthesis are deleted by the Gaon of Wilna
(see Malbim ad loc.). If the emendation is accepted, we
are left with a proper conclusion to the preceding comment, that is, with a verse indicating that it will take
but three days for the people to reach the mountain on
which they will worship God. The concepts embodied
are *'Abodah,* worship, and God's love.

170, ll. 21-24

**Another Interpretation . . . The oath . . . was as yet
too recent . . . (Gen. 21:23) . . . and Abimelech's
grandson was still there.**

See n. 1. Introducing this and all the following comments on "for that was near," the expression "another
interpretation" indicates that a biblical verse may be
given any number of haggadic interpretations. It is an
expression in which is reflected the very character of Haggadah. A haggadic interpretation is not an exegetical
analysis of a text but is rather the product of a creative
imagination, although of an imagination which is canal-
ized. To be specific, a haggadic interpretation always
needs a text as a point of departure, and that text often becomes the channel for the new haggadic idea. On the
other hand, there is no limit on the number of ideas for
which the same text may serve as a point of departure
and, accordingly, the manner in which it serves as a
channel for a new idea is similarly unconfined. Epitomized

by the term "another interpretation," all these things are exemplified in the successive interpretations here of the words "for that was near." In this particular comment the concepts involved are *Shebu'ah,* oath, patriarchs (Abraham), nations of the world (Philistines), and Israel.

170, ll. 24-25

Another Interpretation . . . The first war . . . risk another.

See n. 2. The concept is God's love.

170, ll. 25-27

Another Interpretation . . . The Canaanites had only recently taken possession of the land . . . "And in the fourth generation . . . hither," etc. (Gen. 15:16).

The verse continues with: "for the iniquity of the Amorite is not yet full." See n. 3. Once more "near" is interpreted as near in time, but here it is made to refer to Genesis 15:16. Contained in the literal meaning of that verse, the concepts emphasized are God's justice and the nations of the world ("the Amorite").

171, ll. 27-34

A) Another Interpretation . . . If I bring Israel into the land now . . . his field or his vineyard and neglect Torah.

Here, too, the interpretation hinges on the word "near," but now it means near in respect to space, distance, as in the ordinary rendering of the verse. What the inter-

pretation does is to give a reason different from that given
in the verse itself for not bringing them by the near way.
Does this mean that the Rabbis wish to set aside the reason given in the Bible? We shall return to this problem
shortly. "Neglect of Torah" refers to neglect of the
study of Torah (comp. 'Abot IV.10). This midrash implies that study of Torah ought to be the major occupation of all Jews, but it does not denigrate work or other
necessary activity. Elsewhere the Rabbis laud work (WE,
p. 247, n. 63). At this time, however, the study of Torah
represented a totally new kind of activity for the Israelites,
and it called on all their energies. The emphasis, of
course, is on the concept of *Talmud Torah.*

**But . . . the desert (forty years) . . . the manna to
eat and the water of the well to drink, they will
absorb the Torah.**

See n. 4. The manna and the well are concretizations
of the concept of *Nes,* usually translated "miracle." But
the concept of *Nes* contains two phases, and only one of
them corresponds to what we call miracles or supernatural
events, i.e., refers to changes in *sidre Bereshit,* as the
Rabbis put it. The other phase may refer either to what we
think of as ordinary matters, such as a man's daily sustenance or his restoration to health after illness, or to
extraordinary matters such as the victory of the Macca-
bees. See RM, pp. 152ff., "The Concept of *Nes."* H-R,
p. 76, n. 7, following the Gaon of Wilna, deletes "forty
years." On "they will absorb the Torah," lit., "the Torah
will be absorbed in their body," comp. Psalm 40:9—"Thy
Torah in my inmost parts (lit., in the midst of my intes-
tines)."

On the basis . . . R. Simon . . . who eat manna . . . study the Torah . . . who eat *Terumah*.

See n. 5. R. Simon says, in effect, that the study of Torah demands all of one's energies at all times. On the other hand, he apparently concedes that a person ought to earn his livelihood and not be a mendicant for the sake of studying Torah; the priests are not mendicants.

171-172, ll. 34-42

Another Interpretation . . . straight road?

In this interpretation as well "near" means near in respect to space, as in the ordinary rendering of the verse. This interpretation too, like the preceding one, gives a reason different from that given in the verse itself for not bringing them by the nearer way, but it is "another interpretation."

But . . . the Canaanites . . . burnt the seeds, cut down the trees, destroyed the buildings, and stopped up the wells. God . . . promised Abraham . . . "And houses full of all good things" (Deut. 6:11).

The statement is based not only on Deuteronomy 6:11 but also on the verse which precedes it, and which mentions Abraham.

Therefore I will make them go round about through the desert forty years, so that the Canaanites will arise and repair what they have spoiled.

Here "forty years" is not to be deleted (see the versions in Sifre on Deut., ed. Friedmann, p. 77b; Shemot R. XX.16; Koh. R. III.14, end; Tanḥuma Re'eh, 7). This

reason for the forty years in the desert is entirely different
from the one given in Numbers 14:33f. Surely it was not
the intention of the Rabbis to displace, or set aside, the
reason given in the Bible itself. How was it possible, then,
for them to present an altogether different reason? The
answer is that a haggadic statement was not a matter of
downright belief but of what we have described as indeterminacy of belief (RM, pp. 132ff.), of an attitude of
mind which permitted shadings of belief, an attitude which
has something in common with our own attitude toward
poetry. Haggadic statements are invested with the significance, the meaningfulness, of the rabbinic value concepts
they embody, and that significance alone is responsible
for the degree of belief attaching to those statements,
allowing the shading of belief necessary to make of those
statements genuine teachings. By no means setting aside
the biblical narrative, therefore, the Rabbis at times actually teach things at variance with it. In the biblical narrative, the forty years in the desert constitute God's
punishment of the Israelites; in the rabbinic haggadah
here, the forty years in the desert constitute a delay due
to God's love of Israel, a view which, when contrasted
with the biblical narrative, represents an emphasis on
love.

Indeterminacy of belief and multiple interpretations of
a text are but two facets of the same phenomenon. "Another interpretation" of the word "near" does not imply
that the previous interpretations of that word are now
invalid, and if this is the case, then the attitude toward
the whole series of interpretations is that of indeterminacy
of belief. This applies not only with respect to the haggadot which interpret "near" in the sense of time, and

are thus obviously purely midrashic interpretations. Even when a haggadah takes "near" to refer to space, as in the ordinary meaning of the verse, indeterminacy of belief characterizes the attitude to that haggadah as well; witness the fact that two such haggadot are given consecutively. These haggadot, we may remember, give reasons different from that given in the verse itself for not bringing the Israelites by the nearest way. Evoking no more than indeterminacy of belief, however, neither haggadic reason sets aside the reason given in the Bible. At the same time these haggadot left their own impress, an impress in no way affected by their divergence from the biblical narrative.

172-173, ll. 43-53

A) For God said: 'Lest . . . When They See War,' etc. This refers to the war with the Amalekite . . . (Num. 14:45).

Had they gone the near way, they would have encountered the Amalekites and the Canaanites on that route. Proof is given from Numbers 14:45 which tells of how the Amalekites and the Canaanites did attack them when—as the preceding verses say—the Israelites attempted to go by the near way of their own accord. See the concluding remarks in B) below.

B) Another Interpretation . . . This refers to the war of the sons of Ephraim . . . And it also says: "The children of Ephraim . . . turned back in the day of battle" (Ps. 78:9).

See nn. 6 and 7. According to this interpretation, had they gone the near way they would have encountered "the

men of Gath," that is to say, the Philistines ("by way of
the land of the Philistines"). "When they see war" is made
to refer here to the tradition of the destruction of the
Ephraimites by "the men of Gath," a war that took place
before the proper Exodus but one that indicated the like-
lihood of another such war on that route.

**Why? Because . . . ignored the stipulated term
(*ha-Ḳez*, l. 51) . . . oath.**

See n. 8. *ha-Ḳez* is better rendered here: "the designated time of redemption," *Ḳez* in such contexts being a
value concept; see above, p. 184.

Both A) and B) address themselves to a difficulty
presented by Exodus 14:17, the apprehension expressed
there being seemingly unjustified. The earlier attack by
the Amalekites alone occurred shortly after the Israelites
had left Egypt (Deut. 25:17), yet the people made no
attempt at that time to return to Egypt. But the apprehension in Exodus 14:17, say the Rabbis here, refers to a
different kind of war, one which may come about as a
result of disobeying God, and hence a war in which the
Israelites will suffer a crushing defeat.

**C) Another Interpretation. So . . . bones of their
brethren . . . turn back.**

"When they see war" is interpreted to mean: when
they see the consequences of the war.

173, ll. 53-56

**Another Interpretation . . . should not turn back
. . . had He brought them by a straight road.**

This is not a comment on "when they see war" but on "for that was near" (see H-R, p. 7, n. 2 end).

173-174, ll. 57-69

A) But God Led the People About, by the Way of the Wilderness, by the Red Sea. What for? For the purpose of performing for them miracles and mighty deeds (*Nissim u-Geburot*, l. 58) . . . manna, the quail and the well.

God led the Israelites by way of the wilderness so as to make manifest to them His love through *Nissim* and *Geburot*. On *Nes*, miracle, see above, p. 211. *Geburot* often relates to the giving of rain (e.g., Ta'anit I.1), but the word also has a connotation similar to that of *Nissim* (cf. WE, p. 264, n. 41). This midrash interprets the biblical clause as a whole whereas the midrashim which follow interpret its last phrase word by word.

B) R. Eliezer says: "By the way" indicates that it was for the purpose of tiring them, as it is said: "He weakened my strength in the way" (Ps. 102: 24); "of the wilderness" indicates that it was for the purpose of refining them, as it is said: "Who led thee through the great and dreadful wilderness" etc. (Deut. 8:15);

The interpretation here can be understood only if we recognize that it embodies the concept of *Yissurim shel 'Ahabah,* chastisings of love, sufferings imposed with the purpose of refining and improving a man's character. "Tiring them" had as its purpose, therefore, "refining them." Deuteronomy 8:15, however, does no more than introduce the idea of "refining them." That idea is to be found in the next verse (ibid. v. 16)—"that He might afflict thee, and that He might prove thee, to do thee good at thy latter end"—where the word translated "to do thee good" can also be taken to mean "to make thee better." This is how R. Eliezer interprets the word; instead of expressing the idea of material well-being, the word now conveys the idea of moral improvement, and hence his interpretation is pitched in a different key from that of the literal meaning. (See above, p. 63f, for other examples.) However, the simple meaning, too, seems to imply that the hardships in the wilderness had a positive effect on the character of the Israelites.

"by the Red Sea" . . . of testing them, as it is said: "And they were rebellious . . . at the Red Sea" (Ps. 106:7).

They were tested at the start of the journey, and they failed. That test indicated how much they needed the process of "refining" they were to undergo in the wilderness. The concept embodied is *Nissayon*.

C) R. Joshua says; "By the way" indicates it was for the purpose of giving them the Torah . . . (Deut. 5:30) . . . (Prov. 6:23); "of the wilderness" indicates that it was for the purpose of feeding them the manna . . . (Deut. 8:16); "by the Red Sea" indicates that it was for the purpose of performing for them miracles and mighty deeds (*Nissim u-Geburot*) . . . (Ps. 106:22) . . . (ibid. 106:9).

In addition to the concepts of Torah, *Nissim* and *Ge-*

burot, which are named, the midrash embodies the concept of God's love (giving them Torah, feeding them, performing miracles for them).

174-175, ll. 70-74

A)   And the Children of Israel . . . The word *Ḥamushim* here means armed . . . "But . . . (ḥamushim) armed" (Josh. 1:14).

The context of *ḥamushim* in Joshua 1:14 is as follows: "But ye shall pass over before your brethren *ḥamushim*, all the mighty men of valor, and shall help them." This context obviously justifies the explanation of *ḥamushim* as "armed."

B)   Another Interpretation . . . means zealous . . . (Josh. 4:12-13).

Both A) and B) are evidently attempts at arriving at the literal meaning of the word.

175, ll. 74-85

See above, pp. 125f.

176-181, ll. 86-151

A)   And Moses Took the Bones . . . He took a table of gold on which . . . into the Nile . . . Moses, the master of Elijah do it!

Instead of the entire expression "He took a table of gold on which he engraved the Tetragrammaton," the Oxford MS and the printed editions read: "He took a pebble" (see Apparatus). The reading there, which has been adopted by H-R (p. 78, l. 11), is more in keeping with the analogy which follows. Were it an act involving the use of the Tetragrammaton, it could not have been compared with an act in which this was not the case. Cf. Tos. Soṭah IV.7.

R. Nathan says: They had buried him in the mausoleum of the kings . . . Moses took it and went his way.

The Munich MS and the printed editions do not have "And how did Moses know . . . Moses took it and went his way" (see Apparatus). If these sentences which contain ideas and even phrases so like those of the preceding opinion are to be deleted, then R. Nathan's point is that Joseph's coffin was readily accessible and that its recovery involved no *Nes* (miracle).

B) This is to teach you that with what measure a man metes it is measured unto him. Miriam waited . . . And in the wilderness God caused the ark, the Shekinah, the priests . . . to wait for her . . . (Num. 12:15).

The relevant example here of the principle of "measure for measure" is, of course, the one with respect to Joseph which immediately follows. However, this section B) appears to have been taken from an earlier source in which the principle was exemplified first with respect to Miriam. See Soṭah I.9 and cf. also ibid. I. 7-8.

Why should the *Shekinah* have been mentioned here only after the ark had been mentioned? Because *Shekinah* in this context refers to *Gilluy Shekinah,* a visible manifestation of God, and the ark-cover in the Tabernacle was associated with such a manifestation (Lev. 16:2, and see the discussion in RM, p. 245ff.). *Gilluy Shekinah* is not fully compatible with the other value concepts, for it possesses a feature at variance with them: the other concepts do not refer to phenomena in sensory experience whereas *Gilluy Shekinah* definitely involves visual or auditory sensations. This incompatibility of *Gilluy Shekinah* with the other value concepts prevents it from being used freely, or in the same manner as value concepts in general. It is employed by the Rabbis to depict events in the past or the future but, by and large, not in the present; from this we gather that the type of mysticism for which *Gilluy Shekinah* stands was certainly not encouraged by the Rabbis (ibid., pp. 234ff.). Cf. above, p. 37f.

Joseph than whom none of his brothers was greater, acted meritoriously (*zakah*, l. 113) in burying his father . . . (Gen. 50:7-9). Whom can we find . . . than Moses busied himself.

Joseph was a king (Rashi to Soṭah 9b), and the prooftext indicates that Jacob was buried with the honor due the father of a king. For this Joseph was rewarded in even greater measure since the one who occupied himself with his remains was no less a person than Moses, the greatest in Israel.

Moses, than whom no one in Israel was greater, acted meritoriously (*zakah*, l. 116) in busying himself with the bones of Joseph . . . "And Moses . . . with him."

Joseph, in attending to the burial of Jacob, and Moses, in occupying himself with the bones of Joseph, thereby performed acts of *Gemilut Ḥasadim;* the word *zakah,* used in both instances, refers to acts of that kind (G. Alon,

Toledot ha-Yehudim be-'Erez Yisrael bi-Teḳufat ha-Mish-
nah weha-Talmud [Tel Aviv, 1952] I, p. 333 and n. 68
there). *Gemilut Ḥasadim* is an ethical value concept
which connotes acts of love and personal service to individuals (WE, p. 27, and cf. ibid., p. 21), and among
such acts is burial of the dead (ibid., p. 226). Moses' act,
however, is also designated as a *Miẓwah* (176, ll. 88-89),
and hence in this passage an ethical act is interpreted or
grasped by two concepts at once, by an ethical concept
and by the concept of *Miẓwot*. But this dual characterization of an ethical act is by no means unusual; indeed
every ethical act has this dual character, as we have demonstrated elsewhere (WE, "*Miẓwot* and the Ethical Concepts," pp. 205ff.). Nevertheless, the Rabbis do discriminate between ethical acts and other *Miẓwot*. All acts
which are *Miẓwot* are to be preceded by a *Berakah* (benediction), the *Birkat ha-Miẓwot,* but this rule does not
apply to ethical acts. Omitting the *Berakah* does not, of
course, change their character and make them acts which
are not *Miẓwot,* but it does result in stressing the ethical
concept embodied in each particular act rather than the
concept of *Miẓwot*. Attention is focused on the special circumstances of the particular act, on the human relationships involved in the act, in a word, on the particular
ethical implication of the act. (See ibid., pp. 235ff.)

**Whom . . . than Moses who was attended to by God
Himself, as it is said . . . (Deut. 34:6).**

In Soṭah 14a, Deuteronomy 34:6 is cited as an act
of *Gemilut Ḥasadim*. In all these instances of "measure
for measure" the reward for the deed, though of a similar
character, is greater than the deed itself.

C)   And, what is more, with Jacob . . . while with
Joseph there went up the ark, the Shekinah . . .
clouds of glory.

This is not found in most of the parallels and is obviously based on the statement with regard to Miriam.

D)   Furthermore, the coffin of Joseph went alongside the ark of the Eternal . . . The one lying in
this coffin has fulfilled that which is written on
what lies in that ark.

The ark-cover in the Tabernacle was associated with
Gilluy Shekinah; see B) above. "The Eternal" undoubtedly conveys the general idea of חי העולמים (ll. 123,
125-6, 128); however, the precise meaning of the term
depends on the vowel under חי, and this has not been
altogether established (comp. Tamid VII, end, and Tose-
fot Yom Ṭob a.1., and see Baer, Seder Abodat Yisrael
[ed. Schocken, 1937], p. 568, and the suggestions by
Abudraham quoted there).

Joseph is depicted as one who carried out the Ten
Commandments before they were given at Mount Sinai.
He is thus regarded as not only an ancestor of tribes, but
as a prototype of the entire people, since it is incumbent
upon every member of the people to perform the *Miẓwot.*
A biblical character is here interpreted by means of the
concept of *Miẓwot.*

E)   On the tables lying in this ark is written: "I am
the Lord thy God" (Exod. 20:2) . . . (Gen. 50:19)
. . . "Thou shalt not take the name of the Lord thy
God in vain" (Exod. 20:7), and of Joseph it is

**written "As Pharaoh liveth" (Gen. 42:15) . . .
(Exod. 16:5).**

With regard to Genesis 42:15: The oath was not really
an oath but a threat, hence he avoided taking the name
of God.

**F) It is written: "Honour thy father" (Exod.
20:12), and of Joseph . . . 'Here am I' (Gen. 37:13)**

  The sentence which follows, and translated "He knew
that his brothers hated him . . . orders," is not found in
the basic MSS (see Apparatus) and is an interpolation. It
is omitted in H-R, p. 79.

**G) It is written: "Thou shalt not murder" (Exod.
20:13), and Joseph did not murder Poti-phera.**

There is a legend to the effect that Potiphar's wife offered to murder her husband, an offer from which Joseph
recoiled in horror (Bereshit R., ed. Theodor-Albeck [Ber-
lin, 1927], p. 1067 and Albeck's note there).

**H) It is written: "Thou shalt not commit adultery"
. . . "Thou shalt not steal" . . . "Thou shalt not
bear false witness against thy neighbor" (Exod.
20:13), (and Joseph never told his father what his
brothers had done to him). Now, to reason . . . was
false! It is said, "Thou shalt not covet" . . . wife.**

The words we have put in parenthesis ("and Joseph
never told . . . to him") are, again, not found in the
basic MSS (see Apparatus), and are omitted in the
H-R, p. 80.

I) It is written: "Thou shalt not hate thy brother

in thy heart" (Lev. 19:17), and of Joseph it says:
"And he comforted them, and spoke kindly to
them" (Gen. 50:21) . . . (Lev. 19:18) . . . (Lev.
25:36) . . . and his brethren" (Gen. 47:12)

See n. 16. As in the case of the Ten Commandments,
the other commandments are also given in the order in
which they occur in the Bible. The connection made between Leviticus 19:17 and Genesis 50:21 relates back
to the words of the brothers in ibid. v. 15: "It may be
that Joseph will hate us."

181, ll. 152-162

**A)   For He Had Straitly Sworn the Children of
Israel. This means he had made them swear for
themselves and also . . . upon their children.**

Rather: He made them swear that they would make
their children swear (see R. Judah Najar, op. cit., p. 27b).
"Them" refers to Joseph's brothers, for in these interpretations "the children of Israel" (*bene Yisra'el*) in the
verse is taken to mean, in accordance with Genesis 50:24-
25, literally "the sons of Israel," i.e., the sons of Jacob.
Joseph knew that the redemption would come, not during
his brothers' lifetime, but in the days of their descendents.
The anonymous statement here, however, begins a midrash which interprets the verse as a whole, a midrash
which is broken off at this point so as to make way for
a different interpretation regarding the giving of the oath.

**B) R. Nathan says: Why did he impose the oath
upon his brothers rather than upon his sons? . . .
the Egyptians might not let them fulfill it . . . and
not upon his sons.**

R. Nathan tells why Joseph did not impose an oath on his sons to bring his body to Canaan soon after his death just as he had carried out his father's body (cf. Rashi on the verse). R. Nathan thus explains why Joseph did not address himself to his sons. Instead, he addressed himself to his brothers, for in this midrash, too, the words *bene Yisra'el* in the verse are taken to refer to the sons of Jacob. But R. Nathan's interpretation does not contain the idea in A), namely, that Joseph had his brothers swear to make their children swear. Was it sufficient, then, to have his brothers swear? See the remarks in D).

C) Another Interpretation:

See the Apparatus. H-R, p. 80, does not include these words. Without them, it is clear that what follows is the latter part of R. Nathan's interpretation.

D) Joseph said to them: "My father . . . back . . . I impose an oath upon you that you bring me back to the place whence you stole me." And they did so, for it is said: "And the bones of Joseph which the children of Israel brought up out of Egypt, buried they in Shechem" (Josh. 24:32).

Since not the brothers but their descendents buried Joseph's bones in Shechem, how can it say here that the brothers fulfilled their oath—"And they did so?" In this haggadah, and in others, it is assumed that a man and his descendents constitute a single personality, a corporate personality. (Another example, close by, is on 184, ll. 193ff.) The act of their descendents is therefore conceived to be the fulfillment of the oath taken by the brothers. Notice, however, that according to A) the oath to carry out Joseph's body had to be taken by the descendents, individuals in their own right who presumably would not have been bound by their progenitors' oath. The Rabbis, then, harbor the conception not only of corporate personality but also that of individual personality. They stress the individual so strongly that emphasis on the individual is nothing less than a major trend in rabbinic literature. To give one example, the Rabbis will sometimes interpret a biblical verse addressed to the many as though it were a statement directed to the individual, a shift which may even have halakic implications (see above, p. 104, and cf. ibid., p. 101).

182, ll. 163-171

God Will Surely Remember You. He will remember you in Egypt . . . at the sea . . . in the wilderness . . . at the rivers of Arnon . . . in this world . . . in the world to come.

After presenting R. Nathan's view, the text resumes the interpretation begun in A) above. On the basis of that interpretation, "God will surely remember you" etc. are the words that Joseph addresses, through the brothers, to their descendents, and accordingly the word "you" in this midrash pertains to the generation of the Exodus. This is borne out by the order in which the places named here are mentioned, as well as by their character—Egypt, the sea, the wilderness, the rivers of Arnon. Places at which *Nissim* occurred, they are also successive points in the journey of the generation of the Exodus. Even the note of blessing in this interpretation is more in keeping with words Joseph might direct to his brothers' descendents than with words directed to the brothers themselves. In R. Nathan's interpretation of the giving of the oath, he imparts, with a true artistic touch, a recriminatory tone to what Joseph said to his brothers. We ought to add that Joseph's "blessing" is primarily a prophecy. Here he prefaces the oath with a prophecy that God will perform *Nissim* for Israel, the *Nissim* to occur at the places named, and in that order (on *Nissim,* see above, p. 211). Joseph also assures the generation of the Exodus that after they die they will be resurrected and will inherit the world to come. Elsewhere, he is specifically characterized as a prophet (Tanḥuma, ed. Buber, I, p. 188).

And Ye Shall Carry Up My Bones Away Hence . . . immediately after his death, but it says: "With you" —when you go up.

"With you" relates to the brothers, i.e., when the brothers' bones are carried up out of Egypt by their descendents. See the next comment.

And whence do we know that they also carried up with them the bones of all the other founders of the tribes? From the expression: "Away hence with you."

The expression "away hence," literally "from here," implies a shared locale with those to whom Joseph is talking, and hence that by the words "with you" Joseph is referring to his brothers. Accordingly, "from here with you" means that Joseph's oath concerned not only his own remains, but his brothers' as well. Joseph is thus credited with an act of *Gemilut Ḥasadim* (acts of loving-kindness), a concept which includes, as one of its aspects, acts in behalf of the dead (see WE, p. 21 and the references in n. 13 there). Of course, the concept of *Shebu'ah* (oath) is likewise embodied in the midrash.

The word "tribes" is sometimes used as a designation for the sons of Jacob (cf. e.g., Shabbat 146a), and it is so used in the text here. "Tribes," in that sense, is a concept akin to that of patriarchs and is sometimes equated with the latter (Tosefta Ma'aser Sheni, end; see Ginzberg, Legends, V, p. 378, n.2).

182, ll. 172-177

See above, pp. 155ff.

183, ll. 178-192

And the Lord Went before Them by Day . . . (Num. 14:14) . . . (ibid. 9:19) . . . (Exod. 40:36-38). Thus there were seven clouds, four on the four sides of them, one above them, one beneath them, and one that advanced before them on the road, raising the depressions and lowering the elevations,

The concept of *Middat Raḥamim* (God's love) and *Nes* are combined, both in the midrash and in the biblical verse on which it is based. However, in telling of seven clouds instead of one, the midrash adds the idea of God's encompassing protection; in other words, the combination of the concepts in the midrash results in a greater emphasis on God's love.

as it is said: "Every valley shall be lifted up . . . and the rough places a plain" (Isa. 40:4). It also killed the snakes . . . sprinkled the road before them.

The Rabbis regarded the redemption from Egypt as a paradigm of the expected redemption from Rome in the days of the Messiah (above, p. 157). Here something resembling the converse is implied. Undoubtedly assumed to be a prophecy of what will happen on the journey from the Diaspora in the days of the Messiah, Isaiah 40:4 is given as the proof-text for a *Nes* which the midrash says occurred on the journey from Egypt.

R. Judah . . . thirteen . . . R. Josiah . . . four . . . Rabbi . . . two.

Unlike the other authorities, Rabbi offers no description. According to him, it is enough to say that there was but one additional cloud and thereby, apparently, to express the idea of God's protection.

184-185, ll. 193-208

And the Lord Went before Them by Day. This is to teach you that with what measure a man metes, it is meted out to him. Abraham accompanied . . . and God accompanied his children . . . the well . . . the manna . . . the quail . . . seven clouds of glory . . . (Ps. 105:39).

Embodied here is the concept of *Zekut 'Abot,* merit of the fathers, a concept connoting that God rewards the children for the good deeds of their fathers. The midrash also allows us to see that underlying the concept is the notion of corporate personality. For Abraham's acts of kindness toward the angels God rewards Abraham's children measure for measure, and yet the word *lo* (l. 194) conveys the idea that the reward was given "to him," that is, to Abraham. This can only mean that in this midrash (and elsewhere—cf. above, p. 225f), fathers and children are not differentiated but are regarded as constitutive of a single personality, a corporate personality. The midrash indicates, furthermore, that *Zekut 'Abot,* though a concept in its own right, is also a subconcept of God's justice, the principle of measure for measure being itself an aspect of God's justice. Despite the notion of corporate personality, there is nevertheless an emphasis on the individual in rabbinic thought; see ibid.. and the references there.

And Abraham . . . and the Holy One, blessed be He, protected the houses of his children in Egypt, as it is said: "The Lord will pass over (*u-fasaḥ,* l. 208) the door" (Exod. 12:23).

With sound philological sense, the Rabbis interpret *u-fasaḥ* to mean "and He will protect" rather than "and He will pass over." See above, p. 2f, and cf. 56, ll. 74-77; and 87, ll. 90-93.

185-186, ll. 209-234

And the Lord Went before Them by Day. Is it possible to say so? Has it not already been said: "Do I not fill heaven and earth? Saith the Lord" (Jer. 23:24). And it is written . . . (Isa. 6:3). And it also says: "And behold the glory of the God of Israel . . . and the earth did shine with His glory" (Ezek. 43:2). What then does Scripture mean by saying: "And the Lord went before them by day?" Said Rabbi . . . He Himself went before them so that the nations should treat them with respect.

Although the idea of God's otherness is not represented in rabbinic literature by a specific term, it is nonetheless an idea which the Rabbis do take occasion to teach (RM, p. 311ff.). This midrash, too, contains the idea of God's otherness, but here it is made the background against which is stressed the concept of God's love. On the one hand, the idea of God's otherness is certainly cultivated, as is evident from the following summary of the midrash. "And the Lord went before them by day," yet He had no need to do so, for He fills heaven and earth (Jer. 23:24) and "the whole earth is full of His glory" (Isa. 6:3); similarly, though He led them by night "in a pillar of fire to give them light," He had no need to do so, since Ezekiel 43:2 tells of another occasion when "the earth did shine with His Glory." On the other hand, the point of the midrash is that, because of His love, God did these things notwithstanding His otherness.

There are more midrashim that have the same construction and the same dual purpose (RM, p. 274). We are dealing with a structural stereotype, the elements of which are the following: first, a biblical verse; then, an apprehensive question ("Is it possible to say so?") by the Rabbis; then, the contrasting of the verse in question with other biblical verses, the contrast implying that the Rabbis' apprehension is in reference to the idea of the otherness of God; and finally, the affirmation of the verse in question (in our case, the statement, "He Himself went before them"). Elsewhere we have described other stereotypes with the same dual function (ibid., p. 308ff.; cf. above, p. 189f).

From this midrash it should be obvious that the rabbinic idea of the otherness of God does not stem from a

philosophic aversion to anthropomorphism. An aversion
to anthropomorphisms would not have allowed the Rabbis to adduce Ezekiel 43:2 in order to cultivate the idea
of God's otherness. That verse is not only anthropomor-
phic but vividly so—"And, behold, the glory of the God
of Israel came from the way of the east; and His voice
was like the sound of many waters" (see the text in H-R,
p. 82).

**But . . . put them to death . . . "I will gather all
nations . . . valley of Jehoshaphat"(Joel 4:2). One
might think . . . their practices of idolatry, of incest
and of murder, but it says: "For My people and
My heritage Israel . . . nations" (ibid.).**

"The Sons of Noah," or mankind in general, were, according to the Rabbis, given *Miẓwot,* three of them being
the laws against idolatry, incest and murder. (See above,
p. 95f and the remarks there on idolatry.) Moreover,
in order to save his life, a man may yield on other matters but never on these three, under any circumstances
(WE, p. 25). Not account of these things, however, will
the nations be placed in judgment but on account of their
cruel treatment of Israel.

**It also says: "Egypt . . . and Edom . . . have shed
innocent blood in their land" (Joel 4:19) . . .
"And I will hold as innocent their blood that I have
not held as innocent."**

The latter verse is interpreted to say that even if God
should clear them of their other sins He will not clear
them of the blood of Israel which they shed (Rashi on
Joel 4:21).

When will this be? When "the Lord dwelleth in Zion" (Joel 4:20-21).

That is, in the world to come.

187, ll. 234-238

A) The Pillar of Cloud by Day and the Pillar of Fire by Night Departed Not . . . while the pillar of cloud was still there, the pillar of fire began to gleam.

There was thus no interval of time, however brief, when it was not manifest to the people that God was leading and protecting them. Although the point made by the midrash is clear, there is a question as to how it is derived from the verse. Rashi, Rashbam and Ibn Ezra explain *lo' yamish* (l. 234, translated "departed not") as a transitive verb referring to God, and that is, apparently, also the way in which the midrash employs these words. On this basis, the midrash takes the verse to say that God did not remove the pillar of cloud during day time but at twilight, that is, when the pillar of fire was already visible, and that He did not remove the pillar of fire during nighttime but at dawn, that is, when the pillar of cloud was already visible. A medieval compendium (Midrash Sekel Ṭob, II, ed. Buber, p. 171), however, states that *lo' yamish* is intransitive, a view which would agree with the translation here.

B) Another Interpretation: The Pillar of Cloud . . . proper custom (*Derek 'Erez*, l. 236) on the eve of the Sabbath . . . The pillar of fire . . . pillar of cloud is still present.

See the note. The interpretation of the verse is rather obscure. Apparently this midrash regards *lo' yamish* as intransitive, and as referring to the pillar of cloud. If so, the interpretation of the verse may well be: (When) the pillar of cloud had not (yet) departed, and it was still daytime, the pillar of fire of the night (appeared) before the people.

R. Judah Najar (op. cit., p. 28a) says that *Derek 'Erez* here refers to the custom of lighting the evening lamp while there was still some daylight, and that the midrash teaches, with respect to the Sabbath lamp, that it must be lit while there was still daylight. Accordingly, in this midrash *Derek 'Erez* connotes practical wisdom (WE, p. 40).

CHAPTER II

(Exod. 14:1-9)

187, ll. 1-7

And the Lord Spoke unto Moses, Saying: "Speak unto the Children of Israel . . . Encamp," etc. R. Simon the son of Yoḥai says: When in any commandment to the people . . . "saying," or "and thou shalt say unto them" . . . for all generations. When neither . . . is used, it is only for the time being.

Here "saying" or "and thou shalt say unto them" does not follow "speak unto the children of Israel."

Rabbi says: Even when it does not . . . the commandment is for all generations, with the exception of three instances.

See n. 1. Instead of Exodus 14:15 there, the commentaries (e.g. H-R, p. 83, n. 4) give Exodus 25:2; ibid. 14:15 begins with "And the Lord said" and not with "And the Lord spoke."

For Rabbi, what determines the temporary or permanent character of a commandment is not a formula but the context. A study of the passages, however, proves that for R. Simon, too, the contexts are ultimately decisive; see Friedmann, p. 25b, n. 1. Halakah in general takes into account the context of a verse. Haggadah, too, frequently reckons with the context of a biblical verse, but in Haggadah the verse acts as a channel for a new rabbinic idea, an idea that is the product of creative imagination (RM, p. 99).

188, ll. 8-15

That They Turn Back . . . Pi-hahiroth . . . They were . . . tapering . . . convex . . . square . . . work of Heaven . . . openings. They were a sort of male and female . . . R. Eliezer.

The word translated "slightly convex" means "semi-circular" in Middot II.5 (end), where the entire phrase occurs as well.

R. Joshua says: The Ḥiroth . . . Migdol . . . the sea . . . Egypt behind them.

If the Israelites are commanded to turn back to a place where Egypt would be behind them, then that place was outside of Egypt. It does not say what R. Eliezer's view on that matter was, but presumably he differed from R. Joshua. In that case, R. Joshua would be the only authority to teach that the Israelites did not actually return to Egypt.

188, ll. 15-17

Another Interpretation . . . the place of licentiousness (ḥerutan, l. 16) of the Egyptians, their market place, the place where their idols ('Abodah Zarah, l. 15-16) were.

ḥerutan does not mean "licentiousness," but refers to freedom from taxes. A Roman institution is here retrojected to ancient Egypt. In Roman times, there were certain market places and fairs—some associated with pagan temples and some not—where the goods sold or bought were tax free. (S. Lieberman, עשר מילין, offprint from ירושלים, תשי"ט] [, אשכולות III, pp. 76ff.). If Israel were to return and encamp before such a market place, they would return to a point well within the boundaries of Egypt. God did not want to have it said that they had fled from Egypt.

Ḥerut, freedom, is a value concept. Combined here with three other concepts—*Malkut,* government, (concretized here in the power to tax), *Derek 'Ereẓ* (the phase of that concept which includes business), and *'Abodah Zarah,* idolatry—*Ḥerut* in this midrash has the specific meaning of freedom from taxes. When *Ḥerut* is combined with different concepts, we shall notice soon, it has another specific meaning. A basic characteristic of all value concepts is thus exemplified, namely, that the meaning of a value concept is not something that is given once and for all. Possessed of one meaning when combined with certain concepts, a value concept has another meaning when combined with other concepts, and still another meaning when combined with still different concepts. True, all the various meanings are related by virtue of the conceptual term which they have in common, but this is to say that the conceptual term is only connotative and that it cannot be formally defined. In brief, the idea-content of any value concept is a function of the complex of concepts as a whole, and the conceptual term is merely connotative (WE, p. 4).

188, ll. 17-20

In the past . . . Pithom . . . (Exod. 1:11). After they changed, it was called Pi-hahiroth, because it estranged its worshipers.

"After they changed" ought to be rendered: "After they (i.e., the Israelites) returned"; see 189f, ll. 32-33. In place of "estranged its worshipers" the idea in the text is no doubt more strongly pejorative. But the passage is far from clear. It is not a continuation of the preceding midrash, since it contains a different interpretation of *Pi-haḥiroth*.

188-190, ll. 20-36

The children of Israel journeyed from Raamses to Succoth . . . Pi-hahiroth.

See Numbers 33:5-7. This statement begins still another interpretation of *Pi-haḥiroth*.

They started . . . which was the fourth day . . . to go further.

The text with respect to the days of the week is not certain; see the reading in H-R, p. 83, and also n. 13 there. By stating that it was on "the fourth day of their journey" when the Israelites made preparations for going forth, the midrash indicates that they had gone no farther than a three days' journey. The midrash thereby hints that instead of going on, the Israelites were to return to Egypt in accordance with what Moses had told Pharaoh (Exod. 8:23) about "a three days' journey into the wilderness." Moses' promise was to be kept.

The Egyptian guards . . . (Exod. 8:23). The Israelites . . . "But . . . did we go out by leave of Pharaoh?" . . . (Num. 33:3). The guards . . . "Whether . . . you will have to comply with the orders of the government (*Malkut*, l. 29)." The

Israelites then rose up against them . . . report to Pharaoh.

Powerless to prevent the Exodus, Pharaoh and the Egyptian government were just as powerless to force the Israelites now to return.

Then Moses said to the Israelites: "Turn back lest Pharaoh say that you are fleeing."

The Israelites were not fleeing slaves.

And Moses blew the horn until they returned to the place before Pi-hahiroth . . . those of little faith (*'Amanah,* 1. 34) . . . and tearing their garments

The noun *'Amanah* always means trust, faith in that sense. Instead of "little faith" render: wanting in faith (or trust).

until Moses said to them: "It has been told to me by the word of God (lit., out of the mouth of *Ha-Geburah,* 1. 35) that you are free men (*Bene Ḥorin,* 11. 35f).

According to this midrash, the Israelites achieved the status of free men only now, as they were about to return to Egypt after their three days' journey in the wilderness. Those three days belonged, so to speak, to their period of slavery.

Ha-Geburah (The Strength, The Power) is one of many epithets or appellatives for God. Not being conceptual terms for God but names, these appellatives imply a sense of relationship with God, and therefore a sense of His concern with man, a sense of His nearness (see RM, pp. 204ff., 271). Thus, an appellative is used in this midrash, a midrash which tells of how God now gave to the Israelites, to each one of them, the status of free men. However, we must remember that we are not dealing here with actual religious experience but with Haggadah, a reflection of that experience in literature. Many of the appellatives are solely literary expressions. "Out of the mouth of *Ha-Geburah*" is a stock literary phrase, used not only here but frequently elsewhere as well (e.g. Shabat 88b; Yebamot 72b, 105b; Baba Meẓi'a 58b).

Therefore it says: "That they turn back and encamp" etc.

"etc." stands here for: "before *Pi-haḥirot*"; *ḥirot* is interpreted as *Ḥerut*, freedom, because it was as free men, *Bene Ḥorin* (l. 35), that the Israelites turned back to *Pi-haḥirot*. *Ḥerut* refers to freedom from slavery (comp. Pesaḥim X.5—"He brought us forth from slavery into freedom"), whereas above (188, ll. 15-16) it referred to freedom from taxes. Elsewhere the Rabbis speak of other freedoms, such as freedom from the kingdoms, freedom from the angel of death, freedom from chastisements (Lev. R. XVIII.3, ed. Margulies, p. 407, and the references there).

Bene Ḥorin (singular, *Ben Ḥorin*) is a subconcept of *Ḥerut*—just as *Ḥerut* is the opposite of slavery, so *Ben Ḥorin* ordinarily means a person who is not a slave, as it does in our midrash. But true to its character as a value concept, *Ben Ḥorin* is not limited to that conceptual relationship. It is combined with the concept of *Talmud Torah* in two famous statements: "It is not thy duty to complete the work, but neither art thou free (*Ben Ḥorin*) to desist from it (i.e., from study of Torah)" ('Abot II.16), and "No one is a freeman (*Ben Ḥorin*) but he who is engaged in study of Torah" (ibid. VI.2).

190, ll. 37-40

Between Migdol and the Sea. There was the greatness (*gedullatam*, l. 37) of the Egyptians, there was their glory . . . *mayouma*—festivals . . . all the silver and all the gold . . . (Gen. 47:14).

gedullatam is a play on Migdol. By enlarging on the importance of the place for the Egyptians, this interpretation indicates that the Israelites were commanded to turn back to a place which was definitely within the borders of Egypt. This interpretation, therefore, relates to the preceding midrash. From that midrash alone we should have known only that, after a three days' journey, they turned back as freemen, but not that they were told to return to Egypt. Moses' word was to be fulfilled, but with the Israelites returning to Egypt as freemen instead of as slaves.

There may also have been another consideration in regard to the matter of returning to Egypt. The Rabbis have Moses telling the Israelites, "Turn back lest Pharaoh say that you are fleeing," and they may be taking account in this manner of detractors of Israel in their own day.

190, ll. 41-43

See above, p. 132f.

190-191, ll. 44-56

A) And Pharaoh Will Say . . . Entangled (*Nebu-

kim) in the Land. The word *Nebukim* means perplexed . . . (Joel 1:18). Another Interpretation:
Nebukim . . . confounded . . . (Esth. 3:15).

Both of these interpretations aim at simple meaning,
peshat.

**B)   Another Interpretation: And Pharaoh Will Say.
But he did not know what he was saying.**

That is, Pharaoh's words, as given in this verse, constitute an unwitting prophecy. "But he did not know what
he was saying" is an expression which introduces, from
here on, every interpretation of Pharaoh's words, each
interpretation regarding them as an unwitting prophecy.
Pharaoh's words contain a prophecy because they are
words God says Pharaoh will utter, and hence they are
words of divine origin, as in the case of a prophecy. But
they constitute an unwitting prophecy because, as Pharaoh uttered them, he had in mind the present situation.
On account of its origin, unwitting prophecy is apparently
an aspect of the concept of *Nebu'ah*, prophecy.

**He said: "Moses has led them astray, he did not
know where he was leading them."**

This idea was in Pharaoh's mind when he said, "They
are entangled in the land, the wilderness hath shut
them in."

**For it says: *Nebukim*, etc. . . . alludes to Moses
. . . "Get thee up . . . unto mount Nebo"(Deut.
32:49).**

Moses is to die on Nebo, before the Israelites enter

Canaan (Deut. 32:49-50), and the resemblance of
nebukim to Nebo suggests to the Rabbis that *nebukim*
relates to Moses and his death on Nebo. Interpreted as
an unwitting prophecy, the verse declares therefore:
Moses (= *Nebukim*) is (remains) in the land, the wilderness hath shut him in. Pharaoh, too, connects the
verse with Moses, but that connection is with reference
to the present situation.

Each of the unwitting prophecies is "another interpretation" of the same verse. If it is the verse that gives an
unwitting prophecy its authenticity, how can it give authenticity to an entirely different prophecy? We have here,
however, another indication that haggadic interpretations
evoked not hard-and-fast belief but indeterminacy of belief (above, pp. 209, 213). Incidentally, belief so indistinct
could not have attached to an event predicted in an unwitting prophecy the character of a preordained event.

**C) Another Interpretation: And Pharaoh Will
Say . . . without realizing . . . "The Israelites are
bound to cry in the wilderness."**

Again, that idea was in Pharaoh's mind when he said,
"They are *nebukim* in the land," and meaning by the
word *nebukim* "crying," *bokim*. When the Israelites realized their plight, Pharaoh felt, they would surely weep.

**As it is said: "And all the congregation . . . and
cried " (Num. 14:1).**

It was on this later occasion that they wept, and hence
Pharaoh's words were an unwitting prophecy.

D) Another Interpretation: And . . . Say . . . with-

out realizing . . . "The Israelites are bound to fall in the wilderness."

This idea was in Pharaoh's mind when he said, "The wilderness hath shut them in." Pharaoh thought the Israelites would surely die now.

As it is said: "Your carcasses shall fall in this wilderness" etc. (ibid. 14:29).

After the matter of the spies, God decreed that the generation of the Exodus should die in the wilderness, and hence, once more, Pharaoh's words were an unwitting prophecy.

191, ll. 57-62

The Wilderness Hath Shut (*sagar*, l. 57) Them In.

The midrash which begins here concludes the series telling of the unwitting prophecies by Pharaoh. In this case, what Pharaoh has in mind is no more than the simple meaning of the words, "The wilderness hath shut them in." (For the simple meaning, see Targum Onkelos and Ibn Ezra.) But *sagar* is a transitive verb, and "the wilderness" is therefore personified. The interpretation which follows removes that personification.

As soon as the Israelites saw the sea . . . the enemy . . . they turned toward the wilderness . . . the Holy One, blessed be He, ordered wild beasts to come there . . . as it is said: "He shut the wilderness against them."

sagar without a specific subject means "he shut." Before the *Nes* (miracle) at the Red Sea took place—this was Pharaoh's unwitting prophecy—the Israelites turned to the wilderness as the only possible avenue of escape, but God barred the way with wild beasts. The implication is that everything would have been lost had the Israelites had their way.

For "shutting" . . . wild beasts . . . "My God . . . His angel and hath shut the lions' mouths" (Dan. 6:23).

Support is found in Daniel 6:23 because there, too, the expression "hath shut" is associated with wild beasts.

192, ll. 63-64

And I Will Harden the Heart . . . in his mind whether to pursue or not.

An attempt at explaining the simple meaning. See the remarks below, p. 262.

192, ll. 65-75

See above, p. 92f.

192-193, ll. 75-89

Another Interpretation: And I will Get Me Honour upon Pharaoh. Scripture here tells that when God punishes the nations (*ha-'Ummot*, l. 76), His name becomes renowned (lit., magnified) in the world,

An aspect of *Kiddush ha-Shem,* sanctification of the Name, is taught in this midrash—the phase of the concept characterized by the combination of the concepts of *Kiddush ha-Shem* and God's justice. It is an aspect of the concept in which God Himself sanctifies His Name. When there has been a manifestation of God's justice, either those who have experienced it or others who have witnessed it or have been made aware of it are bound to acknowledge the holiness of God, that is, that He alone is to be worshipped (cf. above, p. 130f).

According to this midrash, those who come to recognize the holiness of God as a result of the experience or awareness of God's justice are the *'Ummot,* the nations of the world. God's Name is thus "magnified," meaning, He is acknowledged by nation after nation, not only by Israel.

We shall return to the interpretation itself later.

as it is said: "And I will work a sign among them, and I will send such as escape of them unto the nations (*ha-Goyim*)" etc. (Isa. 66:19).

The biblical meaning of *Goyim* as nations is retained in the interpretation, since the midrash introducing the verse speaks of *'Ummot,* nations (other examples above, p. 11). "Among them" refers to "all the nations" of the preceding verse, and the entire expression "a sign among them" is taken to mean that they will be punished, in consonance with the phrase "such as escape of them." God will send the latter "unto the nations, to Tarshish, Pul . . . to the isles afar off, that have not heard My fame, neither have they seen My glory; and they shall declare My glory unto the nations" (Isa. 66:19). Inasmuch as the verbs in the verse are in the future tense, the midrash implicitly teaches that this sanctification of the Name will take place in the future, in the days of the Messiah or the world to come.

And it also says: "Thus saith the Lord: 'The labour

of Egypt . . . Ethiopia . . . Sabeans . . . in chains
they shall come over . . . supplication unto thee:
Surely God is in thee and . . there is no other God'"
(ibid. 45:14). And what is said after this? "Verily
Thou art a God that hidest Thyself, O God of Israel,
the Saviour" (ibid. 45:15).

With respect to the nations mentioned, God's justice
will be manifest when their wealth will become the possession of Israel; as for themselves, "they shall go after
thee; in chains they shall come over." They will acknowledge God not only in a "supplication" to Israel but, the
midrash indicates, more directly with the words of Isaiah
45:15: "Verily Thou art a God that hidest Thyself, O
God of Israel, the Saviour." A fuller version is given in
Seder 'Olam, Chap. XXIII. On the basis of both versions
Rashi, on these verses, explains them to be a prophecy
concerning events which later occurred in connection with
Sennacharib's invasion.

**And it also says: "And I will plead against him with
pestilence and with blood," etc. And after this:
"Thus will I magnify Myself, and sanctify Myself"
etc. (Ezek. 38:22-23).**

Ezekiel 38:23 continues with, "And I will make Myself
known in the eyes of many nations, and they shall know
that I am the Lord." Once more the midrash teaches that
there will be a manifestation of God's punitive justice in
the future and that, as a result, "many nations" will
acknowledge God.

The expression "And I will sanctify Myself" identifies
Ezekiel 38:23 as one of a number of biblical verses, all

of them employing expressions of a similar character, which contain the idea of sanctification of the Name (cf. Avraham Holtz, Kiddush Hashem and Hillul Hashem, Judaism, X, No. 4 [1961]). Verses lacking such an expression may likewise contain that idea, as witness the simple meaning of other verses cited in this midrashic passage. Now, in a sense, the verses containing the idea of sanctification of the Name are more than just biblical antecedents of the rabbinic concept. Each of them tells of how God Himself sanctifies His Name. Each of them therefore can be, and is, used by the midrash to concretize the concept of *Ḳiddush ha-Shem*. On the other hand, the rabbinic concept includes other types of *Ḳiddush ha-Shem* as well, those in which man sanctifies God's Name (TE, pp. 64ff. and WE, pp. 131ff.). Furthermore, even when the midrash uses biblical verses as concretizations of the concept, the conceptual element is, so to speak, elicited from them by the midrash, especially through the general statement on *Ḳiddush ha-Shem* that introduces the verses ("When God punishes the nations, His Name is magnified in the world"). *Ḳiddush ha-Shem,* then, but illustrates once more that a rabbinic concept has biblical antecedents (above, p. 6f).

And it is also written: "In Salem . . . There He broke . . . the bow; the shield, and the sword, and the battle . . ." (Ps. 76:3-4), and it is written: "In Judah is God known; His name is great in Israel" (ibid. v. 2).

The idea presented here is, again, that the nations will, in the end, acknowledge God. They will come with full armor, ready to do battle, but God Himself will break their armor. As a result of having thus experienced God's punitive might in the lands of Judah and Israel, it is there that they will acknowledge Him—"In Judah is God known; His Name is great in Israel." But this idea is a midrashic interpretation, achieved by placing Psalm 76:2 after ibid. vv. 3-4. By means of this inversion, the midrash teaches that only after a manifestation of God's justice do the nations acknowledge Him, a teaching conveyed by other verses in the passage merely with the help of the interejction of "And what is said after this," or "And after this." In contrast to its treatment of the other verses, the midrash obviously deviates from the simple meaning of the verses cited here. For the simple meaning, see Ibn Ezra on Psalm 76:2,4.

This example of *Ḳiddush ha-Shem,* like some of those preceding, refers to the future, to the days of the Messiah or the world to come. That is made evident in a version of the midrash. "When will it come to pass that 'in Judah God is known?' When it will be true that 'there He broke the fiery shafts of the bow' " (Yalḳuṭ Shimeʿoni, Psalms, par. 815; comp. ibid., Ezekiel, par. 378).

And . . . it is written here: "And the Egyptians shall know that I am the Lord." In the past they did not know the Lord, but here it is said: "And . . . I am the Lord."

In accord with the preceding examples, this acknowledgment of God by the Egyptians will be a consequence of an experience of God's punitive justice, but such punishment is not mentioned here. It is alluded to in the interpretation of the first half of the verse, that which contains the theme of the entire passage. " 'And I will get

Me honour upon Pharaoh and upon all his host'—Scripture here tells that when God punishes the nations, His Name is magnified in the world." If the last interpretation is thus dependent on the first, then the last interpretation is not just another example of *Kiddush ha-Shem* but is the teaching the passage has aimed at all along.

194, ll. 90-93

A)   And They Did So . . . wisdom of Israel . . . did not say: "How can we turn back," . . . break the hearts of the women and children . . . them.

Despite their great anxiety they had the presence of mind not to utter a protest, and it was this presence of mind that constituted their "wisdom."

B)   Another Interpretation . . . They said: Whether we are willing or not . . . obey the command of the son of Amram.

Literally, "the words of the son of Amram," that is, the words of God transmitted by Moses. "They did so" precisely because they did not feel that Moses issued the command of his own accord.

194, ll. 94-96

And It Was Told the King . . . Who told him? The guards . . . posts of guards . . . some say Amalek told him.

Amalek stands for hatred toward Israel without cause. The guards and the posts merely did their duty.

194, ll. 97-103

That the People Were Fled . . . really fleeing? . . . "On . . . the children of Israel went out with a high hand" (Num. 33:3)? . . . "They smote . . . wounded . . . killed . . . They have no ruler nor chief," . . . "The locusts have no king" etc. (Prov. 30:27).

The Rabbis take every opportunity to teach that the Israelites had not fled from Egypt. The Egyptian guards received the impression that the Israelites possessed no ruler or chief, and hence that no one had led them out of Egypt. Each of them, therefore, must have left Egypt on his own initiative, and thus "fled"; although like locusts, who likewise have no king, they went forth together.

195, ll. 104-118

A) And the Heart of Pharaoh and of His Servants Was Turned, etc. Formerly: "And Pharaoh's servants said . . . 'How long . . . Let the men go ' (Exod. 10:7), but now, "And the heart . . . they said, 'What is this we have done, that we have let Israel go?" . . . They said: If . . . plagued . . . enough . . . let them go without our money . . . enough. But we were plagued, let them go, and our money was taken.

According to this midrash, resentment at having received so "bad a deal" brought about the change of mind.

B) A parable . . . slave went and bought him an ill-smelling fish . . . received the lashes, and paid a hundred *manah* . . . the Egyptians. They were plagued, they let Israel go, and their money was taken.

The slave in the parable had three different kinds of punishment inflicted upon him; the Egyptians, too, had three different kinds of punishment inflicted upon them. In that regard, the analogy of the parable holds, but not in others, for the Egyptians never were given their three kinds of punishment as alternatives to choose from, and the slave was given his three kinds as alternatives. Through the idea of alternatives, however, the point is made that it was the slave's own fault if he was subjected to all three kinds of punishment. The parable implies, therefore, that the Egyptians had only themselves to thank for what happened, that it was not a "bad deal" but a manifestation of God's justice.

Were a parable a complete analogy it would serve no purpose. A parable is told because it includes a factor which is absent in the analogue but which is nonetheless relevant to the analogue. See also above, p. 51.

195-196, ll. 118-120

Another Interpretation: Was Turned . . . the rule (lit., the emipre) of the Egyptians ceased, for it says: "Who are our servants?"

See n. 4. God allowed Egypt to maintain its empire only so long as the Israelites remained in Egypt. When the Egyptians realized this "their heart was turned." The text presents many difficulties; see H-R, p. 86, n. 20.

196-197, ll. 120-142

A)   Another Interpretation: Who Are Our Servants? They said: "Now all the nations . . . will say: 'Even . . . they had to let go.' . . . Now, how . . . officers and taskmasters . . . and Aram-zobah?"

The idea in this midrash is quite different from that of the preceding one. Here the Egyptians regard the Israelites as important not in themselves but because their exodus is bound to have a disturbing effect on the Egyptian empire. The Egyptians were not aware that, had it not been for Israel, they would not have been an empire at all.

This teaches you that Pharaoh ruled from one end of the world to the other . . . for the sake of the honor of Israel . . . "The king . . . even the ruler of peoples . . . free" (Ps. 105:20).

Pharaoh, who set Joseph free, was "the ruler of peoples," hence a cosmocrat. "For the sake of the honor of Israel" is discussed in the remark on the next statement.

B) And . . . every nation or tongue that subjugated Israel ruled from one end of the world to the other for the sake of the honor of Israel.

Although other nations are also cited as examples in the statement to follow, the teaching as a whole undoubtedly relates primarily to Rome, and thus to the situation in the rabbinic period. Subjugated by Rome, Israel in revolt after revolt succeeded only in demonstrating how weak it was in comparison with Rome's might. To counteract that evaluation of Israel and its effect upon possible converts, the Rabbis taught that Rome owed its supreme position in the world indirectly to Israel. The honor of Israel demanded that to dominate Israel a nation would have to dominate the entire world. Furthermore, by telling of nations in the past which in this man-

ner likewise owed their empires indirectly to Israel, the
Rabbis suggested that Rome's position was not at all
unique but that Israel's was.

**What . . . Assyrian Empire? "And . . . have I gath-
ered all the earth . . . chirped" (Isa. 10:14) . . .
Babylonian empire? "And . . . the nation and the
kingdom which will not serve the same Nebuchadnezzar king of Babylon" etc. (Jer. 27:8) . . . the
kingdom of the Medes? "Then king Darius wrote
unto all the peoples" etc. (Dan. 6:26) . . . the Greek
kingdom? "The beast had also four heads; and
dominion was given to it" (ibid. 7:6) . . . the fourth
kingdom? "And shall devour the whole earth, and
shall tread it down and break it in pieces" (ibid.
7:23). Thus . . . for the sake of the honor of Israel.**

We have here a rabbinic interpretation of part of the
vision in the seventh chapter of Daniel, the beast with
four heads being specifically identified as the Greek
kingdom, and "the fourth kingdom" (ibid.) as Rome by
implication, since the Roman empire came after the
Greek empire. In 'Abodah Zarah 2b, the fourth kingdom
is explicitly identified as Rome.

197-198, ll. 142-155

**A)   Another Interpretation: And the Heart of Phar-
aoh and of His Servants Was Turned. They said:
"Has not much good come to us on their account?"**

According to the biblical verse, the Egyptians were
concerned simply because they had now lost their slaves
—"And the heart . . ., and they said: 'What is this we

have done, that we have let Israel go from serving us?' "
(Exod. 14:5). According to the midrash here, however,
the Egyptians were concerned not because of the loss of
a large number of slaves but because they had lost the
benefit of the sheer presence of Israel in Egypt. It was
for the sake of Israel, they recognized, that Egypt had
prospered in so many ways. The midrash, obviously, emphasizes the concept of Israel.

**B)   R. Jose the Galilean, giving a parable says . . .
land which he sold for a trifle . . . seller, seeing
this, began to choke with grief . . . Egyptians who
let go without realizing what they had let go . . .
(Cant. 4:13).**

The parable stresses the idea that only after they had
let Israel go did the Egyptians realize what a prize they
had lost. Of course, the parable does not present a complete analogy; for one thing, because in the parable the
seller had lost the land irretrievably whereas the Egyptians felt that Israel was not lost to them irretrievably.
Rabbinic parables in general, as we have pointed out,
do not present complete analogies (above, p. 252).

**C)   Another Interpretation: R. Simon . . . a resi-
dence in a far off land which he sold for a trifle . . .
seller, seeing this, began to choke with grief . . .
Egyptians who let go without realizing what they let
go . . . "And . . . let Israel go,' " etc.**

Although the authority here is not the same, this parable appears to be another version of the one above, and
our remarks regarding that parable apply here as well.
It is quite likely that these versions reflect different occa-

sions when the Rabbis felt called upon to teach the idea they contain, the idea being an answer to anti-Jewish propaganda according to which Egypt drove out the Israelites as undesirables (cf. Josephus, *Against Apion*, I, 24, 26).

198-199, ll. 156-161

And He Made Ready His Chariot . . . Pharaoh with his own hands . . . When the nobles saw him . . . arranged their own.

This midrash derives from the fact that the verb is in the singular.

This statement and others like it can best be understood against the background of the biblical idea that God hardened Pharaoh's heart. Almost as though to deny that idea, the Rabbis add details to the biblical narrative so as to show that Pharaoh's pursuit of Israel was voluntary. The lengths to which Pharaoh went, these details imply, demonstrate that his pursuit was in keeping with his character. Here Pharaoh goes so far as to assume an egalitarian role, a clever device for making the pursuit a common enterprise.

199-200, ll. 161-176

A) There were four who did their harnessing with joy . . . "And Abraham rose early in the morning . . . ass" (Gen. 22:3) . . . "And Balaam . . . ass" (Num. 22:21) . . . "And Joseph made ready his chariot" (Gen. 46:29) . . . "And he . . . chariot." Let . . . saddling of our father Abraham . . . will of his

**Creator come and stand out . . . Balaam the wicked
. . . Let . . . the chariot . . . Joseph . . . meet his
father . . . stand out . . . Pharaoh the wicked . . .
pursue the Israelites.**

"With joy" because in each case the act was done
eagerly. Both Abraham and Balaam "rose in the morning," indicating eagerness. Both Joseph and Pharaoh evidently made ready their chariots themselves (the verbs in
both cases are in the singular), again an indication of
eagerness. (Abraham and Balaam are also contrasted in
'Abot V.22, or rather their disciples are. See Ginzberg,
Legends, VI, p. 124, n. 722, and p. 144, n. 855, who
denies the contention that the Rabbis identified Jesus
with Balaam.)

Intentions to destroy Israel, manifested in acts of saddling an ass or making a chariot ready, were nullified by
similar acts, but manifesting noble intentions, by Israel's
ancestors. Use of the subjunctive makes similarities and
contrasts alike more striking. Embodied in the passage is
the concept of *Zekut 'Abot*, merit of the fathers, a concept informed by the idea of corporate personality (above,
p. 229f).

**B) Another Interpretation: R. Simon . . . Let the
"sword" and the "hand" . . . our father Abraham
. . . (Gen. 22:10), come and stand out . . . by
Pharaoh the wicked when going to pursue the Israelites . . . (Exod. 15:19).**

See the remarks in A). Here similarity and contrast
are not in the initial acts but in acts meant to be nearly
final ones.

200, ll. 177-185

And Took His People with Him. He attracted them with words . . . "And when Pharaoh drew nigh" (Exod. 14:10). . . . with words.

Pharaoh "brought himself near and hastened in front of his soldiers" (Rashi on the verse).

As in lines 156-161, details are added to the biblical narrative so as to indicate that the pursuit of the Israelites was Pharaoh's own idea. He has to persuade the Egyptians, and does so because he is willing to be in the vanguard himself, to take only a common share of the spoil, and even to distribute his stored up treasures to them. All these things add up to more than just hardening Pharaoh's heart.

201, ll. 186-196

A)   And He Took Six Hundred Chariots. Whose were the beasts that drew the chariots? . . . To those "that feared [the word of] the Lord among the servants of Pharaoh" . . . that (even) those that feared [the word of] the Lord . . . a snare for Israel.

"Even" is not in the text. The words in brackets are omitted in the translation.

There is no doubt an allusion here to the fearers of Heaven in rabbinic times, Gentiles who rejected idolatry, and even observed the Sabbath and moral laws, but who did not convert to Judaism. They often became sects which turned out to be hostile to the Jews (WE, p. 57).

B)   In this connection R. Simon the son of Yoḥai said: "The nicest among the idolaters (*sheba-Goy-*

im, l. 1955),—kill. The best of the serpents—
smash its brains."

Goyim are Gentiles, and not necessarily idolaters
(above, p. 10). A bitter statement by a man hounded
and persecuted by the Romans. Such statements are not
matters of consensus. On the other hand, a conceptual
term is, of course, a necessary element of the value complex and there is a conceptual term reflecting an entirely
different attitude—namely, the term *Ẓaddiḳe 'Ummot ha-
'Olam*, the righteous of the nations of the world (RM,
p. 27f).

201, ll. 196-199

R. Simon b. Gamaliel . . . wealth and greatness of
this wicked empire. Not . . . legions is idle . . . Egypt
. . . idle . . . that.

See n. 10. Despite Rome's wealth and power, its legions were never idle. Egypt's legions were idle, the
proof being that Pharaoh could bring together so many
chariots at once.

202, ll. 200-207

A) And Captains (*Shalishim*) over All of Them
. . . *Shalishim* means mighty men, as in the passage
. . . (Ezek. 23:23).

An attempt at giving the simple meaning. This is also
the rendering in Targum Onkelos.

B) Another Interpretation: *Shalishim* . . . triply
armed. Rabban Simon the son of Gamaliel says: It
refers to the third (man) on the chariot . . . only

two who drove the chariot (lit., who made the chariot to run) . . . added one more . . . Rabbi says: Antoninus added one more . . . four.

The text is somewhat ambiguous, but the parallels (see the references) indicate that the numbers refer to the animals, horses or mules (Targ. Jonathan), which pulled the chariot. In historic times Greeks and Romans did not use chariots in war but did use them in races and processions (Encyc. Brit., 13th ed., V, 860a).

202, ll. 207-213

Another Interpretation: And *Shalishim* over All of Them . . . three of them against each Israelite . . . thirty against each one . . . three hundred . . . But how did Pharaoh know . . . died . . . went out of Egypt? . . . their registers . . . armies against them.

The wicked in Israel died "during the three days of darkness," but the Egyptians were ignorant of that (175, ll. 74-85, and above, p. 126). Pharaoh simply relied on the registers. There can be no doubt that the passage here and the one about Israelites dying during the three days of darkness have a common authorship, both of them exhibiting not only similarity in style but also the same kind of mounting hyperbole with regard to numbers. That would explain why the passage here takes account of the earlier passage.

202-203, ll. 213-215

In a similar way did R. Jeremiah interpret: "And . . . Zerah the Ethiopian with an army of a thousand thousand and three hundred chariots"(II Chr. 14:

8), and the armies which he led out against them were in proportion to the chariots.

This analogy has no bearing on the statement in the text which precedes it, for nothing is said there to suggest that the number of soldiers was in proportion to the chariots. What we have here is an analogy which relates to still another interpretation of the verse, the entire verse, an interpretation that takes *shalishim* to mean "soldiers," or rather triply armed men, somewhat as in an earlier interpretation. Both the interpretation and the analogy are found in Mechilta de-Rabbi Simon b. Jochai, ed. Hoffman, p. 44. "Another interpretation: 'and *shalishim* over all of them'—he brought forth soldiers against them in proportion to the chariots. In a similar way did R. Jeremiah interpret . . . (II Chr. 14:8)—he brought forth soldiers against them in proportion to the chariots." See H-R, p. 90, n. 1. According to this interpretation, then, the verse says: "And he took six hundred chosen chariots, and all the chariots of Egypt, and soldiers in proportion to all of them."

203, ll. 215-218

Another Interpretation: And Captains (*shalishim*, l. 216) over All of Them. In order to destroy all of them. Formerly . . . (Exod. 1:22); but here . . . destroy all of them . . . (Exod. 15:9).

See n. 11, and H-R, p. 90, n. 4. Very likely this interpretation, too, takes *shalishim* to mean soldiers having three weapons.

203, ll. 219-220

And the Lord Hardened the Heart of Pharaoh. For

Pharaoh was not wholly decided in his mind whether to pursue or not.

This interpretation belongs in a different category from that of the preceding midrashim. It is an attempt to teach the simple meaning of the Bible text whereas the other interpretations are purely haggadic in character. In this interpretation the impression is left that even after Pharoah had gathered his chariots and his army, he was still undecided whether to pursue or not. On the other hand, in the haggadot, stress is laid on Pharaoh's cleverness and zeal in the gathering of the army itself, as much as to say that from the very beginning the pursuit was his own idea. He gets his nobles involved through a crafty device, he harnesses his chariot with joy, he succeeds in persuading his people through his promises, he strengthens the power of his chariots, he attempts to make sure of victory by having his army greatly outnumber the Israelites. In fine, though the interpretation here is consistent with the biblical idea that God hardened Pharaoh's heart, the haggadot, without actually saying so, strongly imply that Pharaoh himself was responsible for the pursuit. Pharaoh was a *Rasha'*, a wicked man, and the lesson seems to be that wicked men indulge in wicked deeds through their own volition.

Implicit in an entire series of haggadot, that lesson surely left an impress despite its divergence from the biblical narrative. But do not the Rabbis themselves also present, at the same time, an interpretation consistent with the biblical narrative? On the basis of our theory of indeterminacy of belief, however, both these views can be accounted for. See above, p. 213f, where we discuss another example of a haggadic teaching at variance with a biblical idea.

203, ll. 221-223

And He Pursued . . . the excellence of Israel . . . another people, Pharaoh . . . after them.

No other people was as desirable, in Pharaoh's eyes, as Israel. To counter the calumny that the Israelites in Egypt were undesirables.

203-204, ll. 224-230

And . . . Went Out with a High Hand . . . when pursuing Israel the Egyptians were scorning, reviling and blaspheming. But Israel exalted, glorified . . . adoration . . . to Him . . . of war,

The raising of hands was a gesture of thanksgiving and of praise of God; see Rashi and Ibn Ezra on Nehemiah 8:6. It was naturally accompanied by words and songs of thanksgiving and praise. The two halves of the verse are regarded as contrasts and hence, if Israel praised God, the Egyptians must have blasphemed.

just as it is said: "Let the high praises of God be in their mouth," etc. (Ps. 149:6) . . . (ibid. 57:6) . . . (Isa. 25:1).

These verses are not taken to refer to the Israelites' praise of God here, but are quoted in order to indicate that the raising of hands was symbolic of, and accompanied by, expressions in which God is exalted.

204, ll. 231-232

A)   And . . . with a High Hand. This means with uncovered heads.

In a remark on Targum Onkelos, which translates "with a high hand" in precisely this way, S. D. Luzzatto (Com. to the Pentateuch, on this verse) points out that to them (i.e., to the Rabbis), an uncovered head indicated lack of fear whereas covering the head was a sign of subjection.

B) Another Interpretation: This means that their hand was exalted above the Egyptians.

From Pharaoh's pursuit of the Israelites, we must not conclude that the Israelites were fleeing. Their going forth represented mastery over the Egyptians. See Targum Jonathan and cf. Ibn Ezra on the verse.

CHAPTER III

(Exod. 14:9-14)

204, ll. 1-7

And the Egyptians Pursued After Them. This tells that not one of them stumbled on the way,

Rather: "Not one of them met with an accident (was detained)"—Jastrow, Dictionary, p. 676b. How is this interpretation derived from the verse? The commentators say that since Scripture tells of the pursuit in the preceding verse, the mention of "pursuit" in the present verse is superfluous and thus allows for an interpretation. A far more explicit warrant, however, is contained in that part of the verse which immediately follows what is quoted in the text—"and all the chariot horses of Pharaoh, his horsemen, and his warriors overtook them" (The Torah, Philadelphia, 1962, new J. P. S. translation). If all of them overtook the Israelites, then not one of them met with an accident or was detained.

so that they could not augur evil and turn back.

An accident to any one of them might have been interpreted as an omen of disaster for the entire army, anything interpreted as an omen being regarded as symbolic of a future event. See the discussion above, p. 70. In Rome, augury and divination were not only practiced privately but were also, for a long time, a matter of public law; see W. Fowler, The Religious Experience of the Roman People (London, 1922), pp. 292ff.

And thus we find . . . practice augury . . . "for these nations (*ha-Goyim*, l. 4) . . . hearken . . . unto diviners" (Deut. 18:14).

The midrash takes *ha-Goyim* to refer to Gentiles. Israel is, of course, strictly forbidden to practice any form of divination (ibid. vv. 10-11).

And . . . "And . . . with the rewards of divination in their hand" (Num. 22:7) . . . (Josh. 13:22).

"Means of divination in their hand" (Rashi) is a rendering which would more directly relate to the actual practice of divination.

205, ll. 8-10

And Overtook . . . And Pharaoh Drew Nigh (*hiḳrib*, l. 9). He drew nigh the punishment that was to come upon him.

hiḳrib may also be translated "he caused to draw nigh" or "he brought near." The emphasis, once more, is on Pharaoh's own role, as against, apparently, the idea of the hardening of his heart.

205, ll. 10-15

Another Interpretation: When Pharaoh . . . "Baalzephon approves . . . destroy them in water." He then began to sacrifice . . . to his idol (*'Abodah Zarah*, l. 14). In this sense it is said: "And Pharaoh drew nigh" *hiḳrib*, l. 15) . . . incense.

hiḳrib may also mean "he offered sacrifices." The midrash joins the last words of verse 9, "in front of Baal-
zephon," with the first words of verse 10, "And Pharaoh
offered sacrifices," so as to convey the idea "And Pharaoh offered sacrifices in front of Baal-zephon." Evidently
the midrash regards the phrase "by the sea, beside *Pi-
haḥirot*" as sufficient to describe the place where the Israelites were encamped. In our text the midrash ends
with "to sacrifice and offer incense," but these words are
not found in the Oxford MS (see Apparatus); if kept,
they require *hiḳrib* (l. 15) to mean "he drew nigh"
whereas the entire interpretation here requires that it
mean "he offered sacrifices."

The Rabbis show insight here into the pagan mind.
An omen may lead to worship. The water of the sea
becomes a kind of omen signifying the deity's approval,
an assurance of success which calls for offerings of thanksgiving. Pharaoh's earlier decision to destroy Israel by
means of water (Exod. 1:22) appears to him now as
confirming that omen.

205, ll. 15-18

**Another Interpretation: And Pharaoh Drew Nigh
(*hiḳrib*, l. 15). The distance . . . Pharaoh covered
in one day . . . "And . . . nigh."**

On the problem of the days involved see H-R, p. 91,
n. 9. *hiḳrib* is interpreted, apparently, as a causative—
Pharaoh, because of his swiftness, made what was to
others more distant, appear to be nearer. Once more the
emphasis is on Pharaoh's own role.

205, ll. 19-21

And . . . Lifted Up Their Eyes. After they had beaten the guards they knew that the Egyptians were bound to pursue them.

That is why they kept looking back (R. Moses Frankfort, Zeh Yenaḥamenu, [Amsterdam, 1712] reprinted Warsaw, 1933, p. 203). The Egyptians did not pursue the Israelites because the latter had fled from Egypt. The Israelites were not runaway slaves. The Egyptians pursued because the Israelites had beaten the guards.

206, ll. 22-25

And . . . Marching after Them . . . squadrons, each marching like one man . . . the empire learned . . . squadrons.

By relating Rome (the empire) to Egypt, it is implied that Rome will also be destroyed.

206-209, ll. 26-65

A)   And They . . . Cried Out unto the Lord . . . seized upon the occupation of their fathers . . . of Abraham, Isaac and Jacob.

Targum Onkelos translates "cried out" in the sense of "complained" (Naḥmanides on Exod. 14:11), which is apparently the simple meaning if the mood reflected in Exodus 14:11 is a criterion. Targum Jonathan, however, renders "and they prayed," and that is also what the midrash implies.

What does it say of Abraham? "Having . . . and called upon the name of the Lord" (Gen. 12:8);

"And . . . called there on the name of the Lord, the Everlasting God" (ibid. 21:33).

Targum Onkelos likewise understands both verses to refer to prayer. As to the original meaning, "called upon the Name of the Lord" probably indicates worship (cf. J. Skinner, Com. on Genesis [New York, 1910], p. 127), but very likely not prayer in the sense of petition.

What . . . of Isaac? "And Isaac went out to meditate (*lasuaḥ*) in the field" (Gen. 24:63) . . . prayer . . . (Ps. 55:18) . . . (ibid. 142:3) . . . (ibid. 102:1).

See n. 1. Ibn Ezra on Genesis 24:63 explains *lasuaḥ* as meaning "to walk among the shrubs."

What . . . of Jacob? "And he lighted upon *(vayif-ga‘)* the place" (Gen. 28:11) . . . *(pegi‘ah)* here only means prayer, as in the passage . . . (Jer. 7:16) . . . (ibid. 27:18).

Luzzato (on Gen. 23:8) cites Jeremiah 7:16 among his examples which prove that *pegi‘ah* means "urging."

There are verses which tell explicitly that the patriarchs resorted to prayer—in the case of Abraham, Genesis 20:17, in that of Isaac, ibid. 25:21, and in that of Jacob, ibid, 32:10-13. Why, then, does the midrash employ proof-texts that are certainly not unequivocal? Because, apparently, the midrash is anxious to prove that the patriarchs prayed not only on those occasions of which we are told explicitly, but on many other occasions, indeed that they prayed so often as to deserve to have it said of them that their very "occupation" or "trade" was prayer.

A deeper explanation takes account of the difference

between the explicit texts and the midrashic interpretations of those texts used by the midrash. The explicit texts tell that the patriarchs' prayers were called forth by specific needs. In contrast, the interpretations of the texts used by the midrash mention no specific needs at all, conveying little more than the bare idea that this or the other patriarch prayed. It would seem, according to the midrash, that the patriarchs prayed not just because of a specific need but often because of a reminder of some kind or perhaps because of a mood. Prayer of that kind is bound to be more frequent than that evoked by a specific need, frequent enough so that it could be characterized as an "occupation" or "trade." Obviously the Rabbis are thus relating to the patriarchs one of their own great achievements, making of prayer an "occupation" or "trade" of the Jews (see WE, pp. 97ff.—The Daily Tefillah). A somewhat later midrash actually teaches that the morning, afternoon and evening prayers were first recited by the patriarchs, employing as prooftexts for this purpose a number of verses used by the midrash here (RM, p. 128 and n. 29 there).

Faced with dire danger, the Israelites resorted to prayer. Instead of saying this directly the midrash reports, "They seized upon the occupation of their fathers, the occupation of Abraham, Isaac and Jacob." Why? The midrash does not take prayer for granted. A practice that came down from ancestors who lived a life of prayer, it is nothing less than a heritage. In some such sense, surely, that is what the midrash means when it says, "They seized upon the occupation of their fathers, the occupation of Abraham, Isaac and Jacob." That is the idea this midrash teaches and not the idea of the potency of prayer. But the passage in its present form continues with other midrashim on the subject of prayer, only one of which, the one at the end, is really of a piece with the midrash we have been discussing, and with which the passage begins. The midrashim in between do not speak of prayer as a heritage but contain the idea of the potency of prayer, and therefore appear to be supplementary midrashim.

B) And . . . "Fear not, thou worm Jacob . . . Israel" (Isa. 41:14). Just . . . the cedar with, so Israel has only prayer.

See n. 3. Prayer is Israel's only weapon, and it is a potent one. This interpretation begins the series of midrashim having for their theme the potency of prayer.

And . . . "Moreover . . . with my sword and with my bow (*beharbi u-bekashti*, l. 42)" (Gen. 48:22) . . . (Ps. 44:7)? . . . with prayer.

bekashti is interpreted as though it read *bakashati,* my petition, my prayer, but there is no play on *beharbi,* so far as we can see, either in the reading given in the text or in one in the Apparatus.

And, likewise . . . (Gen. 49:9) . . . "And this . . . 'Hear, Lord, the voice of Judah' " (Deut. 33:7).

"The voice of Judah" refers, of course, to the prayers of the tribe of Judah. But the verse also prophesies that the prayers will not be in vain—"And Thou shalt be a help against his adversaries." Genesis 49:9 is not cited in Mechilta de-Rabbi Simon b. Jochai, ed. Hoffmann, p. 46 and other sources; see H-R, p. 92, n. 13.

And . . . Jeremiah said . . . (Jer. 17:5). But of prayer what does he say? . . . (ibid. 17:7).

As the text reads now there is no specific reference to prayer.

Likewise, David says: "Thou comest . . . a javelin; but I come to thee in the name of the Lord of hosts" (I Sam. 17:45).

"In the name of the Lord of hosts," the midrash implies, refers to prayer. David's prayer was answered for he was victorious over Goliath.

And . . . "Some . . . but we will make mention of the name of the Lord our God. They are . . . fallen; but we are risen and stand upright. Save, Lord; let the King answer us in the day we call" (Ps. 28:8-10).

"Make mention of the name of the Lord" refers to prayer (Rashi on the verse; so also Chajes, Com. on Psalms). That the prayer is answered is implied in the verse which follows, v. 9.

Likewise . . . "And Asa cried (lit., called) unto the Lord his God, and said: 'Lord . . . help us, O Lord our God; for we rely on Thee, and in Thy name are we come against this multitude' " etc. (II Chron. 14:10).

Asa's prayer was answered. "And the Lord smote the Ethiopians before Asa, and before Judah" etc. (ibid. 14:11 ff.).

C) What does it say of Moses? "And Moses . . . king of Edom: 'Thus saith thy brother Israel . . . and

when we cried unto the Lord, He heard our voice' "
etc. (Num. 20:14-16). The Edomites, however, said
to them: . . . what your father bequeathed you, "The
voice is the voice of Jacob," "And the Lord heard
our voice.". . . what our father bequeathed us, . . .
"And by thy sword shalt thou live" . . . "And Edom
said unto him: 'Thou . . . lest I come out with the
sword against thee' " (Num. 20:18). And so also
here you interpret: "And they were sore afraid; and
the children of Israel cried out unto the Lord"—
they seized upon the occupation of their fathers,
the occupation of Abraham, Isaac and Jacob.

"And so also here you interpret" connects this midrash,
and this midrash alone, with the first midrash in the
passage. These midrashim are indeed associated. Both
midrashim describe prayer as Israel's heritage, and this
kinship in idea involves a more specific relationship. Just
as the words "We cried unto the Lord" in Numbers 20:16
indicate that Israel resorted to what was their heritage, so
likewise do the words "And the children of Israel cried
out unto the Lord."

Edom and Esau frequently stand for Rome in rabbinic
literature (above, p. 191). When the Rabbis speak of the
sword as the heritage of Edom, therefore, they may well
be saying of Rome that it endures solely because of its
military power. They seem also to be implying that Israel
will not prevail against Rome if Israel should resort to
war.

209-210, ll. 66-76

And They Said unto Moses: 'Because There Were No
Graves in Egypt.' After they had put leaven into the

dough, they came to Moses and said . . . Behold it says . . . (Exod. 5:20-21). . . . our enslavement in Egypt, then came the death of our brothers during the period of darkness, which was worse . . . now comes our death in this wilderness, which is much worse for us . . . our brothers were buried and mourned for . . . our corpses . . . of the night.

"After (or, since) they had put leaven into the dough" is an expression for which various explanations are given (H-R, p. 93, n. 12). It seems to us, however, that the correct explanation is that of R. Judah Najar (op. cit., p. 31a). He regards it as a pejorative expression, a metaphor of some kind, characterizing the words in the verse just quoted: "Because there were no graves in Egypt, hast thou taken us away to die in the wilderness?"

According to the midrash, after the Israelites had thus complained to Moses, "they came to Moses and said"— "they came," not to upbraid him further, for what they had to say to him now was as much explanation as grievance. They told him of their stages of dejection, each one lower than the previous one: first, their enslavement, then their grief over those who had died during the three days of darkness, and now, finally, their apprehension lest they would have no burial. In a rather elliptic manner, the midrash interprets Exodus 14:12, the verse following the complaint, as successively alluding to these three stages of dejection. When the people said, "Is not this the word that we spoke in Egypt?" they referred to their dejection over their enslavement. When they said, "For it were better for us to serve the Egyptians than that we should die," they referred to their grief over those who had died in the period of darkness. Their present dejection is still greater, and is eliptically referred to by the words, "that we should die in the wilderness." Cf. R. Judah Najar, loc. cit.

210, ll. 77-80

And Moses . . . 'Fear Not' . . . the wisdom of Moses, how he stood there pacifying all these thousands and myriads . . . (Eccl. 7:19).

Moses' wisdom here was not just a matter of wisdom but of patience—"how he stood there pacifying all these thousands and myriads."

210-211, ll. 81-86

Stand Still and See the Salvation of the Lord. The Israelites asked him: "When?" Moses said to them: "Today the Holy Spirit (*Ruah ha-Kodesh*, l. 81) rests upon you."

The word "today" is in the verse being interpreted— "And see the salvation of the Lord, which He will work for you, today." According to a suggestion of the late Prof. Louis Ginzberg, the midrash originally read as follows: "Moses said to them: 'Today.' [Immediately] the Holy Spirit rested upon them."

The concept of *Ruah ha-Kodesh,* the Holy Spirit, has a number of aspects. Sometimes, as here, the term connotes a power given by God to foresee an event, and hence this interpretation of, "Stand still and *see* the salvation of the Lord." Obviously, not prophecy in the sense of a prophetic utterance, this power of foreseeing is nevertheless a prophetic power, and consequently on that day the Israelites could be characterized as prophets. Cf. Bereshit R. LXXV.8, ed. Theodor-Albeck, p. 886.

For the expression "standing" *(yezibah)* everywhere suggests . . . the Holy Spirit. . . . (Amos 9:1) . . . (I Sam. 3:10) . . . (Deut. 31:14).

The examples cited do not represent the aspect of *Ruah ha-Kodesh* just described. The first is a prophecy by Amos, the second is a communication by God to Samuel, and the third refers to a charge to be given by God to Joshua. They are cited together because they are all forms of God's word. On the other hand, all the things told of here, including the foreseeing, embody the concepts of *Ruah ha-Kodesh* and *Nabi* (prophet).

We ought to add that the phenomenon of "speaking with tongues" is not associated with the Holy Spirit by the Rabbis, and that, indeed, it is not even mentioned by them.

211, ll. 86-94

A) To what were the Israelites . . . a dove . . . there is the serpent . . . there is the hawk . . . the sea forming a bar and the enemy pursuing. Immediately they set their minds upon prayer . . . "O my dove that art in the clefts of the rock" etc. (Cant. 2:14) . . . "For sweet is thy voice and thy countenance is comely" (ibid.), it means, for thy voice is sweet in prayer and thy countenance is comely in the study of Torah.

A) relates back to the passage on prayer (206, ll. 26ff.) and to the verse "And the children of Israel cried out unto the Lord." But A) is a rather difficult midrash. The interpretation of the first part of Canticles 2:14 ("O my dove" etc.) definitely refers to Israel at the Red Sea, whereas the interpretation regarding prayer and study of Torah refers to no specific situation, and yet the mention of prayer is not only relevant to the first part of the interpretation but is "required" (cf. H-R, p.94, n. 12). We see nothing wrong, however, with the expression, "Thy countenance is comely in the study of Torah." Koheleth had long ago said, "A man's wisdom maketh his face to shine" (8:1), and people today, too, speak of an intellectual face.

B) Another Interpretation. For thy voice is sweet in prayer and thy countenance is comely in good deeds.

This interpretation of the latter part of Canticles 2:14 likewise refers to no specific situation, and it is attached to A) because it is another interpretation of "For sweet is thy voice and thy countenance is comely." The application here, too, is apt. A person who has a kindly face usually is one who does good deeds.

211-212, ll. 95-106

Another Interpretation: Stand Still and See, etc. "When?" He answered them: "Tomorrow!" . . . "Moses, our Master, we have not the strength to endure."

After the interruption by the passage on prayer, the Mekilta gives another interpretation of "Stand Still," etc. (v. 13). This midrash as well as the earlier interpretation (210, ll. 81ff.) attempts to account for "today" in verse 13, since verse 24 speaks of "the morning watch" and

verse 27 of "the morning," both later verses thus referring
to the next day. "Today" in verse 13, according to these
midrashim, refers not to the destruction of the Egyptians
but to "seeing" today the salvation which God will work
on the next day, the "seeing" being achieved through
the Holy Spirit as told in the earlier midrash, and in a
different manner as given in the sequel here.

**At that moment Moses prayed . . . squadrons of
ministering angels standing before them, just as it
is said . . . (II Kings 6:15-17) . . . before them.**

There is no foretelling here and hence no *Ruaḥ ha-
Ḳodesh,* apparently. What they see are squadrons of
ministering angels standing by them as their protectors.
They are allowed to see the squadrons of angels in order
to allay their fear.

212-213, ll. 106-117

**And thus it says . . . (Ps. 18:13) . . . (ibid. v. 14)
. . . (ibid.) . . . (ibid. v. 15) . . . (ibid.) . . . Another Interpretation . . . Another Interpretation . . .
(Deut. 7:23).**

There is no direct connection between these interpretations of Psalm 18:13ff. and the statement that the fear
of the Israelites was allayed by their being able to see
the presence of the angels. In the interpretations here
the angels do not figure at all. In fact, these interpretations
are presented elsewhere (Yer. Soṭah VIII.3, 22b) as an
independent baraita, and without actual reference to the
Egyptians, although in the present context the baraita is
no doubt intended as a description of how God nullified

the weapons and tactics of that army. There is an escha-
talogical aspect to this baraita.

213-214, ll. 118-128

**For Whereas Ye Have Seen the Egyptians Today,
etc. . . . In three places God warned . . . "For
whereas . . . no more forever." And it says, "Ye
shall . . . no more that way" (Deut. 17:16). And
. . . "By the way . . . thee: 'Thou . . . no more
again' " (ibid. 28:68).**

Because of Deuteronomy 17:16 it is assumed that
what are taken here and elsewhere to be warnings were
given by God, and only transmitted by Moses. However,
there are also sources in which these verses seem to be
represented as a promise by God that the Israelites would
never again return to be enslaved by Egypt (H-R, p. 95,
n. 10). Different concepts inform these divergent interpretations—as a warning, the verses embody the concept of
Miẓwah, whereas as a promise they embody the concept
of God's love. We regard the passage on 93, ll. 47-49
as consistent with the passage here (see above, p. 119).

**But . . . returned three times . . . fell . . . the days
of Sennacharib . . . the days of Johanan, the son
of Kareah . . . the days of Trajan . . . fell.**

On "the days of Trajan," see G. Alon, Toledot ha-
Yehudim be-'Erez Yisrael, I (Tel Aviv, 1952), pp. 245ff.

214, ll. 128-136

**The Israelites at the Red Sea were divided into four
groups . . . throw ourselves into the sea . . . return
to Egypt . . . fight them . . . cry out . . . "Stand**

still . . . the Lord". . . "For whereas . . . today" etc.
"The Lord will fight for you" . . . "And ye shall
hold your peace."

In a general way, the attitudes here may reflect the
attitudes of Jews to Rome even in the pre-Bar Kokeba
period, that is, hopelessness by some and an insistence
on rebellion by others. Apparently the Rabbis attempt
both to encourage the hopeless ("Stand still, and see the
salvation of the Lord") and to calm the rebellion-minded
("The Lord will fight for you").

215, ll. 137-149

**A) The Lord Will Fight for You. Not only at this
time but at all times . . . your enemies.**

These words definitely refer to their own day. But the
verse as it continues is included in the teaching—"And
ye shall hold your peace." The Jews are not to revolt.
In God's good time He Himself will wage war against
the Romans in behalf of Israel.

**B) R. Meir says . . . If even . . . silent . . . how much
more . . . praise to Him!**

R. Meir interprets the entire verse, and to him it is
unthinkable that the Israelites should "hold their peace"
and not be offering praises to God as He fights for them.

**C) Rabbi says: The Lord Will Fight . . . Your Peace.
Shall God perform miracles and mighty deeds for
you and you be standing silent? . . . What is there
for us to do? . . . You should be exalting and praising . . . (Ps. 149:6) . . . (ibid., 57:12) . . . (Isa.
25:1) . . . (Exod. 15:2).**

Rabbi interprets the verse to be a question by Moses: "The Lord will fight for you and you will hold you peace?" According to Rabbi, Moses then tells the Israelites that they ought to be praising God as He fights for them, and that the Israelites did so in the Song of Moses, beginning with Exodus 15:2. Rabbi teaches, then, that the Song of Moses was said at the Red Sea while the Egyptians were being punished.

INDEX

Aaron, as fit as Moses to receive *Dibberot*, 39, 71f; equal to Moses in courage, 39; Moses not given precedence over, 40; showed respect to Moses, 71

'Aberah (transgression), first to commit an, is first to be punished, 92. *See also* Sin

'Abodah Zarah, term refers both to idols and idolatry, 78; Israel in Egypt steeped in, 77ff; practice of, outweighs practice of all *Miẓwot*, 77f; hard for Israel in Egypt to give up, 80f; sacrifice of paschal lamb was negation of, 79; obligatory on all man to abstain from, 95f, 180f, 232; biblical antecedents of concept of, 78. *See also* Idol

'Abot (patriarchs), the, all of equal rank, 41; sometimes included in concept of Israel, 168f; prayers as the occupation of, 268f. *See also* Patriarchs, the

Abraham, plea for justice by, 6; love of God, 72; legend that Isaac was sacrificed by, 100; included in the concept of Israel, 170; acted as escort, 202; acts of kindness of, Israel rewarded measure for measure for, 229f

Abudraham, 222

Adam, did not reckon years by Nisan, 66f; created with male and female bodies, 175; the word as concept, 12f

'Adam ha-Rishon, universalism implied in, 12f, 66f

Against Appion (Josephus), 177, 178, 256

Albeck, C., 177, 223

Alon, G., 220, 279

Altar-building, only Land of Israel fit for, 44

'Amanah, trust, 239. *See also* *'Emunah*

Angels, of lower rank than Israel, 106; as destroyers, 108, 109; came to Abraham on Passover, 183; Israel rewarded for Abraham's kindness to the, 229f; as protectors of Israel at Red Sea, 278

"Another interpretation", implications of, 209f, 213

Anthropomorphism, negation of, not a rabbinic idea, 84, 190, idea of God's otherness not to be identified with, 98f, 232

Aquila, 172

'Arayot (chastity), practiced by Israel in Egypt, 75f. *See also* Chastity

Ark, the, coffin of Joseph carried alongside of, 222; cover of, associated with *Gilluy Shekinah,* 219, 222

Lauterbach's Edition and Translation

of the

MEKILTA DE-RABBI ISHMAEL, Volume I,

Tractate Pisḥa' 1-168

Tractate Beshallaḥ 169-215

SIGLA USED IN APPARATUS CRITICUS

לוח הסימנים בשינויי נוסחאות

TRACTATE PISḤA

CHAPTER I
(Ex. 12.1)

And the Lord Spoke unto Moses and Aaron in the Land of Egypt Saying. From this I might understand that the divine word was addressed to both Moses and Aaron. When, however, it says: "And it came to pass on the day when the Lord spoke unto Moses in the land of Egypt" (Ex. 6.28), it shows that the divine word was addressed to Moses alone and not to Aaron. If so, what does Scripture mean to teach by saying here, "unto Moses and Aaron?" It merely teaches that just as Moses was perfectly fit to receive the divine words, so was Aaron perfectly fit to receive the divine words. And why then did He not speak to Aaron? In order to grant distinction to Moses. Thus you must say that Aaron was not directly addressed in any of the divine communications of the Torah, with the exception of three, for in the case of these three[1] it is impossible to say that they were not directly addressed to him.

Another Interpretation. Why is it said here,

---

[1] The three passages are: Lev. 10.8; Num. 18.1 and 18.8.

1

מסכתא דפסחא

פרשה א (שמות י"ב, א'.)

ו י א מ ר י י א ל מ ש ה ו א ל א ה ר ן
ב א ר ץ מ צ ר י ם ל א מ ר שומע אני שהיה
הדיבור למשה ולאהרן כשהוא אומר ויהי ביום
דבר יי אל משה בארץ מצרים למשה היה הדיבור
5 ולא היה הדיבור לאהרן אם כן מה תלמוד לומר
אל משה ואל אהרן אלא מלמד שכשם שהיה משה
כלול לדברות כך היה אהרן כלול לדברות ומפני
מה לא נדבר עמו מפני כבודו של משה נמצאת
ממעט את אהרן מכל הדברות שבתורה חוץ
10 משלשה מקומות מפני שאי איפשר. דבר אחר אל

---

3 שמות ו', כ'ח. 4—5 ספרא ויקרא ב'. ספרי במדבר נ'ח. 9—6 ת.
בא. 10—16 ש. 6.

3—4 הדיבור] א. הדיבר ד. הדבר. 5 היה הדיבור] ד. / לאהרן[
א"צ. ~ הרי במצרים בסיני מנין הרי הוא אומר ביום דבר יי את משה
בהר סיני באהל מועד מנין הרי הוא אומר ויקרא אל משה וידבר אליו
מאהל מועד נמצא ממעט אהרן מכל וכל. 7 כלול]=א"א: הד'ר ישראל
לוי במחברתו Ein Wort über die Mechilta des R. Simon (Breslau 1889)
p. 38 הניה כלי. מ. ד. כלל. 10 שאי איפשר] ד. שאיפשר.

1

"unto Moses and Aaron"? Because it says,
"And the Lord said unto Moses: See I have set
thee in God's stead to Pharaoh" (Ex. 7.1). From
this I would know only that Moses was a judge[2]
over Pharaoh. How about Aaron? By saying
here, "unto Moses and Aaron," Scripture teaches
that Aaron was equal to Moses: just as Moses
was a judge over Pharaoh, so also was Aaron a
judge over Pharaoh; just as Moses would speak
his words fearlessly, so also would Aaron speak
his words fearlessly. Rabbi says: *unto Moses
and Aaron.* I might understand that the one
preceding in the scriptural text actually had
precedence over the other. But in the passage:
"These are that Aaron and Moses to whom
the Lord said," etc. (Ex. 6.26), Aaron is mentioned first. Scripture thus declares that both
were equal, the one as important as the other.

In like manner you must interpret: "In the
beginning God created the heaven and the
earth" (Gen. 1.1). I might understand that
the one preceding in the scriptural text actually
preceded in the process of creation. But in the
passage: "In the day that the Lord God made
earth and heavens" (Gen. 2.4), the earth is
mentioned first. Scripture thus declares that
both were created simultaneously.

In like manner you must interpret: "I am

---

[2] The word אלהים, designating God, also means "judge"
(see below, *Baḥodesh*, IV, note 10, and *Kaspa*, I, comment
on Ex. 22.27). Hence, the passage in Ex. 7.1 may mean:
"I have set thee in God's stead," and also: "I have set
thee up as judge."

משה ואל אהרן למה נאמר לפי שהוא אומר ויאמר
יי אל משה ראה נתתיך אלהים לפרעה אין לי אלא
משה דיין לפרעה אהרן מנין תלמוד לומר אל
משה ואל אהרן הקיש אהרן למשה מה משה דיין
לפרעה אף אהרן דיין לפרעה מה משה אומר
דבריו ולא ירא אף אהרן אומר דבריו ולא ירא .
רבי אומר אל משה ואל אהרן שומע אני כל הקודם
במקרא הוא קודם במעשה תלמוד לומר הוא אהרן
ומשה מגיד ששניהם שקולין זה כזה . כיוצא בו אתה
אומר בראשית ברא אלהים את השמים ואת הארץ
שומע אני כל הקודם במקרא קודם במעשה תלמוד
לומר ביום עשות יי אלהים ארץ ושמים מגיד
ששניהם שקולין זה כזה . כיוצא בו אתה אומר אנכי

---

11 שמות ז׳, א׳.   23—17 מדרש שמואל ה׳ (56).   18—19 שמות ו׳, כ״ו.
34—19 ב״ר א׳, ט״ו. וי״ר ל״ו, א׳. תוספ׳ כריתות ד׳, ט״ו.   23—19 י׳ חגיגה
ב׳, א׳ (77ᵈ).   20 בראשית א׳, א׳.   22 בראשית ב׳, ד׳.   24—23 שמות ג׳, ו׳.

13—12 ראה נתתיך–תלמוד לומר]א. >.   17 רבי אומר]ד. דבר
אחר ט. > / אל משה ואל אהרן שומע אני] א. מ. > ט. יכול.
23 זה כזה] ד. כאחד זה כזה.   24—23 אנכי אלהיך ד. אנכי האל
אלהי.

the God of thy father, the God of Abraham, the
God of Isaac, and the God of Jacob" (Ex. 3.6).
I might understand that each one who precedes
in the scriptural text was of greater importance
than the one following him. But the order is
reversed in the passage: "Then will I remember
My covenant with Jacob, and also My covenant
with Isaac, and also My covenant with Abraham
will I remember" (Lev. 26.42). Scripture thus
declares that all three were equal.

In like manner you must interpret: "Honour
thy father and thy mother" (Ex. 20.12). I
might understand that the one preceding in the
scriptural text should actually have precedence
over the other. But in the passage: "Ye shall
fear every man his mother and his father"
(Lev. 19.3), the mother precedes. Scripture thus
declares that both are equal.

In like manner you must interpret: "And
Joshua the son of Nun and Caleb the son of
Jephunneh," etc. (Num. 14.6). I might under-
stand that the one preceding in the scriptural
text actually had precedence over the other.
But in the passage: "Save Caleb the son of
Jephunneh the Kenizzite and Joshua the son of
Nun" (Num. 32.12), Caleb is mentioned first.
Scripture thus declares that they were both
equal.

In the Land of Egypt. This means outside of
the city. You say it means outside of the city;
perhaps it means within the city? Since, however, it says: "And Moses said unto him: As
soon as I am gone out of the city I will spread
forth my hands unto the Lord" (Ex. 9.29),

אלהי אביך אלהי אברהם אלהי יצחק ואלהי יעקב
שומע אני כל הקודם במקרא הוא חשוב מחבירו
תלמוד לומר וזכרתי את בריתי יעקב ואף בריתי
יצחק ואף את בריתי אברהם מגיד ששלשתן שקולין.
כיוצא בו אתה אומר כבד את אביך ואת אמך
שומע אני כל הקודם במקרא הוא קודם במעשה
תלמוד לומר איש אמו ואביו תיראו מגיד ששניהם
שקולין זה כזה. כיוצא בו אתה אומר ויהושע בן
נון וכלב בן יפונה וגו' שומע אני כל הקודם במקרא
הוא קודם במעשה תלמוד לומר בלתי כלב בן
יפונה הקנזי ויהושע בן נון וגו' מגיד ששניהם שקולין.
‎ באָרץ מצרים חוץ לכרך לכרך אתה אומר חוץ
לכרך או אינו אלא בתוך הכרך כשהוא אומר
ויאמר אליו משה כצאתי את העיר וגו' והלא

27—26 ויקרא כ"ו, ס"ב. 28 שמות כ', י"ב. 31—28 ספרא קדושים א'.
כריתות ו', ט'. 30 ויקרא י"ט, ג'. 31—32 במדבר י"ד, ו'. 34—33 במדבר
ל"ב, י"ב. 42—35 ת. בא. ש. 5—6. 37 שמות ט', כ"ט. 40—37 שמו"ר י"ב, ה'.

27—26 ואף בריתי יצחק] במקרא כתוב ואף את בריתי יצחק.
27 ששלשתן] ד. ששניהם / שקולין] מ. ט. ~ זה כזה ד. ~ כאחד.
29 שומע אני–קודם במעשה] א. ד. >. 31 זה כזה]מ. כאחת.
34—31 כיוצא בו–ששניהם שקולין] ד. >. 33 בלתי] הנהתי עפ"י ג:
א. מ. זולתי (דברים א', ל"ו) ט. (בראשית רמ"ז, ד') כי אם (במדבר
י"ד, ל"ו). 34 הקנזי ויהושע בן נון] הוספתי עפ"י ס"ח: א. מ. וגו'.
37 וגו'] הוספתי עפ"י ג.

should we not apply the argument of *Kal vahomer?*[3] If with regard to prayer, the less important, Moses would utter it only outside of the city, it is but a logical inference that with regard to the divine word, the more important, He would speak it to him only outside of the city. And why, indeed, did He not speak with him within the city? Because it was full of abominations and idols.

Before the land of Israel had been especially chosen, all lands were suitable for divine revelations; after the land of Israel had been chosen, all other lands were eliminated. Before Jerusalem had been especially selected, the entire land of Israel was suitable for altars; after Jerusalem had been selected, all the rest of the land of Israel was eliminated. For thus it is said: "Take heed to thyself that thou offer not thy burnt offerings in every place that thou seest, but in the place[4] which the Lord shall choose" (Deut. 12.13–14). Before the Temple had been especially selected, the whole of Jerusalem was appropriate for the manifestation of the divine presence; after the Temple had been selected, the rest of Jerusalem was eliminated. For thus it is said: "For the Lord hath chosen Zion, He hath desired it for His habitation: This is My resting-place for ever" (Ps. 132.13–14).

---

[3] *Kal vahomer* is the argument "*a minore ad majus*" or "*a majore ad minus.*" It is the first rule in the hermeneutic system of Hillel, as well as in that of R. Ishmael (see Lauterbach, "Talmud Hermeneutics," in *JE*, XII, 32).

[4] The place chosen by the Lord was Jerusalem.

דברים קל וחמר ומה אם תפלה הקלה לא התפלל
משה אלא חוץ לכרך דבור החמור דין הוא שלא

40 נדבר עמו אלא חוץ לכרך ומפני מה לא נדבר
עמו בתוך הכרך לפי שהיתה מלאה שיקוצים
וגילולים. ועד שלא נבחרה ארץ ישראל היו כל
הארצות כשרות לדברות משנבחרה ארץ ישראל
יצאו כל הארצות עד שלא נבחרה ירושלים היתה

45 כל ארץ ישראל כשרה למזבחות משנבחרה
ירושלים יצאה כל ארץ ישראל שנאמר השמר לך
פן תעלה עולותיך וגו' כי אם במקום אשר יבחר
עד שלא נבחר בית עולמים היתה ירושלים ראויה
לשכינה משנבחר בית עולמים יצאת ירושלים

50 שנאמר כי בחר יי בציון וגו' זאת מנוחתי עדי עד וגו'

57—42 ת. בא. מדרש תהלים קל״ב, נ׳. (רנ״ט).   47—46 דברים י״ב,
י״נ—י״ד.   50 תהלים קל״ב, י״נ—י״ד.

38 תפלה הקלה] א. תפלת הקל.   39 משה] ד. <.   40—39 דין
הוא-לכרך] ד. לא כל שכן.   43 כל ארץ ישראל] ט. כל
הסקוטות/ כשרה למזבחות] ת. כשרה לדבור. א׳צ. ראויה לשכינה.
ט. כשרות להקרבה.   46 כל ארץ ישראל] ט. כל הסקוטות.
46—47 השמר לך-אשר יבחר] א׳צ. כי בחר יי בציון.   47 עולותיך]
א. מ. עולות.   50—51 כי בחר-עדי עד וגו'] א׳צ. השמר לך פן
תעלה עולותיך וגו'.

Before Aaron had been especially chosen, all
Israelites were qualified for the priesthood; after
Aaron had been chosen, all other Israelites were
eliminated. For thus it is said: "It is an everlasting covenant of salt before the Lord, unto
thee and to thy seed with thee" (Num. 18.19);
and again it says: "And it shall be unto him,
and to his seed after him, the covenant of an
everlasting priesthood" (Num. 25.13). Before
David had been chosen, all Israelites were
eligible to the kingship; after David had been
chosen, all other Israelites were eliminated. For
thus it is said: "Ought ye not to know that the
Lord, the God of Israel, gave the kingdom over
Israel to David forever, even to him and to his
sons by a covenant of salt" (II Chron. 13.5).
You could say: "I cite the case of those prophets
with whom He did speak outside of the land of
Palestine." True, He did speak with them
outside of the land, but He did so only because
of the merit of the fathers.[5] For thus it is said:
"A voice is heard in Ramah, lamentation and

---

[5] The expression "merit of the fathers", זכות אבות, here
is not to be taken literally, but rather in the sense of merit
of parents or ancestors, for here it refers to the merit of
Rachel who was regarded as the mother of all Israel (see
Gen. Rab. 71.3). The passage from Jeremiah cited here
as proof was interpreted to mean that Rachel cried to
God about her children who were exiled and God promised
her that He would return them to their own land (see
Pesikta Rabbati, Friedmann, 11b). It was because of Rachel,

עד שלא נבחר אהרן היו כל ישראל ראוים
לכהונה משנבחר אהרן יצאו כל ישראל שנאמר
ברית מלח עולם היא לפני יי וגו' ואומר והיתה לו
ולזרעו אחריו ברית כהונת עולם עד שלא נבחר
55 דוד היו כל ישראל ראוים למלכות משנבחר דוד
יצאו כל ישראל שנאמר הלא לכם לדעת כי יי
אלהי ישראל נתן הממלכה לדוד על ישראל. ואם
תאמר דן אני את הנביאים שנדבר עמהם בחוצה
לארץ אף על פי שנדבר עמהם בחוצה לארץ לא
60 נדבר עמהם אלא בזכות אבות שנאמר קול ברמה

---

53 במדבר י"ח, י"ט.   53–54 במדבר כ"ה,י"נ.   56–57 דהי"ב י"ג, ה'.
57–72 ת. בא. ש. 5.   60–61 ירמיה ל"א, י"ד–ט"ו.

---

51 ראוים] ד. כשרים.   52 משנבחר אהרן-כל ישראל] א .>.
53 לפני יי] א. לו. מ. >.   55 ראוים] ד. כשרים.   56 כי יי]
מ. כי אני יי.   57 הממלכה] במקרא כתוב ממלכה. מ. נ. ל. את
הממלכה. נ. הממלוכה./ על ישראל] נ. על כל ישראל.   58 את] נ.
ל. סן.

---

then, that God communicated with the prophets in the
Babylonian Exile to tell them about the return, when and
how it was to take place.

bitter weeping, Rachel weeping for her children; she refuseth to be comforted for her children, because they are not. Thus saith the Lord: Refrain thy voice from weeping and thine eyes from tears; for thy work shall be rewarded, saith the Lord, and they shall come back from the land of the enemy. And there is hope for thy future saith the Lord" (Jer. 31.15f.). Some say: Even though He did speak with them outside of the land, and because of the merit of the fathers, He did so only at a pure spot, near water, as it is said: "And I was by the stream Ulai" (Dan. 8.2). Again it says: "As I was by the side of the great river, which is Tigris" (Dan. 10.4); "The word of the Lord came expressly unto Ezekiel the priest the son of Buzi, in the land of the Chaldeans by the river Chebar" (Ezek. 1.3).—Some say: He had already spoken with him in the land, and then He spoke with him outside of the land, for thus it is said: "The word of the Lord had come and came to Ezekiel." 'Had come' indicates that He had spoken with him in the land; 'and came'[6] indicates that He spoke with him outside of the land. R. Eleazar the son of Zadok says: Behold it says: "Arise go forth into the plain" (Ezek. 3.22); this declares that the plain was suitable for divine revelation.—You can learn from the following that the Shekinah does not reveal itself outside of the land. It is said:

---

[6] The infinitive absolute היה in this passage is considered as having the force of a pluperfect.

נשמע וגו' כה אמר יי מנעי קולך מבכי וגו' ויש תקוה
לאחריתך וגו' ויש אומרים אף על פי שנדבר עמהם
בחוצה לארץ ובזכות אבות לא נדבר עמהם אלא
במקום טהרה של מים שנאמר ואני הייתי

65 על אובל אולי ואומר ואני הייתי על יד הנהר הגדול
הוא חדקל ואומר היה היה דבר יי אל יחזקאל בן
בוזי הכהן בארץ כשדים על נהר כבר ויש אומרים
נדבר עמו בארץ ונדבר עמו חוצה לארץ שנאמר
היה היה דבר יי היה שנדבר עמו בארץ היה שנדבר

70 עמו חוצה לארץ ר' אלעזר בן צדוק אומר הרי
הוא אומר קום צא אל הבקעה וגו' מגיד שהבקעה
כשרה.   תדע שאין השכינה נגלית בחוצה לארץ

64_65 דניאל–ח', ב'.   65–66 שם י'. ד'.   66–67 יחזקאל א', נ'.
67–70 מו"ק כ"ה, א'.   71 יחזקאל נ', כ"ב.

62 ויש אוטרים] ד. >. / אף על פי] ד. ואף על פי.   63 ובזכות
אבות] א. > מ. ולא נדבר עטהם אלא בזכות אבות.   67 הכהן–נהר
כבר] הוספתי עפ"י ט: מ. א. וגו'.   68 א. נדבר עטו בחוצה לארץ
ונדבר עטו בארץ / שנאמר] א. >.   69 היה היה דבר יי] א. מ. > / היה
שנדבר עטו בארץ] א. > / היה] א. היה היה.   70 א. מ. היה ר' אלעזר
בן צדוק אומר.   72 כשרה] ט. יחזקאל של"ו]. ש"ט. ~ לדיבור / נגלית
בחוצה לארץ] א. מ. נגלה חוצה לארץ.

"But Jonah rose up to flee unto Tarshish from the presence of the Lord" (Jonah 1.3). Could he have thought of fleeing from the presence of God? Has it not been said: "Whither shall I go from Thy spirit? Or whither shall I flee from Thy presence? If I ascend up into heaven Thou art there; if I make my bed in the nether world, behold, Thou art there. If I take the wings of the morning, and dwell in the uttermost parts of the sea; even there would Thy hand lead me," etc.? (Ps. 139.7ff.). And it is also written: "The eyes of the Lord, that run to and fro through the whole earth" (Zech. 4.10); and it is also written: "The Eyes of the Lord are in every place, keeping watch upon the evil and the good" (Prov. 15.3); "Though they dig into the netherworld . . . though they climb up to heaven . . . though they hide themselves in the top of Carmel . . . though they go into captivity," etc. (Amos 9.2–4); "There is no darkness, nor shadow of death, where the workers of iniquity may hide themselves" (Job 34.22). But Jonah thought: I will go outside of the land, where the Shekinah does not reveal itself. For since the Gentiles are more inclined to repent, I might be causing Israel to be condemned.[7]

They[8] give a parable for this: A priest had a

---

[7] By contrast with the Ninevites who would readily listen to the prophet and repent, Israel would stand condemned for not so readily listening to the prophets.

[8] I. e., the sages.

שנאמר ויקם יונה לברוח תרשישה מלפני יי וכי

מלפני יי הוא בורח והלא כבר נאמר אנא אלך

75 מרוחך וגו' אם אסק שמים וגו' אשא כנפי שחר וגו'

גם שם ידך תנחני וגו' וכתיב עיני יי המה משוטטים

בכל הארץ וכתיב בכל מקום עיני יי וגו' אם יחתרו

בשאול וגו' אם יחבאו בראש הכרמל וגו' אם ילכו

בשבי וגו' ואומר אין חשך ואין צלמות וגו' אלא

80 אמר יונה אלך לי חוצה לארץ מקום שאין השכינה

נגלית שהגוים קרובים לתשובה הן שלא לחייב את

ישראל. משלו משל לעבד שהיה לכהן לכהן אמר אברח

---

73 יונה א', ג'. 74—76 תהלים קל"פ, ז'—י'. 76—77 זכריה ד', י'.
77 משלי ט"ו, ג'. 79—77 עמוס ט', ב'—ד'. 79 איוב ל"ד, כ"ב.
80—82 ת. ויקרא, נס סוף פרשת צו. פדר"א י'. י' סנהדרין י"א,
(30b).

---

74 הוא בורח] כ. (יונה א', ב'). מ"ח. יכול לברוח / אנא]
במקרא כתוב אנה. 76 משוטטים] מ. המשוטטות. ד. משוטטות.
78 אם] במקרא כתוב ואם. 81 נגלית] ד. שורה ונגלית. 82 לעבד
שהיה לכהן אמר אברח] א. לעבדו של כהן שברח מרבו אמר
אלך. כ. (יונה א', ב'). מ' ח. לעבדו של כהן שברח ממנו
והלך.

slave who said: "I will run away to the cemetery whither my master cannot follow me."[9] But his master said to him: "I have other heathen slaves like you." Similarly Jonah said: "I will go outside of the land, where the divine presence does not reveal itself, for since the Gentiles are more inclined to repent, I might be causing Israel to be condemned." But the Holy One, praised be He, said unto him: "I have other agents like you," as it is said: "But the Lord hurled a great wind into the sea" (Jonah 1.4). Thus you find that there were three types of prophets. One insisted upon the honor due the Father as well as the honor due the son;[10] one insisted upon the honor due the Father without insisting upon the honor due the son; and one insisted upon the honor due the son without insisting upon the honor due the Father. Jeremiah insisted upon both the honor due the Father and the honor due the son. For thus it is said: "We have transgressed and have rebelled; Thou hast not pardoned"[11] (Lam. 3.42). Therefore his prophecy was doubled, as it is said:

---

[9] A priest is not allowed to enter a cemetery.

[10] God is the father and Israel is the son.

[11] This passage is understood to mean: Thou hast not pardoned as Thou mightest have done. According to the Rabbis, Jeremiah was the author of the book of Lamentations (see B. B. 15a).

לי לבית הקברות מקום שאין רבי יכול לבא אחרי

אמר לו רבו יש לי עבדים כנענים כמותך כך אמר

85 יונה אלך לי לחוצה לארץ מקום שאין השכינה

נגלית שהגוים קרובים לתשובה הן שלא לחייב את

ישראל אמר לו הקב״ה יש לי שלוחין כיוצא בך

שנאמר ויי הטיל רוח גדולה אל הים. נמצאת אומר

שלשה נביאים הם אחד תבע כבוד האב וכבוד הבן

90 ואחד תבע כבוד האב ולא תבע כבוד הבן ואחד

תבע כבוד הבן ולא תבע כבוד האב ירמיה תבע

כבוד האב וכבוד הבן שנאמר נחנו פשענו ומרינו

אתה לא סלחת לפיכך נכפלה נבואתו שנאמר

---

88 יונה א׳, ד׳.   92—93 איכה ג׳, מ״ב.   94 ירמיה ל״ו,

ל״ב.

---

83 לי] ד. > כ. מ״ח. לו/רבי] כ. מ״ח. רבו. 84 עבדים
כנענים] הוספתי עפ״י ג: ט. (יונה תקמ״ט) עבדים. כ. מ״ח. כנענים.
מ. כמותך ד. כיוצא בך. א. כניוח/כמותך]=א. ט: מ. כיוצא
בך. 89 נביאים] א. מ. ט. (ירמיה שכ״ה). ג. בנים. / אחד
תבע–וכבוד הבן] א. >.   93 אתה לא סלחת] הוספתי א. מ.
ונו׳/ שנאמר] א. >.

"And there were added besides unto them many
like words"[12] (Jer. 36.32). Elijah insisted upon
the honor due the Father, but did not insist
upon the honor due the son, as it is said: "And
he said, I have been very jealous for the Lord,
the God of Hosts" (I Kings 19.10). And thereupon what is said? "And the Lord said unto
him: Go return on thy way to the wilderness of
Damascus; and when thou comest, thou shalt
anoint Hazael to be king over Aram; and Jehu
the son of Nimshi shalt thou anoint to be king
over Israel, and Elisha the son of Shaphat of
Abel-meholah shalt thou anoint to be prophet
in thy room" (ibid., vv. 15–16). The expression
"in thy room," used here, can have no purport
other than: I am not pleased with your prophesying. Jonah insisted upon the honor due the son
but did not insist upon the honor due the
Father, as it is said: "But Jonah rose up to
flee unto Tarshish from the presence of the
Lord" (Jonah 1.3). What is written about him?
"And the word of the Lord came to Jonah the
second time, saying" (ibid. 3.1). He spoke with

---

[12] The phrase: "many like words," is understood to
mean as many new prophecies as were contained in the
burned scroll. These new prophecies, according to this
view, however, were not limited to chaps. 37–52, but in
the copy made by Baruch were also interspersed among
the older prophecies. Our present book of Jeremiah,
accordingly, contains two collections of prophecies by
Jeremiah which were originally separate but of equal size.
It is also assumed that the attitude expressed by Jeremiah
in Lamentations which he wrote after the destruction of

ועוד נוסף עליהם דברים רבים כהמה אליהו תבע

95 כבוד האב ולא תבע כבוד הבן שנאמר קנא קנאתי

ליי אלהי צבאות וגו' ומה נאמר שם ויאמר יי אליו

לך שוב לדרכך וגו' ואת יהוא בן נמשי תמשח למלך

על ישראל ואת אלישע בן שפט מאבל מחולה

תמשח לנביא תחתיך שאין תלמוד לומר תחתיך

100 אלא שאי איפשי בנבואתך.   יונה תבע כבוד הבן

ולא תבע כבוד האב שנאמר ויקם יונה לברוח וגו'

מה כתיב ויהי דבר יי אל יונה שנית לאמר שנית

96–95 מלכים א. י״ט, י'.   99–96 שם י״ט, כ״ו–ט״ז.   101 יונה

א, ג'.   102 שם ג', א'.   103–102 יבמות צ״ח, א'.

---

94 נוסף] ק. נ. יוסיף. / רבים כהמה] הוספתי.   96 שם]
א. ק. נ. > כ. ל. לו. א״א. בו/ יי אליו] ד. >.   99–97 תמשח
למלך–לנביא תחתיך] א. וגו'.   98 מאבל מחולה] הוספתי:
ל. וגו'.   99 תחתיך 2] ד. לנביא תחתיך. 100 אלא] א. > / איפשי]
א. מ. כ. איפשר. 101 ויקם יונה לברוח וגו'] ד. >.   102 מה כתיב]
ק. נ. > ל. כ. (יונה נ', א') מה נאמר לו.

Jerusalem had been maintained by him already in his
early activity when he composed his first collection of
prophecies. As a reward for this attitude his prophecy
was doubled, i. e., he was favored with new prophecies
which formed as large a collection as the first one.

him a second time,[13] but did not speak with him
a third time. R. Nathan says: Jonah made his
voyage only in order to drown himself in the
sea, for thus it is said: "And he said unto them:
Take me up and cast me forth into the sea"
(Jonah 1.12).

And so you also find, that the patriarchs and
the prophets offered their lives in behalf of Israel.
As to Moses, what did he say: "Yet now, if
thou wilt forgive their sin; and if not blot me,
I pray Thee, out of the book which Thou hast
written" (Ex. 32.32); "And if Thou deal thus
with me, kill me, I pray Thee, out of hand,
if I have found favour in Thy sight; and let
me not look upon my wretchedness"[14] (Num.
11.15). As to David,[15] what did he say? "And
David spoke unto the Lord, when he saw the
angel that smote the people, and said: Lo, I
have sinned and I have done iniquitously; but

---

[13] The word שנית, "a second time," when the word עוד,
"again," could have been used, is taken literally to mean,
to exclude a third time.

[14] The expression ברעתי, "my wretchedness," found in
the masoretic text represents, according to the Rabbis, a
"correction" or a substitute for another expression which
either actually was or should have been used in the original
text (see below *Shirata* VI, and Rashi to Num. 11.29).
Here it is assumed that the original or correct expression
was ברעתם, "their wretchedness" (so Rashi l.c., *Sifre*,
Num. 91, according to *Yalkuṭ* 756, but comp. Rashi to
Job 32.3; also Albo in '*Ikkarim* III.22 and below *Shirata*,
VI, note 1.

[15] David is here regarded as one of the "Patriarchs."

נדבר עמו ולא נדבר עמו שלישית. רבי נתן אומר
לא הלך יונה אלא לאבד את עצמו בים שנאמר
105 ויאמר אליהם שאוני והטילוני אל הים. וכן אתה
מוצא שהאבות והנביאים נתנו נפשם על ישראל
במשה מה הוא אומר ועתה אם תשא חטאתם ואם
אין מחני נא מספרך אשר כתבת ואם ככה אתה
עושה לי הרגני נא הרוג וגו' בדוד מהו אומר ויאמר
110 דוד אל האלהים הנה אנכי חטאתי ואנכי העויתי

---

105 יונה א' י"ב. 108–107 שמות ל"ב, ל"ב. 109–108 במדבר
י"א, ט"ו. 111–109 שמואל ב. כ"ד, י"ז.

---

103 נתן] ד. יונתן. 106 שהאבות והנביאים] א"צ. במשה
והנביאים / נתנו נפשם] ד. היו נותנים עצמם. 113–107 במשה מה
הוא אומר–נפשם על ישראל] א. >. 108 ואם] ק. נ. אם / 110 ואנכי]
ק. ואני. 110–111 הנה אנכי חטאתי–מה עשו] כ. >.

In Acts 2.29 Peter refers to David as "the patriarch
David." According to the Talmud (Ber. 16b), only
Abraham, Isaac and Jacob are to be called "Patriarchs"
(comp., however, reading in Semaḥot 1.14). In the Midrash to Psalms (18.8 and 25) David is regarded as being
like Abraham. And in later mystic literature David is
regarded as the fourth of the Patriarchs (see *Yalkuṭ Ḥadash*
(Pressburg, 1858), p. 5a (No. 26) and p. 36b (No. 53).

these sheep what have they done? Let Thy hand, I pray Thee, be against me, and against my father's house" (II Sam. 24.17). Thus you find everywhere that the patriarchs and the prophets offered their lives in behalf of Israel.

Saying. This means, go out and tell it to them immediately—these are the words of R. Ishmael—as it is said: "And he came out and spoke unto the children of Israel that which he was commanded" (Ex. 34.34). R. Eliezer says: It means, go out and tell it to them and bring Me back word, as it is said: "And Moses reported the words of the people unto the Lord" (ibid., 19.8). And again it says: "And, behold, the man clothed in linen, who had the inkhorn on his side, reported, saying: I have done according to all that Thou hast commanded me" (Ezek. 9.11). And again it says: "Canst thou send forth lightnings that they may go and say unto thee: Here we are?" (Job 38.35). Thy messengers, O God, are not like the messengers of human beings; for the messengers of human beings must needs return to those who send them before they can report. With Thy messengers, however, it is not so; but, Thou sendest forth lightnings and they go and say—notice, it is not said, "and they return," but "they go and say;"— whithersoever they go they are in Thy presence and can report: we have executed Thy commission. This confirms what has been said in Scripture: "Do not I fill heaven and earth, saith the Lord" (Jer. 23.24). R. Josiah says:

ואלה הצאן מה עשו תהי נא ידך בי וגו' הא בכל
מקום אתה מוצא האבות והנביאים נתנו נפשם על
ישראל.

לאמור צא ואמור אליהם מיד דברי רבי
ישמעאל שנאמר ויצא ודבר רבי אליעזר אומר
צא ואמור אליהם והשיבני דבר שנאמר וישב משה
את דברי העם אל יי ואומר והנה האיש לבוש
הבדים אשר הקסת במתניו משיב דבר ואומר
התשלח ברקים וילכו וגו' שלוחיך לא כשלוחי
בשר ודם ששלוחי בשר ודם צריכין לחזור אצל
שולחיהם אבל שלוחיך אינו כן אלא התשלח ברקים
וילכו וגו' וישובו לא נאמר אלא וילכו ויאמרו הא
בכל מקום שהן הולכין נמצאים לפניך ואומרים
עשינו שליחותך לקיים מה שנאמר הלא את השמים
ואת הארץ אני מלא נאום יי.   רבי יאשיה אומר

115

120

125

115 שמות ל״ד, ל׳. 116—115 לקמן בחורש ד׳, ספרא ויקרא ב׳.
117—116 שמות י״ט, ט׳. 118—117 יחזקאל ט׳, י״א. 124—119 ב׳ב כ״ה,
א׳, ש. 21, סדר רבה דבראשית דר׳ ישמעאל ווערטהיימער, בתי
מדרשות בית א׳) כ״נ. 121—122 איוב ל״ח, ל״ה. 125—124 ירמיה כ״נ, כ״ד.

112 האבות] א׳צ. בט̇שה. 118 אשר הקסת במתניו מש̇יב
דבר] הוספתי עפ״י ט. וא״א: מ. א. ונו'. ד. אשר קסת הסופר
במתניו וגו'. 119 שלוחיך] ד. שלוחי הקב״ה. 121 שלוחיך] ד. לפניך /
אלא] א. >. 122 וגו'] ד. / נאמר] א. ~ כן/ וילכו] מ. א. >/
הא] ד. >. 125 רבי יאשיה אומר] ד. > נ. אמר רבי הושעיא.

When God issues decrees concerning Israel, if
they be beneficent, their execution is reported
back to Him; but if they be for evil it is not
reported back to Him. For thus it is said:
"And, behold, six men came from the way of the
upper gate, which lieth toward the north, every
man with his weapon of destruction in his hand;
and one man in the midst of them clothed in
linen, with a writer's inkhorn on his side . . .
And the glory of the God of Israel was gone up
from the Cherub, whereupon it was, to the
threshold of the house," and it is written: "And
He called to the man clothed in linen, who had
the writer's inkhorn on his side. And the Lord
said unto him: Go through the midst of the
city, through the midst of Jerusalem, and set a
mark upon the foreheads of the men that sigh
and that cry for all the abominations that are
done in the midst thereof. And to the others
he said in my hearing: Go ye through the city
after him, and smite; slay utterly the old man,
the young man and the maiden, and little
children and women, but come not near any
man upon whom is the mark . . . and He said
unto them: Defile the house, and fill the courts
with slain," etc. (Ezek. 9.2–7). All these went
out to execute their commissions. As for those
who were commanded to perform the evil task,
we do not find that they reported back about
their commission, but we do find that the one
who was commanded to perform the good task
reported back about his commission, as it is

כשהמקום גוזר גזירות טובות ורעות על ישראל על

הטובה מחזירים לפניו ועל הרעה אין מחזירים

לפניו שנאמר והנה ששה אנשים באים וגו' וכבוד אלהי

ישראל נעלה מעל הכרוב וכתיב ויאמר יי אליו עבור

130 בתוך העיר וגו' ולאלה אמר באזני וגו' זקן בחור

ובתולה וטף ונשים וגו' ויאמר אליהם טמאו את

הבית ומלאו וגו' יצאו אלו ועשו שליחותן אלו

שנצטוו על הרעה לא למדנו שהחזירו שליחותן

וזה שנצטווה על הטובה למדנו שהחזיר שליחותו

128–132 יחזקאל ט', ב'–ז'.

---

126 טובות ורעות] א. >.   127 לפניו] א. אותו.   128 לפניו] א.
אותו. / וכבוד] ד. וכתוב/ 129 מעל הכרוב] הוספתי: א. מ וגו'.
ד. מעל הכרובים/אליו] ד. אלי. בסקרא כתיב אלו וקרי אלי.
130 העיר] מ. העם/וגו'] ד. ונאסר.   131 וטף] א. טף/ אליהם] ק.נ.
אלהים. 132 ומלאו] ד. הזה.   133 לא למדנו שהחזירו] א. למדנו שלא
החזירו. נ. לא מצינו שהחזירו. 134 למדנו] מ. מצינו.

said: "And, behold, the man clothed in linen who had the inkhorn on his side, reported, saying: I have done according to all that Thou hast commanded me" (ibid., v. 11).

Simon the son of Azzai says: *Saying* means: Teach in the same manner in which you hear. R. Akiba says: *Saying* means: Go and say to them; since it was only for their sake that He was speaking with him. For during all the thirty-eight years in which He was angry with Israel, He did not speak with Moses, as it is said: "So it came to pass, when all the men of war were consumed and dead from among the people, that the Lord spoke unto me, saying"[16] (Deut. 2.16ff.). Said R. Simon the son of Azzai: I am not arguing against the words of my teacher but merely adding to his words. It was not with Moses alone that He spoke only because of Israel, but with all the other prophets, likewise, He spoke only because of Israel, for thus it is said: "And I remained there appalled[17] among them seven days." And it is also written: "And it came to pass at the end of seven days, that the word of the Lord came unto me,

---

[16] See Rashi to this passage in Deut. and Rabad quoted by *Shebut Yehudah* here.

[17] מְשְׁמִים, "desolate" or "appalled," is taken to mean, being without divine communication (see commentaries *Zeh Yenaḥamenu* and Malbim).

135 שנאמר והנה האיש לבוש הבדים משיב וגו'. שמעון
בן עזאי אומר לאמר בקול שאתה שומע בו למד
רבי עקיבא אומר לאמר צא ואמור להם שבזכותם
היה מדבר עמו שכל שלשים ושמונה שנה שהיה
כועס על ישראל לא היה מדבר עם משה שנאמר
140 ויהי כאשר תמו כל אנשי המלחמה וגו' וידבר יי
אלי לאמר. אמר רבי שמעון בן עזאי איני כמשיב
על דברי רבי אלא כמוסיף על דבריו ולא עם
משה בלבד נדבר עמו בזכותן של ישראל אלא עם
שאר כל הנביאים לא נדבר עמהם אלא בזכותן
145 של ישראל שנאמר ואשב שם שבעת ימים משמים
בתוכם וכתיב ויהי מקצה שבעת ימים ויהי דבר יי

136 לקמן בחודש ד'.   129—137 ספרא שם.   140—141 תענית
ל', ב'. דברים ב', ט'ו—י'ז. 146—145 יחזקאל נ', ט'ו—ט'ז.

136 בן עזאי] מ. בן שטח/ לאמור] א. > מ. לסם)קטוע סן
לסשה? (/ בקול=א. ט. א"א. ט. וע'נ ס'ע: מ. בקוו ד. בקו.
137 שבזכותם] א. מ. בזכותה ל. שבזכותכם מ"ח. בזכותכם.
138 היה] א. נ. ל. הוא / עמו] הנהתי עפ"י ט.)ירמיה שס'ט):
א. מ. ד עמי. 140 וידבר] א. ויהי דבר ק. נ. ויאמר. 141 לאמור]
א. ~ אלי היה בדבר./ בן עזאי] א. >. 142 רבי] ט. ~ עקיבא.
143 בלבר] א. >.   145 שם] ד. > / סמסים] מ. > א. וגו' נ.
ל. מסומם.

saying"[18] (Ezek. 3.15–16). And again it is
written: "And it came to pass after ten days,
that the word of the Lord came unto Jeremiah"[19]
(Jer. 42.7). You will also find it so in the case
of Baruch the son of Neriah who was complaining
before God. It is said:[20] "Thou didst say:
Woe is me now! for the Lord hath added sorrow
to my pain" (Jer. 45.3).—"I have been treated
differently from other disciples of the prophets.
Joshua ministered to Moses, and the Holy Spirit
rested upon him. Elisha ministered to Elijah,
and the Holy Spirit rested upon him. But I!
Why have I been differently treated from other
disciples of the prophets?"—"I am weary with
my groaning and I find no rest" (ibid.). "Rest"
here is but a designation for "the spirit of
prophecy," as it is said: "and the spirit rested
upon them . . . and they prophesied in the
camp" (Num. 11.26). And again it says: "The
spirit of Elijah doth rest on Elisha" (II Kings
2.15). Again it says: "And the spirit of the Lord
shall rest upon him" (Isa. 11.2). Now, notice
what God answers him: "Thus shalt thou say
unto him: Thus saith the Lord: Behold, that

---

[18] The passage is interpreted to mean that Ezekiel had
been without communication from God. But after he
dwelled among the people for seven days, the word of
God came to him for the sake of the people.

[19] The passage is understood to mean that the word of God
came to Jeremiah only because the people led by Johanan
and Jezaniah asked for a divine message (ibid. vv. 1–3).

[20] The introductory formula שנאמר has been omitted in
the Hebrew text.

וגו' וכתיב ויהי מקץ עשרת ימים ויהי דבר יי

אל ירמיהו וכן אתה מוצא בברוך בן נריה שהיה

מתרעם לפני המקום אמרת אוי נא לי כי יסף יי

150 יגון על מכאובי וגו' נשתניתי אני מתלמידי הנביאים

יהושע שמש את משה ושרתה עליו רוח הקדש

אלישע שמש את אליהו ושרתה עליו רוח הקודש

ואני מה נשתניתי מתלמידי הנביאים יגעתי באנחתי

ומנוחה לא מצאתי ואין מנוחה אלא נבואה שנאמר

155 ותנח עליהם הרוח ואומר נחה רוח אליהו על

אלישע ואומר ונחה עליו רוח יי בא וראה מה

המקום משיבו כה תאמר אליו כה אמר יי הנה אשר

147—148 ירמיה מ'ב, ז'. 149—150 ירמיה מ'ה, נ'. 153—154 שם.
155 במדבר י'א, כ'ו. 155—156 מלכים ב. ב' ט'ו. 156 ישעיה
י'א, ב'.

147 וכתיב ויהי מקץ עשרת ימים] ד. <. 149 אמרת] א.
ד. אמרתי. 150 מתלמידי] א. ד. מכל תלמידי. 153 מתלמידי] א. ד.
מכל תלמידי. 155—156 ואומר נחה רוח אליהו על אלישע] ד. נחה רוח
יי על אליהו ועל אלישע. 156 ואומר] מ. ד. <.

which I have built will I break down . . . and seekest thou great things for thyself, seek them not" (Jer. 45.4–5). "Great things" here is but a designation for "the spirit of prophecy," as it is said: "Tell me, I pray thee, all the great things that Elisha hath done" (II Kings 8.4). And again it says: "Call unto Me, and I will answer thee, and will tell thee great things, and hidden, which thou knowest not" (Jer. 33.3). "Baruch son of Neriah! There is no vineyard, what need is there of a fence? There is no flock, what need is there of a shepherd?" Why? "For, behold, I will bring evil upon all flesh, saith the Lord; but thy life will I give unto thee for a prey in all places whither thou goest" (Jer. 45.5). Thus you find everywhere that the prophets prophesy only because of Israel.

CHAPTER II
(Ex. 12.2)

This New Moon Shall be unto You. R. Ishmael says: Moses showed the new moon to Israel and said unto them: In this manner shall ye in coming generations observe the new moon and fix the beginning of the month by it. R. Akiba says: This is one of the three things which were

בניתי אני הורם וגו' ואתה תבקש לך גדולות אל
תבקש וגו' ואין גדולות אלא נבואה שנאמר ספרה
160 נא לי את כל הגדולות אשר עשה אלישע ואומר
קרא אלי ואענך ואגידה לך גדולות ובצורות ולא
ידעתם ברוך בן נריה כרם אין כן סייג למה צאן
אין כן רועה למה מפני מה כי הנני מביא רעה אל
כל בשר וגו' ונתתי לך את נפשך לשלל על כל
165 המקומות אשר תלך שם הא בכל מקום אתה מוצא
שאין הנביאים מתנבאים אלא בזכותן של ישראל.

פרשה ב (שמות י"ב, ב'.)

ה ח ד ש הזה לכם וגו' רבי ישמעאל אומר משה
הראה את החדש לישראל ואמר להם כזה היו רואין
וקובעין את החדש לדורות רבי עקיבא אומר זה אחד

159—157 ירמיה מ"ה, ד'-ה'.   160—159 מלכים ב. ח', ד'.
162—161 ירמיה ל"ו, נ'.   165—163 ירמיה מ"ה, ה'.
1—3 ר"ה כ', א'. ת. בא. 7—3 מנחות כ"ט, א'. ספרי במדבר ס"א.
פסדר"כ החדש (נ"ד, ב'). שמו"ר ט"ו, כ"ח. בס"ר ט"ו, ד'. ת. שמיני.

---

159 ספרה] מ. ספרו.   160 ואומר] ד. ונומר.   161 ואגידה]
מ. ואניד.   162 ברוך] ד. אמר ברוך. 162 כן] מ. >.   163—162 כרם
אין-רועה למה] ד. אם אין כרם אין סייג אם אין צאן אין רועה.
163 כן] מ. >./ אל] במקרא כתוב על. 164 וגו'] מ. ד. >./ לך אח]
ד. >.   65—164 על כל המקומות] הגהתי עפ"י א"א: א. וגו'. מ.
את כל המקומות ד. אל המקום.   167 פרשה ב] ק. נ. פרשה א.
3 את החדש] א. מ. בו.

difficult for Moses to understand and all of which
God pointed out to him with His finger. So
also you interpret: "And *these* are they which
are unclean unto you" (Lev. 11.29). So also
you interpret: "And *this* is the work of the
candlestick" (Num. 8.4). Some say, Moses
found it also hard to understand the ritual
slaughtering, for it is said: "Now *this* is what
thou shalt do upon the altar"[1] (Ex. 29.38). R.
Simon the son of Yoḥai says: Is it not a fact
that all the words which He spoke to Moses
He spoke only in the daytime; the new moon,
of course, He showed him at nighttime. How
then could He, while speaking with him at
daytime, show him the new moon, at nighttime?
R. Eliezer says: He spoke with him at daytime
near nightfall, and then showed him the new
moon right after nightfall.

This Month. This means Nisan. You say it is
Nisan, perhaps it might be any month of the
year? But since it says: "and the feast of
ingathering at the end of the year" (Ex. 23.16);
"and the feast of ingathering at the turn of the
year" (ibid., 34.22), you must argue as follows:
Go and see, which month is it in which there
is the feast of ingathering at the turn[2] of the

---

[1] This passage is taken to refer to the slaughtering of
the sacrificial animals, which, according to R. Jose, was
done upon the top of the altar (see below *Baḥodesh*, XI
and note 4).

[2] The word תקופה, "turn," is also used to designate the
solstice as well as the equinox. Hence בתקופת השנה can be

משלשה דברים שנתקשה בהן משה והראהו המקום

כולן באצבע כיוצא בו אתה אומר וזה לכם הטמא

כיוצא בו אתה אומר וזה מעשה המנורה ויש אומרים

אף בשחיטה נתקשה משה שנאמר וזה אשר תעשה

על המזבח רבי שמעון בן יוחאי אומר והלא כל

הדברות שנדבר עם משה לא נדבר עמו אלא ביום

החדש הראהו לו בלילה כיצד מדבר עמו ביום

והראהו החדש בלילה רבי אליעזר אומר נדבר

עמו ביום עם חשכה והראהו את החדש בחשכה.

החדש הזה זה ניסן אתה אומר זה ניסן או אינו

אלא אחד מחדשי השנה כשהוא אומר חג האסיף

בצאת השנה וחג האסיף תקופת השנה אמרת צא

וראה אי זה חדש שיש בו חג האסיף תקופת השנה

---

5 ויקרא י"א, כ"ט.   6 במדבר ח', ד'.   7—8 שמות כ"ט, ל"ח.   8—11 וי"ר
א', י"ג.   13—20 ר"ה ז', א'.   י' ר"ה א', ב' (56d)   שקלים א', א' (45d)
תוספתא ר"ה א', נ'. ת. בא.   14—15 שמות כ"נ, ט"ז. ל"ד, כ"ב.

6 כיוצא בו אתה אומר] מ. ד. <.   7—8 וזה אשר תעשה על
המזבח] ק. נ. וזה הדבר אשר תעשה את המזבח.   8 בן יוחאי]
מ"ח. בן עזאי.   10 בלילה] א. ט. מ"ח. ביום.   11 אליעזר]
ד. אלעזר.   12 בחשכה] א. נ. עם חשיכה מ"ח. ל. משחשיכה.
16 חג האסיף תקופת השנה] ד. <.

---

taken to mean not only "at the turn of the year," but also
at the time of the autumnal equinox of the year.

year, i. e., in which occurs an ingathering and an equinox, in which the year ends and which is called the seventh; you find it to be none other than the month of Tishri. After you have thus ascertained that the seventh month is Tishri, it follows that Nisan must be the first month; and although there be no explicit scriptural proof of the matter, there is a suggestion of it:[3] "In the first month which was the month of Nisan" (Esth. 3.7).

The Beginning of Months. This declares that Nisan is the first in the order of the months. And how do we know that it is also regarded as the beginning of the year in the reckoning of the reign of kings? We learn it from this passage: "In the fourth year of Solomon's reign over Israel, in the month Ziv,[4] which is the second month" (I Kings 6.1). And how do we know that it is likewise so in regard to the succession of the festivals?[5] We learn it from this passage: "On the feast of unleavened bread, and on the feast of weeks, and on the feast of Tabernacles" (Deut. 16.16). We thus learn that

---

[3] The passage in Esther cannot be considered an explicit proof that Nisan is the first month of the year (see R. H. 7a and comp. on the term זכר לדבר W. Bacher, *Die exegetische Terminologie*, I, Leipzig, 1899, p. 51 ff.).

[4] The verse can be interpreted to mean: "In the month of Ziv, which is the second month of the fourth year of Solomon's reign." If Ziv, which is Iyyar, is counted as the second month of the reigning year, Nisan then is the month with which the reigning year begins.

[5] Deut. 23.22 is understood by the Rabbis to mean that

אסיף ותקופה ושנה יוצאה בו וקראוי שביעי אין

אתה מוצא אלא בחודש תשרי לאחר שלמדת

ששביעי תשרי ניסן זה ראשון ואף על פי שאין ראיה

20 לדבר זכר לדבר בחודש הראשון הוא חודש ניסן.

ראש חדשים מגיד שניסן ראש לחדשים ומנין אף

למלכים תלמוד לומר ויהי בשמונים שנה וארבע

מאות שנה לצאת בני ישראל מארץ מצרים בשנה

הרביעית בחדש זו הוא החדש השני למלך שלמה

25 על ישראל ומנין אף לרגלים תלמוד לומר חג

המצות וחג השבועות וחג הסוכות נמצינו למדין

---

20 אסתר ג', ז'.   30—21 ר'ה ב', ב'. ז', א'. י' ר'ה א', א' (56ª).

תוס' שם א', ז'. ש. 7.   25—22 מלכים א. ו', א'.   26—25 דברים

ט'ז, ט'ז.

---

20 חודש ניסן] מ. חודש ראשון ניסן.   24—22 ויהי–בחדש זו]

הוספתי עפ"י ט. וא"א.   25 חג] במקרא בחג.   26 וחג] במקרא

ובחג.

---

vows must be paid before the three festivals *Pesaḥ*, *Shabuot*
and *Sukkot* in the order named have passed (see R. H.
4ab).

Nisan is the beginning of the year as regards
the order of the months, the reign of kings and
the order of the festivals,—R. Isaac and R.
Nathan say: Also as regards the renting of
houses—but not as regards the years in general,
the sabbatical years and Jubilees, nor in regard
to young plants and vegetables.[6] For thus it is
said: "At the end of every seven years, in the
set time of the year of release, in the feast of
tabernacles, when all Israel is come to appear,"
etc. (Deut. 31.10–11); and again it says: "And
the feast of ingathering at the end of the year"
(Ex. 23.16). It is the month in this season
that has been set for you as the beginning of
the year in regard to years in general, sabbatical
years, and Jubilees and plants and vegetables.

Shall Be unto You. Adam did not reckon by
it. You say, "unto you" means that Adam
did not reckon by it; perhaps this only means,
unto you, and not unto the Gentiles, is this
commanded. When it says: "It shall be the first
month of the year *to you*," behold, there it tells
you that it is commanded only to you and not
to the Gentiles. Hence the expression: "unto
you" used here must aim to teach you that
Adam did not reckon by it. We thus learn
that Israel reckons by the moon and that the
Gentiles reckon by the sun.—And the Israelites
are not content with merely reckoning by the
moon, but once every thirty days they lift up

---

[6] With regard to the Law of Lev. 19.23–25 about young
plants and the law of Deut. 14.22–28 and 26.12 about the
tithes.

שניסן ראש לחדשים ולמלכים ולרגלים רבי יצחק
ורבי נתן אומרים אף לשכירות בתים אבל לא
לשנים ולא לשמיטים ולא ליובלות ולא לנטיעה
30 ולא לירקות שנאמר מקץ שבע שנים במועד שנת
השמיטה בחג הסוכות בבוא כל ישראל וגו' ואומר
וחג האסיף בצאת השנה וחג האסיף תקופת השנה
זה הוא האמור לך לשנים לשמיטים וליובלות
לנטיעה ולירקות.

35 ל כם לא מנה בו אדם הראשון אתה אומר לכם
לא מנה בו אדם הראשון או אינו אלא לכם ולא
לגוים אמור כשהוא אומר ראשון הוא לכם הרי לכם
ולא לגוים אמור הא מה תלמוד לומר לכם לא
מנה בו אדם הראשון נמצינו למדין שישראל מונין
40 ללבנה והגוים לחמה ולא דיים לישראל שהם מונין
ללבנה אלא אחת לשלשים יום מגביהים את עיניהם

<hr>

30–31 דברים ל"א, י'–י"א.   32 שמות כ"ג, ט"ז. | שם ל"ד, כ"ב.
35–38 ש. 7.   39–40 ב"ר ו', נ'.   42–40 סנהדרין מ"ב, א'.

<hr>

28 לשכירות] א. מ. לשכור.   31 בחג הסוכות] א. ד. וגו' מ. <.
32 בצאת השנה וחג האסיף] ד. <.   33 זה הוא האמור לך] א"צ. הזה
לזה הוא אמור/ לשנים לשמיטים] ד. ולא לשנים ולא לשמיטים.   37–36 ולא
לגוים] א. מ. ולגוים.   37 אמור] ט. מ"ח. ג. א"א. < / הרי]
ד. משמע.   37–39 ראשון הוא לכם–אדם הראשון] ק. <.   41–40 שהם
מונין ללבנה] הוספתי עפ"י ט. א"א. ג. מ"ה. 41 אלא] מ. ד. <.

their eyes to their Father in heaven.[7]—And so when the sun is eclipsed, it is a bad omen for the Gentiles since they reckon by the sun, and when the moon is eclipsed it is a bad omen for the "enemies of Israel"[8] since they reckon by the moon. R. Meir says: If the sun is eclipsed in the east, it is a bad omen for the inhabitants of the East; if in the west, it is a bad omen for the inhabitants of the west. R. Josiah says: If the planets are eclipsed in the east, it is a bad omen for the inhabitants of the east; if in the west, it is a bad omen for the inhabitants of the west. R. Jonathan says: All these signs may be left to the Gentiles, for thus it is said: "Thus saith the Lord: Learn not the way of the nations, and be not dismayed at the signs of heaven, for the nations are dismayed at them" (Jer. 10.2).

The Beginning of Months. I might understand the word "months" to mean the minimum number of months, i. e. only two. How do we know that it means all the rest of the months? We learn it from the passage: "It shall be unto you the first of the months of the year."

It Shall Be First. Why is this said? Because of the following. It says: "Observe the month of spring (*Abib*), and keep the Passover" (Deut. 16.1), meaning: Keep the Passover near the spring and the spring near the Passover; i. e., see that the spring come in its [Passover's] time.

---

[7] In the performing of the ceremony of Blessing the New Moon (see San. 41b–42a and *JE*, IX, 244).

[8] This is a euphemism for Israel.

לאביהם שבשמים . וכשהחמה לוקה סימן רע לגוים
שהם מונים לחמה וכשהלבנה לוקה סימן רע לשונאי
ישראל שהם מונין ללבנה רבי מאיר אומר כשהחמה
45 לוקה במזרח סימן רע ליושבי מזרח במערב סימן
רע ליושבי מערב רבי יאשיה אומר כשהמזלות
לוקין במזרח סימן רע ליושבי מזרח במערב סימן
רע ליושבי מערב רבי יונתן אומר אילו ואילו נתנו
לגויים שנאמר כה אמר יי אל דרך הגוים אל
50 תלמודו ומאותות השמים אל תחתו.

ראש חדשים שומע אני מיעוט חדשים שנים
מנין לשאר חדשים תלמוד לומר לחדשי השנה.
ראשון הוא, למה נאמר לפי שהוא אומר שמור
את חדש האביב ועשית פסח שמור את הפסח לאביב
55 ואביב לפסח שיבוא אביב בזמנו הא כיצד עבר את

42—48 סוכה כ'ט, א'. תוס' שם ב', ו'.   48—50 סוכה שם. ב'ר ס'ד,
י'ב. נדרים ל'ב, א'. מו'ק כ'ח, א'. שבת קנ'ו, א'.   50—49 ירמיה,
י', ב'.   53—51 מ'ת.   90—89 מדרש סוד העיבור (לקט מדרשים
ווערטהיימער) ב'.   53—54 דברים ט'ז, א'.   55—54 לקמן כספא ד'. ספרי
דברים קכ'ז. סנהדרין י'ג, ב'.

44 מאיר] ד' .>.   46 יאשיה] ד' יוסי.   48 יונתן] מ"ח. נתן /
ואלו] ק' .>.   50 תלמודו] במקרא תלמדו א'. וגו'.   52 לשאר חדשים]
א. מ. .>.   54 ועשית פסח] הוספתי: ד' וגו'.

How so? Add, if necessary, the intercalary Adar
so that the spring should come in its [Passover's]
time.   Now, I might understand that if they
added the intercalary Adar and spring has not
yet come in its time, they may add an intercalary Nisan.   Against this R. Ishmael used to
say: Behold, if you say so, you actually make
a Nisan the second month of the year whereas
the Torah has said: "It shall be the first to
you."   R. Jonathan says: "Observe the month
of the spring," means: intercalate the month
near the spring; and which is it? It is the month
Adar.   But we have not yet learnt how much
one should intercalate. When it says: "Observe
the month," it indicates that it is a whole month
which is intercalated. But the following reasoning would prove it: Since the month is lengthened
by intercalation and the year is lengthened by
intercalation, just as the month is lengthened
by one of its units,[9] so also should the year be
lengthened by one of its units.   As for that,
one might argue that just as the month is
lengthened by one thirtieth thereof so also the
year should be lengthened by one thirtieth
thereof.[10]   Hence Scripture needs to say: "Observe the month," indicating that it is a whole
month which you are to intercalate into the
year and not a thirtieth part of the year. If so,
then, one might argue that just as what is

---

[9] The day is the unit of the month, the month is the
unit of the year.

[10] I.e., about 12 days, which would amply make up the
difference between the lunar and solar years.

אדר כדי שיבוא אביב בזמנו הרי שעיברו את אדר

ולא בא אביב בזמנו שומע אני יעברו את ניסן היה

ר' ישמעאל אומר הא אם אמרת כן נמצאת עושה

ניסן שיני ואמרה תורה ראשון הוא לכם. ר' יונתן

60 אומר שמור את חדש האביב חדש הסמוך לאביב

אתה מעבר ואיזה זה זה חדש אדר אבל לא שמענו

מכמה מעבר כשהוא אומר שמור את חדש חדש

אתה מעבר והדין נותן הואיל והחודש מתעבר

והשנה מתעברת מה החדש אחד ממנויו אף שנה אחד

65 ממנויה אי מה החודש אחד מל' בו אף שנה אחד

מל' בה תלמוד לומר שמור את חדש חדש אתה

מעבר ואין אתה מעבר אחד מל' בה אי מה שנה

59—61 סנהדרין י"ב, א'–ב'. תוס' שם ב' י"א. י'. פסחים ט', א'. (36c) ש. 7. 63—64 ר"ה כ', א'. מגלה ה', א'. 66—67 סנהדרין י"א, א'. תוס' שם ב', ח'. ר"ה י"ט, ב'. ערכין ט', ב'.

---

56 כדי] א. ד. > / את אדר] א. כ"ז באדר. 57 ולא בא–בזמנו] א. > / את] מ. > ד. ר"ח 58 ישמעאל] ד. שמעון. 59 יונתן] ד. נתן. 65 אי] א. מ. >. 66—67 ת"ל שמור–אחד מל' בה] א. >.

intercalated into the year is one twelfth thereof, so also what is intercalated into the month should be one twelfth thereof. But the scriptural passage: "And on the fifteenth day of this month shall be a feast" (Num. 28.17), teaches that it is only a day which you may intercalate into the month and not one twelfth of the month.—R. Isaac says: Behold, if you should say so, the moon would at the beginning of the month already be well up in the sky.—Hence it is impossible for you to argue as in the latter version, but you must argue as in the first version, viz. since the month is lengthened by intercalation and the year is lengthened by intercalation, just as the month is lengthened by one of its units, so also the year by one of its units. And just as, in the case of the month, its intercalary addition is put only at its end, so also in the case of the year its intercalary addition is to be put only at its end. R. Jeremiah says: Since ritual impurity delays the passover celebration, and the lateness of the spring delays the passover celebration, it follows that just as in the case of ritual impurity the delay caused by it is not less than thirty days,[11] so also in the case of the lateness of the spring, the delay caused by it must be for not less than thirty days. Perhaps, "Observe the month of the spring and keep the Passover," means also to celebrate the Passover earlier if the spring happens to

---

[11] According to Num. 9.10, persons ritually unclean on the 14th of Nisan had to keep the Passover 30 days later, on the 14th day of Iyyar.

אחד משנים עשר בה אף חדש אחד משנים עשר בו

תלמוד לומר ובחמשה עשר יום לחדש הזה וגו' יום

70 לחדש אתה מעבר ואין אתה מעבר אחד משנים

עשר בו ר' יצחק אומר הא אם אמרת כן כבר לבנה

באמצע הרקיע הא אין עליך לומר כלשון אחרון

אלא כלשון ראשון הואיל והחדש מתעבר והשנה

מתעברת מה החדש אחד ממנויו אף שנה אחד

75 ממנויה מה החודש אין תוספת עיבורו אלא בסוף

אף שנה אין תוספת עיבורה אלא בסוף רבי ירמיה

אומר הואיל וטומאה מעכבת ואביב מעכב מה

טומאה אין פחות משלשים יום אף אביב אין פחות

משלשים יום או אפילו ביחל אביב ובא תלמוד

---

69 ויקרא כ"ג, ו'. ספרא אמור ט'.

---

68 אחד] ד. >. ‏ 69–71 תלמוד לומר– משנים עשר בו] א. >.
69 הזה וגו'] ד. חג שבעת ימים. ‏ 71 ר' יצחק] ד. ור' יצחק.
74 אחד 1] מ. אינו/ אחד 2] מ. אינה. ‏ 79 או] מ. אום' (קטיע מן
אותר)/ ביחל]–מ"ת. ראב"ד בפירושו לספרא אמור פ"ט. ל: מ.
בוחיל ק.נ. כי חל א. חל.

come earlier. But the scriptural passage: "Thou shalt therefore keep this ordinance in its season from year to year" (Ex. 13.10), teaches that you may increase the interval between two Passovers but never reduce it.

It Shall be the First Month of the Year to You: This means that no second Nisan shall be declared. R. Josiah says: Whence can you prove that the year can be intercalated only by the Great Court at Jerusalem? From the passage: "It shall be the first unto you, speak ye unto all the congregation of Israel" (Ex. 12.2–3).

CHAPTER III
(Ex. 12.3–4)

Speak Ye unto All the Congregation of Israel. R. Ishmael says: Did actually both of them speak? Has it not been said: "Speak thou unto the children of Israel," etc. (Ex. 31.13)? What then does Scripture mean by saying here: "Speak ye"? Simply this: Whenever Moses spoke Aaron inclined his ear to listen with awe, and Scripture accounts it to him as if he had heard it directly from the mouth of the Holy One.

R. Aḥai the son of R. Josiah says: Did both

80 לומר ושמרת את החוקה למועדה מימים ימימה
מוסיף את ואין את גורע.

ר א ש ו ן הוא לכם לחדשי השנה שלא יעשה
ניסן שיני רבי יאשיה אומר מנין אתה אומר שאין
מעברין את השנה אלא בבית דין הגדול שבירושלים
85 תלמוד לומר ראשון הוא לכם וגו' דברו אל כל
עדת ישראל.

פרשה ג (שמות י"ב, ג'–ד'.)

ד ב ר ו אל כל עדת ישראל וגו' רבי ישמעאל
אומר וכי שניהם היו מדברים והלא כבר נאמר
ואתה דבר אל בני ישראל וגו' ומה ת"ל דברו אלא
כיון שהיה משה מדבר היה אהרן מרכין אזנו לשמוע
5 באימה ומעלה עליו הכתוב כאילו שומע מפי
הקודש ר' אחי ב"ר יאשיה אומר וכי שניהם היו

80 שמות י"ג, י'. 81 ש. 8. 7–8. 82–83 סנהדרין י"א, ב'. כ"ו, א'.
י' שם א', ב' (18d–19a). מנלה י"ח, ב'. תוס' שם ב', ה'. י' ר"ה
ב', ו' (56ab). יבמות קט"ו, א'. מ"ת 90. שמו"ר ט"ו, כ'. וי"ר כ"ט,
ד'. פדר"א ח'. מדרש סוד העיבור שם ב', ב'.
3 שמות ל"א, י"ג.

80 הזאת למועדה מימים ימימה] הוספתי=ל: א. וגו' ק. נ. הזאת
במועדה במועדה. 81 גורע] א. מונע. 83 שיני] ד. אחר. 84 דין]
מ. </> הגדול] א. גדול. 85 עדת ישראל] ק. נ. עדת בני ישראל.
1 עדת ישראל] א. ק. נ. עדת בני ישראל. 3 ואתה דבר] א. ואתה
תדבר.

of them actually speak? Has it not been said: "Speak thou unto the children of Israel?" What then does Scripture mean by saying here: "Speak ye"? Simply this: Whenever Moses spoke Aaron was at his right hand—and Eleazar at his left and Ithamar at the right hand of Aaron—so that the word went forth from among them as if both of them were speaking.

R. Simon the son of Yoḥai says: Moses would show respect to Aaron, saying to him, "Teach me," and Aaron showed respect to Moses, saying to him, "Teach me;" and thus the word went forth from between them as if both of them were speaking.

Speak Ye unto All the Congregation of Israel, Saying: In the Tenth Day. The command was given on the first of the month, the purchase of the lamb was made on the tenth, and the slaughtering on the fourteenth. You say that the command was given on the first of the month and the purchase was made on the tenth and the slaughtering on the fourteenth. Perhaps it is not so, but both the command and the purchase occurred on the tenth, and the slaughtering on the fourteenth? It says, however: "This new moon shall be unto you . . . speak ye." When, then, was the command given? On the new moon. Consequently it is impossible for you to argue as in the latter version, but you must say as in the former, viz., the command was given on the

מדברים והלא כבר נאמר ואתה דבר אל בני
ישראל ומה ת"ל דברו אלא כיון שהיה משה מדבר
היה אהרן מימינו ואלעזר משמאלו ואיתמר מימינו
10   של אהרן והיה הדיבור יוצא מביניהם כאילו שניהם
מדברים ר' שמעון בן יוחי אומר משה היה חולק
כבוד לאהרן ואומר לו למדני ואהרן היה חולק
כבוד למשה ואומר לו למדני והדבור יוצא מביניהם
כאלו שניהם מדברים.

15   דברו אל כל עדת ישראל לאמר בעשור
הדבור בראש חדש ולקיחה בעשור ושחיטה
בארבעה עשר אתה אומר הדיבור בר"ח ולקיחה
בעשור ושחיטה בי"ד או אינו אלא הדבור ולקיחה
בעשור ושחיטה בי"ד תלמוד לומר החודש הזה
20   לכם דברו אימתי היה הדיבר בר"ח הא אין עליך
לומר בלשון אחרון אלא בלשון ראשון הדיבר

8—10 עירובין נ'ד, ב'.   16 פסחים ו', ב'.   שבת פ'ו, ב'.

---

7 ואתה דברו] א. ד. ואתה תדבר (ק. נ. ~ אל כל ישראל).
10 מביניהם] ט. מבין שניהם נ. מבין שלשתן.   11—10 כאלו שניהם מדברים]
הנהתי=ל. מ"ח. ש"ט. א"א: ט. > א. כאלו יוצא מפי שלשתן מ.
ק. נ. כאלו השלשה (מ.   שלשתן) מדברים.   11 שמעון] מ. ישמעאל.
12 למדני] ד. ~והדיבור יוצא מביניהם.   15 עדת ישראל] ק. נ. ש.
עדת בני ישראל.   16 הדיבור] ד. ~ הזה.   17 הדיבור] ד. ~ היה
20 דברו] א. ~ הא. 21 לוטר] ק. נ. >.

first, the purchase was made on the tenth and the slaughtering on the fourteenth of the month.

R. Aḥai the son of R. Josiah says: The command was given on the first of the month, the purchase was made on the tenth and the slaughtering on the fourteenth. You interpret it so. Perhaps it is not so, but both the command and the purchase took place on the first of the month, and the slaughtering on the fourteenth? This is refuted by the scriptural passage: "Speak ye unto all the congregation of Israel . . . saying." For, the word "saying" here has no other purport than to divide the subject. Consequently it is impossible for you to argue as in the latter version but you must accept the former version, viz., that the command was given on the first of the month, the purchase was made on the tenth and the slaughtering on the fourteenth.

R. Jose the Galilean says: The command was given on the first of the month, the purchase was made on the tenth, and the slaughtering on the fourteenth. You interpret it so. Perhaps it is not so, but the command was given on the first and both the purchasing and the slaughtering were done on the tenth of the month? This is refuted by the scriptural passage: "And ye shall keep it until the fourteenth day" (v. 6). Thus, if you should reason this way you would be distorting this whole passage. Consequently it is impossible for you to argue as in the latter version but you must accept the former statement.

In the Tenth Day of the Month They Shall Take. From this I know only that the tenth of the

בר״ח ולקיחה בעשור ושחיטה בי״ד ר׳ אחי ב״ר
יאשיה אומר הדיבור בר״ח ולקיחה בעשור ושחיטה
בארבעה עשר אתה אומר כן או אינו אלא הדבור

25 ולקיחה בר״ח ושחיטה בי״ד תלמוד לומר דברו
אל כל עדת ישראל לאמר שאין ת״ל לאמר אלא
להפסיק את העניַן הא אין עליך לדון בלשון אחרון
אלא בלשון ראשון הדיבור בר״ח ולקיחה בעשור
ושחיטה בי״ד רבי יוסי הגלילי אומר הדיבור בר״ח

30 ולקיחה בעשור ושחיטה בי״ד אתה אומר כן או
אינו אלא הדיבור בר״ח ולקיחה ושחיטה בעשור
תלמוד לומר והיה לכם למשמרת עד ארבעה עשר
יום הא אם אמרת כן עקרת את כל הכתוב הא אין
עליך לומר בלשון אחרון אלא בלשון ראשון.

35 ב ע ש ו ר לחדש הזה ויקחו אין לי אלא עשירי

---

32 שמות י״ב, ו׳.

---

22 אחי] ק. נ. אחא ל. אחאי.   26 אל כל עדת ישראל] א. >
ק. נ. אל כל עדת בני ישראל מ. אל כל עדת וגו׳ ~ אלא כל דבר
הדבר בראש חדש ולקיחה בעשור ושחיטה בארבעה עשר / לאמר
1] הוספתי=ז״י. א׳א׳. / לאמר 2] א. ק. נ. >.

month is the proper time for the purchase of the paschal lamb. How about the fourteenth? You reason by using the method of *Kal vaḥomer*: If on the tenth, which is not fit for slaughtering, purchase is permitted, is it not but logical that on the fourteenth, which is fit for slaughtering, purchase should be permitted? How about the thirteenth? You may reason by using the method of *Kal vaḥomer*. If the tenth, which is not so near to the time of slaughtering, is a proper time for the purchase, it is but logical that the thirteenth which is close to the time of slaughtering, should be a proper time for the purchase. And the same reasoning holds good for the eleventh and the twelfth.

In the Tenth Day of This Month. "This" is to exclude the paschal sacrifice of subsequent generations. For only the paschal sacrifice in Egypt had to be purchased from the tenth of the month on. But the paschal lamb of subsequent generations may be purchased at any time.

They Shall Take to Themselves. Were all of them actually to attend to the purchase? This is simply to indicate that the agent of a man is as the man himself. It is on the basis of this passage that the sages said: A man's agent is like the man himself.

Every Man a Lamb (Seh). In the term *Seh* are included kids as well as lambs, for thus it is said: "The *Seh* of the sheep and the *Seh* of the goats" (Deut. 14.5).

שהוא כשר ללקיחה ארבעה עשר מנין אמרת קל
וחמר ומה עשירי שאינו כשר לשחיטה כשר ללקיחה
י"ד שהוא כשר לשחיטה אינו דין שיהא כשר
ללקיחה י"ג מנין אמרת ק"ו ומה אם עשירי שאינו
40 קרוב לשחיטה כשר ללקיחה י"ג שהוא קרוב
לשחיטה דין הוא שכשר ללקיחה והוא הדין לאחד
עשר ולשנים עשר.

ב ע ש ו ר לחדש הזה להוציא פסח דורות שפסח
מצרים מקחו מבעשור ופסח דורות מקחו בכל זמן.

45 ו י ק ח ו להם וכי כולם היו לוקחין אלא לעשות
שלוחו של אדם כמותו מכאן אמרו שלוחו של
אדם כמותו.

א י ש ש ה בכלל שה טלה וגדי שנאמר שה
כשבים ושה עזים.

43—44 לקמן פ"ה ופט"ו. ש. 8. פסחים צ"ו, א'. 47—46 לקמן
פ"ה, ש. שם, ספרי זוטא 279. קידושין ט"א, ב' וש"נ. י' שם ב',
א' (62ª). 49—48 דברים י"ד ד'. לקמן פ"ד.

38 אינו דין] א. דין הוא. 40 קרוב] מ. כשר/י"נ] א. אף י"נ.
43 הזה] הוספתי עפ"י ט. 46 אסרו] א. נ. ~ חכמים. 49 עזים] נ.
ל. ~ שומע אני שה אחד לכולן ת"ל.

According to Their Fathers' Houses. The term "father's houses" merely means families, as it is said: "By their families, by their fathers' houses" (Num. 1.2). But suppose there were ten families belonging to one father's house. I might understand that in such a case one lamb only should be required for all of them. Scripture therefore says: "A lamb for a household."

And if the Household be Too Little for a Lamb. Scripture aims to teach you that until it is slaughtered, people may enroll for partnership in the paschal lamb or withdraw from it, so long as they leave the paschal lamb intact. R. Judah says: Provided there be one of the original company left, so that the original group should not be entirely replaced by subsequent additions.

Then Shall He and His Neighbour . . . Take One. R. Ishmael says: Whence can you prove that if a man desire to enroll others for partnership in his own paschal lamb he is permitted to do so? From the scriptural passage: Let him take one with his neighbor. R. Akiba says: Whence can you prove that if a man desire to have his paschal lamb for himself alone he is permitted to do so? From the scriptural passage: Let him take.

50 ל ב י ת א ב ו ת אין לבית אבות אלא למשפחות
שנאמר למשפחותם לבית אבותם והרי שהיו עשר
משפחות לבית אב אחד שומע אני שה אחד לכולם
תלמוד לומר שה לבית.

ו א ם י מ ע ט ה ב י ת מ ה י ו ת מ ש ה ב א
55 הכתוב ללמד שלעולם נמנין על הפסח ומושכין
את ידיהם ממנו עד שישחט ובלבד שיניח את הפסח
כל שהוא ר' יהודה אומר בלבד שיהיה שם אחד
מחבורה הראשונה שלא לעשות עיקר טפלה וטפלה
עיקר.

60 ו ל ק ח ה ו א ו ש כ נ ו ר' ישמעאל אומר מנין
אתה אומר שאם ירצה אדם למנות עמו אחרים על
פסחו שהוא רשאי ת"ל ולקח הוא ושכנו ר' עקיבא
אומר מנין אתה אומר שאם ירצה אדם לעשות פסחו
יחידי שהוא רשאי ת"ל ולקח הוא.

51 במדבר א', ב'. לקטן פי"א. ש. שם. פסחים פ"ט, א'. צ"ט, א'.
תוס' שם ז', ז', י' שם ח', ד' (36ᵇ).   60—62 פסחים צ', א'. ש. שם.
62—64 ספרי דברים קל"ב. פסחים צ"א, א'. י' שם ח', ז' (36ᵃ).

53 שה לבית] מ. ד. ~ אבות.   56 ובלבד]= ל. ט. מ"ח:
א. מ. ק. נ. בלבד/ שיניח] ד. ט. שלא יניח.   57 כל שהוא] ד.
כמות שהוא/ שיהיה]=א. ט. ש"ט. ש"י. מ"ח: מ. שלא. ד. שלא
יהא.   60—64 נ. ל. הסדר מהופך ומאמר ר' עקיבא קודם למאמר
ר' ישמעאל.   60 ישמעאל] א. עקיבא.   62 ושכנו] נ. ל. >.
64 שהוא] א"צ. שאינו/ הוא] נ. ל. ~ ושכנו.

And His Neighbour. I understand this to mean the neighbor under the same roof. Perhaps this is not so, but it means his neighbor near his field? It says, however, further on: "Next unto his house." Scripture accordingly speaks only of the neighbor in the usual sense. R. Simon the son of Yoḥai says: It means his neighbor in any way.

According to the Number of the Souls. The word *miksat* simply means number. It thus indicates that the lamb must be slaughtered for those enrolled as partners in it. I might, however, understand that if one has slaughtered it for others than those enrolled as partners in it and thus transgressed the command, it should nevertheless be ritually fit. But it is said further on: "According to every man's eating ye shall make your count for the lamb." Scripture has purposely repeated this command about the paschal lamb in order to declare it ritually unfit if the command be transgressed.

Another interpretation: *According to the Number of the Souls.* Why is this said? Because it has been said "every man," from which I know only that a man may be enrolled as a partner in the paschal lamb. How about a woman, a *tumtum*[1] and a hermaphrodite? It says: "According to the number of the souls," which means to be inclusive. Perhaps it means to include not only these but also the sick and the little ones who are not able to eat of it even as much as the size

---

[1] A *Tumtum* is one whose sex is unknown (see Jastrow, *Dictionary*, s. v., p. 524).

65 ו ש כ נ ו שומע אני שכנו שבגגו או אינו אלא שכנו

שבשדו ת״ל הקרוב אל ביתו דבר הכתוב בהווה

ר' שמעון בן יוחי אומר שכנו מכל מקום.

ב מ כ ס ת אין מכסת אלא מנין שישחטנו למנויו

ואם שחטו שלא למנויו ועבר על מצוה שומע אני

70 שיהיה כשר תלמוד לומר איש לפי אכלו תכוסו

שנה עליו הכתוב לפסול דבר אחר ב מ כ ס ת

נ פ ש ו ת למה נאמר לפי שנאמר איש אין לי אלא

איש אשה וטומטום ואנדרוגינוס מנין תלמוד לומר

במכסת נפשות ריבה משמע מביא את אלו ומביא

75 את החולה ואת הקטן שאינן יכולין לאכול כזית

65—67 תוס' פסחים ח', י״ב–י״ג. ש. 9.	68—70 פסחים ס״א א'.
ש. שם.	74—71 ספרי במדבר ע'. פסחים ע״ט, א'. צ״א, ב'. י' שם
ח', א' (35d). תוספתא שם א' ל״ג. ז' י״א. ח', י'. אהלות נ', ט'.
ש. שם.	76—74 פסחים ס״א, א'. צ״א, א'. י' שם ה',ג'. (32a).
סוכה מ״ב, ב'. תוספתא חגיגה א', ב'.

---

65 שבננו] ק. שכננדו מ״ח.	נ. שבביתו.	66 שבשדו] ד.
שבשדה. ט. א״א שבצדו/ דבר הכתוב בהוה] א״צ. >.	67 מכל
מקום] מ״ח. א״צ. ~ ומה ת״ל (א״צ א״כ לסה נאסר) הקרוב אל
ביתו דיבר הכתוב בהווה. ונראה כי כן היתה נ״כ נירסת נ.	69 ואם]
א. אבל/ ועברו ד. עבר.

of an olive? But the expression: "According to his eating," eliminates the sick and the little ones. Since they cannot consume of it as much as the size of an olive, the paschal lamb may not be slaughtered for them.

Ye Shall Make Your Count (*Takossu*): R. Josiah says: This (*Takossu*) is a Syriac expression,[2] as e. g. when one says to his neighbor: Slaughter (*kos*) for me this lamb.

For the Lamb. R. Ishmael says: Scripture aims to teach you that until it is slaughtered, people may enroll for partnership in the paschal lamb or withdraw from it, so long as they leave the paschal lamb intact. R. Isaac says: Of what does Scripture speak here? Of the living lamb.

CHAPTER IV
(Ex. 12.5)

Lamb (*Seh*). In the term *Seh* are included young kids as well as young lambs, for thus it is said: "The *seh* of the sheep and the *seh* of the goats" (Deut. 14.5).

Perfect. To exclude one that has a blemish.

A Male. To exclude a *Tumtum*, hermaphrodite and a female.

---

[2] It accordingly means: Ye shall slaughter the lamb.

תלמוד לומר לפי אכלו יצאו החולה והקטן שאינן
יכולין לאכול כזית אין שוחטין עליהן.

תכוסו ר' יאשיה אומר לשון סורסי הוא זה
כאדם שאומר לחבירו כוס לי טלה זה.

80   על השה ר' ישמעאל אומר בא הכתוב
ללמדך שנמנים על הפסח ומושכים את ידיהם ממנו
עד שישחט ובלבד שיניח את הפסח כל שהוא ר'
יצחק אומר במי הכתוב מדבר בחי.

פרשה ד   (שמות י"ב, ה'.)

שה בכלל שה גדי וטלה שנאמר שה כשבים
ושה עזים.

תמים להוציא בעל מום.

זכר להוציא טומטום ואנדרוגינוס ונקבה.

1–2 דברים י"ד, ד'.   3 חוס' פסחים ח', י"א. י' שם ט', ד' (36^d).
4 ספרא ויקרא, נדבה ג'. בכורות ס"א, א'.

---

76 לפי אכלו] מ. ד. איש לפי אכלו/יצאו] א. ג. סכאן
אסרו.   77 כזית] מ"ח. ~ סכאן אסר ר' החולה והקטן שאינן יכולין
לאכול כזית.   78 ר' יאשיה] מ"ח. רבי ש"ט. רבי יוחנן/ סורסי]
א. סרסי מ. פרסי.   82 שיניח] ד. ט. שלא יניח/ כל שהוא] ד.
כמות שהוא.   83 במי] מ"ח. בפירוש.

Of the First Year.   From this I know only that
it must be a lamb born during the current
calendar year. How about a lamb during the
entire first year of its life? R. Ishmael used to
say: it can be determined by using the method
of *Kal vaḥomer*: If for the more important burnt-
offering an animal during the entire first year
of its life is as fit as one born during the current
calendar year,[1] is it not but logical to conclude
that for the less important passover sacrifice an
animal during the entire first year of its life
should be as fit as one born during the current
calendar year? R. Jose the Galilean says: If the
ram, though not fit at the beginning of its term,
its second year,[2] is fit at the end of it, is it not
but logical to conclude that the lamb which even
at the beginning of its first year is already fit,
should be considered fit up to the end of its
first year?

From the Sheep and from the Goats.   From the
one species [sheep] alone or from the other species
[goats] alone. You interpret it so. Perhaps this
is not so, but it means that one must bring the
sacrifice from both of them together.[3] It says
however: "And if his offering be of the flock

---

[1] In the case of the burnt-offering the Law (Lev. 12.6)
expressly says that an animal during the entire first year
of its life, even though it be in the second calendar year
after its birth, is fit for the sacrifice. For it says there
בן שנתו, which is understood to mean: "Its own year, not
the calendar year," שנתו שלו לא שנה למנין עולם (see *Sifra
Tazri'a* III, Weiss 59b and comp. Talm. 'Ar. 18b. On
the question of the age of the lamb for the sacrifice, see

5   בן שנה אין לי אלא בן שנה כל שנתו מנין היה

ר' ישמעאל אומר ק"ו ומה אם עולה חמורה כשרה

לבא כל שנתה כבת שנתה פסח שהוא קל אינו דין

שיוכשר לבוא כל שנתו כבן שנתו ר' יוסי הגלילי

אומר ומה איל שתחלתו פסול סופו כשר שה

10   שתחלתו כשר אינו דין שיהא סופו כשר.

מן הכשבים ומן העזים מזה בפני עצמו

ומזה בפני עצמו אתה אומר כן או אינו אלא שיביא

משניהם כאחת תלמוד לומר ואם מן הצאן קרבנוֹ

---

5 ערכין י"ח, ב'. נדה ס"ו, ב'.   8 פרה א', נ'.   14–13 ויקרא א', י'.

---

5 כל שנתו] ק. בן שנתו.   7 כל שנתה] מ. ש"ט. כל שנתו.
8 כבן שנתו] ש"ט. כבן שנה.

Geo. Buchanan Gray, *Sacrifices in the Old Testament*
(Oxford, 1925), pp. 348 ff.).

[2] אַיִל "ram," according to the Rabbis, is the designation
for a sheep during the second year of its life after one
month of its second year has elapsed. During the first
month of its second year, however, i. e., during the thirteenth month of its life, it is designated as *palges* פלגס,
and is not fit for a sacrifice which requires an *ayyil* (see
M. Parah 1.3).

[3] The *Vav* in ומן העזים can mean "and" as well as "or."

whether of the sheep or of the goats for a burnt-offering'' (Lev. 1.10), where it is expressly stated that one should bring from the one species [sheep] by itself or from the other species [goats] by itself. Now, then, by using the method of *Kal vahomer* we say it is to be reasoned: If the more important burnt-offering may be brought from one species alone, is it not but logical to assume that the less important passover sacrifice may surely be brought from one species alone? Hence what must be the meaning of the expression: "from the sheep and from the goats?" Either from this species alone or from that species alone.

It Shall Be for You. This is to include the passover sacrifice of subsequent generations, that it also should be brought only from sheep or from goats—these are the words of R. Eliezer. R. Josiah says: "Ye shall take it." Why is this said? Because of the following: It is said: "And thou shalt sacrifice the passover-offering unto the Lord thy God, of the flock and the herd" (Deut. 16.2), which means of the flock for the passover sacrifice, and of the herd for the festal sacrifice. So you interpret it. Perhaps it is not so, but it means that the one [flock] as well as the other [herd] is to be used for the passover sacrifice; and as for the expression: "A lamb perfect, a male," I apply it only to the passover sacrifice in Egypt; but the passover sacrifice of subsequent generations one may bring from either the one or the other. It says, however: "From the sheep and from the goats ye shall take it" (Ex. 12.5). Apparently there is no need for again saying, "ye shall take it"; what then is the purport of the

מן הכשבים או מן העזים לעולה מזה בפני עצמו

15 ומזה בפני עצמו והרי דברים קל וחמר ומה אם

עולה חמורה כשרה לבוא מין אחד פסח שהוא קל

אינו דין שיוכשר לבוא מין אחד הא מה תלמוד

לומר מן הכשבים ומן העזים מזה בפני עצמו ומזה

בפני עצמו.

20 יהיה לכם להביא פסח דורות שלא יבוא

אלא מן הכשבים ומן העזים דברי רבי אליעזר ר'

יאשיה אומר תקחו למה נאמר לפי שנאמר וזבחת

פסח ליי אלהיך צאן ובקר צאן לפסח ובקר לחגיגה

אתה אומר כן או אינו אלא אחד זה ואחד זה בפסח

25 ומה אני מקיים שה תמים זכר וגו' פסח מצרים אבל

פסח דורות יביא מזה ומזה תלמוד לומר מן

הכשבים ומן העזים תקחו שאין ת"ל תקחו ומה ת"ל

41—21 מ'ת 90.   23—22 דברים ט'ז, ב'.

---

14 מן הכשבים–לעולה] הוספתי: א. מ. ונו'.   17 הא] ד. >.
18 מ. ד. הכבשים.   20 יהיה]=מ"ח. א"א: מ. ד.   והיה. 27 א.
הכשבים.

words "ye shall take it?" To include the passover sacrifice of the subsequent generations, that it likewise must be brought only from the sheep or from the goats. These are the words of R. Josiah. R. Jonathan says: The flock is for the passover sacrifice and the herd is for the festal sacrifice. So you interpret it. Perhaps it is not so, but it means that the one [flock] as well as the other [herd] is to be used for the passover sacrifice. And as for the expression, "a lamb perfect, a male," I apply it only to the passover sacrifice in Egypt; but the passover sacrifice of subsequent generations one may bring from the one as well as from the other. It says, however: "That thou shalt keep this service in this month" (Ex. 13.5), which means: In the same way as you performed the service in Egypt so shall you perform it in subsequent generations—These are the words of R. Jonathan. R. Eliezer says: The flock is for the passover sacrifice and the herd is for the festal sacrifice. So you interpret it. Perhaps this is not so, but it means that the one [flock] as well as the other [herd] is to be used for the passover sacrifice; and as for the expression, "a lamb perfect, a male," I apply it only to the passover sacrifice in Egypt; but the passover sacrifice of subsequent generations one may bring either from the one or from the other. It says, however: "And ye shall observe this thing for an ordinance to thee and to thy sons for ever" (Ex. 12.24). Behold, then, here the passover sacrifice of subsequent generations is also prescribed. If so, what must be the meaning of the passage: "Thou shalt sacrifice . . . of the

תקחו להביא פסח דורות שלא יבוא אלא אלא מן

הכבשים ומן העזים דברי ר' יאשיה ר' יונתן אומר

30 צאן לפסח ובקר לחגיגה אתה אומר כן או אינו

אלא אחד זה ואחד זה בפסח ומה אני מקיים שה

תמים זכר וגו' פסח מצרים אבל פסח דורות יביא

מזה ומזה תלמוד לומר ועבדת את העבודה הזאת

בחדש הזה כעבודה שעבדת במצרים כך עשה

35 לדורות דברי ר' יונתן ר' אליעזר אומר צאן לפסח

ובקר לחגיגה אתה אומר כן או אינו אלא אחד זה

ואחד זה בפסח ומה אני מקיים שה תמים וגו' פסח

מצרים אבל פסח דורות יביא מזה ומזה תלמוד

לומר ושמרתם את הדבר הזה לחק לך ולבניך עד

40 עולם הרי פסח דורות אמור אם כן מה ת"ל וזבחת

33—34 שמות י"ג, ה'. 34—35 לקמן י"ו. 35—36 לקמן י"א.

39—40 שמות י"ב, כ"ד.

---

28 להביא—אלא] ד. שלא יביא פסח דורות אלא. 29 יונתן] ד. נתן.

39—40 לחק לך ולבניך עד עולם] מ. וגו' ועפי"ז הוספתי.

flock and the herd" (Deut. 16.2)? Of the flock
for the passover sacrifice and of the herd for the
festal sacrifice.

R. Akiba says: One scriptural passage says:
"And thou shalt sacrifice the passover-offering
unto the Lord thy God, of the flock and the
herd" (Deut. 16.2), and another scriptural passage says: "from the sheep or from the goats
shall ye take it" (Ex. 12.5). How can both these
verses be maintained? You must say: This is a
rule about the interpretation of the Torah: Two
passages opposing one another and conflicting
with one another stand as they are, until a third
passage comes and decides between them.[4] Now,
the passage: "Draw out and take you lambs
according to your families, and kill the passover
lamb" (Ex. 12.21) decides in this case, declaring
that from the flock only and not from the herd
may the passover sacrifice come.[5]

R. Ishmael says: The scriptural passage (Deut.
16.2) speaks of the festal sacrifice which is
brought on the Passover. So you interpret it.
Perhaps it speaks only of the passover sacrifice
itself? When it says: "A lamb perfect, a male"
(Ex. 12.5), behold, the passover sacrifice itself is
already there prescribed. What then does the
passage: "Thou shalt sacrifice the passover-

---

[4] This is the thirteenth rule in the hermeneutic system
of R. Ishmael (see *JE*, XII, 33).

[5] The passage in Deut. 16.2 was understood by some
Alexandrian Jews to mean that the passover sacrifice may
be brought from the herd, בקר, as well as from the flock,
i. e., sheep or goats (see Graetz, *Gesch.*, III, 5 (1906),

פסח ליי אלהיך צאן ובקר צאן לפסח ובקר לחגיגה
רבי עקיבא אומר כתוב אחד אומר וזבחת פסח
ליי אלהיך צאן ובקר וכתוב אחד אומר מן הכשבים
ומן העזים תקחו כיצד יתקיימו שני כתובים הללו
45 אמרת זו מדה בתורה שני כתובים זה　נגד זה
וסותרים זה על ידי זה ומתקיימים במקומן עד
שיבא הכתוב השלישי ויכריע ביניהן תלמוד לומר
משכו וקחו לכם צאן למשפחותיכם ושחטו הפסח
צאן לפסח ולא בקר לפסח רבי ישמעאל אומר
50 בחגיגה הבאה בפסח הכתוב מדבר אתה אומר כן
או אינו מדבר אלא בפסח עצמו כשהוא אומר שה
תמים זכר וגו' הרי פסח עצמו אמור ומה ת"ל וזבחת

44–54 מ'ת שם.　48 שמות י"ב, כ"א.　49–54 ספרי דברים קכ'ט.
פסחים ע', ב'.　י' שם ו', א' (33a).

---

44 כתובים] ד. מקראות.　46 זה על ידי זה] מ"ח. זה את זה./
ומתקיימים] א. יתקיימו ד. עד שיתקיימו.　47–46 עד שיבא הכתוב
השלישי] ד. יבא כתוב שלישי.　47 תלמוד לומר] א. > ונ. מוחקו.
51 בפסח–ט. ל. מ"ח: א. מ. ק. נ. בפני.

---

p. 608). I Esdras 1.6–9 also presupposes such an interpretation of the passage in Deut. Against such an interpretation
the arguments of the Rabbis here are directed.

offering unto the Lord thy God of the flock and the herd" (Deut. 16.2) deal with? Evidently it deals with the festal sacrifice which is brought on the Passover.

Rabbi says: The scriptural passage (Deut. 16.2) deals with a sacrifice which may come from the herd as well as from the flock; and which is it? It is the peace offering. On the basis of this passage they said: "The "leftovers" of peace offerings are to be offered up as peace offerings and also the "leftovers" of the passover sacrifice are to be offered up as peace offerings."

Chapter V
(Ex. 12.6)

And Ye Shall Keep It until the Fourteenth Day of the Same Month. Why did the Scripture require the purchase of the paschal lamb to take place four days before its slaughter? R. Matia the son of Ḥeresh used to say: Behold it says: "Now when I passed by thee, and looked upon thee, and, behold, thy time was the time of love" (Ezek. 16.8). This means, the time has arrived for the fulfillment of the oath which the Holy One, blessed be He, had sworn unto Abraham, to deliver his children. But as yet they had no religious duties to perform by which to merit redemption, as it further says: "thy breasts were fashioned and thy hair was grown; yet thou wast naked and bare" (ibid.), which means bare of any religious deeds. Therefore the Holy One, blessed be He, assigned them two duties, the

פסח ליי אלהיך וגו' בחגיגה הבאה בפסח הכתוב
מדבר רבי אומר בזבח שהוא בא מן הבקר ומן
הצאן הכתוב מדבר ואי זה זה זה שלמים מכאן 55
אמרו מותר שלמים לשלמים ומותר פסח לשלמים.

פרשה ה (שמות י"ב, ו'.)

ו ה י ה   ל כ ם   ל מ ש מ ר ת וגו' מפני מה הקדים
הכתוב לקיחתו של פסח קודם לשחיטתו ארבעה
ימים היה רבי מתיא בן חרש אומר הרי הוא אומר
ואעבור עליך ואראך והנה עתך עת דודים הגיע
שבועה שנשבע הקב"ה לאברהם אבינו שהוא גואל 5
את בניו ולא היו בידם מצות שיתעסקו בהם כדי
שיגאלו שנאמר שדים נכונו ושערך צמח ואת ערום
ועריה ערים מכל מצות נתן להם הקב"ה שתי מצות

54–56 שקלים ב', ח'. מנחות פ"ב, א'–ב'. פ"נ ב'.
4 יחזקאל ט"ז, ח'.   7 שם ט"ז, ז'.   8–12 שמו"ר ט"ו, י"ב. י"ט, ה'.
שהש"ר א', ה'. י"ב, נ', ו'. ה', ב'. מדרש תהלים קי"ד, ה'. פדר"א כ"ט.

2 הכתוב] ד. / < קודם] ד. <.   3 הרי הוא אוטר] ד. <.
5 שבועה] ד. שבועתו מ"ח. עח.

duty of the paschal sacrifice and the duty of circumcision, which they should perform so as to be worthy of redemption. For thus it is said: "And when I passed by thee, and saw thee wallowing in thy blood, I said unto thee: In thy blood live[1]" (ibid., 6). And again it is said: "As for thee also, because of the blood of thy covenant I sent forth thy prisoners out of the pit wherein is no water" (Zech. 9.11). For this reason Scripture required that the purchase of thé paschal lamb take place four days before its slaughter. For one cannot obtain rewards except for deeds.

R. Eliezer ha-Kappar says: Did not Israel possess four virtues than which nothing in the whole world is more worthy: that they were above suspicion in regard to chastity and in regard to tale bearing, that they did not change their names and that they did not change their language.—And how do we know that they were above suspicion in regard to chastity? It is said: "And the son of an Israelitish woman whose father was an Egyptian, went out" (Lev. 24.10). This actually proclaims the excellence of Israel.

---

[1] The Hebrew text has the dual form בְּדָמַיִךְ, thus referring to "two bloods," the blood of the passover-sacrifice and the blood of circumcision, by both of which the Israelites were freed from Egypt. In support of the statement that the Israelites in Egypt observed the ceremony of circumcision, the passage from Zech. 9.11 is cited, which was taken to imply that because of the blood of the covenant God sent forth the Israelites from the Egyptian bondage.

מצות פסח ומצות מילה שיתעסקו בהם כדי שינאלו

10 שנאמר ואעבור עליך ואראך מתבוססת בדמיך

וגו' ואומר גם את בדם בריתך שלחתי אסיריך מבור

אין מים בו לכך הקדים הכתוב לקיחתו של פסח

קודם לשחיטתו ארבעה ימים שאין נוטלין שכר אלא

על המעשה רבי אלעזר הקפר אומר וכי לא היה

15 בידם של ישראל ארבע מצות שאין כל העולם

כדאי בהן שלא נחשדו על העריות ולא נחשדו על

לשון הרע ולא שינו את שמם ולא שינו את לשונם

ומנין שלא נחשדו על העריות שנאמר ויצא בן אשה

ישראלית והוא בן איש מצרי להודיע שבחן של

---

10 יחזקאל ט"ז, ו'.   12—11 זכריה ט', י"א.   25—14 וי"ר ל"ב, ה'.
פסדר'כ ויהי בשלח (פ'נ, א'—ב'). מדרש תהלים קי"ד, ד'. קכ"ב, ה'.
שהש"ר ד', י"ב. שמו"ר א', כ"ח. במ"ר כ', כ"ב. ת. בלק ט"ו. ת. בובער
בלק כ"ה. סדא"ר כ"א—כ"ב (פריעדמאן 125—123). יומא ע"ה, א'.
19—18 ויקרא כ"ד, י'.

---

9 מצות פסח] מ. פסח ד. דם פסח / ומצות]—ט: מ. ד. ודם.
14 על המעשה] ד. על ידי המעשה/ אלעזר] מ. ד. אליעזר/ הקפר]
מ"ח. < ד. ~ ברבי. 15 של ישראל] א. שלש.   19 ישראלית]—ל:
מ. וגו' א. ק. נ. הישראלית/והוא בן איש מצרי] א. וגו' ועפי"ז
הוספתי.

The covenant, ברית, here is understood to refer to the rite
of circumcision, the covenant of Abraham (Gen. 17.13).

This was the only instance among them of unchastity[2]; hence Scripture makes special mention of it. Of them it is stated in the traditional sacred writings:[3] "A garden shut up is my sister, my bride; a spring shut up, a fountain sealed" (Cant. 4.12). "A garden shut up," refers to the men; "a spring shut up," refers to the women. R. Nathan says: "a garden shut up," refers to the married women, "a fountain sealed," refers to the betrothed women.

Another interpretation: "a garden shut up, a spring shut up," means, shut up with respect to the two modes of cohabitation.[4]

And how do we know that they were above suspicion in regard to tale bearing and that they loved one another? It is said: "But every woman shall ask of her neighbour," etc. (Ex. 3.22). They had had this order for twelve months, and you do not find that one of them informed against the other.

And whence do we know that they did not change their names? From the fact that just as Scripture records their genealogies at their going down to Egypt by the names: Reuben, Simeon,

---

[2] I. e., sexual intercourse with a person whom one could not legally marry. It is assumed that the Israelites were forbidden intermarriage with the Egyptians. Such an older prohibition is presupposed in Deut. 23.8. It is also possible that the unchastity here referred to means adultery and the Mekilta has in mind an old legent (comp. Lev. Rab. 32.4–5), according to which the mother of the blasphemer, Shelomith the daughter of Dibri, was married to an Israelite, and her son, the blasphemer, whose father was an Egyp-

20 ישראל שלא היה ביניהם אלא זה בלבד ופרטו
הכתוב עליהם מפורש בקבלה גן נעול אחותי כלה
גל נעול מעין חתום גן נעול אילו הזכרים גל נעול
אילו הנקבות ורבי נתן אומר גן נעול אלו הנשואות
מעין חתום אלו הארוסות דבר אחר גן נעול וגל

25 נעול שתי ביאות ומנין שלא נחשדו על לשון הרע
והיו אוהבין זה את זה שנאמר ושאלה אשה משכנתה
וגו' כבר היה בידם שנים עשר חדש ואין אתה מוצא
אחד מהם שהלשין על חבירו ומנין שלא שינו את
שמם שכשם שמיחסן בירידתן ראובן שמעון לוי

21–22 שה"ש ד', י"ב.   26 שמות ג', כ"ב.   29 שם א', ב'.

---

20 זה] א. זו / ופרטו] ד. ופרסמו ופרטו א. ט. ופירסמה.
21 עליהם מפורש] א. ופרש.   21 בקבלה] ק. ~ שנאמר.
21–22 אחותי כלה גל נעול מעין חתום] מ. וגו' ועפי"ז הוספתי.
22 גל נעול] ד. ~ מעין חתום.   23–24 ט. (תהלים תת"פ) ר' נתן אומר גל
נעול אלו הנשואות גן נעול אלו הארוסות.   24 מעין חתום] ד. גל נעול
מעין חתום / וגל] ד. גל.   25 שתי ביאות] ד. אלו שתי ביאות.
26 שנאמר] ד. ת"ל.   29 בירידתן] ד. ~ שנאמר.

---

tian, was born in adultery. Comp. also Rashi and Ramban
in their commentaries to Lev. 24.10–11.

3 קבלה, "Traditional sacred writings," is the designation
for the extra-Pentateuchal works of the Bible, both the
Prophets and the Hagiographa (see Bacher, *Terminologie*,
I, 155).

4 Comp. Gen. Rab. 60.5.

Levi, Judah, etc. (Gen. 46.8f.), so also it records their genealogies after they had come up from Egypt by the names: Reuben, Simeon, Levi, Judah, etc., as it is said: "And they declared their pedigrees after their families by their fathers' houses" (Num. 1.18). And again it says: "The angel who hath redeemed me from all evil, bless the lads; and let my name be named in them" (Gen. 48.16).

And whence do we know that they did not change their language? It is said: "Who made thee a ruler and a judge over us,"[5] etc. (Ex. 2.14). From this it is evident that they were speaking Hebrew. And it is also said: "That it is my mouth[6] that speaketh unto you" (Gen. 45.12). And again it says: "And they said; the God of the Hebrews[7] hath met with us" (Ex. 5.3). And it is also said: "And there came one that had escaped, and told Abram the Hebrew" (Gen. 14.13).—Why then was the purchasing of the paschal lamb to precede its slaughtering by four days? Because the Israelites in Egypt were steeped in idolatry. — And the law against idolatry outweighs all other commandments in the Torah. For it is said: "Then it shall be, if it be done in error by the congregation, it being

---

[5] It is assumed that the Torah reports the original words addressed by the Israelite to Moses.

[6] "My mouth" is taken here in the sense of "my native tongue," i. e., "Hebrew." So it was also understood by Onkelos ad loc. and Gen. Rab. 93.11.

[7] "Hebrews" is taken to mean, people who speak Hebrew, the language of Abraham the Hebrew.

30 ויהודה כך מייחסן בעלייתן ראובן שמעון לוי

ויהודה שנאמר ויתילדו על משפחותם לבית אבותם

וגו' ואומר המלאך הגואל אותי מכל רע הוא יברך

את הנערים ויקרא בהם שמי וגו' ומנין שלא שינו

את לשונם שנאמר מי שמך לאיש שר ושופט וגו'

35 מיכן שהיו מדברים עברית ונאמר כי פי המדבר

אליכם ואומר ויאמרו אלהי העברים נקרה עלינו

וגו' ואומר ויבא הפליט ויגד לאברם העברי ומפני

מה הקדים לקיחתו של פסח לשחיטתו ארבעה

ימים לפי שהיו ישראל שטופין בעבודה זרה

40 במצרים ועבודה זרה שקולה כנגד כל המצות

שבתורה שנאמר והיה אם מעיני העדה נעשתה

31 במדבר א', י"ח.   32–33 בראשית מ"ח, ט"ז.   34 שמות ב', י"ד

35 בראשית מ"ה, י"ב. 36 שמות ה', נ'.   37 בראשית י"ד, י"נ.   39 שמו"ר

ט"ו, ב'. 54–39 ספרי במדבר קי"א. ספרי זוטא 284. הוריות ח', א'.

42–41 במדבר ט"ו, כ"ד.

30–31 ראובן שמעון לוי ויהודה] ד. >.   32–33 הוא יברך את

הנערים ויקרא בהם שמי] הוספתי=מ"ח.   33 וגו']א. ט. ג. ~ ולא

היה בהם זנות שנאמר ששם עלו שבטים שבטי יה אמר הקב"ה שמי מעיד

על ישראל שלא נטמאו במצרים בזנות.   33 שינו] א. ט. חלפו.

34–35 מי שמך–ונאמר] מ. ד. >.   34 וגו'] ט. ~ שני אנשים עברים

נצים.   41 שבתורה] ד. >.

hid from their eyes," etc. (Num. 15.24). Scripture here singles out one law, mentioning it
separately. And which law is it? It is the law
against idolatry. You say, it refers to idolatry;
perhaps this is not so, but it refers to any one of
the commandments mentioned in the Torah?
When it says, however: "And when ye shall err,
and not observe all these commandments"[8]
(ibid., 15.22), "all these commandments," indicates the character of the one commandment.
Just as the transgression of all the commandments breaks off the yoke,[9] annuls the covenant
between God and Israel, and misrepresents the
Torah, so also the transgressor of this one commandment breaks off the yoke, annuls the
covenant between God and Israel, and misrepresents the Torah.[10]   Now what can this one
commandment be? The one against idolatry.
For one who worships idols breaks off the yoke,
annuls the covenant and misrepresents the
Torah.   And whence do we know that he who
transgresses all the commandments breaks off

---

[8] v. 24 speaks of one sin, for it uses the singular נעשתה
"it be done," while v. 22 speaks of "all these commandments" being disregarded. Hence, the one sin referred to
in v. 24 must be such a one as equals the disregard of all
the commandments, i. e., idolatry.

[9] I. e., "the yoke of the commandments," עול מצות, or
"the yoke of the Torah," עול תורה.

[10] I take מגלה פנים בתורה here to be an abbreviated form
for מגלה פנים בתורה שלא כהלכה meaning, to misrepresent or
misinterpret the Torah (cf. however, Bacher, *Terminologie*,
I, 149–151).

לשגגה ייחד הכתוב המצוה הזאת ואמרה ענין בפני

עצמה ואיזה זה זה עבודה זרה אתה אומר זו עבודה

זרה או אינו אלא אחת מכל מצות האמורות בתורה

45 כשהוא אומר וכי תשגו ולא תעשו את כל המצות

האלה באו כל המצות ללמד על מצוה אחת מה

העובר על כל מצות פורק עול ומפר ברית ומגלה

פנים בתורה אף העובר על מצוה אחת פורק עול

ומפר ברית ומגלה פנים בתורה ואיזו זו עבודה זרה

50 שפורק עול ומפר ברית ומגלה פנים בתורה שנאמר

לעבור בריתו ומנין לעובר על כל המצות שהוא

46—45 במדבר ט״ו, כ״ב.   50—49 מ״ת 99.   51 דברים י״ז, ב׳.

---

42 לשגגה]=ל: א. מ. וגו׳. ק. נ. בשגגה.   43—45 אתה אומר—
כשהוא אומר] ז״י. ובה״מ. גורסין דבר אחר.   44 בתורה] ד. ~
סתם.   46—45 את כל המצות האלה] הוספתי: א. מ. ד. וגו׳.
46 אחת] מ״ח. ~ שקולה ככולן.   49—46 מה העובר—בתורה] הנהתי
עפ״י ט. מ״ח. ג. א״א.   50—49 ואיזו זו עבודה זרה שפורק עול
ומפר ברית ומגלה פנים בתורה] הנהתי=מ״ע. מ״ה.   51—50 שנאמר
לעבור בריתו]=מ״ח. מ״ע. ומ״ה.

the yoke, annuls the covenant,[11] and misrepresents the Torah? From the scriptural passage: "That thou shouldest enter into the covenant of the Lord thy God" (Deut. 29.11), for "the covenant" here simply means the Torah, as it is said: "These are the words of the covenant which the Lord commanded Moses" (Deut. 28.69). —Therefore he said to them: withdraw your hands from idol worship and adhere to the commandments.

R. Judah the son of Bathyra says: Behold it says: "But they hearkened not unto Moses for impatience of spirit," etc. (Ex. 6.9). Can you imagine a man receiving good tidings and not rejoicing; being told, "a male child is born unto thee," and not rejoicing; being told, "your master sets you free," and not rejoicing? What, then, does Scripture mean by saying: "But they hearkened not unto Moses?" (Ex. 6.9). Merely that it was hard for them to part with their idols. And so it is also said: "And I said unto them: Cast ye away every man the detestable things of his eyes, and defile not yourselves with the idols of Egypt" (Ezek. 20.7); and it says further: "But they rebelled against Me and would not hearken, etc. . . . But I wrought for My name's sake," etc. (ibid., 20.8-9). This is what is meant by the passage: "And the Lord spoke unto Moses and unto Aaron, and gave them a charge unto the children of Israel" (Ex. 6.13)— charging them to give up idol worship.

----

[11] I. e., the covenant which was made for the commandments to be kept (see Ex. 24.7–8; Deut. 28.69 and 29.8, 11, 13.

פורק עול ומפר ברית ומגלה פנים בתורה שנאמר
לעברך בברית יי אלהיך ואין ברית אלא תורה
שנאמר אלה דברי הברית וגו' אמר להם משכו
ידיכם מעבודה זרה והדבקו במצות רבי יהודה בן

55

בתירה אומר הרי הוא אומר ולא שמעו אל משה
מקוצר רוח וגו' וכי יש לך אדם שהוא מתבשר
בשורה טובה ואינו שמח נולד לך בן זכר ואינו שמח
רבך מוציאך לחרות ואינו שמח ואם כן מה תלמוד
לומר ולא שמעו אל משה אלא שהיה קשה בעיניהם

60

לפרוש מעבודה זרה וכן הוא אומר ואומר אליהם
איש שקוצי עיניו השליכו ובגילולי מצרים   אל
תטמאו ואומר וימרו בי ולא אבו וגו' ואעש למען
שמי וגו' הדה היא דכתיב וידבר יי אל משה ואל
אהרן ויצום אל בני ישראל ציום לפרוש מעבודה

65

זרה.

---

53 דברים כ'ט, י'א.   54 דברים כ'ח, ס'ט.   54—55 לקטן י'א.
56—57 שמות ו', ט'.   61 יחזקאל כ', ז'—ח'—ט'.   64—65 שמות
ו', י'ב.

---

52 בתורה] א. מ. ~ והעובר על מצוה אחת.   58 נולד] ד.
שנאמר וירמיה כ', ט'ו) יולד/ואינו שמח] ד. שמח שמחהו.   59 ד. רבו
מוציאו.   59—60 מה ת'ל] ד. לטה נאמר.   61 וכן הוא אומר] ד. שנאמר
63 ולא אבו וגו'] ד. בית ישראל בסרבר.   65 אל בני ישראל]=ל:
מ. וגו' א. ד. על בני ישראל.

And Ye Shall Keep It. Why was this said?
Because when it was said: "Draw out and take
you lambs," etc. (Ex. 12.21), the Israelites said
unto Moses: Moses our teacher, lo, if we sacrifice
the abomination of the Egyptians before their
eyes will they not stone us?[12] Then he said to
them: From the miracle which He will perform
for you at its acquisition, you will know what
He will do for you at its slaughtering.

And Ye Shall Keep It, etc. This means keep
it until the fourteenth and slaughter it on the
fourteenth. Perhaps it means, keep it and
slaughter it on any day, but not later than the
fourteenth? It says, however: "In the first
month on the fourteenth day of the month"
(Num. 9.5). Scripture has thus fixed the slaughtering on the fourteenth as an obligation. Consequently it is impossible for you to argue as in the
latter version, but you must argue as in the
former version, i. e., keep it until the fourteenth
and slaughter it on the fourteenth.

And Ye Shall Keep It. Scripture here tells
that they should examine it four days before
slaughtering it. From this you can argue concerning the *Tamid* offering: "Keeping" is prescribed for the passover offering, and "keeping"
is also prescribed for the *Tamid.* Just as the
"keeping" said with regard to the passover offering implied that they should examine it four

---

[12] They quoted to Moses the very words which he himself
said to Pharaoh (Ex. 8.22).

והיה לכם למשמרת למה נאמר לפי
שנאמר משכו וקחו לכם צאן וגו' אמרו ישראל
למשה רבינו משה הן נזבח את תועבת מצרים וגו'
אמר להן מן הנס שהוא עושה לכם במשיכתו אתם 70
יודעים מה בשחיטתו.

והיה לכם למשמרת וגו' שמרוהו עד
ארבעה עשר ושחטוהו בארבעה עשר או שמרוהו
ושחטוהו עד ארבעה עשר תלמוד לומר בראשון
בארבעה עשר יום קבעו הכתוב חובה הא אין 75
עליך לדון בלשון אחרון אלא בלשון ראשון שמרוהו
עד י"ד ושחטוהו בי"ד.

והיה לכם למשמרת מגיד הכתוב שהיו
מבקרין אותו ד' ימים קודם לשחיטתו מכאן אתה
דן על התמיד נאמרה שמירה בפסח ונאמרה שמירה 80
בתמיד מה שמירה האמורה בפסח מבקרין אותו ד'

---

68 שמות י"ב, כ"א.   69 שמות ח', כ"ב.   74—75 במדבר ט', ה'.
78—83 ספרי במדבר קמ"ב. פסחים צ"ו, א'. מנחות מ"ט, ב'. ערכין י"ג, ב'.

---

71 סה] ד' <.   72 וגו'] מ.   עד ארבעה עשר יום שוחטיהו בי"ד
או שומריהו עד י"ד ושוחטיהו בארבע אתה אומר ד. שחטוהו בי"ד
ושטרוהו עד י"ד אתה אומר.   73 או] מ. >/ שמרוהו] מ. ד. ט. ~
עד י"ד ומשכהו.   74 עד ארבעה עשר] ט. > מ. ד. בארבעה עשר
מ"ח. ש"י. (ר' סולימאן) בחמשה עשר ז"י. בה"מ. מ"ס. מ"ע.
מ"ה. בעשור.   80 שמירה] מ. שחיטה.

days before it was slaughtered, so the "keeping"
said with regard to the *Tamid* must also be
understood as implying that they should examine
it four days before it is slaughtered. Hence they
said: They should keep in the lambfold no less
than six examined lambs, sufficient for a Sabbath
followed by two days of the New Year's festival,[13]
but they may always have more.

Ye Shall Keep It. This excludes the paschal
sacrifice of subsequent generations, for only the
passover sacrifice in Egypt had to be purchased
from the tenth of the month on; but the paschal
lamb of subsequent generations may be purchased
at any time.

And They Shall Kill It. And did all of them
really do the slaughtering? It merely implies
that a man's agent is like the man himself. On
the basis of this passage the sages said: A man's
agent is like the man himself.

They Shall Kill It. Whether the day be a
weekday or the Sabbath. To what then am I to
apply: "Every one that profaneth it, shall surely
be put to death" (Ex. 31.14)? To any other

---

[13] The expression ולשני ימים טובים של ראש השנה, if not a
later interpolation, is not to be taken strictly as referring
to the case of a Sabbath day followed by the *Rosh Hashanah*
festival lasting for two days (cf. 'Ar. 13ab and Men. 49b).
There was only one slight possibility of two days being
practically observed as *Rosh Hashanah*, and this was during
the period when the rule, subsequently abolished by
R. Johanan b. Zakkai, of limiting the time for receiving
the witnesses for the New Moon up to the *Minḥah* time
of the day (M. R. H. 4.4) still prevailed. But even in such

ימים קודם לשחיטתו אף שמירה האמורה בתמיד
מבקרין אותו ד' ימים קודם לשחיטתו מכאן אמרו
אין פוחתים מששה טלאים המבוקרין מלשכת
הטלאים כדי לשבת ולשני ימים טובים של ראש   85
השנה ומוסיפין לעולם.

והיה לכם למשמרת להוציא פסח דורות
שפסח מצרים מקחו מבעשור ופסח דורות מקחו
בכל זמן.

ושחטו אותו וגו' וכי כולם היו שוחטין אותו   90
אלא לעשות שלוחו של אדם כמותו מכאן אמרו
שלוחו של אדם כמותו.

ושחטו אותו בין בחול בין בשבת ומה אני
מקיים מחלליה מות יומת בשאר מלאכות חוץ

86–83 ערכין ב', ה'.   92–87 לעיל פ'נ.   105–93 ספרי במדבר
ס'ה וקמ'ב. פסחים ס'ו, א'. תוספתא שם ד', ב'. י' שם ו', א' (33ª).

83 לשחיטתו] נ. ~ מכאן אתה דן על התמיד נאמר שמירה ובפסח
נאמר שמירה מה שמירה האמורה בפסח מכין אותו ד' ימים קודם
שחיטתו אף שמירה האמורה בתמיד מבקרין אותו ד' ימים קודם
לשחיטתן.   91–92 מכאן–כמותו] מ. >.   91 אמרו] א. ~ חכמים.

---

a case there was really only one day *Rosh Hashanah*,
though people might have refrained from work on the
day preceding it (see Commentaries). In Mishnaic times
one could hardly speak of two days *Rosh Hashanah*.

work except the slaughtering of the paschal sacrifice. But perhaps it applies also to the slaughtering of the paschal sacrifice; and as for the commandment: "and they shall slaughter it," it holds good for all other days but the Sabbath? However, the passage: "Let the children of Israel keep the Passover in its due season" (Num. 9.2) teaches that it should be slaughtered even on the Sabbath—these are the words of R. Josiah. Said R. Jonathan to him: Still we cannot learn this from the interpretation of the passage. Said R. Josiah to him: Behold it says: "Command the children of Israel, and say unto them: My food which is presented unto Me . . . shall ye observe to offer unto Me in its due season" (Num. 28.2). If this were merely intended to teach that the *Tamid* should set aside the sabbath law, it would be superfluous; for it has been expressly stated: "And on the sabbath day two he-lambs of the first year . . . this is the burnt-offering for every sabbath besides the continual burnt-offering" (ibid., vv 9-10). What then is the purport of the words: "in its due season?" It is merely to enable us to make a comparison, and to formulate a *Gezerah Shavah*:[14] Here, in the case of the paschal sacrifice, it is said: "in its due season" (Num. 9.2), and there, in the case of the *Tamid*, it is also said, "in its due season" (ibid. 28.2). Just as there the phrase "in its due season" means that the *Tamid* sacrifice should set aside the sabbath law, so also here the phrase "in its due season" means that the paschal sacrifice should set aside the sabbath law.

---

[14] "*Gezerah shavah*" is the second rule in the hermeneutic

95 משחיטת פסח או אף בשחיטת פסח ומה אני מקיים

ושחטו אותו בשאר כל הימים חוץ מן השבת תלמוד

לומר ויעשו בני ישראל את הפסח במועדו אפילו

בשבת דברי רבי יאשיה נם לו רבי יונתן ממשמע

זה עדיין לא שמענו נם לו ר' יאשיה הרי הוא אומר

100 צו את בני ישראל ואמרת אליהם את קרבני וגו'

אם ללמד על התמיד שידחה את השבת והלא כבר

נאמר וביום השבת שני כבשים וגו' ומה ת"ל במועדו

אלא להקיש לדין גזירה שוה נאמר כאן במועדו

ונאמר להלן במועדו מה להלן דוחה את השבת

105 אף כאן דוחה את השבת.

94 שמות ל'א, י'ד.   97 במדבר ט', ב'.   100 במדבר כ'ח, ב'.
102 שם כ'ח, ט'.

96 השבת] ד. ~ או אף בשבת. 98 יונתן] ד. נתן.   98–99 ממשמע
זה]=ט. מ'ח: א. טר שמע זה מ. מה שמע זה ד. >.   99 עדיין]
ד. ועדיין מ. עניין.   104 מה להלן] ק. נ. מה כאן.   105 אף כאן]
ק. נ. אף להלו.

system of Hillel and in that of R. Ishmael. It is the argument by analogy based upon the similarity of expression used in two laws (see *JE*, XII, 32–33).

And the Whole Assembly of the Congregation of Israel Shall Kill It. R. Eliezer says: Whence can you prove that if all Israel had only one paschal lamb, all of them can fulfill their duty with it? From the passage: And the whole assembly of the Congregation of Israel shall kill it.

And the Whole Assembly of the Congregation of Israel Shall Kill It. On the basis of this passage the sages said: The rite of slaughtering the paschal lamb is performed by three successive groups, an assembly, a congregation, and Israel.

At Dusk. I might understand this to mean at the morning twilight, but it is said: "There thou shalt sacrifice the Passover offering at even" (Deut. 16.6). If "at even," I might say that it means after it is already dark. But it is said: "At the going down of the sun" (ibid.). Perhaps "at the going down of the sun" goes with "thou shalt roast and eat it." But the intervening words: "At the season that thou camest forth out of Egypt" (ibid.), close the subject of the time for the slaughtering. The commandment following: "And thou shalt roast and eat it," is to be observed only after it is already dark.

Rabbi says: Behold it says: "There thou shalt sacrifice the passover-offering at even." I might take this literally, i. e. in the evening. But Scripture goes on to say: "at the time that thou camest forth out of Egypt." When did Israel go

ו ש ח ט ו   א ו ת ו   כ ל   ק ה ל   ע ד ת   י ש ר א ל
ר' אליעזר אומר מנין אתה אומר שאם אין להם
לישראל אלא פסח יחידי שכולם יוצאין בו ידי
חובתן ת"ל ושחטו אותו וגו'.

110   ו ש ח ט ו   א ו ת ו   כ ל   ק ה ל   ע ד ת   י ש ר א ל
מכאן אמרו הפסח נשחט בשלש כתות קהל ועדה
וישראל.

ב י ן   ה ע ר ב י ם   שומע אני עם דמדומי חמה
ת"ל שם תזבח את הפסח בערב אי בערב יכול
115 משתחשך ת"ל כבוא השמש או כבוא השמש ובשלת
ואכלת ת"ל מועד צאתך ממצרים הפסיק הענין
ובשלת ואכלת משחשיכה רבי אומר הרי הוא אומר
שם תזבח את הפסח בערב שומע אני כמשמעו ת"ל
מועד צאתך ממצרים אימתי יצאו ישראל ממצרים

106—109 קידושין מ'א, ב'—ס'ב, א. פסחים ע'ח, ב'. י' שם ז', ה'
(34b). 111—112 פסחים ס'ד, א'. תוס' שם ד', י'. ח', י'ט. י' שם
ה', ה'. ש. 10. (32c). 113—124 י' פסחים ה', א' (31ab). מ'ח
92. ש. 10. 114—116 דברים ט'ז, ו'—ז'.

107 ר' אליעזר אומר] ד. >.   110 כל קהל עדת ישראל]
הוספתי: ד. וגו'.   114 שם תזבח את הפסח] הוספתי.   115 משתחשך]
מ. מ'ח. ~ חמה / או] הנהתי עפ'י מ'ח: א. מ. ד. אי.
119 ישראל] ד. אלו.

forth out of Egypt? After the sixth hour of the day.[15] And so it says: "And it came to pass the selfsame day that the Lord did bring the Children of Israel out of the Land of Egypt" (Ex. 12.51). R. Nathan says: Whence can we prove that "dusk" here means from the time after the sixth hour of the day? Although there is no direct proof for it, there is at least a suggestion[16] of it in the passage: "for the day declineth, for the shadows of the evening are stretched out" (Jer. 6.4).

R. Simon the son of Yoḥai says: The scriptural passage: "At even at the going down of the sun, at the time that thou camest forth out of Egypt" (Deut. 16.6), puts first in the order of the text what is last in the actual process, and last in the order of the text what is first in the actual process: "at the time [17] that thou camest forth out of Egypt," is the time set for the slaughtering; "at the going down of the sun," is the time set for the roasting; "at even," is the time set for the eating of the paschal sacrifice.

The son of Bathyra says: Between the evenings slaughter it, says the law. This means, fix one evening time for its slaughtering and another evening time for its eating.

---

[15] I. e., after the noon hour. The daytime is divided into 12 equal parts called hours. At the time of the equinoxes these hours are equal to our hours. Rabbi takes the expression מועד צאתך in Deut. 16.6 to designate the time of the day when they came out, and not the season.

[16] See above ch. II, note 3.

[17] Like Rabbi (see above note 15) R. Simon b. Yoḥai

¹²⁰ משש שעות ולמעלה וכן הוא אומר ויהי בעצם היום

הזה יצאו וגו' רבי נתן אומר מנין ראיה לבין הערבים

שהוא משש שעות ולמעלה אף על פי שאין ראיה

לדבר זכר לדבר שנאמר כי פנה היום כי ינטו

צללי ערב רבי שמעון בן יוחי אומר בא הכתוב

¹²⁵ להשוות ראשון לאחרון ואחרון לראשון מועד צאתך

לשחיטתו כבוא השמש לצלייתו בערב לאכילתו

בן בתירה אומר בין הערבים שחטהו תן ערב

לשחיטתו ותן ערב לאכילתו.

121–120 שמות י״ב, נ״א.   124–123 ירמיה ו׳, ד׳.   128–127 ספרי
דברים קל״נ. זבחים י״א, ב׳. פסחים ק״ח, א׳.

---

121 ראיה] מ״ח. א״צ. >.   125 ד. להשית ראשון אחרון ואחרון
ראשון.

---

also interprets מועד צאתך (Deut. 16.6) as referring to the
time of the day when they came out, i. e., in the afternoon, and not to the season.

CHAPTER VI
(Ex. 12.7-10)

And They Shall Take of the Blood. I might understand this to mean of the blood that is in the hand or in a vessel; therefore it says (v. 22): "which is near the threshold (*ba-saf*)". Scripture thus tells that one would scoop out a hole, near the threshold, over which he slaughtered. For *saf* here means threshold, as in the passage: "In their setting of their thresholds by My threshold" (Ezek. 43.8). And it is also written: "And the posts of the thresholds were moved" (Isa. 6.4) —these are the words of R. Ishmael. R. Akiba says: *Saf* here means vessel, as in the passage: "And the cups,[1] and the snuffers, and the basins, and the pans" (I Kings 7.50).

And Put It on the Two Side-Posts and on the Lintel. This means, on the inside. You interpret it to mean on the inside. But perhaps it means only on the outside? It says however: "And when I see the blood" (v. 13), i. e., the blood that would be seen by Me and not by others[2]— these are the words of R. Ishmael. R. Jonathan says: This means, on the inside. You interpret it to mean on the inside. But perhaps it means only on the outside? It says however: "And the blood shall be to you for a token" (ibid.), i. e., a sign to you but not a sign to others. R. Isaac says: Still I say it means on the outside, so that the Egyptians, seeing it, would be cut to the quick.

---

[1] In Hebrew: *sippim*, plural of *saf*.

[2] I. e., non-Israelites.

פרשה ו (שמות י"ב, ז'–י'.)

ו ל ק ח ו מ ן ה ד ם שומע אני בין ביד בין בכלי
ת"ל אשר בסף מגיד הכתוב שעוקה חוקק בצד
האסקופה ושוחט בתוכה ואין סף אלא אסקופה
שנאמר בתתם ספם את ספי וגו' וכתיב וינועו אמות
5 הספים דברי ר' ישמעאל ר' עקיבא אומר אין סף
אלא כלי שנאמר והספים והמזמרות והמזרקות
והכפות וגו'.

ו נ ת נ ו ע ל ש ת י ה מ ז ו ז ו ת ו ע ל ה מ ש ק ו ף
מבפנים אתה אומר מבפנים או אינו אלא מבחוץ
10 ת"ל וראיתי את הדם הנראה לי ולא לאחרים דברי
ר' ישמעאל ר' יונתן אומר מבפנים אתה אומר
מבפנים או אינו אלא מבחוץ ת"ל והיה הדם לכם
לאות לכם לאות ולא לאחרים לאות ר' יצחק
אומר לעולם מבחוץ כדי שיהו המצריים רואים
15 ומעיהם מתחתכין.

7–1 י' פסחים ט', ה' (b37a).   15–1 לקמן י"א.   4 יחזקאל מ"ג, ח'.
5–4 ישעיה ו', ד'. 7–6 מלכים א. ז', נ'. 10 שמות י"ב, י"ג. 13–12 שמות שם.
לקמן ד'.

2 שעוקה] ד. שעוקר/ חוקק] א. מ. חוצץ ד. וחוקק.   3 ושוחט
בתוכה ואין סף אלא אסקופה] א. <.   5 שנאמר] א. מ. כשהוא אומר./
והספים] א. > במקרא והספות.   11 ישמעאל] ד. שמעון/ יונתן] ד.
נתן.   14 לעולם] מ"ח. ג. <.   15 מתחתכין] מ"ח. מתהפכים.

And Put It on the Two Side-Posts and on the Lintel. I might understand that if one put it first on the latter, he has not fulfilled his duty. But the scriptural passage: "And strike the lintel and the two side-posts" (v. 22), clearly shows that no matter which he does first, he fulfills his duty. We thus learn that our forefathers in Egypt had three altars, the lintel and the two side-posts. R. Ishmael says: They had four, the threshold, the lintel and the two side-posts.

Upon the Houses Wherein They Shall Eat It. This means only the houses in which they ate it. How about the houses in which they slept? Scripture says: "Upon the houses where ye are" (v. 13), meaning, no matter for what purpose you are in them.

And They Shall Eat the Flesh. The flesh but not the sinews, nor the bones, nor the horns, nor the hoofs.

In that Night. I might understand this to mean, all night, i. e., up to daytime. There is, however, a teaching against this in the scriptural passage: "And ye shall let nothing of it remain until the morning; but that which remaineth of it until the morning ye shall burn with fire" (v. 10). It could have said merely: But that which remaineth of it ye shall ,burn with fire. Why is "until the morning" repeated? Scripture

ו נ ת נ ו ע ל ש ת י ה מ ז ו ז ו ת ו ע ל ה מ ש ק ו ף
שומע אני אם הקדים זה לזה לא יצא ת"ל והגעתם
אל המשקוף ואל שתי המזוזות הא אם הקדים זה
לזה יצא נמצינו למידין ששלשה מזבחות היו
לאבותינו במצרים המשקוף ושתי המזוזות ר'
ישמעאל אומר ארבעה היו הסף והמשקוף ושתי
המזוזות.

ע ל ה ב ת י ם א ש ר י א כ ל ו א ו ת ו ב ה ם א י ן
לי אלא בתים שהיו אוכלין אותו בהם בתים שהיו
ישנים בהם מנין ת"ל על הבתים אשר אתם שם מכל
מקום.

ו א כ ל ו א ת ה ב ש ר בשר ולא גידים ולא
עצמות ולא קרנים ולא טלפים.

ב ל י ל ה ה ז ה שומע אני כל הלילה ת"ל לא
תותירו ממנו עד בוקר אני אקרא והנותר ממנו באש
תשרופו עד בוקר למה נאמר לא בא הכתוב אלא

18—17 שמות י"ב, כ"ב.   26—23 לקמן ז'.   28—27 פסחים פ"ד,
א'. ש. 11.

---

16 ועל המשקוף]=ט. מ"ח: ד. וגו'.   18 ואל שתי המזוזות]
הוספתי עפ"י ט: ד. וגו'/הא אם] מ. שומע אני.   21 ישמעאל]
ד. שמעון.   25 ישנים] מ"ח. ל"ט. יושבים.   30 ממנו 2] ד.~עד
בקר.   31—30 באש תשרופו] א. וגו' מ. באש תשרף.

aims thereby to fix its limit only up to the very break of morning, and what is this? It is the early dawn. Hence, they said: The duty of eating the paschal lamb, eating the sacrifices, and burning the fat and the parts of the sacrifices can be performed up to the rise of dawn. Likewise, all sacrifices that are to be eaten for only one day, can be eaten up to the rise of dawn the next day. Why then have the sages said: "Up to midnight?" To prevent the possibility of a transgression of the law, and to make a fence around the Torah. And thus they fulfilled the words of the men of the Great Synagogue, who had said three things: Be deliberate in judgment raise up many disciples, and make a fence round the Torah.

R. Eliezer says: The word "night" is used here: "And they shall eat the flesh in that night," and the word "night" is also used there: "For I will go through the land of Egypt in that night" (v. 12). Just as there, "night" means not later than midnight, so the word "night" used here also means only up to midnight.

Roast with Fire. But not roast by the heat of the spit, or of the grate, or of the earthen body of the oven.

ליתן תחום לבוקרו של בוקר ואיזה זה זה עמוד
השחר מכאן אמרו אכילת פסחים ואכילת זבחים
והקטר חלבים ואיברים מצותן עד שיעלה עמוד
השחר כל הנאכלין ביום אחד מצותן עד שיעלה
עמוד השחר ולמה אמרו חכמים עד חצות להרחיק
מן העבירה ולעשות סייג לתורה ולקיים דברי אנשי
כנסת הגדולה שהיו אומרים שלשה דברים הוו
מתונין בדין והעמידו תלמידים הרבה ועשו סייג
לתורה ר' אליעזר אומר נאמר כאן לילה ואכלו
את הבשר בלילה הזה ונאמר להלן לילה ועברתי
בארץ מצרים בלילה הזה מה לילה האמור להלן
עד חצות אף כאן עד חצות.

צ ל י א ש ולא צלי שפוד ולא צלי אסכלה ולא
צלי חרסו של תנור.

33 ברכות א', א'. י' שם א', ג' (א3). — 40–38 אבות א', א'.
40–43 לקמן י"ג. ברכות ט', א'. וש"נ. י' שם (א3) ש. 11. — 42 41–42 שמות י"ב,
י"ב. 44–45 פסחים ע"ד. א'. ע"ה, א'–ב'. י' שם ז', ב' (א34).

35

40

45

32 תחום] א. קבע תחום / של בקר] מ"ח. של לילה.
36 להרחיק] ד. ~ אדם. 3 אנשי] א. מ. >. 40 אליעזר] א.
מ"ח. אלעזר. א'א. ש"י. אלעזר בן עזריה. 40–41 ואכלו את הבשר
בלילה הזה] הוספתי עפ"י נ. וא'א. 42–41 ועברתי בארץ מצרים
בלילה הזה] הוספתי עפ"י נ. וא'א. 45 תנור] מ. ד. ~ אלא. מ"ח.
~ אלא צלי אש.

Roast with Fire. This means, roasted raw. You interpret it to mean roasted raw. Perhaps it is not so, but it means roasted after having been boiled? But Scripture says: "But roast with fire" (v. 9). Hence, what must be the meaning of "roast with fire" here? Roasted raw.

Roast with Fire and Unleavened Bread; *with Bitter Herbs They Shall Eat It.* Scripture prescribes in connection with the paschal lamb two additional commandments, besides the one prescribed with regard to its body. And what is the latter? "Neither shall ye break a bone thereof" (v. 46).

Roast with Fire and Unleavened Bread. Scripture tells that the duty regarding the paschal sacrifice consists of eating unleavened bread, roast and bitter herbs. Whence can you prove that when they have no unleavened bread and bitter herbs, they can discharge their obligation by the eating of the paschal lamb alone? From the scriptural passage: "They shall eat it." From this I know only that when they have no unleavened bread and bitter herbs, they can discharge their obligation by the eating of the paschal lamb alone. One might think that just as when they have no unleavened bread and bitter herbs they can discharge their obligation by eating the paschal lamb alone, so also when they have no

צלי אש הצלוי מן החי אתה אומר הצלוי מן
החי או אינו אלא הצלוי מן המבושל ת״ל כי אם
צלי אש הא מה ת״ל צלי אש הצלוי מן החי.

צלי אש ומצות על מרורים יאכלוהו
50 הוסיף לו הכתוב שתי מצות חוץ מן המצוה האמורה
בגופו ואיזה זה זה ועצם לא תשברו בו.

צלי אש ומצות מגיד הכתוב שמצות הפסח
מצה צלי ומרור מנין אתה אומר שאם אין להם מצה
ומרור הן יוצאין ידי חובתן בפסח ת״ל יאכלוהו
55 אין לי אלא בזמן שאין להם מצה ומרור יוצאין
ידי חובתן בפסח יכול כשם שאם אין להם מצה
ומרור יוצאין י״ח בפסח כך אם אין להם פסח

46–48 פסחים מ״א, א׳. 47–48 שמות י״ב, ט׳. 49–51 ספרי במדבר
ס״ט. 52–62 פסחים ק״כ, א׳. תוס׳ שם א׳, ל״ד.

---

46 אש] מ. > / הצלוי] הוספתי עפ״י א״א. נ. (מ״ח. צלי).
47 מן המבושל]=ל.נ.מ״ח:א״א. כמבושל א.מ.ק.נ. במבושל.
49 ומצות על מרורים] ק.נ. על מצות ומרורים (במדבר ט׳, י״א).
51 בגופו] א.נ. כאן בנופו. 52–53 שמצות הפסח-אתה אומר] א. >/
53 מצהו]ק. >/ ומרור] ק.נ. ~ צלי אש ומצות מ. ~ צלי אשה ומצה
מגיד הכתוב שאם אין להם מצה ומרור הן יוצאין ידי חובתן בפסח ת״ל
צלי אש. 55 יוצאין] ק. אין יוצאין. 55–56 אין לי אלא-ידי חובתן
בפסח] נ. מוחקן וחסר ג״כ בספר המצות להרמב״ם עשין נ״ו ובמ״ח.
56 יכול] א.מ. > ט. א״צ. ומנין. 57 כשם שאם-י״ח בפסח]
הוספתי עפ״י סה״מ שם (הוצאת העליר) וספר מעשה נסים (הוצאת ב״נ.
פאריש תרכ״ו) צד 66–57,67 כך אם] ט. א״צ. שאם.

paschal lamb they can discharge their obligation by eating unleavened bread and bitter herbs alone. And one could argue thus: To eat the paschal lamb is a mandatory duty, and to eat unleavened bread and bitter herbs is also a mandatory duty. Now, inasmuch as you have proved that when they have no unleavened bread and bitter herbs they can discharge their obligation by eating the paschal lamb alone, it follows that when they have no paschal lamb they can discharge their obligation by eating unleavened bread and bitter herbs. Against this Scripture says: "They shall eat it."

Another Interpretation. *They Shall Eat It with Unleavened Bread and Bitter Herbs.* On the basis of this passage they said: The paschal lamb alone must be eaten only after one is already satiated[3] but it is not necessary that the unleavened bread and bitter herbs be eaten only after one is already satiated.

Eat Not of It Raw (na). The word *na* simply means raw.

Nor Sodden At All. This condemns eating it either raw or boiled. You interpret it either raw or boiled. Perhaps it merely means to condemn eating it boiled too much? But Scripture says: "But roast with fire." Hence what is the purport of saying: "Nor sodden at all?" To condemn eating it either raw or boiled.

---

[3] The word על, rendered "with", is interpreted here to mean "after" or "following upon."

יוצאין ידי חובתן במצה ומרור הרי אתה דן הואיל

והפסח מצות עשה ומצה ומרור מצות עשה אם

60 למדת שאם אין להם מצה ומרור יוצאין ידי חובתן

בפסח כך אם אין להם פסח יוצאין ידי חובתן

במצה ומרור ת״ל יאכלוהו. דבר אחר על מצות

ומרורים יאכלוהו מכאן אמרו הפסח נאכל אכילת

שובע ואין מצה ומרור נאכלין אכילת שובע.

65 אל תאכלו ממנו נא אין נא אלא חי.

ובשל מבושל לחייב על החי ועל המבושל

אתה אומר לחייב על החי ועל המבושל או אינו

אלא לחייב על המבושל ביותר ת״ל כי אם צלי

אש הא מה ת״ל ובשל מבושל לחייב על החי ועל

70 המבושל.

62—64 פסחים ע׳, א׳. קי״ט, ב׳. 66—82 פסחים מ״א, א׳—ב׳. י׳ שם
ב׳, ז׳ (29b), ז׳, ב׳ (34b), ש. 12.

---

58 יוצאין] נ. ל. אין יוצאין. 62—58 הרי אתה דן-במצה ומרור]
א. מ״ח. >. 59 אם] ד. הא. 60 שאם] ד. כמו שאם. 62 ת״ל
יאכלוהו] נ. ל. >. 66 החי] א׳ צ. הצלי. 67 החי] א׳ צ. הצלי.
68 המבושל] א. ~ ועל החי. 70—68 ביותר-ועל המבושל] א. >.

Nor Sodden at All with Water. From this I know only that it is forbidden to boil it in water. How about boiling it in other liquids? R. Ishmael used to say: You can reason by using the method of *Kal vaḥomer.* If it is forbidden to boil it in water, which has no taste to impart, it is but logical to assume that it should be forbidden to boil it in other liquids, which have a taste of their own to impart. R. Akiba says: From this I know only that it is forbidden to boil it in water. How about boiling it in other liquids? The scriptural expression: "nor sodden at all," includes all other liquids in the prohibition. Rabbi says: It could have read: Eat not of it but roast with fire. What is the purport of saying: "raw nor sodden at all?" For one might think that only during the time when one is under the obligation to eat it roasted is one forbidden to eat it raw or sodden. How about eating it raw or boiled during the day? The expression: "nor sodden at all," teaches that by eating it raw or boiled even during the day one is guilty of violating the law.

And Cooked—(ubashel). The word *bashel* by itself would mean only roast, as when it is said: "And thou shalt roast *(ubishalta)* and eat it" (Deut. 16.7). And it also says: "And they roasted the passover with fire according to the ordinance; and the holy offerings sod they in pots, and in caldrons, and in pans, and carried them quickly to all the children of the people" (II Chr. 35.13). Hence R. Josiah said: If one vows to abstain from eating what is cooked, he is also forbidden to eat roast.

ו ב ש ל מ ב ו ש ל ב מ י ם אין לי אלא מים שאר
כל המשקין מנין היה ר' ישמעאל אומר אמרת קל
וחמר הוא ומה מים שאינן מפיגין את טעמן הרי
הן אסורין בבישול שאר המשקין שהן מפיגין את
75 טעמן דין הוא שיהיו אסורין בבישול ר' עקיבא
אומר אין לי אלא מים שאר כל המשקין מנין ת"ל
ובשל מבושל להביא שאר המשקין רבי אומר אני
אקרא אל תאכלו ממנו כי אם צלי אש ומה ת"ל נא
ובשל מבושל שיכול אין לי אלא בשעה שהוא באכול
80 צלי שהוא בבל תאכל נא ומבושל מבעוד יום מנין
ת"ל ובשל מבושל לחייב עליו מבעוד יום.

ו ב ש ל אין בשל אלא צלי שנאמר ובשלת
ואכלת ואומר ויבשלו את הפסח באש כמשפט
85 והקדשים בשלו בסירות ובדודים ובצלחות ויריצו
לכל בני העם מכאן היה ר' יאשיה אומר הנודר מן
המבושל אסור בצלי.

83–84 דברים ט"ז, ז'.   87–83 מ"ת 92. נדרים מ"ט, א'.   86–84 דה"ב,
ליה, י"ג.

---

79 ממנו] מ. ט. ~ נא מ"ח. ~ נא ובשל / נא] מ"ח. ט. >.
80 ובשל] א. מ. > / מבושלו] א. מ. ומבושל.   81 שהוא בבל
תאכל]=ט. א"א. ג: א. מ. ד. ובשעה שהוא.   84 את] במקרא >.

But Roast with Fire, etc. Why is this said? I might have thought what is fit for boiling one may boil, and only what is fit for roasting should one roast. Therefore Scripture says: "But roast with fire; its head with its legs and with the inwards thereof," i. e., both the inner and the outer parts—these are the words of R. Akiba. R. Eliezer says: It should be barbecued.

Ye Shall Let Nothing of It Remain until the Morning. I might understand that if one let some of it remain until the morning, thus transgressing the commandment, it would still be ritually fit. Therefore Scripture says: "Ye shall let nothing of it remain until the morning; but that which remaineth of it until the morning ye shall burn with fire."

It could have read: But that which remaineth of it, ye shall burn with fire. Why is: "until the morning" repeated? Scripture aims thereby to fix its limit, only up to the very break of morning.

Another Interpretation. What is the purport of the words: "Until the morning?" It is to tell that it was not to be burned before the morning of the sixteenth. R. Ishmael says: Scripture need not tell us this here, for it is said: "No manner of work shall be done in them" (v. 16), and burning is a kind of work. What then is the purport of the words: "Until the morning?" It is merely to tell us that if the sixteenth falls on a Sabbath, it should not be burned before the

כי אם צלי אש וגו' למה נאמר הייתי אומר
הראוי לשלוק ישלוק הראוי לצלות יצלה ת"ל כי
90 אם צלי אש ראשו על כרעיו ועל קרבו תוך ובר
דברי ר' עקיבא ר' אליעזר אומר מקולס.

לא תותירו ממנו עד בקר הא אם הותיר
ועבר על מצוה שומע אני יהיה כשר ת"ל לא תותירו
ממנו עד בקר והנותר ממנו עד בוקר באש תשרופו.

95 אני אקרא והנותר ממנו באש תשרופו עד בוקר
למה נאמר אלא בא הכתוב ליתן תחום לבוקרו
של בוקר דבר אחר מה ת"ל עד בקר מגיד שאינו
נשרף אלא אור ששה עשר רבי ישמעאל אומר אינו
צריך הרי הוא אומר כל מלאכה לא יעשה בהם
100 שריפה מעין מלאכה היא ומה ת"ל עד בקר אלא
אם חל אור ששה עשר להיות בשבת מגיד שאינו

88—91 פסחים ע"ד, א'. י' שם ז', א' (34b) תוס' ביצה ב', ט"ו. ש. שם.
93—98 פסחים פ"ג א', ב'. י' שם ז', ט' (35a). י' שבת ב', א' (4d).
ש. שם. 99 שמות י"ב, ט"ז.

90 ראשו על כרעיו ועל קרבו] הוספתי עפ"י ט. מ"ח: א. מ. וגו'.
91 עקיבא] ט> א"א. אליעזר א"צ. ישמעאל ש. טרפון / אליעזר]
ד. <ט. א"א. עקיבא א"צ. טרפון. 92 לא תותירו] במסקרא ולא
תותירו. 94 והנותר סמנו עד בוקר באש תשרופו] הוספתי: א. וגו'.
95 והנותר סמנו] ד. מ. ~ עד בקר. 96 אלא בא הכתוב] מ"ח. זהו
שאמרנו. 98 אלא] ד. עד. 100 סעין] מ"ח. <. 101 ד. מ"ח. שאם
חל ששה עשר.

morning of the seventeenth. R. Jonathan says: Scripture need not specially tell us this. Even the holiday, though its laws may be disregarded in order to prepare food, cannot be disregarded for the sake of burning the "left-overs" of the sacrifice. Is it not logical then to assume that the Sabbath, the laws of which cannot be disregarded even for the sake of preparing any food at all, should surely not be disregarded in order to burn the "left-overs" of the sacrifice. What then is the purport of the words: "Until the morning?" Scripture aims thereby to fix its limits, only up to the very break of morning. R. Isaac says:[4] Scripture need not tell us this here. Even the unleavened bread, though it is under the prohibition of being seen or found, cannot be burned in disregard of the holiday. Is it not logical then to assume that the "left-overs" of the sacrifice, to which the prohibition of being seen or found does not apply, should surely not be burned in disregard of the holiday. Hence what must be the purport of the words: "Until the morning?" What we have said above.

CHAPTER VII
(Ex. 12.11-14)

And Thus Shall Ye Eat It with Your Loins Girded, etc. Like people starting on a journey. R. Jose the Galilean says: This passage teaches you that according to the Torah it is proper for people starting on a journey to be alert.

---

[4] R. Isaac does not argue against R. Jonathan but against "Another Interpretation."

נשרף אלא אור שבעה עשר ר' יונתן אומר אינו
צריך ומה אם במקום שכל אוכל נפש דוחה את
יום טוב אין שריפת נותר דוחה את יום טוב מקום
105 שאין מקצת אוכל נפש דוחה את השבת אינו דין
שלא תהא שריפת נותר דוחה את השבת ומה ת"ל
עד בקר בא הכתוב ליתן תחום לבוקרו של בקר
ר' יצחק אומר אינו צריך ומה אם חמץ שהוא בבל
יראה ובבל ימצא אין שריפתו דוחה את יום טוב
110 נותר שאינו בבל יראה ובבל ימצא אינו דין שלא
תהא שריפתו דוחה את יום טוב הא מה ת"ל עד
בקר לענין שאמרנו.

פרשה ז (שמות י"ב, י"א,–י"ד.)

וככה תאכלו אותו מתניכם חגורים
וגו' כיוצאי דרכים רבי יוסי הגלילי אומר בא
הכתוב ללמדך דרך ארץ מן התורה על יוצאי
דרכים שיהיו מזורזין.

_____

111–108 לקמן ח'. שבת כ"ד, ב'. פסחים פ"ג, ב' וש"נ.
14–1 ספרי דברים ק"ל. ברכות ט', א'. מ"ת. 91.

_____

102 אלא] ד. ~ עד/ אור] מ. >.
2–1 מתניכם חגורים וגו'] הוספתי: ג. וגו'.   3 דרך ארץ מן התורה]
ג. >.

And Ye Shall Eat It in Haste. This refers to
the bustle of the Egyptians.[1] You interpret it as
referring to the bustle of the Egyptians. Perhaps
this is not so, but it refers to the bustle of the
Israelites? It says, however: "But against any
of the children of Israel shall not a dog whet his
tongue" (Ex. 11.7). The bustle of Israel is
already referred to there.[2] To what then must
I apply: "And ye shall eat it in haste?" To the
bustle of the Egyptians. R. Joshua, the son of
Korḥah says: "And ye shall eat it in haste."
This refers to the bustle of Israel. You interpret
it as referring to the bustle of Israel. Perhaps
it is not so, but it refers to the bustle of the
Egyptians. But it says: "Because they were
thrust out of Egypt and could not tarry" (v. 39).
The bustle of the Egyptians is referred to there.
Hence, what must Scripture refer to by saying:
"And ye shall eat it in haste?" To the bustle of
the Israelites. Abba Ḥanin in the name of R.
Eliezer says: It refers to the haste of the Shekinah.
And though there is no proof for this, there is a
hint of it: "Hark! my beloved! Behold He
cometh,[3] etc. Behold He standeth behind our
wall" (Cant. 2.8-9). One might think that in the
future also the deliverance will be in haste. But
it says: "For ye shall not go out in haste, neither

---

[1] The word בחפזון is interpreted to mean not "in haste"
but, during the confusion and bustle of the Egyptians.

[2] The verse is taken to mean that the dogs will not bark
at the Israelites even though the latter will be in a bustle.

[3] This verse in Song of Songs is interpreted as referring
to God who hastens to deliver Israel (cf. Midrash Cant.

ואכלתם אותו בחפזון זה חפזון מצרים   5

אתה אומר חפזון מצרים או אינו אלא חפזון ישראל

כשהוא אומר ולכל בני ישראל לא יחרץ כלב

לשונו הרי חפזון ישראל אמור הא מה אני מקיים

ואכלתם אותו בחפזון זה חפזון מצרים רבי יהושע

בן קרחה אומר ואכלתם אותו בחפזון זה חפזון   10

ישראל אתה אומר חפזון ישראל או אינו אלא חפזון

מצרים כשהוא אומר כי גורשו ממצרים ולא יכלו

להתמהמה הרי חפזון מצרים אמור הא מה תלמוד

לומר ואכלתם אותו בחפזון זה חפזון ישראל אבא

חנין אומר משום רבי אליעזר זה חפזון שכינה אף   15

על פי שאין ראיה לדבר זכר לדבר קול דודי הנה

זה בא וגו' ואומר הנה זה עומד אחר כתלנו יכול

אף לעתיד לבא יהיה בחפזון תלמוד לומר. כי לא

8—7 שמות י"א, ז'.   13—12 שמות י"ב, ל"ט.   16—17 שה"ש ב' ח'—ט'.

20—18 ישעיה נ"ב י"ב. שמו"ר י"ט, ו'. מ"ת שם.

---

8 מה אני מקיים] א. מ. מה ת"ל.   10 בן קרחה] ד. <.   12—13 ולא

יכלו להתמהמה] הוספתי עפ"י א"צ.   15 חנין] ד. חנן/ אליעזר] ד.

אלעזר.   17—18 יכול אף] א. מ. ואף.   18 ת"ל] ד. שנאמר.

Rab., *Sidra Tinyana* to II.8–9; on the term זכר לדבר see
above, chap. II, note 3).

shall ye go by flight; for the Lord will go before you" (Isa. 52.12).

It Is the Lord's Passover. All work done in connection with it should be in the name of Heaven.

For I Will Go Through the Land of Egypt. R. Judah says: Like a king who passes from one place to another. Another interpretation. I shall put My wrath[4] and My terror in Egypt. For the word *'ebrah* means only anger, as in the passage: "He sent forth upon them the fierceness of His anger, wrath and indignation and trouble" (Ps. 78.49). And it also says: "That day is a day of wrath" (Zeph. 1.15). And it also says: "Behold the day of the Lord cometh, cruel, and full of wrath and fierce anger" (Isa. 13.9).

And Will Smite. I might understand this to mean, through an angel or through an agent. But it says: "that the Lord smote all the first-born" (v. 29)—not through an angel nor through an agent.

And Will Smite All the First-Born in the Land of Egypt. Even those who hailed from other places. And how about Egyptian first-born who were in other places? Scripture says: "To Him that smote Egypt in their first-born" (Ps.

---

[4] The Hebrew word ועברתי is interpreted as if it read "*ve'ebrati*," meaning, "and My anger."

בחפזון תצאו ובמנוסה לא תלכון כי הולך לפניכם

20 יי וגו'.

פ ס ח ה ו א ל י י שיהו כל מעשיו לשם שמים.

ו ע ב ר ת י ב א ר ץ מ צ ר י ם רבי יהודה אומר

כמלך שהוא עובר ממקום למקום דבר אחר נותן

אני עברתי ויראתי במצרים אין עברה אלא זעם

25 שנאמר ישלח בם חרון אפו עברה וזעם וצרה ואומר

יום עברה היום ההוא וגו' ואומר הנה יום יי בא

אכזרי ועברה וחרון אף וגו'.

ו ה כ ת י שומע אני על ידי מלאך או על ידי

שליח תלמוד לומר ויי הכה כל בכור לא על ידי

30 מלאך ולא על ידי שליח.

ו ה כ ת י כ ל ב כ ו ר ב א ר ץ מ צ ר י ם אפילו

ממקומות אחרים ובכורי מצרים שהן במקומות

אחרים מנין תלמוד לומר למכה מצרים בבכוריהם

---

21 ספרי דברים קכ"ח.   23—22 לקטן י"א. ש. 13.   25 תהלים ע"ח,
מ"ט.   26 צפניה א', ט"ו.   27—26 ישעיה י"ג, ט'.   29 שמות י"ב,
כ"ט. לקמן י"ג.   35—31 ש.   33 תהלים קל"ו, י'.

---

21 מעשיו] ק. נ. מעשיהם / שמים] א"צ. פסח ק. נ. ~ ונוטר.
23 כמלך] מ"ח. כאדם.   24 ויראתי] ד. >.   25—26 ואומר יום עברה
היום ההוא] ד. >.   26 יי] ד. >.   27 אף] ד. ואף.   28 מלאך]
א. המלאך מ. המלך.   31 בארץ מצרים] הוספתי—ט.   32 ממקומות
ק. במקומות / במקומות] א. ממקומות.

136.10). And how about the first-born of Ham, Cush, Put and Lud?[5] Scripture says: "And smote all the first-born in Egypt, the first-fruits of their strength in the tents of Ham" (Ps. 78.51).

Both Man and Beast. He who was first to sin was also the first to be punished. In like manner you must interpret: "And blotted out every living substance . . . both man and cattle" (Gen. 7.23). He who was first to sin was also the first to be punished. In like manner you must interpret: "And they smote the men that were at the door of the house with blindness, both small and great" (Gen. 19.11). He who was first to sin was also the first to be punished. In like manner you must interpret: "And I will get Me honor upon Pharaoh and upon all his host" (Ex. 14.4). He who was first to sin was also the first to be punished. In like manner you must interpret: "Thou shalt surely smite the inhabitants of that city . . . and the cattle thereof" (Deut. 13.16). He who was first to sin was also the first to be punished. In like manner you must interpret: "And her belly shall swell," etc. (Num. 5.27). That part of the body which was first to sin was also the first to be punished. And so also here you interpret: "And will smite all the first-born in the land of Egypt, both man and beast." He who was first to sin was also the first to be punished. Now, by using the method of *Kal vaḥomer*, you reason: If with regard to

---

[5] Lud here refers not to Lud the son of Shem (Gen. 10.11) but to the Ludim who like Cush and Put were descendants of Ham (ibid. vv. 6 and 13).

ובכורי חם וכוש ופוט ולוד מנין ת״ל ויך כל בכור

במצרים ראשית אונים באהלי חם.   35

מ א ד ם   ו ע ד   ב ה מ ה   מי שהתחיל בעבירה
תחלה ממנו התחילה הפורענות כיוצא בדבר אתה
אומר וימח את כל היקום וגו׳ מי שהתחיל בעבירה
תחלה ממנו התחילה הפורענות כיוצא בדבר אתה

אומר ואת האנשים אשר פתח הבית הכו בסנורים   40
וגו׳ מי שהתחיל בעבירה תחלה ממנו התחילה
הפורענות כיוצא בדבר אתה אומר ואכבדה
בפרעה ובכל חילו וגו׳ מי שהתחיל בעבירה
תחלה וגו׳ כיוצא בדבר אתה אומר הכה תכה וגו׳

מי שהתחיל בעבירה וגו׳ כיוצא בדבר אתה אומר   45
וצבתה בטנה וגו׳ אבר שהתחיל בעבירה וגו׳ אף
כאן אתה אומר והכתי כל בכור וגו׳ מי שהתחיל
בעבירה וגו׳ והרי הדברים קל וחמר ומה אם מדת

35—34 שם ע״ח, נ״א.   50—36 לקמן בשלח ב׳. ספרי במדבר י״ח.
חוס׳ סוטה ד׳, י׳—ט׳ו.   38 בראשית ז׳, כ״ג.   40 שם י״ט, י״א.
43—42 שמות י״ד, י״ז.   44 דברים י״ג, ט״ו.   46 במדבר ה׳, כ״ז. סוטה
ט׳, ב׳. י׳ שם א׳, ז׳ (17ª).

39—37 כיוצא בדבר–הפורענות] א. >.   42—39 כיוצא בדבר–
הפורענות] ד. >.

meting out evil, which is of less importance, the rule is that he who sins first is first punished, how much more should this be the rule with regard to meting out good which is of greater importance!

And Against All the Gods of Egypt I Will Execute Judgments: I Am the Lord. Judgments differing one from the other. The stone idols melted, the wooden ones rotted away, the metal ones corroded, as it is said: "While the Egyptians were burying," etc. (Num. 33.4). Some say: Those of stone rotted away and those of wood melted. R. Nathan says: Judgments—not one, not two, but four judgments.[6] They became soft, they became hollow, they were chopped down, they were burned. We thus learn that the idols were smitten in four ways, and those who worshiped them in three ways, by affliction, by injury, and by plague.

I Am the Lord. What flesh and blood cannot say.

I Am the Lord. I affirm under oath that I shall exact punishment from them. Now, by using the method of *Kal vaḥomer*, you reason: If with regard to meting out evil, which is of less importance, the Holy One, blessed be He, acts when He says that He will act, how much more is it so with regard to meting out good, which is of greater importance.

---

[6] See Introduction and comp. commentaries.

הפורענות מעוטה מי שהתחיל בעבירה לוקה תחלה
קל וחומר למדת הטוב שמרובה.

וּבְכָל אֱלֹהֵי מִצְרַיִם אֶעֱשֶׂה שְׁפָטִים
אֲנִי יְיָ שפטים משונים זה מזה של אבן היתה נמסת
של עץ היתה נרקבת של מתכת נעשת חלודה
שנאמר ומצרים מקברים וגו' ויש אומרים של אבן
היתה נרקבת של עץ נימסת רבי נתן אומר שפטים
שפוט שופטי שפטים נרככים נבקקים נגדעים
נשרפים נמצינו למידין שעבודה זרה לוקה בארבעה
דרכים ועובדיה בשלשה במכה ובהשחתה ובמגפה.

אֲנִי יְיָ מה שאי איפשר לבשר ודם לומר כן.

אֲנִי יְיָ בשבועה אני נפרע מהם והרי הדברים
קל וחומר ומה אם מידת הפורענות מעוטה אמר
הקב״ה לעשות ועשה מידת הטובה שמרובה על
אחת כמה וכמה.

51—52 ש. שם.   54 במדבר ל׳נ, ד׳.

---

52 של אבן] ד. צלם של אבן / היתה נמסת] ד. היה ניתוח.
53 חלודה] ק. מ. חררה נ. חרדה.   55 שפוט] ש״ט. שפט ט. מ׳ח.
ש׳י. </ שופטי] מ׳ח. שפטי ט. ושפטי/ שפטים מ. שופטים/ נרככים]
א. ד. נרקבים.   59 שאי איפשר] מ. שאיפשר.   60 בשבועה]
א׳צ. בשמי.

And the Blood Shall Be to You for a Token. A sign to you and not to Me, a sign to you and not to others.

Upon the Houses. Why is this said? Has it not already been said: "Upon the houses wherein they shall eat it?" From the latter I know only about the houses in which they ate it. But how do I know about the houses in which they dwelled? It says here: "Upon the houses where ye are," no matter for what purposes you are there.

And When I See the Blood. R. Ishmael used to say: Is not everything revealed before Him, as it is said: "He knoweth what is in the darkness and the light dwelleth with Him" (Dan. 2.22)? And it also says: "Even the darkness is not too dark for Thee," etc. (Ps. 139.12). What then is the purport of the words: "And when I see the blood?" It is only this: As a reward for your performing this duty I shall reveal Myself and protect you, as it is said: "And I will pass over you". Passing over merely means protecting, as it is said: "As birds hovering, so will the Lord of Hosts protect Jerusalem; He will deliver it, as He protecteth it, He will rescue it, as He passeth over" (Isa. 31.5).

והיה הדם לכם לאות לכם לאות ולא לי

לאות לכם ולא לאחרים לאות. 65

על הבתים למה נאמר והלא כבר נאמר על
הבתים אשר יאכלו אותו בהם אין לי אלא בתים
שהן אוכלים אותו בהם בתים שהן יושבים בהם
מנין ת״ל על הבתים אשר אתם שם מכל מקום.

וראיתי את הדם היה רבי ישמעאל אומר 70
והלא הכל גלוי לפניו שנאמר ידע מה בחשוכא
ונהורא עמה שרא ואומר גם חשך לא יחשיך ממך
וגו׳ ומה ת״ל וראיתי את הדם אלא בשכר מצוה
שאתם עושים אני נגלה וחס עליכם שנאמר ופסחתי
עליכם אין פסיחה אלא חיים שנאמר כצפרים 75
עפות כן יגן יי צבאות על ירושלם גנון והציל פסוח
והמליט.

64–65 לעיל ו׳. לקמן י״א. 67–66 שמות י״ב, ז׳. 82–70 לקמן י״א.
72–71 דניאל ב׳, כ״ב. 72 תהלים קל״ט, י״ב. 75–77 ישעיה ל״א, ה׳.

66 והלא כבר נאמר] מ״ח. לפי שנאמר. 67–66 על הבתים] א. ועל
הבתים. 68 יושבים] ט. מ״ח. א״א. ישנים. 69 על הבתים] א. ועל
הבתים ק. נ. סן הבתים. 71 בחשוכא] מ. ק. נ. בחשוכה. 72 עמה
שרא] ק. נ. עמיה שריה. 73 מצוה] א. ט. ~ אחת. 75 חיים] ט.
מ״ח. חסות.

And When I See the Blood. I see the blood of
the sacrifice of Isaac.[7] For it is said: "And
Abraham called the name of that place Adonai-
jireh" (The lord will see), etc. (Gen. 22.14).
Likewise it says in another passage: "And as He
was about to destroy, the Lord beheld and He
repented Him," etc. (I. Chr. 21.15). What did He
behold? He beheld the blood of the sacrifice of
Isaac, as it is said: "God will Himself see the
lamb," etc. (Gen. 22.8).

I Will Pass Over You. R. Josiah says: Do
not read *ufasaḥti* (I will protect) but *ufasa'ti*
(I will step over). God skipped over the houses
of His children in Egypt, as it is said: "Hark!
my beloved! behold, He cometh leaping upon the
mountains," and it continues: "Behold, He
standeth behind our wall," etc. (Cant. 2.8–9).
R. Jonathan says: "I will pass over you." This
means, you alone will I protect but I will not
protect Egyptians. Suppose an Egyptian was in
the house of an Israelite. I might understand
that he also would be saved on account of the
Israelite. Therefore it says: "I will pass over

---

[7] I. e., the readiness of Isaac to give his blood as a
sacrifice, for actually no blood of Isaac was offered in
sacrifice and according to Gen. Rab. on Gen. 22.12,
Abraham was not allowed to shed even one drop of Isaac's
blood. It is, however, possible that our *Mekilta* here
follows R. Joshua according to whom, one-fourth of a
log, רביעית, of Isaac's blood was actually offered upon the
altar. See *Mekilta d. R. Simon b. Yoḥai*, ed. Hoffmann,
p. 4. Comp. also Joshua Finkel: "Old Israelitish Traditions in the Koran," in *Proceed. Amer. Acad. for Jew. Res.*

וראיתי את הדם רואה אני דם עקידתו של

יצחק שנאמר ויקרא אברהם שם המקום ההוא יי

80 יראה וגו' ולהלן הוא אומר ובהשחית ראה יי וינחם

וגו' מה ראה ראה דם עקידתו של יצחק שנאמר

אלהים יראה לו השה וגו'.

ופסחתי עליכם ר' יאשיה אומר אל תקרי

ופסחתי אלא ופסעתי שהמקום מדלג על בתי בניו

85 במצרים שנאמר קול דודי הנה זה בא מדלג על

ההרים ואומר הנה זה עומד אחר כתלנו וגו' ר'

יונתן אומר ופסחתי עליכם עליכם אני חס

ואיני חס על מצרים הרי שהיה מצרי בתוך ביתו

של ישראל שומע אני ינצל בנינו ת"ל ופסחתי עליכם

79–80 בראשית כ'ב, י'ד.   80 דהי'א. כ'א, ט'ו.   82 בראשית כ'ב,
ח'.   85–86 שה'ש ב', ח'–ט'.

78 מ"ח. ד'א וראיתי את הדם / רואה אני] ט. דבר אחר.
79 מ. את שם המקום.   80 ובהשחית] במקרא וכהשחית מ. וכשהשחית
יי בעם.   81–82 שנאמר–השה וגו'] ד. <.   84 בניו] ד. בני ישראל.
89 בנינו] א. סבנינו של ישראל ד. <.

(1931), p. 20. Likewise: "God will Himself see the lamb
for the sacrifice" (Gen. 22.5), is interpreted to mean: God
will see that Isaac was ready to be the lamb for the sacrifice. Comp. however, Gen. Rab. on Gen. 22.13.

you," you alone will I protect, but I will not protect Egyptians. Suppose an Israelite was in the house of an Egyptian. I might understand that he would also be smitten because of the Egyptian. But it says: "And there shall no plague be upon you to destroy you, when I smite the land of Egypt."

Another Interpretation: When I smite the land of Egypt, there will be no plague upon you, but there will be at some future time.

And this Day Shall Be unto You for a Memorial, and Ye Shall Keep it a Feast, etc. You must keep as a feast the day which is a memorial to you. But we have not learned which day it is. Even when it says: "And Moses said unto the people: Remember this day, in which ye came out from Egypt" (Ex. 13.3), it still remains undecided. But it says: "And they journeyed from Raamses in the first month, on the fifteenth day of the first month; on the morrow after the passover the children of Israel went out with a high hand" (Num. 33.3). When did the Israelites eat the passover? On the night of the holiday. Hence they did not go out until the very day of the holiday.

And Ye Shall Keep It a Feast to the Lord. From this I know only that the first day of the festival requires a festal offering. How about the last day of the festival? Scripture says: "Six

עליכם אני חס ואיני חס על המצרים הרי שהיה 90
ישראל בתוך ביתו של מצרי שומע אני ילקה בגללו
ת"ל ולא יהיה בכם נגף למשחית בהכתי בארץ
מצרים בכם אינו הווה אבל הווה במצרים דבר
אחר בהכותי בארץ מצרים אינו הווה אבל הווה
לאחר זמן. 95

והיה היום הזה לכם לזכרון וחגתם
וגו' יום שהוא לך לזכרון אתה חוגגו אבל לא שמענו
איזה יום הוא כשהוא אומר ויאמר משה אל העם
זכור את היום הזה אשר יצאתם ממצרים וגו' עדיין
הדבר שקול כשהוא אומר ויסעו מרעמסס בחדש 100
הראשון בחמשה עשר יום לחדש הראשון ממחרת
הפסח יצאו בני ישראל ביד רמה אימתי אכלו
ישראל את הפסח בלילי יום טוב והם לא יצאו
אלא ביום טוב עצמו.

104—96 ש. 14.   98—99 שמות י"ג, נ'.   100—102 במדבר ל"נ, נ'.
102—104 לקמן ט'. ספרי דברים קכ"ח.

91 בגללו] א. מ. סביניו ט. בינינו מ"ח. סבינו.   93—94 דבר
אחר] ט.>.   100 בלילי יום טוב] א. בלילי טוב [אולי צ"ל בליל י
טוב] בדפוסי ווילנא ולעמבערג הגיהו בליל יום טוב.

days thou shalt eat unleavened bread; and on the seventh day shall be a solemn assembly to the Lord thy God" (Deut. 16.8). Now I know that both the first day of the festival and the last one require a festal offering. How about the intervening days of the festival? Behold, you reason thus: Since the first day and the last day of the festival are called "Holy Convocation," and the intervening days of the festival are likewise called "Holy Convocation," it is but logical, inasmuch as you have proved that the first and last day of the festival, which are called "Holy Convocation," require a festal offering, to assume that the intervening days, which are also called "Holy Convocation," should likewise require a festal offering. Furthermore, it can be argued by using the method of Kal vaḥomer: If the first and last days of the festival, neither one of which is both preceded and followed by holy days, require a festal offering, is it not but logical to assume that the intervening days, being both preceded and followed by holy days, should all the more require a festal offering? Another way: If the first and last days, neither one of which is both preceded and followed by days requiring a festal offering, require a festal offering, is it not but logical to assume that the intervening days, which are both preceded and followed by days requiring a festal offering, should themselves require a festal offering? R. Jose the Galilean says: Behold it says:

וחגותם אותו חג ליי אין לי אלא יום טוב 105
ראשון שהוא טעון חגיגה יום טוב האחרון מנין ת"ל
ששת ימים תאכל מצות וביום השביעי עצרת ליי
אלהיך אין לי אלא יום טוב ראשון ואחרון שהם
טעונין חגיגה חולו של מועד מנין הרי אתה דן הואיל
ויום טוב ראשון ואחרון קרואין מקרא קדש וחולו 110
של מועד קרוי מקרא קדש אם למדת על יום טוב
הראשון והאחרון שהן קרואין מקרא קדש הרי הן
טעונין חגיגה חולו של מועד שהוא קרוי מקרא קדש
דין הוא שיטען חגיגה ועוד קל וחומר ומה אם יום
טוב הראשון והאחרון שאין לפניהם ולאחריהם 115
מקודשין הרי הן טעונין חגיגה חולו של מועד
שמקודש לפניו ולאחריו דין הוא שיטען חגיגה דבר
אחר אם יום טוב הראשון והאחרון שאין לפניהם
ולאחריהם טעונין חגיגה הרי הן טעונין חגיגה
חולו של מועד שלפניו ואחריו טעון חגיגה דין 120
הוא שיטען חגיגה ר' יוסי הגלילי אומר הרי הוא

"Seven days shalt thou keep a feast unto the Lord thy God" (Deut. 16.15). This includes the seven days of the passover festival, indicating that they all require a festal offering. Perhaps this passage refers only to the feast of Tabernacles. But when it says: "And ye shall keep it a feast (ḥag) to the Lord," the festal offerings for the feast of Tabernacles are already prescribed. What then must be the purport of the words: "Seven days shalt thou keep a feast unto the Lord thy God?" It must be to include the seven days of the passover festival, indicating that they all require festal offerings.

Throughout Your Generations. This means that this practice should obtain for all generations. But I might understand "throughout your generations" to mean, the minimum number of generations, i. e., two generations. Scripture, therefore, says: Ye shall keep it a feast by an ordinance forever.

CHAPTER VIII
(Ex. 12.15)

Seven Days Shall Ye Eat Unleavened Bread. I might understand this to mean, unleavened bread of any kind. But it says: "Thou shalt eat no leavened bread with it" (Deut. 16.3). The law, then, applies only to such kinds as could be leavened as well as unleavened. And which are those that can be leavened as well as unleavened? They are the five species, namely, wheat, barley, spelt, oats, and rye. Rice, millet, poppyseed,

אומר שבעת ימים תחוג ליי אלהיך להביא שבעת
ימי הפסח שיטענו חגיגה או אינו מדבר אלא בחג
כשהוא אומר וחגותם אותו חג ליי הרי חג אמור
125 ומה תלמוד לומר שבעת ימים תחוג ליי להביא
שבעת ימי הפסח שיטענו חגיגה.

לדורותיכם שינהוג הדבר לדורות או
לדורותיכם שומע אני מיעוט דורות שנים
תלמוד לומר חקת עולם תחגהו.

פרשה ח (שמות י״ב, ט״ו.)

שבעת ימים מצות תאכלו שומע אני כל
מצה במשמע ת״ל לא תאכל עליו חמץ לא אמרתי
אלא בדבר שהוא בא לידי מצה וחמץ ואיזה דבר
שהוא בא לידי מצה וחמץ אלו חמשת המינים ואלו
5 הן החטים והשעורים והכוסמים ושבולת שועל
והשיפון יצאו האורז והדוחן והפרגים והשומשמין

---

122 דברים ט״ז, ט״ו. 127 לקטן שבתא א׳. ספרי במדבר ס״ט וק״ט.
ב״ב ק״כ, א׳.

3–1 לקטן י׳ וי״ז. ספרי במדבר ק״י וקס״ו. פסחים ל״ה, א׳. י׳ שם ב׳,
ד׳ (29b). י׳ חלה א׳, א׳ (57a). 2 דברים ט״ז, ג׳.

---

125 ומה ת״ל] ד. ומה אני מקיים.
2 במשמע] ק. כמשמעו.

sesame and legumes, which cannot be leavened as well as unleavened, but which decay, are thus excluded.

Seven Days Shall Ye Eat Unleavened Bread. I might understand this to mean even such as is prepared in a pot.[1] Therefore Scripture says: "even the bread of affliction" (ibid.).

Seven Days Shall Ye Eat Unleavened Bread. Seven days, including the first day of the festival. You interpret it to mean including the first day of the festival. Perhaps this is not so, but it means exclusive of the first day of the festival? But Scripture says: "until the one and twentieth day of the month" (v. 18). Perhaps, however, "until the one and twentieth day of the month," means to exclude the day next to the twentieth. But Scripture says: "Seven days."

Seven Days Shall Ye Eat Unleavened Bread. That is, it is obligatory to eat unleavened bread the first day only, but the remaining days it is optional. You interpret it to mean that it is obligatory the first day only but on the remaining days it is optional. Perhaps this is not so, but it means, to make it optional for the first day and obligatory for the remaining days? The scriptural passage: "In the first month, on the fourteenth day of the month at even, ye shall eat unleavened bread," however, fixes it as an obligation for the first day. Hence, it is impossible for you to argue as in the latter statement,

---

[1] I. e., richly prepared, like pudding.

והקטניות שאינן באין לידי מצה וחמץ אלא לידי
סירחון.

שבעת ימים מצות תאכלו שומע אני אף
10 מעשה קדרה במשמע תלמוד לומר לחם עוני.

שבעת ימים מצות תאכלו עם יום טוב
הראשון אתה אומר עם יום טוב הראשון או אינו
אלא חוץ ליום טוב הראשון ת״ל עד יום האחד
ועשרים לחדש אי עד יום האחד ועשרים אוציא
15 סמוך לעשרים תלמוד לומר שבעת ימים.

שבעת ימים מצות תאכלו לעשות
הראשון חובה ושאר הימים רשות אתה אומר לעשות
הראשון חובה ושאר הימים רשות או אינו אלא
לעשות הראשון רשות ושאר הימים חובה תלמוד
20 לומר בראשון בארבעה עשר יום לחדש קבעו
הכתוב חובה הא אין עליך לומר בלשון אחרון

---

10 דברים שם, לקמן י׳. פסחים ל״ז, ב׳. מ״א, א׳. תוס׳ שם א׳, ל״א–ל״ב.
11–15 י׳ פסחים א׳, א׳ (27ᵇ).   14–13 שמות י״ב, י״ח.   15 לקמן י׳ וי״ו.
20 שמות י״ב, י״ח.

10 עוני] א. מ. נ. ל. >.   11 מ. שבעת ימים תאכלו מצות.
15 סמוך לעשרים] א׳צ. יום אחד ועשרים. מ״ח והר״ר״ס בש״י
סמוך לעשרים ואחד.   16 שבעת ימים מצות תאכלו] הגהתי עפ״י
מ״ח. ומ״ה.

but you must say as in the former: It means to
make it obligatory for the first day and optional
for the remaining days.

Seven Days Shall Ye Eat Unleavened Bread.
One scriptural passage says: "Seven days shall
ye eat unleavened bread," and one passage says:
"Six days thou shalt eat unleavened bread"
(Deut. 16.8). How can both these passages be
maintained? The seventh day had been included
in the more inclusive statement and then was
taken out of it. Now, that which is singled out
from a more inclusive statement means to teach
us something about that whole statement,[2]
Hence, just as on the seventh day it is optional,
so on all the other days it is optional. May it not
be that just as on the seventh day it is optional,
so on all the rest, including even the first night,
it is optional? The scriptural passage: "In the
first month, on the fourteenth day of the month,
at even ye shall eat unleavened bread," fixes it
as an obligation to eat unleavened bread on the
first night. It is therefore impossible for you to
argue as in the latter version, but you must
argue as in the former version: The seventh day
had been included in the more inclusive statement and then was taken out of it. Now that
which is singled out from a more inclusive statement means to teach us something about that

---

[2] See rule 8 of the Thirteen Rules of R. Ishmael (*JE*,
X, 512). The general or more inclusive statement here
(Ex. 12.15) speaks of seven days. The statement, "Six
days," etc. (Deut. 16.8), however, excludes the seventh
day. This statement could not have meant to change the
law from seven days to six, thus entirely eliminating the

אלא בלשון ראשון לעשות הראשון חובה ושאר
הימים רשות.

שבעת ימים מצות תאכלו כתוב אחד
אומר שבעת ימים מצות תאכלו וכתוב אחד אומר
ששת ימים תאכל מצות כיצד יתקיימו שני מקראות
הללו השביעי היה בכלל ויצא מוצא מן הכלל
ללמד על הכלל מה שביעי רשות אף כולם רשות
או מה השביעי רשות אף לילה הראשון רשות
תלמוד לומר בראשון בארבעה עשר יום לחדש
בערב תאכלו מצות קבעו. הכתוב חובה הא אין
עליך לומר בלשון אחרון אלא בלשון ראשון
השביעי היה בכלל ויצא מוצא מן הכלל ללמד

24—34 לקמן י׳ז. ספרא אמור י״א. פסחים ק׳כ, א׳. מדרש תנאים 92.
25 דברים ט׳ז, ח׳. 31—30 שמות שם. פסחים כ׳ח, ב׳.

27 היה בכלל] ד. הזה בכלל היה / מוצא] א. מ״ח. <.
28 כולם] ד. כל. 30 יום לחדש] א. <. 31 בערב] מ. ק.
נ. < ל. וו׳/. תאכלו מצות] הוספתי.

seventh day, for then the Torah would contradict itself.
It evidently only meant to exclude the seventh day from
being obligatory and to make it merely optional. But it
must have meant more than this, according to rule 8 of
R. Ishmael. It meant to imply that like the seventh day
all the others—excepting the first day, which has been
specified as obligatory—are also merely optional.

whole statement, that is, just as on the seventh
day it is optional, so on all the other days it is
optional.

Another Interpretation: One scriptural passage
says six, and one says seven. How can both
these two passages be maintained? Six days if
it is from the new crop and seven days if it is
from the old crop.[3]

*Howbeit, the First Day Ye Shall Put Away
Leaven Out of Your Houses.* This means, on the day
preceding the holiday. You interpret it to mean
on the day preceding the holiday. Perhaps this
is not so, but it means on the first day of the
festival itself. But Scripture says: "Thou shalt
not offer the blood of My sacrifice with leavened
bread" (Ex. 34.25), meaning, thou shalt not
slaughter the paschal lamb while leaven is still
around[4]—these are the words of R. Ishmael.
R. Jonathan says: There is no need of this proof.
It has already been said: "No manner of work
shall be done in them" (v. 16), and burning is a
kind of work.[5] Hence what must the passage:
"Ye shall put away leaven out of your houses,"
apply to? To the day preceding the holiday. R.

---

[3] Before the *Omer*, or the first sheaf of barley, was
offered, the new crop was forbidden to be eaten (Lev.
23.14). The offering of the *Omer* took place "on the
morrow after the sabbath" (ibid. v. 11), which, according
to the Rabbis, means, the morrow after the first day of
the passover festival. Hence, the unleavened bread for
the first day of the passover festival had to be prepared
from the old crop, while for the remaining six days it
could be prepared from either the old or the new crop.

על הכלל מה שביעי רשות אף כולם רשות. דבר
35 אחר כתוב אחד אומר ששה וכתוב אחד אומר
שבעה כיצד יתקיימו שני כתובים הללו ששה מן
החדש ושבעה מן הישן.

אך ביום הראשון וגו' מערב יום טוב אתה
אומר מערב יום טוב או אינו אלא ביום טוב עצמו
40 ת"ל לא תשחט על חמץ דם זבחי לא תשחט את
הפסח ועדיין חמץ קיים דברי רבי ישמעאל רבי
יונתן אומר אינו צריך והלא כבר נאמר כל מלאכה
לא יעשה בהם מעין מלאכה היא הא מה
ת"ל תשביתו שאור מבתיכם מערב יום טוב רבי

37—34 לקמן י"ו. ספרי דברים קל"ד. מנחות ס"ו, א'. י' פסחים ו',
א' (33ᵃ).   47—38 פסחים ה', א'.   40 שמות ל"ד, כ"ה. לקמן כספא ד'.
43—42 שמות י"ב, מ"ו. ש. 15.   61—42 פסחים כ"ז, ב'. י' שם ב' א' (28ᵈ),
ש. שם.

---

36 כתובים] ד. מקראות.   41 ועדיין חמץ] א. מ. ט. וחמץ.
42 יונתן] א"צ. עקיבא/ כל] א. וכל.   46—44 ר' יוסי הגלילי–מבערב
יו'ט] א. ט. <.

---

[4] The paschal lamb was slaughtered on the fourteenth day in the afternoon; hence the leaven had to be removed previously on that day.

[5] "Putting away the leaven," was understood to mean, "burning it," which could not be done on the day of the festival.

Jose the Galilean says: "Ye shall put away leaven out of your houses," that is on the day preceding the holiday. You interpret it to mean on the day preceding the holiday. Perhaps this is not so, but it means on the first day of the festival itself? Against this Scripture says: "But (ak) on the day," thus dividing the day.[6]

R. Jose says: "Ye shall put away leaven out of your houses." This means by burning it. You interpret it to mean by burning. Perhaps this is not so, but it means in any way at all? Behold, you must reason thus: That which is left over of the sacrifice may not be eaten, and leaven may not be eaten.[7] Now, then, if, as you have learned, the "left-overs" of the sacrifice must be destroyed only by burning,[8] then leaven likewise must be destroyed only by burning. But the law regarding a carcass would disprove this. For a carcass may not be eaten, and yet need not be burned; this should prove that leaven, likewise, though it may not be eaten need not necessarily be burned. But you must say, there is a difference. The "left-overs" of the sacrifice are forbidden for any use at all, and leaven, likewise, is forbidden for any use at all. Now, then, if, as you have learned, the "left-overs" of the sacrifice must be destroyed only by burning, then leaven, likewise, should be destroyed only by burning. But the law regarding the stoned ox would disprove this. For the stoned

_____

[6] The word אך, "but," according to the Rabbis, implies a limitation. In this case then "the day" is limited to mean only part of the day. Hence, it can refer only to

45 יוסי הגלילי אומר תשביתו שאור מבתיכם מבערב

יום טוב אתה אומר מערב יום טוב או אינו אלא

ביום טוב עצמו ת״ל אך ביום חלק רבי יוסי אומר

תשביתו שאור מבתיכם בשריפה אתה אומר

בשריפה או אינו אלא בכל דבר הרי אתה דן נותר

50 אסור באכילה וחמץ אסור באכילה אם למדת על

נותר שאינו אלא בשריפה אף חמץ לא יהיה אלא

בשריפה הרי נבילה תוכיח שהיא אסורה באכילה

ואינה בשריפה היא תוכיח על חמץ אף על פי שהוא

אסור באכילה לא יהיה בשריפה אמרת הפרש

55 נותר אסור בהנאה וחמץ אסור בהנאה אם

למדת על נותר שאינו אלא בשריפה אף חמץ לא

יהיה אלא בשריפה והרי שור הנסקל יוכיח שהוא

---

47 אך ביום] מ. ד. אך. / יוסי] ט. מ״ח. א׳צ. יהודה.

50 וחמץ אסור באכילה] ד. ~ מה נותר בשריפה אף חמץ בשריפה.

57—62 והרי שור הנסקל—לא יהא אלא בשריפה] מ. >.

---

the day preceding the holiday, for on the Holiday itself
the leaven must be out of the house all of the day and not
merely part of it.

⁷ I. e., during the time of the passover festival.

⁸ See Lev. 7.17.

ox is likewise forbidden for any use at all and
yet need not be burned; this should prove that
leaven likewise, even though it is forbidden for
any use at all, need not necessarily be burned.
But you must say, there is a difference. The
"left-overs" of the sacrifice are forbidden to be
eaten under the penalty of extermination, and
leaven is also forbidden to be eaten under the
penalty of extermination. Now, then, if as you
have learned, the "left-overs" of the sacrifice
must be destroyed only by burning, then leaven,
likewise, should be destroyed only by burning.
But the law regarding the tallow of the stoned ox
would disprove this. For the tallow, likewise, is
forbidden to be eaten under the penalty of
extermination, and yet need not be burned; this
should prove that leaven, likewise, even though
it is forbidden to be eaten under the penalty of
extermination need not necessarily be burned.
You must say, I can judge one case which has
four qualifications from another which has the
same four qualifications. That which is left over
of the sacrifice may not be eaten, may not be
used at all, can make one incur the penalty of
extermination, and it is all conditioned by the
element of time. Leaven, likewise, may not be
eaten, may not be used at all, can make one incur
the penalty of extermination, and it is all conditioned by the element of time. So you cannot
cite in argument the law regarding a carcass, for
although the carcass is forbidden to be eaten,
yet it is not forbidden to be used otherwise. Nor
can the case of an ox that has been stoned prove

אסור בהנאה ואינו בשריפה הוא יוכיח על חמץ

אף על פי שהוא אסור בהנאה לא יהיה בשריפה

אמרת הפרש נותר חייבין עליו כרת וחמץ חייבין

עליו כרת אם למדת על נותר שאינו אלא בשריפה

אף חמץ לא יהא אלא בשריפה והרי חלב של שור

הנסקל יוכיח שחייבין עליו כרת ואינו בשריפה הוא

יוכיח על חמץ שאף על פי שחייבין עליו כרת לא

יהא בשריפה אמרת ארבעה אדון ארבעה לשונות כאחת

מארבעה לשונות כאחת נותר אסור באכילה ואסור

בהנאה וחייבין עליו כרת והזמן גורם וחמץ אסור

באכילה ואסור בהנאה וחייבין עליו כרת והזמן

גורם ואל תאמר נבילה תוכיח שאף על פי שאסורה

באכילה אינה אסורה בהנאה ולא שור הנסקל

62—84 פסחים שם.

---

65 אמרת] א. ט. ~ הפרש / אדון] ט. הדין. 66 מארבעה
לשונות כאחת] א. ט. >. 67 כרת] א. >. 69—67 וחמץ–והזמן
גרם] א. >. 70—69 שאסורה באכילה אינה אסורה בהנאה] מ. שהיא
אסורה בהנאה.

anything, for although that ox is forbidden for any use at all, yet it cannot make one incur the penalty of extermination. Nor can the case of the tallow of the stoned ox prove anything. For although it can make one incur the penalty of extermination, yet the element of time plays no part in it. For I learn about one thing only from another thing exactly like it. I learn about one thing which has four characteristics from another thing that is exactly like it in all these four characteristics. But I can not argue about a thing that has four characteristics by comparing it with another thing that differs from it in one or two or three of its four characteristics. Therefore, inasmuch as you have learned that the "left-overs" of the sacrifice must be destroyed only by burning, it follows that leaven also must be destroyed only by burning it.

Said R. Judah to him: You think you are making it harder for one, but you really are making it easier. For if one could not find a fire, he would sit there without burning it. You should rather put it this way: Before the time limit set for its removal, it is one's duty to destroy it by burning, but after the time limit for its removal, it is one's duty to destroy it by any means available. Rabbi says: It should be destroyed by such means as would make it impossible for one to see it or to find it. And by what means could it be destroyed so that one could never again see it or find it? You conclude that it can be done only by burning.

יוכיח שאף על פי שהוא אסור בהנאה אין חייבין

עליו כרת ולא חלב שור הנסקל יוכיח שאף על פי

שחייבין עליו כרת אין הזמן גורם אלמד דבר מדבר

ואדון דבר מדבר אלמד דבר שהוא שווה בארבעה

75 דרכים מדבר שהוא שווה בארבעה דרכים ולא

אלמד דבר שהוא שווה בארבעה דרכים מדבר

שאינו שווה לא בדרך אחד ולא בשנים ולא בשלשה

אם למדת על נותר שאינו אלא בשריפה אף חמץ

לא יהיה אלא בשריפה אמר לו רבי יהודה סבור

80 אתה שאתה מחמיר עליו ואינך אלא מקיל עליו

הא אם לא מצא אור ישב לו ולא ישרוף אלא בלשון

זה הוי אומר עד שלא תגיע שעת הביעור מצות

כיליוו בשריפה משתגיע שעת הביעור מצות כיליוו

בכל דבר רבי אומר בדבר שהוא בל יראה ובל

85 ימצא ואיזה הוא דבר שהוא בל יראה ובל ימצא

אין אתה מוצא אלא בשריפה.

84—86 י' פסחים שם.

---

73 אלמד] ד. אלא אלמור]   77 שאינו שווה] ט. שהוא שווה/ לא]
ט. > בה'מ היה לו. מ"ע היה אלא/ ולא] ט. או.   79 לו]
ד. >/ יהודה] ד. מ. ~ בן בתירה.   83 כיליוו] מ. כולו.

For Whosoever Eateth Leavened Bread. I might understand this to mean fermented food of any kind. But it says: "Thou shalt eat no leavened bread with it; seven days shalt thou eat unleavened bread therewith" (Deut. 16.3). The law, then, applies only to such kinds as could be leavened as well as unleavened. And which are those that can be leavened as well as unleavened? They are the five species, namely, wheat, barley, spelt, oats and rye. Rice, millet, poppyseed, sesame and legumes, which cannot be leavened as well as unleavened, but which decay, are thus excluded.

Shall Be Cut Off. To be cut off merely means to cease to exist.

That Soul. This means the soul acting presumptuously—these are the words of R. Akiba.

From Israel. I might understand it to mean: that soul shall be cut off from Israel, but go to live among other people. But it says: "From before Me; I am the Lord" (Lev. 22.3). My dominion is everywhere.

From the First Day until the Seventh Day. During the seven days the penalty attaches to the act, but thereafter there is only a prohibition against it. For the following argument might have been advanced: The eating of tallow is punishable by extermination, and the eating of leavened bread is punishable by extermination. Now, since you have learned that the prohibition

כי כל אוכל חמץ ונכרתה שומע אני
כל חמץ במשמע ת"ל לא תאכל עליו חמץ שבעת
ימים תאכל עליו מצות לא אמרתי אלא דבר שהוא
באלמין מצה וחמץ ואיזה הוא דבר שהוא בא לידי

90 מצה וחמץ אילו חמשת המינין ואילו הן החטים
והשעורים והכוסמים ושבולת שועל והשיפון יצאו
האורז והדוחן והפרגין והשומשמין והקטניות שאין
באין לידי מצה וחמץ אלא לידי סירחון.

95 ונכרתה אין הכרתה אלא הפסקה. הנפש
ההיא מזידה דברי רבי עקיבא.

מישראל שומע אני ונכרתה מישראל ותלך
לה אל עם אחר תלמוד לומר מלפני אני יי
בכל מקום הוא רשותי.

100 מיום הראשון עד יום השביעי עונשו
שבעה ואזהרתו לעולם שהיה בדין הואיל והחלב
חייבין עליו כרת וחמץ חייבין עליו כרת אם למדת

89–88 דברים ט"ז, ג'.   96–95 לקמן י' ושבתא א'. ספרי בסדבר
ע' וקי"ב.   98 ויקרא כ"ב, ג'. לקמן י'.

87 מ. כי כל אוכל מחמצת.   98ד. מלפני יי.   102 וחמץ חייבין
עליו כרת] מ. ד. <.

against tallow always carries the penalty with it, one would think that the prohibition against leavened bread likewise always carries the penalty with it. Therefore Scripture says: "From the first day until the seventh day." Only during the seven days the penalty is attached to the act, but thereafter there is merely a prohibition against it. We have heard the penalty for it, but we have not yet heard the prohibition against it. It says: "Ye shall eat nothing leavened" (v. 20).

CHAPTER IX
(Ex. 12.16-17)

And in the First Day there Shall Be to You a Holy Convocation and in the Seventh Day a Holy Convocation. Honor the festival by food, drink and clean garments. From here I know only that the first and last day of the festival are called "holy convocation." How about the intervening days of the festival? Scripture says: "The appointed seasons of the Lord, which ye shall proclaim to be holy convocations" (Lev. 23.2).

No Manner of Work Shall Be Done. From this I know only that on the last day of the festival work is forbidden.[1] How about the first

---

[1] I. e., by connecting "no manner of work shall be done" with "in the seventh day a holy convocation."

על החלב שעונשו ואזהרתו לעולם יכול אף חמץ
עונשו ואזהרתו לעולם תלמוד לומר מיום הראשון
105 עד יום השביעי עונשו שבעה ואזהרתו לעולם עונש
שמענו אזהרה לא שמענו תלמוד לומר כל מחמצת
לא תאכלו.

פרשה ט (שמות י"ב, ט"ז,-י"ז.)

ביום הראשון מקרא קודש וביום
השביעי מקרא קודש וגו' כבדהו במאכל
ובמשתה ובכסות נקייה אין לי אלא יום טוב הראשון
והאחרון שהם קרואין מקרא קדש חולו של מועד
5 מנין ת"ל אלה מועדי יי אשר תקראו אותם מקראי
קדש.

כל מלאכה לא יעשה אין לי אלא יום
טוב האחרון שהוא אסור בעשיית מלאכה יום טוב

107–106 שמות י"ב, כ'.

3–1 ספרי במדבר קמ"ו. ספרא אמור פרשה י"ב. ש. 16. 6–5 ויקרא
כ"ג, ב'.

---

103 שעונשו ואזהרתו] מ. ד. שעשה עונשו כאזהרתו / יכול]
א. >/ חמץ] ד. על החמ/. 104 עונשו ואזהרתו] מ. ד. יעשה עונשו
כאזהרתו. 105 לעולם] מ. ד. >.
2–1 וביום השביעי-וגו'] ד. >. 2 כבדהו] א. מ. ארעם ט. קדשהו.
5 אלה] ליתא במקרא. 7 לא יעשה] א. מ. ~ בהם. 9–7 אין לי
אלא-מקרא קודש] א'צ. >.

day of the festival? Scripture says: "in the first
day there shall be to you a holy convocation."
Thus far I know only that on the first and the
last day of the festival work is forbidden, as it is
said: "in the first day there shall be to you a
holy convocation and in the seventh day a holy
convocation." How about the intervening days
of the festival? Scripture says: "The feast of
unleavened bread shalt thou keep seven days"
(Ex. 23.15), i. e., including all the days of the
festival—these are the words of R. Josiah. R.
Jonathan says, there is no need for this proof.
If on the first and last day of the festival, neither
one of which is both preceded and followed by
holiness,[2] it is forbidden to work, is it not but
logical to assume that on the intervening days of
the festival, which are both preceded and followed by holiness, work should be forbidden.
But the case of the six days of the week[3] would
disprove this. For they are both preceded and
followed by holiness and yet work is not forbidden on them. This should prove that on the
intervening days of the festival, even though
they are both preceded and followed by holiness,
work should not be forbidden. No! If you cite
the instance of the six weekdays—they have no
Musaf sacrifice and, therefore, work is not for-

---

[2] I. e., a Holiday.

[3] The six days of the week are designated in Hebrew,
"the days of creation," ששת ימי בראשית, since the acts of
creation took place on these days. The week days are
preceded and followed by a holy day, a Sabbath.

הראשון מניין ת״ל ביום הראשון מקרא קדש אין לי

10 אלא יום טוב הראשון והאחרון שהן אסורין בעשיית

מלאכה שנאמר ביום הראשון מקרא קדש וביום

השביעי מקרא קדש חולו של מועד מנין תלמוד

לומר את חג המצות תשמר שבעת ימים מכל מקום

דברי רבי יאשיה רבי יונתן אומר אינו צריך אם

15 יום טוב הראשון והאחרון שאין קדושה לפניהם

ולאחריהם הרי הן אסורין בעשיית מלאכה חולו

של מועד שיש קדושה לפניו ולאחריו אינו דין שיהא

אסור בעשיית מלאכה ששת ימי בראשית יוכיחו

שיש קדושה לפניהם ולאחריהם ומותרים בעשיית

20 מלאכה הם יוכיחו על חולו של מועד אף על פי

שיש קדושה לפניו ולאחריו שיהא מותר בעשיית

מלאכה לא אם אמרת בששת ימי בראשית שאין

בהם קרבן מוסף לפיכך מותרין בעשיית מלאכה

33־9 ספרא שם. ספרי דברים קל״ה. ש. שם. מ״ת   93־92. חנינה

י״ח, א׳.   13 שמות כ״ג, ט״ו.

22־20 הם יוכיחו־בעשיית מלאכה] א. <.

bidden on them. But will you argue the same
about the intervening days of the festival? They
have a *Musaf* sacrifice and therefore work should
be forbidden on them. But the case of the new-
moon days would disprove this. For they have
a *Musaf* sacrifice and yet work is permitted on
them. This should prove that on the intervening
days of the festival, even though they have a
Musaf sacrifice, work should not be forbidden.
No! If you cite the case of new-moons—they
are not called "holy convocations," and therefore work is not forbidden on them. But will
you argue the same about the intervening days
of the festival? They are called "holy convocations," and therefore work should be forbidden
on them. Behold we have thus learned that work
is forbidden during the intervening days of the
festival.

No Manner of Work Shall Be Done in Them.
This means, neither you nor your fellow-Jew
shall do any work, nor shall a non-Jew do your
work. So you interpret it. But perhaps it means
rather: Neither you nor your fellow-Jew shall do
any work, and the non-Jew shall not do even
his own work? But Scripture says: "Six days

תאמר בחולו של מועד שיש בו קרבן מוסף|לפיכך

25 יהא אסור בעשיית מלאכה והרי ראשי חדשים
יוכיחו שיש בהן קרבן מוסף ומותרין בעשיית מלאכה
הם יוכיחו על חולו של מועד שאף על פי שיש בו
קרבן מוסף יהיה מותר בעשיית מלאכה לא אם
אמרת בראשי חדשים שאינן קרואין מקרא קדש

30 לפיכך מותרין בעשיית מלאכה תאמר בחולו של
מועד שהוא קרוי מקרא קדש לפיכך יהא אסור
בעשיית מלאכה הא למדנו על חולו של מועד שהוא
אסור בעשיית מלאכה.

כל מלאכה לא יעשה בהם לא תעשה

35 אתה ולא יעשה חברך ולא יעשה גוי מלאכתך אתה
אומר כן או אינו אלא לא תעשה אתה. ולא יעשה
חברך ולא יעשה גוי מלאכתו תלמוד לומר ששת

39—37 ויקרא כ״ג, ג׳.

27—28 הם יוכיחו–בעשיית מלאכה] א <. 35 חברך] מנדול עוז ריש
פ״א מהלכות שביתת יום טוב נרס בדברך / ולא יעשה גוי מלאכתך]
ט. א״א. א״צ. ור׳ ישעיה הראשון מובא בברכי יוסף או׳חׂׂסִי׳ רס״נ.
אבל יעשה גוי מלאכתך. 37—35 אתה אומר כן–גוי מלאכתו] מ. ור׳
ישעיה שם >. 42—35 אתה אומר כן–עושה גוי את מלאכתו] א. <.
37 ולא יעשה גוי מלאכתו] הגהתי עפ״י הרמב״ן בפירושו על החורה
ומ״ח. והר״ר״ס בש״י: ד. ויעשה גוי מלאכתו ט. ולא יעשה גוי
מלאכתך א. ולא יעשה גוי מלאכתך אבל עושה גוי את מלאכתו.

shall work be done but on the seventh day is a
sabbath of solemn rest, a holy convocation; ye
shall do no manner of work" (Lev. 23.3). Thus
you learn that, "no manner of work shall be
done in them," means neither you nor your
fellow-Jew shall do any work, nor shall the non-
Jew do your work, but a non-Jew may do his
own work—these are the words of R. Josiah.
R. Jonathan says, there is no need of this proof.
Has it not already been said: "Remember the
sabbath day, to keep it holy. Six days shall
thou labour, and do all thy work; but the seventh
is a sabbath unto the Lord thy God" (Ex. 20.10).
Now, by using the method of *Kal vaḥomer* it
can be reasoned: If on the Sabbath, in regard to
which the law is more rigorous, you are not warned
against the non-Jew's work as you are against
your own work, it is but logical to assume that
on holidays, in regard to which the law is less
rigorous, you surely are not warned against the
non-Jew's work as you are against your own work.

No Manner of Work Shall Be Done in Them.
From this I know only with respect to a holiday
that you are warned against the work of your
fellow-Jew as you are against your own. How
about the Sabbath? It can be reasoned by
using the method of *Kal vaḥomer*: If on a holiday
in regard to which the law is not so rigorous,

ימים תעשה מלאכה וביום השביעי שבת שבתון
מקרא קדש כל מלאכה לא תעשו הא למדת כל
מלאכה לא יעשה בהם לא תעשה אתה ולא יעשה   40
חברך ולא יעשה הגוי מלאכתך אבל עושה גוי את
מלאכתו דברי רבי יאשיה רבי יונתן אומר אינו
צריך והלא כבר נאמר זכור את יום השבת לקדשו
ששת ימים תעבוד ועשית כל מלאכתך והרי דברים
קל וחמר ומה אם שבת חמורה אין אתה מוזהר על   45
מלאכת הגוי כמלאכתך יום טוב הקל דין הוא שלא
תהא מוזהר על מלאכת הגוי כמלאכתך.

כל מלאכה לא יעשה בהם אין לי אלא
יום טוב שאתה מוזהר על מלאכת חברך כמלאכתך
שבת מנין קל וחמר ומה אם יום טוב הקל אתה   50

43—44 שמות כ', ח'—ט'.

38—39 וביום השביעי שבת שבתון מקרא קדש כל מלאכה לא תעשו]
הוספתי: א. מ. ד. וגו'. מ"ח. והרר"ס וביום השביעי יהיה לכם
קודש.   39—40 כל מלאכה] ד. וכל מלאכה.   41 ולא יעשה הגוי
מלאכתך] ט. א"א. אבל יעשה הגוי מלאכתך.   41—42 אבל עושה גוי
את מלאכתו] הוספתי—רמב"ן.   44 ועשית כל מלאכתך] הוספתי: א. וגו'.
46 כמלאכתך] ד. במלאכתך.   47 כמלאכתך] ד. במלאכתך.
48 ד. ח"ל כל מלאכה לא יעשה בהם.   48—50 אין לי אלא—ק"ו ומה]
ק. >.   48—52 כל המאמר נמחק בא"צ.   49—50 שאתה מוזהר—ק"ו
ומה] נ. ל. >.   49 כמלאכתך] מ. במלאכתך.

you are warned against the work of your fellow-
Jew as you are against your own work, it is but
logical to assume that on the Sabbath in regard
to which the law is more rigorous, you surely are
warned against the work of your fellow-Jew as
you are against your own work.

Save that which Every Man Must Eat. Any
work necessary for the preparation of food may
be done in disregard of the holiday, but not any
work upon the altar may be done in disregard of
the holiday. For the following argument could
be advanced: If the Sabbath, which may not be
disregarded for any work necessary for the preparation of food, is disregarded for some work upon
the altar, is it not but logical to assume that the
holidays, which may be disregarded for any work
necessary for the preparation of food, should be
disregarded for any work upon the altar. But
Scripture says: "Save that which every man must
eat, that alone may be done by you," i. e., any
work necessary for the preparation of food, but
not any work upon the altar, may be done in
disregard of the holiday. Then let it be permitted
to do some work necessary for the preparation
of food in disregard of the Sabbath. And the
following argument would favor it: If the holiday, which may not be disregarded for all work
upon the altar, may be disregarded for all work
necessary for the preparation of food, the Sabbath, which may be disregarded for some work
upon the altar, should also be disregarded for
some work necessary for the preparation of food.
But Scripture says: "Save that which every man

מוזהר על מלאכת חברך כמלאכתך שבת חמורה

דין הוא שתהא מוזהר על מלאכת חברך כמלאכתך.

אך אשר יאכל לכל נפש כל אוכל נפש

דוחה את יום טוב ואין כל עבודה דוחה את יום

55 טוב שהיה בדין מה אם במקום שאין מקצת אוכל

נפש דוחה את השבת מקצת עבודה דוחה את השבת

מקום שכל אוכל נפש דוחה את יום טוב אינו דין

שתהא כל עבודה דוחה את יום טוב תלמוד לומר

אך אשר יאכל לכל נפש וגו' כל אוכל נפש דוחה

60 את יום טוב ואין כל עבודה דוחה את יום טוב ויהא

מקצת אוכל נפש דוחה את השבת והדין נותן מה

אם במקום שאין כל עבודה דוחה את יום טוב כל

אוכל נפש דוחה את יום טוב מקום שמקצת עבודה

דוחה את השבת אינו דין שיהא מקצת אוכל נפש

65 דוחה את השבת תלמוד לומר אך אשר יאכל

53—54 ביצה כ', ב'. י' שם ב' ד' (61bc). ספרי במדבר קמ'ו.

52 כמלאכתך] א. מ. נ. ל. במלאכתך.   58—60 ת'ל אך–דוחה את
יום טוב] א. >.   64—65 אינו דין–דוחה את השבת] א. >.   65 אך]
ק. ורמב'ן בפרשת אמור >.   66—65 אשר יאכל–לבדו וגו'] מ'ח.
א'צ. מ'ה. >.

must eat, that alone may be done by you," i. e.,
only the holiday may be disregarded for any
work necessary for the preparation of food, but
the Sabbath is not to be disregarded for any
work necessary for the preparation of food.

Save that which Every Living Being⁴ Must Eat,
etc. I might understand this to include the
preparation of food for cattle and for strangers.
But it says *lakem*, meaning for yourselves and
not for cattle, for yourselves and not for strangers
—these are the words of R. Ishmael. R. Jose
the Galilean says: "Save that which every living
being must eat." This includes cattle. May be
it includes strangers as well as cattle. But
Scripture says: "Save" (*ak*), which makes some
distinction. R. Akiba says: "Save that which
every living being must eat." This includes
cattle. May be it includes strangers as well as
cattle. But Scripture says *lakem*, meaning for
yourselves and not for strangers. Why do you
see fit to make such a distinction between cattle
and strangers? Because you are under obligation
to feed the former but you are not commanded
to feed the latter.⁵

*And Ye Shall Observe the (Feast of) Unleavened
Bread*. Watch it [the dough] so as not to let it
become unfit. In connection with this the sages
said: If the dough tends to rise it should be beaten
down with cold water. If it is already *sior*, it

---

⁴ This rendering of the Hebrew word נפש here is required
by the *Mekilta*.

⁵ I. e., because the stranger can prepare his own food
while the cattle cannot.

לכל נפש הוא לבדו וגו' כל אוכל נפש דוחה
את יום טוב ואין מקצת אוכל נפש דוחה את השבת.

אך אשר יאכל לכל נפש וגו' שומע אני
אף נפשות בהמה ונפשות אחרים במשמע תלמוד
70 לומר לכם ולא לבהמה לכם ולא לאחרים
דברי רבי ישמעאל רבי יוסי הגלילי אומר אך אשר
יאכל לכל נפש אף נפשות בהמה במשמע משמע
מביא נפשות בהמה ומביא נפשות אחרים ת"ל אך
חלק רבי עקיבא אומר אך אשר יאכל לכל נפש
75 אף נפשות בהמה במשמע משמע מביא נפשות בהמה
ומביא נפשות אחרים ת"ל לכם ולא לאחרים מה
ראית לחלוק שאתה מוזהר על הבהמה ואין אתה
מוזהר על הגוי.

ושמרתם את המצות שמרהו שלא תביאהו
80 לידי פסול מכאן אמרו תפח תלטוש בצונן שיאור

66—74 ביצה כ"א, א'—ב'. י' שם ד', א' (62ᵃ). ש. 17.   74—78 ביצה
כ"א, ב'. י' שם א', י"א (61ᵃ).   85—79 פסחים מ"ח, ב'.

66 וגו'] נ. ל. ~ אך אשר יאכל.   66—67 כל אוכל נפש דוחה
את יו"ט] הנהח~ט. א'א. א'צ.וم'ה: א. מ. ד. מקצת עבודה
דוחה שבת.   79 ד. עד שלא תביאהו.   80 תלטוש] א. תרבה (תכבה?)
מ. תכבה./ בצונן] מ. בצונים.

must be burned, but one who eats it incurs no penalty. If it is already *siduk* it must be burned and one who eats it incurs the penalty of extermination. When is it *sior*? When it is so leavened that the cracks on its surface spread like the horns of a locust; and it is *siduk* when the cracks run into one another—these are the words of R. Judah. But the other sages say: One who eats dough leavened to either of these degrees, incurs the penalty of extermination. When, then, is it *sior*? When its surface becomes pale like a man whose hair stands up from fright.

And Ye Shall Observe the (Feast of) Unleavened Bread (ha-mazzot). R. Josiah says: Do not read it so, but: "Ye shall observe the commandments (*ha-mizvot*).[6] Just as one should not be slow when making the *mazzah*, lest it leaven, so should one not be slow to perform a religious duty. But if a religious duty comes your way, perform it immediately.

For in This Selfsame Day, etc. This tells that they went out of Egypt in the daytime.

Have I Brought Your Hosts Out. These are the hosts of Israel. You say these are the hosts of Israel. Perhaps this is not so, but it means the hosts of the ministering angels? When it says: "All the hosts of the Lord went out from the Land of Egypt" (v. 41), behold, the hosts of ministering angels are there spoken of. Hence what must "I brought your hosts out" refer to? To the hosts of Israel.

---

[6] The word המצות in Hebrew can be read both ways. Comp. Hayyim Heller, הנוסח השמרוני (Berlin, 1924), p. 206.

ישרף והאוכלו פטור סידוק ישרף והאוכלו חייב
כרת איזהו שיאור כקרני חגבים סידוק שנתערבו
סדקיו זה בזה דברי רבי יהודה וחכמים אומרים
זה וזה האוכלו חייב איזהו שיאור כל שהכסיפו
85 פניו כאדם שעמדו שערותיו.

ושמרתם את המצות רבי יאשיה אומר אל
תקרא כן אלא ושמרתם את המצוות כדרך שאין
מחמצין את המצה כך לא יחמיצו את המצוה אלא
אם באת מצוה לידך עשה אותה מיד.

90 כי בעצם היום הזה וגו' מגיד שלא יצאו
אלא ביום.

הוצאתי את צבאותיכם אלו צבאות
ישראל אתה אומר אלו צבאות ישראל או אינו אלא
צבאות מלאכי השרת כשהוא אומר יצאו כל צבאות
95 יי מארץ מצרים הרי צבאות מלאכי השרת אמור
הא מה ת"ל הוצאתי את צבאותיכם אלו צבאות
ישראל.

---

89 יומא ל"ג, א'. מגלה ו', ב'.   91—90 לעיל ז'. ספרי דברים קכ"ח.
95—94 שמות י"ב, ס"א. לקמן י"ד.

---

82 כרת] מ. ד. סיחה.   84 חייב] ד. ~ סיחה ט. ~ כרת.
96 צבאותיכם] א. צבאותי מ. צבאות.

Therefore Shall Ye Observe this Day. Why is this said? Has it not already been said: "no manner of work shall be done in them" (v. 16)? From this I would know only about work that can be regarded as labor.[7] How about activities that can be regarded only as detracting from the restfulness of the day? Scripture says: "Therefore, shall ye observe this day," thus prohibiting even such work as only detracts from the restfulness of the day. Perhaps such work should be forbidden on the intervening days of the festival also? And the following argument would favor it: The first day and the last day of the festival are called "holy convocation," and the intervening days of the festival are likewise called "holy convocation." Now, then, inasmuch as you have proved that on the first day and on the last day of the festival, which are called "holy convocation," such activities as only detract from the restfulness of the day are forbidden, it follows that on the intervening days, which are also called "holy convocation," such activities should also be forbidden. But Scripture says: "On the first day shall be a solemn rest, and on the seventh[8] day shall be a solemn rest" (Lev. 23.39).

---

[7] By the term מלאכה, "labor," is meant one of the 39 classes of work forbidden on the Sabbath (see M. Shab. 7.2). By the term שבות is meant such activity as does not come under any of these 39 classes, but nevertheless is not compatible with the restfulness of the day.

[8] Our text reads: "And on the eighth," dealing as it does with the *Sukkot* festival which extends over eight days (see Introduction).

ושמרתם את היום הזה למה נאמר והלא

כבר נאמר כל מלאכה לא יעשה בהם אין לי אלא

100 דברים שהם משום מלאכה דברים שהם משום שבות

מנין ת״ל ושמרתם את היום הזה להביא דברים

שהן משום שבות ואף חולו של מועד יהיה אסור

משום שבות והדין נותן הואיל ויום טוב הראשון

והאחרון קרויין מקרא קדש וחולו של מועד קרוי

105 מקרא קדש אם למדת על יום טוב הראשון והאחרון

שהן קרויין מקרא קדש הרי הן אסורין משום שבות

אף חולו של מועד שהוא קרוי מקרא קדש יהיה

אסור משום שבות ת״ל ביום הראשון שבתון וביום

השביעי שבתון.

100–102 ביצה ל״ו, ב׳. ש. 16.   109–108 ויקרא כ״ג, ל״ט.

---

107 אף] ד. <./ יהיה] ד. אינו דין שיהא.   109–108 וביום השביעי
שבתון] מ. ~ וגו׳ ד. > במקרא כתוב וביום השטיני שבתון.

CHAPTER X
(Ex. 12.18-20)

In the First Month, on the Fourteenth Day of the Month at Even, Ye Shall Eat Unleavened Bread. Scripture fixes this as an obligation.

Until the One and Twentieth Day of the Month at Even. Why is this said? Since it says: "Seven days shall ye eat unleavened bread" (v. 15), I know only about the days. How about the nights? Scripture says here: "until the one and twentieth day of the month at even," to include the nights.

Seven Days Shall There Be No Leaven Found. From this I know only that it is under the prohibition of being found. How do we know that it is also under the prohibition of being seen? Scripture says: "And there shall be no leaven seen with thee" (Deut. 16.4). So far I know only that leaven is under the prohibition of being seen and of being found. How about leavened bread? The scriptural passage: "And there shall no leavened bread be seen with thee, neither shall there be leaven seen with thee" (Ex. 13.7), compares leaven to leavened bread and leavened bread to leaven: Just as the one, leaven, is under the prohibition of being seen and of being found, so also is the other, leavened bread, under the prohibition of being seen and of being found. And just as the one, leavened bread, is forbidden only when it is made of one of the five species, so also is the other, leaven, forbidden only when it comes from one of the five species.

פרשה י (שמות י״ב, י״ח,–כ׳.)

בראשון בארבעה עשר יום לחדש
בערב תאכלו מצות קבעו הכתוב חובה.

עד יום האחד ועשרים לחדש בערב
למה נאמר לפי שהוא אומר שבעת ימים מצות
5 תאכלו אין לי אלא ימים לילות מנין תלמוד לומר
עד יום האחד ועשרים וגו׳ לרבות את הלילות.

שבעת ימים שאור לא ימצא אין לי אלא
בל ימצא בל יראה מנין תלמוד לומר לא יראה לך
שאור אין לי אלא שאור שהוא בבל יראה ובבל
10 ימצא חמץ מנין ת״ל לא יראה לך חמץ ולא יראה
לך שאור הקיש שאור לחמץ וחמץ לשאור מה זה
בבל יראה ובבל ימצא אף זה בבל יראה ובבל
ימצא ומה זה מחמשת המינין אף זה מחמשת המינין.

2–1 לעיל ח׳. פסחים כ״ח, ב׳.   4–5 שמות י״ב, ט״ו.   7–11 ספרי
דברים קל״א. ביצה ז׳, ב׳.   8–9 דברים ט״ז, ד׳.   11–10 שמות י״ג, ז׳.

2–1 לחדש בערב תאכלו מצות] הוספתי: א. מ. וני׳.   6 לרבות]
מ״ח. לפרש.   7 אלא] א. ~ דברים שהן משום.   8 לא יראה]
במקרא כתוב ולא יראה.   10 לא יראה] במקרא ולא יראה.

In Your House. Why is this said? Because it is said: "Neither shall there be leaven seen with thee in all thy borders" (Ex. 13.7), which I might understand literally, Scripture here says "in your houses": Just as what is in your houses is under your full control, so also what is in "thy borders" must be under your full control. Hence, there is excluded from this prohibition leavened bread actually owned by a Jew but subject to the control of a non-Jew; for even though the Jew could destroy it, he may not do so, not having complete control over it. There is also excluded leavened bread actually owned by a non-Jew but under the control of a Jew, as well as leavened bread buried under debris; for although it is under the control, or within the territory of the Jew, he has not the right, in the one case, nor the physical possibility, in the other case, of actually destroying it. You say it is intended for this purpose. Perhaps it only comes to teach that in houses the prohibition holds for seven days, while in territories it holds for all times? But the scriptural passage: "And there shall be no leaven seen with thee in all thy borders seven days" (Deut. 16.4), declares that just as in houses the prohibition holds only for seven days, so also in territories it holds only for seven days.

For Whosoever Eateth that which is Leavened, that Soul Shall Be Cut Off. Why is this said? Since it says: "For whosoever eateth leavened bread that soul shall be cut off" (v. 15), I know only that for eating leavened bread one incurs the penalty of extermination. How about

ב ב ת י כ ם למה נאמר לפי שנאמר בכל גבולך

15 שומע אני כמשמעו ת״ל בבתיכם מה בתיכם

ברשותכם אף גבולך ברשותך יצא חמצו של ישראל

שהוא ברשות נכרי אף על פי שהוא יכול לבערו

אבל אינו ברשותו יצא חמצו של נכרי שהוא ברשות

ישראל וחמץ שנפלה עליו מפולת אף על פי שהוא

20 ברשותו אבל אינו יכול לבערו אתה אומר לכך

בא או לא בא אלא ללמד בבתים שבעה ובגבולין

לעולם תלמוד לומר ולא יראה לך שאור בכל

גבולך שבעת ימים מה בבתים שבעה אף בגבולין

שבעה.

25   כי כל אוכל מחמצת ונכרתה למה

נאמר לפי שהוא אומר כי כל אוכל חמץ ונכרתה

אין לי אלא חמץ שחייבין עליו כרת שאור מנין

---

14 דברים ט״ז, ד׳.   14—20 ספרי שם. פסחים ה׳, ב׳. ש. 18—19.

22—23 דברים ט״ז, ד׳.   25—42 פסחים ס׳, א׳. ביצה ז׳, ב׳. ש. 19.

20 אבל] ד. >.   22 לעולם] א׳ צ. יום אחד. / ולא יראה] א. ק.

נ. לא יראה.   26 שהוא אומר] ד. שנאמר.

leaven? Therefore, Scripture says here: "For whosoever eateth that which is leavened, that soul shall be cut off." But even if Scripture had not said this, I could have argued: If for leavened bread, which cannot leaven other things, one incurs the penalty of extermination, it is but logical to assume that for leaven, which can leaven other things, one should surely incur the penalty of extermination. No! If you cite the case of leavened bread—that is fit for eating. Therefore one incurs for it the penalty of extermination. But will you argue the same for leaven? It is not fit for eating and therefore one should not incur for it the penalty of extermination. Hence Scripture had to say: "For whosoever eateth that which is leavened, that soul shall be cut off." Then, let me read in Scripture only the law about leaven, and by using the method of *Kal vaḥomer* I would reason about leavened bread thus: If for leaven, which is not fit for eating, one incurs the penalty of extermination, it is but logical that for leavened bread, which is fit for eating, one should surely incur the penalty of extermination. No! If you cite the case of leaven—that can leaven other things and therefore one incurs for it the penalty of extermination. But will you argue the same for leavened bread? The latter cannot leaven other things and therefore one should not incur for it the penalty of extermination. Scripture therefore had to say: "For whosoever eateth leavened

ת״ל כי כל אוכל מחמצת ונכרתה עד שלא יאמר

יש לי בדין מה אם חמץ שאינו מחמיץ לאחרים

30 חייבין עליו כרת שאור שמחמיץ לאחרים דין הוא

שיהיו חייבין עליו כרת לא אם אמרת בחמץ שהוא

ראוי לאכילה חייבין עליו כרת תאמר בשאור

שאינו ראוי לאכילה לפיכך לא יהו חייבין עליו

כרת ת״ל כי כל אוכל מחמצת ונכרתה אני אקרא

35 את השאור קל וחמר לחמץ מה אם השאור שאינו

ראוי לאכילה חייבין עליו כרת חמץ שהוא ראוי

לאכילה דין הוא שיהו חייבין עליו כרת לא אם

אמרת בשאור שהוא מחמיץ לאחרים חייבין עליו

כרת תאמר בחמץ שאינו מחמיץ לאחרים לפיכך

40 לא יהו חייבין עליו כרת ת״ל כי כל אוכל חמץ

---

32 לאכילה] ד. ~ לפיכך יהו.

bread, that soul shall be cut off", and "For whosoever eateth that which is leavened, that soul
shall be cut off." Both verses had to be said,
for otherwise we could not have known.[1]

Shall Be Cut Off. To be cut off merely means
to cease to exist.

That Soul. This means the soul acting presumptuously—these are the words of R. Akiba.

From Israel. I might understand it to mean,
that soul shall be cut off from Israel, but go to
live among another people. But it says: "From
before Me; I am the Lord" (Lev. 22.3). My
dominion is everywhere.

*Whether He Be a Sojourner or One that is Born
in the Land.* Since this is an act prescribed for
Israelites, Scripture had to mention that strangers
are included. Wherever an act is prescribed for
Israelites, strangers must be especially included.

Ye Shall Eat Nothing Leavened. Why is this
said? Since it says: "For whosoever eateth
leavened bread, that soul shall be cut off" (v. 15),
and, "Whosoever eateth that which is leavened,
that soul shall be cut off" (v. 19), I know only
that one incurs the penalty of extermination
when eating these things themselves. How about
their compounds? Scripture says: "Ye shall eat
nothing leavened," in any form whatever.

---

[1] I. e., that the law applies in both cases.

ונכרתה כי כל אוכל מחמצת ונכרתה עד שיאמרו
שני כתובים ואם לאו לא שמענו.

ונכרתה אין הכרתה אלא הפסקה.　הנפש
ההיא מזידה דברי רבי עקיבא.

מעדת ישראל שומע אני תכרת מעדת ישראל 45
ותלך לה אל עם אחר ת״ל מלפני אני יי בכל מקום
רשותי.

בגר ובאזרח הארץ לפי שהוא מעשה
בישראל צריך להביא את הגרים בכל מקום שהוא
מעשה בישראל צורך להביא את הגרים. 50

כל מחמצת לא תאכלו למה נאמר לפי
שהוא אומר כי כל אוכל חמץ ונכרתה כי כל אוכל
מחמצת ונכרתה אין לי אלא אלו תערובתן מנין
ת״ל כל מחמצת לא תאכלו מכל מקום.

43—47 לעיל ח׳.　46 ויקרא כ״ב, ג׳.　48—50 ספרי במדבר ק״ט
וקי״א.　51—54 פסחים מ״נ, א׳. י׳ שם נ׳, א׳ (29d).

46 מקום] ק.~ הוא נ. ל. ~ שהוא.　49 בכל מקום שהוא] ד. אף
בכל שהוא.　50 צורך להביא את הגרים] מ. נ. ל. >.　51 נאמר]
א. בא.　52 שהוא אומר] א. ד. שנאמר.　53 ונכרתה] א׳ צ.
~ הרי עונש אזהרה מנין ת״ל לא תאכל וכו׳ / אלו] א׳ צ. הם.　54 מכל
מקום] א. ד. >.

In All Your Habitations Shall Ye Eat Un-leavened Bread. Why is this said? Since it says: "And thou shalt eat before the Lord, thy God . . . the tithe of thy corn," etc. (Deut. 14.23), I might understand that if one brings the second tithe to Jerusalem he can use it there to discharge his obligation to eat unleavened bread. Therefore, it says here: "in all your habitations," thus excluding this kind of unleavened bread, since it cannot be eaten in all places. And how do we know that one cannot discharge his obligation with the showbread, the remnants of meal offerings, the cakes of a thanksgiving sacri-fice, the wafers of a nazirite, or the unleavened bread made of the first fruit offerings? Scripture says: "in all your habitations,"[2] thus excluding all these, since they cannot be eaten in all habitations. It does mean to exclude these. May it not also mean to include sponge cakes, honey cakes, pastry, pudding and pancakes? Scripture says: "even the bread of poverty"[3] (Deut. 16.3), thus excluding all these, for they are not the bread of poverty—these are the words of R. Ishmael. The other sages, however, say, one can discharge his obligation to eat

---

[2] The second tithe, the remnants of a meal offering, the cakes that come with a thanksgiving sacrifice, the wafers of a nazirite, and the first fruit offering must be eaten within the walls of Jerusalem and cannot be eaten in any habitation outside of Jerusalem.

[3] This rendering of the word עני is required by our Midrash.

בכל מושבותיכם תאכלו מצות למה
נאמר לפי שהוא אומר ואכלת לפני יי אלהיך מעשר
דגנך וגו' הרי שהעלה מעשר שני לירושלם שומע אני
יוצא בו ידי חובתו משום מצה ת"ל בכל מושבותיכם
יצא זה שאינו נאכל בכל מקום ומנין שלא יצא
לא בלחם הפנים ולא בשירי מנחות ולא בחלות
תודה ולא ברקיקי נזיר ולא בבכורים ת"ל בכל
מושבותיכם תאכלו מצות יצאו אלו שאינן נאכלין
בכל מושבותיכם משמע מוציא את אלו ומביא את
האספנין ואת הדבשנין ואת האסקריטין וחלת משרת
ואשישה ת"ל לחם עני יצאו אלו שאינן לחם עני
דברי רבי ישמעאל וחכמים אומרים יוצא בם

76—55 ספרי דברים ק"ל. פסחים ל"ו, א', ב'. י' שם ב', ד' (29b).
תוס' שם א', ל"ב–ל"ג. ש. 20—19.   57—56 דברים י"ד, כ"נ.   65 דברים
ט"ז, ג'.

56 אלהיך] במקרא ~ במקום אשר יבחר לשכן שמו שם.   58 משום
מצה] ט. משום מצוה מ"ח. משום לפני יי.   59–58 ידי חובתו–שלא
יצא] א. <, ח'ל בכל מקום] א. מ. ט. מ"ח. <.   60 לא בלחם
הפנים] א. לא בשתי הלחם ולא בלחם הפנים.   מ. לא משום שתי
הלחם ולא בלחם הפנים. מ"ח. בו ולא בלחם הפנים.   64 האספנין]
א. הספגנים. ט. הסופנין. מ"ח. הסופנין.   65 עני] מ. ד.
עוני/ יצאו אלו שאינן לחם עני] ד. <./ עני 2] מ. עוני. מ"ח. <.

unleavened bread with any of these as well as
with unleavened bread made of second tithe.
What then is the purport of the words: "bread of
poverty?" That one should not use wine, oil or
any other fruit juice to knead it with. One may,
however, use all liquids to smear and mold it
with. R. Eliezer says: One can discharge his
obligation to eat unleavened bread with any of
these as well as with unleavened bread made of
second tithe. What then is meant by the words:
"bread of poverty?" Simply this: How is the
bread of the poor man prepared throughout the
whole year? His wife kneads while he heats
the oven. So also must this be prepared: while
his wife kneads, he should prepare the oven. R.
Jose the Galilean says: Behold it says: "Thou
shalt eat no leavened bread with it; seven days
shalt thou eat unleavened bread therewith"
(Deut. 16.3). I might understand this to mean
even unleavened bread made of second tithe.
But Scripture says: "even bread of affliction,"
thus excluding second tithe which may not be
eaten except when one is joyful.[4]

CHAPTER XI.
(Ex. 12.21-24)

Then Moses Called for All the Elders of Israel.
This tells that he constituted them a court.
And Said unto Them. The word came from
the mouth of Moses, telling it to all Israel—these
are the words of R. Josiah. R. Jonathan says:

---

[4] See Deut. 26.14 and M. Bik. 2.2 and M. Ma'as. 5.12.

ובמעשר שני ומה ת"ל לחם עני שלא ילוש לא ביין
ולא בשמן ולא בשאר כל המשקים אבל מקטף
הוא מכולם רבי אליעזר אומר יוצא בם ובמעשר

70 שני ומה תלמוד לומר לחם עני אלא מה לחמו של
עני כל ימות השנה אשתו לשה והוא מסיק בתנור
אף כאן אשתו לשה והוא מסיק בתנור רבי יוסי
הגלילי אומר הרי הוא אומר לא תאכל עליו חמץ
שבעת ימים תאכל עליו מצות שומע אני אף מעשר

75 שני במשמע ת"ל לחם עני יצא מעשר שני שאינו
נאכל אלא בשמחה.

פרשה יא (שמות י"ב, כ"א,–כ"ד.)

ויקרא משה לכל זקני ישראל מגיד
שעשאן בית דין ויאמר אליהם הדבר יצא
מפי משה לאמר לכל ישראל דברי רבי יאשיה רבי

67 עני] מ. ד. עוני.   69 אליעזר] א. אלעזר.   71 ימות] ד. >.
73 הגלילי] ד. >/ לא תאכל עליו חמץ] ד. >.   74 תאכל עליו
מצות] א. מ. וגו'. ד. תאכלו מצות.   75 עני] מ"ח. אוני.
1 מגיד] ד. מלמד.

The word came from the mouth of Moses, telling
it to the elders, and the elders were to tell it to
all Israel. Said R. Josiah to him: Why distinguish
this commandment from all the other commandments in the Torah? In the case of every other
commandment in the Torah the word came out
from the mouth of Moses, telling it to all Israel.
Here, too, the word came out from the mouth of
Moses telling it to all Israel. What then is
meant by: "And said unto them?" Simply, that
Moses showed respect to the elders. For so God
had told him: "Show respect to the elders," as
it is said: "Go and gather the elders of Israel
together" (Ex. 3.16). And Moses did so, as it is
said: "And Moses and Aaron went and gathered
together all the elders of the children[1] of Israel"
(Ex. 4.29).

Draw Out and Take You. Those of you who
own a lamb draw it out, and those who do not
own it, get one. R. Jose the Galilean says:
Withdraw your hands from idol worship and
adhere to the commandments. R. Ishmael says:
The Scripture aims to teach you that until it is
slaughtered people may enroll for partnership in
the paschal lamb or withdraw from it; so long

---

[1] The *Mekilta* text omits in this citation the word בני
found in the masoretic text.

יונתן אומר הדבר מפי משה לאמר לזקנים וזקנים

5 לאמר לכל ישראל נם לו רבי יאשיה מה נשתנה
הדבר הזה מכל הדברות שבתורה שכל הדברות
שבתורה הדבר מפי משה לאמר לכל ישראל אף
כאן הדבר מפי משה לאמר לכל ישראל ומה ת״ל
ויאמר אליהם אלא שמשה חלק כבוד לזקנים

10 וכן הקב״ה אמר לו חלוק כבוד לזקנים שנאמר לך
ואספת את זקני ישראל וכן עשה משה שנאמר וילך
משה ואהרן ויאספו את כל זקני ישראל.

משכו וקחו לכם משכו מי שיש לו וקחו מי
שאין לו ורבי יוסי הגלילי אומר משכו ידיכם מעבודה

15 זרה והדבקו במצוות רבי ישמעאל אומר בא הכתוב
ללמדך שלעולם נימנין על הפסח ומושכין את
ידיהם ממנו עד שישחט ובלבד שיניח את הפסח

12—9 ספרי במדבר צ״ב. שמו״ר ה׳, י״ב, וי״ר י״א. ח׳. תנחומא סוף
פרשת שמות. בובער שם ט׳, א׳. ש. 20. 11—10 שמות ג׳, ט״ז. 12—11 שמות
ד׳, כ״ט. 13 ש. 20. 15—13 לעיל ה. ש. שם. 18—15 לעיל ג׳.

5 נם לו] א. בטלו מ. נמולו/ יאשיה] מ. > / מה נשתנה] מ. ד.
אחד זה ואחד זה מה נשתנה. 8 ומה ת״ל] ק. > נ. ~ ויאמר וגו׳ ל.
~ לאמר מ״ח. והרר״ס בש״י ~ לכל זקני ישראל. 11 וכן עשה
משה] מ. ד. וגו׳ / שנאמר] מ. ד. וכתיב. 12 כל זקני ישראל]
במקרא כתוב כל זקני בני ישראל. 14 ידיכם] ד. >. 16 שלעולם
נמינין] ד. על כל העולין למנין א״צ. שעולין למנין. 17 שיניח]
ט. א״א. א״צ. שלא יניח.

as they leave the paschal lamb intact. R. Isaac says: Scripture aims to teach you about small cattle that they are acquired by the act of pulling.[2]

And Kill the Passover. The commandment is that it should be slaughtered as such. But if one slaughters it for another purpose, he transgresses the command. I might think that it should nevertheless be ritually fit. But it says: "Draw out and take you." Scripture has purposely repeated this commandment about the paschal lamb to declare it ritually unfit if this commandment is not complied with. Hence, they said: All sacrifices which have been slaughtered for a purpose other than the one designated for them are ritually fit, though not considered as having fulfilled the obligation resting upon the owner, except the paschal sacrifice and the sin offering.

And Ye Shall Take a Bunch of Hyssop. From this you judge every "taking" prescribed in the Torah.[3] Since the "takings" prescribed in the Torah are undefined with the exception of this one, where Scripture specifies that it must be "a bunch," I apply this specification to every other "taking"—that it also must be "a bunch."

Hyssop. But not Greek hyssop, nor Roman hyssop, nor hyssop of *Koḥalit,* nor desert hyssop, nor any hyssop that is qualified by an epithet.

---

[2] See M. Kid. 1.4.

[3] I. e., where the expression לקח is used, or where taking of hyssop is prescribed, as in Lev. 14.4 and Num. 19.6 (see commentaries).

כל שהוא רבי יצחק אומר בא הכתוב ללמדך על
בהמה דקה שתהא נקנית במשיכה.

20   ו ש ח ט ו ה פ ס ח מצוה שישחטנו לשמו אבל
אם שחטו שלא לשמו עבר על מצוה שומע אני יהא
כשר ת״ל משכו וקחו לכם שנה עליו הכתוב לפסול
מכאן אמרו כל הזבחים שנזבחו שלא לשמן כשרין
אלא שלא עלו לבעלים לשום חובה חוץ מן הפסח
25 ומן החטאת.

ו ל ק ח ת ם א ג ו ד ת א ז ו ב מכאן אתה דן כל
הלקיחות שבתורה הואיל ונאמרו כל הלקיחות
שבתורה סתם ופרט לך הכתוב באחת מהן שאינה
אלא אגודה אף פורט אני כל הלקיחות שאינן אלא
30 אגודות.

א ז ו ב ולא אזוב׳יון ולא אזוב רומי ולא אזוב
כחלית ולא אזוב מדברית ולא כל אזוב שיש לו
שם לווי.

---

19 י׳ קידושין א׳, ד׳ (60^b).   20—25 תוס׳ פסחים ד׳, ג׳–ד׳. י׳ שם ה׳,
ב׳ (31^d). זבחים ב׳, א׳. ז׳ ב׳.   26—30 ספרי במדבר קכ״ד וקכ׳ט. ש. 20.
31—33 ספרי שם. פרה י״א, ז׳. ספרא מצורע א׳. סוכה י׳נ א׳. ש. שם.

---

18 כל שהוא] א׳ א׳. כמות שהוא.   19 א. במשיחה.   20 ק. נ.
ושחטו את הפסח.   22 ת״ל משכו וקחו לכם] מ״ח. והר״ר״ס בש״י.
א׳ צ׳. ת״ל ואטרתם זבח פסח הוא.   26 ק. נ. ולקחתם לכם אגודת אזוב.
28—29 סתם—כל הלקיחות] א. >.   29 אגודה] ד. אגודת אזוב.

And Dip It in the Blood. There must be blood enough for dipping.

Which is Near the Threshold (ba-saf). Scripture thus tells that he would scoop out a hole near the threshold, over which he slaughtered. *Saf* here means threshold, as in the passage: "In their setting of their thresholds by My threshold" (Ezek. 43.8). And it also says: "And the posts of the thresholds were moved" (Isa. 6.4). R. Akiba says: *Saf* here means vessel, as in the passage: "And the cups, and the snuffers, and the basins" (I Kings 7.50).

And Strike the Lintel. This means, on the inside. You interpret it to mean on the inside. Perhaps it means only on the outside? But Scripture says: "And when I see the blood" (v. 13), i. e., the blood that would be seen by Me and not by others—these are the words of R. Ishmael. R. Jonathan says: This means on the inside. You interpret it to mean on the inside. Perhaps it means only on the outside? But Scripture says: "And the blood shall be to you for a token" (ibid.), i. e., a sign to you but not a sign to others. R. Isaac says: Not so! But it was on the outside, so that the Egyptians, seeing it, would be cut to the quick.

And Strike the Lintel and the Two Side-posts. I might understand that if one strikes the latter first, he has not fulfilled his duty. But the

וטבלתם בדם שיהא בדם כדי טבילה.

אשר בסף מגיד הכתוב שעוקה חוקק בצד
האסקופה ושוחט בתוכה אין סף אלא אסקופה
שנאמר בתתם ספם את ספי וגו' ואומר וינועו אמות
הספים דברי רבי ישמעאל רבי עקיבא אומר אין
סף אלא כלי שנאמר והספים והמזרות והמזרקות.

והגעתם אל המשקוף מבפנים אתה אומר
מבפנים או אינו אלא מבחוץ ת"ל וראיתי את הדם
הנראה לי ולא לאחרים דברי רבי ישמעאל רבי
יונתן אומר מבפנים אתה אומר מבפנים או אינו
אלא מבחוץ תלמוד לומר והיה הדם לכם לאות
לכם לאות ולא לאחרים לאות רבי יצחק אומר לא
כי אלא מבחוץ כדי שיהו המצרים רואים ומעיהם
מתחתכים.

והגעתם אל המשקוף ואל שתי
המזוזות שומע אני אם הקדים זה לזה לא יצא

---

34 ספרי במדבר קכ"ט. זבחים צ"ג, ב'. ש. 21.   39–35 לעיל ו'.
ש. שם.   37 יחזקאל מ"ג, ח'.   38–37 ישעיה ו', ד'.   39 מלכים א. ז', נ'.
41 שמות י"ב, י"ג.   42–54 לעיל ו'.   44 שמות י"ב, י"ג.

---

35 שעוקה חוקק] הנהתי=מ"ח. א"צ: א. מ. ק. נ. שעוקה
חוצק ל. שעוקה וחוקק. א"א. שעוקר וחוקק/ בצד] א"צ. בתוך.
37 ספם] א. > ד. את ספם/ את ספי] מ. וגו' ד. תחת ספי א"א.
אל ספי.   49–48 ואל שתי המזוזות] הוספתי: א. ונו'.

scriptural passage: "And put it on the two side-posts and upon the lintel" (v. 7), clearly shows that no matter which he does first, he fulfills his duty. We thus learn that our forefathers in Egypt had three altars, the lintel and the two side-posts. R. Ishmael says: They had four, the threshold, the lintel and the two side-posts.

From the Blood that is in the Basin (ba-saf). Why is this said again? Has it not already been said: "And dip it in the blood that is in the basin?" What need, then, is there of saying: "With the blood that is in the basin?" Because it says: "And they shall take of the blood and put it," etc. (v. 7), which I might understand to mean that one dipping is sufficient for all of them, Scripture says here: "And strike the lintel and the two side-posts with the blood," etc. There must be a dipping for every striking.

And None of You Shall Go Out, etc. This tells that the angel, once permission to harm is given him, does not discriminate between the righteous and the wicked, as it is said: "Come, My people, enter thou into thy chambers," etc. (Isa. 26.20). And it also says: "Behold, I am against thee, and will draw forth My sword out of its sheath, and will cut off from thee the righteous and the wicked" (Ezek. 21.8). And it further says: "And it shall come to pass, while My glory passeth by," etc. (Ex. 33.22).

תלמוד לומר ונתנו על שתי המזוזות ועל המשקוף   50
הא אם הקדים זה לזה יצא נמצינו למדין שלשה
מזבחות היו לאבותינו במצרים המשקוף ושתי
המזוזות רבי ישמעאל אומר ארבעה הסף והמשקוף
ושתי המזוזות.

מן הדם אשר בסף עוד למה נאמר והלא   55
כבר נאמר וטבלתם מן הדם אשר בסף ומה תלמוד
לומר מן הדם אשר בסף לפי שהוא אומר ולקחו
מן הדם ונתנו וגו' שומע אני טבילה אחת לכולם
ת"ל והגעתם אל המשקוף ואל שתי המזוזות מן הדם
וגו' על כל הגעה טבילה.   60

ואתם לא תצאו וגו' מגיד משנתנה רשות
למלאך לחבל אינו מבחין בין צדיק לרשע שנאמר
לך עמי בא בחדריך וגו' ואומר הנני אליך והוצאתי
חרבי מתערה והכרתי ממך צדיק ורשע ואומר
והיה בעבור כבודי וגו'.   65

57–58 שמות י"ב, ז'.   61–65 ב'ק ס', א'–ב'. תענית י', ב'. ש. 21.
63 ישעיה כ"ו, כ'.   63–64 יחזקאל כ"א, ח'.   65 שמות ל"ג, כ"ב.

51 יצא] א. לא יצא.   53 המזוזות] א. המזבחות.   53–54 ר' ישמעאל–
המזוזות] ד. וכו'.   55 עוד] ד. >.   56–57 ומה ת"ל–אשר בסף] ד. >.
57–58 ולקחו מן הדם] מ. ולקחתם מן הדם א"צ. וטבלתם בדם.
58 ונתנו וגו'] מ. ד. >.   59–60 ואל שתי המזוזות מן הדם וגו'] ד. >.
62 למלאך] ד. למשחית.   65 וגו'] ד. ואומר ואתם לא תצאו וגו'.

Until the Morning. This is to teach you that you should come in to a place or leave it only in the daytime.[4] And you also find that the patriarchs and the prophets observed this as a custom. For, it is said: "And Abraham rose early in the morning" (Gen. 22.3); "And Jacob rose up early in the morning" (Gen. 28.18); "And Moses rose up early in the morning" (Ex. 34.4); "And Joshua rose up in the morning" (Josh. 3.1); "And Samuel rose early to meet Saul in the morning" (I Sam. 15.12). Now by using the method of *Kal vaḥomer* you reason: If the patriarchs and the prophets, who went to carry out the will of Him by whose word the world came into being, observed this as a custom, how much more should all other people observe it? And thus it says: "Thou makest darkness and it is night," etc.; "The young lions roar after their prey" (Ps. 104.20–21). And it says: "Thou givest it unto them, they gather it," etc. (ibid., v. 28). And it says: "The sun ariseth, they slink away," etc. (ibid., v. 22). From then on, "man goeth forth unto his work and to his labour until the evening" (v. 23). And it says: "How manifold are Thy works, O Lord," etc. (v. 25).

For the Lord Will Pass Through to Smite the Egyptians, etc. R. Judah says: Like a king who passes from one place to another. Another

---

[4] The expression כי טוב, "that it was good," is used in Gen. 1.3 with reference to daylight. Hence it became a designation for daytime.

עד בבקר ללמדך שתהא נכנס בכי טוב ויוצא

בכי טוב וכן אתה מוצא שהאבות והנביאים נהגו

בדרך ארץ שנאמר וישכם אברהם בבקר וישכם

יעקב בבקר וישכם משה בבקר וישכם יהושע בבקר

70 וישכם שמואל לקראת שאול בבקר והרי דברים

קל וחמר ומה אם האבות והנביאים שהלכו לעשות

רצונו של מי שאמר והיה העולם נהגו בדרך ארץ

שאר בני אדם על אחת כמה וכמה וכן הוא אומר

תשת חשך ויהי לילה וגו' הכפירים שואגים לטרף

75 ואומר תתן להם ילקטון וגו' ואומר תזרח השמש

יאספון וגו' מכאן ואילך יצא אדם לפעלו ולעבודתו

עדי ערב ואומר מה רבו מעשיך יי וגו'.

ועבר יי לנגוף את מצרים וגו' רבי יהודה

אומר כמלך שהוא עובר ממקום למקום דבר אחר

68 בראשית כ"ב, נ'. 68—69 בראשית כ"ח, י"ח. 69 שמות ל"ד, ד'. /
יהושע נ', א'. 70 שמואל א. ט"ו, י"ב. 74 תהלים ק"ד, כ'—כ"א. 75 שם
ק"ד, כ"ח./ שם ק"ד, כ"ב. 77—76 שם ק"ד, כ"ג. 77 שם ק"ד, כ"ד.

66 עד בקר] ד. >/ ללמדך] ד. ~ כשתצא לדרך/ שתהא] ד.
(תהלים ק"ד) שהוא. 67 שהאבות והנביאים] ד. האבות הראשונים.
68 בדרך ארץ] מ"ח. כ. כן בדרך ארץ. 71 ומה אם] ק. נ. והלא.
79—84 דבר אחר—נאום ה'] ד. >.

Interpretation is: And the Lord will be angry.
He will put His wrath and His terror in Egypt.
For the word 'ebrah means only anger, as in the
passage: "He sent forth upon them the fierceness
of His anger, wrath and indignation and trouble"
(Ps. 78.49). And it is also written: "That day is
a day of wrath" (Zeph. 1.15). And it is also
written: "Behold the day of the Lord cometh,
cruel, and full of wrath and fierce anger" (Isa.
13.9). And it is also written: "And in all vine-
yards shall be lamentation; for I will pass[5]
through the midst of thee, saith the Lord" (Amos
5.17).

And When He Seeth the Blood. R. Ishmael
used to say: Is not everything revealed and
known before Him, as it is said: "He knoweth
what is in the darkness, and the light dwelleth
with Him" (Dan. 2.22)? And it also says:
"Even the darkness is not too dark for Thee,"
etc. (Ps. 139.12). What then is the purport of
the words: "And when He seeth the blood?"
It is only this: As a reward for their performing
these duties He will reveal Himself and protect
them as it is said: "And the Lord will pass over
the door." Passing over merely means protecting,
as it is said: "As birds hovering so will the Lord
of Hosts protect Jerusalem; He will deliver it, as
He protecteth it, He will rescue it, as He passeth
over" (Isa. 31.5).

Another Interpretation: *And When He Seeth*

---

[5] The Midrash, however, takes the word אעבור to mean
not "I will pass," but "I will get angry" (see above, VII,
note 4).

80 ועבר יי נותן הוא עברתו ויראתו במצרים אין עברה

אלא זעם שנאמר ישלח בם חרון אפו עברה וזעם

וצרה וכתיב יום עברה היום ההוא וכתיב הנה יום

יי בא אכזרי ועברה וגו' וכתיב ובכל כרמים מספד

כי אעבור בקרבך נאום יי.

85   וראה את הדם היה רבי ישמעאל אומר

והלא הכל גלוי וידוע לפניו שנאמר ידע מה בחשוכא

ונהורא עמיה שרי ואומר גם חשך לא יחשיך ממך

וגו' ומה תלמוד לומר וראה את הדם אלא בשכר

מצות שהם עושים הוא נגלה וחס עליהם שנאמר

90 ופסח יי על הפתח ואין פסיחה אלא חיים שנאמר

כצפרים עפות כן יגן יי צבאות על ירושלם גנון

והציל פסוח והמליט דבר אחר וראה את הדם

81—82 תהלים ע"ח, מ"ט.   82 צפניה א', ט"ו.   82—83 ישעיה י"ג, ט'.
83—84 עמוס ה', י"ז.   85—96 לעיל ז'.   86—87 דניאל ב', כ"ב.   87 תהלים
קל"ט, י"ב.   92—91 ישעיה ל"א, ה'.

84 נאום] במקרא שלפנינו אמר.   88 בשכר] הגהתי—ל. מ"ח.
א"צ: א. מ. ק. נ. לשכר.   92—91 כן יגן-והמליט] מ. וגו'./ צבאות]
ק. נ. >.   92 דבר אחר] הגהתי עפ"י מ"ח. א"צ.

the Blood. He seeth the blood of the sacrifice of Isaac, as it is said: "And Abraham called the name of that place *Adonai-jireh*" (the Lord will see), etc. (Gen. 22.14). And it is also written: "And as He was about to destroy, the Lord beheld and He repented Him" (I Chron. 21.15). What did He behold? He beheld the blood of the scarifice of Isaac, as it is said: "God will Himself see the lamb for a burnt-offering" (Gen. 22.8).

And the Lord Will Pass Over the Door. Behold, by using the method of *Kal vaḥomer* we can reason as follows: With respect to the performance of the rite with the blood of the paschal sacrifice in Egypt, the less important—since it was only for the time being, was not to be observed both by day and by night, and was not to be observed in subsequent generations—it is said: "And He will not suffer the destroyer to come in." The *Mezuzah,*[6] the more important —since it contains the name of God ten times and is prescribed for day and night and for all generations—should all the more be the cause of God's not suffering the destroyer to come in to our houses. But what caused it to be otherwise? Our sins. As it is said: "Our iniquities have turned away these things" (Jer. 5.25). And it is

---

[6] *Mezuzah*, literally "door-post," designates a piece of parchment, containing the biblical verses Deut. 6.4–9 and 11.13–20, and attached to the door-post. In the biblical verses contained in the *Mezuzah*, the Name of God occurs ten times, the tetragrammaton seven times and אלהים with a suffix three times. According to this passage in the *Mekilta* then, the term "specific name," שם המיוחד, applies

רואה הוא דם עקדתו של יצחק שנאמר ויקרא

אברהם שם המקום ההוא יי יראה וכתיב ובהשחית

בעם ראה וגו' מה ראה ראה דם עקדתו של יצחק

שנאמר אלהים יראה לו השה לעולה.

ו פ ס ח יי ע ל ה פ ת ח והרי דברים קל וחמר

ומה אם דם פסח מצרים הקל שאינו אלא לשעה

ואינו נוהג ביום ובלילה ואינו נוהג לדורות נאמר בו

ולא יתן המשחית מזוזה שהיא חמורה שיש בה עשרה

שמות מיוחדין ונוהגת ביום ובלילה ונוהגת לדורות

על אחת כמה וכמה שלא יתן המשחית וגו' ומי גרם

עונותינו שנאמר עונותינו הטו אלה וכתיב כי אם

93–94 בראשית כ"ב, י"ד.   94–95 דהי"א. כ"א, ט"ו.   96 פראשית
כ"ב ח'.   102–100 מנחות ל"ג, ב'. ע"ז י"א, א'.   103 ירמיה ה'. כ"ה.
105–103 ישעיה נ"ט, ב'.

94 ובהשחית] במקרא כתוב וכהשחית.   103 עונותינו הטו אלה]
ד. > ט. מ"ח. עונותיכם הטו אלה, כאשר הוא במקרא שלפנינו / אם]
מ. ד. >.

---

also to the name אלהים and not exclusively to the tetragrammaton (as maintained by W. Bacher, *Terminologie*,
I, 159).

also written: "But your iniquities have separated between you and your God, and your sins have hid His face from you, that He will not hear" (Isa. 59.2).

And Ye Shall Observe this Thing. This is to include the passover sacrifice of subsequent generations—it should also be brought only from sheep or from goats—these are the words of R. Eliezer.

For an Ordinance to Thee and to Thy Sons. Why is this said? Since it says: "And they shall take of the blood" (v. 7), I might understand that women are also meant. Scripture therefore says: "For an ordinance to thee and to thy sons"—men and not women.

CHAPTER XII
(Ex. 12.25-28)

And It Shall Come to Pass, When Ye Be Come to the Land. Scripture stipulates that this service be observed only after the time of ·their coming into the land.

According as He Hath Promised. And where did He promise? "And I will bring you in unto the land," etc. (Ex. 6.8). In like manner you interpret: "This is that which the Lord hath spoken: Tomorrow is a solemn rest, a holy sabbath" (Ex. 16.23). And where had He spoken? "And it shall come to pass on the sixth day that they shall prepare" (ibid., 16.5) In like manner you interpret: "This is it that the

עונותיכם היו מבדילים ביניכם ובין אלהיכם
105 וחטאתיכם הסתירו מכם פנים משמוע.

ושמרתם את הדבר הזה להביא פסח
דורות שלא יביא אלא מן הכבשים ומן העזים דברי
רבי אליעזר.

לחק לך ולבניך למה נאמר לפי שהוא
110 אומר ולקחו מן הדם שומע אני אף הנשים במשמע
תלמוד לומר לחק לך ולבניך האנשים ולא הנשים.

פרשה יב (שמות י״ב, כ״ה,-כ״ח.)

והיה כי תבואו אל הארץ תלה הכתוב
לעבודה זו מביאתן לארץ ולהלן.

כאשר דבר והיכן דבר והבאתי אתכם אל
הארץ וגו' כיוצא בדבר אתה אומר הוא אשר דבר
5 יי שבתון שבת קדש והיכן דבר והיה ביום הששי
והכינו כיוצא בדבר אתה אומר הוא אשר דבר יי

108—106 לעיל ד'.   111—109 קידושין ל״ו, א'.
2—1 ספרי במדבר ס״ז וק״ג. קידושין ל״ז א' ב'.   4—3 שמות ו', ח'.
5—4 שמות ט״ז, כ״ג.   6—5 שם ט״ז, ה'.   7—6 ויקרא י', נ'. ספרא שמיני
(מלואים). זבחים קט״ו ב'.

104 היו] א. הם.   105 מכם פנים] במקרא, פנים מהם.

Lord spoke, saying: Through them that are
nigh unto Me, I will be sanctified," etc. (Lev.
10.3). And where had He said it? "And there
I will meet with the children of Israel and it shall
be sanctified by My glory" (Ex. 29.43). In like
manner you interpret: "The Lord your God shall
lay the fear of you and the dread of you . . . as
He hath spoken" (Deut. 11.25). And where had
He spoken? "I will send My terror before thee,
and will discomfort all the people," etc. (Ex.
23.27). In like manner you interpret: "When
the Lord thy God shall enlarge thy border, as
He hath promised thee" (Deut. 12.20). And
where had He promised? "For I will cast out
nations before thee, and enlarge thy borders"
(Ex. 34.24). And it also says: "And I will set
thy border from the Red Sea," etc. (Ex. 23.31).
In like manner you interpret: "For the Lord
thy God will bless thee, as He promised thee"
(Deut. 15.6). And where had He promised?
"Thou shalt be blessed above all peoples" (ibid.,
7.14). In like manner you interpret: "And the
Lord hath avouched thee this day to be His own
treasure, as He hath promised thee" (Deut.
26.18). And where had He promised? "Then ye
shall be Mine own treasure," etc. (Ex. 19.5).
In like manner you interpret: "And to make you
high above all nations that He hath made, in
praise, and in name, and in glory; and that thou
mayest be a holy people unto the Lord thy God,

לאמר בקרבי אקדש וגו' והיכן דבר ונועדתי שמה

לבני ישראל ונקדש בכבודי כיוצא בדבר אתה

אומר פחדכם ומוראכם יתן יי וגו' כאשר דבר

10 והיכן דבר את אימתי אשלח לפניך והמותי את כל

העם וגו' כיוצא בדבר אתה אומר כי ירחיב יי

אלהיך את גבולך כאשר דבר לך והיכן דבר כי

אוריש גוים מפניך והרחבתי את גבולך ואומר ושתי

את גבולך מים סוף וגו' כיוצא בדבר אתה אומר

15 כי יי אלהיך ברכך כאשר דבר לך והיכן דבר

ברוך תהיה מכל העמים כיוצא בדבר אתה אומר

ויי האמירך היום להיות לו לעם סגולה כאשר דבר

לך והיכן דבר והיתם לי סגולה וגו' כיוצא בדבר

אתה אומר ולתתך עליון על כל הגוים אשר עשה

20 לתהלה לשם ולתפארת ולהיותך עם קדש ליי

7—8 שמות כ״ט, כ״ג.   9 דברים י״א, כ״ה.   10—11 שמות כ״ג, כ״ז.
ספרי דברים נ״ב.   11—12 דברים י״ב, כ'.   14—11 ספרי שם ע״ה.
12—13 שמות ל״ד, כ״ד.   13—14 שם כ״ג, ל״א.   15 דברים ט״ו, ו'.
16 דברים ז', י״ד. ספרי שם קט״ז.   16—18 מ״ח 57.   17 דברים כ״ו, י״ח.
18 שמות י״ט, ה'.   19—21 דברים כ״ו, י״ט.

---

7 לאמר] ק. נ. <.   8 ונקדש בכבודי] הוספתי: ד. וגו'.   9 וגו']
הוספתי—ל.   11 העם] ק. נ. הגויים.   14 אתה אומר] הוספתי.
17 להיות לו לעם סגולה] הוספתי עפ״י מ״ח.   18 והייתם לי סגולה]
הגהתי—מ״ח. א׳א. א״צ. ומהר״ס בש״י: מ. ד. את יי האמרת
היום.   19—21 על כל הגוים—כאשר דבר] הוספתי: ד. וגו'.

as He hath spoken" (Deut. 26.19). And where
had He spoken? "And ye shall be holy unto
Me" (Lev. 20.26). In like manner you interpret:
"Hear, O heavens, and give ear, O earth, for the
Lord hath spoken" (Isa. 1.2). And where had
He spoken? "Give ear, ye heavens, and I will
speak" (Deut. 32.1). In like manner you interpret: "And the Glory of the Lord shall be
revealed, and all flesh shall see it together; for
the mouth of the Lord hath spoken it" (Isa.
40.5). And where had He spoken it? "See now
that I, even I, am He" (Deut. 32.39). In like
manner you interpret: "But if ye refuse and
rebel, ye shall be devoured with the sword; for
the mouth of the Lord hath spoken" (Isa. 1.20).
And where had He spoken? "And I will bring
a sword upon you, that shall execute the vengeance," etc. (Lev. 26.25). In like manner you
interpret: "He will swallow up death forever . . .
for the Lord hath spoken it" (Isa. 25.8). And
where had He spoken it? "I kill, and I make
alive," etc. (Deut. 32.39). In like manner you
interpret: "Then shalt thou delight thyself in
the Lord, and I will make thee to ride upon the
high places of the earth . . . for the mouth of the
Lord hath spoken it" (Isa. 58.14). And where
had He spoken it? "He maketh him ride upon the
high places of the earth," etc. (Deut. 32.13).

אלהיך כאשר דבר והיכן דבר והייתם לי קדושים

וגו' כיוצא בדבר אתה אומר שמעו שמים והאזיני

ארץ כי יי דבר והיכן דבר האזינו השמים ואדברה

כיוצא בדבר אתה אומר ונגלה כבוד יי וראו

25 כל בשר יחדיו כי פי יי דבר והיכן דבר ראו

עתה כי אני אני הוא כיוצא בדבר אתה אומר ואם

תמאנו ומריתם חרב תאכלו כי פי יי דבר והיכן

דבר והבאתי עליכם חרב נוקמת וגו' כיוצא בדבר

אתה אומר בלע המות לנצח וגו' כי יי דבר והיכן

30 דבר אני אמית ואחיה וגו' כיוצא בדבר אתה אומר

אז תתענג על יי והרכבתיך על במותי ארץ וגו'

כי פי יי דבר והיכן דבר ירכיבהו על במותי ארץ

---

21 ויקרא כ', כ"ו.   22—23 ישעיה א', ב'.   23—24 דברים ל"ב, א'.
24—25 ישעיה מ', ה'.   26—26 דברים ל"ב, ל"ט.   26—27 ישעיה א', כ'.
28 ויקרא כ'ו, כ"ה.   29 ישעיה כ"ה, ח'.   30—29 ספרי דברים שכ"ה.
30 דברים ל"ב, ל"ט.   32—31 ישעיה נ"ח, י"ד.   32 דברים ל"ב, י"ג.

---

21 והיכן דבר] ד. ~ ונתנך יי אלהיך לראש ולא לזנב ואומר / והייתם
לי קדושים] ק. והייתם קדושים.   22 וגו'] כ. (יואל נ', ה') ט. (שופטים
ס"נ) מ"ח. ~ כיוצא בו כה אמר יי שימו איש חרבו על יריכו (שמות
ל"ב, נ"ז) והיכן דבר זובח לאלהים יחרם (שמות כ"ב, י"ט).   27 חרב
תאכלו כי פי יי דבר] הוספתי: מ. ד. וגו'.   29 כי יי דבר] הוספתי.
32—31 והרכבתיך–כי פי יי דבר] הוספתי: ד. וגו'.

In like manner you interpret: "Behold, it
cometh, and it shall be done, saith the Lord
God; this is the day whereof I have spoken"
(Ezek. 39.8). And where had He spoken? "And
I will make Mine arrows drunk with blood,"
etc. (Deut. 32.42). In like manner you interpret:
"But they shall sit every man under his vine
and under his fig-tree; and none shall make
them afraid; for the mouth of the Lord of Hosts
hath spoken" (Micah 4.4). And where had He
spoken? "And I will give peace in the land,"
etc. (Lev. 26.6). In like manner you interpret:
"And there shall not be any remaining of the
house of Esau; for the Lord hath spoken" (Obad.
1.18). And where had He spoken? "And out of
Jacob shall one have dominion, and shall destroy
the remnant from the city" (Num. 24.19). In
like manner you interpret: "And the Lord
remembered Sarah as He had said" (Gen. 21.1).
And where had He said it? "Nay, but Sarah thy
wife shall bear thee a son" (ibid., 17.19). In
like manner you interpret: "And the Lord did
unto Sarah as He had spoken" (ibid., 21.1).
And where had He spoken? "In that day the
Lord made a covenant with Abram, saying:
Unto thy seed have I given this land" (ibid.,
15.18). In like manner you interpret: "And I
will sell your sons and your daughters . . . for
the Lord hath spoken" (Joel 4.8). And where
had He spoken? "And he said: Cursed be
Canaan," etc. (Gen. 9.25). In like manner you

וגו׳ כיוצא בדבר אתה אומר הנה באה ונהייתה
נאום יי אלהים הוא היום אשר דברתי והיכן דבר
35 אשכיר חצי מדם וגו׳ כיוצא בדבר אתה אומר
וישבו איש תחת גפנו ותחת תאנתו ואין מחריד כי
פי יי צבאות דבר והיכן דבר ונתתי שלום בארץ
וגו׳ כיוצא בדבר אתה אומר ולא יהיה שריד לבית
עשו כי יי דבר והיכן דבר וירד מיעקב והאביד
40 שריד מעיר כיוצא בדבר אתה אומר ויי פקד את
שרה כאשר אמר והיכן אמר אבל שרה אשתך וגו׳
כיוצא בדבר אתה אומר ויעש יי לשרה כאשר דבר
והיכן דבר ביום ההוא כרת יי את אברם ברית
לאמר לזרעך נתתי את הארץ הזאת כיוצא
45 בדבר אתה אומר ומכרתי את בניכם ואת בנותיכם
כי יי דבר והיכן דבר ויאמר ארור כנען וגו׳

33—35 ספרי שם של״ב.   33—34 יחזקאל ל״ט, ח׳.   35 דברים
ל״ב, מ״ב.   36—37 מיכה ד׳, ד׳.   37 ויקרא כ״ו, ו׳.   38—39 עבדיה
א׳, י״ח.   39—40 במדבר כ״ד, י״ט.   40—41 בראשית כ״א, א׳.   41 שם
י״ז, י״ט.   42 שם כ״א, א׳.   43—44 שם ט״ו, י״ח.   45—46 יואל ד׳, ח׳.
46 בראשית ט׳, כ״ה.

34 אלהים] ד. < / דברתי] ד. וגו׳.   36—37 ותחת תאנתו–צבאות
דבר] הוספתי: מ. ד. וגו׳.   38—39 לבית עשו כי יי דבר] הוספתי:
מ. ד. וגו׳.   40 מעיר] הוספתי: ד. וגו׳.   41 כאשר אמר] הוספתי: מ.
ד. וגו׳ / והיכן אמר] ד. והיכן דבר.   42 כאשר דבר] הוספתי: מ. ד.
וגו׳.   44 לאמר לזרעך–הזאת] הוספתי: ד. וגו׳.

interpret: "Forasmuch as the Lord hath said unto you: Ye shall henceforth return no more that way" (Deut. 17.16). And where had He said it? "For whereas ye have seen the Egyptians today, ye shall see them again no more" (Ex. 14.13). In like manner you interpret: "The wolf and the lamb shall feed together . . . they shall not hurt nor destroy in all My holy mountain, saith the Lord" (Isa. 65.25). And where had He said it? "And I will cause evil beasts to cease out of the land" (Lev. 26.6). In like manner you interpret: "Of the nations concerning which the Lord said unto the children of Israel: Ye shall not go among them, neither shall they come among you" (I Kings 11.2). And where had He said it? "Neither shalt thou make marriages with them" (Deut. 7.3). In like manner you interpret: "Then spoke Solomon: The Lord hath said that He would dwell in the thick darkness" (I Kings 8.12). And where had He said it? "For I appear in the cloud upon the ark-cover" (Lev. 16.2). In like manner you interpret: "Then they shall be Mine, saith the Lord of Hosts, in the day that I do make, even Mine own treasure" (Mal. 3.17). And where had He said it? "Then ye shall be Mine own treasure" (Ex. 19.5). In like manner you interpret: "And it shall come to pass, that whoever shall call on the name of the Lord shall be delivered; for in mount Zion and in Jerusalem there shall be those that escape as the Lord hath said" (Joel 3.5). And where had He said it? "And all the peoples of the earth shall see," etc. (Deut. 28.10). In like manner

כיוצא בדבר אתה אומר ויי אמר לכם לא תוסיפון

וגו' והיכן אמר כי אשר ראיתם את מצרים היום

לא תוסיפו לראותם כיוצא בדבר אתה אומר זאב

50 וטלה ירעו כאחד וגו' לא ירעו ולא ישחיתו בכל

הר קדשי אמר יי והיכן אמר והשבתי חיה רעה מן

הארץ כיוצא בדבר אתה אומר מן הגוים אשר אמר

יי והיכן אמר לא תתחתן בם כיוצא בדבר אתה

אומר אז אמר שלמה יי אמר לשכון בערפל והיכן

55 אמר כי בענן אראה על הכפרת כיוצא בדבר אתה

אומר והיו לי אמר יי צבאות ליום אשר אני עושה

סגולה והיכן אמר והייתם לי סגולה כיוצא בדבר

אתה אומר והיה כל אשר יקרא בשם יי ימלט כי

בהר ציון ובירושלים תהיה פליטה כאשר אמר יי

60 והיכן אמר וראו כל עמי הארץ וגו' כיוצא בו וגם

---

47 דברים י״ז, ט״ז. 48—49 שמות י״ד, י״ג. 49—50 ישעיה, ס״ה, כ״ה.
51—52 ויקרא כ״ו, ו'. 52—53 מלכים א. י״א, ב'. 53 דברים ז', ג'.
54 מלכים א. ח', י״ב. 55 ויקרא ט״ז, ב'. 56—57 מלאכי ג', י״ז. 57 שמות
י״ט, ה'. 58—59 יואל ג', ה'. 60 דברים כ״ח, י'. 60—61 ישעיה ס״ו, כ״א.

48—49 היום לא תוסיפו לראותם] הוספתי: ד. וגו'. 50—51 לא
ירעו—אמר יי] הוספתי. 53 לא תתחתן] במקרא כתוב ולא תתחתן.
58—59 ימלט—אמר יי] הוספתי: ד. וגו'.

you interpret "And of them also will I take for the priests and for the Levites, saith the Lord" (Isa. 66.21). And where had He said it? "The secret things belong unto the Lord our God," etc. (Deut. 29.28). So also here you interpret: "And it shall come to pass, when ye be come to the Land," etc. Scripture stipulates that this service be observed only after the time of their coming into the Land.

And It Shall Come to Pass, When Your Children Shall Say unto You. Evil tidings were announced to Israel at that time, namely that the Torah would ultimately be forgotten. But some say, it was good tidings that were announced to Israel at that time, that they were destined to see children and children's children; for it is said: "And the people bowed the head and worshipped[1]."

That Ye Shall Say: It is the Sacrifice of the Lord's Passover . . . and Delivered Our Houses. R. Jose the Galilean says: Until the last one of them finished his paschal sacrifice, the "enemies of Israel"[2] were liable to be destroyed in Egypt, as it is said: "That ye shall say: It is the sacrifice of the Lord's passover," etc.

---

[1] I. e., they gave thanks.

[2] "Enemies of Israel," euphemistic for Israel (see above, chap. II, note 7).

מהם אקח לכהנים הלויים אמר יי והיכן אמר
הנסתרות ליי אלהינו וגו' אף כאן אתה אומר והיה
כי תבואו אל הארץ וגו' תלה הכתוב לעבודה
הזאת מביאתן לארץ ולהלן.

65   והיה כי יאמרו אליכם בניכם בשורה
רעה נתבשרו ישראל באותה שעה שסוף התורה
עתידה להשתכח ויש אומרים בשורה טובה נתבשרו
ישראל באותה שעה שהן עתידין לראות בנים ובני
בנים להם שנאמר ויקוד העם וישתחוו.

70   ואמרתם זבח פסח הוא ליי וגו' ואת
בתינו הציל רבי יוסי הגלילי אומר ראויין היו
שונאיהם של ישראל כלייה במצרים עד שנגמר
האחרון שבהם את פסחו שנאמר ואמרתם זבח פסח
הוא וגו'.

---

62 דברים כ"ט, כ"ח.   67–65 ספרי דברים מ"ח. תוס' עדיות א',
א'. שבת קל"ח, ב'.

---

61 הלויים] במקרא כתוב ללוים.   64–62 אף כאן–ולהלן] ט. א"צ.
> ש"י. מ"ח. אף כאן אתה אומר (מ"ח ~ כי תבואו אל הארץ) והיכן
דבר והבאתי אתכם אל הארץ וגו'.   69 שנאמר] ט. מ"ח. ש"ט. > /
וישתחוו] ד. ~ וגו'.   70–71 ואת בתינו הציל] הוספתי.   73 האחרון]=ט.
מ"ח. א"א. א"צ. ש"ט: ד. אחר/ שנאמר]=ט. מ"ח. א"א: ד.
>. 74 וגו'] הוספתי עפ"י ט.

And the People Bowed the Head and Worshipped.
This is to teach you that whoever hears these
miracles which the Holy One, blessed be He, did
for Israel in Egypt should give praise, as it is
said: "And Moses told his father-in-law . . . And
Jethro rejoiced . . . And Jethro said: Blessed be
the Lord" (Ex. 18.8-10).

And Worshipped. Why did they worship?
Because of the following: It is said: "And the
children of Israel went up armed (*ḥamushim*)
out of Egypt" (Ex. 16.18), this means, one out
of five³ went up. Some say, one out of fifty,
and some say, one out of five hundred. R.
Nehorai says: By the worship!⁴ Not even one
out of five hundred went up. For it is said:
"I caused thee to increase, even as the growth
of the field" (Ezek. 16.7). It also says: "And
the children of Israel were fruitful and increased
abundantly" (Ex. 1.7)—a woman would give
birth to six children at one time. And you say,
one out of five hundred went up!⁵ When did
all the others die? During the three days of
darkness, of which it is said: "They saw not
one another" (Ex. 10.23). They then buried
their dead and thanked and praised God that
their enemies could not see their losses and
rejoice over them.

---

³ The word חמושים here is taken as derived from חמש
"five" and meaning, reduced to one-fifth.

⁴ "By the worship," is equal to "by God" (see Jastrow,
Dictionary, p. 1036, s. v. עבודה).

⁵ At such a rate of increase there must have been more
than 500 times the number of those who came out.

ויקוד העם ללמדך שכל מי ששומע הנסים
האלו שעשה הקב"ה לישראל במצרים צריך ליתן
שבח שנאמר ויספר משה לחתנו וגו' ויחד יתרו וגו'
ויאמר יתרו ברוך יי.

וישתחו למה השתחוו משום שנאמר וחמשים
עלו בני ישראל עלו אחד מחמשה ויש אומרים אחד
מחמשים ויש אומרים אחד מחמש מאות רבי נהוראי
אומר העבודה ולא אחד מחמש מאות עלו שנאמר
רבבה כצמח השדה נתתיך ואומר ובני ישראל פרו
וישרצו שהיתה אשה יולדת ששה בכרס אחד ואתה
אומר אחד מחמש מאות עלו ואימתי מתו בשלשת
ימי אפילה שנאמר לא ראו איש את אחיו שהיו
קוברין את מיתיהן והודו ושבחו שלא ראו אויבים
ושמחו במפלתם.

77—78 שמות י"ח, ח'—י'.   79—80 שמות י"ג, י"ח.   לקטן בשלח א'.
83 יחזקאל ט"ז, ז'.   83—84 שמות א', ז'.   86 שמות י', כ"ג.

75 ויקוד העם] הוספתי עפ"י מ"ח: א"צ. ~ וישתחוו ד. מ. > /
ששומע] מ. מ"ח. ט. ש"ט. שרואה ושומע א"א. ששומע ורואה.
76 במצרים] מ"ח. א"א. >.   77 שנאמר] ק. נ. ונומר. ל. ואומר
מ"ח. ל"ט. וכן הוא אומר א"א. כענין שנאמר.   79 וישתחוו
הוספתי—מ"ח: א"צ. ל"ט. דבר אחר ויקוד וגו'.   79—88 למה
השתחוו—ושמחו במפלתם] ד. מ. הפכו הסדר והביאו המאמר הזה
למעלה קודם הדרש על ואמרתם זבח פסח ואנכי תקנתי הסדר
וערכתי המאמרים לפי סדר המקראות—מ"ח. וא"צ. וכן הניה רמא"ס.
84 אשה] ד. ~ אחת. / ששה] ד. ~ בנים.

And the Children of Israel Went and Did. This indicates that reward is given for setting out to perform a religious duty as well as for actually performing it.

And Did So. And had they already done so? No, but once they undertook to do it it is accounted to them as if they had already done it.

As the Lord had Commanded Moses and Aaron so They Did. This makes known the excellency of Israel, that they did exactly as Moses and Aaron told them. Another Interpretation: What is the purport of the words, "so they did?" Simply, that Moses and Aaron also did so.

CHAPTER XIII
(Ex. 12.29–36)

And It Came to Pass at Midnight. The Creator of the night divided it exactly. Why is this said? Because it is said: "And Moses said: Thus saith the Lord: About midnight will I go out," etc. (Ex. 11.4). For, is it possible for a human being to fix the exact time of midnight? None but the Creator could have divided the night exactly.[1] R. Judah b. Bathyra says: He who knows its hours and its fractions divided it.

---

[1] See Lauterbach, "Abbreviations and their Solutions," in *Studies in Jewish Bibliography and Related Subjects*, New York, 1929, p. 145.

וילכו ויעשו ליתן שכר להליכה ושכר
לעשייה.

ויעשו וכי כבר עשו אלא משקבלו עליהם
לעשות מעלה עליהם כאלו עשו.

כאשר צוה יי וגו' להודיעך שבחן של ישראל
שכשם שאמרו להם משה ואהרן כן עשו דבר אחר
מה תלמוד לומר כן עשו אלא שאף משה ואהרן
עשו כן.

פרשה יג (שמות י״ב, כ״ט,–ל״ו.)

ויהי בחצי הלילה יוצרו חלקו למה נאמר
לפי שנאמר ויאמר משה כה אמר יי כחצות הלילה
אני יוצא וגו' וכי אפשר לבשר ודם לעמוד על חציו
של לילה אלא אם כן יוצרו חלקו רבי יהודה בן
בתירה אומר היודע שעותיו ועתותיו הוא חלקו

93–96 ספרי במדבר א'. ספרא שמיני סוף מכילתא דמילואים.
6–1 ברכות ג', ב'. ד'. א'. פסדר״כ ז' (ס״ב, א'. ס״ג, ב'). פס״ר
י״ז (פ״ה, א'. פ״ז, ב'). ב״ר ס״ג, נ'. ש. 22.   3–2 שמות י״א, ד'.

92 כאלו עשו] ק. נ. ~ וגו'.   93 וגו'] הוספתי.   94 דבר אחר]
א״צ. ז״י. >.

1 יוצרו חלקו] כ. (תהלים קל״ו, ט״ו) מ״ח. >. 5–1 למה נאמר–
בתירה אומר] א״צ. >.   3 וכי אפשר] כ. (שם) מ״ח. שאי איפשר.
4 אלא] כ. מ״ח. אבל/ אם כן] ט. סכאן כ. מ״ח. כאן. 4–5 ר״י בן
בתירה אומר] כ. מ״ח. >.   5 היודע] כ. מ״ח. שיודע/ ועתותיו] כ.
מ״ח. ורעיו/ הוא חלקו] כ. מ״ח.>.

R. Eliezer says: The word "night" is used here, and the word "night" is used there (v. 12). Just as the word "night" used here means not later than midnight, so the word "night" used there means not later than midnight.

And the Lord Smote All the First-Born. I might understand this to mean through an angel or through an agent, therefore it says: "And I will smite" (v. 12)—not through an angel nor through an agent.

That the Lard Smote All the First-Born in Egypt. Even those who hailed from other places. And how about Egyptian first-born who were in other places? Scripture says: "To Him who smote Egypt in their first-born" (Ps. 136.10). And how about the first-born of Ham, Cush, Put and Lud? Scripture says: "And smote all the first-born in Egypt, the first fruit of their strength in the tents of Ham"² (Ps. 78.51).

From the First-Born of Pharaoh that Sat on His Throne. Scripture comes to teach that Pharaoh himself was a first-born. You say that it is to teach you that Pharaoh was a first-born. Perhaps it is merely to teach that his son was a first-born? But when it says, "that sat on his

---

² Ham is the ancestor of Cush, Put and Lud (see Gen. 10.5 and 13 and cf. above, chap. VII, note 5).

רבי אליעזר אומר נאמר כאן לילה ונאמר להלן
לילה מה לילה האמור כאן עד חצות אף לילה
האמור להלן עד חצות.

וייי הכה כל בכור שומעני על ידי מלאך
או על ידי שליח תלמוד לומר והכתי כל בכור לא
על ידי מלאך ולא על ידי שליח.

וייי הכה כל בכור בארץ מצרים
אפילו ממקומות אחרים ובכורי מצרים שהן
במקומות אחרים מנין תלמוד לומר למכה מצרים
בבכוריהם בכורי חם כוש ופוט ולוד מנין תלמוד
לומר ויך כל בכור במצרים ראשית אונים באהלי
חם.

מבכור פרעה היושב על כסאו בא
הכתוב ללמד על פרעה שהוא בכור אתה אומר
ללמדך על פרעה שהוא בכור או אינו בא אלא
ללמד על בנו שהוא בכור כשהוא אומר היושב על

8—6 לעיל פ״ו.   9—17 לעיל פ״ו.   10 שמות י״ב. י״ב.   15—14 תהלים
ק״ו, י׳.   17—16 תהלים ע״ח, נ״א.   20—18 פסדר״כ שם (ס״ה, א׳). ש. 23.

6 אליעזר] ט. אליה.   7—6 להלן לילה] ד. להלן חצות.   8—7 מה
לילה-להלן עד חצות] ד. מה להלן עד חצות אף כאן עד חצות.
17—16 אונים באהלי חם] הוספתי: מ. ונו׳.   22—18 מבכור פרעה-תלמוד
לומר] מ. >.   20—19 אתה אומר-שהוא בכור] ד. >.

throne," behold then his son is there referred to. Hence, what does Scripture mean by saying: "From the first-born (of) Pharaoh?" Scripture comes to teach that Pharaoh himself was a first-born. He alone was left of all the first-born, and referring to him Scripture says: "But in very deed for this cause, have I made thee to stand," etc. (Ex. 9.16). Baal-Zephon was left of all the deities to mislead the minds of the Egyptians. Referring to it, Scripture says: "He misleadeth the nations and destroyeth them" (Job 12.23).

Unto the First-Born of the Captive. But how did the captives sin? It was only that the captives should not say: "Our deity brought this visitation upon the Egyptians. Our deity is strong, for it stood up for itself. Our deity is strong, for the visitation did not prevail over us." Another Interpretation: This is to teach you that the captives used to rejoice over every decree which Pharaoh decreed against Israel. For it is said, "He that is glad at calamity shall not be unpunished" (Prov. 17.5). It also says: "Rejoice not when thy enemy falleth" (ibid., 24.17). And it is written: "Son of man, because that Tyre hath said against Jerusalem Aha," etc. (Ezek. 26.2). What does it then say? "Behold, I am against thee, O Tyre, and will cause many nations to come up against thee as the sea

כסאו הרי בנו אמור הא מה תלמוד לומר מבכור
פרעה בא הכתוב ללמד על פרעה שהוא בכור
והוא נשתייר מכל הבכורות ועליו הכתוב אומר
ואולם בעבור זאת העמדתיך וגו' בעל צפון נשתייר
מכל היראות בשביל לפתות לבן של מצרים עליו
הוא אומר משגיא לגוים ויאבדם.

ע ד ב כ ו ר ה ש ב י וכי שבויין מה חטאו אלא
שלא יהיו השבויין אומרים יראתינו הביאה עליהם
את הפורענות קשה יראתינו שעמדה לעצמה קשה
יראתינו שלא שלטה בנו הפורענות. דבר אחר
ללמדך שכל גזירות שהיה פרעה גוזר על ישראל
היו השבויין שמחין בהם שנאמר שמח לאיד לא
ינקה ואומר בנפול אויבך אל תשמח וכתיב בן אדם
יען אשר אמרה צר על ירושלים האח וגו' מה הוא
אומר הנני אליך צר והעליתי עליך גוים רבים

---

25 שמות ט', ט'ז.　27 איוב י'ב, כ'נ.　33—34 משלי י'ז, ה'.
34 שם כ'ד, י'ז.　37—34 יחזקאל כ'ו, ב'—ג'.

---

23 על פרעה] ד. <.　24 והוא] א. פרעה.　26 עליו] ד. עליהם.
27 משגיא] מ. משנה.　29 עליהם] ד. עליו.　30 יראתינו שעמדה
לעצמה] ד. יראתן שעמדה לעצמן.　31 בנו הפורענות] מ. בהם את
הפורענות./דבר אחר] הוספתי עפ"י מ"ח.　32 ללמדך] א' צ. וללמדך,
33 שמחין בהם] מ"ח. ~ לפיכך לקו עליהם לקיים מה.　34 וכתיב] א.
וכן.　36—35 מה הוא אומר הנני] מ. ד. וכתיב לכן כה אמר יי צבאות
(במקרא כתוב אדני ה'). 36 אליך] במקרא כתוב עליך.

causeth its waves to come up" (ibid. v.3). And not the captives alone acted thus but also the Egyptian menservants and maidservants, for it is said: "even unto the first-born of the maid-servant" (Ex. 11.5).

And All the First-Born of the Cattle. But how did the cattle sin? It was only that the Egyptians should not say: "Our own deity has brought this visitation upon us. Our deity is strong, for it stood up for itself. Our deity is strong, for this visitation did not prevail over it."[3]

And Pharaoh Rose Up. I might understand this to mean after the third hour of the day, for such is the custom of kings that they get up after the third hour. But Scripture says: "in the night." If "in the night" I might understand that he was awakened by the princes and the princesses, but the passage: "He and all his servants, and all the Egyptians," tells that it was Pharaoh who went around to the houses of all his servants and to the houses of all the Egyptians and aroused every one from his place.

And There Was a Great Cry. Just as it had been said: "And there shall be a great cry" (Ex. 11.6).

For There Was Not a House Where There Was Not One Dead. R. Nathan says: And were there not houses in which there was no first-born? It

---

[3] There is here an allusion to the animal worship of the Egyptians.

כהעלות הים לגליו ולא שבויים בלבד אלא אפילו
עבדים ושפחות שנאמר עד בכור השפחה.

וכל בכור בהמה וכי בהמה מה חטאה
40 אלא שלא יהו המצרים אומרים יראתינו הביאה
עלינו את הפורענות קשה יראתינו שעמדה על
עצמה קשה יראתינו שלא שלטה בה הפורענות.

ויקם פרעה שומע אני בשלש שעות שכן דרך
מלכים לעמוד בשלש שעות תלמוד לומר לילה אי
45 לילה שומע אני על ידי שרים ושרות תלמוד לומר
הוא וכל עבדיו וכל מצרים מגיד שהיה פרעה
מחזיר על בתי כל עבדיו ועל בתי כל מצרים
ומעמידן כל אחד ואחד ממקומו.

ותהי צעקה גדולה כענין שנאמר והיתה
50 צעקה גדולה וגו׳.

כי אין בית אשר אין שם מת שם רבי נתן
אומר וכי לא היו שם בתים אשר אין שם בכור אלא

---

38 שמות י״א, ה׳.   42—39 פסדר׳כ שם (ס׳ה, ב׳).   44—43 ברכות
א׳, ב׳.   50—49 שמות י״א, ו׳.   60—51 פסדר׳כ שם. פס׳ר שם (פ׳ז,
ב׳). ש. 23.   70—52 מדרש שה׳ש (הוצאת גרינהוט) ב׳, י׳ (כ׳ד, א׳).

---

42 הפורענות] ד. ~ קשה יראתינו שהביאה עלינו את הפורענות.
45 שרים ושרות] א. שדים ושדות. ת. שדה ושדות.   46 וכל מצרים]=ט:
מ. ד. >.   47 בתי כל מצרים] ד. כל בתי ישראל.

means simply this: When the first-born of one of the Egyptians died, they would make a statue of him and set it up in the house. On that night such statues were crushed, ground and scattered. And in their eyes that day was as sad as though they had just then buried their first-born. Furthermore, the Egyptians used to bury the dead in their houses. The dogs, entering through the gutters, dug out and dragged forth the first-born out of their niches and sported with them. And this was as hard on the Egyptians as though they had just buried them on that day.

And He Called for Moses and Aaron. This tells that Pharaoh went around in the whole land of Egypt, asking: Where does Moses dwell, where does Aaron dwell?

And said: Rise Up, Get You Forth. Moses, however, said to him: "We are warned not to go out except in broad daylight," as it is said: "And none of you shall go out of the door of his house until the morning" (v. 22).

Another Interpretation. *And He Called for Moses and Aaron.* Why is this said? Because it is said: "And Pharaoh said unto him: Get thee

כיון שהיה הבכור מת לאחד מהן היה עושה לו
איקונין שלו ומעמידה בתוך ביתו ואותו הלילה
נשחקת ונידקת ונזרת והיה אותו היום קשה בעיניהם
כאילו אותו היום קברוהו ולא עוד אלא שהיו
המצרים קוברים בתוך בתיהם והיו הכלבים נכנסין
דרך הביבין ומחטטין ומוציאין את הבכורות מתוך
כוכיהם ומתעתעין בהם וקשה היה בעיניהם כאילו
אותו היום קברוהו.

ויקרא למשה ולאהרן מגיד שהיה פרעה
מחזר ושואל בכל ארץ מצרים היכן משה שרוי
היכן אהרן שרוי.

ויאמר קומו וצאו אמר לו משה מוזהרין
אנו שלא לצאת אלא בפרהסיא שנאמר ואתם לא
תצאו וגו' דבר אחר ויקרא למשה ולאהרן
למה נאמר לפי שהוא אומר ויאמר לו פרעה לך

65—64 מדרש תהלים קי"נ (רל"ה, א'). 66—65 שמות י"ב, כ"ב.
68—67 שמות י', כ"ח-כ"ט.

---

54 הלילה] ד. היום. 55 ונזרת] א. ונידרת. 56 כאילו אותו
היום קברוהו] מ. ד. כיום הקבורה. 57 קוברים] מ"ח. ~ מיתיהם
ד. מקוברים / נכנסין] ד. באין לשם. 58 דרך הביבין] ד. > מ. ט.
מ"ח. דרך הכוכין. 59—58 מתוך כוכיהם]ק. > ל. מתוך כוביהם א.
מתוך המתים. 59 וקשה היה בעיניהם]—ט: מ"ח. והיה בעיניהם. מ.
ד. והיה אותו היום קשה בעיניהם. 65 אלא] מ. אפילו. 67 שהוא
אומר ויאמר לו]ק. נ. שהיה אומר לו ל. שאמר לו.

from me," etc. (Ex. 10.28). "And Moses said:
Thou hast spoken well,"—you have spoken
appropriately and you have spoken in time,—"I
will see thy face again no more" (ibid., v. 29),
but "all these thy servants shall come down,"
etc. (Ex. 11.8). The purpose of saying "these"
was none other than to imply: "You yourself
will ultimately come down leading them."[4]
Moses, however, showed respect to royalty. For
so the Holy One, blessed be He, had told him:
"Show respect to royalty," as it is said: "And
the Lord spoke unto Moses and unto Aaron,
and gave them a charge," etc. (Ex. 6.13)—He
charged them to show respect to royalty. And
so we find that Joseph, likewise, showed respect
to royalty, as it is said: "It is not in me; God will
give Pharaoh an answer of peace" (Gen. 41.16).
And we also find that our father Jacob showed
respect to royalty, as it is said: "And Israel
strengthened himself and sat upon the bed"[5]
(ibid., 48.2). And we find that Elijah, likewise,
showed respect to royalty, as it is said: "And he
girded up his loins, and ran before Ahab"
(I Kings 18.46). And so we find that Hananiah,
Mishael and Azariah also showed respect to,

---

[4] "All these," implies all these people present here,
including Pharaoh himself.

[5] This refers to an old midrash to the effect that Jacob
sat up before Joseph to show him the honor due to a ruler
(cf. *Tanḥuma, Vayeḥi*, 6).

מעלי וגו' ויאמר משה כן דברת וגו' יפה דברת

ובזמנה דברת לא אוסיף עוד ראות פניך אלא

70 וירדו כל עבדיך אלה וגו' שאין תלמוד לומר אלה

אלא שסופך עתיד לירד בראשם אלא שמשה חלק

כבוד למלכות וכן הקדוש ברוך הוא אמר לו חלוק

כבוד למלכות שנאמר וידבר יי אל משה ואל אהרן

ויצום וגו' ציום לחלוק כבוד למלכות וכן מצינו

75 ביוסף שחלק כבוד למלכות שנאמר בלעדי אלהים

יענה את שלום פרעה וכן מצינו באבינו יעקב שחלק

כבוד למלכות שנאמר ויתחזק ישראל וישב על

המטה וכן מצינו באליהו שחלק כבוד למלכות

שנאמר וישנס מתניו וירץ לפני אחאב וכן מצינו

80 בחנניה מישאל ועזריה שחלקו כבוד למלכות שנאמר

---

70 שמות י"א, ח'. 70—72 זבחים ק"ב, א'. מנחות צ"ח, א'. שמו"ר
י"ח, א'. 73—74 שמות ו', י"נ. 75—76 בראשית מ"א, ט"ז. 77—78 בראשית
מ"ח, ב'. 79 מלכים א. י"ח, מ"ו. מנחות שם.

70—71 שאין ת"ל אלה אלא] א. <. 71 שסופך] ט. שסופו/ לירד
בראשם] א. ט. לירד בראשונה ד. להיות בראשם (נ. ל. ~ ולירד
בראשונה) / שמשה]מ. ד. מלמד שמשה. 72—73 וכן הקב"ה־כבוד
למלכות] ק. <. 74 וגו'] ל. ~ואל פרעה] ק. נ. אל פרעה (במקרא
כתוב אל בני ישראל ואל פרעה)/וכן] ד. שכן. 79 לפני אחאב] א.
מ. ונו' ועפ"ז הוספתי כמו במקרא: ד. לקראת אחאב.

royalty, as it is said: "Then Nebuchadnezzar came near to the mouth the burning fiery furnace; he spoke and said: 'Shadrach, Meshach, and Abed-nego, ye servants of God Most High, come forth and come hither.' Then Shadrach, Meshach and Abed-nego came forth" (Dan. 3.26). And we find that Daniel, likewise, showed respect to royalty, as it is said: "And when he came near unto the den," etc. (Dan. 6.21). And what does it then say? "Then said Daniel unto the King: 'O King, live forever'" (ibid., v. 22).

And Said: Rise Up, Get You Forth. I had said: "Who are they that shall go?" (Ex. 10.8). And you had said: "We will go with our young and with our old," etc. (ibid., v. 9). "Rise up, get you forth from my people, both ye and the children of Israel; and go, serve the Lord, as ye have said." I had said: "Only let your flocks and your herds be stayed" (ibid., v. 24). And you had said: "Our cattle also shall go with us" (ibid., 26). "Take both your flocks and your herds." You had said: "Thou must also give into our hand sacrifices and burnt-offerings" (ibid., v. 25). "Take . . . as you have said and be gone; and bless me also." Pray for me that this visitation may cease from me.

באדין קרב נבוכדנצר לתרע אתון נורא יקדת ענה

ואמר שדרך מישך ועבד נגו עבדוהי די אלהא

עליא פוקו ואתו באדין נפקין שדרך מישך ועבד

נגו וכן מצינו בדניאל שחלק כבוד למלכות שנאמר

85 וכמקרביה לגובא וגו' ומה הוא אומר אדין דניאל

עם מלכא מליל מלכא לעלמין חיי.

ויאמר קומו צאו אני אמרתי   מי ומי

ההולכים ואתם אמרתם בנערינו ובזקנינו

נלך וגו' קומו צאו מתוך עמי גם אתם גם בני

90 ישראל ולכו עבדו את יי כדברכם אני אמרתי

רק צאנכם ובקרכם יצג ואתם אמרתם

וגם מקנינו ילך עמנו גם צאנכם גם

בקרכם קחו אתם אמרתם גם אתה תתן

בידינו זבחים ועולות קחו כאשר

95 דברתם ולכו וברכתם גם אותי והתפללו עלי

שתכלה ממני הפורענות.

84–81 דניאל ג', כ'ו.   86–85 שם ו', כ'א-כ'ב.   89–87 שמות י',
ח'-ט'.   91 שם י', כ'ד.   92 שם י', כ'ו.   94–93 שם י', כ'ה.

---

81 באדין קרב] ד.   באדין נפקין שדרך מישך וגו' כד קרב.
84–81 יקדת-נפקין שדרך מישך ועבד נגו] א. מ. וגו' ועפי'ז הוספתי-א'א.
90–89 מתוך עמי-כדברכם] הוספתי: א. וגו'.   91–93 ואתם אמרתם-
בקרכם קחו] ד. <.

And the Egyptians Were Urgent upon the People, etc. This tells that they hurried and rushed them to go out.

For They Said: "We Are All Dead Men." They said: This is not according to the decree of Moses, Moses having said only: "And all the first born in the land of Egypt shall die," etc. (Ex. 11.5). They thought if a man had four or five sons, only the oldest of them would die. But they did not know that their wives were guilty of adultery, and that all of the sons were first-born, each having a different bachelor for his father. These women had done wrong in secret but God exposed them. Now by using the method of *Kal vaḥomer* you argue: If with regard to meting out evil, which is of less importance, the rule is that God makes public the deeds done in secret, how much more should this be the rule with regard to meting out good, which is of greater importance?

And the People Took Their Dough before it Was Leavened. This tells that they had kneaded their dough but had not sufficient time to let it leaven before they were redeemed. You also find the same said about the future. What does it say? "Who ceaseth to stir from the kneading of the dough until it be leavened. On the day of our king the princes make him sick" (Hos. 7.4–5).

ותחזק מצרים על העם וגו' מגיד שהיו
מבהלין אותן וטורדין אותן לצאת.

כי אמרו כלנו מתים אמרו לא בגזירת
משה הוא משה אמר ומת כל בכור וגו' והיו
סבורין שכל מי שיש לו ארבעה או חמשה בנים אין
מת אלא הבכור שבהם והם לא היו יודעין שנשיהם
חשודות על העריות והיו כולן בכורות מרווקין
אחרים הן עשו בסתר והמקום פרסמן בגלוי והרי
הדברים קל וחמר ומה אם מדת הפורענות מעוטה
העושה בסתר המקום מפרסמו בגלוי מדה טובה
מרובה על אחת כמה וכמה.

וישא העם את בצקו טרם יחמץ מגיד
שלשו את העיסה ולא הספיקו לחמצה עד שנגאלו
וכן אתה מוצא לעתיד לבא מה הוא אומר ישבות
מעיר מלוש בצק עד חומצתו יום מלכנו החלו
שרים.

100

105

110

103—99 ש. 24.   100 שמות י"א, ה'.   112—108 לקטן פנ'ד.
112—110 הושע ז', ד'—ה'.

99 בגזירת] ד. כמדת.   100 הוא] מ. ד. > / משה אמר] מ.
שמשה גזר.   102—100 והיו סבורין—שבהם] א. היו אומרים ד' ה' בנים
לאחד מהם ואחד מהם מת הותרה.   109 עד שנגאלו] ד. >.

Their kneading-troughs (Mish'arotam). This refers to the "left-overs"[6] of the unleavened bread and bitter herbs. You interpret it so. Perhaps this is not so, but it means the left-overs of the paschal sacrifices? When it says: "And ye shall let nothing of it remain until the morning" (v. 10), behold then it forbids having "left-overs" of the paschal-sacrifice. Hence what is meant by "their kneading-troughs (*Mish'arotam*) being bound up in their clothes?" The "left-overs" of the unleavened bread and bitter herbs.

Being Bound up in Their Clothes upon Their Shoulders. R. Nathan says: And were there no beasts of burden there? Has it not been said: "And a mixed multitude went up also with them; and flocks and herds even very much cattle?" What then is the purport of saying here: "being bound up in their clothes upon their shoulders?" Simply that the Israelites cherished their religious duties.

And the Children of Israel Did according to the Word of Moses. But what had Moses told Israel in Egypt? Behold, it says: "Speak now in the ears of the people,"[7] etc. (Ex. 11.2). And so the children of Israel did.

---

[6] The Hebrew word for "their kneading-troughs," משארתם, is connected by the Midrash with שאר, meaning "to remain," "to be left over." In the citation of the biblical passage I retained the usual translation, "their kneading-troughs," because the midrashic comments may mean to imply that they used their kneading-troughs as containers in which they carried the "left-overs".

משאֵרותם אלו שיירי מצה ומרור אתה אומר

כן או אינו אלא שירי פסחים כשהוא אומר לא

תותירו ממנו עד בוקר הרי שירי פסחים 115

אמור הא מה תלמוד לומר משארותם צרורות

בשמלותם אלו שיירי מצה ומרור.

צרורות בשמלותם על שכמם רבי נתן

אומר וכי לא היתה שם בהמה והלא כבר נאמר

וגם ערב רב עלה אתם וצאן ובקר ומה תלמוד 120

לומר צרורות בשמלותם על שכמם אלא שהיו

ישראל מחבבין את המצוות.

ובני ישראל עשו כדבר משה וכי מה

אמר להם משה לישראל במצרים הרי הוא אומר

דבר נא באזני העם וגו' וכן עשו בני ישראל. 125

---

113 ש. שם. 114—115 שמות י"ב, י'. 120 שמות י"ב, ל"ח.
123—125 ברכות ט', א'–ב'. 125 שמות י"א, ב'.

114—115 לא תותירו] במקרא כתוב ולא תותירו.

---

[1] It is assumed that Moses carried out God's command
and told the Israelites to borrow things from the Egyptians.

And They Asked of the Egyptians Jewels of Silver, and Jewels of Gold, and Raiment. There would be no purpose in saying "and raiment," except to indicate that garments were more precious to them than silver and gold.

And the Lord Gave the People Favour, etc. This is to be taken literally. No sooner had the Israelite said: "Lend me," than the Egyptian brought forth the article and gave it to him— these are the words of R. Ishmael. R. Jose the Galilean says: They trusted the Israelites because of their experience with them during the three days of darkness. For they said: If at the time when we were in darkness and they had light they proved above suspicion, shall they now be suspected? R. Eliezer the son of Jacob says: The Holy Spirit rested upon the Israelites. And every one of them could say to the Egyptians: "Lend me your article which you have put away in such and such a place." The Egyptians would then bring it forth and give it to him. The word "favour" (*Ḥen*) here only means, "the Holy Spirit," as in the passage: "And I will pour upon the house of David, and upon the inhabitants of Jerusalem, the spirit of grace" (*Ḥen*), etc. (Zech. 12.10). R. Nathan says: There would be no

וישאלו ממצרים כלי כסף וכלי זהב
ושמלות שאין תלמוד לומר ושמלות אלא הכסות
היתה חביבה עליהם יותר מן הכסף ומן הזהב.

ויי נתן את חן העם וגו' כמשמעו לא
130 הספיק לומר לו השאילני עד שהוא מוציא ונותן לו
דברי רבי ישמעאל רבי יוסי הגלילי אומר האמינו
בהם משלשת ימי האפילה שהיו אומרים ומה אם
בשעה שהיינו באפילה והם באורה לא נחשדו
ועכשיו נחשדין רבי אליעזר בן יעקב אומר רוח
135 הקדש שרתה על ישראל והיה אומר לו השאילני
כליך המונח לך במקום פלוני והוא מוציא ונותן לו
ואין הן אלא רוח הקדש שנאמר ושפכתי על בית
דוד ועל יושב ירושלים רוח חן וגו' רבי נתן אומר

---

131 דברי ר' ישמעאל] הצנתי כאן עפ"י ט. כ. «זכריה י"ב,
י"א) א"צ. ום"ח: בכת"י וד. נמצא אחר תיבת כמשמעו.
132 משלשת ימי האפילה] ד. >.   133 בשעה שהיינו] ד. / והם
באורה] ד. < / נחשדו] ד. עשו.   134 נחשדין] מ. עשין/ אליעזר]
ט. אליה/ בן יעקב] א. מ. ט. כ. (שם) >.   135 על ישראל] ד.
עליהם.   136 והוא] א. מ. יהלא ט. מ"ח. יהלה.   137 ושפכתי]
ד. ונתתי.   138 דוד] ד. ~ רוח חן/ועל יושב ירושלים] א. מ.
וגו' ועפי"ז הוספתי כמו במקרא שלפנינו: ד. ועל ירושלים. א"א.
כ. (שם) ועל יושבי ירושלים.

need of saying: "So they let them have" (*vaya-sh'ilum*),[8] except to indicate that they let them have even what they did not ask for. The Israelite would say to an Egyptian: "Let me have such and such a thing." And the Egyptian would say to him: "Take it, and here is another one like it."

And They Despoiled the Egyptians. This means that their idols melted, thus ceasing to be idols and returning to their former state.

And how do we know that the plunder at the sea was greater than the plunder in Egypt? It is said: "And thou didst increase and grow up and camest to the ornament of ornaments"[9] (Ezek. 16.7). "To the ornament," refers to the plunder in Egypt. "Of ornaments," refers to the plunder at the sea. "The wings of the dove are covered with silver" (Ps. 68.14), refers to the plunder in Egypt. "And her wings with the shimmer of gold" (ibid.), refers to the plunder at the sea. "We will make thee circlets of gold" (Cant. 1.11), refers to the plunder at the sea. "With studs of silver" (ibid.), refers to the plunder in Egypt.

---

[8] The *Hif'il* form of the verb has causative force. Hence, וישאילום is interpreted as meaning, the Egyptians urged the Israelites to borrow things which the Israelites themselves never asked for.

[9] The rendering "excellent beauty" as given in the Bible Translations would not furnish the basis for the interpretation of our Midrash.

אין צריך לומר וישאילום אלא מה שלא שאלו היו

140 משאילין אותם היה אומר לו תן לי חפץ פלוני והיה

אומר לו טול לך ואחר כיוצא בו.

ויצלו את מצרים מגיד שעבודה זרה

שלהם נתכת ובטלה וחוזרת לתחלתה ומנין שביזת

הים גדולה מביזת מצרים שנאמר ותרבי ותגדלי

145 ותבואי בעדי עדיים בעדי זו ביזת מצרים עדיים

זו ביזת הים כנפי יונה נחפה בכסף זו ביזת מצרים

ואברותיה בירקרק חרוץ זו ביזת הים תורי זהב

נעשה לך זו ביזת הים עם נקודות הכסף זו ביזת

מצרים.

143—149 ש. 25.   144—145 יחזקאל ט"ז, ז'.   146—147 תהלים ס"ח,

י"ד.   147—148 שה"ש א', י"א.

139 לומר] ד. כך אלא/ אלא] ד. <.   141 טול לך] א. טול

ולך מ ד.   142 מניד] ד. טלטד.   144 מביזת מצרים] ד. מזו.

145 ביזת] מ. ד. <.

Chapter XIV
(Ex. 12.37–42)

And the Children of Israel Journeyed from Rameses to Succoth. From Rameses to Succoth was a distance of a hundred and sixty miles, forty parasangs. Moses' voice traveled the distance of a forty days' journey.[1] This need not surprise you. Behold, it says: "And the Lord said unto Moses and unto Aaron: Take to you handfuls of soot of the furnace . . . and it shall become small dust over all the land of Egypt," etc. (Ex. 9.8–9). Now by using the method of *Kal vaḥomer* you reason: If dust, the nature of which is not to move, traveled the distance of a forty days' journey, how much the more could the voice, whose very nature it is to travel, do so! In the twinkling of an eye did the children of Israel travel from Rameses to Succoth. This confirms what has been said: "I bore you on eagles' wings," etc. (Ex. 19.4).

---

[1] Egypt, according to the Rabbis, covers an area of 400 parasangs in length and 400 parasangs in width (Pes. 94a). An average traveler on foot covers only 10 parasangs a day (ibid. l. c.). The distance then from one end of Egypt to the other is a 40 days' journey. The Israelites, it is assumed here, were scattered all over the land of Egypt. Yet they all heard the call of Moses and came to Rameses (cf. below, *Baḥodesh*, II, l. 19ff.). Hence, Moses' voice must have traveled the distance of a 40 days' journey, i. e., 400 parasangs, the length and width of the land of Egypt.

פרשה יד   (שמות י״ב, ל״ז,_מ״ב.)

ויסעו בני ישראל מרעמסס סכתה
מרעמסס לסוכות מאה וששים מיל מהלך ארבעים
פרסה הלך קולו של משה מהלך ארבעים יום ואל
תתמה הרי הוא אומר ויאמר יי אל משה ואל אהרן

5   קחו לכם מלא חפניכם וגו' והיה לאבק על כל ארץ
מצרים וגו' והרי הדברים קל וחמר ומה אם אבק
שאין דרכו להלוך והלך מהלך ארבעים יום קל
וחמר לקול שדרכו להלוך כהרף עין נסעו בני
ישראל מרעמסס לסכות לקיים מה שנאמר ואשא

10   אתכם על כנפי נשרים וגו'.

1—22 ש. 26.   3 י' פסחים ה', ה' (32c).   4—6 שמות ט', ח'—ט'.
שמו"ר י"א, ה'. ת. וארא. מ"ת. 57.   8—10 לקמן עמלק פ"ד.   9—10 שמות
י"ט, ד'.

---

2 מאה וששים] הנהתי=ט. ש: ת. > א. מ. מ"ח. מאה ושלשים.
ד. מאה ועשרים/ מיל] א. ת. ד. פרסה.   2—3 ארבעים פרסה]=א.
ט. ת. א"א: מ. מיל פרסה. ד. מ"ח. ארבעה מיל פרסה.
3 הלך] ד. הולך. א"א. והיה הולך א"צ. כיוצא בו הולך/ יום]
ט. >.   6 מצרים וגו'] א"א. ~ ומצרים מהלך ארבעים יום.   8 נסעו]
א. באו.

To Succoth, to the place where they actually put up booths, as it is said: "And Jacob journeyed to Succoth, and built him a house and made booths for his cattle" (Gen. 33.17)—these are the words of R. Eliezer. But the other sages say: Succoth is merely the name of a place, for it is said: "And they journeyed from Succoth, and pitched in Etham" (Num. 33.7). Just as Etham is the name of a place, so also is Succoth. R. Akiba says: Succoth here means only clouds of glory, as it is said: "And the Lord will create over the whole habitation of Mount Zion, and over her assemblies, a cloud and smoke by day, and the shining of a flaming fire by night; for over all the glory shall be a canopy. And there shall be a pavilion for a shadow in the daytime" (Isa. 4.5–6). So far I know only about the past. How about the future? Scripture says: "And the ransomed of the Lord shall return and come with singing into Zion, and everlasting joy shall be upon their heads" (ibid., 35.10). R. Nehemiah says: "To Succoth" (*sukkotah*). Instead of prefixing a *lamed* to indicate "to," a *he* is appended at the end of the word.

About Six Hundred Thousand Men on Foot. Sixty myriads—these are the words of R. Ishmael. For when it says: "Behold, it is the litter of

סוכותה סוכות ממש היו שנאמר ויעקב נסע
סוכותה ויבן לו בית ולמקנהו עשה סכת דברי רבי
אליעזר וחכמים אומרים אין סוכות אלא מקום
שנאמר ויסעו מסוכות ויחנו באיתם מה איתם מקום

15 אף סוכות מקום רבי עקיבא אומר אין סוכות אלא
עניי כבוד שנאמר וברא יי על כל מכון הר ציון
ועל מקראיה ענן יומם ונוגה אש להבה לילה כי
על כבוד חופה וסכה תהיה לצל יומם אין לי אלא
לשעבר לעתיד לבא מנין תלמוד לומר וסוכה

20 תהיה לצל ואומר ופדויי יי ישובון וגו' ושמחת עולם
על ראשם רבי נחמיה אומר סוכותה לפי שצריך
למד מתחלתו נותן לו הא בסופו.

כ ש ש מ א ו ת א ל ף ר ג ל י הגברים ששים
ריבוא דברי רבי ישמעאל שנאמר הנה מטתו

12—11 בראשית ל'ג, י'ז.   15—11 ספרא אמור פ', י'ז. לקמן בשלח
א'. סוכה י'א, ב'.   14 במדבר ל'ג, ו'.   18—16 ישעיה ד', ד'-ו'.
20—19 ישעיה שם.   20—21 ישעיה ל'ה, י'.   22—21 יבמות י'ג, ב'. ב'ר
ס'ח, ח'.   25—24 שה'ש נ', ז'-ח'.

12 ויבן לו בית–סכה] הוספתי: מ'ח. ויבן וגו'.   17 סקראיה] ק.
מקרש/ יומם ונוגה] במקרא כתוב יומם ועשן ונוגה.   18 וסכה תהיה לצל
יומם] הוספתי=א'א.   20—21 ושמחת עולם על ראשם] הוספתי=מ'ח.
23 הגברים] הוספתי: א. מ. וגו'.   24 דברי רבי ישמעאל] מ'ח.
א'צ. >/ שנאמר] מ. >.

Solomon; three score mighty men are about it,"
it means, behold the litter of Him who is the
possessor of peace, sixty myriads of mighty men
are about it "of the mighty men of Israel. They
all handle the sword, and are expert in war"
(Cant. 3.7–8). And it says: "Wherefore it is
said in the book of the Wars of the Lord" (Num.
21.14). And it is written: "Let the saints exult
in glory . . . Let the high praises of God . . .
To execute vengeance . . . To bind their kings
. . . To execute upon them the judgment written," etc. (Ps. 149.5–9).

Beside Children. That is, beside women, children and little ones. R. Jonathan says: Besides
women, children and old men.

And a Mixed Multitude Went up Also. A
hundred and twenty myriads—these are the
words of R. Ishmael. R. Akiba says: Two
hundred and forty myriads. R. Jonathan says:
Three hundred and sixty myriads.

And Flocks and Herds even Very Much Cattle.
All these were implied in what God said to our
father Abraham: "And afterward shall they come
out with great substance" (Gen. 15.14)—at their
going out from Egypt I will fill them with silver
and gold.

25 שלשלמה ששים גבורים סביב וגו' הנה מטתו של מי
שהשלום שלו ששים ריבוא גבורים מגבורי ישראל
כולם אחוזי חרב מלומדי מלחמה וגו' על כן יאמר
בספר מלחמות יי וכתיב יעלזו חסידים וגו' רוממות
אל וגו' לעשות נקמה וגו' לאסור מלכיהם וגו'
30 לעשות בהם משפט כתוב וגו'. לבד מטף לבד מנשים
טף וקטנים רבי יונתן אומר לבד מנשים טף וזקנים.

וגם ערב רב וגו' מאה ועשרים ריבוא דברי
רבי ישמעאל רבי עקיבא אומר מאתים וארבעים
ריבוא רבי יונתן אומר שלש מאות וששים ריבוא.

35 וצאן ובקר מקנה כבד מאד עליהם
אמר המקום לאברהם אבינו ואחרי כן יצאו ברכוש
גדול עם יציאתן ממצרים אני ממלאן כסף וזהב.

26–25 שהש"ר ג', ד'. 27 שה'ש שם. 27–28 במדבר כ"א, י"ד.
30–28 תהלים קט"ט, ה'–ט'. 37–36 בראשית ט"ו, י"ד. בכורות ה', ב'.

---

25 הנה מטתו] ד. > מ"ח. הנה מטותיו. 26–25 מי שהשלום
שלו] ט. מי שאסר והיה העולם. 28 סלחמות יי] מ. וגו'/ וכתיב]
א. ט. >. 31–30 מנשים טף וקטנים] ד. מנשים וקטנים א"צ.
מקטנים ~ דברי רבי ישמעאל/ יונתן] ד. יוחנן א"צ. עקיבא/ אומר]
א. מ. ט. ~ סאה וששים רבוא/ לבד מנשים] מ. לבד מטף לבד
מנשים/ טף וזקנים] מ. וטפי קטנים. א. טף וקטנים. 31–32 ר' יונתן
אומר–ערב רב וגו'] מ"ח. >. 34 יונתן] ד. נתן./ שלש מאות] ד.
מאתים.

And They Baked Unleavened Cakes of the Dough, etc. This tells that they had kneaded the dough but had not sufficient time to let it leaven before they were redeemed. You also find the same said about the future. What does it say? "Who ceaseth to stir from the kneading of the dough until it be leavened. On the day of our King," etc. (Hos. 7.4–5).

Cakes (*'Ugot*). '*Ugot* merely means cakes baked on coal, as it is said: "And thou shalt eat it as barley cakes" (Ezek. 4.12). And it also says: "But make me thereof a little cake first" (I Kings 17.13). A great miracle was performed for the Israelites with that cake. They kept on eating of it for thirty days until the manna came down for them.

Because They Were Thrust Out of Egypt. I might understand this to mean that they hurried out of their own accord, but Scripture says: "and could not tarry," as soon as they were freed, they had to get out.

Neither Had They Prepared for Themselves Any Victual. This proclaims the excellence of Israel, for they did not say to Moses: How can we go out into the desert, without having provisions for the journey? But they believed in Moses and followed him. Of them it is said in the traditional sacred writings: "Go and cry in the ears of Jerusalem saying," etc. (Jer. 2.2). What reward did they receive for this? "Israel was the Lord's hallowed portion," etc. (ibid. 2.3).

ויאפו את הבצק וגו' מגיד שלשו את העיסה
ולא הספיקו לחומצה עד שנגאלו וכן אתה מוצא
לעתיד לבא מה הוא אומר ישבות מעיר וגו' יום
מלכנו וגו'.

עוגות אין עוגות אלא חררה שנאמר ועוגת
שעורים תאכלנה ואומר אך עשי לי משם עונה
קטנה בראשונה נס גדול נעשה להם בחררה שאכלו
ממנה שלשים יום עד שירד להם המן.

כי גורשו ממצרים שומע אני מאליהם
תלמוד לומר ולא יכלו להתמהמה עד שנגאלו.

וגם צדה לא עשו להם להודיע שבחן של
ישראל שלא אמרו למשה היאך אנו יוצאין למדבר
ואין בידנו צדה לדרך אלא האמינו בו והלכו אחרי
משה ועליהם מפורש בקבלה הלוך וקראת באזני
ירושלם לאמר וגו' ומה שכר נטלו על כך קדש
ישראל ליי וגו'.

38—41 לעיל י"נ.   40—41 הושע ז', ד'—ה'.   42—43 ש. 27. יחזקאל ד',
י"ב.   43—44 מלכים א. י"ז, י"נ.   44—45 לקמן ויסע א'.   51—52 ירמיה
ב', ב'.   52—53 שם ב', נ'.

---

39 אתה מוצא] ד. >.   40 מה הוא אומר] ד. >.   43 תאכלנה]
ד. תאכל/ אך] ק. נ. אף.   45 שלשים יום] ד. לחם.   47 ת"ל]
ד. שנאמר/ עד] מ"ח. על.   48 להודיע] ד. ~ הקב"ה.   49 שלא]
ד. עד שלא.   52 על כך] ד. >.   53 וגו'] ד. לכך נאמר.

Now the Time that the Children of Israel Dwelt in Egypt Was Four Hundred and Thirty Years. One passage says: "Four hundred and thirty years," and one passage says: "And shall serve them; and they shall afflict them four hundred years" (Gen. 15.13). How can both these passages be maintained? Thirty years before Isaac was born the decree[2] was issued at the covenant between the parts. Rabbi says: One passage says: "And shall serve them; and they shall afflict them four hundred years," and one passage says: "And in the fourth generation they shall come back hither" (Gen. 15.16). How can both these passages be maintained? The Holy One, blessed be He, said: If they repent I will redeem them after the number of generations, and if not, I will redeem them after the number of years.

Now the Time that the Children of Israel Dwelt in Egypt and in the Land of Canaan and in the Land of Goshen Was Four Hundred and Thirty Years. This is one of the passages which they changed when writing the Torah for king Ptolemy.[3] Likewise they wrote for him: "God created in the beginning" Gen. 1.1); "I will make a man according to an image and a likeness" (ibid., 1.26); "A male with corresponding female

---

[2] I. e., that the children of Israel should sojourn in Egypt. And counting from that time it was 430, but counting from the date of the birth of Isaac it was only 400 years. (See note 3a).

[3] Comp. Geiger, *Urschrift*, p. 439 ff.

ומושב בני ישראל וגו' כתוב אחד אומר

שלשים שנה וארבע מאות שנה וכתוב אחד אומר

ועבדום וענו אותם ארבע מאות שנה כיצד יתקיימו

שני כתובים הללו שלשים שנה עד שלא נולד יצחק

נגזרה גזרה בין הבתרים רבי אומר כתוב אחד אומר

ועבדום וענו אותם ארבע מאות שנה וכתוב אחד

אומר ודור רביעי ישובו הנה כיצד יתקיימו שני

כתובים הללו אמר הקדוש ברוך הוא אם עושין

תשובה אני גואלם לדורות ואם לאו אני גואלם

לשנים.

ומושב בני ישראל אשר ישבו במצרים

ובארץ כנען ובאבץ גושן שלשים שנה

וארבע מאות שנה זה אחד מן הדברים שכתבו

לתלמי המלך כיוצא בו כתבו לו אלהים ברא

בראשית. אעשה אדם בצלם ובדמות. זכר ונקוביו

54—58 סע'ר פ'נ. פדר'א מ'ה. ש. שם.   56 בראשית ט'ו, י'ד.
60 בראשית שם ט'ז.   60—63 תוס' עדיות א', י'ד.   66—75 מנלה
ט', א'–ב'. י' שם א', ט' (71d). סופרים א', ט'. ת. שמות.
67—68 בראשית א', א'.   68—69 בראשית א', כ'ו–כ'ז. ב'ר ח', י'א.

61 אמר הקב'ה] א. ט. מ'ח. >.   65 ובארץ כנען ובארץ נושן]
א'צ. ובשאר ארצות. מ'ח. עם שאר מקומות.   68 ונקוביו] מ.
מ'ח. ונקיבה.

parts created He him" (ibid., 5.2); "And God finished on the sixth day . . . and rested on the seventh day" (ibid., 2.2); "Now I will go down and there confound their language" (ibid., 11.7); "And Sarah laughed among her relatives" (ibid., 18.12); "For in their anger they slew an ox and in their selfwill they tore up a stall" (ibid., 49.6); "And Moses took his wife and his sons and set them upon a carrier of man" (Ex. 4.20); "I have not taken any desirable thing from them" (Num. 16.15); "Which the Lord thy God hath allotted to give light unto all the peoples" (Deut. 4.19); "Which I have commanded the nations not to worship them" (ibid., 17.3); "And the slender-footed" (Lev. 11.6). And so also they wrote for him: "Now the time that the children of Israel dwelt in Egypt and in the land of Canaan and in the land of Goshen was four hundred and thirty years."

And It Came to Pass at the End of Four Hundred and Thirty Years, etc. This tells that as soon as the designated time came, God did not delay them an instant. On the fifteenth of Nisan did He speak with our father Abraham at the covenant between the parts. On the

בראו. ויכל ביום הששי וישבות ביום השביעי. הבה

70 ארדה ואבלה שם שפתם. ותצחק שרה בקרוביה.

כי באפם הרגו שור וברצונם עקרו אבוס. ויקח

משה את אשתו ואת בניו וירכיבם על נושא אדם.

לא חמוד אחד מהם נשאתי. אשר חלק יי אלהיך

אותם להאיר לכל העמים. אשר לא צויתי לאומות

75 לעבדם. ואת צעירת הרגלים. וכן כתבו לו ומושב

בני ישראל אשר ישבו במצרים ובארץ כנען ובארץ

גושן שלשים שנה וארבע מאות שנה.

ויהי מקץ שלשים שנה וגו' מגיד שמכיון

שהגיע הקץ לא עכבן המקום כהרף עין בחמשה

80 עשר בניסן נידבר עם אברהם אבינו בין הבתרים

69 בראשית ב', ב'. ב"ר י', ט'. 69–70 בראשית י"א, ז'. ב"ר
ל"ח, י'. 70 בראשית י"ח, י"ב. ב"ר מ"ח, י"ז. 71 בראשית מ"ט, ו'.
ב"ר צ"ח, ה'. 71–72 שמות ד', כ'. שמו"ר ה', נ'. 73 במדבר
ט"ז, ט"ו. 73–74 דברים ד', י"ט. 74–75 דברים י"ז, נ'. 75 ויקרא
י"א, ו'. דברים י"ד, ז'. 78–84 ת. בא ט'. סע"ר ה'. ר"ה י"א, א'.

69 בראו] ד. בראם / ויכל ביום הששי וישבות ביום השביעי]
א. > מ. מ"ח. ויכל בששי וישבות בשביעי. 70 ותצחק] א. ותכחק/
שרה] מ. שם/ בקרוביה] א. בקרביה. 71 שור] ד. איש. 73 חמוד]
ד. חמור מ"ח. חמד. 74 אותם] א. >/ לכל] מ. על. / לא]
מ"ח. >. 75 צעירת] מ. שעירת. 79 המקום] ד. הכתוב.
79–80 בט"ו בניסן–בין הבתרים] ד. >.

fifteenth of Nisan the ministering angels came to bring good tidings to our father Abraham. On the fifteenth of Nisan Isaac was born. On the fifteenth of Nisan it was decreed at the covenant between the parts, for it is said: "And it came to pass at the end." There was one date designated for all of them.[3a]

Even the Selfsame Day It Came to Pass, that All the Hosts of the Lord Went Out from the Land of Egypt. The hosts of the Lord are the ministering angels. And so you find that whenever Israel is enslaved the Shekinah, as it were, is enslaved with them, as it is said: "And they saw the God of Israel; and there was under His feet[4]," etc. But after they were redeemed what does it say? "And the like of the very heaven for clearness" (Ex. 24.10). And it also says: "In all their affliction He was afflicted" (Isa. 63.10). So far I know only that He shares in the affliction of

---

[3a] The expression "at the end" implies that it was exactly at the end of 430 years, counting from the covenant between the parts (Gen. 15.10–18). Hence, that covenant must have been made on the 15th day of Nisan. The end of the 430 years, as counted from the covenant between the parts, coincides with the end of 400 years counting from the birth of Isaac. Hence, Isaac must have been born on the 15th of Nisan. On the 15th day of Nisan of the year before Isaac was born, the angels came to Abraham to bring him the good tidings that Sarah would have a son. For it is said, "When the season cometh round, and lo Sarah thy wife shall have a son" (Gen. 15.10). Hence, there was one date for all these events.

בחמשה עשר בניסן באו מלאכי השרת אצל אברהם
אבינו לבשרו בחמשה עשר בניסן נולד יצחק
בחמשה עשר בניסן נגזרה גזרה בין הבתרים
שנאמר ויהי מקץ קץ אחד לכולם.

85   ויהי בעצם היום הזה יצאו כל צבאות
ה' וגו' אלו מלאכי השרת וכן אתה מוצא שכל
זמן שישראל משועבדין כביכול שכינה משועבדת
עמהם שנאמר ויראו את אלהי ישראל ותחת
רגליו וגו' וכשנגאלו מה הוא אומר וכעצם השמים
90   לטוהר ואומר בכל צרתם לו צר אין לי אלא

91—86 תענית ט"ו, א'.   112—86 ספרי במדבר פ'ד. ש. 27.
89—88 שמות כ"ד, י'.   90 ישעיה ס"נ, ט'.

---

82 לבשרו] מ"ח. לבשר את שרה/ בט"ו בניסן נולד יצחק] ד. <.י
83 בחמשה עשר-בין הבתרים] מ"ח. ומנין שבחמשה עשר-בין הבתרים.
ש"ט. ת. בחמשה עשר בניסן נגאלו. (ת. ~ בט"ו בניסן עתידין להגאל
משעבוד מלכיות). 84 לכולם] א. ט. מ"ח. ~וכן הוא אומר. 86 אלו
מלאכי השרת] הוספתי עפ"י מ"ח. ז"י. וא"צ. 87 משועבדת]
ד. <.

---

[4] The expression כמעשה לבנת in Ex. 24.10 is taken to
refer to the work in bricks in which the Israelites were
engaged in Egypt. God, as it were, was with them in
this work (see Introduction and cf. Yer. Suk. 4.4 (54c)
and Lev. Rab. 23.8).

the community. How about the affliction of the
individual? Scripture says: "He shall call upon
Me, and I will answer him; I will be with him in
trouble" (Ps. 91.15). It also says: "And Joseph's
master took him," etc. (Gen. 39.20). And
what does it say then? "But the Lord was with
Joseph" (ibid., 39.21). And thus it says: "From
before Thy people, whom Thou didst redeem to
Thee out of Egypt, the nation and its God"[4a]
(II Sam. 7.23). R. Eliezer says: An idol crossed
the sea with Israel, as it is said: "And a rival[5]
passed through the sea" (Zech. 10.11). And
which idol was it? The idol of Micah.[6] R. Akiba
says: Were it not expressly written in Scripture,
it would be impossible to say it. Israel said to
God: Thou hadst redeemed Thyself, as though
one could conceive such a thing.[7] Likewise you
find that whithersoever Israel was exiled, the
Shekinah, as it were, went into exile with them.
When they went into exile to Egypt, the Shekinah
went into exile with them, as it is said: "I

[4a] This rendering of the verse in II Samuel 7.23 is
required by our Midrash which presupposes the reading גוי
(also found in some Bible Mss.; see R. Kittel's edition of
Biblia Hebraica, Stuttgart, 1913) instead of גוים found in
the masoretic text. In the Hebrew text I have given the
reading of the masoretic text on the basis of the 'וו found
in the two Mss. though the printed editions have גוי. See
Apparatus and comp. Introduction p. lxi.

[5] This rendering of the verse is required by the *Mekilta*,
which takes the word צרה to mean "rival," not "affliction."
By "rival" is meant an idol which the superstition of the
people regarded as a rival to God (cf. Yoma, 9b).

צרת ציבור צרת יחיד מנין תלמוד לומר יקראני

ואענהו עמו אנכי בצרה ואומר ויקח אדני יוסף

וגו' ומה הוא אומר ויהי יי את יוסף וכן הוא

אומר מפני עמך אשר פדית לך ממצרים גוים

95 ואלהיו רבי אליעזר אומר עבודה זרה עברה עם

ישראל בים שנאמר ועבר בים צרה ואיזה זה זה

צלמו של מיכה רבי עקיבא אומר אלמלא מקרא

כתוב אי איפשר לאומרו כביכול אמרו ישראל

לפני המקום עצמך פדית וכן את מוצא שבכל

100 מקום שגלו ישראל כביכול שכינה גלתה עמהם גלו

למצרים גלתה שכינה עמהם שנאמר הנגלה נגליתי

91—92 תהלים צ׳א, ט׳ו.   92—93 בראשית ל׳ט, כ׳-כ׳א.
94—95 שמואל ב. ז׳, כ׳ג.   95—97 מ׳ת. 2.   96 זכריה י׳, י׳א.
97—99 שמו׳ר ט׳ו, י׳ב.   99—112 ספרי בסדבר קס׳א. מגלה כ׳ט, א׳.
101—102 שמואל א. ב׳, כ׳ו.

---

94 לך] ק. נ. > / גוים ואלהיו] א. מ. וגו'. ד. גוי ואלהיו.
100 כביכול] ד. >/נלתה] ד. >.   101 נלתה] א. ד. >.

---

[6] See Jud. 17.1 ff. and cf. *JE*, VIII, 533–4.

[7] On the expression כביכול, "as if it were possible," i. e.,
to speak of God in such terms, see N. Brüll in Kobak's
Jeshurun, VII (Hebrew part), pp. 1–6 and cf. W. Bacher,
Terminologie, I, p. 72.

exiled[8] Myself unto the house of thy fathers
when they were in Egypt" (I Sam. 2.27). When
they were exiled to Babylon, the Shekinah went
into exile with them, as it is said: "For your
sake I ordered Myself to go[9] to Babylon" (Isa.
43.14). When they were exiled to Elam, the
Shekinah went into exile with them, as it is said:
"I will set My throne in Elam" (Jer. 49.38).
When they were exiled to Edom, the Shekinah
went into exile with them, as it is said: "Who is
this that cometh from Edom," etc. (Isa. 63.1).
And when they return in the future, the Shekinah,
as it were, will return with them, as it is said:
"That then the Lord thy God will return with
thy captivity" (Deut. 30.3). Note that it does
not say: "The Lord will bring back" (veheshib),
etc., but it says: "He will return" (ve-shab). And
it is also said: "With me from Lebanon, my
bride" (Cant. 4.8). Was she really coming from
Lebanon? Was she not rather going up to
Lebanon? What then does Scripture mean by
saying: "With me from Lebanon?" Merely
this: You and I, as it were, were exiled from
Lebanon; you and I will go up to Lebanon.

A Night of Watching unto the Lord, etc. In
that night were they redeemed and in that night
will they be redeemed in the future—these are
the words of R. Joshua, as it is said: "This same

---

[8] This is the interpretation given by our Midrash to the
expression הנגלה נגליתי. It ignores the interrogative *He*
and takes נגלה to be the *Nif'al*, from גלה, meaning "to go
into exile."

[9] This rendering is required by the Midrash which

אל בית אביך בהיותם במצרים גלו לבבל גלתה
שכינה עמהם שנאמר למענכם שלחתי בבלה גלו
לעילם גלתה שכינה עמהם שנאמר ושמתי כסאי
בעילם גלו לאדום גלתה שכינה עמהם שנאמר מי 105
זה בא מאדום וגו' וכשעתידין לחזור כביכול שכינה
חוזרת עמהם שנאמר ושב יי אלהיך את שבותך וגו'
והשיב יי אלהיך את שבותך אינו אומר כן אלא ושב
ואומר אתי מלבנון כלה וכי מלבנון היא באה והלא
ללבנון היא עולה מה תלמוד לומר אתי מלבנון 110
אלא כביכול אני ואת מלבנון גלינו אני ואת ללבנון
עולים.

ליל שמורים הוא ליי וגו' בו נגאלו ובו
עתידין להגאל דברי רבי יהושע שנאמר הוא הלילה

---

103 ישעיה מ'נ, י'ד.   103—112 שהש'ר ד', ח'.   104—105 ירמיה
מ'ט, ל'ח.   105—106 ישעיה ס'נ, א'.   107 דברים ל', נ'.   109 שה'ש
ד', ז'.   109—112 שמו'ר כ'נ, ה'.   113—121 ר'ה י'א, ב'. ש. 28.

103 שלחתי] ד. שולחתי.   104 נלתה] א. ד. >.   105 נלתה]
א. ד. >.   106 כביכול] א. >.   107 חוזרת] ד. >.   111 אני
ואת מלבנון גלינו] הוספתי עפ'י מ'ח.

---

interprets the word שלחתי as if it read שָׁלַחְתִּי "I was sent,"
i. e., I caused myself to go.

night is a night of watching unto the Lord[10]."
R. Eliezer says: In that night they were redeemed; in the future, however, they will not be
redeemed in that night but in the month of
Tishri, as it is said: "Blow the horn at the new
moon[11]," etc. Why? "For it is a statute for
Israel," etc. (Ps. 81.4–5). What then does
Scripture mean by saying: "This same night is a
night of watching unto the Lord?" Merely
this: This is the night referred to by God, when
He said to our father Abraham: "Abraham, on
this night I will redeem your children." And as
soon as the designated time came, God did not
delay them an instant.

*Watching unto the Lord for All the Children of
Israel.* This tells that all the Israelites need
watchful protection on that night.[12]

---

[10] R. Joshua evidently derives his proof from the rest
of the verse which reads: "for all the children of Israel
throughout their generations." (See commentary *Shebut
Yehudah*, ad. loc.).

[11] The "New moon" in this passage is understood to
mean the new moon of Tishri, i. e., the New Year on
which the *Shofar* is blown (see Talm. R. H. 8ab). Here
it is assumed that the blowing of the *Shofar* for the redemption of Israel in the future, at the coming of the Messiah,
will also take place in the month of Tishri.

[12] See commentary *Shebut Yehudah*. The passage may
also mean that the Israelites need to be watchful on that
evening and careful with regard to the observances of
the laws in connection with the Passover.

115 הזה ליי שמורים רבי אליעזר אומר בו נגאלו אבל

לעתיד לבא אינם נגאלים אלא בתשרי שנאמר תקעו

בחדש שופר וגו' מפני מה כי חק לישראל הוא וגו'

ומה תלמוד לומר הוא הלילה הזה ליי אלא הוא

הלילה שאמר המקום לאברהם אבינו אברהם

120 בלילה הזה אני גואל את בניך וכשהגיע הקץ לא

עיכבן המקום אפילו כהרף עין.

שמורים לכל בני ישראל מגיד שכל

ישראל צריכין להשתמר בו.

116—117 תהלים פ״א, ד׳–ה׳.   122—123 ר״ה שם. פסחים ק״ט, ב׳.

120 בלילה הזה] ד. >/ בניך] ד. ~ לעתיד לבא.   121 עיכבן]
ד. עיכבו.   123 צריכין] ז״י. בשם הילקוט. מ״ח. עתידין.

Chapter XV
(Ex. 12.43–49)

And the Lord Said unto Moses and Aaron: This is the Ordinance of the Passover. There are some sections in which the general statement comes first and the particular follows, and some in which the particular comes first and the general follows. "And ye shall be unto Me a kingdom of priests and a holy nation" (Ex. 19.6), is a particular statement. "These are the words which thou shalt speak unto the children of Israel" (ibid.), is a general statement. "This is the statute of the Law" (Num. 19.2), is a general statement. "That they bring thee a red heifer, faultless" (ibid.), is a particular statement. "This is the ordinance of the passover," is a general statement. "There shall no alien eat thereof," is a particular statement. When a general statement is followed by a particular, it does not include more than is contained in the particular.[1]

This is the Ordinance of the Passover. Scripture here deals with both the Passover of Egypt and the Passover of subsequent generations—these are the words of R. Josiah. R. Jonathan says: This passage deals with the Passover of Egypt, and hence I would know only about the Passover of Egypt. How do I know about the Passover of subsequent generations? Scripture says: "Ac-

---

[1] This is the 4th rule of the 13 rules of R. Ishmael (see *JE*, X, 512; cf. also "Talmud Hermeneutics," ibid., XII, 33).

פרשה טו (שמות י"ב, מ"ג–מ"ט.)

ויאמר יי אל משה ואל אהרן זאת
חקת הפסח יש פרשיות שהוא כולל בתחלה
ופורט בסוף פורט בתחלה וכולל בסוף ואתם
תהיו לי ממלכת כהנים וגוי קדוש פרט אלה
הדברים אשר תדבר אל בני ישראל כלל זאת חקת
התורה כלל ויקחו אליך פרה אדומה תמימה פרט
זאת חקת הפסח כלל כל בן נכר לא יאכל בו פרט
כלל ופרט אין בכלל אלא מה שבפרט.

זאת חקת הפסח בפסח מצרים ובפסח
דורות הכתוב מדבר דברי רבי יאשיה רבי יונתן
אומר בפסח מצרים הכתוב מדבר אין לי אלא
פסח מצרים פסח דורות מנין תלמוד לומר ככל

5

10

8–1 ספרי במדבר קכ"ג.   3–5 שמות י"ט, ו'.   6–5 במדבר י"ט, ב'.
13–12 במדבר ט', ד'.

2 פרשיות] א. פרשות/ שהוא] ד. <.   10 יונתן] ש"ט. נתן.

cording to all the statutes of it, and according to all the ordinances thereof, shall ye keep it" (Num. 9.3). Said R. Josiah to him: This passage as well as that one deals with both the Passover of Egypt and the Passover of subsequent generations. Why, then, does Scripture have to say: "According to all the statutes of it, and according to all the ordinances thereof?" It merely aims to teach thereby that even those laws which are omitted[2] in the regulations for the Passover of subsequent generations are applicable to it. R. Isi the son of Akiba says: This ordinance prescribed for the Passover applies only to the body of the paschal lamb.

There Shall No Alien Eat Thereof, meaning both an apostate Jew and a Gentile, for it is said: "Thus saith the Lord God: No alien, uncircumcised in heart and uncircumcised in flesh, shall enter into My sanctuary, even any alien that is among the children of Israel" (Ezek. 44.9).

But Every Man's Servant. From this I would know only about the servant of a man. How about the servant of a woman or a minor? Scripture says: "That is bought for money," no matter who owns him.

---

[2] I. e., not specifically mentioned in Ex. 12.43–49 and in Num. 9.2–3, but prescribed in the regulations about the first Passover in Egypt (Ex. 12.3–6, 8–10).

חקותיו וככל משפטיו תעשו אותו נם לו רבי יאשיה

אחד זה ואחד זה בפסח מצרים ובפסח דורות

15 הכתוב מדבר ומה תלמוד לומר ככל חקותיו וככל

משפטיו אלא בא הכתוב ללמד בו דברים

המחוסרים בו רבי איסי בן עקיבא אומר חוקה

האמורה בפסח אינה אלא גופו.

כל בן נכר לא יאכל בו אחד ישראל

20 משומד ואחד גוי במשמע שנאמר כה אמר יי אלהים

כל בן נכר ערל לב וערל בשר לא יבא אל מקדשי

לכל בן נכר אשר בתוך בני ישראל.

וכל עבד איש אין לי אלא עבד איש עבד

אשה וקטן מנין תלמוד לומר מקנת כסף מכל מקום.

17—18 ספרי במדבר ס"ט. פסחים צ"ה, א'.   19—26 ש. 28.
20—22 יחזקאל ס"ד, ט'.

13—16 נם לו—וככל משפטיו] מ. מ"ח. >.   14 אחד זה ואחד זה]—
א. ט: ד. >.   16 ללמד בו] ד. ולללמד מ"ח. ללמדו.   17 המחוסרים
בו] מ"ח. המחוסרים כאן/רבי] ט. > / איסי] ט. > / איסי] א. אסי/ עקיבא]
א. ט. עקביא ש"ט. יהודה.   18 גופו]=ט. ש"י: ד. נופה מ.
נופיה.   20—21 שנאמר כה אמר... לא יבא] מ. שנאמר כל ערל לא
יאכל בו (שמות י"ב, מ"ח) ק. נ. שנאמר וכל בן נכר (נ. ~ ערל לב).
22 אל מקדשי לכל בן נכר אשר בתוך בני ישראל] א. ט. הוספתי: א. וגו'.
23—24 עבד אשה וקטן] ד. אשה וקטן.

When Thou Hast Circumcised Him, Then Shall He Eat Thereof. "He" refers to the master. This tells that failure to circumcise one's slaves debars one from partaking of the paschal lamb. So far I know only about the circumcision of slaves. How about the circumsicion of free males? You can reason as follows: The expression "then" (*az*) is used here and the expression "then" (*az*) is used further on (v. 48). Just as further on it refers to the circumcision of free males, so here it refers also to the circumcision of free males. And just as here it refers to the circumcision of slaves, so there it refers also to the circumcision of slaves—these are the words of R. Eliezer. R. Ishmael says: Failure to circumcise one's slaves does not debar one from partaking of the paschal lamb. Why then is it said: "When thou hast circumcised him?" Suppose a man has uncircumcised slaves. How would you know that if he wishes to circumcise them and let them partake of the paschal lamb, he is permitted to do so? Scripture, therefore, says: "When thou hast circumcised him; then shall he eat thereof." And we do find that one is permitted to keep uncircumcised slaves, for it is

ומלתה אותו אז יאכל בו רבו מגיד 25

שמילת עבדיו מעכבתו מלאכול בפסח אין לי אלא

מילת עבדים מילת זכרים מנין הרי אתה דן נאמר

כאן אז ונאמר להלן אז מה להלן מילת זכרים אף

כאן מילת זכרים ומה כאן מילת עבדים אף להלן

מילת עבדים דברי רבי אליעזר רבי ישמעאל אומר 30

אין מילת עבדים מעכבתו מלאכול בפסח ומה

תלמוד לומר ומלתה אותו הרי שהיו לפניו עבדים

ערלים מנין אתה אומר שאם רצה למולן ולהאכילן

בפסח שהוא רשאי תלמוד לומר ומלתה אותו אז

יאכל בו ומצינו שהוא רשאי לקיים לו עבדים ערלים 35

27—29 יבמות ע', ב'. חוס' פסחים ח', י"ח. ש. 25. 41—35 יבמות מ"ח, ב'.

---

25 אז יאכל בו] ד. >/רבו] ק. ~רבי אוטר. 27 ד. עבדיו/
ד. זכריו. 29 ומה כאן]=מ"ח. א"א. א"צ. ז"י: א. מה כאן. מ.
ד. אי מה להלן/ אף להלן] ד. אף כאן. 31—30 דברי רבי אליעזר—
אין מלת עבדים] א. >/ דברי רבי אליעזר]=מ. ט. מ"ח.
ל"ט. ש"ט: ד. < ש"י. מ"ע. דברי רבי יהושע/ ר' ישמעאל]=
מ. ט: ד. תוספות יבמות ע', ב' ד"ה אי מה פסח. ר' אליעזר. מ"ח.
ר' שמעון. 34 בפסח שהוא] ד. > 35 יאכל בו] מ. ד. ~ רבו
ומוחקו א"א. וליחא ב ט. ומ"ח.) א"צ. ~ העבד זכ"ה ברש"י עיין
מ"ע./ ומצינו]=ל: מ"ח. וכן מצינו א. מ. ד. מצינו.

said: "And the son of thy handmaid, and the
stranger may be refreshed" (Ex. 23.12). R.
Eliezer says: One is not permitted to keep
uncircumcised slaves, for it says: "And thou
shalt circumcise him." If so, why then does
Scripture need to say: "And the son of thy
handmaid, and the stranger may be refreshed?"
It is merely for this: Suppose his master bought
him Friday afternoon towards nightfall, so that
he had not sufficient time to circumcise him
before it got dark. It is for such a case that
Scripture says: "And the son of thy handmaid
. . . may be refreshed."

Another Interpretation: *When Thou Hast Circumcised Him, Then Shall He Eat Thereof.* Why
is this said? To include one upon whom circumcision had been performed though without
permanent effect. Even though the flesh has
again covered the corona he is not debarred from
partaking of the paschal lamb or of *terumah*.[3]
On this question our teachers in Lud took a vote
and decided that such a regrowth does not constitute an interposition in regard to uncleanness.[4]

---

[3] *Terumah* is the portion of the crop given to the priest.
See *JE*, XII, 111–112, s. v. *Terumot*.

[4] I. e., in regard to removing uncleanness by taking a
ritual bath. When taking a ritual bath the water must
touch the whole body. If there be anything sticking to
any part of the body, thus preventing the water from
touching the body on that part, the ritual bath is not
effective and the unclean person remains unclean. A
"regrowth," however, is considered part of the body and
not something foreign to it.

שנאמר וינפש בן אמתך והגר. רבי אליעזר אומר

אינו רשאי לקיים לו עבדים ערלים שנאמר ומלתה

אותו אם כן מה תלמוד לומר וינפש בן אמתך והגר

אלא הרי שלקחו רבו ערב שבת עם חשיכה ולא

40 הספיק למולו עד שהחשיך לכך נאמר וינפש בן

אמתך דבר אחר ומלתה אותו אז יאכל בו למה

נאמר להביא את שנתקיימה בו מצות מילה אפילו

שעה אחת אף על פי שחזר הבשר וחפה את העטרה

אינו מעכבו לא לאכול בפסח ולא לאכול בתרומה

45 על זה נמנו רבותינו בלוד ואמרו אין חוצץ לטומאה.

---

36 שמות כ״ג, י״ב. לקטן בחודש ז׳. כספא נ׳. 43—45 יבמות ע״ב, א׳. י׳ שם ח׳, א׳. (8d).

---

36 ר׳ אליעזר] ד. ר׳ אליעזר אומר אינו רשאי לקיים לו עבדים ערלים שנאמר וינפש בן אמתך והגר. ר׳ אליעזר נ. ר׳ יאשיה. א״צ. ר׳ עקיבא. ש״י. ר׳ יהושע. 36—38 ר׳ אליעזר אומר–אמתך והגר] א. >. 39 אלא] ד. לומר לך. 42—41 למה נאמר] ד. >. 45 בלוד] א. בדור/ לטומאה] א״צ. לתרומה.

A Sojourner and a Hired Servant Shall Not Eat Thereof. "Sojourner" means a resident alien.[5] "Hired servant" here means a Gentile. R. Eliezer says: "A sojourner and a hired servant shall not eat thereof." Why is this said? So that we may be able to prove from the law about the paschal lamb that an uncircumcised person is disqualified from eating *terumah.* But even if Scripture had not said this, I could have reasoned: If in the case of the paschal lamb, the less weighty, an uncircumcised person is disqualified from partaking of it, is it not a logical inference that in the case of *terumah,* the more weighty, an uncircumcised person should be disqualified from eating it? No! If you cite the case of the paschal lamb— Scripture limits the time of eating it even for those who are to eat it, and therefore it disqualifies the uncircumcised person from eating it. But will you argue the same about *terumah,* in the case of which Scripture does not limit the time of eating it for those who may eat it? Since Scripture does not put any limit to the time in which it may be eaten, it is but logical to assume that we should not disqualify the uncircumcised from eating it. However, Scripture uses the expression "a sojourner and a hired servant," in the case of the paschal lamb and in the case of *terumah.* Hence, just as the expression "a sojourner and a hired servant," used in the case of the paschal

---

[5] A resident alien, *Ger Toshab,* is a heathen who has foresworn idolatry (see Ab. Zarah 64b). He may be a potential proselyte but as yet not a proselyte. He is contrasted with the righteous proselyte who is fully like

תושב ושכיר לא יאכל בו תושב זה גר

חושב שכיר זה הגוי רבי אליעזר אומר תושב ושכיר

לא יאכל בו למה נאמר לדון מן הפסח על התרומה

לפסול בה את הערל עד שלא יאמר יש לי בדין

50 מה אם הפסח הקל פסל בו את הערל תרומה

חמורה אינו דין שיפסל בה את הערל לא אם אמרת

בפסח שמיעט בו הכתוב זמן אכילתו לאוכליו

לפיכך פסל בו את הערל תאמר בתרומה שריבה

הכתוב זמן אכילתה לאוכליה והואיל וריבה הכתוב

55 זמן אכילתה דין הוא שלא ניפסל בה את הערל

תלמוד לומר תושב ושכיר בפסח תושב ושכיר

בתרומה מה תושב ושכיר האמור בפסח פסל בו

<hr />

49—47 שם ע', א'. י' שם (80). ספרא אמור ד' (97a). ש. 29.
57—56 חושב ושכיר בתרומה] ויקרא כ״ב, י'.

<hr />

55—54 והואיל וריבה הכתוב זמן אכילתה]=א: מ. ד. <. 55 דין
הוא שלא ניפסל] ד. אינו דין שניפסול. ט. אינו דין שלא נפסול. א״צ.
יכול שלא נפסל. ש״י. לכך לא יפסול. 56 תלמוד לומר] מ. שאין
ת׳ל/חושב ושכיר בפסח]א.<. 57—56 תושב ושכיר בתרומה] מ.ק.
נ.ל. (מ. ק. נאמר תושב ושכיר בתרומה) ~ אלא מפנה (ק. נ. ואפנה
א״צ. ל. ומופנה) להקיש ולדון נ׳ש נאמר תושב ושכיר בפסח ונאמר
תושב ושכיר בתרומה. 58—57 מה-פסל בו את הערל]=ט. ש״י: מ. ד.
מה להלן (מ״ח. מה כאן) פוסל בו את הערל אף כאן (מ״ח. להלן)
פוסל בו את הערל.

<hr />

an Israelite. (See on the *Ger Toshab*, G. F. Moore, *Judaism*,
I, 338 ff. and III, 112; and cf. also *JE*, X, 220 ff.).

lamb, disqualifies an uncircumcised person, so also the expression "a sojourner and a hired servant," used in the case of the *terumah* disqualifies an uncircumcised person. R. Isaac says: "A sojourner and a hired servant shall not eat thereof." Why is this said? Has it not already been said: "There shall no alien eat thereof?" Answer. From the latter I might understand that a circumcised[6] Arabian or a circumcised Gibeonite is qualified to partake of the paschal lamb. Therefore Scripture says: "A sojourner and a hired servant shall not eat thereof."

In One House Shall It Be Eaten. Scripture here means in one group. You interpret it to mean in one group, perhaps "in one house" is to be taken literally? When it says: "Upon the houses wherein ye shall eat it" (v. 12), we learn that it may be eaten in more than one house. Hence, what does Scripture mean by saying here "in one house shall it be eaten?" Scripture here means in one group. And how am I to maintain the expression: "Upon the houses wherein ye shall eat it?" They said on the basis of this expression, that the paschal lamb may be eaten in two places,

---

[6] The term "alien," בן נכר, might have been understood to refer only to one who is both uncircumcised in heart and uncircumcised in flesh (cf. Ezek. 44.9.

את הערל אף תושב ושכיר האמור בתרומה פסל

בו את הערל רבי יצחק אומר תושב ושכיר לא

60 יאכל בו למה נאמר והלא כבר נאמר כל בן נכר

לא יאכל בו אבל אם היה ערבי מהול וגבעוני מהול

שומע אני יהיה כשר לאכול בפסח תלמוד לומר

תושב ושכיר לא יאכל בו.

בבית אחד יאכל בחבורה אחת הכתוב

65 מדבר אתה אומר בחבורה אחת או בבית אחד

כמשמעו כשהוא אומר על הבתים אשר יאכלו

אותו בהם הא למדנו שהוא נאכל בבתים הרבה

הא מה תלמוד לומר בבית אחד יאכל בחבורה

אחת הכתוב מדבר ומה אני מקיים על הבתים אשר

70 יאכלו אותו בהם מכאן אמרו הפסח נאכל בשני

64—75 פסחים פ"ו, א'. תוס' שם ו', א'.   64—79 פסחים פ"ה, ב'.

י' שם ז', י"ב (35be).   66—67 שמות י"ב, ז'.

60 כל בן נכר] א"צ. וכל ערל.   61 אבל] מ"ח. הרי.
א"צ. יכול מ"ע. אלא/ ונבעוני] א. ט. ונבנוני/ מהול]–א. א"א.
א"צ: מ. ד. כשר.   64 יאכל] א"צ. ~ ר' שמעון בן יוחאי אומר.
67—66 אשר יאכלו אותו בהם] מ. אשר יאמר.   67 הא למדנו] מ.
מ"ח. למדנו. ד. שומע אני.   69 הכתוב סדבר] ד. >.   70—69 ומה
אני מקיים–אותו בהם] ט. מ"ח. א"צ. >.

but may not be eaten in two companies—these are the words of R. Simon the son of Yoḥai. In two places! How? If they are inside the house and a beam over their heads breaks, they go out to the yard. If they are in the yard and rain comes down upon them, they go inside. Thus they may eat it in two places.

Thou Shalt Not Carry Forth . . . Out of the House. This means outside the group. You interpret it to mean outside the group. Perhaps this is not so, but merely means outside of the house. But Scripture says: "Abroad" (*ḥuzah*). which can only mean outside of where it must be eaten. Now, if one takes it outside he violates a commandment. I might understand that it should nevertheless be ritually fit. But the following argument is against it: Peace offerings belong to the class of minor sacrifices and the paschal lamb also belongs to the class of minor sacrifices. Now, inasmuch as you have learned that peace offerings become ritually unfit if taken outside, it follows that the paschal lamb must likewise become ritually unfit if taken outside.[7]

---

[7] I. e., outside of the territory in which it is allowed to be eaten (see M. Zeb. 5.7–8).

מקומות ואין נאכל בשני חבורות דברי רבי שמעון
בן יוחאי בשני מקומות כיצד היו בתוך הבית ובקעה
עליהם קורה יוצאין לחצר היו בחצר וירדו עליהם
גשמים נכנסין לתוך הבית נמצאו אוכלים אותו בשני
75 מקומות.

לא תוציא מן הבית וגו' חוץ לחבורה אתה
אומר חוץ לחבורה או אינו אלא חוץ לבית תלמוד
לומר חוצה חוץ לאכילתו הא אם הוציא עבר על
מצוה שומע אני יהיה כשר והדין נותן הואיל ושלמים
80 קדשים קלים והפסח קדשים קלים אם למדת על
השלמים שאם הוציאן לחוץ פסלן אף הפסח אם
הוציאו לחוץ פסלו.

76—82 פסחים פ'ה, א'.

71 ואין נאכל] א. מ. מ"ח. ואין אוכליו אוכלין אותו / בשני
חבורות] א. מ. בשני מקומות/ דברי רשב"י] הגהתי עפ"י ש"י. וש"ט.
בש"ט. מוסיף שרשב"י אומר: מ"ח. דברי ר' ישמעאל. א. מ. ד.
רשב"י אומר ובא"צ. מוחקו.   73 יוצאין לחצר] מ. ד. ויוצאין לחוץ.
74 אוכלים אותו] א. מ. מ"ח. אוכליו אוכלין אותו.   76—77 אתה
אומר חוץ לחבורה] מ"ח. א"צ. > ד. אתה אומר חוצה חוץ לחבורה.
א. אתה אומר לא מן הבית מן הבשר חוצה.   77—78 או אינו–חוץ
לאכילתו] א. מ. >.   81 פסלן] ק. ~ אכל. א. מ. נ. ל.
~ יכול. והשמטתי–ט. מ"ח. ש"י. א"צ. נ. ז"י.   82 פסלו] א. מ.
ק. נ. ל.~.(ק. יאכל) הא מה ת"ל לא תוציא מן הבית מן הבשר חוצה
חוץ לחבורה: והשמטתי–מ"ח. ש"י. ז"י. נ. א"צ. ומ'ע.

Thou Shalt Not Carry Forth . . . Out of the House. This passage deals with the meat. You interpret it as dealing with the meat, perhaps it deals with both, the meat and the bones? But the words, "Thou shalt not carry forth aught of the flesh," etc., teach that the passage deals only with the meat.

Neither Shall Ye Break a Bone Thereof. Why is the word "thereof" said here? Has it not already been said: "And they shall eat the flesh in that night" (v. 8), which means the meat on the outside of the bones? You interpret it to mean the meat on the outside of the bones. Perhaps this is not so, but it means also the meat inside the bones? And as for the passage: "Neither shall ye break a bone thereof", I apply it only to such bones as have no meat inside them. But it may just as well apply to bones which have meat inside. The word "thereof" in the passage, "neither shall ye break a bone thereof," shows that it applies to any bone thereof, whether it has meat in it or not.[8]

---

[8] See Lauterbach on שבירת עצם בפסח, in *Hazofeh*, IX (Budapest, 1925).

לא תוציא מן הבית וגו' בבשר הכתוב
מדבר אתה אומר בבשר הכתוב מדבר או אחד
בשר ואחד עצם תלמוד לומר לא תוציא מן הבשר
וגו' בבשר הכתוב מדבר.

ועצם לא תשברו בו למה נאמר בו והלא
כבר נאמר ואכלו את הבשר בלילה הזה הבשר
שבחוצה לעצם אתה אומר הבשר שחוצה לעצם
או אינו אלא הבשר שבתוך העצם ומה אני מקיים
ועצם לא תשברו בו עצם שאין בו בשר או עצם
שיש בו בשר תלמוד לומר ועצם לא תשברו בו בין
שיש בו בשר בין שאין בו בשר.

85—90 שם פ"ד, ב'—פ"ה א'. י' שם (35b) זבחים צ"ו ב', ספרי
זוטא (260). 88 שמות י"ב, ח'.

---

85 עצם] מ. ד. ~ פסל ומוחקו בא"צ. וליתא במ"ח./ לא
תוציא] מ"ח. >/ מן הבשר] מ. > ד. מן הבית. 87 בו 2]=מ.
א"צ: א. ד. >. 88 בלילה הזה] מ. וגו'. מ. ~ לפי שנאמר ואכלו
את הבשר וליתא בט. ובמ"ח. 89 שבחוצה לעצם] א. שבתוך
העצם. 89—90 אתה אומר—או אינו אלא] א. מ. ט. או. 90 שבתוך
העצם] א. שבחוצה לעצם/ ומה] ד. הא מה. 91 שאין בו בשר]—
ט. מ"ח. ז"י. ש"י: מ. ד. שיש בו בשר. א. בין שיש בו בשר.
91—92 או עצם שיש בו בשר]—ט. ש"י: מ"ח. > ז"י. אבל עצם
שיש בו בשר שובר ואוכל. מ. ד. או עצם שאין בו בשר. א. בין
שאין בו בשר. 92—93 בין שיש בו—שאין בו בשר]—א. מ. ט. מ"ח. ש"י:
ד. עצם שיש בו בשר.

Thereof. This does not apply to any other sacrifice. For the following argument could be advanced: If in the case of the paschal lamb, the less weighty, one is subject to the prohibition against breaking the bones, is it not but logical to assume that in the case of the more weighty sacrifices one should be subject to the prohibition against breaking the bones? But the word "thereof" teaches that this law applies only to the paschal lamb and not to any other sacrifice.

All the Congregation of Israel Shall Keep It. Why is this said? Since it says: "Draw out and take your lambs according to your families" (v. 21), one might think that just as the paschal lamb of Egypt could be offered only by a family, so the paschal lamb of all subsequent generations could be brought only by a family. Therefore, Scripture says: "All the congregation of Israel shall keep it," declaring thereby that the paschal lamb of subsequent generations may be brought by a mixed group.[9]

And When a Stranger Shall Sojourn with Thee and Will Keep the Passover to the Lord. I might understand this to mean that as soon as one becomes a proselyte he should forthwith offer a paschal sacrifice. But the scriptural passage: "And he shall be as one that is born in the land," teaches that just as the one born a Jew offers it on the fourteenth, so the proselyte offers

---

[9] I. e., a group made up of members of different families.

ב ו ולא בשאר כל הקדשים שהיה בדין ומה אם

הפסח הקל הרי הוא עובר עליו משום בל תשבור

קדשים החמורים אינו דין שיעבור עליהם משום

בל תשבור תלמוד לומר בו ולא בשאר כל

הקדשים.

כל עדת ישראל יעשו אותו למה נאמר

לפי שהוא אומר משכו וקחו לכם צאן למשפחותיכם

יכול כשם שפסח מצרים אינו כשר אלא למשפחה

כך פסח דורות לא יהיה כשר אלא למשפחה

תלמוד לומר כל עדת ישראל יעשו אותו מגיד

שפסח דורות בא בערבוביא.

וכי יגור אתך גר ועשה פסח ליישומע

אני כיון שנתגייר יעשה פסח מיד תלמוד לומר והיה

כאזרח הארץ מה אזרח בארבעה עשר אף הגר

99—102 חוס' פסחים ח', ט'ו.   100 שם י'ב, כ'א.   105—112 ספרי
במדבר ע'א. פסחים צ'ג, א'. תוס' שם ח', ד'.

---

94 בו] א'צ. דבר אחר בו.   95 עובר—תשבור] ד. עובר עליו
משום ועצם לא תשברו בו.   97 בל תשבורו] ד. בל תשברו בו./
ת'ל] ד. הא מה ת'ל.   101 יכול] הוספתי=מ'ח. ז'י. וא'צ.
104 דורות] ק. >/ בערבוביא] א. בעבובייה. מ. בערבויה.

it only on the fourteenth. R. Simon the son of
Eleazar says: I might think that one who became
a proselyte in the interval between the two
Passovers,[10] should celebrate the second Passover. But the scriptural passage: "And he shall
be as one that is born in the land," teaches that
just as the one born a Jew celebrates the second
Passover only when he omitted to celebrate the
first, so also the proselyte should celebrate the
second Passover only if he could have celebrated
the first but failed to do so.

*Let All His Males Be Circumcised and Then
Let Him Come Near and Keep It.* This tells that
failure to circumcise his free males debars one
from partaking of the paschal lamb. So far I
know only about the circumcision of free males.
How about the circumcision of slaves? You can
reason as follows: The expression "then" (*az*) is
used here, and the expression "then" (*az*) is used
above (v. 44). Just as there it refers to the
circumcision of slaves, so here it refers to the
circumcision of slaves. And just as here it refers
to the circumcision of free males so also there it
refers to the circumcision of free males—these
are the words of R. Eliezer. R. Ishmael says:
Failure to circumcise one's free males does not
debar one from partaking of the paschal lamb.
Why then is it said: "Let all his males be circumcised and then let him come near to keep it?"

---

[10] I. e., between the 14th of Nisan and the 14th of Iyyar.

בארבעה עשר רבי שמעון בן אלעזר אומר הרי
שנתגייר בין שני פסחים שומע אני יעשה פסח שני
תלמוד לומר והיה כאזרח הארץ מה אזרח שלא
עשה את הראשון יעשה את השני כך גר כל שלא
עשה את הראשון יעשה השני.

המול לו כל זכר ואז יקרב לעשותו מגיד
שמילת זכרים מעכבתו מלאכול בפסח אין לי אלא
מילת זכרים מילת עבדים מנין הרי אתה דן נאמר
כאן אז ונאמר להלן אז מה להלן מילת עבדים אף
כאן מילת עבדים ומה כאן מילת זכרים אף להלן
מילת זכרים דברי רבי אליעזר רבי ישמעאל אומר
אין מילת זכרים מעכבתו מלאכול בפסח ומה
תלמוד לומר המול לו כל זכר ואז יקרב לעשותו

108 בן אלעזר]=ט. ש"ט. מ"ח: א. בן אליעזר. ד. >.
110—111 שלא עשה]=מ"ח. א"צ: מ. ד. עד שלא עשה. מ"ע. על
שלא עשה.   111 כל] מ"ח. א"צ. >.   111—112 כך גר–יעשה השני] א.
ט. >.   113 המול לו] מ. המול לכם.   114 זכרים] א. זכוריו. ט.
מ"ח. זכריו.   115—116 הרי אתה דן–ונאמר להלן אז] מ"ח. ת"ל אז אז
למירה שוה.   116 אז] ד. >.   117 ומה כאן]=מ"ח. ט: מ. אי מה כאן
ד. או מה להלן/ אף להלן] ד. אף כאן.   118 רבי אליעזר] הגהתי עפ"י
מ"ח. ומהר"ס בש"י: א. מ. ד. רבי ישמעאל. ז"ר. ש"י.
בה"מ.ומ"ע. ר' יהושע.   מ"ס. ר' יאשיה/ רבי ישמעאל]=מ"ח.
ומהר"ס שם. ובה"מ: א. מ. ד. רבי יונתן. ט. עקיבא.

Suppose one has two commandments to fulfill, that of the Passover and that of circumcision, I would not know which of them has precedence. But when it says: "Let all his males be circumcised and then let him come near to keep it," it indicates that the commandment of circumcision has precedence over that of the Passover. R. Nathan says: There would be no purpose in Scripture's saying: "Let all his males be circumcised and then let him come near to keep it," except to include the slave who took the ritual bath in the presence of his master and thereby became a free man.[11]

It happened to Valeria that some of her handmaids took the ritual bath in front of her and some took it behind her. The case then came before the sages and they declared that those who submerged themselves in front of her were free and those who bathed behind her were still slaves. Nevertheless they all continued to serve her till the day of her death.

But No Uncircumcised Person Shall Eat Thereof. Why is this said? Has it not already been said: "There shall no alien eat thereof" (v. 43)? But I might understand from the latter that if an

---

[11] A slave when freed by his master must, like a proselyte, take a ritual bath before he can acquire the status of an Israelite (Yeb. 47b and *Sh. 'Ar. Yoreh De'ah* 267.7). Hence, if the slave takes the ritual bath in the presence of the master without the latter's objection, it is taken for granted that the master consented to give him his freedom and therefore permitted him to take the ritual bath, the final step in acquiring the status of an Israelite.

הרי שהיו לפניו שתי מצות מצות פסח ומצות מילה
איני יודע איזה מהם תקדים כשהוא אומר המול לו
כל זכר ואז יקרב לעשותו תקדים מצות מילה
למצות הפסח רבי נתן אומר שאין תלמוד לומר
125 המול לו אלא להביא את העבד שטבל לפני רבו
ויצא בן חורין מעשה בבלוריא שטבלו מקצת
שפחותיה לפניה ומקצתן לאחריה ובא מעשה לפני
חכמים ואמרו את שטבלו לפניה בנות חורין ושטבלו
לאחריה משועבדות ואף על פי כן משמשות היו
130 אותה עד יום מותה.

ו כ ל   ע ר ל   ל א   י א כ ל   ב ו   למה נאמר והלא
כבר נאמר כל בן נכר לא יאכל בו אבל אם היה

121—124 י' פסחים ג', ז' (30‏b).   126—130 יבמות ס"ו, א'. נזרים ב', ד'.

121 הרי שהיו] א. אלא הרי שהיו. ט. אלא שאם היו.   121—123 הרי
שהיו–ואז יקרב לעשותו] ק. >.   122 איני]=מ"ח: א. ואינו. ד. אינו/
תקדים] א. יקדים.   122—123 המול לו–תקדים] מ. המול ל:ם
תקדים לכם. 123 תקדים] א. הקדים.   124 שאין] מ"ח. סה.
125 להביא] א"צ. להוציא. 126 ויצא] ט. מ"ח. שיצא/ ד. לבן
חורין/ בבלוריא] מ"ח. ~ הניורת.   131 וכל ערל] מ. ק. נ. כל
ערל.   131—132 והלא כבר נאמר]א"צ. לפי שנאמר. 132 אבל]א.
אלא/ אם היה]ד. >.

Israelite be uncircumcised he is nevertheless qualified to partake of the paschal lamb. Therefore Scripture says: "But no uncircumcised person shall eat thereof."

One Law Shall Be to Him that is Homeborn. Why is this said? Has it not already been said: "And he shall be as one that is born in the land" (v. 48)? What purpose then is there in saying here: "One law shall be to him that is homeborn and unto the stranger"? Since it says: "And when a stranger shall sojourn with thee," etc. (v. 48), I might understand that the proselyte is like the born Jew only with respect to the Passover. How about all the other commandments of the Torah? Scripture says: "One law shall be to him that is homeborn, and unto the stranger." This passage comes to declare the proselyte equal to the born Jew with respect to all the commandments of the Torah.

CHAPTER XVI
(Ex. 13.1–4)

And the Lord Spoke unto Moses, etc. *Sanctify unto Me All the First-Born.* This is one of the rules for interpreting the Torah. There are instances in which not only does the general term need its specific term, but the specific term also needs its general term. "Sanctify unto Me all the first-born, whatsoever openeth the womb," etc., is the general term, including in its meaning

ישראל ערל שומע אני יהיה כשר לאכול בפסח
תלמוד לומר כל ערל לא יאכל בו.

135 　　תורה אחת יהיה לאזרח למה נאמר
והלא כבר נאמר והיה כאזרח הארץ ומה תלמוד
לומר תורה אחת יהיה לאזרח לפי שהוא אומר וכי
יגור אתך גר אין לי אלא פסח שהשוה בו את הגר
לאזרח שאר כל המצות שבתורה מנין תלמוד לומר
140 תורה אחת יהיה לאזרח ולגר בא הכתוב והשוה
את הגר לאזרח בכל המצות שבתורה.

פרשה טז　(שמות י"ג, א'–ד'.)

וידבר יי אל משה וגו' קדש לי כל
בכור　זו אחת מן י"ג מדות שהתורה נדרשת בהן
כלל שהוא צריך לפרטו ופרט שהוא צריך לכללו
קדש לי כל בכור פטר כל רחם וגו' כלל אחד

135–141 לעיל י'. ספרי שם.
17–1 בברייתא דר"י בריש ח"כ (2bc). מ"ת 87. בכורות י"ט, א'.

---

133 ערל] מ. >.　137–138 וכי יגור] א. כי יגור　138 שהשוה]
מ. שהוא שוה. א. שהשוו.　140 ולגר]=מ"ח: א. ד. >.
2 זו] ק. הא. נ. יהא/ י'נ] א. ט. >/ א. ט. המדות/ שהתורה-
בהן] מ. שבתורה נדרשת הן.　3 כלל] ד. בכלל/ לפרטו] ד. לפרט.
4 פטר כל רחם] ק. נ. פטר רחם.

both males and females. "All the firstling males that are born of thy herd and of thy flock thou shalt sanctify unto the Lord thy God" (Deut. 15.19), is a specific term, the meaning of which excludes females. Now, once I read the general statement, what need is there of making the specific statement? Because if I read merely the general statement without the specific, I might understand it to mean that whatsoever is born first, whether male or female, is to be considered a "first-born." Scripture therefore says: "All the firstling males that are born of thy herd and of thy flock," etc.—males but not females. Then, let me read only the specific statement. What need is there of making the general statement? Because if I read only the specific statement without the general statement, I might understand it to mean that as long as it is the first male offspring whether it is the one that first opened the womb or not, it is to be considered a "first-born." Therefore, Scripture says: "Sanctify unto Me all the first-born, whatsoever openeth the womb"—it must be both a male and first to open the womb. This confirms what has been said: "All that openeth the womb is Mine; and every firstling among thy cattle, whether ox or sheep, that is male" (Ex. 34.19).

Both of Man and of Beast. Those who are subject to the law as regards the human first-born are also subject to the law as regards their beasts. The Levites are thus excluded. Since they are not subject to the law as regards their human

זכרים ואחד נקבות במשמע כל הבכור אשר יולד   5

בבקרך וצאנך הזכר תקדיש ליי אלהיך פרט יצאו

נקבות ממשמע אני אקרא את הכלל מה תלמוד

לומר את הפרט שאם אני קורא את הכלל אבל

לא את הפרט שומע אני כל שיולד ראשון בין זכר

ובין נקבה יהיה בכור תלמוד לומר כל הבכור   10

אשר יולד וגו' הזכר זכרים אבל לא נקבות אני

אקרא את הפרט מה תלמוד לומר את הכלל שאם

קורא אני את הפרט אבל לא את הכלל שומע אני

כל שהוא זכר בין שהוא פותח רחם ובין שאינו פותח

רחם יהיה בכור תלמוד לומר קדש לי כל בכור   15

פטר כל רחם עד שיהיה זכר ופותח רחם לקיים

מה שנאמר כל פטר רחם לי וכל מקנך תזכר.

באדם ובבהמה את שיש לו באדם יש לו

בבהמה יצאו הלוים שאין להם באדם ולא יהיה

5–6 דברים ט"ו, י"ט.   10–11 שמות ל"ד, י"ט.   20–18 בכורות ד',
א'. תוס' שם א', ב'. ספרי במדבר קי"ח. ספרי זוטא (295). ש. 31.

---

5 במשמע] מ. ד. >.   6 בבקרך–ליי אלהיך] הוספתי: א. מ.
ד. וגו'.   11 אשר יולד] מ. ד. > / וגו'] ד. > / הזכר]–ט. מ"ח:
מ. ד. >.   12–13 שאם קורא–את הכלל] מ. >.   14 שהוא]
מ. ט. מ"ח. > א. שיולד / זכר]א. > ט. ~ שיולד.   19 ולא יהיה]
ד. אין.   23 נותנו] א. מ. אתה רשאי ליתנו / לכהן] ד. לו.

first-born, they are likewise not subject to the law as regards their beasts.

Another Interpretation: The first-born of human beings are compared to the first-born of beasts and the first-born of beasts are compared to the first-born of human beings. Just as in the case of beasts a premature birth frees the one born after it from the law about the first-born, so also in the case of human beings, a miscarriage frees the one born after it from the law about the first-born. And just as one may give the first-born of human beings to the priest wherever one pleases, so also may one give the first-born of beasts to the priest wherever one pleases. Since it says: "And thither ye shall bring your burnt-offerings . . . and the firstlings of your herd and of your flock" (Deut. 12.6), I might understand that even if one is in a far-off place it is incumbent upon him to bring them to the Temple. But Scripture says: "Both of man and of beasts," indicating thereby—the first-born of men and the first-born of beasts are alike: Just as one may give the first-born of man to the priest wherever one pleases, so also may one give the first-born of beasts to the priest wherever one pleases. And just as one must tend the first-born of man for thirty days, so also must one tend the first-born of beasts for thirty days.

It Is Mine. Why is this said? Because when it says: "All the firstling males thou shalt sanctify unto the Lord thy God" (Deut. 15.19), it merely means, consecrate it only for the sake of receiving reward for doing so. But perhaps

²⁰ להם בבהמה דבר אחר הקיש בכור אדם לבכור
בהמה ובכור בהמה לבכור אדם מה הבהמה
הנפלים פוטרים בה את הבכורה אף האדם הנפלים
פוטרים בו את הבכורה ומה בכור אדם נותנו לכהן
בכל מקום שירצה אף בכור בהמה נותנו לכהן
²⁵ בכל מקום שירצה לפי שהוא אומר והבאתם שמה
עולותיכם וגו' ובכורות בקרכם וצאנכם שומע אני
אפילו הוא במקום רחוק יהיה חובה עליו להביאו
לבית הבחירה תלמוד לומר באדם ובבהמה הקיש
בכור אדם לבכור בהמה מה בכור אדם נותנו
³⁰ לכהן בכל מקום שירצה אף בכור בהמה נותנו
לכהן בכל מקום שירצה ומה בכור אדם אתה
מיטפל בו שלשים יום אף בכור בהמה תהא מיטפל
בו שלשים יום.

לי הוא למה נאמר לפי שהוא אומר הזכר
³⁵ תקדיש ליי אלהיך הקדישו כדי שתקבל שכר או

33–20 לקטן כספא א'. ספרי במדבר שם. מ"ת 77.   26–25 דברים
י"ב, ו'.   38–34 ספרא בחוקותי ח' (114°). ערכין כ"ט, א'. תמורה
כ"ה, א'. נדרים י"ג, א'. מ"ת 87. ש. 30.

---

24 לכהן] ד. לו.   26 ובכורות בקרכם וצאנכם] הוספתי–ט.
31 אתה]–ט: מ"ח. מ. ד. >.   33 בו]–ט. מ"ח: א. בה. ד. לו.

it means, only if you consecrate it does it
become consecrated; but if you do not, it does
not become so? Against this Scripture says: "It
is Mine"—in any event. Hence what does "All
the firstling males thou shalt sanctify unto the
Lord thy God" mean? Consecrate it merely in
order that you may receive reward for doing so.
In like manner you interpret: "And the priest
shall kindle wood on it," etc. (Lev. 6.5). Why
has this been commanded? Has it not been
said: "And Lebanon is not sufficient fuel?" (Isa.
40.16). What then is the purport of the commandment: "And the priest shall kindle wood
on it?" Merely to enable you to receive reward
for fulfilling it. In like manner you interpret:
"The one lamb thou shalt offer in the morning"
(Ex. 29.39). Why has this been commanded?
Has it not been said: "Nor the beast thereof
sufficient for burnt-offerings" (Isa. 40.16)? What
then is the purport of the commandment: "The
one lamb thou shalt offer in the morning?" To
enable you to receive reward for fulfilling it. In
like manner you interpret: "And let them make
Me a sanctuary, that I may dwell among them"
(Ex. 25.8). Why has this been commanded? Has
it not been said: "The heaven is My throne . . .
where is the house that ye may build unto Me?"
(Isa. 66.1)? What then is the purport of the
commandment: "And let them make Me a
sanctuary"? To enable them to receive reward
for fulfilling it.

Once the disciples spent the Sabbath in Jabneh.
R. Joshua, however, was not there on that

אם הקדשתו מקודש ואם לאו אינו מקודש תלמוד

לומר לי הוא מכל מקום הא מה תלמוד לומר

הזכר תקדיש הקדישו כדי שתקבל שכר כיוצא בו

אתה אומר ובער עליה הכהן עצים וגו' למה נאמר

40 והלא כבר נאמר ולבנון אין די בער הא מה תלמוד

לומר ובער עליה הכהן עצים כדי שתקבל שכר

כיוצא בו אתה אומר את הכבש האחד תעשה בבקר

למה נאמר והלא כבר נאמר וחיתו אין די עולה

הא מה תלמוד לומר את הכבש האחד תעשה

45 כדי שתקבל שכר כיוצא בו אתה אומר ועשו

לי מקדש ושכנתי בתוכם למה נאמר והלא

כבר נאמר השמים כסאי וגו' אי זה בית אשר תבנו

לי הא מה תלמוד לומר ועשו לי מקדש כדי לקבל

שכר כבר שבתו תלמידים ביבנה ולא שבת שם רבי

---

39 ויקרא ו', ה'.   40 ישעיה מ', ט"ו.   42 במדבר כ"ח, ד'.

43 ישעיה שם.   45—46 שמות כ"ה, ח'.   47—48 ישעיה ס"ו, א'.

49—62 אדר'נ י"ח. חגיגה נ', א'. י' שם א', א' (75d). תוס' סוטה ז', ט'.

---

36 ואם לאו] ד. ואם לא הקדישו.   38—39 בו אתה אומר] ק. נ.

בואתה תצוה אותר.   41 כדי שתקבל] א. ד. שיקבל.   42 הכבש

האחד] במקרא כתוב הכבש אחד.   44—45 תעשה כדי] ק.נ. למה נאמר.

47 השמים כסאי וגו'] א. ד. ט"כ. הלא (ד. >) את השמים ואת הארץ

אני מלא (ירמיה כ"ג, כ"ד) / אי זה בית אשר תבנו לי] הוספתי.

48 לקבל]א.מ. שתקבל.   49 שכר] ד. ~ על העשייה/ א. התלמידים.

Sabbath. When the disciples came to visit him, he said to them: "What new lesson did you have in Jabneh?" They said to him: "After you, master." He then said to them: "And who was there for the Sabbath?" They said to him: "R. Eleazar the son of Azariah." Then he said to them: "Is it possible that R. Eleazar the son of Azariah was there for the Sabbath and did not give you anything new?" So they said to him: "He brought out this general idea in his exposition of the text: 'Ye are standing this day all of you . . . your little ones,' etc. (Deut. 29.9). Now what do the little ones know about distinguishing between good and evil? It was but to give the parents reward for bringing their children, thus increasing the reward of those who do His will. This confirms what has been said: 'The Lord was pleased for His righteousness' sake[1]," etc. (Isa. 42.21). Then R. Joshua exclaimed and said to them: "Is not this a new teaching? Behold, I am nearly eighty years old, and I never had the good fortune to get this teaching until this day. Happy thou, our father Abraham, in that Eleazar the son of Azariah is a descendant of yours. Surely the generation in which there is an Eleazar b. Azariah is not to be considered orphaned." Then they said to him: "Master, he also brought out this general idea in the exposition of the text: 'Therefore, behold,

---

[1] See interpretation of R. Hananiah b. Akashya (Mak. 3.16).

50 יהושע וכשבאו התלמידים אצלו אמר להם מה
דבר חדש היה לכם ביבנה אמרו לו אחריך רבי
אמר להם ומי שבת שם אמרו לו רבי אלעזר בן
עזריה אמר להם אפשר ששבת שם רבי אלעזר בן
עזריה ולא חידש לכם דבר אמרו לו כלל זה דרש
55 אתם נצבים היום כלכם וגו' טפכם וגו' וכי מה טף
זה יודע להבין בין טוב לרע אלא ליתן שכר בנים
לאבות לרבות שכר עושי רצונו לקיים מה שנאמר
יי חפץ למען צדקו וגו' אמר להם אין זה דבר חדש
והרי אני כבן שמנים שנה ולא זכיתי לדבר זה בלתי
60 היום אשריך אברהם אבינו שאלעזר בן עזריה
יצא מחלציך אין הדור יתום שרבי אלעזר בן עזריה
שרוי בתוכו אמרו לו רבי עוד כלל זה דרש לכן

55 דברים כ"ט, ט'–י'.　　　58 ישעיה מ"ב, כ"א.　　　62–64 ירמיה ט"ז,
י"ד–ט"ו.　　　62–76 ברכות י"ג, א'. י' שם א', ט' (4ᵃ). תוס' שם א',
י"א–י"ג.

50 התלמידים] מ. ק. נ. תלמידיו.　　　51 דבר חדש] ד. דברים/
ביבנה] מ. שם ביבנה.　　　53 אפשר] ט. אי אפשר.　　　54 דבר] א. ~
כלל. מ. שם דבר/ כלל זה] א. דבר כלל זה. ט. רבי כלל זה.
55 וגו'ב'] ק. נ. >/ וגו'ב'] ק. נ. נשיכם/מה] ד. >.　　　56 זה] ד. הזה/להבין]
מ. להבחין.　　　57–56 בנים לאבות] ד. למביאיהם.　　　57 עושי] א. מ.
עושה.　　　58 אין זה דבר חדש]=ט: ד. אי זה דבר חדש יתר על זה. מ. אי
זה דבר חדש.　　　59 והרי אני] ט. והלא אני ד. הריני/ שמונים]=ט: ד.
שבעים.　　　60 אברהם] א. >/. שרבי אלעזר ב'ע] א. שאליעזר בן עזריה.

the days come, saith the Lord, that they shall
no more say: "As the Lord liveth, that brought
up the children of Israel . . . " but: "As the
Lord liveth, that brought up and that led," ' etc.
(Jer. 23.7–8). One can illustrate it by a parable.
To what can it be compared? To the following:
One was very desirous of children.   After a
daughter had been born to him, he would swear
by the life of the daughter.   When again a son
was born to him, he left off swearing by the
daughter and swore only by the life of the son."
—R. Simon b. Yoḥai says: One can illustrate
it by a parable. To what can it be compared?
To the following: One was traveling along the
road.   He encountered a wolf and was saved
from him. So he kept on telling the story of the
wolf. Then he encountered a lion and was saved
from him. So he forgot the story of the wolf and
kept on telling the story of the lion. He then
encountered a serpent and was saved from him.
So he forgot the story of both of them and kept
on telling the story of the serpent. So it is with
Israel. Later troubles cause the former ones to
be forgotten.—In like manner he interpreted:
"And he called the name of that place Beth-el"
(Gen. 28.19). The first name was given up and
the second came into permanent use. In like
manner he interpreted: "Neither shall thy name

הנה ימים באים נאום יי ולא יאמרו עוד חי יי אשר
העלה וגו' כי אם חי יי אשר העלה ואשר הביא וגו'
מושלו משל למה הדבר דומה לאחד שהיה מתאוה
לבנים ונולדה לו בת והיה נודר בחיי הבת חזר
ונולד לו בן הניח את הבת והיה נודר בחיי הבן רבי
שמעון בן יוחי אומר מושלו משל למה הדבר דומה
לאחד שהיה מהלך בדרך ופגע בו זאב וניצל ממנו
והיה הולך ומספר מעשה הזאב פגע בו ארי וניצל
הימנו שכח מעשה הזאב והיה הולך ומספר מעשה
ארי פגע בו נחש וניצל ממנו שכח מעשה שניהם
והיה הולך ומספר מעשה נחש כך ישראל צרות
האחרונות משכחות הראשונות כיוצא בו דרש ויקרא
שם המקום ההוא בית אל עבר שם הראשון ונתקיים
שם השני כיוצא בו דרש ולא יקרא עוד את שמך

65 ... 70 ... 75

74—75 בראשית כ"ח, י"ט. 76—77 שם י"ז, ה'.

63 נאום יי] הוספתי: א. מ. ונו'/ ולא יאמרו] ד. לא יאמר (ירמיה
ט"ז, י"ד) ובמקרא שם כתוב ולא יאמר. 65 מושלו משל] ד. >. 66 חזר]
א. >. 68 אומר] א. >/ מושלו משל] ד. >. 69 ממנו]=ט: א.
מ"ח. סידו ד. >. 70 הולך ומספר מעשה הזאב] א. ט. מ"ח. סתנה
נסים שנעשו לו בזאב. 71הימנו] א. מ"ח. סידו. 72—71 הולך-ארי] א.
מתנה נסים שנעשו לו בארי. 72—74 פגע בו נחש—משכחות הראשונות] מ.
ד. >. 74—76 כיוצא בו—שם השני] א. >. 75—74 ויקרא שם] במקרא
כתוב ויקרא את שם. 76 את] ד. >.

anymore be called Abram," etc. (Gen. 17.5).
The first name was given up and the second one
came into use. In like manner he interpreted:
"As for Sarai thy wife, thou shalt not call," etc.
(Gen. 17.15). The first name was given up and
the second came into use. He also interpreted:
"And he said: 'Thy name shall be called no more
Jacob'," etc. (Gen. 32.29). The first name
continued to be used and the second was merely
an additional one. As for Isaac, his name was
not changed because it was given to him by the
Holy One, blessed be He. And there were three
whose names were given to them by the Holy
One, blessed be He: Isaac, Solomon and Josiah.
In the case of Isaac, what does it say? "Nay, but
Sarah thy wife shall bear thee a son; and thou
shalt call his name Isaac" (Gen. 17.19). In the
case of Solomon, what does it say? "For his
name shall be Solomon" (I Chron. 22.9). In
the case of Josiah, what does it say? "Behold, a
son shall be born unto the house of David, Josiah
by name" (I Kings 13.2).—Some say, Among
the Gentiles there was also one, Ishmael[2].—We
find that the names of the righteous and their

---

[2] I. e., whose name was given to him by God (Gen.
16.11).

אברם וגו' עבר שם הראשון ונתקיים שם השני כיוצא
בו דרש שרי אשתך לא תקרא וגו' עבר שם הראשון
ונתקיים שם השני כיוצא בו דרש ויאמר לא יעקב
80 יאמר עוד שמך וגו' הראשון נתקיים לו והשני
נתוסף לו יצחק לא נשתנה שמו שנקרא מפי הקדוש
ברוך הוא ושלשה הם שנקראו מפי הקדוש ברוך
הוא יצחק ושלמה ויאשיה ביצחק מהו אומר אבל
שרה אשתך יולדת לך בן וקראת את שמו יצחק
85 בשלמה מהו אומר כי שלמה יהיה שמו ביאשיהו
מהו אומר הנה בן נולד לבית דוד יאשיה שמו ויש
אומרים אף ישמעאל בגוים מצינו שמותן של צדיקים

79—77 ברכות י"נ, א'. תוס' שם א', י"ב. י' שם א', ט' (4a).
78 בראשית י"ז, ה'. 80—79 בראשית ל"ב, כ"ט. 81—79 ברכות
שם. תוס' שם א', י'. י' שם. 86—81 י' ברכות שם. פדר"א ל"ב.
84—83 בראשית י"ז, י"ט. 85 דברי הימים א. כ"ב, ט'. 86 מלכים א.
י"ג, ב'. 91—86 י' שם.

---

79 כיוצא בו דרש] א"צ. >. 80—79 ויאמר לא יעקב—וגו'] ד.
ולא יקרא שמך עוד יעקב (בראשית ל"ה. י') אך במקרא שם כתוב לא.
80 הראשון נתקיים]=ט. א"א: מ. מ"ח. עבר שם הראשון ונתקיים. ד.
עבר הראשון נתקיים. 80 לו] ד. >/ והשני] ד. השני. 81 יצחק]
מ. ר' יצחק אומר. 84 יולדת לך—יצחק] א. מ. וגו' ועפ"ז הנהתי
כמו במקרא. ד. וקראת שמו. 85 כי שלמה יהיה שמו] א. הנה בן יולד
לך והוא וגו' כי שלמה יהיה שמו ובמקרא כתוב הוא. 86 לבית דוד] מ.
לבן דוד.

deeds are revealed before God even before they are born, as it is said: "Before I formed thee in the belly I knew thee," etc. (Jer. 1.5). We thus learn that the names of the righteous and their deeds are revealed before God. How about those of the wicked? Scripture says: "The wicked are estranged from the womb," etc. (Ps. 58.4).

And Moses Said unto the People: 'Remember This Day,' etc. From this I know only that the exodus from Egypt should be mentioned during the daytime.[3] How about the nighttime? Scripture says: "That thou mayest remember the day when thou camest forth out of the land of Egypt all the days of thy life" (Deut. 16.3). Had it said only "the days of thy life," it would have meant only the daytime. "All the days of thy life," means during the nighttime also—according to the words of Ben Zoma. But the other sages say, "The days of thy life," would have meant only in this present world; "All the days of thy life," includes the days of the Messiah. Said Ben Zoma to the sages: In the future Israel will leave off mentioning the exodus from Egypt, as it is said: "Therefore, behold, the days come, saith the Lord, that it shall no more be said: 'As the Lord liveth, that brought up the children of Israel out of the land of Egypt' but, 'As the Lord liveth that brought up the children of Israel from the land of the North'" (Jer. 16.14–15). R. Nathan says the words: "That

---

[3] I. e., in the recitation of the *Shema'* (see *JE*, XI, 266, s. v. Shema').

ומעשיהם גלויים לפני המקום עד שלא נוצרו שנאמר
בטרם אצרך בבטן ידעתיך וגו' למדנו ששמותן
של צדיקים ומעשיהן גלוים לפני המקום של רשעים
מנין תלמוד לומר זורו רשעים מרחם וגו'.

ויאמר משה אל העם זכור את היום
הזה וגו' אין לי מזכירים יציאת מצרים אלא בימים
בלילות מנין תלמוד לומר למען תזכור את יום
צאתך מארץ מצרים וגו' ימי חייך בימים כל ימי
חייך בלילות כדברי בן זומא וחכמים אומרים ימי
חייך בעולם הזה כל ימי חייך להביא את ימות
המשיח אמר להם בן זומא עתידים ישראל שלא
להזכיר יציאת מצרים לעתיד לבא שנאמר לכן
הנה ימים באים נאם יי ולא יאמר עוד חי יי אשר
העלה את ישראל ממצרים כי אם חי יי אשר העלה
את ישראל מארץ צפון רבי נתן אומר אשר העלה

90

95

100

───────────

89 ירמיה א', ה'.   91 תהלים נ'ח, ד'.   92–102 ספרי דברים ק'ל.
ברכות שם. י' שם.   95–94 דברים ט'ז, ג'.   102–99 ירמיה ט'ז, י'ד-ט'ו.

───────────

89 ששמותן] מ. ד. שמותן.   90 ומעשיהן גלוים לפני המקום]
מ. ד. > ט. גלוים/ של רשעים] ד. שמותיהן של רשעים.   91 תלמוד
לומר] ד. שנאמר.   96 כדברי] א. דברי.   97 את ימות] א. ד. ליםות.
101 ישראל ממצרים] במקרא כתוב בני ישראל מארץ מצרים.
102–101 העלה את ישראל] א. העלה וגו' במקרא כתוב העלה את בני
ישראל.   103–101 את ישראל-ואשר הביא] א. >.

brought up and that led" (ibid., 23.8), show that
even in the future they will mention the exodus
from Egypt.[4]   And how do we know that one
should say: "Blessed be Thou, O Lord, our God
and God of our fathers, God of Abraham, God of
Isaac, God of Jacob?" It is said: "And God said
moreover unto Moses: 'Thus shalt thou say unto
the children of Israel: The Lord, the God of your
fathers, the God of Abraham, the God of Isaac
and the God of Jacob'," etc.   (Ex. 3.16).   And
how do we know, that one must say grace after
meals? It is said: "And thou shalt eat and be
satisfied and bless the Lord thy God for the good
land which He hath given thee" (Deut. 8.10).
"And bless," indicates the first benediction. "For
the land," indicates the second benediction. "The
good," indicates the benediction closing with
"who rebuilds Jerusalem[5]," as it is said, "that
goodly hill-country[6] and Lebanon" (Deut. 3.25).
"What He hath given thee," indicates the benediction for having bestowed upon us all good.[7]
R. Ḥiyya the son of Naḥamani said in the name

---

[4] According to R. Nathan, the expression "that brought
up" in v. 8 still refers, as in the preceding verse, to the
deliverance from Egypt.   The expression "that led," etc.,
however, refers to the deliverance from the other countries.

[5] The grace after meal consists of three benedictions.
The third benediction closes with the words "who rebuilds
Jerusalem." To these a fourth was added, thanking God for
all the good He has bestowed upon us (see *JE*, VI, 61–62).

[6] "The goodly hill-country," according to the Rabbis,
refers to Jerusalem (see *Sifre*. Num. 134).

[7] This is the fourth benediction (see above, note 5).

ואשר הביא מגיד שמזכירים יציאת מצרים לעתיד

לבא ומנין שהם אומרים ברוך אתה יי אלהינו ואלהי

105 אבותינו אלהי אברהם אלהי יצחק ואלהי יעקב

שנאמר ויאמר עוד אלהים אל משה כה תאמר אל

בני ישראל יי אלהי אבותיכם אלהי אברהם אלהי

יצחק ואלהי יעקב וגו' ומנין שמברכין על המזון

שנאמר ואכלת ושבעת וברכת את יי אלהיך על

110 הארץ הטובה אשר נתן לך וברכת זו ברכה ראשונה

על הארץ זו ברכה שנייה הטובה זו בונה ירושלים

שנאמר ההר הטוב הזה והלבנון אשר נתן לך שגמלנו

כל טוב רבי חייא בר נחמני אמר משום רבי

108—106 שמות ג', ט'ו.   124—108 ברכות מ'ח, ב'. תוס' שם ז',
א'. י' שם ז', א' (11a).   110—109 דברים ח', י'.   112 דברים
ג', כ'ה.

---

103 מגיד] ד. >.   106 שנאמר] א. כענין שנאמר.   108—107 אלהי
יצחק ואלהי יעקב] הוספתי.   108 שמברכין]=ט. ז"י: מ. ד. שהן
מברכין.   110—109 את יי אלהיך–אשר נתן לך] הוספתי: א. וגו'.
110 וברכת] הוספתי–מ"ע.   111 בונה]=ט. א"א: א. ד. >.
112 שגמלנו] ד. שגמלם.

of R. Ishmael: Behold it says: "And thou shalt
eat and be satisfied and bless the Lord thy God
for the good land" (Deut. 8.10). What need is
there of saying: "Which He hath given thee?"
To indicate, for whatever He gives you, good or
bad.[8] So far we know only that one is required
to say a benediction after the meal. How about
before it? R. Ishmael used to say it can be
determined by using the method of *Kal vaḥomer*:
If one is required to say a benediction after he
has eaten and is satisfied, how much the more
when he desires to eat? R. Nathan says: Behold
it says: "As soon as ye are come into the city, ye
shall straightway find him before he go up to the
high place to eat; for the people will not eat
until he come, because he doth bless the sacrifice[9]," etc. (I Sam. 9.13). R. Isaac says: Behold
it says: "And ye shall serve the Lord your God,
and He will bless thy bread" (Ex. 23.25). When
is it "thy bread?" Before thou hast eaten it. So
far we know only that one is required to say a
benediction before and after partaking of food.
How about before and after the reading of the
Torah? R. Ishmael used to say, it can be
determined by using the method of *Kal vaḥomer*:
If a meal, which is only for the ephemeral life,
requires a benediction before and after it, it is
but logical to assume that the reading from the
Torah, which is for life eternal, should require a

---

[8] See M. Ber. 9.5.

[9] The sacrifice was also the meal. To bless the sacrifice
accordingly means to recite the blessing over the meal.

ישמעאל הרי הוא אומר ואכלת ושבעת וברכת וגו'

115 מה זה מחוסר אשר נתן לך בין מדת הטוב ובין מדת

הפורענות אין לי אלא מזון שהוא טעון ברכה

לאחריו לפניו מנין היה רבי ישמעאל אומר קל

וחמר הוא אם כשאכל ושבע הרי הוא טעון ברכה

קל וחמר כשהוא תאב לאכול רבי נתן אומר הרי

120 הוא אומר כבאכם העיר כן תמצאון אותו בטרם

יעלה הבמתה לאכול כי לא יאכל העם עד בואו

כי הוא יברך הזבח וגו' רבי יצחק אומר הרי הוא

אומר ועבדתם את יי אלהיכם וברך את לחמך

אימתי הוא לחמך עד שלא אכלתו אין לי אלא

125 מזון שהוא טעון ברכה לפניו ולאחריו תורה מנין

היה רבי ישמעאל אומר קל וחמר מה אם מזון שאינו

אלא חיי שעה הרי הוא טעון ברכה לפניו ולאחריו

תורה שהיא חיי עולם דין הוא שתטעון ברכה לפניה

117–131 ברכות שם. תוס' שם. י' שם. 122–120 שמואל א. ט', י"ג.
123 שמות כ"נ, כ"ה.

117–116 אלא מזון–לאחריו] ז"י. אלא שהוא טעון ברכת המזון
לאחריו. ד. אלא ברכת המזון שהוא טעון ברכה לאחריו. 118 הוא]
ד. </ הרי הוא] ד. >. 119 קל וחמר] ד. / לאכול] ד. לא כל
שכן. 120 כבואכם העיר] ד. כבואכם אל העיר. 122–120 בטרם
יעלה –וגו'] א. מ. וגו'. 121 לא יאכל] ד. לא יאכלו. 125–127 תורה
מנין–ולאחריו] א. >. 128 שהיא חיי עולם] ד. שיש בה עולם הבא.

benediction before and after it. R. Judah the son
of Bathyra says: Behold it says: "And thou
shalt eat and be satisfied and bless the Lord thy
God for the good land." What need is there of
using the adjective "good?" It is merely to refer
to the Torah, as it is said: "For I give you good
doctrine" (Prov. 4.2). R. Ḥanina the nephew of
R. Joshua says: Behold it says: "For I will proclaim the name of the Lord; ascribe ye greatness,"
etc. (Deut. 32.3). "For I will proclaim," refers
to the one who recites the benediction. "Ascribe
ye greatness," refers to those who respond after
him. And what do they respond after the one
who recites the benediction? "Praised be the
Lord who is to be praised for ever and ever."
And whenever he mentions His name they shall
exclaim and say: "Praised be His name, whose
glorious kingdom is for ever and ever." For so
David also says: "O magnify the Lord with me
and let us exalt His name together" (Ps. 34.4).
Rabbi says: "The memory of the righteous shall
be for a blessing" (Prov. 10.7), means, whenever
one mentions the Righteous One, the Righteous
One who lives eternally—as it is said: "The Lord
is righteous in all His ways" (Ps. 145.17),—
give Him praise by saying Amen.

ולאחריה רבי יהודה בן בתירה אומר הרי הוא

130 אומר ואכלת ושבעת וברכת מה זה מחוסר טובה

אלא זו תורה שנאמר כי לקח טוב נתתי לכם וגו'

רבי חנינא בן אחי רבי יהושע אומר הרי הוא אומר

כי שם יי אקרא הבו גודל וגו' כי שם יי אקרא זה

המברך הבו גודל לאלהינו אלו העונים אחריו ומה

135 הן עונין אחרי המברך ברוך יי המבורך לעולם

ועד וכשהוא קורא בשמו יהיו עונין אחריו ואומרין

ברוך שם כבוד מלכותו לעולם ועד וכן דוד אומר

גדלו ליי אתי ונרוממה שמו יחדו רבי אומר זכר

צדיק לברכה כשהוא מזכיר את הצדיק צדיק חי

140 העולמים שנאמר צדיק יי בכל דרכיו תן לו ברכה

אמן.

131 משלי ד', ב'.   137—132 ספרי דברים ש'ו. ס'ת 186.
133 דברים ל'ב, נ'.   138 תהלים ל'ד, ד'.   139—138 משלי י', ז'.
141—138 יומא ל'ח, ב'. ס'ת 186.   140 תהלים קמ'ה, י'ז.

130 מה זה מחוסר טובה] ט. א'א. ז'י. מהו הטובה.   131 אלא]
א. מ. <.   132 חנינא] א. חנניה.   133—132 הרי הוא אומר–גודל וגו']
ד. <.   133 י'י] ד. השם.   137 דוד אומר] ד. <.   139 את הצדיק
צדיק] ט. > ט'כ. צדיק.   140 שנאמר] א. <. / תן לו ברכה]–ט:
א. מ. ד. וגו' לברכה.

There Shall No Leavened Bread Be Eaten. This makes one who gives others leavened bread to eat as guilty of violating the law as one who eats it himself. You interpret it as making one who gives others to eat like one who eats it. Perhaps this is not so, but it means that any enjoyment of leaven is forbidden? When it says: "Thou shalt eat no leavened bread with it" (Deut. 16.3), behold, we learn that any enjoyment thereof is forbidden. Hence what is the purpose of saying: "There shall no leavened bread be eaten?" To make one who gives others to eat like one who eats it himself—these are the words of R. Josiah. R. Isaac says: Scripture would not need to tell us this here. Even in the case of reptiles, where the law is less severe, it regards one who gives others to eat like one who eats them himself. Is it not logical to assume that in the case of leaven, where the law is more severe, we should regard one who gives others to eat like one who eats it himself? Hence what is the need of saying: "There shall no leavened bread be eaten?" Scripture merely comes to forbid any enjoyment of it.

R. Jose the Galilean says: "There shall no leavened bread be eaten this day." This tells that the Israelites in Egypt ate unleavened bread only one day.

This Day Ye Go Forth in the Month Abib. In adding the words: "In the month Abib," Scripture merely means to say: A month convenient

לא יאכל חמץ לעשות את המאכיל כאוכל

אתה אומר לעשות את המאכיל כאוכל או אינו

אלא לאסרו בהנאה כשהוא אומר לא תאכל עליו

145 חמץ הא למדנו שהוא אסור בהנאה הא מה תלמוד

לומר לא יאכל חמץ לעשות את המאכיל כאוכל

דברי רבי יאשיה רבי יצחק אומר אינו צריך מה

אם שרצים קלים עשה בהם את המאכיל כאוכל

חמץ החמור אינו דין שנעשה בו את המאכיל כאוכל

150 הא מה תלמוד לומר לא יאכל חמץ לא בא הכתוב

אלא לאסרו בהנאה רבי יוסי הגלילי אומר לא

יאכל חמץ היום מגיד שלא אכלו ישראל מצה

במצרים אלא יום אחד בלבד.

היום אתם יוצאים בחדש האביב

155 שאין תלמוד לומר חדש האביב אלא חדש שהוא

142—149 י' פסחים ב', א' (28c).   144—145 דברים ט'ז, ג'.
148 ת'כ שמיני ה' (50b).   151—153 פסחים כ'ח, ב'.
צ'ו, ב'. י' שם ט', ה' (37a). ש. 32.   154—159 ספרי דברים קכ'ח.

---

143 אתה אומר—כאוכל] א. ד. >.   145 האו] מ. ד. >/ שהוא
אסור] א'צ. מ'ע. שמותר.   149 בו את] ק. נ. כזאת. ט. בו
כן/ המאכיל כאוכל] ט. >.   152 שלא אכלו ישראל מצה] א'צ.
שלא נאסרו בחמץ.

for you. The sun was not too hot and there were
no rains. Likewise when it says: "God maketh
the solitary to dwell in a house; He bringeth out
the prisoners with convenience"[10] (*Bakosharot*)
(Ps. 68.7), Scripture uses the word *Bakosharot*
merely to indicate that it was in a convenient
month. The sun was not too hot and there
were no rains. R. Jonathan says: *Bakosharot*
means: There were those who wept and those
who sang.[11] The Egyptians wept, as it is said:
"While the Egyptians were burying," etc. (Num.
33.4). The Israelites sang, as it is said, "The
voice of rejoicing and salvation is in the tents of
the righteous . . . The right hand of the Lord
is exalted" (Ps. 118.15–16), because the Lord
was exalted over the Egyptians. R. Nathan says:
Bakosharot means, by the conduct of the pious
women among them. And so it also says: "Of
the mirrors of the serving women that did
service," etc. (Ex. 38.8). R. Eleazar the son of
Azariah says: Because of the merit of our father
Abraham did God bring Israel out of Egypt, as it
is said: "For He remembered His holy word
unto Abraham His servant," and, "And He
brought forth His people with joy" (Ps. 105.
42–43). R. Simon b. Yoḥai says: Because of
their observing the rite of circumcision did God

[10] So the word בכושרות is understood by the Midrash.
The Bible translations render it differently.

[11] R. Jonathan divides the words into two, viz., בכו
and שרות.

כשר לכם לא חמה קשה ולא גשמים וכן הוא אומר
אלהים מושיב יחידים ביתה מוציא אסירים
בכושרות שאין תלמוד לומר בכושרות אלא חדש
שהוא כשר לכם לא חמה קשה ולא גשמים רבי
160 יונתן אומר בכושרות אלו בוכים ואלו משוררים
מצריים בוכים שנאמר ומצרים מקברים וגו' וישראל
משוררים שנאמר קול רנה וישועה באהלי צדיקים
ימין יי רוממה שהמקום מתרומם על מצרים רבי
נתן אומר בכושרות במעשה הכשרות שלהם וכן
165 הוא אומר במראות הצובאות אשר צבאו וגו' רבי
אלעזר בן עזריה אומר בזכות אברהם אבינו הוציא
המקום את ישראל ממצרים שנאמר כי זכר את
דבר קדשו את אברהם עבדו ואומר ויוצא עמו
בששון וגו' רבי שמעון בן יוחי אומר בזכות המילה

157–158 תהלים ס"ח, ז'.   161 במדבר ל"ג, ד'.   162–163 תהלים
קי"ח, ט"ו, ט"ז.   163–165 סוטה י"א, ב'. שמו"ר א', י"ב.   165 שמות
ל"ח, ח'.   165–180 לקמן בשלח פ"ד.   167–168 תהלים ק"ה, מ"ב.
168–169 שם ק"ה, מ"ג.   169–171 לעיל פ"ה.   170–171 יחזקאל ט"ז, ו'.

156 לכם] ט. כ. (תהלים ס"ח, י"נ) ד. >.   158 שאין ת"ל בכושרות]
ד. ~ סה ת"ל בכושרות.   160 יונתן]=ט. כ. (שם) מ"ח.: מ. ד.
נתן / משוררים] ד. שוחקים.   161 מצריים] ד. שבמצרים.   163 ימין יי
רוממה] הוספת=כ. (שם): א. מ. ד. וגו'/ מתרומם] כ. (שם) סרומם
ידו.   164 בכושרות] כ. (שם) ~ בכשריות. מ"ח. ~ בכשרות..
164–165 וכן הוא אומר]=ט. כ. (שם) א"א. מ"ח: א. מ. ד. ר' אומר

bring the Israelites out of Egypt, as it is said:
"And when I passed by thee and saw thee wal-
lowing in thy blood, I said unto thee: In thy
blood live," etc. (Ezek. 16.6). Rabbi says:
Through the strength of God Israel went out of
Egypt, as it is said: "By strength of hand the
Lord brought us forth out of Egypt" (v. 16).

Another Interpretation: With an alertness of
their own Israel went out of Egypt, as it is said:
"And thus shall ye eat it; with your loins girded,"
etc. (Ex. 12.11). Rabbi says: "God maketh the
solitary to dwell in a house; He bringeth out the
prisoners into prosperity; but the rebellious dwell
in a parched land" (Ps. 68.7). They were rebellious but He dealt with them charitably. And
so it also says: "And I said unto them: Cast ye
away every man the detestable things of his eyes
. . . But they rebelled against Me and would
not hearken . . . But I wrought for My name's
sake, that it should not be profaned," etc. (Ezek.
20.7–9). "But the rebellious"—they were indeed
rebellious but He dealt with them charitably.

This Day Ye Go Forth, etc. There seems to be
no need of saying: "In the month Abib." What
then is the purport of saying: "In the month
Abib?" To declare that the year in which Israel
went out of Egypt did not have to be intercalated.

הוציא המקום את ישראל ממצרים שנאמר ואעבור 170
עליך ואראך מתבוססת בדמיך וגו' רבי אומר
בזריזות יצאו ישראל ממצרים שנאמר בחוזק יד
הוציאנו יי וגו' דבר אחר בזריזות עצמן יצאו ישראל
ממצרים שנאמר וככה תאכלו אותו מתניכם חגורים

וגו' רבי אומר אלהים מושיב יחידים ביתה מוציא 175
אסירים בכושרות אך סוררים שכנו צחיחה סוררים
היו אלא שנהג עמהם בהכשרות וכן הוא אומר
ואומר להם איש שקוצי עיניו וגו' וימרו בי ולא אבו
לשמוע וגו' ואעש למען שמי לבלתי החל וגו' אך
סוררים סוררים היו אלא שנהג עמהם בהכשרות. 180

היום אתם יוצאים וגו' שאין תלמוד לומר
בחדש האביב ומה תלמוד לומר בחדש האביב
מגיד שהשנה שיצאו בה ישראל ממצרים לא היתה
צריכה לעבר.

174—171 לעיל פ״ז. 173—172 שמות י״ג, י״ד. 174 שמות י״ב, י״א.
178—179 יחזקאל כ', ז'-ט'.

171 רבי אומר]־ד. ד׳א. 173 הוציאנו יי וגו']־ד. הוציא ד' אתכם
מארץ מצרים (שמות י״ג, נ׳) ובמקרא שם כתוב הוציא ד' אתכם מזה/
עצמן] ד. עצמו. 175 רבי אומר] ד. ד׳א כ. (שם) ואומר. 176 אך]
מ״ח. אף. 177—176 סוררים היו] כ. (שם) מ״ח. אף סוררים היו.
178 להם]=מ: במקרא כתוב אלהם. מ״ח. אליהם כ. (שם) עליהם. ט.
להן. א. ד. אליכם/ שקוצי] במקרא כתוב את שקוצי. 181 א״צ. דבר
אחר היום אתם יוצאים. 182 ומה ת׳ל בחודש האביב] מ. ד. > ט. אלא.

Chapter XVII
(Ex. 13.5–10)

And It Shall Be When the Lord Shall Cause Thee to Come into the Land of the Canaanite, etc. Scripture here speaks of the land of the five nations. Perhaps this is not so, but it refers to the land of the seven nations?[1] You must, however, reason as follows: Here the expression, "come into the land," is used and there (Deut. 26.1) the expression, "come in unto the land," is used. Just as there Scripture deals with the land of the five nations[2] which in another passage (Deut. 7.1) is referred to as the land of the seven,[3] so also here Scripture speaks of the land of the five nations, which in another passage is referred to as the land of seven. R. Jose the Galilean says: "Which He swore unto thy fathers to give thee." Why is this said? Because when it says: "Thou shalt take of the first of all the fruit of the ground," etc. (Deut. 26.2), one

---

[1] I. e., including Transjordania, the land which they took from Sihon and Og, and which Moses gave to the children of Gad, and to the children of Reuben, and unto the half-tribe of Manasseh (Num. 32.33).

[2] From Deut. 1.4 it is evident that the law of Deut. 26.1 can refer only to Palestine west of the Jordan.

[3] Before the Israelites entered Palestine, the land, exclusive of Transjordania, belonged to seven nations, as stated in Deut. 7.1. Two of these seven nations, however, according to rabbinic tradition, voluntarily abandoned the country when they heard that the Israelites were coming to it.

פרשה יז (שמות י"ג, ה',–י'.)

והיה כי יביאך יי אל ארץ הכנעני
וגו' בארץ חמשת העממים הכתוב מדבר אתה אומר
בארץ חמשת העממים הכתוב מדבר או אינו אלא
בארץ שבעת העממים הרי אתה דן נאמר כאן
5 ביאה ונאמר להלן ביאה מה להלן בארץ חמשת
העממים שהן שבעה במקום אחר הכתוב מדבר
אף כאן בארץ חמשת העממים שהן שבעה במקום
אחר הכתוב מדבר רבי יוסי הגלילי אומר אשר
נשבע לאבותיך לתת לך למה נאמר לפי שהוא
10 אומר ולקחת מראשית כל פרי האדמה וגו' שומע

1—19 ספרי דברים ש"א. מ"ת 171.   10 דברים כ"ו, ב'.

---

2 חמשת]— ט. ל'ט. ש"ט: ד. ר א'מ. שבעת/ העממים] ט. ~
שהן שבעה במקום אחר.   3 בארץ חמשת העמים הכתוב מדבר] ד. >
א. בארץ הכנעני. ר א'מ. מ"ע. כן.   4 שבעת העמטים] ד. ר א'מ.
חמשת עטמין.   5–6 בארץ חמשת העממים] ק. מ"ח. בארץ שבעת
עממין.   6 במקום אחר] ברכי יוסף. או'ח סי' תפ"ט מוחקו. נ. במקום אחר.
7 חמשת]מ"ח. שבעה/ במקום אחר] ד . וברכי יוסף שם >.

These two nations were the Girgashite (see Lev. Rab.
17.6) and the Canaanite (see below, ch. XVIII). Accordingly, when the Israelites entered the land, it actually
belonged only to five nations whom the Israelites had to
conquer.

might take it literally, as meaning all fruits.⁴
Now, however, you reason thus: Here the oath is
mentioned and there (Deut. 26.3) the oath is
mentioned. Just as the oath mentioned there has
reference to the land of the five nations, which in
another passage is referred to as the land of
seven, so also the oath mentioned here has reference to the land of the five nations, which in
another passage is referred to as the land of seven.
R. Josiah says: Here it is said: "A land flowing
with milk and honey," and there it is said: "A
land flowing with milk and honey" (Deut. 26.9).
Just as there it deals with the land of the five
nations, which in another passage is referred to as
the land of seven, so here also it deals with the
land of the five nations which in another passage
is referred to as the land of seven.

Which He Swore unto Thy Fathers. And where
did He swear? In the case of Abraham what does
it say? "In that day the Lord made a covenant
with Abram," etc. (Gen. 15.18). In the case of
Isaac what does it say? "Sojourn in this land,"
etc. (Gen. 26.3). In the case of Jacob what does
it say? "The land whereon thou liest," etc. (Gen.
28.13).

---

⁴ There is probably something missing in the text.
Possibly the equivalent of the following sentence: "But it
says: 'Unto the land which the Lord swore unto our
fathers to give us' (ibid., v. 3)" was omitted from the text
by a mistake of a copyist (see Introduction and cf.
Commentaries).

אני כל הפירות במשמע הרי אתה דן נאמר כאן
שבועה ונאמר להלן שבועה מה שבועה האמורה
להלן בארץ חמשת העממים שהן שבעה במקום
אחר אף כאן בארץ חמשת העממים שהן שבעה

15 במקום אחר רבי יאשיה אומר נאמר כאן ארץ
זבת חלב ודבש ונאמר להלן ארץ זבת חלב ודבש
מה להלן בארץ חמשת העממים שהן שבעה במקום
אחר אף כאן בארץ חמשת העממים שהן שבעה
במקום אחר.

20   **אשר נשבע לאבותיך** והיכן נשבע
באברהם מהו אומר ביום ההוא כרת יי את אברם
ברית וגו׳ ביצחק מה הוא אומר גור בארץ הזאת
וגו׳ ביעקב מהו אומר הארץ אשר אתה שוכב עליה
וגו׳.

19—15 ש 32,.   24—20 לקטן י״ח.   22—21 בראשית ט״ו, י״ח.
22 בראשית כ״ו, ג׳.   23 שם כ״ח ,י׳ג.

---

11 הפירות] מ״ח. הארצות. א״צ. הארץ.   12 שבועה] ק·
ז׳/ שבועה האמורה] ד. >.   15 אחר] ק. נ. ברכי יוסף שם אחד.
19—17 מ״ח. מה כאן ארץ שבעה עמסים אף להלן ארץ שבעה עמסים.
18—17 במקום אחר] ק. נ. במקום אחד.   19 אחר] ק. נ. אחד.
20 והיכן נשבע] ד. ~ לאבותיך.

Thou Shalt Keep this Service, etc. Exactly as you performed the service in Egypt, so shall you perform it in subsequent generations—these are the words of R. Jonathan.

Seven Days Thou Shalt Eat Unleavened Bread. I might understand this to mean unleavened bread of any kind; therefore it says: "Thou shalt eat no leavened bread with it" (Deut. 16.3). The law, then, applies only to such kinds as could be leavened as well as unleavened. And which are those? They are the five species, namely: wheat, barley, spelt, oats, and rye. Rice, millet, poppy-seed, sesame and legumes, which cannot be leavened as well as unleavened, but which decay, are thus excluded.

Seven Days Shalt Thou Eat Unleavened Bread. That is, the first day only is it obligatory to eat unleavened bread, but the remaining days it is optional. Perhaps, however, it rather means to make it optional for the first day and obligatory for the last day? But the scriptural passage: "In the first month, on the fourteenth of the month at even" (Ex. 12.18), fixes it as an obligation for the first day. Hence it is impossible for you to argue as in the latter version, but you must say as in the former.

ועבדת את העבודה הזאת וגו' כעבודה 25
שעבדת במצרים כך עשה לדורות דברי רבי יונתן.

שבעת ימים תאכל מצות שומע אני כל
מצה במשמע תלמוד לומר לא תאכל עליו חמץ
וגו' לא אמרתי אלא דברים שבאים לידי מצה וחמץ

ואיזה זה חמשת המינין ואילו הן החטים והשעורים 30
והכוסמים ושבולת שועל והשיפון יצאו האורז
והדוחן והפרגין והשומשמין והקטניות שאינן באין
לידי מצה וחמץ אלא לידי סרחון.

שבעת ימים תאכל מצות לעשות הראשון
חובה ושאר הימים רשות או אינו אלא לעשות 35
הראשון רשות והאחרון חובה תלמוד לומר בראשון
בארבעה עשר יום לחדש בערב קבעו הכתוב
חובה הא אין עליך לומר בלשון אחרון אלא בלשון
ראשון.

25—26 לעיל פ"ד.   26—27 לעיל פ"ח וש"נ.   28 דברים ט"ז, ג'.
36—37 שמות י"ב, י"ח.

---

26 יונתן] ד. נתן.   27 תאכל] ד. תאכלו.   29 דברים שבאים] א.
מ"ח. דבר שהוא בא.   34 תאכל] ק. נ. תאכלו/ לעשות] מ"ח.
לילה   36 והאחרון חובה]מ"ח.>.   37 לחדש]ק. נ.>.

Seven Days Shalt Thou Eat Unleavened Bread.
One scriptural passage says: "Seven days shalt
thou eat unleavened bread," and one passage
says: "Six days shalt thou eat unleavened bread,"
(Deut. 16.8). How can both these passages be
maintained? The seventh day had been included
in the more inclusive statement and was then
taken out of it. Now that which is singled out
from a more inclusive statement means to teach
us something about that whole statement. Hence
just as on the seventh day it is optional, so on all
the other days it is optional. Perhaps, however,
just as on the seventh day it is optional, so on
all the rest, including even the first night, it is
optional? The scriptural passage: "In the first
month, on the fourteenth day of the month, at
even ye shall eat unleavened bread," fixes it as an
obligation to eat unleavened bread on the first
night. It is therefore impossible for you to argue
as in the latter version, but you must argue as
in the former version: The seventh day had been
included in the more inclusive statement and
was taken out of it. Now, that which is singled
out from a more inclusive statement means to
teach us something about the whole statement,
that is, just as on the seventh day it is optional,
so on all the other days it is optional.

Another Interpretation: One scriptural passage
says six, and one says seven. How can both
these passages be maintained? Six days if it is
from the new crop, and seven days if it is from
the old crop.

40   שבעת ימים תאכל מצות כתוב אחד

אומר שבעת ימים תאכל מצות וכתוב אחד אומר

ששת ימים תאכל מצות כיצד יתקיימו שני כתובים

הללו השביעי היה בכלל יצא מוצא מן הכלל

ללמד על הכלל מה שביעי רשות אף כולן רשות

45 או מה שביעי רשות אף לילה הראשון רשות תלמוד

לומר בראשון בארבעה עשר יום וגו' בערב תאכלו

מצות קבעו הכתוב חובה הא אין עליך לומר בלשון

אחרון אלא בלשון ראשון השביעי היה בכלל יצא

מוצא מן הכלל ללמד על הכלל מה שביעי רשות

50 אף כולם רשות דבר אחר כתוב אחד אומר ששת

ימים וכתוב אחד אומר שבעת ימים כיצד יתקיימו

שני מקראות הללו ששה מן החדש ושבעה מן הישן.

40—52 לעיל פ"ח.   42 דברים ט"ז, ח'.   46 שמות י"ב, י"ח.

---

43 השביעי] ד. ~ הזה / מוצא] ד. >.   47—46 בראשון–מצות] ד.
בארבעה עשר.   50—48 השביעי היה בכלל–אף כולם רשות] ד. לילה
הראשון חובה ושאר כל הימים רשות השביעי הזה מן הכלל יצא וכו'.
50 דבר אחר]=מ"ח. א"צ: מ. ק. נ. >.

And in the Seventh Day Shall Be a Feast to the Lord. Why is this said? Since it says: "And ye shall keep it a feast to the Lord" (Ex. 12.14), I know only that the first day of the festival requires a festal offering. How about the last day of the festival? Scripture says here: "And in the seventh day shall be a feast to the Lord." Now I know that both the first day of the festival and the last one require a festal offering. How about the intervening days of the festival? Behold, you reason thus: Since the first day and the last day of the festival are called "holy convocation," and the intervening days of the festival are likewise called "holy convocation," it is but logical, inasmuch as you have proved that the first and last day of the festival, which are called "holy convocation," require a festal offering, to assume that the intervening days, which are also called "holy convocation," should likewise require a festal offering. Furthermore, it can be argued by using the method of *Kal vaḥomer*: If the first and last days of the festival, neither one of which is both preceded and followed by holy days, require a festal offering, is it not but logical to assume that the intervening days, being both preceded and followed by holy days, should all the more require a festal offering? Another way: If the first and

ו ב י ו ם ה ש ב י ע י חג ליי למה נאמר לפי

שהוא אומר וחגותם אותו חג ליי אין לי אלא יום

טוב הראשון שהוא טעון חגיגה יום טוב האחרון

מנין תלמוד לומר וביום השביעי חג ליי אין לי אלא

יום טוב ראשון ואחרון שהן טעונין חגיגה חולו של

מועד מנין הרי אתה דן הואיל ויום טוב הראשון

והאחרון קרואין מקרא קדש וחולו של מועד קרוי

מקרא קדש אם למדת על יום טוב הראשון והאחרון

שהם קרויים מקרא קדש שהם טעונים חגיגה אף

חולו של מועד שהוא קרוי מקרא קדש דין הוא

שיטעון חגיגה ועוד קל וחמר ומה אם יום טוב

הראשון והאחרון שאין לפניהם ולאחריהם מקודשין

הרי הן טעונין חגיגה חולו של מועד שלפניו ולאחריו

מקודשין דין הוא שיטעון חגיגה דבר אחר אם יום

53—72 לעיל פ"ז.

---

54 לי] ק. נ. לך.   55 טעון] ק. נ. טעין.   56 וביום השביעי
חג ליי] מ. ד. שבעת ימים תאכל מצות (ל. ~ וגו').   57 יום טוב
ראשון ואחרון] א. יו'ט האחרון.   64 שאין לפניהם ולאחריהם מקודשין]
מ. ד. שאין קדוש לא לפניהם ולא לאחריהם.   66—65 שלפניו ואחריו
מקודשין] מ. ד. שיש קדושה לפניו ולאחריו.

last days, neither one of which is both preceded
and followed by days requiring a festal offering,
require a festal offering, is it not but logical to
assume that the intervening days, which are both
preceded and followed by days requiring a festal
offering, should themselves require a festal offering? Perhaps it means to say that the obligation
to eat unleavened bread obtains only as long as
the institution of the festal offering exists, but
when there is no festal offering[5] no unleavened
bread need be eaten? Against this Scripture says:
"Unleavened bread shall be eaten throughout
the seven days."

*Unleavened Bread Shall Be Eaten Throughout
the Seven Days; and There Shall No Leavened
Bread Be Seen with Thee.* Why is this said?
Because we have not yet learned that unleavened
bread is forbidden on the fourteenth day after
the sixth hour of the day. And, indeed, how do
we know that it is forbidden after the sixth hour
of the day? Scripture says: "Unleavened bread
shall be eaten throughout the seven days; and
there shall no leavened bread be seen with thee,
neither shall there be leaven seen with thee." In
this connection R. Judah the son of Bathyra used
to say: One should search for the leavened bread
at three periods; on the night before the fourteenth, on the fourteenth in the morning, and at
the hour when it is actually to be burned.

---

[5] I. e., after the destruction of the Temple, when sacrifices could not be offered.

טוב הראשון והאחרון שאין לפניהם ולאחריהם
טעונין חגיגה הרי הן טעונין חגיגה חולו של מועד
שלפניהם ולאחריהם טעון חגיגה דין הוא שיטעון
חגיגה או כל זמן שיש חגיגה יש מצה ואם אין חגיגה
אין מצה תלמוד לומר מצות יאכל את שבעת
הימים.

מצות יאכל את שבעת הימים ולא
יראה לך חמץ למה נאמר לפי שלא למדנו
על החמץ שאסור משש שעות ולמעלן ומנין שהוא
אסור משש שעות ולמעלן תלמוד לומר מצות יאכל
את שבעת הימים ולא יראה לך חמץ ולא יראה לך
שאור מכאן היה רבי יהודה בן בתירה אומר
בשלשה פרקים בודקין את החמץ אור ארבעה
עשר ובארבעה עשר שחרית ובשעת הביעור.

77—70 ש. 33.　　80—75 פסחים י', ב'. י' שם א', נ' (27c).

68—67 שאין לפניהם ולאחריהם טעונין חגיגה] ק. נ. שאין קדושה
לפניו ולאחריו ואין טעונין חגיגה לפניהם ולאחריהם.　　69—68 חולו של
מועד—דין הוא] ד. חולו של מועד שהוא טעון חגיגה לפניו ולאחריו
לא דין הוא.　　70 ואם אין] מ"ח. א. אם אין. ד. כל זמן שאין.
73 מצות יאכל את שבעת הימים] מ. מ"ח. >.　　74—73 ולא יראה
לך חמץ] הוספתי: ל. וגו'. מ"ח. לא יראה לך חמץ.　　76—75 מצות
יאכל-הימים] מ"ח. > ל. ~ וגו'.　　77—78 ולא יראה לך חמץ ולא
יראה לך שאור] הנהתי—מ"ח. וש"י.　　78 בן בתירה] ד. >.

And There Shall No Leavened Bread Be Seen with Thee, etc. This compares leaven to leavened bread and leavened bread to leaven. Just as the one, leaven, is under the prohibition of being seen, so also is the other, leavened bread, under the prohibition of being seen; just as the one is under the prohibition of being found, so also is the other under the prohibition of being found. And just as the one, leavened bread, is forbidden only when it is made of one of the five species, so also is the other, leaven, forbidden only when it comes from one of the five species.

In All Thy Borders. Why is this said? Because when it is said: "Seven days shall there be no leaven found in your houses" (Ex. 12.19), I might understand it to mean even if it is not under your full control. Scripture therefore says here: "In all thy borders": Just as what is in your borders is under your full control, so also what is in your house must be under your full control. Hence there is excluded from this prohibition leavened bread actually owned by a Jew but subject to the control of a non-Jew; for even though the Jew could destroy it, he may not do so, not having complete control over it. There is also excluded leavened bread actually owned by a non-Jew, but under the control of a Jew, as well as leavened bread buried under debris; for although it is under the control or within the territory of the Jew, he has not the right, in the one case, nor the physical possibility, in the other case, actually to destroy it. You say it comes for this purpose. Perhaps it only comes to teach

ו ל א י ר א ה ל ך ח מ ץ וגו' הקיש שאור לחמץ

וחמץ לשאור מה זה בל יראה אף זה בל יראה מה

זה בל ימצא אף זה בל ימצא מה זה מחמשת המינין

אף זה מחמשת המינין.

ב כ ל ג ב ו ל ך למה נאמר לפי שנאמר שאור 85

לא ימצא בבתיכם שומע אני אף שאין ברשותך

תלמוד לומר בכל גבולך מה גבולך ברשותך אף

ביתך ברשותך יצא חמצו של ישראל שהוא ברשות

נכרי אף על פי שהוא יכול לבערו אבל אינו

ברשותו יצא חמצו של נכרי שהוא ברשות ישראל 90

וחמץ שנפלה עליו מפולת אף על פי שהוא ברשותו

אבל אינו יכול לבערו אתה אומר לכך בא או לא

86–85 למה נאמר לפי שנאמר–בבתיכם] ד. למה נאמר בבתים.
ש"י. מ"ע. >/ שאור לא ימצא] הוספתי עפ"י מ"ח. ש"ט. 86 אף
שאין ברשותך] א. ד. מ"ח. ש"י. כשטועו. 87 בכל גבולך]
מ"ח. ~ אם כן למה נאמר בבתיכם. ש"י. שאור לא ימצא בבתיכם.
מ"ע. בבתיכם. 88–87 מה גבולך–ביתך ברשותך] מ"ח. ש"י.
מ"ע. מה בתיכם ברשותכם (מ"ח. ביתך ברשותו) אף גבולך
ברשותך. 89 אף על פי–אבל] א. >/ אינו] א. שאינו.

that in the territories the prohibition holds for seven days, while in the house it holds for all time? But the scriptural passage: "And there shall be no leaven seen with thee in all thy borders seven days" (Deut. 16.4), declares that just as in the territories the prohibition holds only for seven days, so also in the houses it holds only for seven days.

And Thou Shalt Tell Thy Son. I might understand this to mean from the first day of the month on, but Scripture says: "In that day." If "in that day," I might understand it to mean in the daytime; but Scripture says: "It is because of that," etc., indicating that it should be at the time when unleavened bread and bitter herbs are placed upon your table before you.

Because of That Which the Lord Did for Me. Why is this said? Because it says: "What mean ye by this service?" (Ex. 12.26), which is but the question of the wicked son who excludes himself from the group. And because he excludes himself from the group, do thou also exclude him from the group. Say to him: "Because of that which the Lord did for me"—for me but not for you. Had you been there you would not have been redeemed.

בא אלא ללמד בגבולין שבעה ובבתים לעולם
תלמוד לומר לא יראה לך שאר בכל גבולך שבעת
ימים מה בגבולין שבעה אף בבתים שבעה. 95

והגדת לבנך שומע אני מראש חדש תלמוד
לומר ביום ההוא אי ביום ההוא שומע אני מבעוד
יום תלמוד לומר בעבור זה בשעה שמצה ומרור
מונחים לפניך על שולחנך.

בעבור זה עשה יי לי למה נאמר לפי 100
שהוא אומר מה העבודה הזאת לכם אלא זה בן
רשע שהוציא את עצמו מן הכלל ולפי שהוציא את
עצמו מן הכלל אף אתה הוציאו מן הכלל אמור
לו בעבור זה עשה יי לי ולא לך אלו היית שם
לא היית נגאל. 105

—————————

95–94 דברים ט״ז, ד׳.   97 שטות י״ב, י״ד.   105–100 לקמן פ׳ י״ח.
101 שטות י״ב, כ״ו.

—————————

93 בגבולין שבעה ובבתים לעולם] ש״י. מ״ע. בבתים שבעה
ובגבולין לעולם. מ״ח. בבתים ובגבולין לעולם.   94 לא] במסקרא כתוב
ולא.   95–94 בכל נבולך שבעת יטים] מ. ד. ונו׳.   95 בגבולין שבעה אף
בבתים שבעה] מ״ח. ש״י. מ״ע. בבתים שבעה אף בגבולין שבעה.
96 שומע אני] ד. יכול.   102 רשע] ד. ~ הוא/ מן הכלל] א. ~ וכפר
בעיקר.   103–102 ולפי שהוציא–הוציאו מן הכלל] א. >.   104–103 אמור
לו]—ט: מ. ד. >.   104 לך] א. לו ד. ~ ולפי שהוצאת את עצך
מן הכלל.

And It Shall Be for a Sign unto Thee upon Thy Hand. One roll containing all four scriptural sections.[6] For the following argument might have been advanced: The Torah says: Put phylacteries upon the head, put phylacteries upon the hand. Just as the one put on the head contains the four sections on four separate rolls of parchment, so the one put on the hand should also contain four separate rolls of parchment. But Scripture says: "And it shall be for a sign unto thee upon thy hand"—one roll containing all the four scriptural sections. Now, one might think, that just as the one on the hand contains only one roll, so also the one on the head should contain only one roll. And the following argument might be advanced: The Torah says: Put phylacteries upon the hand, put phylacteries upon the head. Just as the one on the hand contains only one roll so the one on the head should contain only one roll. But Scripture says "frontlet" (here), "frontlet" (Deut. 6.8), "frontlets"[7] (Deut. 11.18), thus four separate rolls are mentioned. Perhaps, then, one should make four separate containers for the scriptural sections? Against this Scripture says: "And for a memorial between thine eyes" (v. 9), meaning one container for all the four sections.

---

[6] The phylacteries contain four sections from the Pentateuch: Ex. 13.1–10; Ex. 13.11–16; Deut. 6.4–9; and Deut. 11.13–20. The phylactery put on the hand contains only one roll of parchment on which all these four sections are written. The phylactery put on the head contains four separate rolls of parchment, on each one of which one of the four sections is written.

והיה לך לאות על ידך כרך אחד של
ארבע פרשיות והדין נותן הואיל ואמרה תורה תן
תפילין בראש תן תפילין ביד מה בראש ארבע
טוטפות אף ביד ארבע טוטפות תלמוד לומר והיה

110 לך לאות על ידך כרך אחד של ארבע פרשיות יכול
כשם שביד כרך אחד כך בראש כרך אחד והדין
נותן הואיל ואמרה תורה תן תפילין ביד תן תפילין
בראש מה ביד כרך אחד אף בראש כרך אחד
תלמוד לומר לטוטפת לטוטפת לטוטפות הרי

115 ארבע טוטפות אמורות או יעשה ארבעה כיסין
של ארבע פרשיות תלמוד לומר ולזכרון בין עיניך
כיס אחד של ארבע פרשיות.

106—117 ספרי דברים ל״ה. מנחות ל״ד, ב׳. ש. 4.:   114 לטוטפת
לטוטפת לטוטפות] כאן ודברים ו׳, ח׳; י״א, י״ח.

---

110 כרך אחד של ארבע פרשיות] ק. ידך אחד של ארבע
טוטפות/ יכול] א. מ. ק.>.   114 לטוטפת לטוטפת לטוטפות]—מ"ח:
מ. לטוטפות לטוטפות לטוטפות. ד. לטוטפות לטוטפות.

---

7 Here and in Deut. 6.8, the word טוטפת is read in the
singular form. Each passage thus mentions one frontlet.
In Deut. 11.18 the same word is read in the plural, as
vocalized. This passage thus mentions at least two frontlets. In all three passages then four frontlets are mentioned
which refer to four separate rolls.

Upon Thy Hand. This means on the upper arm. You interpret it to mean on the upper arm. Perhaps it means, literally, on your hand? The following reasoning disproves it. The Torah says: Put phylacteries upon the head, put phylacteries upon the hand. Just as the one on the head is put on the upper part of the head, so the one on the hand should be put on the upper part of the arm. R. Eliezer says: "Upon thy hand," this means on the upper arm. You interpret it to mean on the upper arm. Perhaps it means literally, on your hand? But Scripture says: "And it shall be for a sign unto thee"—it is to be a sign unto you and not a sign unto others. R. Isaac says: It means on the upper arm. Perhaps this is not so, but it means literally, upon thy hand? Against this Scripture says: "Therefore shall ye lay these My words in your heart" (Deut. 11.18). I can interpret this only as pointing to something that is directly opposite the heart. And what is it that is directly opposite the heart? It is the upper arm.

Upon Thy Hand. This means the left. You interpret it to mean the left, but perhaps this is not so, but it means the right? Although there is no direct proof for it, there is at least a suggestion of it in the passage: "Yea, My hand hath laid the foundation of the earth, and My right hand hath spread out the heavens" (Isa. 48.13). And it also says: "Her hand she put to the tent-pin, and her right hand," etc. Judg. 5.26). Hence "hand" everywhere means the left.

עַל יָדְךָ עַל גּוֹבַהּ שֶׁל יַד אַתָּה אוֹמֵר עַל גּוֹבַהּ
שֶׁל יַד אוֹ עַל יָדְךָ כְּשֶׁמּוּעוֹ וְהַדִּין נוֹתֵן הוֹאִיל וְאָמְרָה
120 תוֹרָה תֶּן תְּפִילִּין בָּרֹאשׁ תֶּן תְּפִילִּין בַּיָּד מַה בָּרֹאשׁ
עַל גּוֹבַהּ שֶׁל רֹאשׁ אַף בַּיָּד עַל גּוֹבַהּ שֶׁל יַד רַבִּי
אֱלִיעֶזֶר אוֹמֵר עַל יָדְךָ עַל גּוֹבַהּ שֶׁל יַד אַתָּה אוֹמֵר
עַל גּוֹבַהּ שֶׁל יַד אוֹ עַל יָדְךָ כְּשֶׁמּוּעוֹ תַּלְמוּד לוֹמַר
וְהָיָה לְךָ לְאוֹת לְךָ הִיא לְאוֹת וְאֵינָהּ אוֹת לַאֲחֵרִים
125 רַבִּי יִצְחָק אוֹמֵר עַל גּוֹבַהּ שֶׁל יַד אוֹ אֵינוּ אֶלָּא עַל
יָדְךָ כְּשֶׁמּוּעוֹ תַּלְמוּד לוֹמַר וְשַׂמְתֶּם אֶת דְּבָרַי אֵלֶּה
עַל לְבַבְכֶם לֹא אָמַרְתִּי אֶלָּא דָּבָר שֶׁהוּא מְכֻוָּן כְּנֶגֶד
הַלֵּב וְאֵיזֶהוּ דָּבָר שֶׁהוּא מְכֻוָּן כְּנֶגֶד הַלֵּב זוֹ גּוֹבַהּ
שֶׁל יַד.

עַל יָדְךָ זֶה שְׂמֹאל אַתָּה אוֹמֵר זֶה שְׂמֹאל אוֹ אֵינוּ
130 אֶלָּא יָמִין אַף עַל פִּי שֶׁאֵין רְאָיָה לַדָּבָר זֵכֶר לַדָּבָר
אַף יָדִי יָסְדָה אֶרֶץ וִימִינִי טִפְּחָה שָׁמַיִם וְגוֹ' וְאוֹמֵר
יָדָהּ לַיָּתֵד תִּשְׁלַחְנָה וִימִינָהּ וְגוֹ' הָא אֵין יַד בְּכָל מָקוֹם

118–129 ספרי שם. מנחות ל״ז, ב'. ש. 33.   127–126 דברים י״א, י״ח.
139–130 ספרי שם. מנחות ל״ז, ב'; ל״ז, א'.   132 ישעיה ס״ח, י״ג.
133 שופטים ה', כ״ו.

118 ידך] ק. נ. ידכה.   119 או על ידך] ד. או אינו אלא על יד.
128 ואיזהו דבר שהוא מכוון] ד. ואיזהו מכוון.

R. Nathan says: "And thou shalt bind them,"
"and thou shalt write them" (Deut. 6.8–9). Just
as writing is done with the right hand, so also the
binding must be done with the right hand.[8] Abba
Jose says: We do find that the right hand is also
called simply "hand." Although there is no
direct proof for it, there is at least a suggestion
of it in the passage: "And Israel stretched out
his right hand and laid it," etc . . . "And he
held up his father's hand," etc. (Gen. 48.14–17).
What then is the purpose of Scripture's saying:
"upon thy hand," to include a lefthanded man,
who should put the phylactery on the right hand.

*And It Shall Be for a Sign unto Thee upon Thy
Hand*, etc. When the phylactery of the hand is
on the hand, put the one of the head upon the
head. On the basis of this interpretation the
sages said: The law in regard to the phylacteries
is: In putting them on, one puts on that of the
hand first and then puts on that of the head.
And when taking them off one must first take
off that of the head and then that of the hand.

Between Thine Eyes. This means upon the
upper part of the head. You interpret it to mean
upon the upper part of the head. Perhaps this is
not so, but "between thine eyes," is to be taken
literally. But Scripture teaches otherwise by
saying: "Ye are the children of the Lord your
God: Ye shall not cut yourselves nor make any

---

[8] Hence, it must be put on the left hand.

אלא שמאל רבי נתן אומר וקשרתם וכתבתם מה

135 כתיבה בימין אף קשירה בימין אבא יוסי אומר
מצינו שהימין קרואה יד אף על פי שאין ראיה
לדבר זכר לדבר וישלח ישראל את ימינו וישת
וגו' ויתמוך יד אביו וגו' ומה תלמוד לומר על ידך
להביא את הגידם שיהיה נותן בימין.

140 והיה לך לאות על ידך וגו' כל זמן
שתפילין של יד ביד תן את של ראש בראש מכאן
אמרו מצות תפילין כשהוא נותן נותן את של יד
ואחר כך נותן את של ראש וכשהוא חולץ חולץ
את של ראש ואחר כך חולץ את של יד.

145 בין עיניך על גובה של ראש אתה אומר על
גובה של ראש או אינו אלא בין עיניך כשמועו
תלמוד לומר בנים אתם ליי אלהיכם לא תתגודדו

---

134 וקשרתם וכתבתם] דברים י"א, י"ח–כ'.   137 בראשית מ"ח, י"ד.
138 שם מ"ח, י"נ.   153–140 ספרי שם. מנחות ל"ו, א'.   150–145 מ"ח 72.
ש. 34.   148–147 דברים י"ד, א'.

---

134 נתן] ד. יונתן.   135–134 מה כתיבה בימין אף קשירה
בימין] ק. נ. מה קשירה בימין אף כתיבה בימין.   135 אבא יוסי]
מ. אבא יוסף החרם.   137 וישלח ישראל את ימינו וישת וגו'] ק. נ.
וישלח ישראל את יד ימינו. ל. וירא יוסף כי ישית אביו יד ימינו.
138 ויתמוך יד אביו וגו'] הוספתי–א"א.   141 שתפילין] הוספתי–
ט. א"א./ תן את] מ. >/ של ראש] מ. ושל ראש.

baldness between your eyes" (Deut. 14.1)—
Just as the expression, "between your eyes,"
used there, means upon the upper part of the
head, so the expression "between thine eyes"
used here, means upon the upper part of the
head. R. Judah says: The Torah says: Put
phylacteries upon the hand, put phylacteries
upon the head. Hence, just as the spot on the
hand is one that is subject to uncleanness by one
of the symptoms of leprosy, so the spot on the
head must be one subject to uncleanness by one
of the symptoms of leprosy.

*That the Law of the Lord May Be in Thy
Mouth.* Why is this said? Because it says: "And
it shall be for a sign unto thee," which I might
understand to include women. And the following
argument could be advanced for it: The law
about the *Mezuzah* is a positive commandment
and the law about the phylacteries is a positive
commandment. Now, having learned that the
law about the *Mezuzah* applies to women as well
as to men, one might think that the law about
the phylacteries should likewise apply to women
as well as to men. But Scripture says: "That the
law of the Lord may be in thy mouth." I must
therefore interpret this law as applying only to
those who are under the obligation of studying
the Torah. On the basis of this interpretation
the sages said: All are subject to the law of
phylacteries except women and slaves. Michal

ולא תשימו קרחה בין עיניכם מה בין עיניכם האמור
להלן על גובה של ראש אף בין עיניך האמור כאן
על גובה של ראש רבי יהודה אומר הואיל ואמרה 150
תורה תן תפלין ביד תן תפילין בראש מה ביד
מקום שהוא ראוי להטמא בנגע אחד אף בראש
מקום שהוא ראוי להטמא בנגע אחד.

ל מ ע ן ת ה י ה ת ו ר ת יי ב פ י ך למה נאמר
לפי שהוא אומר והיה לך לאות שומע אני אף הנשים 155
במשמע והדין נותן הואיל ומזוזה מצות עשה ותפילין
מצות עשה אם למדת על המזוזה שהיא נוהגת בנשים
כבאנשים יכול אף תפילין ינהגו בנשים כבאנשים
תלמוד לומר למען תהיה תורת יי בפיך לא אמרתי
אלא במי שהוא חייב בתלמוד תורה מכאן אמרו 160
הכל חייבין בתפילין חוץ מנשים ועבדים מיכל

193—155 ש. 34.   159—158 קידושין ל״ד, א׳. ברכות כ׳, ב׳. י׳ שם
נ׳, נ׳ (6b).   164—158 י׳ ברכות שם וב׳, ג׳ (4c). עירובין צ״ו, א׳. י׳ שם
י׳, א׳ (26a). י׳ סוכה ב׳, א׳ (52d).

148 ולא תשימו קרחה בין עיניכם] הוספתי: א. מ. ונו׳ / בין עיניכם2]
א. עיניכם ק. נ. בעיניכם.   152 אחד]=א׳א׳. ל: א. ק. נ. >.
161 בתפילין] הנהתי=א״צ. מ״ח. ספר העיטור חלק שני כ״ו, ע״ג: א.
מ. ד. בתלמוד תורה.

the daughter of Kushi used to put on phylac-
teries. The wife of Jonah used to go up to
Jerusalem for the festivals. Tobi the slave of
R. Gamaliel used to put on phylacteries.

*And for a Memorial between Thine Eyes, that
the Law of the Lord May Be in Thy Mouth.* On the
basis of this passage the sages said: Whoever
puts on phylacteries is like one who studies the
Torah, and one who studies the Torah is not
obligated to put on phylacteries.

*Thou Shalt Therefore Keep this Ordinance in Its
Season.* Why is this said? Because it says: "And
it shall be for a sign unto thee upon thy hand,"
which I might understand to include minors.
And the following argument could be advanced
for it: The law about the *Mezuzah* is a positive
commandment and the law about the phylacteries is a positive commandment. Now, having
learned that the law about the *Mezuzah* applies
to minors as well as to adults, one might think
that the law about the phylacteries should likewise apply to minors as well as to adults. But
Scripture says: "Thou shalt therefore keep this
ordinance." I must therefore interpret this law
as applying only to one who knows how to take
care of the phylacteries. Hence, the sages said:
Any minor who knows how to take care of the
phylacteries, may have phylacteries made for
himself.

בת כושי היתה מנחת תפילין אשתו של יונה היתה
עולה לרגלים טבי עבדו של רבן גמליאל היה מניח
תפילין.

165 ולזכרון בין עיניך למען תהיה
תורת יי בפיך מכאן אמרו כל המניח תפילין
כאלו קורא בתורה וכל הקורא בתורה פטור מן
התפילין.

ושמרת את החקה הזאת למועדה
170 למה נאמר לפי שהוא אומר והיה לך לאות על ידך
שומע אני אף הקטנים במשמע והדין נותן הואיל
ומזוזה מצות עשה ותפילין מצות עשה אם למדת
על המזוזה שהיא נוהגת בקטנים ובגדולים יכול אף
התפילין ינהגו בקטנים ובגדולים תלמוד לומר
175 ושמרת את החקה הזאת לא אמרתי אלא במי שהוא
יודע לשמור תפילין מכאן אמרו כל קטן שהוא
יודע לשמור תפילין הרי זה עושה לו תפילין.

168—165 מדרש תהלים א', י"ז. 173—175 י' ברכות ג', ג'. (5b),
177—176 ערכין ב', ב'.

177 הרי זה] ק.נ. הרי הוא. ל. ט. מ"ח. העיטור שם, אביו.

Thou Shalt Therefore Keep this Ordinance. This means the law about the phylacteries. You interpret it as meaning the law about the phylacteries. Perhaps this is not so, but it means the law about all the observances?[9] You must, however, reason: What subject is here dealt with? The phylacteries.

From Year to Year. Why is this said? Because it says: "And it shall be for a sign unto thee," which I might understand to mean, even during the night time. And the following argument could be advanced for it: The law about the *Mezuzah* is a positive commandment and the law about the phylacteries is a positive commandment. Now, having learned that the law of the *Mezuzah* holds during the night time as well as during the day, one might think that the law of the phylacteries should likewise hold during the night as well as during the day. Scripture therefore, says: "From days to days,"[10] indicating thereby that you should put them on during the day and not during the night.

Another Interpretation. *From Year to Year.* Why is this said? Because it says: "And it shall be for a sign unto thee," which I might understand to mean, even on Sabbaths and holidays. And the following argument could be advanced for it: The law of the *Mezuzah* is a positive commandment and the law of the phylacteries is a positive commandment. Now, having learned that the law of the *Mezuzah* holds even on

---

[9] I. e., the observances of the Passover mentioned in this section.

ו ש מ ר ת א ת ה ח ו ק ה ה ז א ת זו חוקת תפילין

אתה אומר זו חוקת תפילין או אינו אלא חוקת כל

180 המצות אמרת במי העגין מדבר בתפילין.

מ י מ י ם י מ י מ ה למה נאמר לפי שהוא אומר

והיה לך לאות שומע אני אף הלילות במשמע והדין

נותן הואיל ומזוזה מצות עשה ותפילין מצות עשה

אם למדת על המזוזה שהיא נוהגת בלילות כבימים

185 יכול אף תפילין ינהגו בלילות כבימים תלמוד

לומר מימים ימימה בימים אתה נותן ואין את נותן

בלילות דבר אחר מימים ימימה למה נאמר לפי

שהוא אומר והיה לך לאות שומע אני אף שבתות

וימים טובים במשמע והדין נותן הואיל ומזוזה מצות

190 עשה ותפילין מצות עשה אם למדת על מזוזה שהיא

180—178 ברכות מ״ד, ב׳. י׳ שם ב׳, נ׳ (4c).   209—181 מנחות ל״ו,

ב׳. עירובין צ״ו, א׳. י׳ שם י׳, א׳ (26a). ש. 34.

---

[10] This interpretation takes the expression ימים, in the phrase מימים ימימה, rendered in the Bible translation by "from year to year," literally as the plural of יום, hence it simply means "days" and is not a designation for "year."

Sabbaths and holidays, one might think that the law about the phylacteries should likewise hold even on Sabbaths and holidays. But Scripture says: "From days to days."[10] Sabbaths and holidays are thus excluded. R. Josiah says: *From Year to Year.* Why is this said? Because it says: "And it shall be for a sign unto thee," which I might understand to mean, even on Sabbaths and holidays. And the following argument could be advanced for it: The law of the *Mezuzah* is a positive commandment and the law of the phylacteries is a positive commandment. Now, having learned that the law of the *Mezuzah* holds even on Sabbaths and holidays, one might think that the law about the phylacteries should likewise hold even on Sabbaths and holidays. But Scripture says: "From days to days," indicating thereby that there are days in which you must put them on and days in which you should not put them on. Sabbaths and holidays are thus excluded. R. Isaac says: Since the Sabbath is called a sign and the phylacteries are called a sign, one should not add one sign to another. But perhaps one rather should add one sign to another? You must say: The Sabbath which is called both a sign and a covenant should set aside the phylacteries which are called a sign only. R. Eliezer says: Since the Sabbath is called a sign and the phylacteries are called a sign,

נוהגת בשבתות ובימים טובים יכול אף תפילין
ינהגו בשבתות ובימים טובים תלמוד לומר מימים
ימימה יצאו שבתות וימים טובים רבי יאשיה אומר
מימים ימימה למה נאמר לפי שהוא אומר והיה לך
לאות שומע אני אף שבתות וימים טובים במשמע   195
והדין נותן הואיל ומזוזה מצות עשה ותפילין מצות
עשה אם למדת על המזוזה שהיא נוהגת בשבתות
ובימים טובים יכול אף תפילין כן תלמוד לומר
מימים ימימה יש ימים שאתה נותן ויש ימים שאין
אתה נותן יצאו שבתות וימים טובים רבי יצחק אומר   200
הואיל ושבת קרואה אות ותפילין קרואות אות לא
יתן אות בתוך אות או יתן אות בתוך אות אמרת
תדחה שבת שהיא קרואה אות וברית לתפילין
שאינן קרואות אלא אות בלבד רבי אליעזר אומר
הואיל ושבת קרואה אות ותפילין קרואות אות לא   205

193—199 יצאו שבתות—ח״ל מימים ימימה] א׳ ﬧ. מוחק.   193 רבי
יאשיה אומר] מ״ח. ז״י. דברי ר׳ יאשיה.   194—199 מימים ימימה
למה נאמר—ח״ל מימים ימימה] ﬑. מימים ל.   > ובמ״ח. חסר כל
המאמר עד ר׳ יצחק אומר וכו׳ (200) ומוחקו נ״כ בז״י.   199 מימים
ימימה] א. מ. ק. נ. ~ (א. יצאו שבתות וימים טובים) דבר אחר
מימים ימימה וא﬑א. מוחקו.   202—206 אמרת תדחה שבת—או יתן
אות בתוך אות=﬑. מ״ח: ד. >.   204 אליעזר]=מ״ח: ﬑. אליה.
מ״ע. עזריה.

one should not add one sign to another. But perhaps one rather should add one sign to another? You must, however, reason: The Sabbath, for the violation of whose laws one may incur the penalty of extermination or even of death by order of the court, should set aside the phylacteries for the disregard of whose laws one incurs neither the penalty of extermination nor of death by order of the court.

Another Interpretation: *From Year to Year.* This tells that one should examine the phylacteries once in twelve months. Here it says: "From year to year," and there it says: "For a full year shall he have the right of redemption" (Lev. 25.29). Just as "year" there means fully twelve months, so "year" here also means fully twelve months—these are the words of the School of Hillel. The School of Shammai say: One need never examine them. Shammai the Elder said: These are the phylacteries of my mother's father.

CHAPTER XVIII
(Ex. 13.11–16)

And It Shall Be When the Lord Shall Bring Thee into the Land of the Canaanite. Canaan merited that the land should be called by his name. But what did Canaan do? Simply this: As soon as he heard that the Israelites were about to enter the land, he got up and moved away from before them. God then said to him: You have moved away from before My children; I,

יתן אות בתוך אות או יתן אות בתוך אות אמרת
תדחה שבת שחייבין עליה כרת ומיתת בית דין
לתפילין שאינן חייבין עליהם לא כרת ולא מיתת
בית דין דבר אחר מימים ימימה מגיד שאדם צריך
210 לבדוק את התפילין אחת לשנים עשר חדש נאמר
כאן מימים ימימה ונאמר להלן ימים תהיה גאולתו
מה ימים האמור להלן אין פחות משנים עשר חדש
אף ימים האמור כאן אין פחות משנים עשר חדש
דברי בית הלל בית שמאי אומרים אינו צריך
215 לבודקן עולמית שמאי הזקן אומר אלו תפילין של
אבי אימא.

פרשה יח   (שמות י״ג, י״א,–ט״ז.)

ו ה י ה   כ י   י ב י א ך   י י   א ל   א ר ץ   ה כ נ ע נ י
זכה כנען שתקרא הארץ על שמו וכי מה עשה כנען
אלא כיון ששמע כנען שישראל נכנסין לארץ עמד
ופינה מפניהם אמר לו המקום אתה פנית מפני בני

209–216 י׳ עירובין שם.   211 ויקרא כ״ה, כ״ט.
5–1 תוס׳ שבת ז׳, כ״ה. ד״ר ה׳, י״ה.

---

211 מימים] א. מ. מ׳ח. >.   213 אף ימים האמור כאן] א. אף
ימימה שנאמר כאן. ד. אף ימים האמורים כאן. מ׳ח. העיטור שם, אף
כאן.   215 שמאי הזקן] סמ״נ עשׂין כ״ב. הלל הזקן.

in turn, will call the land by your name and will give you a goodly land in your own country.[1] And which is it? It is Africa. Likewise, it says: "And Canaan begat Zidon his first-born and Heth" (Gen. 10.15). And it is written: "And the children of Heth answered Abraham, saying unto him: 'Hear us my Lord'" (Gen. 23.5–6). God then said to them: You have honored My friend. I, in turn, will call the land by your name and give you a goodly land in your own country. And which is it? It is Africa.

As He Swore unto Thee. And where did He swear unto thee? "And I will bring you in into the land concerning which I lifted up my hand," etc. (Ex. 6.8).

And to Thy Fathers. Where did He swear to thy fathers? In the case of Abraham what does it say? "In that day the Lord made a covenant with Abram," etc. (Gen. 15.18). In the case of Isaac what does it say? "Sojourn in this land," etc. (Gen. 26.3). In the case of Jacob what does it say? "The land whereon thou liest," etc. (Gen. 28.13).

---

[1] The original country of the Canaanites, descendants of Canaan, the son of Ham (Gen. 10.6) was Africa. The Canaanites, however, in the course of time conquered Palestine, taking it away from the sons of Shem to whom Palestine belonged (see Rashi to Gen. 12.6 and cf. *Sifra, Kedoshim* II, Weiss 95c). The Canaanites (or the Amorites with whom they are identified, see below *Besh.* I, note 3 and *Tosefta Shab.* 8.25) now were going back to their original country, Africa. In this Midrash there may be an allusion to the settlement of Carthage by the Phoenicians

5   אף אני אקרא את הארץ על שמך ואתן לך ארץ
יפה בארצך ואי זו זו זו אפריקי וכן הוא אומר וכנען
ילד את צידון בכורו ואת חת וכתיב ויענו בני חת
את אברהם לאמר לו שמענו אדני וגו' אמר להם
המקום אתם כבדתם את ידידי אף אני אקרא את
10   הארץ על שמכם ואתן לכם ארץ יפה בארצכם
ואיזו זו זו אפריקי.

כ א ש ר נ ש ב ע   ל ך והיכן נשבע לך והבאתי
אתכם אל הארץ אשר נשאתי את ידי וגו'.

ו ל א ב ו ת י ך   היכן נשבע לאבותיך באברהם
15   מהו אומר ביום ההוא כרת יי את אברם וגו' ביצחק
מהו אומר גור בארץ הזאת וגו' ביעקב מהו אומר
הארץ אשר אתה שוכב עליה וגו'.

6—7 בראשית י', ט'ו   7—8 שם כ'נ, ה'—ו'.   12—13 שמות ו', ח'.
12—17 לעיל י'ז.   15 בראשית ט'ו, י'ח.   16 שם כ'ו, נ'.   17 שם כ'ח, י'נ.

---

6 בארצך] ק. נ. כארצך.   10 בארצכם] ק. נ.כארצכם.   11 ואיזו
זו זו אפריקי] ד. < ז'י. בשם מהר'ם נגארי ~ דבר אחר על שכיבדו את
אברהם.   12 לך 2]=מ'ח: א. < ד. לו.   14 ולאבותיך] ק. נ. כאשר
נשבע לאבותיך / לאבותיך] מ. ד. < ט. לאבות.   15 מהו אומר]
ק. נ. הוא כתיב. מ. ל. כתיב.   16 מהו אומר] מ. ד. כתיב.

---

or Canaanites. Comp. also M. Mieses in *Hatekufah*, XVIII
(Warsaw, 1923), pp. 229 ff.

And Shall Give It to Thee. You should not look upon it as something inherited from your fathers but as something that has been given to you on that day.

Thou Shalt Cause to Pass unto the Lord All that Openeth the Womb. "Causing to pass unto" (*Ha'abarah*) means, "setting apart for." Similarly, it says: "Then shall ye cause his inheritance to pass unto his daughter" (Num. 27.8). Simon the son of Azzai says: "Thou shalt cause to pass all that openeth the womb." Why does Scripture need to say this? Because it says: "Whatsoever passeth under the rod" (Lev. 27.32). For I might understand the latter to mean even the orphaned animal. And the following reasoning would favor it: If a defective animal, which is not fit for the altar, is brought into the shed among the animals to be tithed, it is but logical to assume that an orphaned animal, which is fit for the altar, should surely be brought into the shed among the animals to be tithed. But the case of the bought animal would disprove this. For a bought animal is fit for the altar and yet is not brought into the shed among the animals to be tithed. This would prove that the orphaned animal, although it is fit for the altar, should nevertheless not be brought into the shed among the animals to be tithed. No! If you cite the case of the bought animal—it was not born on the premises of its present owner. Therefore it is not brought into the shed among the animals to be tithed. But will you argue the same about the

ונתנה לך שלא תהא בעיניך כירושת אבות

אלא תהא בעיניך כאלו אותו היום נתנה לך.

20　　　והעברת כל פטר רחם אין העברה אלא

הפרשה וכן הוא אומר והעברתם את נחלתו לבתו

שמעון בן עזאי אומר והעברת כל פטר רחם וגו'

מה תלמוד לומר לפי שהוא אומר כל אשר יעבור

תחת השבט שומע אני אף היתום במשמע והדין

25　נותן ומה אם בעל מום שאינו כשר על גבי המזבח

הרי הוא נכנס לדיר להתעשר יתום שהוא כשר על

גבי המזבח דין הוא שיכנס לדיר להתעשר והרי

הלקוח יוכיח שהוא כשר על גבי המזבח ואינו נכנס

לדיר להתעשר הוא יוכיח על היתום אף על פי

30　שהוא כשר על גבי המזבח לא יהא נכנס לדיר

להתעשר לא אם אמרת בלקוח שלא נולד ברשותו

לפיכך אינו נכנס לדיר להתעשר תאמר ביתום

19—18 ש. 35.　21 במדבר כ"ז, ח'.　22—37 לקמן כספא א'. בכורות

נ"ז, א'. חולין ל"ח, א'.　24—23 ויקרא כ"ז, ל"ב.

19 אותו היום נתנה] ד. היום נתונה.

orphaned animal? It was born on the premises of its present owner. Therefore it should be brought into the shed among the animals to be tithed. Thus, by mere logical reasoning I could not decide this question. However, here, in the law about the first-born, the expression "pass" is used and there, in the law about tithing (Lev. 27.32), the expression "pass" is used. Just as "pass" used here deals with an animal that can become consecrated only when its mother is alive, so "pass" used there must deal only with an animal that becomes consecrated while its mother is still alive. If so, then, just as here the law applies only to male animals, so also there the law should apply only to males? But Scripture says: "Whatsoever passeth under the rod" (Lev. 27.32), meaning both males and females.

Every Firstling . . Coming From a Beast. The expression, "Firstling coming from a beast," here, means a firstling which the mother cast prematurely. Such a one is exempt from the law regarding first-born. And yet the one born after it is not regarded as a first-born either.

Which Thou Hast. This excludes him who sells to a non-Jew the young of his cattle while still in embryo.[2] But this may mean to exclude one who sells to a non-Jew the young of his cattle while still in embryo and to include him who buys from a non-Jew the young of his cattle while still in embryo. Therefore Scripture says: "That

---

[2] I. e., selling it for future delivery.

שנולד ברשותו לכך יהא נכנס לדיר להתעשר לא

זכיתי מן הדין נאמר כאן העברה ונאמר להלן

35 העברה מה העברה האמורה כאן אין קדושה חלה

עליו אלא בחיי אמו אף העברה האמורה להלן

דין הוא שלא תהא קדושה חלה עליו אלא בחיי

אמו אי מה כאן זכרים אף להלן זכרים תלמוד

לומר כל אשר יעבור וגו' אחד זכרים ואחד נקבות

40 במשמע.

וכל פטר שגר בהמה אין פטר שגר בהמה

אלא ששיגרתו אמו יהיה פטור מן הבכורה והבא

אחריו אינו בכור.

אשר יהיה לך להוציא את המוכר עובר

45 בהמתו לגוי משמע מוציא את המוכר עובר בהמתו

לגוי ומביא את הלוקח עובר בהמתו של גוי תלמוד

41—43 לקמן כספא א'. ספרי במדבר קי״ח. בכורות ג', א'.
44—48 בכורות ב', א'. נ׳ה, ב'. מ׳ת 87.

---

34 העברה]=ט. ל׳: א. מ. עברה. ק. נ. עבודה.
35 העברה]=ט. ל׳: א. מ. עברה. ק. נ. עבודה/ האמורה כאן]=ל׳.
ט. א׳צ. ז״י: א. מ. ק. נ. להלן. 36 העברה]=ט. ל׳: א. מ.
עברה. ק. נ. עבודה/ האמורה להלן]=ל׳. ט. א׳צ. ז״י: א. מ. ק.
נ. כאן. 41 וכל] מ. ק. נ. כל. 45 לגוי] נ. ~ אשר יולד.
46—48 ת׳ל אשר יולד–בהמתו של גוי] מ. >.

are born of thy herd and of thy flock" (Deut. 15.19), thereby excluding one who buys from a non-Jew the young of his cattle while still in embryo.

The Males Shall Be the Lord's. On the basis of this passage R. Jose the Galilean used to say: If a ewe that had never before given birth gives birth to two males and their two heads come out simultaneously, both belong to the priest, for it is said: "The males shall be the Lord's." But the other sages say: It is impossible to ascertain exactly whether they came out simultaneously. Hence, only one of them belongs to the priest and the other belongs to the owner.

And Every Firstling of an Ass Thou Shalt Redeem with a Lamb. But not with a calf nor with a wild beast, nor with a slaughtered animal, nor with a diseased animal, nor with a hybrid, nor with a *Koy*.[3] And why is it said again: "And the firstling of an ass thou shalt redeem with a lamb" (Ex. 34.20)? Since it says: "Howbeit, the first-born of man shalt thou surely redeem, and the firstling of unclean beasts" (Num. 18.15), I might understand it to mean all unclean beasts, but Scripture says: "Every firstling of an ass."

---

[3] *Koy* is an animal of which the Rabbis were in doubt as to whether it belongs to the genus of cattle, בהמה, or beast of chase, חיה (see Jastrow, *Dictionary*, s. v.).

לומר אשר יולד בבקרך ובצאנך להוציא את
הלוקח עובר בהמתו של גוי.

הזכרים ליי מכאן היה רבי יוסי הגלילי
50 אומר רחל שלא בכרה וילדה שני זכרים ויצאו שני
ראשיהם כאחת שניהם לכהן שנאמר הזכרים ליי
וחכמים אומרים אי איפשר לצמצם אלא אחד לו
ואחד לכהן.

וכל פטר חמור תפדה בשה ולא בעגל
55 ולא בחיה ולא בשחוטה ולא בטרפה ולא בכלאים
ולא בכוי ופטר חמור תפדה בשה למה
נאמר לפי שהוא אומר אך פדה תפדה את בכור
האדם ואת בכור הבהמה הטמאה תפדה שומע אני
כל בכור בהמה טמאה במשמע תלמוד לומר כל

47 דברים ט'ו, י'ט.   49—53 בכורות י'ז, א'.   54—56 שם י'ב, א'.
ש. 36.   56 שמות ל'ד, כ'.   66—66 בכורות ה', א'. תוספתא שם א'
נ'. ספרי במדבר קי'ח.   57—58 במדבר י'ח, ט'ו.

51 כאחת] א. ט. כאחד.   52 לצמצם] הוספתי—ט. ל: מ'ח.
לומר כן.   57—58 את בכור האדם ואת בכור הבהמה הטמאה תפדה]
הוספתי: א. מ. וגו'.   59—60 ח'ל כל פטר חמור] הנהתי—ל. מ'ח:
א. מ. ק. נ. ט. ח'ל ופטר חמור (א. ~ וגו') מ. ק. נ. ט. ~
תפדה בשה חמור אתה פודה ואי אתה פודה כל בכור בהמה טמאה.

Still I might say, the firstling of an ass you redeem with a lamb and the firstling of any other unclean beast you redeem with clothing or other articles, therefore it is said again: "And the firstling of an ass"—only the firstling of an ass you have to redeem, but you do not have to redeem the firstling of any other unclean beast. If so what purpose is there in saying: "Howbeit . . . shalt thou surely redeem," etc.? If it has no bearing upon the subject of redeeming the firstling of unclean beasts, consider it as bearing upon the subject of consecrating unclean beasts for the Temple repair—that one should redeem them if they have been so consecrated.

And If Thou Wilt Not Redeem It, Then Thou Shalt Break Its Neck. On the basis of this passage the sages said: The duty of redemption has precedence over the duty of breaking the neck. Another Interpretation: "And if thou wilt not redeem it, then thou shalt break its neck." If you do not redeem it, break its neck, for since you have caused the priest a loss of property, your property should be destroyed. And how do

60 פטר חמור ועדיין אני אומר פטר חמור אתה פודה

בשה ושאר בהמה טמאה בכסות וכלים תלמוד

לומר ופטר חמור פטר חמור אתה פודה ואי אתה

פודה בכור שאר בהמה טמאה אם כן מה תלמוד

לומר אך פדה תפדה אם אינו ענין שפודין בכור

65 בהמה טמאה תנהו ענין שמקדישין בהמה טמאה

לבדק הבית ופודין אותה מהקדש בדק הבית.

ואם לא תפדה וערפתו מכאן אמרו

מצות פדייה קודמת למצות עריפה דבר אחר ואם

לא תפדה וערפתו אם אין אתה פודהו ערפהו

70 הואיל ואיבדת נכסי כהן אף גכסיך יאבדו ומנין

68 בכורות י"ג, א'.   70–68 שם י', ב'. ש. 36.

60 ועדיין אני אומר] הנהתי=מ"ח. ומ"ה: א"א. ש"י. ט.
(דפוס ווילנא) או א. ט. < מ. ד. דבר אחר ~ (מ.) ופטר חמור תפדה
בשה. (ק.) כל פטר חמור תפדה בשה. (נ. ל.) כל פטר חמור תפדה
בשה יכול.   61 בשה] א. מ. ק. < / ושאר בהמה טמאה בכסות וכלים]
מ. ואין אתה פודה שאר בהמה טמאה בכסות וכלים ד"א ופטר חמור
תפדה בשה ושאר בהמה טמאה בכסות וכלים. ק. ואי אתה פודה כל
בכור בהמה טמאה אלא בכסות וכלים ד"א ופטר חמור תפדה בשה ושאר
בהמה טמאה בכסות וכלים/ ח"ל] מ. ק. < נ. ~אך. א"א ש"י. ~
עוד במקום אחר.   62–63 ופטר חמור–שאר בהמה טמאה]=מ"ח. מ"א.
ש"י: א. מ. ד. < ט. דפוס קושטא חסר כל המאמר מן: ועדיין אני
אומר '60 עד: שאר בהמה טמאה (63).   63 אם כן מה ת'ל] א. אם כן
למה נאמר ת'ל.   64 אך] ק. נ. >.   67 ואם] מ. ק. נ. אם.

we know that it is forbidden for any use at all?
Here the term "breaking the neck" is used and
there (Deut. 21.4) the term "breaking the neck"
is used. Just as the breaking of the neck prescribed there makes the animal forbidden for
any use at all, so the breaking of the neck prescribed here makes the animal forbidden for
any use at all.

*And All the First-Born of Man Among Thy
Sons Shalt Thou Redeem.* Why is this said?
Because of the following: It says: "And their
redemption money—from a month old shalt
thou redeem them" (Num. 18.16), which is a
general statement. "According to thy valuation,
five shekels of silver" (ibid.), is a specific statement. Now, a general statement followed by a
specific cannot include more than the specific
statement. But when it says: "And all the first-
born of man among thy sons shalt thou redeem,"
it again makes a general statement. Perhaps,
however, the second general statement is to be
considered identical with the first general statement? You must say: No! It is a case of a
general statement followed by a specific statement and by another general statement, which
must be interpreted as including only things
similar to those mentioned in the specific statement. Now, in this case, the specific statement
specifies movable property not possessing the
quality of serving as permanent surety, though
of intrinsic value in itself. I can, therefore,
include in the general statement only movable
property not possessing the quality of serving as

שהוא אסור בהנאה נאמר כאן עריפה ונאמר להלן
עריפה מה עריפה האמורה להלן אסורה בהנאה
אף עריפה האמורה כאן אסורה בהנאה.

וכל בכור אדם בבניך תפדה למה
נאמר לפי שהוא אומר ופדוייו מבן חדש תפדה כלל
בערכך כסף חמשת שקלים פרט כלל ופרט אין
בכלל אלא מה שבפרט וכשהוא אומר וכל בכור
אדם בבניך תפדה חזר וכלל או כלל בכלל
הראשון אמרת לאו אלא כלל ופרט וכלל אין אתה
דן אלא כעין הפרט מה הפרט מפורש בנכסים
מטלטלין שאין להם אחריות וגופן ממון אף אני
איני מרבה אלא נכסים מטלטלין שאין להם אחריות

74–84 בכורות נ׳א, א׳. תוס׳ שם ו׳, י׳נ.   75 במדבר י׳ח, ט׳ו.

72 עריפה האמורה]=ט:׳ מ. ד. >.   74 וכל] מ. ק. נ. כל.
77 וכל] מ. ק. נ. כל.   79 וכלל] מ. >.   80 כעין הפרט] א. ~
לומר לך.   81 וגופן ממון] א. ט.   82 איני מרבה] מ. אין לי/
מטלטלין] מ. ד. >.

permanent surety. On the basis of this interpretation the sages said: The first-born of man may be redeemed with any thing except with slaves, notes, and lands, or consecrated property. Rabbi says: One may redeem the first-born of man with anything.

Another Interpretation: "And all the first-born of man among thy sons shalt thou redeem." Suppose one has five first-born sons, each from a different wife. How do we know that he is obligated to redeem them all? Scripture says: "And all the first-born of man among thy sons shalt thou redeem."

But All the First-Born of My Sons I Redeem. How do we know that the first-born whom his father has not redeemed must redeem himself? Scripture says: "And all the first-born of my sons I redeem."[4]

R. Jose the Galilean says: The Torah says: Redeem your son, and teach your son Torah. Having learned that one whom his father had not taught must teach himself, you conclude that likewise one whom his father had not redeemed must redeem himself. No! If you cite the case of the study of the Torah—it is as important as all other religious duties together.

---

[4] See Commentaries.

מכאן אמרו בכל פודין בכורי אדם חוץ מעבדים
ושטרות וקרקעות והקדשות רבי אומר בכל פודין
בכורי אדם דבר אחר וכל בכור אדם בבניך תפדה   85
הרי שהיו לו חמשה בכורות מחמש נשים מנין שחייב
לפדות את כולם תלמוד לומר וכל בכור אדם
בבניך תפדה.

וכל בכור בני אפדה מנין אם לא פדאו
אביו הוא יפדה את עצמו תלמוד לומר כל בכור   90
בני אפדה רבי יוסי הגלילי אומר הואיל ואמרה תורה
פדה את בנך ולמד את בנך תורה אם למדת על
תלמוד תורה שאם לא למדו אביו מלמד הוא את
עצמו כך אם לא פדאו אביו הוא יפדה את עצמו
לא אם אמרת בתלמוד תורה שהוא שקול כנגד   95

84—85 קידושין כ"ט, ב'.   89—91 קידושין כ"ט, א'.   95—96 פאה א', א'.

---

83 בכל] מ. ק. נ. ~ מקום.   84—85 רבי אומר בכל פודין בכורי
אדם]=מ"ח. ט: ד. > מ"ח. ~ חוץ משטרות.   85 דבר אחר]=ט:
מ. ד. > / וכל] מ. ד. כל.   86 חמשה] ד. > / מנין] א. מ. / >
שחייב] א. היו לו.   87—88 ת"ל וכל בכור אדם בבניך תפדה]
ט. > / וכל] מ. ק. נ. כל.   89 וכל בכור בני אפדה] מ. א. ד"א
(אולי צ"ל רבי אומר) וכל (מ. כל) בכור בני אפדה. ק. רבי אומר
מכאן וכל בכור בני אפדה. ט. דבר אחר וכל בכור בני אפדה (דפוס
ווילנא דבר אחר וכל בכור בניך תפדה)/ מנין] א. ומנין.   92—93 אם
למדת על תלמוד תורה] א. > מ. אם לא למדת על תלמוד תורה.

Hence one must teach himself if his father has not taught him. But will you argue the same about redemption? It is not as important as all other religious duties together. Hence a first-born need not redeem himself if his father has not redeemed him. But the law about circumcision would disprove this. For circumcision likewise is not as important as all other religious duties together and yet one whom his father has not circumcised must circumcise himself. And so also one whom his father has not redeemed should be obliged to redeem himself. No! If you cite the case of circumcision—one incurs the penalty of extermination for neglecting it; and, therefore, one has to circumcise himself if his father has not circumcised him. But will you argue the same about redemption? One does not incur the penalty of extermination for neglecting it. Therefore one need not redeem himself if his father has not redeemed him. You argue the differences, so let me establish a general rule on the basis of what is common to all these three instances: The peculiar aspect of the duty of circumcision is not like the peculiar aspect of the duty of study, and the peculiar aspect of the duty of study is not like the peculiar aspect of the duty of circumcision. Neither have both of them the same peculiar aspect as the duty of redemption, nor has the duty of redemption the peculiar aspect of either. What is common to all three of them is that each is a religious duty affecting the son which should be performed by the father. And if the father does not perform it,

הכל שאם לא למדו אביו מלמד הוא את עצמו

תאמר בפדייה שאינה שקולה כנגד הכל לפיכך

אם לא פדאו אביו לא יפדה את עצמו והרי מילה

תוכיח שאינה שקולה כנגד הכל ואם לא מלו אביו

100 הוא מל את עצמו כך אם לא פדאו אביו הוא יפדה

את עצמו לא אם אמרת במילה שחייבין עליה כרת

שאם לא מלו אביו הוא מל את עצמו תאמר בפדייה

שאין חייבין עליה כרת לפיכך אם לא פדאו אביו

לא יפדה את עצמו אמרת הפרש ואדון בנין אב

105 מבין שלשתן לא הרי מילה כהרי תלמוד ולא הרי

תלמוד כהרי מילה ולא זה וזה כהרי פדייה ולא

הרי פדייה כהרי זה וזה הצד השוה שבהן שהוא

מצות האב על הבן אם לא עשה אביו יעשה הוא

---

104 ואדון בנין אב] א. הדין בנין. מ. ועדיין ((נידיין!) בנין אב.
105 הרי] מ. ראי/ כהרי] מ. כראי.

the son himself must do it. So also any religious
duty affecting the son which should be performed
by the father must be performed by the son
himself if the father fails to do it. In this
connection the sages said: By the law of the
Torah a man is obligated to circumcise his son,
to redeem him if he be a first-born, to teach him
Torah, and to get him a wife. R. Akiba says:
Also to teach him to swim. Rabbi says: Also to
teach him civics.

*And It Shall Be When Thy Son Asketh Thee
Tomorrow.* Sometimes "tomorrow" means the
next day and sometimes "tomorrow" means in
time to come. In "tomorrow, saying: What is
this," "tomorrow" means in time to come. In
"By tomorrow shall this sign be" (Ex. 8.19),
"tomorrow" means the next day. In "Tomorrow
I will stand," etc. (Ex. 17.9), "tomorrow" means
the next day. In "Tomorrow your children
might speak unto our children," etc. (Josh.
22.24), "tomorrow" means in time to come.

What Mean the Testimonies and the Statutes,
etc. (Deut. 6.20). You find that you have to say:
There are four types of sons: the wise, the
simpleton, the wicked, and the one who does not
know enough to ask. The wise—what does he
say? "What mean the testimonies and the
statutes and the ordinances which the Lord our
God hath commanded you?" (Deut. 6.20). You
explain to him, in turn, the laws of the Passover

לעצמו אף כל שהוא מצות האב על הבן אם לא

110 עשה לו אביו הוא יעשה לעצמו מכאן אמרו מן

התורה חייב אדם למול את בנו ולפדותו וללמדו

תורה וללמדו אומנות ולהשיאו אשה רבי עקיבא

אומר אף ללמדו שיט רבי אומר אף ישוב מדינה.

והיה כי ישאלך בנך מחר יש מחר

115 עכשיו ויש מחר לאחר זמן מחר לאמור מה זאת

הרי מחר לאחר זמן מחר יהיה האות הזה הרי מחר

עכשיו מחר אנכי נצב הרי מחר עכשיו מחר יאמרו

בניכם לבנינו הרי מחר לאחר זמן מה העדות

והחקים וגו' נמצאת אומר ארבעה בנים הם אחד

120 חכם אחד טפש אחד רשע אחד שאינו יודע לשאול

חכם מה הוא אומר מה העדות והחקים והמשפטים

אשר צוה יי אלהינו אתכם אף אתה פתח לו בהלכות

110—113 קידושין פ"ב, א'. י' שם א', ז' (61ᵃ). תוס' שם א', ב'.
ה', ט'ו. 116 שמות ח', י"ט. 117 שם י"ז, ט'. 118—117 יהושע כ"ב,
כ"ד. 130—119 י' פסחים. י', ד' (37ᵈ). 122—121 דברים ו', כ'.

111—110 מן התורה] א. מ"ח. >. 116 מחר יהיה] במקרא כתוב
למחר יהיה. 117 מחר אנכי נצב הרי מחר עכשיו]=ט. מ"ח: א.
ד. >. 118 מה העדות] מ"ח. להלן הוא אומר מה העדות.
119 והחקים] מ"ח. > ק. נ. החקים. 120 אחד טפש אחד
רשע] ד. ואחד רשע ואחד תם. 121 והחקים] ק. נ. החקים.
122—121 והמשפטים-אתכם] א. > ט. וגו' ק. נ. והמשפטים-אותנו.
123—122 פתח לו בהלכות הפסח] ט. מ"ח. אמור לו כהלכות הפסח.

and tell him that the company is not to disband immediately after partaking of the paschal lamb. There should follow *Epikomon*.⁵ The simpleton— what does he say? "What is this? And thou shalt say unto him: By strength of hand the Lord brought us out from Egypt, from the house of bondage." The wicked one—what does he say? "What mean ye by this service?" (Ex. 12.26). Because he excludes himself from the group, do thou also exclude him from the group, and say unto him: "It is because of that which the Lord did for me" (v. 8)—for me but not for you. Had you been there, you would not have been redeemed. As for him who does not know enough to ask, you should begin and explain to him. For it is said: "And thou shalt tell thy son in that day" (v. 8). Another Interpretation: *What Mean the Testimonies and the Statutes and the Ordinances,*" etc. R. Eliezer says: How can you prove that even a company of teachers or disciples of the wise should be sitting and discussing the laws of the Passover until midnight? It is for this that it says: "What mean the testimonies and statutes."

And It Came to Pass When Pharaoh Would Hardly Let Us Go. I might understand this to mean that Pharaoh became hard of his own accord, but Scripture says: "And the Lord hardened the heart of Pharaoh," etc. (Ex. 9.12).

---

⁵ See L. Löw, *Lebensalter* (Szegedin, 1875), p. 318; Krauss, *Lehnwörter*, II, p. 107; also Jastrow, *Dictionary*, p. 104; and cf. Strack, *Der Misnatraktat Passafest* (Leipzig, 1911), p. 34, note 27; and Beer, *Pesaḥim* (1912), p. 62 and 74, note 4. Comp. also Hans Lietzmann, "Jüdische Passahritten," in *ZNTW*, 1926, pp. 1–5.

הפסח ואמור לו אין מפטירין אחר הפסח אפיקומן
טיפש מהו אומר מה זאת ואמרת אליו בחוזק יד
125 הוציאנו יי ממצרים מבית עבדים רשע מהו אומר
מה העבודה הזאת לכם לפי שהוציא את עצמו מן
הכלל אף אתה הוציאו מן הכלל ואמור לו בעבור
זה עשה יי לי בצאתי ממצרים לי ולא לך אלו היית
שם לא היית נגאל ושאינו יודע לשאול את פתח לו
130 שנאמר והגדת לבנך ביום וגו' דבר אחר מה העדות
והחקים והמשפטים וגו' רבי אליעזר אומר מנין אתה
אומר שאם היתה חבורה של חכמים או של תלמידי
חכמים שצריכין להיות יושבין ועוסקין בהלכות
פסח עד חצות לכך נאמר מה העדות והחקים וגו'.
135 ויהי כי הקשה פרעה לשלחנו שומע
אני מאליו תלמוד לומר ויחזק יי את לב פרעה.

_____

126 שמות י"ב, כ"ו.   128–127 שמות י"ג, ח'.   130 שמות שם.
134–130 תוס' פסחים י', י"ב.

_____

123 ואמור לו] ט. מ"ח. מ. ד. / > / אין מפטירין-אפיקומן]
מ. > / אחר הפסח] א. > / אפיקומן] ק. אפיקומין. מ"ח. אפיקימון.
124 טיפש]ד. חם.   126–127 מן הכלל]ד. ט. ~ כפר בעיקר.
127 אף אתה הוציאו מן הכלל]=ט. מ"ח: ד. אף אתה הקהה את שיניו.
130 דבר אחר] א. >.   133–132 תלמידי חכמים] ד. תלמידים.
133 להיות יושבין ועוסקין] ד. לעסוק. מ. לעשות.

That the Lord Slew All the First-Born, etc. On the basis of this passage the sages said: We sacrifice the firstlings of cattle because of what happened to the firstlings of cattle in Egypt. And we redeem the first-born of man because of what happened to the first-born of man in Egypt.

And It Shall Be for a Sign, etc. In four places Scripture records the section of the phylacteries: "Sanctify unto me," etc. (Ex. 13.2–10); "And it shall be when the Lord shall bring thee," etc. (ibid., 13.11–16); "Hear," etc. (Deut. 6.4–9); "And it shall come to pass, if ye shall hearken," etc. (ibid. 11.13–20). On the basis of this passage the sages said: The law in regard to the phylacteries is: The phylactery of the hand contains the four sections on one roll of parchment. The phylactery of the head contains the four sections on four separate rolls of parchment. And these are the four sections: "Sanctify unto Me"; "And it shall be when the Lord shall bring thee"; "Hear"; "And it shall come to pass, if ye shall hearken." They must be written in their order. And if they are written not in this order they must be hidden away.

End of the Tractate Pisḥa.

ויהרג יי כל בכור מכאן אמרו זובחין
בכורי בהמה כנגד בכורי בהמה ופודין בכורי אדם
כנגד בכורי אדם.

והיה לאות וגו' בארבעה מקומות מזכיר
פרשת תפילין קדש לי והיה כי יביאך שמע והיה
אם שמוע מכאן אמרו מצות תפילין ארבע פרשיות
של יד הן כרך אחד ארבע פרשיות של ראש הן
ארבע טוטפות ואלו הן קדש לי והיה כי יביאך
שמע והיה אם שמוע כותבן כסדרן ואם כותבן שלא
כסדרן הרי אלו ינגזו.

חסלת מסכתא דפסח ואית בה פרשייתא
י"ח וסימניהון מיצריא הדין לאומר וסה למינטר
למיסב מיכולתא לשובעה יומין קודם לארבעת
עשר ותיקדש ותיעול בליליא מפלוסיו פסחה
ותקדש ארעא דמעאלנא. ח'ז'ק'. ואית בהת
מסכתא הלכות ת'ס 'ו'.

---

136 שמות ט', י"ב.   146—140 מנחות ל'ד, ב'.

140 מזכיר] א. מ'ח. > ד. מזכירין.   142 תפלין] ד. <.
143 כרך אחד] א. ~ של.   147 דפסחן מ. ד. דפסחא (ד. ~
והיתה הרוחה).   152—147 ואית בה פרשייתא-הלכות תס'ו]=א: מ.
ד. > ועיין מאמרי "The Arrangement and the Divisions of the
Mekilta" in *Hebrew Union College Annual*, I, pp. 448ff.

MEKILTA TRACTATE BESHALLAH

CHAPTER I
(Ex. 13.17–22)

And It Came to Pass When Pharaoh Had Let the People Go. "Letting go," *Shiluah*, means escorting, as it is said: "And Abraham went with them to bring them on the way" (Gen. 18.16); "And Isaac sent them away" (ibid., 26.30). The mouth that had said: "And moreover I will not let Israel go" (Ex. 5.2), that same mouth said: "I will let you go" (ibid., 8.24). What was the reward for this? "Thou shalt not abhor an Egyptian" (Deut. 23.8). The mouth that had said: "I know not the Lord" (Ex. 5.2), that same mouth said: "Let us flee from the face of Israel; for the Lord fighteth for them against the Egyptians" (ibid., 14.25). What was the reward for this? "In that day shall there be an altar to the Lord in the midst of the land of Egypt, and a pillar at the border thereof to the Lord" (Isa. 19.19). The mouth that had said: "Who is the Lord, that I should hearken to His voice?" (Ex. 5.2), that same mouth said: "The Lord is righteous, and I and my people are wicked" (ibid., 9.27). What reward did they receive for this? A place to be buried in was given to them, as it is said: "Thou stretchedst out Thy right hand—the earth swallowed them" (ibid., 15.12).

169

מסכתא ויהי בשלח

פרשה א (שמות י"ג, י"ז,–כ"ב.)

ויהי בשלח פרעה אין שלוח בכל מקום
אלא ליווי שנאמר ואברהם הולך עמם לשלחם
וישלחם יצחק וגו'. הפה שאמר וגם את ישראל לא
אשלח הוא הפה שאמר אנכי אשלח אתכם מה שכר
נטלו על כך לא תתעב מצרי הפה שאמר לא ידעתי
את יי הוא הפה שאמר אנוסה מפני ישראל כי יי
נלחם להם במצרים מה שכר נטלו על כך ביום
ההוא יהיה מזבח ליי בתוך ארץ מצרים ומצבה
אצל גבולה ליי הפה שאמר מי יי אשר אשמע בקולו
10 הוא הפה שאמר יי הצדיק ואני ועמי הרשעים ומה
שכר נטלו על כך שניתן להם מקום קבורה שנאמר
נטית ימינך תבלעמו ארץ.

42–1 ח. בשלח.   4–1 שמו"ר כ', נ'. ש. 37.   2 בראשית י"ח, ט"ז.
3 בראשית כ"ו, ל"א.   4–3 שמות ה', ב'.   4 שם ח', כ"ד.   5 דברים כ"ג, ח'.
6–5 שמות ה', ב'.   6–7 שם י"ד, כ"ה.   9–7 ישעיה י"ט, י"ט.   9 שמות ה', ב'.
12–9 לקטן שירה פ"ט.   10 שמות ט', כ"ז.   12 שמות ט"ו, י"ב.

פרשה א.] הוספתי.   4 אשלח אתכם] א. ק. נ. ~ ואת טפכם.
11–10 ומה שכר–שניתן] ד. על כן נתן.

That God Led Them Not. The expression *"nihuy"* can only mean "leading." And thus it says: "Thou didst lead Thy people like a flock" (Ps. 77.21). And it is written: "By day also He led them with a cloud" (ibid., 78.14).

By the Way of the Land of the Philistines, for That Was Near. That which the Holy One, blessed be He, had said to Moses: "When thou hast brought forth the people out of Egypt, ye shall serve God upon this mountain" (Ex. 3.12), was soon to be.

Another Interpretation: "For that was near." That would have been a nearer way to return to Egypt. As it is said: "We will go three days' journey into the wilderness" (ibid., 8.23).

Another Interpretation: "For that was near." That oath which Abraham had sworn to Abimelech was as yet too recent, for it is said: "Now therefore swear unto me here by God that thou wilt not deal falsely with me, nor with my son, nor with my son's son" (Gen. 21.23), and Abimelech's grandson was still there.[1]

Another Interpretation: "For that was near." The first war[2] was too recent to risk another.

Another Interpretation: "For that was near."

---

[1] The Israelites could therefore not march through the land of the Philistines where Abimelech's grandson was ruling.

[2] I. e., the war of the Ephraimites mentioned below.

ולא נחם אלהים אין נחוי בכל מקום אלא
נהוג וכן הוא אומר נחית כצאן עמך וגו' וכתיב וינחם
בענן יומם.

דרך ארץ פלשתים כי קרוב הוא
קרוב הוא הדבר שאמר הקב"ה למשה בהוציאך
את העם ממצרים תעבדון את האלהים על ההר
הזה דבר אחר כי קרוב הוא קרוב הדרך לשוב
למצרים שנאמר דרך שלשת ימים נלך במדבר
דבר אחר כי קרוב הוא קרובה השבועה שנשבע
אברהם לאבימלך שנאמר ועתה השבעה לי
באלהים הנה אם תשקור לי ולניני ולנכדי ועדיין
נכדו קיים דבר אחר כי קרוב הוא קרובה מלחמה
ראשונה לשנייה דבר אחר כי קרוב הוא בקרוב

---

14 תהלים ע"ז, כ"א.   15—14 שם ע"ח, י"ד.   19—17 שמות נ' י"ב.
20 שם ח', כ"נ.   24—21 פסדר"כ פיסקא ויהי בשלח (פ"ה א') ש. 37.
מדרש אגדה בשלח קמ"נ.   23—22 בראשית כ"א, כ"נ.   24—37 ש. 37.

---

13 נחוי]=מ"ח: א. מ. ד. נחום. ש"ט. ורפוס ווילנא נחם / בכל
מקום] ד. זה.   17—19 קרוב הוא הדבר-דבר אחר כי קרוב הוא] מ. <.
19 דבר אחר]—ט. ל: ק. נ. <.   23 הנה אם תשקור-ולנכדי]
א. מ. וגו' ק. נ. אם תשקור-ולנכדי.   24 קרובה מלחמה] ק.
נ. קרובה השבועה מלחמה.   26—25 בקרוב ירשו] מ. בקרוב חרשו
(חדשו!) א'א. קרוב הוא שירשו.

The Canaanites had only recently taken possession of the land. For it is said: "And in the
fourth generation they shall come back hither,"[3]
etc. (Gen. 15.16).

Another Interpretation: Should God not all
the more have brought them in by the straight
road? But God said: If I bring Israel into the
land now, every one of them will immediately
take hold of his field or his vineyard and neglect
the Torah. But I will make them go round about
through the desert forty years, so that, having
the manna to eat and the water of the well[4] to
drink, they will absorb the Torah. On the basis
of this interpretation R. Simon the son of
Yohai said: Only to those who eat manna is it
given really to study the Torah. Like them are
those who eat *Terumah*.[5]

Another Interpretation: Should God not all the
more have brought them in by the straight road?

----

[3] The Canaanites who took possession of Palestine in
the days of Abraham (see above, note 1) are here identified
with the Amorites (see above Pisha, XVII, note 3 and
XVIII, note 1) whose iniquity was not full before the time
of the fourth generation of the Israelites in Egypt (Gen.
15.16; cf. Rashi ad loc.). Hence, the Israelites could not go
straight from Egypt to Palestine to dispossess the Amorites
but had to wander about in the desert, waiting for the time
when the iniquity of the Amorites would become full.

[4] This refers to the so-called well of Miriam, a miraculous
well, which accompanied the Israelites on their wanderings
through the desert (see Ta'an. 9a and Rashi, ibid., s. v.
באדה של מרים; cf. also *JE*, VIII, 609 and Israel S. Horowitz,
Palestine, Vienna, 1923, p. 105 f.).

ירשו כנענים את הארץ שנאמר ודור רביעי ישובו
הנה וגו' דבר אחר כל שכן לא הביאן המקום
בפשוטה אלא אמר המקום אם אני מכניס את
ישראל לארץ עכשיו מיד הם מחזיקים אדם בשדהו
ואדם בכרמו והן בטלים מן התורה אלא הרי אני 30
מקיפן במדבר ארבעים שנה כדי שיהיו אוכלין מן
ושותין מי באר והתורה נבללת בגופן מכאן היה
רבי שמעון בן יוחי אומר לא נתנה התורה לדרוש
אלא לאוכלי המן ושוין להם אוכלי תרומה דבר
אחר כל שכן לא הביאן המקום בפשוטה אלא כיון 35

26—27 בראשית ט"ו, ט"ז. 32—34 לקטן ויסע פ"נ. 34—42 ספו"ר כ', ט"ז.

27 וגו'] ת. א"א. ועדיין לא היה להם דור רביעי/ דבר אחר]=ט:
מ. ד. > / א"צ. ~ כי קרוב הוא/ כל שכן]=ט. מ"ח: מ"ח. אם
הביאן] ק. א"א. ולמה לא הביאן. ל. לכך לא הביאן. מ"ח. אם
הביאן. ט. אלו הביאן (בהוצאות מאוחרות למה לא הביאן)/ הטקום]
ק. הכתוב. 28 בפשוטה] א. > ד. דרך פשוטה לארץ ישראל/ אלא]
ד. ~ דרך המדבר / אמר המקום] מ"ח. כך אמר המקום. ל. דבר
אחר אמר הקב"ה. 30—31 הרי אני מקיפן]=ט. מ"ח: מ"ח. מ. סעכבן. ד.
אקיפם. 32 נבללת]=ט: ד. נכללת. 33 בן יוחי] ד. > / לדרוש]
מ"ח. לידרש. 34 ושוין] א"א. ט. ל. שניים. 35 כל שכן] ד. כי
קרוב הוא/ לא]=ט: מ"ח. אם ל. ולא/ בפשוטה] ק. נ. בפישוטן.

---

[5] I. e., priests who get their portion or share in the crop,
תרומה, without any effort on their part to produce it.

But, as soon as the Canaanites heard that the Israelites were about to enter the land, they arose and burnt the seeds, cut down the trees, destroyed the buildings, and stopped up the wells. God, then, said: I promised Abraham to bring them not into a desolate land, but into a land full of all good things, as it is said: "And houses full of all good things" (Deut. 6.11). Therefore I will make them go round about through the desert forty years, so that the Canaanites will arise and repair what they have spoiled.

For God Said: 'Lest Peradventure the People Repent When They See War,' etc. This refers to the war with the Amalekite, as it is said: "Then the Amalekite . . . came down," etc. (Num. 14.45).

Another Interpretation: "For God said: 'Lest peradventure the people repent when they see war'." This refers to the war of the sons of Ephraim,[6] as it is said: "And the sons of Ephraim: Shuthelah—and Bered was his son . . . whom the men of Gath that were born in the

---

[6] According to an old tradition, there was an exodus from Egypt sometime before the Exodus under the leadership of Moses took place. This first exodus under the leadership of the sons of Ephraim is, according to the Midrash, referred to in I Chron. and alluded to in Ps. 78.9. The Ephraimites failed, and their undertaking resulted in disaster for them and their followers (see *Pirḳe de R. Eliezer*, ch. 48, *Sefer ha-Yashar, Shemot*, ed. L. Goldschmidt, Berlin, 1923, pp. 256–7; Ex. Rab. 20.11, Cant. Rab. to 1.7, end of *Sidra Ḳamma*).

ששמעו כנעניים שישראל נכנסים לארץ עמדו ושרפו
את הזרעים וקצצו את האילנות וסתרו את הבנינים
וסתמו את המעיינות אמר הקב"ה לא הבטחתי
לאברהם אביהם שאני מכניסן לארץ חריבה אלא
40 לארץ מלאה כל טוב שנאמר ובתים מלאים כל
טוב אלא הרי אני מקיפן במדבר ארבעים שנה כדי
שיעמדו כנענים ויתקנו מה שקלקלו.

כי אמר אלהים פן ינחם העם בראותם
מלחמה וגו' זו מלחמת עמלקי שנאמר וירד
45 העמלקי וגו' דבר אחר כי אמר אלהים פן ינחם
העם בראותם מלחמה זו מלחמת בני אפרים שנאמר
ובני אפרים שותלח וברד בנו וגו' והרגום אנשי גת

---

38. ש. 42—38 ד. 40—41 דברים ו', י"א. 45—44 במדבר י"ד, ס"ה.
45—53 שמו"ר כ', י"א. שהש"ר ב', ז' סוף סדרא קמא. פדר"א מ"ח.
ש. 38—37. פסדר"כ ויהי בשלח (פ"ה, א', ב'). מדרש אגדה שם.
47—48 דהי"א ז', כ'—כ"א.

---

36 נכנסים] ק. נ. נכנסו / לארץ] ק. נ. <.   38 הבטחתי] ק.
נ. הבטחתם. 39 לאברהם אביהם] ד. לאבותם. 40 ובתים] א. בחים.
41 כדי] ד. עד.   43 כי אמר] ק. נ. ד"א כי אמר.   44—43 ינחם העם
בראותם מלחמה] הוספתי עפ"י מ"ח: א. מ. ד. וגו'. 46—45 פן ינחם-
מלחמה] הוספתי-ט.   47 ובני אפרים] מ. ד. אלה בני אפרים / וברד
בנו] הנגהתי=מ"ח. וכמו שהוא במקרא. א. בנו ובדד (ובדד!) בנו מ.
בנו ד. > ט. בנו זכר (ובד!) בנו.   48—47 והרגום אנשי נת וגו' מאתים
אלף בני אפרים] מ. ד. <.

land slew" (I Chr. 7.20–21)—two hundred thousand children of Ephraim.[7]   And it also says:
"The children of Ephraim were archers, handling
the bow, they turned back in the day of battle"
(Ps. 78.9). Why? Because "they kept not the
covenant of God and refused to walk in His law"
(ibid., 78.10), that is, because they ignored the
stipulated term, because they violated the oath.[8]

Another Interpretation: So that they should
not see the bones of their brethren lying around
in Philistia and turn back.

Another Interpretation: It was in order that
they should not turn back. This can be argued
by the method of *Kal vaḥomer*: If after He had
made them go round about a long way they said:
"Let us make a captain and let us return into
Egypt" (Num. 14.4), how much more would
they have said so, had He brought them by a
straight road.

*But God Led the People About, by the Way of the
Wilderness, by the Red Sea.* What for? For the
purpose of performing for them miracles and
mighty deeds, by giving them the manna, the
quail and the well.[9]   R. Eliezer says: "By the

---

[7] The phrase מאתים אלף בני אפרים, "two hundred thousand children of Ephraim," is not found in our masoretic
text, but is presupposed in *Targum Rab Joseph* (Wilna,
1816), p. 9 to this passage in Chronicles.

[8] I. e., the term stipulated for their deliverance from
Egypt and the oath imposed upon them not to attempt to
leave Egypt before the time fixed by God (see Cant. Rab.
l. c. and cf. *Pseudo-Jonathan* to Gen. 50.25).

[9] I. e., the miraculous well (see above, note 4).

וגו' מאתים אלף בני אפרים ואומר בני אפרים

נושקי רומי קשת הפכו ביום קרב מפני מה על שלא

50 שמרו ברית אלהים ובתורתו מאנו ללכת על שעברו

על הקץ על שעברו על השבועה דבר אחר כדי

שלא יראו עצמות אחיהם מושלכין בפלשת ויחזרו

להם דבר אחר כדי שלא יחזרו לאחוריהם והרי

דברים קל וחמר ומה אם כשהקיפן דרך רחוקה

55 אמרו נתנה ראש ונשובה מצרימה אלו הביאן

בפשוטה על אחת כמה וכמה.

ויסב אלהים את העם דרך המדבר

ים סוף מפני מה כדי לעשות להם נסים וגבורות

במן ובשליו ובבאר רבי אליעזר אומר דרך כדי

49—48 תהלים ע'ח, ט'—י'.　　55 במדבר י'ד, ד'.　　85—57 ש. 38.

---

48 ואומר]=מ'ח: א. שנאמר ד. וכתיב.　　51—50 על שעברו—על
השבועה] ט. מ. ד. עברו על הקץ ועל (מ. ועברו על) השבועה.
51 דבר אחר] מ'ח. א'צ. >.　　53 דבר אחר] ד. ~ כי אמר
אלהים.　　54 רחוקה]=ט. מ'ח: ק. ל. עקומה. נ. עטוקה.
57—58 דרך המדבר ים סוף] הוספתי: א. מ. וגו'.　　59 במן ובשליו
ובבאר] א. מ. ט. מ'ח. >/ דרך] ק. נ. >.

way," indicates that it was for the purpose of tiring them, as it is said: "He weakened my strength in the way" (Ps. 102.24); "of the wilderness," indicates that it was for the purpose of refining them, as it is said: "Who led thee through the great and dreadful wilderness," etc. (Deut. 8.15); "by the Red Sea," indicates that it was for the purpose of testing them, as it is said: "And they were rebellious at the sea, even at the Red Sea" (Ps. 106.7). R. Joshua says: "By the way," indicates that it was for the purpose of giving them the Torah, as it is said: "Ye shall walk in all the way which the Lord your God hath commanded you" (Deut. 5.30). And it also says: "For the commandment is a lamp, and the teaching (Torah) is light and a way of life" (Prov. 6.23); "of the wilderness," indicates that it was for the purpose of feeding them the manna, as it is said: "Who fed thee in the wilderness with manna," etc. (Deut. 8.16); "by the Red Sea," indicates that it was for the purpose of performing for them miracles and mighty deeds, as it is said: "Terrible things by the Red Sea" (Ps. 106.22), and it also says: "And He rebuked the Red Sea, and it was dried up; and He led them through the depths, as through a wilderness" (ibid., 106.9).

And the Children of Israel Went Up Armed (Ḥamushim). The word *Ḥamushim* here means armed, as in the passage: "But ye shall pass over before your brethren (*ḥamushim*) armed" (Josh. 1.14).

Another Interpretation: The word *Ḥamushim* only means zealous, as in the passage: "And the

60 לינען שנאמר ענה בדרך כחי המדבר כדי לצרפן
שנאמר המוליכך במדבר הגדול וגו' ים סוף כדי
לנסותם שנאמר וימרו על ים בים סוף רבי יהושע
אומר דרך כדי ליתן להם את התורה שנאמר בכל
הדרך אשר צוה יי אלהיכם אתכם תלכו ואומר כי

65 נר מצוה ותורה אור ודרך חיים המדבר כדי
להאכילם את המן שנאמר המאכילך מן במדבר
וגו' ים סוף כדי לעשות להם נסים וגבורות שנאמר
נוראות על ים סוף ואומר ויגער בים סוף ויחרב
ויוליכם בתהומות כמדבר.

70 וחמושים עלו בני ישראל אין חמושים
אלא מזוינין שנאמר ואתם תעברו חמושים דבר
אחר אין חמושים אלא מזורזין שנאמר ויעברו בני

---

60 תהלים ק"ב, כ"ד. 61 דברים ח', ט"ו. 62 תהלים ק"ו, ז'.
63—64 דברים ה', ל'. 64—65 משלי ו', כ"ג. 66 דברים ח', ט"ז.
68 תהלים ק"ו, כ"ב. 68—69 שם ק"ו, ט'. 70—71 שמו"ר כ', י"ט. י'
שבת ו', ד' (8b). 71 יהושע א', י"ד. 72—74 שם ד', י"ב–י"נ.

62 בים] א. >. 64 צוה יי אלהיכם] א. מ. וגו' ק. נ. צוה יי
אלהינו. 65 ודרך חיים] הוספתי=ט. מ"ח. (מ"ח. ~ תוכחות מוסר).
67 וגבורות] ד. ונפלאות. 71 מזוינין] מ. מזורזין/ שנאמר] ק. נ. ~
וחמושים עלו בני ישראל. 71—72 דבר אחר אין חמושים אלא
מזורזין]=ט: ד. > מ. ואין חמושים אלא מזורין. 72 שנאמר] ד.
וכתיב. 73—72 ויעברו בני ראובן ובני גד] ק. נ. ויעברו ראובן ובני גד
ט. ויעברו בני גד ובני ראובן.

children of Reuben, and the children of Gad, and the half-tribe of Manasseh passed on zealously[10] (ḥamushim) before the children of Israel . . . about forty thousand ready armed for war" (Josh. 4.12–13).

Another Interpretation: They went up *Ḥamushim*; This means only one out of five came out. Some say only one out of fifty. And some say only one out of five hundred. R. Nehorai says: By the worship! Not even one out of five hundred came out. It says: "I cause thee to increase, even as the growth of the field" (Ezek. 16.7), and it also says: "And the children of Israel were fruitful, and increased abundantly," etc. (Ex. 1.7), which means that a woman would give birth to six children at one delivery; and you would say that one out of five hundred came out? By the worship! Not even one out of five hundred came out, but very many Israelites died in Egypt.[11] And when did they die? During the three days of darkness, when, as it is said: "They saw not one another," etc. (Ex. 10.23), so that they could bury their dead, thanking and praising God that their enemies could not see and rejoice at their downfall.

---

[10] So our Midrash understands the word חמושים in this passage, not "armed" as rendered by the Bible Translations.

[11] Cf. above, *Pisḥa*, XII, notes 3–5.

ראובן ובני גד וחצי שבט המנשה חמושים לפני בני

ישראל ואומר כארבעים אלף חלוצי צבא דבר

אחר וחמושים עלו אחד מחמשה ויש אומרים אחד ⁷⁵

מחמשים ויש אומרים אחד מחמש מאות רבי נהוראי

אומר העבודה ולא אחד מחמש מאות עלו שנאמר

רבבה כצמח השדה נתתיך וגו' ואומר ובני ישראל

פרו וישרצו וגו' שהיתה אשה יולדת ששה בכרס

אחד ואתה אומר אחד מחמש מאות עלו העבודה ⁸⁰

ולא אחד מחמש מאות עלו אלא שמתו הרבה

מישראל במצרים ואימתי מתו בשלשת ימי אפלה

שנאמר לא ראו איש את אחיו וגו' שהיו קוברים את

מתיהם והודו ושבחו שלא ראו אויביהם וששו

במפלתם. ⁸⁵

---

⁸⁵–⁷⁶ לעיל פסחא י"ב. פסדר"כ ויהי בשלח (פ"ה, ב'). ⁷⁸ יחזקאל
ט"ז, ז'. ⁷⁹–⁷⁸ שמות א', ז'. ⁸³ שם י', כ"ג.

---

⁷⁴–⁷³ וחצי שבט המנשה חמושים לפני בני ישראל] א. מ. וגו'. ק.
נ. וחצי שבט המנשה חלוצים. ⁷⁴ ואומר] מ. ד. / כארבעים]
ד. ארבעים / צבא] במקרא כתוב הצבא. ⁸²–⁷⁷ שנאמר רבבה–
מישראל במצרים] מ. >.

And Moses Took the Bones of Joseph with Him.
This proclaims the wisdom and the piety of
Moses. For all Israel were busy with the booty
while Moses busied himself with the duty of
looking after the bones of Joseph. Of him Scripture says: "The wise in heart takes on duties"
(Prov. 10.8). But how did Moses know where
Joseph was buried? It is told that Seraḥ, the
daughter of Asher, survived from that generation
and she showed Moses the grave of Joseph.[12] She
said to him: The Egyptians put him into a metal
coffin which they sunk in the Nile. So Moses
went and stood by the Nile. He took a table of
gold on which he engraved the Tetragrammaton,
and throwing it into the Nile, he cried out and
said: "Joseph son of Jacob! The oath to redeem
his children, which God swore to our father
Abraham, has reached its fulfillment. If you
come up, well and good. But if not, we shall be
guiltless of your oath."[13] Immediately Joseph's

---

[12] See on this legend M. Güdemann, *Religionsgeschicht-
liche Studien* (Leipzig, 1876), p. 26 ff. and B. Heller, *Die
Sage vom Sarge Josephs*, etc., in *MGWJ*, 70 (1926), p. 271 ff.
[13] See Gen. 50.25.

ויקח משה את עצמות יוסף עמו
להודיע חכמתו וחסידותו של משה שכל ישראל
עוסקין בבזה ומשה עוסק במצות עצמות יוסף עליו
הכתוב אומר חכם לב יקח מצות וכי מנין היה משה

90 יודע היכן היה קבור יוסף אמרו סרח בת אשר
נשתיירה מאותו הדור והיא הראתה למשה קברו
של יוסף אמרה לו ארון של מתכת עשו לו מצרים
ושקעוהו בתוך הנילוס בא משה ועמד על הנילוס
נטל לוח של זהב וחקק בה שם המפורש וזרקה

95 לתוכו צעק ואמר יוסף בן יעקב הגיעה השבועה
שנשבע הקב"ה לאברהם אבינו שהוא גואל את בניו
אם אתה עולה מוטב ואם לאו נקיים אנו משבועתך

86–151 סוטה י"נ, א'. חוס' שם ד', ז'. שמו'ר כ', י"ט. פסדר'כ שם
(פ"ה, ב'. פ'ו, א'). ש. 39. ת. בשלח ב'.   87–98 ד'ר י"א, ז'.   89 משלי
י', ח'.   92–98 מדרש אגדה שם.

87 וחסידותו] א. מ. </ של משה] ק. >.   87–88 שכל ישראל
עוסקין] א. שהיו הכל עסוקין.   90–89 וכי מנין–יודע] ד. ומשה מהיכן
היה יודע.   91 הראתה] א. ~ ואמרה.   92–91 קברו של יוסף] ד. קבר
יוסף. א. היכן יוסף קבור.   92 אמרה לו] ד. ~ במקום הוה שמוהו. א.
ולא עוד אלא.   94–95 נטל לוח של זהב–וזרקה לתוכו] א. ד. נטל
צרור וזרק לתוכו.   95 יוסף בן יעקב] א. ד. יוסף יוסף/ השבועה]
מ"ח. העת.   97 אם אתה עולה מוטב ואם לאו] א. > מ"ח. ש.
אם אתה מראה את (ש. מנלה) עצמך מוטב ואם לאו. ד. חן כבוד
ליי אלהי ישראל ואל תעכב את נאולתך (ל. נאולחן) כי בגללך אנו
מעוכבים ואם לאו/ משבועתך] א. ~ שהשבענו מ"ח. משבועתינו.

coffin came to the surface, and Moses took it.
And you need not be surprised at this. Behold
it says: "But as one was felling a beam . . . and
the man of God said: 'Where fell it' "? etc.
(II Kings 6.5–6). Now, to apply the method of
Kal vaḥomer, if Elisha, the disciple of Elijah,
could make the iron come to the surface, how
much more could Moses, the master of Elijah,
do it! R. Nathan says: They had buried him in
the capitol of Egypt in the mausoleum of the
kings, as it is said: "And they embalmed him,
and he was put in a coffin in Egypt" (Gen. 50.26).
And how did Moses know which was Joseph's
coffin? Moses went and stood among the coffins.
He cried out and said: "Joseph, Joseph! The
oath to redeem his children which God has sworn
to our father Abraham has reached its fulfillment," etc. Immediately Joseph's coffin began
to move and Moses took it and went his way.
This is to teach you that with what measure a
man metes it is measured unto him. Miriam
waited for her brother a while, as it is said:
"And his sister stood afar off" (Ex. 2.4). And

מיד צף ארונו של יוסף ונטלו משה ואל תתמה
בדבר הזה הרי הוא אומר ויהי האחד מפיל הקורה
וגו' ויאמר איש האלהים אנה נפל וגו' והרי דברים 100
קל וחמר ומה אם אלישע תלמידו של אליהו הציף
הברזל קל וחמר למשה רבו של אליהו רבי נתן
אומר בקפיטולין של מצרים קברוהו בין המלכים
שנאמר ויחנטו אותו וייסם בארון במצרים וכי מנין
היה יודע משה איזה הוא ארונו של יוסף הלך משה 105
ועמד בין הארונות צעק ואמר יוסף יוסף הגיעה
השבועה שנשבע המקום לאברהם אבינו וגו' מיד
נזדעזע ארונו של יוסף ונטלו ובא לו ללמדך
שבמדה שאדם מודד בה מודדין לו מרים המתינה
למשה שעה אחת שנאמר ותתצב אחותו מרחוק וגו' 110

99—100 מלכים ב. ו', ה'-ו'.   104 בראשית נ', כ'ו.   110 שמות
ב', ד'.

---

99 בדבר הזה] א. מ"ח. > מ. בדבר / האחד] מ. אחד / הקורה]
ד. את הקורה.   100 וגו'] ד. והברזל נפל למים ויצעק ויאמר אהה יי
והוא שאול / ויאמר איש האלהים-וגו'] ק. נ. > ל. ויאמר אנה נפל
ויקצב עץ יישליך ויצף הברזל.   103 בקפיטולין] ק. בקפיטולין. נ. ל.
בקיפוסולין / של מצרים] ל. של סלכים / קברוהו בין המלכים]
מ. ד. היה קבור יוסף.   104 שנאמר ויחנטו] מ. וגו' ד. > / אותו
וייסם בארון במצרים] הוספתי: א. וגו'.   108—104 וכי מנין היה
יודע-ונטלו ובא לו] מ. ד. >.

in the wilderness God caused the ark, the Shekinah, the priests, all Israel and the seven clouds of glory to wait for her, as it is said: "And the prople journeyed not till Miriam was brought in again" (Num. 12.15). Joseph, than whom none of his brothers was greater, acted meritoriously in burying his father, as it is said: "And Joseph went up to bury his father . . . and there went up with him," etc. (Gen. 50.7–9). Whom can we find greater and more honored than Joseph with whom no less a person than Moses busied himself. Moses, than whom no one in Israel was greater, acted meritoriously in busying himself with the bones of Joseph, as it is said: "And Moses took the bones of Joseph with him." Whom can we find greater and more honored than Moses, who was attended to by God Himself, as it is said, "And He buried him in the valley" (Deut. 34.6). And, what is more, with Jacob there went up the servants of Pharaoh and the elders of his house, while with Joseph there went up the ark, the Shekinah, the priests, the Levites, all Israel and the seven clouds of glory. Furthermore, the coffin of Joseph went alongside of the ark of the Eternal.[14]   And the nations

---

[14] I. e., not only during their wanderings through the desert but also after they entered Palestine, up to the time when they buried it at Shechem (Josh. 24.32). The nations to whom it was pointed out that Joseph had kept the Torah were the nations of Palestine (see below, note 16).

והמקום עכב לה במדבר הארון והשכינה והכהנים
וכל ישראל ושבעת ענני הכבוד והעם לא
נסע עד האסף מרים יוסף זכה לקבור את אביו
שאין באחיו גדול ממנו שנאמר ויעל יוסף לקבור
115 את אביו וגו' ויעל עמו וגו' מי לנו גדול מיוסף שלא
נתעסק בו אלא משה משה זכה בעצמות יוסף שאין
בישראל גדול ממנו שנאמר ויקח משה את עצמות
יוסף עמו מי לנו גדול ממשה שלא נתעסק בו אלא
הקב"ה שנאמר ויקבור אותו בגיא ולא עוד אלא
120 שעם יעקב עלו עבדי פרעה וזקני ביתו ועם יוסף
עלו הארון והשכינה והכהנים והלויים וכל ישראל
ושבעת ענני הכבוד ולא עוד אלא שהיה ארונו של
יוסף מהלך עם ארון חי העולמים והיו אומות

112–113 במדבר י"ב, ט"ז.   114–115 בראשית נ', ז'–ט'.   119 דברים
ל"ד, ו'.

---

112 ושבעת ענני הכבוד] ד. שבעת יסים עם ענני כבור.   114 שאין]
א. מ"ח. ואין.   115 מיוסף] ק. כאסף נ. ל. כיוסף/ שלא] מ"ח. ולא.
116 וכה] ד. נתעסק/ שאין] מ"ח. ואין.   118 ממשה] ד. כמשה/ שלא]
מ"ח. ולא.   119 הקב"ה] ד. שכינה.   120 וזקני ביתו] א. ~ וגו'. מ. ~
שנאמר ויעלו עמו עבדי פרעה וזקני ביתו (בראשית נ', ז') ובמקרא כתוב
ויעלו אתו כל עבדי פרעה זקני ביתו.   123–124 והיו אומות העולם
אומרים=ט. מ"ח: א. אומרים. מ. ואומרים היו אומות העולם. ד.
והיו עוברים ושבים אומרים.

would say to the Israelites: What are these two
chests? And the Israelites would say to them:
The one is the ark of the Eternal, and the other
is a coffin with a body in it. The nations then
would say: What is the importance of this coffin
that it should go alongside of the ark of the
Eternal? And the Israelites would say to them:
The one lying in this coffin has fulfilled that
which is written on what lies in that ark. On the
tablets lying in this ark is written: "I am the
Lord thy God" (Ex. 20.2), and of Joseph it is
written: "For, am I in the place of God?" (Gen.
50.19). On the tablets in this ark is written:
"Thou shalt have no other gods before Me"
(Ex. 20.3), and of Joseph it is written: "For I
fear God" (Gen. 42.18). It is written: "Thou
shalt not take the name of the Lord thy God in
vain" (Ex. 20.7), and of Joseph it is written:
"As Pharaoh liveth"[15] (Gen. 42.15). It is written:
"Remember the Sabbath day" (Ex. 20.8), and
of Joseph it is written: "And kill the beasts and
prepare" (Gen. 43.16), which can only mean
"preparing" for the Sabbath, as it is said: "And
it shall come to pass on the sixth day that they
shall prepare" (Ex. 16.5). It is written: "Honour
thy father" (Ex. 20.12), and of Joseph it is
written: "And Israel said unto Joseph: 'Do not

---

[15] He did not take the Name of God in vain (see Gen.
Rab. 91.6).

העולם אומרים להן לישראל מה טיבן של שני

125 ארונות הללו והם אומרים להם זה ארונו של חי
העולמים וזה ארונו של מת והיו אומרים להם אומות
העולם מה טיבו של ארונו של מת שמהלך עם ארון
חי העולמים אמרו להן המונח בארון זה קיים מה
שכתוב במונח בארון זה במונח בארון זה כתיב

130 אנכי יי אלהיך וביוסף כתיב התחת אלהים אני
במונח בארון זה כתיב לא יהיה לך אלהים אחרים
וביוסף כתיב את האלהים אני ירא כתיב לא תשא
וביוסף כתיב חי פרעה כתיב זכור את יום השבת
וביוסף כתיב וטבוח טבח והכן ואין הכן אלא שבת

135 שנאמר והיה ביום הששי והכינו וגו' כתיב כבד את
אביך וביוסף כתיב ויאמר ישראל אל יוסף הלא

130 שמות כ', ב'./ בראשית נ', י"ט.   130—141 סא"ר כ"ד (131).
131 שמות כ', ג'.   132 בראשית מ"ב, י"ח/ שמות כ', ז'.   133 בראשית
מ"ב, ט"ו—ט"ז./ שמות כ', ח'.   134 בראשית מ"ג, ט"ז.   134—135 ב"ר
צ"ב, ד'. עירובין ל"ח, ב'.   135 שמות ט"ז, ה'.   135—136 שם כ', י"ב.
136—138 בראשית ל"ז, י"ג.

124 להן לישראל] א. ט. להן ד. >.   125 והם אומרים להם]
א. אומרים ישראל לאומות העולם ~ שני ארונות הללו.   125—126 והיו
אומרים להם אומות העולם–אסרו להן] א. >.   128 המונח] א.
המת המונח.   130 התחת אלהים אני] א. מ. התחת אלהים אנכי.
134 שבת]–ט. מ"ח: ד. ערב שבת. א"צ. לשבת. ש. לצורך השבת.
135 שנאמר] ד. כתיב הכא והכן וכתיב התם.

thy brethren feed the flock in Shechem? Come,
and I will send thee unto them.' And he said to
him: 'Here am I' " (Gen. 37.13)—he knew that
his brothers hated him and yet he would not
disobey his father's orders. It is written: "Thou
shalt not murder" (Ex. 20.13), and Joseph did
not murder Poti-phera. It is written: "Thou
shalt not commit adultery" (ibid.)—he did not
commit adultery with Poti-phera's wife. It is
written: "Thou shalt not steal" (ibid.)—he did
not steal, as it is said: "And Joseph gathered up
all the money . . . and Joseph brought the
money into Pharaoh's house" (Gen. 47.14). It is
written: "Thou shalt not bear false witness
against thy neighbour" (Ex. 20.13), and Joseph
never told his father what his brothers had done
to him. Now, to reason by the method of *Kal
vaḥomer*, if he would not tell his father even
things that were true about his brothers, how
much less would he tell against them what was
false! It is said: "Thou shalt not covet" (Ex.
20.14)—he did not covet Poti-phera's wife. It is
written: "Thou shalt not hate thy brother in thy
heart" (Lev. 19.17), and of Joseph it says: "And
he comforted them, and spoke kindly unto them"
(Gen. 50.21). It is written: "Thou shalt not take
vengeance, nor bear any grudge" (Lev. 19.18),
and [of Joseph] it is written: "And as for you, ye
meant evil against me; but God meant it for good"

אחיך רועים בשכם לכה ואשלחך אליהם ויאמר
לו הנני יודע היה שאחיו שונאים אותו ולא רצה
לעבור על דברי אביו כתיב לא תרצח ויוסף לא
רצח לפוטיפרע כתיב לא תנאף לא נאף אשתו 140
של פוטיפרע כתיב לא תגנוב לא גנב כענין
שנאמר וילקט יוסף את כל הכסף וגו' כתיב לא
תענה ברעך ויוסף לא הגיד לאביו מה שעשו לו
אחיו והרי דברים קל וחמר ומה דברים של אמת
לא הגיד לאביו של שקר על אחת כמה וכמה כתיב 145
לא תחמוד לא חמד אשתו של פוטיפרע כתיב לא
תשנא את אחיך בלבבך וביוסף אומר וינחם אותם
וידבר על לבם כתיב לא תקום ולא תטור וכתיב
ואתם חשבתם עלי רעה אלהים חשבה לטובה

139 שמות כ', י"ג./ ב"ר פ"ד, י"נ.   140 שמות כ', י"ד./ ב"ר פ"ז, ה'.
141 שמות כ', ט"ו.   142 בראשית מ"ז, י"ד.   142—143 שמות כ', ט"ז.
146 שם כ', י"ז.   146—147 ויקרא י"ט, י"ז.   147—148 בראשית נ', כ"א.
148 ויקרא י"ט, י"ח.   149 בראשית נ', כ'.

139—138 יודע היה-דברי אביו] א. מ. ט. מ"ח. <.   141 גנב]
ק. נ. ~ פרעה. ל. לפרעה. א"צ. של פרעה.   141—142 כענין
שנאמר]—ט: מ. דכתיב. ד. שנאמר.   143—144 ויוסף לא הגיד
לאביו מה שעשו לו אחיו] א. מ. ט. מ"ח. <.   145 הגיד לאביו]
ד. ענה.   146 אשתו של פוטיפרע] ד. אשת פוטיפר.

(Gen. 50.20). It is written: "That thy brother may live with thee"[16] (Lev. 25.36), and of Joseph it is written: "And Joseph sustained his father, and his brethren" (Gen. 47.12).

For He Had Straitly Sworn the Children of Israel. This means he had made them swear for themselves and also that they would impose the oath upon their children.[17]   R. Nathan says: Why did he impose the oath upon his brothers rather than upon his sons?   He thought, if I impose the oath upon my sons the Egyptians might not let them fulfill it. And if they would say to the Egyptians: "Our father has carried his father out," the Egyptians might answer them: "Your father was a king." Therefore he imposed the oath upon his brothers and not upon his sons.

Another Interpretation: Joseph said to them: "My father came down here of his own free will and yet I took him back. I came down here against my will. I impose an oath upon you that you bring me back to the place whence you stole me." And they did so, for it is said: "And the bones of Joseph which the children of Israel brought up out of Egypt, buried they in Shechem"[18] (Josh. 24.32).

---

[16] The last three commandments are not from the Ten Commandments but from the book of Leviticus.   It is assumed that in the ark alongside of the two tablets containing the Ten Commandments there was placed also the whole Book of the Law (see Deut. 31.9 and 26; and cf. B. B. 14a and esp. Yer. Sotah 8.3 (22d), ויש אומרים מצד (הלוחות היה מונח בארון.

כתיב וחי אחיך עמך וביוסף כתיב ויכלכל יוסף ¹⁵⁰
את אביו ואת אחיו.

כי ה ש ב ע ה ש ב י ע השביעם שישביעו לבניהם
רבי נתן אומר מפני מה השביע את אחיו ולא השביע
את בניו אמר אם אני משביע את בני אין המצרים
מניחים אותם ואם אומרים להם אבינו העלה את ¹⁵⁵
אביו הם אומרים להם אביכם מלך היה לפיכך
השביע את אחיו ולא השביע את בניו דבר אחר
אמר להם יוסף אבי ירד כאן לרצונו ואני העלתיו
אני ירדתי על כרחי משביע אני אליכם שממקום
שגנבתוני לשם תחזירוני וכן עשו לו שנאמר ואת ¹⁶⁰
עצמות יוסף אשר העלו בני ישראל ממצרים קברו
בשכם.

---

¹⁵⁰ ויקרא כ״ה, ל״ו.   151—150 בראשית מ״ז, י״ב.   162—152 סוטה
שם. ב״ר כ׳, י״ט. ת. בשלח ב. ש. שם.   162—160 יהושע כ״ד, ל״ב.

---

¹⁵¹ את אביו ואת אחיו] א. מ. ונו׳. ד. את אביו.   ¹⁵⁷ דבר
אחר]=ט: מ. ד. >.   ¹⁵⁹ אני ירדתי] הוספתי=ט. א׳א. א׳צ.
מ״ה./ על כרחי] ד. ~ כי הוא השביעני.

---

[17] The infinitive absolute השבע is interpreted as referring
to another act besides the one in the finite verb.

[18] It was in the neighborhood of Shechem that Joseph
was sold by his brethren (see Gen. 37.12–14 and cf. Sanh.
102a).

God Will Surely Remember You. He will remember you in Egypt and He will also remember you at the sea.[19] He will remember you at the sea and He will also remember you in the wilderness. He will remember you in the wilderness and He will also remember you at the rivers of Arnon. He will remember you in this world and He will also remember you in the world to come.

And Ye Shall Carry Up My Bones Away Hence. I might understand this to mean immediately after his death, but it says: "With you"— when you go up. And whence do we know that they also carried up with them the bones of all the other founders of the tribes? From the expression: "Away hence with you."

And They Took Their Journey from Succoth and Encamped in Etham. Just as Etham is the name of a place so also is Succoth the name of a place. R. Akiba says: Succoth here means only clouds of glory, as it is said: "For over all the glory shall be a canopy" (Isa. 4.5). So far I know only about the past. How about the future? Scripture says: "And there shall be a pavilion for a shadow," etc. (ibid., 4.6). And it also says: "And the ransomed of the Lord shall return and come with singing into Zion, and everlasting joy shall be upon their heads" (ibid., 35.10).

---

[19] The infinitive absolute פקוד is interpreted as indicating another act besides the one indicated in the finite verb.

פ ק ו ד   י פ ק ו ד   א ל ה י ם   א ת כ ם   פקד אתכם
במצרים ויפקוד אתכם על הים פקד אתכם על
165 הים ויפקוד אתכם במדבר פקד אתכם במדבר
ויפקוד אתכם בנחלי ארנון פקד אתכם בעולם הזה
ויפקוד אתכם בעולם הבא.

ו ה ע ל י ת ם   א ת   ע צ מ ו ת י   מ ז ה   שומע אני
מיד תלמוד לומר אתכם כשתהיו עולים ומנין שאף
170 עצמות שאר השבטים העלו עמהם שנאמר מזה
אתכם.

ו י ס ע ו   מ ס כ ו ת   ו י ח נ ו   ב א י ת ם   מה איתם
מקום אף סוכות מקום רבי עקיבא אומר אין סוכות
אלא ענני כבוד שנאמר כי על כבוד חופה אין לי
175 אלא לשעבר לעתיד לבא מנין תלמוד לומר וסוכה
תהיה לצל וגו' ואומר ופדויי יי ישובון ובאו ציון
ברנה ושמחת עולם על ראשם.

167—163 ת. שם.   171—166 סוטה ז', ב'. ב'ר ק', י'א. ש. 40.
177—172 לעיל פסחא י'ד. ש. שם.   174 ישעיה ד', ה'.   176—175 שם
ד', ו'.   177—176 שם ל'ה, י'.

167 בעולם הבא] ט. ~ פקידה במצרים פקידה בסיני פקידה
בניסן פקידה בתשרי.   170 שאר] א. מ. ק. >.   171—170 מזה
אתכם] מ. ט. ת. מובא בש"י. ~ זה שנים עשר.   174 שנאמר]
ד. ~ ובורא יי על מכון הר ציון וכתיב.

And the Lord Went before Them by Day. You will have to say: There were seven clouds: "And the Lord went before them by day in a pillar of cloud;" "And Thy cloud standeth over them, and Thou goest before them in a pillar of cloud" (Num. 14.14); "And when the cloud tarried upon the tabernacle" (ibid., 9.19); "And whenever the cloud was taken up . . . But if the cloud was not taken up . . . For the cloud of the Lord was upon the tabernacle" (Ex. 40.36–38). Thus there were seven clouds, four on the four sides of them, one above them, one beneath them, and one that advanced before them on the road, raising the depressions and lowering the elevations, as it is said: "Every valley shall be lifted up, and every mountain and hill shall be made low; and the rugged shall be made level, and the rough places a plain" (Isa. 40.4). It also killed the snakes and the scorpions, and swept and sprinkled the road before them. R. Judah says: There were thirteen clouds, two on every side, two over them, two beneath them, and one that advanced before them. R. Josiah says: There were four, one in front of them, one behind them, one above them, and one beneath them. Rabbi says: There were only two.

ויי הולך לפניהם יומם נמצאת אומר
שבעה עננים הם ויי הולך לפניהם יומם וגו' ועננך
180 עומד עליהם ובעמוד ענן וגו' ובהאריך הענן
ובהעלות הענן ואם לא יעלה הענן כי ענן יי על
המשכן הא שבעה עננים מארבע רוחותם
ואחד למעלה ואחד למטה ואחד שהיה מהלך
לפניהם כל הנמוך מגביהו וכל הגבוה משפילו
185 שנאמר כל גיא ינשא וכל הר וגבעה ישפלו והיה
העקוב למישור והרכסים לבקעה והיה מכה נחשים
ועקרבים מכבד ומרבץ לפניהם רבי יהודה אומר
שלשה עשר עננים היו שנים לכל רוח ורוח שנים
מלמעלה ושנים מלמטה ואחד שהיה מהלך לפניהם
190 רבי יאשיה אומר ארבעה אחד לפניהם ואחד
לאחריהם אחד למעלה ואחד למטה רבי אומר
שנים.

_____

178–192 ספרי במדבר פ'נ. תנחומא בשלח נ'. ש. שם.   179 במדבר
י"ד, י"ד.   179–180 שם ט', י"ט.   180–181 שמות מ', ל"ו.   181 שמות
מ', ל"ז./ שם מ', ל"ח.   185–187 ישעיה מ', ד'.

_____

179 עננים הם ויי] ד. עננים הם והשם.   179–180 ועננך עומד] ק. נ.
ועננך בעמוד ענן ועננך עומד.   180 וגו'] מ. יומם ד. >.   181 ובהעלות
הענן] א. ובהעלות הארון.   182 הא] ד. >.   184 משפילו] ק. ~
מניכו. א. מ"ח. מסיכו. מ. מסכו. ה. מנסיכו.   192 שנים] מ. ~
שנאמר. א'צ.~ שנאסר ועננך עומד עליהם. עיין ב ב ה"מ.

And the Lord Went Before Them by Day. This is to teach you that with what measure a man metes, it is meted out to him. Abraham accompanied the ministering angels, as it is said: "And Abraham went with them to bring them on the way" (Gen. 18.16), and God accompanied his children in the wilderness forty years, as it is said: "And the Lord went before them by day in a pillar of cloud." About Abraham it is written: "Let now a little water be fetched" (Gen. 18.4), and the Holy One, blessed be He, caused the well to come up for his children in the wilderness, as it is said: "Then sang Israel this song: 'Spring up O well—sing ye unto it' " (Num. 21.17). About Abraham it is written: "And I will fetch a morsel of bread" (Gen. 18.5), and God sent down the manna to his children in the wilderness, as it is said: "Behold, I will cause to rain bread from heaven for you" (Ex. 16.4). About Abraham it is written: "And Abraham ran unto the herd" (Gen. 18.7), and the Holy One, blessed be He, drove up the quail for his children in the wilderness, as it is said: "And there went forth a wind from the Lord and brought across quails from the sea" (Num. 11.31). About Abraham it is written: "And recline yourselves under the tree" (Gen. 18.4), and the Holy One, blessed be He, spread out seven clouds of glory for his children, as it is said: "He spread a cloud for a screen" (Ps. 105.39). About Abraham it is written: "And he

ויי הולך לפניהם יומם ללמדך שבמדה
שאדם מודד בה מודדין לו אברהם ליוה את מלאכי
195 השרת שנאמר ואברהם הולך עמם לשלחם והמקום
ליוה את בניו במדבר ארבעים שנה שנאמר ויי הולך
לפניהם יומם בעמוד ענן באברהם כתיב יוקח נא
מעט מים והקב"ה העלה לבניו את הבאר במדבר
שנאמר אז ישיר ישראל את השירה הזאת עלי באר
200 ענו לה באברהם כתיב ואקחה פת לחם והקב"ה
הוריד לבניו את המן במדבר שנאמר הנני ממטיר
לכם לחם באברהם כתיב ואל הבקר רץ אברהם
וגו' והקב"ה הגיז לבניו את השליו במדבר שנאמר
ורוח נסע מאת יי ויגז שלוים מן הים באברהם כתיב
205 והשענו תחת העץ והקב"ה פרש לבניו שבעה ענני
כבוד שנאמר פרש ענן למסך באברהם כתיב והוא

193—208 תוס' סוטה ד', א'—ו'. ב'ם פ'ו, ב'. ב'ר מ'ח, י'. ת. שם ד'.
195 בראשית י'ח, ט'ז. 195—197 שם י'ח, ד'. 199—200 במדבר כ'א, י'ז.
200 בראשית י'ח, ה'. 201—202 שמות ט'ז, ד'. 202 בראשית י'ח, ז'.
204 במדבר י'א, ל'א. 205 בראשית י'ח, ד'. 206 תהלים ק'ה, ל'ט.
206—207 בראשית י'ח, ח'.

197—202 ד. הסדר מהופך והדרש על ואקחה פת לחם קודם
לוה שעל יוקח נא מעט מים. 201 במדבר] ק. שנה פ'. נ. ל.
ארבעים שנה.

stood by them" (Gen. 18.8), and the Holy One, blessed be He, protected the houses of his children in Egypt, so that they should not be smitten, as it is said: "The Lord will pass over the door" (Ex. 12.23).

And the Lord Went before Them by Day. Is it possible to say so? Has it not already been said: "Do not I fill heaven and earth? Saith the Lord" (Jer. 23.24)? And it is written: "And one called unto another, and said: 'Holy, holy, holy, is the Lord of hosts; the whole earth is full of His glory' " (Isa. 6.3). And it also says: "And, behold, the glory of the God of Israel . . . and the earth did shine with His glory" (Ezek. 43.2). What then does Scripture mean by saying: "And the Lord went before them by day?" Said Rabbi: Antoninus would sometimes continue his court sessions, sitting on the platform, till after dark, and his sons would stay with him there. When leaving the platform, he himself would take a torch and light the way for his sons. The great men of the Empire would approach him saying: "We will take the torch and light the way for your sons." But he would say to them: "It is not that I have no one to take the torch and light the way for my sons. It is merely to show

עומד עליהם והקב״ה הגין על בתי בניו במצרים

כדי שלא יגפו שנאמר ופסח יי על הפתח וגו'.

ו י י ה ו ל ך ל פ נ י ה ם י ו מ ם איפשר לומר כן

210 והלא כבר נאמר הלא את השמים ואת הארץ אני

מלא נאם יי וכתיב וקרא זה אל זה ואמר קדוש

קדוש קדוש יי צבאות מלא כל הארץ כבודו ואומר

והנה כבוד אלהי ישראל וגו' והארץ האירה מכבודו

ומה תלמוד לומר ויי הולך לפניהם אמר רבי

215 אנטונינוס פעמים שהוא דן על הבימה ומחשיך והיו

בניו מחשיכין אצלו אחר שנפטר מן הבימה היה

נוטל את הפנס ומאיר לבניו והיו גדולי מלכות

קרובין אצלו ואומרים לו אנו   נוטלין את הפנס

ונאיר לפני בניך והוא אומר להן לא מפני שאין לי

220 מי שיטול אותו ויאיר לפני בני אלא הרי אני מודיע

---

208 שמות י״ב, כ׳ג.   233–209 ת. שם ה׳.   211–210 ירמיה כ׳ג, כ׳ד.
  212–211 ישעיה ו׳, נ׳.   213 יחזקאל מ׳ג, ב׳.

207 בתי] ק. נ. בני. ל.>.   209 איפשר] מ. אי איפשר.   213 והנה כבוד אלהי ישראל] מ. והנה כבוד יי ישראל. ד. הנה כבוד יי אלהי ישראל.   214 אמר רבי] א. ט. רבי אומר.   215 אנטונינוס] כ. (יואל ד׳, ב') א׳צ. אנטונינוס/ פעמים] ד. לטלך. מ׳ח. א׳צ. הטלך פעמים/ שהוא] ט. שהיה.   218 קרובין] מ׳ח. כ. (שם) קרבין.

you how dear my sons are to me, so that you should treat them with respect." In the same way, God showed the nations of the world how dear the children of Israel were to Him, in that He Himself went before them so that the nations should treat them with respect. But it is not enough that they do not treat them with respect, they even put them to death in all sorts of cruel and strange ways. In accordance with this it says: "I will gather all nations, and will bring them down to the valley of Jehoshaphat" (Joel 4.2). One might think that this is to be on account of their practices of idolatry, of incest and of murder, but it says: "For My people and My heritage Israel whom they have scattered among the nations" (ibid.). It also says: "Egypt shall be a desolation, and Edom shall be a desolate wilderness, for the violence against the children of Judah, because they have shed innocent blood in their land" (ibid., 4.19). At that time "Judah shall be inhabited for ever," etc. . . . "And I will hold as innocent their blood that I have not held as innocent." When will this be? When "the Lord dwelleth in Zion" (ibid., 4.20–21).

לכם חבתם של בני שתהיו נוהגים עמהם בכבוד

כך הודיע הקב״ה חבתן של ישראל לאומות העולם

שהוא בעצמו הלך לפניהם שיהיו נוהגין עמהם

בכבוד ולא דיין שאינם נוהגין עמהם בכבוד אלא

225 שממיתים אותם מיתות חמורות משונות זו מזו ולענין

כן הוא אומר וקבצתי את כל הגוים והורדתם אל

עמק יהושפט יכול על עבודה זרה ועל גילוי עריות

ועל שפיכות דמים תלמוד לומר על עמי ונחלתי

ישראל אשר פזרו בגוים ואומר מצרים לשממה

230 תהיה ואדום למדבר שממה תהיה מחמס בני יהודה

אשר שפכו דם נקי בארצם באותה שעה ויהודה

לעולם תשב וגו׳ ונקתי דמָם לא נקתי אימתי ויי

שוכן בציון.

226—227 יואל ד׳, ב׳.   228—233 שם ד׳, י״ט-כ״א.

222 לאומות העולם] א. מ. לפני כל אומות העולם.   223 שהוא
בעצמו הלך לפניהם] א. מ. ט. >.   224 ולא דיין שאינם]–ט.
מ״ח: מ. > א. ואינם/נוהגין עמהם בכבוד]– ט. מ״ח: מ. > ד.
עושים.   224—225 ולענין כן]מ. לענין כך. א. ולענין מהו מ״ח. לכך.
226 והורדתם] ד. > ט. והורדתים.   227 יהושפט] ד. ~ ונשפטתי
אותם שם. ובמקרא שלפנינו ונשפטתי עמם שם.   229 מצרים] ד.
ומצרים./ לשממה] מ. ט. ד. לשמה.   232 לא נקיתי] ק. נ. ~ ויי
שוכן בציון.   232—233 איתמי ויי שוכן בציון] ל. > ק. ~ונקתי דמם
כשינקם מהם. נ. ~ ונקתי דמם לא נקתי.

The Pillar of Cloud by Day and the Pillar of Fire by Night Departed Not. This scriptural passage tells that while the pillar of cloud was still there, the pillar of fire began to gleam.

Another Interpretation: *The Pillar of Cloud . . . Shall Not Depart.* This passage suggests that you can learn from the Torah what the proper custom on the eve of the Sabbath should be. The pillar of fire should shine forth while the pillar of the cloud is still present.[20]

CHAPTER II
(Ex. 14.1–9)

And the Lord Spoke unto Moses, Saying: "Speak unto the Children of Israel, that They Turn Back and Encamp," etc. R. Simon the son of Yoḥai says: When in any commandment to the people Scripture uses the expression "saying," or "and thou shalt say unto them," that commandment is for all generations. When neither "saying" nor "and thou shalt say unto them" is used, it is only for the time being. Rabbi says: Even when it does not use the expression "saying" or "and thou shalt say unto them" the commandment is for all generations, with the exception of three instances.[1]

---

[20] I. e., the Sabbath light should be kindled on Friday when there is still daylight.

[1] These are: Exod. 14.2; 14.15; and Num. 17.16–17 (see, however, Commentaries).

לא ימיש עמוד הענן מגיד הכתוב עד

235 שעמוד הענן קיים היה עמוד האש צומח דבר אחר

לא ימיש בא הכתוב ללמדך דרך ארץ מן התורה

על ערבי שבתות עד שעמוד הענן קיים יהיה עמוד

האש צומח.

פרשה ב (שמות י"ד, א'.–ח'.)

וידבר יי אל משה לאמר דבר אל

בני ישראל וישובו ויחנו וגו' רבי שמעון

בן יוחאי אומר בכל מקום שהוא אומר לאמר

ואמרת אליהם הרי זה לדורות ובכל מקום שאינו

5 אומר לאמר ואמרת אליהם הרי זה לשעה רבי

אומר אפילו בכל מקום שאינו אומר לאמר ואמרת

אליהם הרי זה לדורות חוץ משלשה מקומות.

238–234 תוס' סוטה ד' ב'. שבת כ"ג, ב'. ש. 40.

231–1 ש. 43–41.

234–235 עד שעמוד הענן. מ. ד. שעדיין עמוד הענן. 237 יהיה]

ד. היה.

3–4 לאמור ואמרת] מ"ח. אמור ואמרת. 4 אליהם] מ"ח. <.

5 לאמר ואמרת] מ"ח. אמור ואמרת.

That They Turn Back and Encamp before Pi-hahiroth. What were those *Ḥiroth?* They were not leaning but tapering to the apex. They were not rectilinear but slightly convex. They were not round but square. They were not the work of man but the work of Heaven. They had eyes as openings. They were a sort of male and female. These are the words of R. Eliezer. R. Joshua says: The *Ḥiroth* were on the one side and Migdol on the other, the sea before them and Egypt behind them.

Another Interpretation: *Pi-hahiroth.* *Ḥiroth* only means the place of the licentiousness of the Egyptians, their market place, the place where their idols were. In the past it had been called Pithom, as it is said, "And they built for Pharaoh store-cities, Pithom and Raamses" (Ex. 1.11). After they changed, it was called Pi-hahiroth, because it estranged its worshipers.—The children of Israel journeyed from Raamses to Suc-

וישובו ויחנו לפני פי החירות מה היו
חירות הללו לא היו משופעות אלא גדודיות לא
10 היו תרטוטות אלא מוקפות לא היו עגולות אלא
מרובעות לא היו מעשה אדם אלא מעשה שמים
ועינים היו להם לפותחות כמין זכר וכמין נקבה
היו דברי רבי אליעזר רבי יהושע אומר החירות
מצד זה ומגדול מצד זה הים   לפניהם ומצרים
15 מאחריהם דבר אחר פי החירות אין חירות אלא
מקום חירותן של מצרים מקום אטלס מקום עבודה
זרה שלהם לשעבר היתה נקראת פיתום שנאמר
ויבן ערי מסכנות לפרעה את פיתום ואת רעמסס
חזרו להם נקראת פי החירות שהיא מאחרת את
20 עובדיה נסעו בני ישראל מרעמסס לסכות ומסכות

18 שמות א', י"א.

8 מה] מ"ח. ל. >. / היו] הוספתי–ט. א"א.   9 חירות] ל. מ"ח.
החירות / נדודיות] ק. נדוריות.   10 תרטוטות] ט. טרטוטות / מוקפות]
ש"ט. משוקעות.   12 לפותחות] ל. פותחות. ט. פתוחות. א"א.
ופתוחות. ל"ט. ש. ספותחות.   16 מצרים] נ. ל. ישראל/ אטלס]=ט:
מ. מ"ח. אטלין (צ"ל אטלין) ש. עטלין (צ"ל עטלין) ש"ט. אטליי.
ד. סובחר להם.   19–17 פיתום–נקראת] א. >.   19 להם נקראת]=
ק. ט: נ. ל. להם להקראות. מ. להקראות. מ"ח. לה ונקראת.
19–20 שהיא מאחרת את עובדיה] ד. שהיא מאחרת לעובדיה.
א"צ. שם נעשו בני ישראל חורין.   20 נסעו] ד. ויסעו.

coth and from Succoth to Etham and from
Etham to the place before Pi-hahiroth. They
started their journey on the day before the
Sabbath, continuing through the Sabbath and
the first day of the week. On the second day of
the week, which was the fourth day of their
journey, they began arranging their things and
preparing their animals to go further. The
Egyptian guards then said to them, "The time
fixed for your return to Egypt has arrived," as
it is said: "We will go three days' journey"
(Ex. 8.23). The Israelites, however, said to
them: "But when we actually went out, did we
go out by leave of Pharaoh?" It says: "On the
morrow after the passover the children of Israel
went out with a high hand" (Num. 33.3). The
guards, however, said to them: "Whether you
are willing or not, you will have to comply with
the orders of the government." The Israelites
then rose up against them, some of them they
smote, some of them they wounded, some of
them they killed. The guards then went back
to report to Pharaoh. Then Moses said to the
Israelites: "Turn back lest Pharaoh say that you
are fleeing." And Moses blew the horn until
they returned to the place before Pi-hahiroth.

לאיתם ומאיתם לפני פי החירות נסעו מערב שבת
ובשבת ובאחד בשבת בשני בשבת שהוא רביעי
לנסיעתן התחילו ישראל מתקנין את כליהם ומציעין
בהמתם לצאת אמרו להם האקטורין הגיעה
25   פרותיזמיה שלכם לחזור למצרים שנאמר דרך
שלשת ימים וגו' אמרו להם ישראל וכשיצאנו ברשות
פרעה יצאנו שנאמר ממחרת הפסח יצאו בני ישראל
ביד רמה אמרו להם האקטורין רוצין ולא רוצין
סופכם לקיים דברי מלכות עמדו עליהם ישראל
30   הכו מהם פצעו מהם הרגו מהם הלכו והגידו לפרעה
אמר להם משה חזרו לאחוריכם שלא יאמר פרעה
שאתם בורחין תקע משה קרן עד שחזרו לפני פי

21—23 לקמן ויסע ב'. סע"ר ה'. סע"ר ה'. שבת פ"ו, ב'. פ"ח, א'. פס"ר
החודש (ע"ח, א.) פסדר"כ החודש (נ"ד, ב'.)   25—26 שמות ח', כ"נ.
27—28 במדבר ל"ג, נ'.

21—22 נסעו מערב שבתובשבת]=ט. מ"ח: ד. יום חמישי נסעו ממצרים
ובאו עד רעמסס וביום ששי ובשבת שבתו שם. 22 בשני בשבת] הוספתי~
ט. ש./ שהוא רביעי] מ. שהוא שלישי. מ"ח. וברביעי. 23 ומציעין]
מ"ח. ומסיעין. 25 פרותיזמיה] א. פרותזומיא. ד. פרותימיה. מ"ח.
פריטנמה. 26 וכשיצאנו] ק. ל. כשיצאנו. נ. כשיצאו. ש. כיון שיצאנו
ממצרים. 27—26 ברשות פרעה יצאונו] ט. ברשות מי יצאנו. ש. יצאנו
ברשות פרעה. 31 חזרו] א. וחזרו/ לאחוריכם]=ט. מ"ח. ל: ק. נ.
לאחוריכם. א. לאחוריהם. 33—31 שלא יאמר-פי החירות] א. מ. ט.
מ"ח. ˂.

As soon as the horn began to blow for the return, those of little faith among the Israelites began plucking their hair and tearing their garments until Moses said to them: "It has been told to me by the word of God that you are free men." Therefore it says: "That they turn back and encamp," etc.

Between Migdol and the Sea. There was the greatness of the Egyptians, there was their glory, there they celebrated their *mayouma*[2]-festivals, there Joseph had brought together all the silver and all the gold, as it is said: "And Joseph gathered up all the money," etc. (Gen. 47.14).

Before Baal-zephon. Baal-zephon alone was left of all the deities, to mislead the minds of the Egyptians. To him applies the scriptural passage: "He misleadeth the nations and destroyeth them" (Job 12.23).

And Pharaoh Will Say of the Children of Israel: They Are Entangled (Nebukim) in the Land. The word *Nebukim* means perplexed, as in the passage: "How do the beasts groan! The herds of cattle are perplexed" (Joel 1.18). Another Interpretation: *Nebukim.* The word

---

[2] See S. Krauss, *Lehnwörter*, I, p. 95 and II, p. 334; also Böhmer in *Kerem Ḥemed*, VIII, p. 13.

החירות כיון שתקעה קרן לחזור התחילו מחוסרי
אמנה שבישראל מתלשין שערן ומקרעין כסותן עד
35 שאמר להם משה מפי הגבורה נאמר לי שאתם בני
חורין לכך נאמר וישובו ויחנו וגו׳.

ב י ן מ ג ד ו ל ו ב י ן ה י ם שם היתה גדולתן
של מצריים שם היתה תפארתם שם היתה מיומס
שלהם שם כנס יוסף את הכסף ואת הזהב שנאמר
40 וילקט יוסף את כל הכסף וגו׳.

ל פ נ י ב ע ל צ פ ו ן בעל צפון נשתייר מכל
היראות בשביל לפתות לבן של מצרים ועליו הוא
אומר משגיא לגוים ויאבדם.

ו א מ ר פ ר ע ה ל ב נ י י ש ר א ל נבוכים
45 ה ם ב א ר ץ אין נבוכים אלא מטורפים שנאמר מה
נאנחה בהמה נבוכו עדרי בקר דבר אחר נבוכים

---

40 בראשית מ״ז, י״ד.   43 איוב י״ב, כ״נ.   45—46 יואל א׳, י״ח.

---

33 שתקעה] ד. שתקע / קרן לחזור] ד. >.   34 שבישראל]
ד. >.   38 מיומס] ט. מקום מיומס. ק. מקום מיומס. נ. ל. מקום
מרומם.   42 היראות] ד. ~ שלהן נכחו תחנו על הים/ של מצרים] ד. ~
להטעותם שהוא הציל את עצמו.   42—43 ועליו הוא אומר משגיא לגוים
ויאבדם] מ. > א. ט. מ״ח. ~נכחו תחנו על הים בשביל לפתות לבן
של מצרים.   44 ואמר פרעה] מ. שנאמר ואמר פרעה.   46 נבוכו עדרי
בקר] א. נבוכו כל וגו׳. ד. נבוכה וגו׳. מ״ח. נבוכו עדרי צאן.

Nebukim means confounded, as in the passage:
"And the king and Haman sat down to drink; but
the city of Shushan was confounded" (Esth. 3.15).
Another Interpretation: *And Pharaoh Will Say.*
But he did not know what he was saying. He
said: "Moses has led them astray, he did not
know where he was leading them." For it says:
Nebukim, etc. and *Nebukim* here only alludes to
Moses, for it says: "Get thee up into this
mountain of Abarim, unto mount Nebo"[3] (Deut.
32.49).

Another Interpretation: *And Pharaoh Will Say*
—but without realizing what he was saying—:
"The Israelites are bound to cry in the wilderness." As it is said: "And all the congregation
lifted up their voice, and cried" (Num. 14.1).

Another Interpretation: *And Pharaoh Will Say*
—but without realizing what he was saying—:
"The Israelites are bound to fall in the wilderness." As it is said: "Your carcasses shall fall
in this wilderness," etc. (ibid., 14.29).

The Wilderness Hath Shut Them In. As soon
as the Israelites saw the sea storming and the
enemy pursuing them, they turned towards the
wilderness. Immediately the Holy One, blessed
be He, ordered wild beasts to come there and
they did not let them cross, as it is said: "He
shut the wilderness against them." For "shutting" here can only mean by wild beasts. As it
says: "My God hath sent His angels and hath
shut the lions' mouths" (Dan. 6.23).

---

[3] The first part of the Hebrew word נבוכים was taken as
an allusion to Nebo, the place where Moses was buried.

אין נבוכים אלא מעורבבין שנאמר והמלך והמן
ישבו לשתות והעיר שושן נבוכה דבר אחר ואמר
פרעה ולא ידע מה אמר משה הטען ולא היה
יודע להיכן מוליכן שנאמר נבוכים וגו' ואין נבוכים ₅₀
אלא משה שנאמר עלה אל הר העברים הזה הר
נבו דבר אחר ואמר פרעה ולא ידע מה אמר
עתידין ישראל לבכות במדבר שנאמר ותשא כל
העדה ויתנו את קולם ויבכו דבר אחר ואמר פרעה
ולא ידע מה אמר עתידין לישראל לנפול במדבר ₅₅
שנאמר במדבר הזה יפלו וגו'.

סגר עליהם המדבר כיון שראו ישראל
הים סוער ושונא רודף הפכו פניהם למדבר מיד
זימן הקב"ה חיות רעות ולא היו מניחות אותם
לעבור שנאמר סגר עליהם המדבר ואין סגירה ₆₀
אלא רעה חיה שנאמר אלהי שלח מלאכיה וסגר
פום אריותא.

47—48 אסתר נ', ט'ו.   51 דברים ל"ב, פ"ט.   53—54 במדבר י"ד, א'.
56 שם י"ד, כ"ט.   57—62 שמו"ר כ"א, ה'.   61—62 דניאל ו', כ"ג.

48 דבר אחר]=ט. מ"ח: מ. ד. <.   49 אמר 2] א. ד. <.
53 עתידין] א. שעתידין/לבכות] מ. ליפול.   55 עתידין] א. שעתידין.
58 סוער] מ. ש. סוגר / ושונא רודף] ד. < / מיד] א. ד. <.
59 זימן] א. ד. ~ להם.

And I Will Harden the Heart of Pharaoh, etc.
For Pharaoh was not wholly decided in his mind
whether to pursue or not.

*And I Will Get Me Honour upon Pharaoh and
upon All His Host.* Pharaoh was the first to sin
and he was also the first to be punished. In like
manner you interpret: "And He blotted out every
living substance," etc. (Gen. 7.23). In like
manner you interpret: "And I will smite all the
first-born in the land of Egypt," etc. (Ex. 12.12).
In like manner you must interpret: "Thou shalt
surely smite," etc. (Deut. 13.16). Likewise also:
"And her belly shall swell," etc. (Num. 5.27)—
that part of the body which was first to sin was
also the first to be punished. And so also here,
you interpret: "And I will get Me honour upon
Pharaoh," etc. Pharaoh was first to sin and he
was also the first to be punished. Now by using
the method of *Kal vaḥomer*, you argue: If in the
case of punishing evil deeds, which is of less
importance, the rule is that he who sins first is
first punished, how much the more should this be
the rule in rewarding good deeds, which is of
greater importance.

Another Interpretation: *And I Will Get Me*

וחזקתי את לב פרעה וגו' שהיה לבו
חלוק אם לרדוף אם לא לרדוף.

‎65   ואכבדה בפרעה ובכל חילו פרעה
התחיל בעבירה תחלה וממנו התחילה הפורענות
כיוצא בו וימח את כל היקום וגו' כיוצא בו אתה
אומר והכתי כל בכור בארץ מצרים וגו' כיוצא
בו הכה תכה וגו' כיוצא בו וצבתה בטנה אבר
‎70   שהתחיל בעבירה תחלה ממנו התחילה הפורענות
ואף כאן אתה אומר ואכבדה בפרעה פרעה התחיל
בעבירה תחלה ממנו התחילה הפורענות והרי
דברים קל וחמר ומה אם מדת הפורענות מעוטה
מי שהתחיל בעבירה תחלה ממנו התחילה הפורענות
‎75   קל וחומר למדת הטובה מרובה דבר אחר ואכבדה

‎75—65 לעיל פסחא ז'.   ‎67 בראשית ז', כ'ג.   ‎68 שמות י'ב, י'ב.
‎69 דברים י'ג, ט'ו. / במדבר ה', כ'ז.

‎66 בעבירה תחלה] ד. בעברה שנאמר כל הבן הילוד / הפורענות]
ד. ~ טבע הוא וכל חילו.   ‎67—68 כיוצא בו אתה-בארץ מצרים וגו'] ד. >.
‎68—69 כיוצא בו הכה תכה וגו'] ד. כיוצא בו ואת האנשים אשר פתח
הבית וגו' מי שהתחיל בעבירה בו וגו'.   ‎69—70 כיוצא בו וצבתה-התחילה
הפורענות] ק. וכן אבר שהתחילה מסנו וגו'. נ. ל. >.   ‎74 בעב'רה] מ.
בעולם.   ‎75 ק'ו למדת הטובה מרובה] ק. נ. ל. סדה ל. ~ טובה)
מרובה לא כל שכן/ דבר אחר] א'צ. >.

Honour upon Pharaoh. Scripture here tells that when God punishes the nations, His name becomes renowned in the world, as it is said: "And I will work a sign among them, and I will send such as escape of them unto the nations," etc. (Isa. 66.19). And it also says: "Thus saith the Lord: 'The labour of Egypt, and the merchandise of Ethiopia, and of the Sabeans, men of stature shall come unto thee, and they shall be thine; they shall go after thee, in chains they shall come over; and they shall fall down unto thee, they shall make supplication unto thee: Surely, God is in thee and there is none else, there is no other God'" (ibid., 45.14). And what is said after this? "Verily Thou art a God that hidest Thyself, O God of Israel, the Saviour" (ibid., 45.15). And it also says: "And I will plead against him with pestilence and with blood," etc. And after this: "Thus will I magnify Myself and sanctify Myself," etc. (Ezek. 38.22–23). And it is also written: "In Salem also is set His tabernacle," etc. "There He broke the fiery shafts of the bow; the shield, and the sword, and the battle. Selah" (Ps. 76.3–4), and it is written: "In Judah is God known; His name is great in Israel" (ibid., v. 1). And thus also it is written here: "And the Egyptians shall know that I am the Lord." In the past they did not know the Lord, but here it is said: "And the Egyptians shall know that I am the Lord."

בפרעה מגיד הכתוב שכשהמקום נפרע מן האומות

שמו מתגדל בעולם שנאמר ושמתי בהם אות ושלחתי

מהם פלטים וגו' ואומר כה אמר יי יגיע מצרים

וסחר כוש וסבאים אנשי מדה עליך יעבורו ולך

80 יהיו אחריך ילכו בזיקים יעבורו ואליך ישתחוו

ואליך יתפללו אך בך אל ואין עוד אפס אלהים

ואחריו מה הוא אומר אתה אל מסתתר אלהי

ישראל מושיע ואומר ונשפטתי אתו בדבר ובדם

וגו' ואחר כך והתגדלתי והתקדשתי וגו' וכתיב ויהי

85 בשלם סכו וגו' שמה שבר רשפי קשת מגן וחרב

ומלחמה סלה וכתיב נודע ביהודה אלהים בישראל

גדול שמו ולכך כתיב וידעו מצרים כי אני יי לשעבר

לא היו יודעין את יי אבל כאן וידעו מצרים כי אני

יי.

77–78 ישעיה ס'ו, י'ט.   78–81 שם מ'ה, י'ד.   82–83 שם מ'ה, ט'ו.
83–84 יחזקאל ל'ח, כ'ב–כ'נ.   84–86 תהלים ע'ו, נ'–ד'.   86–87 שם
ע'ו, ב'.

---

76 שכשהמקום] ט. שכשיבא הקב'ה/ נפרע] ד. פורע. ט. לפרוע/
מן האומות] א. מן המצריים. מ. מן האומה זו. ט. ל'ט. מן האומה.
ש. מן הרשעים.   79–81 וסבאים–אפס אלהים] א. מ. וגו'.   81 ק. נ.
ואליך יתפללו בך ואין עוד.   82 אתה אל] מ. אכן אל.   83 ואומר]
ד. וכתוב אחר אומר. א. ואחריו מהו אומר. ט. וכן הוא אומר.
86 וכתיב] א. אחריו מהו אומר. ד. <.   87 גדול] ק. נ. קדוש.

And They Did So. This is to proclaim the wisdom of Israel in that they did not say: "How can we turn back," for fear lest they break the hearts of the women and children that were with them.

Another Interpretation: *And They Did So.* They said: Whether we are willing or not there is nothing else for us to do but to obey the command of the son of Amram.

And It Was Told the King of Egypt. Who told him? The guards whom he had sent with them. Some say he had regular posts of guards. And some say, Amalek told him.

That the People Were Fled. And were they really fleeing? Has it not already been said: "On the morrow after the passover the children of Israel went out with a high hand" (Num. 33.3)? Why then does it say: "that the people were fled"? Merely because the guards, beaten by the Israelites, went and reported to Pharaoh, saying: "They smote some of us, they wounded some of us and they killed some of us, without any man restraining them. They have no ruler nor chief," just as it is said, "The locusts have no king" (Prov. 30.27).

90   ויעשו כן להודיע חכמתם של ישראל שלא
אמרו היאך אנו חוזרין לאחורינו שלא לשבור לב
טף ונשים שעמהם דבר אחר ויעשו כן אמרו רוצין
ולא רוצין אין לנו אלא דברי בן עמרם.

ויוגד למלך מצרים מי הגיד לו האקטורין
95 שלו ויש אומרים דידכיות היו לו ויש אומרים עמלק
הגיד לו.

כי ברח העם וכי בורחים היו והלא כבר
נאמר ממחרת הפסח יצאו בני ישראל ביד רמה
ומה תלמוד לומר כי ברח העם אלא מתוך שהכו
100 את האקטורין שלו הלכו והגידו לפרעה ואמרו לו
הכו ממנו פצעו ממנו והרגו ממנו ולא מיחה אדם
בידם אין להם לא מושל ולא שר כענין שנאמר
מלך אין לארבה וגו'.

---

98 במדבר ל"ג, נ'.   103 משלי ל', כ"ז.

---

93 לנו] ד. ~ לעשות.   95 דידכיות]=ט"כ: מ. ק. דורביות.
נ. ל. דורכיות. ט. דידכאות. ש. דידבאות. מ"ח. דיתכאות.
99 בני] ק. נ. <.   100 ואמרו לו] ד. ~ ראה ישראל.   103 לארבה]
מ. לו לארבה.

And the Heart of Pharaoh and of His Servants Was Turned, etc. Formerly: "And Pharaoh's servants said unto him: 'How long shall this man be a snare unto us? Let the men go' " (Ex. 10.7), but now, "And the heart of Pharaoh and of his servants was turned, and they said: 'What is this we have done, that we have let Israel go?' " They said: If we had been plagued without letting them go, it would have been enough. But we were plagued and let them go. Or, if we had been plagued and let them go without our money being taken, it would have been enough. But we were plagued, let them go, and our money was taken. A parable. To what can this be compared? To one who said to his slave: "Go get me a fish from the market." The slave went and brought him an ill-smelling fish. He said to the slave: "I decree that you eat the fish or receive a hundred lashes, or you pay a hundred *manah*." The slave said: "I will eat it." He began to eat, but could not finish. He, therefore, said: "I will take the lashes." After receiving sixty lashes, he could stand no more. He therefore said: "I will pay the hundred *manah*." The result was that he ate the fish, received lashes, and paid a hundred *manah*. So also it was done to the Egyptians. They were plagued, they let Israel go, and their money was taken.

ויהפך לבב פרעה וגו' לשעבר ויאמרו

105 עבדי פרעה אליו עד מתי יהיה זה לנו למוקש שלח

את האנשים ועכשיו ויהפך לבב פרעה ועבדיו

ויאמרו מה זאת עשינו כי שלחנו את ישראל אמרו

אלו לקינו ולא שלחנו כדי הוא אלא לקינו ושלחנו

או אלו לקינו ושלחנו ולא ניטל ממוננו כדי הוא

110 אלא לקינו ושלחנו וניטל ממוננו משל למה הדבר

דומה לאחד שאמר לעבדו צא והבא לי דג מן השוק

יצא והביא לו דג מן השוק מבאיש אמר. לו בגזירה

שתאכל את הדג או שתלקה מאה מכות או שתתן

מאה מנה אמר הריני אוכל התחיל לאכול ולא

115 הספיק לגמור עד שאמר הריני לוקה לקה ששים

לא הספיק לגמור עד שאמר הריני נותן מאה מנה

נמצא אוכל את הדג ולוקה מכות ונותן מאה מנה

כך נעשה למצרים לקו ושלחו וניטל ממונם דבר

104—106 שמות י', ז'.

105—106 שלח את האנשים] הוספתי: א. מ. וגו'.   107 כי שלחנו]
הוספתי: ד. וגו'.   108 אלא לקינו ושלחנו] ד. >.   109 או אילו] ד.
או לא.   113 שתתן] ד. ~ לי.   115—116 עד שאמר-הספיק לגמור]
מ. >.

Another Interpretation: *Was Turned.* This passage tells that when the Israelites went out of Egypt, the rule of the Egyptians ceased, for it says: "Who are our servants?"[4]

Another Interpretation: *Who Are Our Servants?* They said: "Now all the nations will noise it abroad against us like a bell and will say: 'Even those who were in their power they had to let go' —Now, how will we be able to send officers and taskmasters to bring us male and female slaves from Aram-naharaim and Aram-zobah?" This teaches you that Pharaoh ruled from one end of the world to the other and had governors from one end of the world to the other, for the sake of the honor of Israel.[5] Of him it is said: "The king sent and loosed him; even the ruler of peoples and set him free" (Ps. 105.20). And so you will find that every nation or tongue that subjugated Israel ruled from one end of the world to the other for the sake of the honor of Israel. What does it say of the Assyrian empire? "And my

---

[4] The Hebrew word מעבדנו is interpreted as if it read מִי עֲבָדֵינוּ.

[5] It is less of an humiliation to be oppressed by a mighty empire.

אחר ויהפך מגיד הכתוב שכשיצאו ישראל ממצרים
120 בטלה מלכותם של מצרים שנאמר מעבדינו דבר
אחר מעבדינו אמרו עכשיו יהיו כל אומות העולם
מקישות עלינו כזוג ואומרים ומה אם אלו שהיו
ברשותם הניחום והלכו להם עכשיו היאך אנו
שולחים לארם נהרים ולארם צובא פקידים ושרי
125 מסים להביא לנו עבדים ושפחות ללמדך שהיה
פרעה שולט מסוף העולם ועד סופו והיו לו שלטונים
מסוף העולם ועד סופו בשביל כבודן של ישראל
עליו הוא אומר שלח מלך ויתירהו מושל עמים
ויפתחהו וכן אתה מוצא שכל אומה ולשון ששיעבדה
130 את ישראל שלטה מסוף העולם ועד סופו בשביל
כבודן של ישראל במלכות אשור מהו אומר ותמצא

128–129 תהלים ק"ה, כ'.   131–134 ישעיה י', י"ד.

---

120 מעבדינו]=ט: כ. (ישעיה י', י"ד) מ"ח. ויאמרו מה זאת
עשינו כי שלחנו את ישראל מעבדנו. מ. ד. ססי נעמת רדה והשכבה
את ערלים (יחזקאל ל"ב, י"ט)   120–121 ד"א מעבדינו אמרו] מ. כי
שלחנו את ישראל מעבדנו אמרו ד. >.   122 כזוג] א. >.   123 ברשותם
הניחום] כ. (שם) מ"ח. ברשותנו הנחנום / עכשיו] ד.>./ אנו] ל. הם.
124–125 פקידים ושרי מסים] ד. להעלות להם מס.   125 להביא לנו]
ד. ולהביא להם.   127 126– שלטונים–ועד סופו] א. שלטונות על העולם
כולו.   129–130 ששיעבדה את] ד. ששלטה על.   131 במלכות]=ט:
מ"ח. במלך. מ. ד. במלכי.

hand hath found as a nest the riches of the peoples; and as one gathereth eggs that are forsaken, have I gathered all the earth; and there was none that moved the wing, or that opened the mouth, or chirped" (Isa. 10.14). What does it say of the Babylonian empire? "And it shall come to pass, that the nation and the kingdom which will not serve the same Nebuchadnezzar king of Babylon," etc. (Jer. 27.8). What does it say of the kingdom of the Medes? "Then king Darius wrote unto all the peoples," etc. (Dan. 6.26). What does it say of the Greek kingdom? "The beast had also four heads; and dominion was given to it" (ibid., 7.6). What does it say of the fourth kingdom? "And shall devour the whole earth, and shall tread it down and break it in pieces" (ibid., 7.23). Thus you learn that every nation or kingdom that subjugated Israel ruled from one end of the world to the other for the sake of the honor of Israel.

Another Interpretation: *And the Heart of Pharaoh and of His Servants Was Turned.* They said: "Has not much good come to us on their account?" R. Jose the Galilean, giving a parable, says: To what can this be compared? To a man to whom there has fallen as an inheritance a *bet-kor*[6] of land which he sold for a trifle. The buyer, however, went and opened up wells in it,

---

[6] Measurements of fields are usually indicated by the amount of seed that can be sowed on them. A *bet-kor* of land, then, is a field requiring a *kor* of seed. See Jastrow, *Dictionary*, p. 625 and cf. *JE*, XII, 487–489, s. v. Weights and Measures.

כָכֵן ידי לחיל העמים וכאסוף ביצים עזובות כל
הארץ אני אספתי ולא היה נודד כנף ופוצה פה
ומצפצף במלכות בבל מהו אומר והיה הגוי

135 והממלכה אשר לא יעבדו את נבוכדנצר וגו'
במלכות מדי מהו אומר באדיין דריוש מלכא כתב
לכל עממיא וגומר במלכות יון מהו אומר וארבעה
ראשין לחיותא ושולטן יהיב לה במלכות רביעית
מהו אומר ותיכול כל ארעא ותדושנה ותדקינה

140 הא למדת שכל אומה ומלכות ששעבדה את ישראל
שלטה מסוף העולם ועד סופו בשביל כבודן של
ישראל דבר אחר ויהפך וגו' אמרו לא בשבילן
היתה טובה באה עלינו רבי יוסי הגלילי אומר משל
למה הדבר דומה לאדם שנפלה לו בית כור בירושה

145 ומכרה בדבר מועט הלך הלוקח ופתח בה מעיינות

134—135 ירמיה כ"ו, ח'.   135—136 דניאל ו', כ"ו.   137—138 דניאל
ז', ו'.   139 דניאל ז', כ"ג.   143—154 שהש"ר ד', י"נ. שמו"ר כ', ב'.

135 יעבדו את] במקרא שלפנינו, יעבדו אותו את.   136 כתב]
א. שלח.   138 ושולטן] מ. די שולטן / רביעית] מ"ח. חייבת.
142 דבר אחר] א. א'צ. > / לא] נ. לו. ט. >. / עלינו] ד. ~
בתסיהה.

and planted gardens, trees and orchards in it. The seller, seeing this, began to choke with grief. So it happened to the Egyptians who let go without realizing what they let go. Of them it is stated in the traditional sacred writings: "Thy shoots[7] are a park of pomegranates," etc. (Cant. 4.13).

Another Interpretation: R. Simon the son of Yoḥai, giving a parable, says: To what can this be compared? To a man to whom there had fallen as an inheritance a residence in a far off country which he sold for a trifle. The buyer, however, went and discovered in it hidden treasures and stores of silver and of gold, of precious stones and pearls. The seller, seeing this, began to choke with grief. So also did the Egyptians, who let go without realizing what they let go. For it is written: "And they said: 'What is this we have done that we have let Israel go'," etc.

And He Made Ready His Chariot. Pharaoh with his own hands made it ready. It is customary for kings to stand by while others arrange for them the equipment of the chariot and make it ready. But here Pharaoh with his own hands made ready his chariot and arranged its equipment. When the nobles of the kingdom saw him

---

[7] The Hebrew word for "shoots," שלחיך, can also be interpreted to mean, "Those whom thou hast sent away."

ונטע בה גנות ואילנות ופרדסים התחיל המוכר
נחנק כך נעשה למצרים ששלחו ולא ידעו מה שלחו
עליהם מפורש בקבלה שלחיך פרדס רמונים וגו'
דבר אחר רבי שמעון בן יוחאי אומר משל למה

150 הדבר דומה לאחד שנפלה לו פלטרית במדינת הים
בירושה ומכרה בדבר מועט והלך הלוקח ומצא
בה מטמוניות ואוצרות של כסף ושל זהב ושל אבנים
טובות ומרגליות התחיל המוכר נחנק כך עשו מצרים
ששלחו ולא ידעו מה שלחו דכתיב ויאמרו מה זאת

155 עשינו כי שלחנו וגו'.

ויאסור את רכבו הוא בידו אסרו דרך
מלכים להיות עומדים ואחרים מציעין להם תשמיש
המרכבה ואוסרין אותה אבל כאן הוא בידו אסרו
והציע תשמישי רכבו כיון שראו גדולי מלכות שהוא

---

148 שה"ש ד', י"נ.

---

147 נחנק] ד. ליחנק ~ על שנתן ירושתו בדבר מועט.
148—154 עליהם מפורש-מה שלחו] מ. >.   151 הלוקח] ד. ~
וחפרה.   154—155 דכתיב ויאמרו-וגו'] מ. ואמרו מה זאת עשית לנו וגו'.
157—158 תשמיש המרכבה ואוסרין אותה] א. מ. ט. >.   158 כאן] ד.
פרעה הרשע.   159 והציע תשמישי רכבו] א. מ. ט. >.   159—160 שהוא
עומד ומציע לעצמו] מ. ד. >.

getting up and arranging his own, every one of them got up and arranged his own.

There were four who did their harnessing with joy. Abraham harnessed with joy, as it is said: "And Abraham rose early in the morning, and saddled his ass" (Gen. 22.3). Balaam harnessed with joy, as it said: "And Balaam rose up in the morning, and saddled his ass" (Num. 22.21). Joseph harnessed with joy, as it is said: "And Joseph made ready his chariot" (Gen. 46.29). Pharaoh harnessed with joy, as it is said: "And he made ready his chariot." Let the work of saddling which our father Abraham did in order to go and do the will of his Creator come and stand out against the work of saddling which Balaam, the wicked, did in order to go and curse Israel. Let the work of making ready the chariot done by Joseph in order to go to meet his father come and stand out against the work of making ready the chariot done by Pharaoh in order to go and pursue the Israelites.

Another Interpretation: R. Simon the son of Yoḥai says: Let the "sword" and the "hand"

עומד ומציע לעצמו עמד כל אחד ואחד והציע 160
לעצמו ארבעה אסרו בשמחה אברהם אסר בשמחה
שנאמר וישכם אברהם בבקר ויחבש את חמורו
בלעם אסר בשמחה שנאמר ויקם בלעם בבקר
ויחבש את אתונו יוסף אסר בשמחה שנאמר ויאסר
יוסף מרכבתו וגו' פרעה אסר בשמחה שנאמר 165
ויאסור את רכבו תבא חבשה שחבש אברהם אבינו
לילך לעשות רצון קונו ותעמוד על חבשה שחבש
בלעם הרשע לילך לקלל את ישראל תבא אסרה
שאסר יוסף לעלות לקראת אביו ותעמוד על אסרה
שאסר פרעה הרשע לילך לרדוף את ישראל דבר 170
אחר רבי שמעון בן יוחאי אומר תבא חרב יד ותעמד

161–174 ב"ר נ"ה, ח'.   161–164 סנהדרין ק"ה, ב'.   162 בראשית
כ"ב, נ'.   163–164 במדבר כ"ב, כ"א.   164–165 בראשית מ"ו, כ"ט.
165–166 במ"ר כ', י"ב. ת. בלק ח'. ת. בובער שם י"א.

160–161 עמד כל אחד–לעצמו] ק. נ. ל. עמדו כולם ואסרו
(ל. והציעו) מרכבותיהם והציעו לעצמן.   162 חמורו] ד. ~ ולא
היו לו כמה עבדים אלא לכבוד המקום.   165 וגו'] ד. ולא היו לו כמה
עבדים אלא לכבוד אבא.   166–167 שחבש א'א לילך] ד. של אברהם
שהלך.   167 קונו] ד. המקום.   167–168 שחבש–לילך] ד. של בלעם
שהלך.   171–172 תבא חרב יד ותעמוד על חרב יד] ד. >.

come and stand out against the sword and the hand. Let the sword and the hand used by our father Abraham when going to slay his son, as it is said: "And Abraham stretched forth his hand and took the knife to slay his son" (Gen. 22.10), come and stand out against the sword and the hand used by Pharaoh when going to pursue the Israelites, as it is said: "I will draw my sword, my hand shall destroy them" (Ex. 15.9).

And Took His People with Him. He attracted them with words. He said to them: "It is the custom of kings to direct from the rear while their armies advance before them; but I will advance before you," as it is said: "And when Pharaoh drew nigh" (Ex. 14.10). "It is the custom of kings to plunder for themselves and to take their share first; but I will share with you equally in the spoil," as it is said: "I will divide the spoil" (ibid., 15.9). "And what is more, I will open to you the treasures of silver and gold, of precious stones and pearls and distribute them among you." In this sense it is said: "And took his people with him." He got them with words.

על חרב יד תבא חרב יד שעשה אבינו אברהם

לילך לשחוט את בנו שנאמר וישלח אברהם את

ידו ויקח את המאכלת לשחוט את בנו ותעמד על

175 חרב יד שעשה פרעה הרשע לילך לרדוף אחרי

ישראל שנאמר אריק חרבי תורישמו ידי.

ואת עמו לקח עמו לקחם עמו בדברים

אמר להם דרך מלכים להיות מנהגין בסוף

וחיילותיהם מקדמין לפניהם אבל אני אקדם

180 לפניכם שנאמר ופרעה הקריב דרך מלכים להיות

בוזזין לעצמן ונוטלין חלק בראש אני אשוה לכם

בבזה שנאמר אחלק שלל ולא עוד אלא שאני פותח

לכם אוצרות של כסף ושל זהב ושל אבנים טובות

ומרגליות ומחלק לכם לכך נאמר ואת עמו לקח

185 עמו לקחם עמו בדברים.

173—174 בראשית כ״ב, י׳.   176 שמות ט״ו, ט׳.   180 שם י״ד, י׳.

172—173 שעשה אבינו אברהם לילך לשחוט את בנו] ד. >.
173—174 שנאמר וישלח—את בנו] א. מ. > ד. דכתיב באברהם ויקח את
המאכלת.   177 לקחם עמו] ד. שלקחם.   178 מלכים] ק. נ. בני
מלכים.   180 מלכים] ק. נ. בני מלכים.   180—181 להיות בוזזין לעצמן
ונוטלין] ד. כל העם בוזזין ונוטנין לפניו והוא נטל.   182 ולא עוד—
פותח] ד. ועוד שאני אפתח.   184 ומחלק] ד. ואתן.

And He Took Six Hundred Chosen Chariots.
Whose were the beasts that drew the chariots?
Should you say they belonged to the Egyptians—
has it not already been said: "And all the cattle
of Egypt died" (Ex. 9.6)? Should you say they
belonged to Pharaoh—has it not already been
said: "Behold, the hand of the Lord is upon thy
cattle" (ibid., 9.3)? Should you say they belonged to the Israelites—has it not already been
said: "Our cattle also shall go with us; there
shall not a hoof be left behind" (ibid., 10.26)?
To whom then did they belong? To those "that
feared of the Lord among the servants of Pharaoh."[8] We thus learn that even those that feared
the Lord among the servants of Pharaoh became
a snare for Israel. In this connection R. Simon
the son of Yoḥai said: "The nicest among the
idolaters,—kill![9] The best of serpents—smash its
brains." R. Simon b. Gamaliel says: Come and
see the wealth and the greatness of this wicked
empire.[10] Not one of its numerous legions is idle,
for all of them are running about day and night.
Compare with them those of Egypt, and all of
them were idle at that.

---

[8] Their cattle was spared, since they heeded the warning
of Moses (Ex. 9.20).

[9] See on this saying M. Joel, *Gutachten über den Talmud*
(Breslau, 1877), p. 26; and Lauterbach, *The Attitude of
the Jew towards the Non-Jew* (1921, reprinted from the
CCAR Yearbook, vol. XXXI), p. 30.

[10] This is an allusion to Rome. Comp. Frankel in
MGWJ, 1854, p. 194 and J. Perles, *Etymologische Studien
zur Kunde der rabbinischen Sprache und Literatur* (Breslau,
1871), pp. 90–91.

ויקח שש מאות רכב בחור משל מי היו
הבהמות שהיו טוענין המרכבות אם תאמר משל
מצרים היו והלא כבר נאמר וימת כל מקנה מצרים
ואם תאמר משל פרעה היו והלא כבר נאמר הנה
190 יד יי הויה במקנך וגו' ואם תאמר משל. ישראל היו
והלא כבר נאמר וגם מקנינו ילך עמנו לא תשאר
פרסה אלא משל מי היו של הירא את דבר יי
נמצינו למדין שהיראים את דבר יי מעבדי פרעה
הם היו תקלה לישראל מכאן היה רבי שמעון בן
195 יוחאי אומר היפה שבגוים הרוג והטוב שבנחשים
רצץ את מוחו רבן שמעון בן גמליאל אומר בא וראה
עושרה וגודלה של מלכות חייבת זו שאין לה נומירן
אחת בטלה שכולן רצות ביום ובלילה וכנגדן של
מצרים וכולן עומדות בטילות.

186—196 ת. בשלח ח'.   188 שמות ט', ו'.   189—190 שם ט', נ'.
191—192 שם י', כ'ו.   192 שם ט', כ'.

---

187 הבהמות שהיו טוענין המרכבות] א. מ. >.   193 שהיראים
את–פרעה]= א.א.מ.מ"ח. (א. הם שיראו. מ.מ"ח.
הירא) את–פרעה. ד. הסקנה שהנים הירא את–פרעה. ט. >.   194 הם
היו] ט. שמהן היתה.   195 היפה] ד. טוב.   197 שאין] ד. ואין/ לה]–
מ"ח: א. לכם א'א. ט. להם. ד. >.   198 רצות] מ. ~ שם.
199 וכולן] א. ט. מ"ח. ל. ושלהן.

And Captains (Shalishim) over All of Them.
The word *Shalishim* here means mighty men, as
in the passage, "Captains (*Shalishim*) and coun-
cillors, all of them riding upon horses" (Ezek.
23.23).

Another Interpretation: *Shalishim* means that
they were triply armed. Rabban Simon the son
of Gamaliel says: It refers to the third man on the
chariot. Formerly there had been only two who
drove the chariot, but Pharaoh added one more
so as to pursue Israel faster.   Rabbi says:
Antoninus added one more to them so that
there were four.

Another Interpretation: *And Shalishim over
All of Them.* This means that there were three
of them against each Israelite. Some say there
were thirty against each one. And some say
three hundred against each one. But how did
Pharaoh know how many of the Israelites had
died during the three days of darkness and how
many of them went out of Egypt? He got out
their registers and on the basis of these registers
he sent forth armies against them. In a similar
way did R. Jeremiah interpret: "And there came

ו ש ל י ש י ם ע ל כ ו ל ו אין שלישים אלא גבורים
שנאמר שלישים וקרואים רוכבי סוסים כלם דבר
אחר ושלישים שהיו משולשים בזיין רבן שמעון בן
גמליאל אומר זה השלישי שעל המרכבה לשעבר
לא היו אלא שנים שהיו מריצים המרכבה ופרעה
הוסיף עליהם עוד אחד בשביל למהר לרדוף
אחרי ישראל רבי אומר אנטונינוס הוסיף עליהם
עוד אחד והיו ארבעה דבר אחר ושלישים על כולו
שלשה על כל אחד ואחד ויש אומרים שלשים על
כל אחד ואחד ויש אומרים שלש מאות על כל אחד
ואחד ומנין היה פרעה יודע כמה מתו מישראל
בשלשת ימי אפילה וכמה היוצאים ממצרים אלא
הוציא טומסין שלהן ולפי הטומסין הוציא עליהן
חיילות כיוצא בדבר דרש רבי ירמיה ויצא אליהם

201 יחזקאל כ״נ, כ׳ן.   201—206 י׳ כלאים ח׳, ב׳ (31c).   מדרש שה״ש
הוצ׳ גרינהוט י״א, ב׳,   214—213 דהי״ב י״ד, ח׳.

201 שלישים וקרואים] ק. נ. שלישים קרואים לבושי.   202 משולשים]
נ. משוללים.   204 שהיו טריאים המרכבה] א. מ׳ח. מ. ט. <.
206 רבי אומר אנטונינוס הוסיף עליהם] ד. ר׳ אנטונינוס אומר נ׳ היו
הוסיף עליהם / אנטונינוס] מ. אנטנינוס.   207 והיו ארבעה] א.
ט. </ דבר אחר] א. <.   209—208 ויש אומרים שלשים על כל אחד
ואחד[−ט: א. ד. <.   211 וכמה היוצאים ממצרים] א. ט.
ט. </ אלא] ד. <.   212 הוציא טומסין שלהן] ד. הוסיף עליהם
טומסין/הוציא] ד. הוסיף.   213 ירמיה] ד. ~ טאי דכתיב.

out against them Zerah the Ethiopian with an army of a thousand thousand and three hundred chariots" (II Chr. 14.8), and the armies which he led out against them were in proportion to the chariots.

Another Interpretation: *And Captains over All of Them*. In order to destroy[11] all of them. Formerly he had decreed only: "Every son that is born ye shall cast into the river" (Ex. 1.22); but here it says: "And captains over all of them" —in order to destroy all of them, as it is said: "I will draw my sword, my hand shall destroy them" (Ex. 15.9).

And the Lord Hardened the Heart of Pharaoh. For Pharaoh was not wholly decided in his mind whether to pursue or not.

And He Pursued after the Children of Israel. This is to proclaim the excellence of Israel. For had it been another people, Pharaoh would not have run after them.

For the Children of Israel Went Out with a High Hand. Scripture tells that when pursuing Israel the Egyptians were scorning, reviling and blaspheming. But Israel exalted, glorified, praised, and uttered songs of praise and adoration, of laudation and glorification to Him in whose hands are the fortunes of war, just as it is said:

---

[11] In this interpretation there is a play on the word כלו, which is taken as if it were derived from the root כלה, "to destroy."

זרח הכושי בחיל אלף אלפים ומרכבות שלש מאות
215 ולפי מרכבות הוציא עליהם חיילות דבר אחר
ושלישים על כלו על מנת לכלות לשעבר כל הבן
הילוד וגו' אבל כאן ושלישים על כלו על מנת
לכלות שנאמר אריק חרבי תורישמו ידי.

ויחזק יי את לב פרעה שהיה לבו חלוק
220 אם לרדוף אם לא לרדוף.

אחרי בני ישראל להודיע שבחן של ישראל
שאלו היתה אומה אחרת לא היה פרעה רודף
אחריה.

ובני ישראל יוצאים ביד רמה מגיד
225 הכתוב שכשהיו המצרים רודפים אחרי ישראל
היו מנאצים ומחרפים ומגדפים אבל ישראל
מרוממים ומפארים ומשבחים ונותנים שיר שבח
וגדולה ותהלה תפארת למי שהמלחמה שלו כענין

216—217 שמות א', כ"ב.   218 שמות ט"ו, ט'.

"Let the high praises of God be in their mouth,"
etc.   (Ps. 149.6).   And it also says: "Be thou
exalted, O God, above the heavens" (ibid.,
57.6). And it also says: "O Lord, Thou art my
God, I will exalt Thee" (Isa. 25.1).

*For the Children of Israel Went Out with a High
Hand.* This means with uncovered heads.

Another Interpretation: This means that their
hand was exalted above the Egyptians.

CHAPTER III
(Ex. 14.9–14)

And the Egyptians Pursued after Them. This
tells that not one of them stumbled on the way,
so that they could not augur evil and turn back.
And thus we find everywhere that the idolaters
practice augury. For it says: "For these nations,
that thou art to dispossess, hearken unto sooth-
sayers, and unto diviners" (Deut. 18.14). And
it is also written: "And the elders of Moab and
the elders of Midian departed with the rewards
of divination in their hand" (Num. 22.7), and:
"Balaam also the son of Beor, the soothsayer,"
etc. (Josh. 13.22).

שנאמר רוממות אל בגרונם וגו' ואומר רומה על
230 שמים אלהים ואומר יי אלהי אתה ארוממך וגו'.

וּבני ישראל יוצאים ביד רמה בראש
גלוי דבר אחר שהיתה ידן רמה על מצרים.

פרשה ג (שמות י״ד, ט׳–י״ד.)

וירדפו מצרים אחריהם מגיד שלא
נכשל אחד מהם בדרך שמא ינחשו ויחזרו להם
לאחוריהם וכן מצינו בכל מקום שהגוים מנחשים
שנאמר כי הגוים האלה אשר אתה יורש אותם אל
5 מעוננים ואל קוסמים ישמעו וכתיב וילכו זקני מואב
וזקני מדין וקסמים בידם ואת בלעם בן בעור
הקוסם וגו'.

---

229 תהלים קמ״ט, ו'.   229–230 תהלים נ״ו, י״ב.   230 ישעיה כ״ה, א'.
8–1 ש. 45.   4–5 דברים י״ח, י״ד.   5–6 במדבר כ״ב, ז'.   6–7 שם
ל״א, ח', יהושע י״ג, כ״ב.

---

229 וגו'] ד. במקום חרב פיפיות בידם.   230 שמים] מ. ד.
השמים.   231 מ״ח. ד״א ובני ישראל יוצאים.   231–232 בראש נלוי]
ד. בריש נלי /ידן] ש. ידו.
4 האלה] ק. נ. ההם. מ. הם.   7 וגו'] מ. ~ מגיד שלא נכשל אחד
מהם שמא ינהגם ויחזרו לאחוריהם. ק. הרנו בחרב מגיד שלא נכשל אחד
שלא ינחשו ויחזרו לאחוריהם. נ. ל. הרנו בחרב וזקני מדין נחשו וחזרו
לאחוריהם.

And Overtook Them Encamping by the Sea, beside Pi-hahiroth, in Front of Baal-zephon. And Pharaoh Drew Nigh. He drew nigh the punishment that was to come upon him.

Another Interpretation: When Pharaoh saw the Israelites encamping by the sea, he said: "Baal-zephon approves of my decision. I had planned to destroy them in water and now Baal-zephon approves of my decision to destroy them in water." He then began to sacrifice, offer incense and libations and to prostrate himself to his idol. In this sense it is said: "And Pharaoh drew nigh"—to sacrifice and offer incense.

Another Interpretation: *And Pharaoh Drew Nigh.* The distance which the Israelites covered in three days, the guards covered in a day and a half; and what the guards covered in a day and a half Pharaoh covered in one day. In this sense it says: "And Pharaoh drew nigh."

And the Children of Israel Lifted Up Their Eyes. After they had beaten the guards they knew that the Egyptians were bound to pursue them.

וישיגו אותם חונים על הים וגו' לפני
בעל צפון ופרעה הקריב הוא הקריב את
הפורענות לבא עליו דבר אחר כיון שראה פרעה
שישראל חונים על הים אמר בעל צפון הסכים על
גזרתי אני חשבתי לאבדם במים ובעל צפון הסכים
על גזרתי לאבדם במים התחיל מזבח ומקטר ומנסך
ומשתחוה לעבודה זרה שלו לכך נאמר ופרעה
הקריב לזבח ולקטר דבר אחר ופרעה הקריב מה
שהלכו ישראל בשלשה ימים הלכו האקטורין ביום
ומחצה ומה שהלכו האקטורין ביום ומחצה הלך
פרעה ביום אחד לכך נאמר ופרעה הקריב.
וישאו בני ישראל את עיניהם כיון
שהכו את האקטורין היו יודעין שסופן לרדוף
אחריהם.

10–14 ת. בשלח ח'.

8–9 לפני בעל צפון] הוספתי–ש.   10–9 ופרעה הקריב–
עליו] ש. דבר אחר ופרעה הקריב–עליו, ונורסו למטה בשורה ט'ו קודם
ד'א ופרעה הקריב מה שהלכו וגו'. ובא״צ. גורסו למטה בשורה י'ח
אחר ופרעה הקריב.   10 דבר אחר] הוספתי עפ'י מ'ח.ובה'מ.
ומ'ה.   11 שישראל חונים על הים–] ט: א. מ. ק. > מ'ח. אותם כן.
נ. ל. שנשארו (ל. שנשאר) בעל צפון.   12 לאבדם במים] ד. >.
12–13 ובעל צפון הסכים על גזרתי] ט. והוא התחיל.   14 לע'ז שלו]
מ'ח. לפניו.   15 לזבח ולקטר] א. >/ ופרעה הקריב] ד. ~ קרב
עצמו ומיהר ללכת ולרדוף אחריהם.

And Behold, the Egyptians Were Marching after Them. It really does not say "were marching" (*Nose'im*) but "was marching" (*Nose'a*). This tells that the Egyptians all formed squadrons, each marching like one man. From this the empire learned to lead its armies in squadrons.

And They Were Sore Afraid; and the Children of Israel Cried Out unto the Lord. Immediately they seized upon the occupation of their fathers, the occupation of Abraham, Isaac and Jacob. What does it say of Abraham? "Having Beth-el on the west and Ai on the east; And he builded there an altar unto the Lord, and called upon the name of the Lord" (Gen. 12.8); "And Abraham planted a tamarisk-tree in Beer-sheba, and called there on the name of the Lord, the Everlasting God" (ibid., 21.33). What does it say of Isaac? "And Isaac went out to meditate in the field" (ibid., 24.63), and meditation here only means prayer, as it is said: "Evening, and morning, and at noonday will I complain,[1] and moan; and He hath heard my voice" (Ps. 55.18). And it is written: "I pour out my complaint before Him," etc. (ibid., 142.3). And it is also written: "A prayer of the afflicted, when he fainteth, and poureth out his complaint before the Lord" (ibid., 102.1). What does it say of Jacob? "And he

---

[1] I. e., in prayer. In all these passages the root of the Hebrew word is שׂיח.

והנה מצרים נוסע אחריהם נוסעים אין
כתיב כאן אלא נוסע מגיד שנעשו כולן תורמיות
תורמיות כאיש אחד מכאן למדה מלכות להיות
מנהגת תורמיות תורמיות.   25

וייראו מאד ויצעקו וגו' מיד תפסו להם
אומנות אבותיהם אומנות אברהם יצחק ויעקב
באברהם מהו אומר בית אל מים והעי מקדם ויבן
שם מזבח ליי ויקרא בשם יי ויטע אשל בבאר שבע
ויקרא שם בשם יי אל עולם ביצחק מהו אומר ויצא   30
יצחק לשוח בשדה ואין שיחה אלא תפלה שנאמר
ערב ובקר וצהרים אשיחה ואהמה וישמע קולי
וכתיב אשפוך לפניו שיחי וגו' וכתיב תפלה לעני
כי יעטוף ולפני יי ישפך שיחו ביעקב מהו אומר

35—26 ת. שם ט'.   29—28 בראשית י"ב, ו'.   35—28 ברכות כ"ו, ב'.
י' שם ד', א' (7ª).   29—30 מדרש תהלים נ"ה, ב'.   30—29 בראשית כ"א, ל"נ.
31—30 שם כ"ד, ס"נ.   35—31 ב"ר ס', י"ד. ס"ח, ט'. ע"ז ז', א'. פדר"א
ט"ז. מדרש תהלים ק"ב, י"ב.   32 תהלים נ"ה, י"ח.   33 תהלים קס"ב, ג'.
34—33 שם ק"ב, א'.

---

23 מניד] מ. מלמד.   26 מיד] א. ט. מ"ח. >.   29—28 ויבן שם
מזבח ליי ויקרא בשם יי] הוספתי: א. מ. וגו' ק. נ. ויבן שם מזבח
ויקרא בשם ד'.   30 ויקרא שם-עולם] הוספתי: א. מ. ד. וגו'.

lighted upon (vayifga') the place" (Gen. 28.11).
"Lighting upon" (pegi'ah) here only means
"prayer,"[2] as in the passage: "Therefore, pray
not thou for this people, neither lift up cry nor
prayer for them, neither make intercession to
Me" (Jer. 7.16). And it is also written: "Let
them now make intercession to the Lord of
hosts" (ibid., 27.18). And in this sense it also
says: "Fear not, thou worm Jacob, and ye men
of Israel" (Isa. 41.14). Just as the worm has
only its mouth to smite the cedar with, so Israel
has only prayer.[3] And thus it says: "Moreover,
I have given to thee one portion above thy
brethren, which I took out of the hand of the
Amorite, with my sword and with my bow"
(Gen. 48.22). And did he really take it with his
sword and his bow? Has it not already been said:
"For I trust not in my bow, neither can my
sword save me" (Ps. 44.7)? Hence, what must
be the meaning of the words: "With my sword
and with my bow"? With prayer. And, likewise, it says: "Judah is a lion's whelp," etc.
(Gen. 49.9), but it also says: "And this for
Judah, and he said: 'Hear, Lord, the voice of
Judah'" (Deut. 33.7). And, likewise, Jeremiah
said: "Cursed is the man that trusteth in man"
(Jer. 17.5). But of prayer what does he say?
"Blessed is the man that trusteth in the Lord,

---

[2] Cf. Ḥul. 91b.
[3] I. e., as a weapon against its oppressors.

35 ויפגע במקום ואין פגיעה אלא תפלה שנאמר ואתה
אל תתפלל בעד העם הזה ואל תשא בעדם רנה
ותפלה ואל תפגע בי וכתיב יפגעו נא ביי צבאות
וכן הוא אומר אל תראי תולעת יעקב מתי ישראל
מה התולעת אינה מכה את הארז אלא בפה כך
40 אין להם לישראל אלא תפלה וכן הוא אומר ואני
נתתי לך שכם אחד על אחיך אשר לקחתי מיד
האמורי בחרבי ובקשתי וכי בחרבו ובקשתו לקחה
והלא כבר נאמר כי לא בקשתי אבטח וגו' הא מה
תלמוד לומר בחרבי ובקשתי זו תפלה וכן הוא
45 אומר גור אריה יהודה וגו' ואומר וזאת ליהודה
ויאמר וגו' וכן ירמיה אמר ארור הגבר אשר יבטח
באדם אבל בתפלה מהו אומר ברוך הגבר אשר

---

35 בראשית כ"ח, י"א. ספרי דברים כ"ו. 35—37 ירמיה ז', ט"ז.
35—65 ת. שם. 35—71 ש. 46—45. 37 ירמיה כ"ז, י"ח. 38 ישעיה מ"א,
י"ד. 42—40 בראשית מ"ח כ"ב. 42—44 ב"ב קכ"ג, א'. 43 תהלים
מ"ד, ז'. 45 בראשית מ"ט, ט'. במ"ר כ', כ'. 46—45 דברים ל"ג, ז'.
46—47 ירמיה י"ז, ה'. 48—47 שם י"ז, ז'.

---

43 והלא כבר נאמר–אבטח וגו']–ט: מ. ד. >. 43—44 הא
מה ח'ל–זו תפלה[=]–ט: מ. ד. אלא לומר לך חרבי זו תפלה
בקשתי זו בקשה. 45 גור אריה יהודה וגו' ואומר] מ"ח. >. 47 אבל
בתפלה]=מ"ח: א. ומן התפלה. ד. ובתפלה. ט. >.

and whose trust the Lord is" (ibid., 17.7). Likewise, David says: "Thou comest to me with a sword and with a spear and with a javelin; but I come to thee in the name of the Lord of hosts" (I Sam. 17.45). And it is also written: "Some trust in chariots, and some in horses; but we will make mention of the name of the Lord our God. They are bowed down and fallen; but we are risen and stand upright. Save, Lord; let the King answer us in the day that we call" (Ps. 20.8–10). Likewise, it says: "And Asa cried unto the Lord his God, and said: 'Lord, there is none beside Thee to help, between the mighty and him that hath no strength; help us, O Lord our God; for we rely on Thee, and in Thy name are we come against this multitude,'" etc. (II Chr. 14.10). What does it say of Moses? "And Moses sent messengers from Kadesh unto the king of Edom: 'Thus saith thy brother Israel: Thou knowest all the travail that hath befallen us; how our fathers went down into Egypt, and we dwelt in Egypt a long time; and the Egyptians dealt ill with us, and our fathers; and when we cried unto the Lord, He heard our voice,'" etc. (Num. 20.14–16). The Edomites, however, said to them: You pride yourselves upon what your father

יבטח ביי והיה יי מבטחו וכן דוד אומר אתה בא
אלי בחרב ובחנית ובכידון ואני בא אליך בשם יי
50 צבאות אלהי ישראל וכתיב אלה ברכב ואלה
בסוסים ואנחנו בשם יי אלהינו נזכיר המה כרעו
ונפלו ואנחנו קמנו ונתעודד יי הושיעה המלך יעננו
ביום קראנו וכן הוא אומר ויקרא אסא אל יי אלהיו
ויאמר יי אין עמך לעזור בין רב לאין כח עזרנו
55 יי אלהינו כי עליך נשעננו ובשמך באנו אל ההמון
הזה וגו' במשה מהו אומר וישלח משה מלאכים
מקדש אל מלך אדום וגו' ונצעק אל יי וישמע קולינו
אמרו להם אתם מתגאים עַל מה שהוריש לכם

48—50 שמואל א. י"ז, מ"ה.   50—53 תהלים כ', ח'—י'.   53—56 דה"ב
י"ד, י'.   56—57 במדבר כ', י"ד—ט"ז.   58—61 שמו"ר כ"א, א'. ב"ר
ס"ה, כ'.

48 מבטחו] ד. ~ מבטחן של ישראל בשעה שמתפללין לו והוא
(ק. הוא) קרוב להם שנאמר קרוב יי לכל קוראיו / דוד אומר] ד.
אמר דוד לנגית.   50—49 ואני בא—צבאות אלהי ישראל] א. מ. וגו'.
מ"ח. ואני באתי. ובמקרא שלפנינו ואנכי בא—צבאות אלהי מערכות
ישראל.   53 הוא אומר] א. מ. אסא אומר / אל יין] ק. נ. בשם
יי/ אלהיו] מ. >.   54 בין רב לאין כח] א. וגו'. ק. נ. בין רב לסעט.
ט. כ. בין רב ללא כח.   55 אלי אלהינו] ק. נ. אלהי ישענו/ נשעננו]
ט. כ.=בסקרא נשענו/ אל] במקרא על.   57 אל יין] א. מ. ~
אלהי אבותינו / קולינו] א. את קולינו.   58 אמרו להם] ד. אמר
להם משה.

bequeathed you, "The voice is the voice of Jacob,"[4] "And the Lord heard our voice."[5] And we pride ourselves upon what our father bequeathed us, "The hands are the hands of Esau,"[6] "And by thy sword shalt thou live."[7] That is why it is written: "And Edom said unto him: 'Thou shalt not pass through me, lest I come out with the sword against thee' " (Num. 20.18). And so also here you interpret: "And they were sore afraid; and the children of Israel cried out unto the Lord"—they seized upon the occupation of their fathers,[8] the occupation of Abraham, Isaac and Jacob.

And They Said unto Moses: 'Because There Were No Graves in Egypt.' After they had put leaven into the dough,[9] they came to Moses and said: "Is not this the word that we spoke to thee in Egypt?" And what was it the Israelites said unto Moses in Egypt? Behold it says: "And they met Moses and Aaron, who stood in the way, as they came forth from Pharaoh; and they said unto them: 'The Lord look after you and judge'," etc. (Ex. 5.20–21). We had been grieving over

---

[4] Gen. 27.22.

[5] Deut. 26.7.

[6] Gen., l. c.

[7] Ibid. 27.40.

[8] I. e., prayer.

[9] I. e., after having stirred up excitement.

אביכם הקול קול יעקב וישמע יי את קולינו ואנו
60 מתגאים על מה שהוריש לנו אבינו והידים ידי עשו
ועל חרבך תחיה הדא היא דכתיב ויאמר אליו
אדום לא תעבור בי פן בחרב אצא לקראתך ואף
כאן אתה אומר וייראו מאד ויצעקו בני ישראל אל
יי תפסו להם אומנות אבותיהם אומנות אברהם
65 יצחק ויעקב.

ויאמרו אל משה המבלי אין קברים
במצרים מאחר שנתנו שאור בעיסה באו אל
משה ואמרו לו הלא זה הדבר אשר דברנו אליך
במצרים וכי מה אמרו ישראל למשה במצרים הרי
70 הוא אומר ויפגעו את משה' ואת אהרן וגו' ויאמרו
אליהם ירא יי עליכם וישפוט וגו' היינו מצטערים

---

59 בראשית כ"ז, כ"ב./דברים כ"ז, ז'. 60 בראשית כו, מ. 61 שם
כ"ז, מ'. 61–62 במדבר כ', י"ח. 70–71 שמות ה', כ'–כ"א.
71–145 ש. 46–48.

---

59 אביכם] ד. ~ יצחק/הקול] מ. ד. דכתיב הקול/קולינו] ד.
קול ישראל/ואנו] ד. ואלו. 60 לנו אבינו] ד. להם אבינו יצחק
דכתיב. 61 הדא היא דכתיב] א. ט. ומהו אומר. 62 לקראתך]
ד. ~ שאינן בטוחים אלא בחרב אבל ישראל תפסו להם אומנות
אבותיהם אומנות אברהם יצחק ויעקב. 62–63 ואף כאן אתה אומר]
ד. שנאמר. 63 מאד] ק. נ. מצרים. 64–65 תפסו–ויעקב] ד. <.
70 ואת אהרן] ק. ואת אחיו.

our enslavement in Egypt, then came the death of our brothers during the period of darkness, which was worse for us than our enslavement in Egypt. We have been grieving over the death of our brothers in the period of darkness, now comes our death in this wilderness, which is much worse for us than the death of our brothers during the period of darkness. For our brothers were buried and mourned for, but we—our corpses will be exposed to the heat of the day and the cold of the night.

And Moses Said unto the People: 'Fear Ye Not.' Behold! Moses is rallying them. This is to proclaim the wisdom of Moses, how he stood there pacifying all these thousands and myriads. Of him it is stated in the traditional sacred writings: "Wisdom is a stronghold to the wise man," etc. (Eccl. 7.19).

Stand Still and See the Salvation of the Lord. The Israelites asked him: "When?" Moses said to them: "Today the Holy Spirit rests upon you." For the expression "standing" (*yezibah*) everywhere suggests the presence of the Holy Spirit, as in the passages: "I saw the Lord standing beside the altar" (Amos 9.1). "And the Lord came, and stood, and called as at other times: 'Samuel, Samuel' " (I Sam. 3.10). And it also

על שיעבודינו במצרים מיתת אחינו באפלה קשה
לנו משעבודנו במצרים היינו מצטערים על מיתת
אחינו באפלה מיתתנו במדבר הזה קשה לנו ממיתת

75 אחינו באפלה שאחינו נספדו ונקברו ואנחנו תהיה
נבלתינו מושלכת לחורב ביום ולקרח בלילה.

ויאמר משה אל העם אל תיראו הרי
משה מזרזן להודיע חכמתו של משה היאך היה
עומד ומפייס לכל אותם האלפים והרבבות ועליו

80 מפורש בקבלה והחכמה תעוז לחכם וגו'.

התיצבו וראו וגו' אמרו לו ישראל אימתי
אמר להם משה היום שרתה עליכם רוח הקדש
שאין יציבה בכל מקום אלא רוח הקדש שנאמר
ראיתי את יי נצב על המזבח וגו' ויבא יי ויתיצב

85 ויקרא כפעם בפעם שמואל שמואל ואומר קרא

---

80 קהלת ז', י"ט.   86—83 לקטן שירתא י'. סוטה י"א, א'; י' שם א',
ט' (17b). שמו"ר א', כ"ב. מדרש משלי י"ד (ל"ח, א'). מ"ת 180.
84 עמוס ט', א'.   85—84 שמואל א. ג', י'.   86—85 דברים ל"א, י"ד.

79 והרבבות] ד. ~והיו נשמעין לו.   80 והחכמה] מ. חכמה.
במקרא החכמה.   82 שרתה] נ. ל. השרתה. א"א. מ"ח. תשרה.
א. ט. ישלח/ עליכם] ק. שכינה עליכם. נ. ל. שכינה עליהם.
84 ויבא יי] ד. ויבא לו.

says: "Call Joshua and stand in the tent of meeting that I may give him a charge" (Deut. 31.14). To what were the Israelites at that moment like? To a dove fleeing from a hawk, and about to enter a cleft in the rock where there is a hissing serpent. If she enters, there is the serpent! If she stays out, there is the hawk! In such a plight were the Israelites at that moment, the sea forming a bar and the enemy pursuing. Immediately they set their mind upon prayer. Of them it is stated in the traditional sacred writings: "O my dove that art in the clefts of the rock," etc. (Cant. 2.14). And when it further says: "For sweet is thy voice and thy countenance is comely" (ibid.), it means, for thy voice is sweet in prayer and thy countenance is comely in the study of the Torah. Another Interpretation: For thy voice is sweet in prayer and thy countenance is comely in good deeds.

Another Interpretation: *Stand Still and See*, etc. The Israelites asked Moses: "When?" He answered them: "Tomorrow!" Then the Israelites said to Moses: "Moses, our Master, we have not the strength to endure." At that moment Moses prayed and God caused them to see squadrons upon squadrons of ministering angels

את יהושע והתיצבו באהל מועד ואצונו למה היו
ישראל דומין באותה שעה ליונה שברחה מפני הנץ
ונכנסה לנקיק הסלע והיה נחש נושף בו תכנס לפנים
הרי הנחש תצא לחוץ הרי הנץ כך היו ישראל
90 באותה שעה הים סוגר ושונא רודף מיד נתנו עיניהם
בתפלה עליהם מפורש בקבלה יונתי בחגוי הסלע
וגו' ונאמר כי קולך ערב ומראך נאוה כי קולך
ערב בתפלה ומראך נאוה בתלמוד תורה דבר אחר
כי קולך ערב בתפלה ומראך נאוה במעשה הטוב
95 דבר אחר התיצבו וראו וגו' אמרו לו אימתי אמר
להם למחר אמרו לו ישראל למשה רבינו משה אין
בנו כח לסבול התפלל משה באותה שעה והראה
להם המקום תורמיות תורמיות של מלאכי השרת

93—86 שהש"ר ב', י"ד. שמו"ר כ"א, ה'. 92—91 שה"ש ב', י"ד.
103—99 מלכים ב. ו', ט"ו—י"ז.

---

86 באהל מועד ואצונו] א. וגו' מ. ותו' ותתצב אחותו מרחוק ד. ~
ואומר ותתצב אחותו מרחוק שרתה עליו (ל. עליה) רוח הקודש.
88 נושף] ק. נושך./ בו] ק. > מ. נ. ל. ט. בה / תכנס] ד. אם
תכנס א. ט. ונכנסה ט"כ. ונכנס. 89 הרי הנחש] א. ט. > מ"ח.
הרי כאן נחש./ תצא] ד. ואם תצא א. ט. וכשיצאה./ הנץ] א. ט.
בן הנץ (ט. בא בן הנץ) לתופשה. מ"ח. כאן נץ/ ישראל] א. ט.
מ"ח. ~ דומין. 93—94 דבר אחר–במעשה הטוב] א. ט. >.
97 לסבול] מ. לסבר. 98 להם המקום] ד. לו הקב"ה/ תורמיות]
א. ט. טורסיות.

standing before them, just as it is said: "And when the servant of the man of God was risen early, and gone forth, behold, a host with horses and chariots was round about the city. And his servant said unto him: 'Alas, my master! how shall we do?' And he answered: 'Fear not: for they that are with us are more than they that are with them.' And Elisha prayed, and said: 'Lord I pray Thee, open his eyes, that he may see.' And the Lord opened the eyes of the young man; and he saw; and, behold, the mountain was full of horses and chariots of fire round about Elisha" (II Kings 6.15–17). And so also here Moses prayed at that moment and God caused them to see squadrons upon squadrons of ministering angels standing before them. And thus it says: "At the brightness before Him, there passed through His thick clouds, hailstones and coals of fire" (Ps. 18.13)—"His thick clouds," as against their squadrons; "hailstones," as against their catapults; "coals," as against their missiles; "fire," as against their naphtha. "The Lord also thundered in the heavens" (ibid., v. 14)—as against the clasping of their shields and the noise of their trampling shoes. "And the Most High gave forth His voice" (ibid.), as against their

עומדין לפניהם כענין שנאמר וישכם משרת איש

100 האלהים לקום וגו' ויאמר אל תירא כי רבים אשר

אתנו מאשר אותם ויתפלל אלישע ויאמר יי פקח

נא את עיניו ויראה ויפקח יי את עיני הנער וירא

והנה ההר מלא סוסים ורכב אש סביבות אלישע

כך התפלל משה באותה שעה והראה להם המקום

105 תורמיות תורמיות של מלאכי השרת עומדים

לפניהם וכן הוא אומר מנוגה נגדו עביו עברו ברד

וגחלי אש עביו כנגד תורמיות שלהם ברד כנגד

בלסטראות שלהם גחלי כנגד טורמנטא שלהם

אש כנגד נפט שלהם ירעם מן שמים יי כנגד הגפת

110 תריסין ושפעת עקלגוסין שלהם ועליון יתן קולו

107–106 תהלים י"ח, י"ג.   117–106 י' סוטה ח', נ' (22b).

109 שמואל ב. כ"ב, י"ד.   110 שם. שם.

---

99 לפניהם] ד. עליהם.   100 וגו'] ק. נ. ~ ויראו והנה חיל
סביבות העיר סוס ורכב ויאמר נערו אליו אהה אדני איכה
נעשה, ובמקרא שלפנינו, ויצא והנה חיל סובב את העיר וסוס וגו'.
100–101 אשר אתנו מאשר אותם] א. ט. וגו' מ. אתם אשר אתנו וגו'./
אותם]ק. נ. אתם.   103 ורכב]ק. נ. >.   104 להם]ד. לו.
105 טורמנטא] הגנתי–ש: א. טרמינה. מ. סרסנה. ד. טרמנסנה. ט.
טרמנ'. כ. (תהלים י"ח, ל"ז) תורמסא. מ"ח. טרמנסה.   109 נפט] ש.
ט. א. נטפת. ל. מ"ח.הנפט. מ. ק. נ. הנפש.   110 ושפעת] א.
ושיפת/ עקלגוסין] מ. ל. ט. עקלגסין. א. קולוסין. ק. נ. עקלנסין.

whetting the swords. "And He sent out His arrows and scattered them" (ibid., v. 15), as against their arrows. And He shot forth lightnings and discomfited them" (ibid.), as against their shouting. Another Interpretation: *And He Sent Out His Arrows.* The arrows would scatter them, and the lightnings would huddle them together. *"And Discomfited Them."* He confounded them and brought confusion among them. He took away their signals so that they did not know what they were doing. Another Interpretation: *And Discomfited Them.* Discomfiture here means by pestilence, as in the passage: "And shall discomfit them with a great discomfiture until they be destroyed"[10] (Deut. 7.23).

For Whereas Ye Have Seen the Egyptians Today, etc. In three places God warned the Israelites not to return to Egypt. For it says: "For whereas ye have seen the Egyptians today, ye shall see them again no more for ever." And it says: "Ye shall henceforth return no more that way" (Deut. 17.16). And it also says: "By the way whereof I said unto thee: 'Thou shalt see it no more again'" (ibid., 28.68). But in spite of these three warnings, they returned three times and in all three times they fell. The first time was in the days of Sennacherib, as it is said: "Woe to

---

[10] The "discomfiture" mentioned in the passage of Deut. 7.23 was understood to mean pestilence caused by "the mighty hand" mentioned in v. 19 (cf. *Sifre,* Num. 115, Friedmann, 35b) and by the hornet mentioned in v. 20 (cf. Sotah 36a).

כנגד צחצוח חרבות שלהן וישלח חציו ויפיצם
כנגד חצים שלהם וברקים רב ויהומם כנגד צוחה
שלהם דבר אחר וישלח חציו שהיו חצים מפזרים
אותם וברקים מכנסין אותם ויהומם המם וערבבם
115 נטל סגניות שלהם ולא היו יודעים מה הם עושים
דבר אחר ויהמם אין הממה אלא מנפה כענין
שנאמר והמם מהומה גדולה עד השמדם.

כ י א ש ר ר א י ת ם א ת מ צ ר י ם וגו' בשלשה
מקומות הזהיר המקום לישראל שלא לחזור
120 למצרים שנאמר כי אשר ראיתם את מצרים היום
לא תוסיפו לראותם עוד עד עולם ואומר לא
תוסיפון לשוב בדרך הזה עוד ואומר בדרך אשר
אמרתי לך לא תוסיף עוד לראותה בשלשתם חזרו
שם ובשלשתם נפלו הראשונה בימי סנחריב שנאמר

111 תהלים י"ח, ט"ו.   112 שם. שם.   117—114 לקמן פ"ו.
117 דברים ז', כ"ג.   128—118 י' סוכה ה', א' א' (5b). אסתר רבה
א', נ'.   122—121 דברים י"ז, ט"ז.   123—122 שם כ"ח, ס"ח.

111 חרבות] א. ט. הזיין.   113—112 כנגד חצים–וישלח חציו]
א. >.   113 חצים] מ. ד. ~ של פרעה. / מפזרים] א. ט.
מפזרן.   114 אותם] א. ט. > ד. ~ לישראל. / אותם 2] א. >.
115 סגניות] א. סננות. נ. ל. מנפות.   117 מהומה] ק. מקומה.
נ. מהומם.   122 תוסיפון] ד. תוסיפו.   124 שם] א. ט. >.

them that go down to Egypt for help" (Isa. 31.1). The second time was in the days of Johanan, the son of Kareah, as it is said; "Then it shall come to pass, that the sword, which ye fear, shall overtake you there in the land of Egypt" (Jer. 42.16). The third time was in the days of Trajan. These three times they returned and in all of these three times they fell.

The Israelites at the Red Sea were divided into four groups. One group said: Let us throw ourselves into the sea. One said: Let us return to Egypt. One said: Let us fight them; and one said: Let us cry out against them. The one that said: "Let us throw ourselves into the sea," was told: "Stand still, and see the salvation of the Lord." The one that said: "Let us return to Egypt," was told: "For whereas ye have seen the Egyptians today," etc. The one that said: "Let us fight them" was told: "The Lord will fight for you." The one that said: "Let us cry out against them," was told: "And ye shall hold your peace."

125 הוי היורדים מצרים לעזרה השנית בימי יוחנן בן

קרח שנאמר והיתה החרב אשר אתם יראים ממנה

שם תשיג אתכם בארץ מצרים השלישית בימי

טרגינוס בשלשתן חזרו ובשלשתן נפלו ארבע כתות

נעשו לישראל על הים אחת אומרת ניפול לים

130 ואחת אומרת נחזור למצרים ואחת אומרת נעשה

מלחמה כנגדן ואחת אומרת נצווח כנגדן זאת

שאמרה ניפול לים נאמר לה התיצבו וראו את

ישועת יי זו שאמרה נחזור למצרים נאמר לה כי

אשר ראיתם את מצרים וגו' וזו שאמרה נעשה

135 מלחמה כנגדן נאמר לה יי ילחם לכם וזו שאמרה

נצווח כנגדן נאמר לה ואתם תחרישון.

---

125 ישעיה ל"א, א'.   126—127 ירמיה מ"ב, ט"ז.   128—136 י' תענית ב', ה' (65d).

---

125 מצרים] א. ד. למצרים.   127 בארץ מצרים] ד. ~ והחרב אשר אתם דואגים ממנו שם ידבק אחריכם מצרים ושם תמותו (ק. ~ אסר להם נביא לישראל יראתם מחרב נבוכדנצר וברחתם לפרעה לעזרה שם תהא ממשלתכן).   128 טרגינוס] א. טרניאנוס. מ"ח. סרניאנוס. ד. טורנינוס./ נפלו] ד. ~ הדא היא דכתיב אפרים יונה פותה אין לב וגו' (הושע ז', י"א).

The Lord Will Fight for You. Not only at this time, but at all times will He fight against your enemies.   R. Meir says: *The Lord Will Fight for You.* If even when you stand there silent, the Lord will fight for you, how much more so when you render praise to Him!   Rabbi says: *The Lord Will Fight for You and Ye Shall Hold Your Peace.* Shall God perform miracles and mighty deeds for you and you be standing there silent?   The Israelites then said to Moses: Moses, our teacher, what is there for us to do? And he said to them: You should be exalting, glorifying and praising, uttering songs of praise, adoration and glorification to Him in whose hands are the fortunes of wars, just as it is said: "Let the high praises of God be in their mouth" (Ps. 149.6).   And it also says: "Be Thou exalted, O God, above the heavens; Thy glory be above all the earth" (ibid., 57.12).   And it also says: "O Lord, Thou art my God, I will exalt Thee" (Isa. 25.1).

At that moment the Israelites opened their mouths and recited the song: "I will sing unto the Lord, for He is highly exalted," etc.   (Ex. 15.2).

יי ילחם לכם לא לשעה זו בלבד אלא

לעולם ילחם כנגדן של אויבכם רבי מאיר אומר יי

ילחם לכם אם כשתהיו עומדים ושותקין יי ילחם

140 לכם קל וחמר כשתהיו נותנין לו שבח רבי אומר

יי ילחם לכם המקום יעשה לכם נסים וגבורות

ואתם תהיו עומדין ושותקין אמרו ישראל למשה

רבינו משה מה עלינו לעשות אמר להם אתם תהיו

מרוממים ומפארים ומשבחין ונותנין שיר ושבח

145 וגדולה ותפארת למי שהמלחמות שלו כענין שנאמר

רוממות אל בגרונם ואומר רומה על השמים אלהים

על כל הארץ כבודך ואומר יי אלהי אתה ארוממך

אודה שמך וגו' באותה שעה פתחו ישראל פיהם

ואמרו שירה אשירה ליי כי גאה גאה וגו'.

---

146 תהלים קמ'ט, ו'.   147—146 שם נ'ז, ו'.   148—147 ישעיה כ'ה, א'.

---

140 רבי אומר] ד. רבי מאיר אומר.